HOWLIN'
WOLF
PHOTOS
More Real Than Real



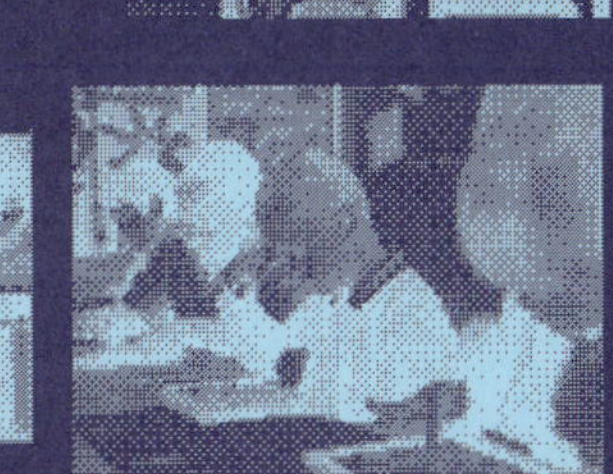
REALSIM
MORE
TIME
FOR
YOU

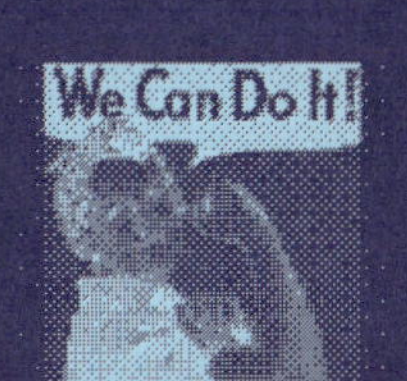

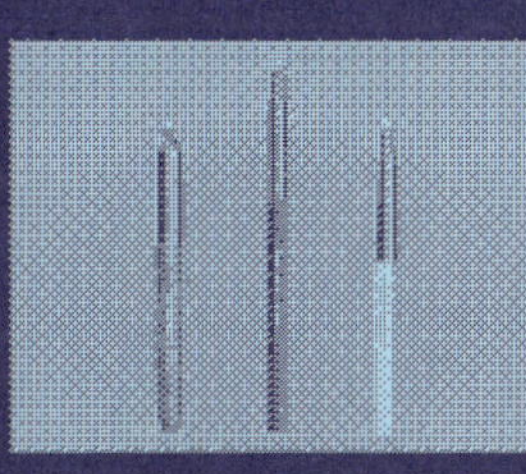

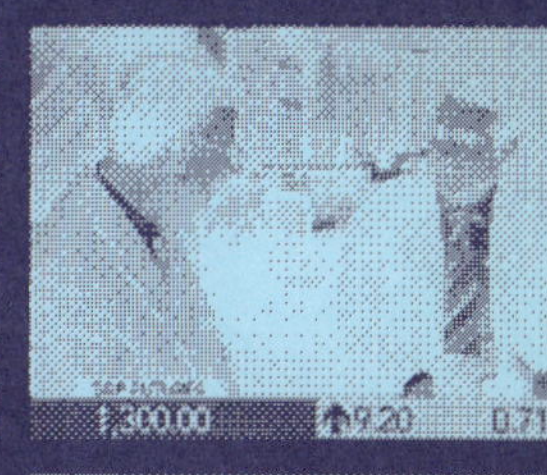

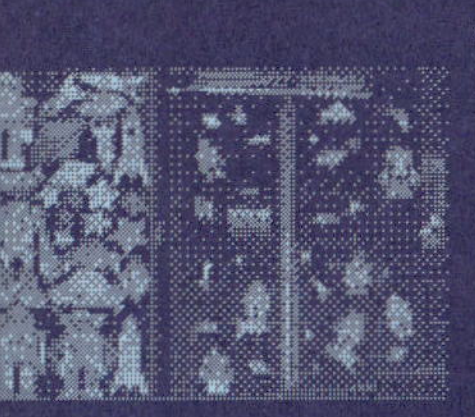
We Can Do It!

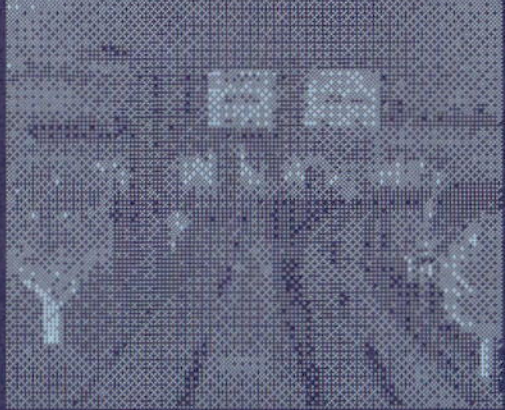

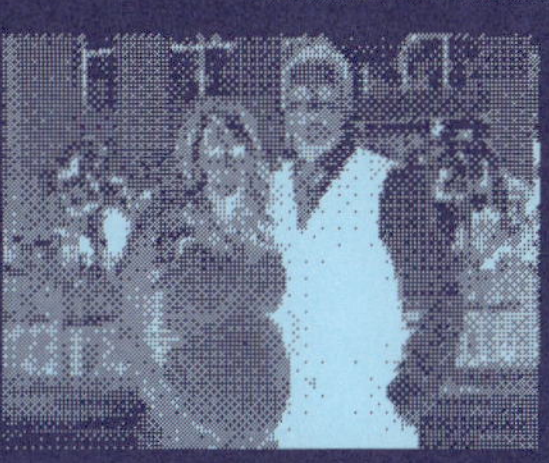

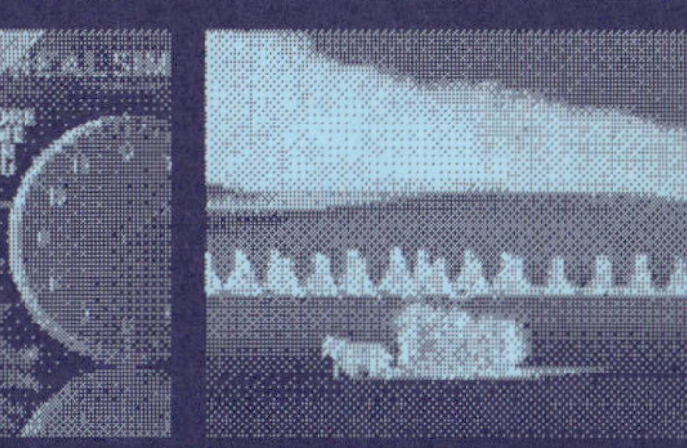
1,300.00    9.20    0.71

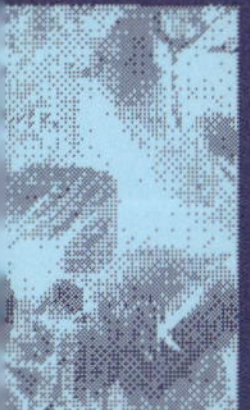

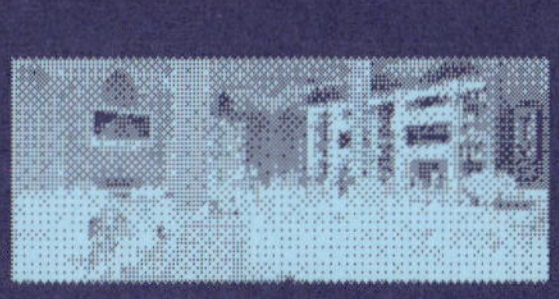

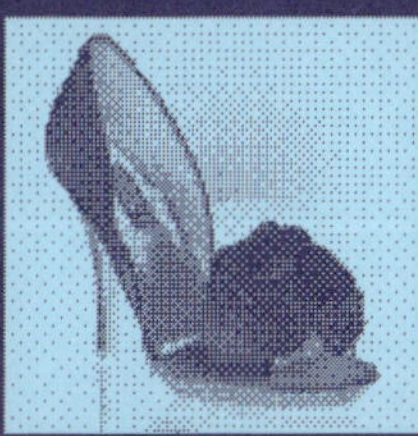

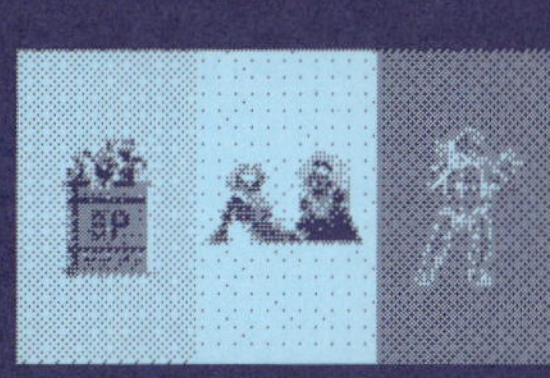
REALSIM

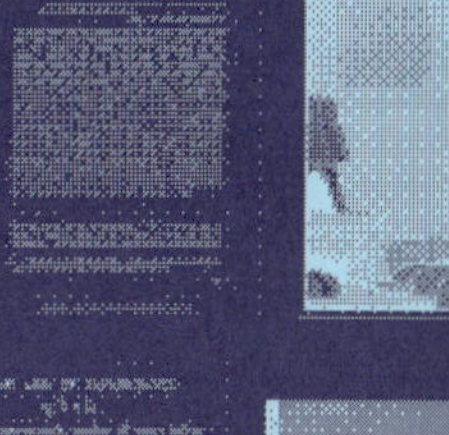

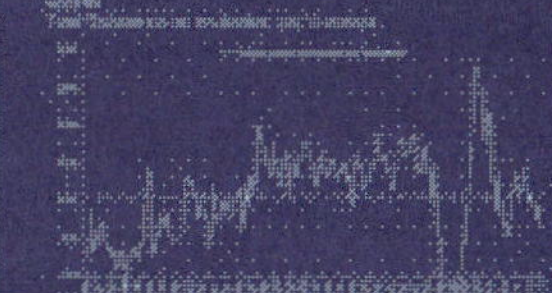

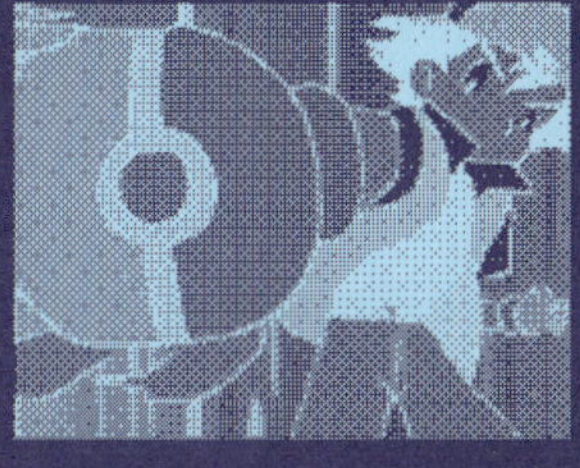

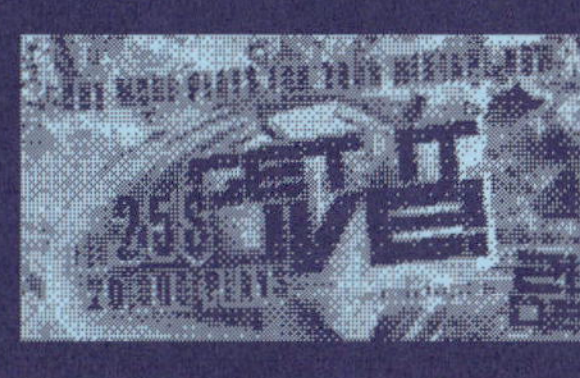
25$
GET IT

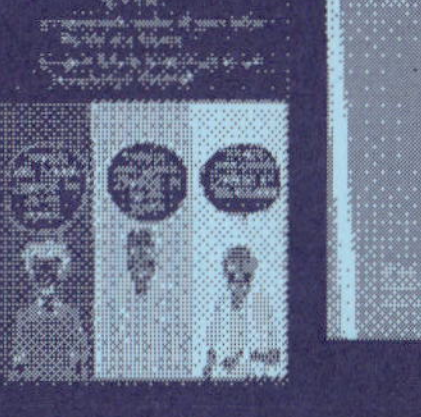

IN THE NEWS ▶ Gay 12-Year-Old  |  Apple Announcement  |  Super Tuesday  |  Contraception Sabotage   Last Updated 8:36 PM      Search

# NEWS

# Manifesto Coming Along Fine

APRIL 14, 1999 | ISSUE 35·14

LIBBY, MT —Ken Hausch, a Libby-area Luddite separatist and conspiracy theorist, announced Monday that his much-anticipated manifesto, *My Lonely Battle Against The Mind-Control Slavery Of The Illuminati And Its Footmen In The CIA, KGB, U.N., Vatican, NASA, IRS, AT&T, Federal Reserve, Disney, The Order Of Skull & Bones, And The Rosicrucians*, is "coming along fine" and should be completed by fall of this year.

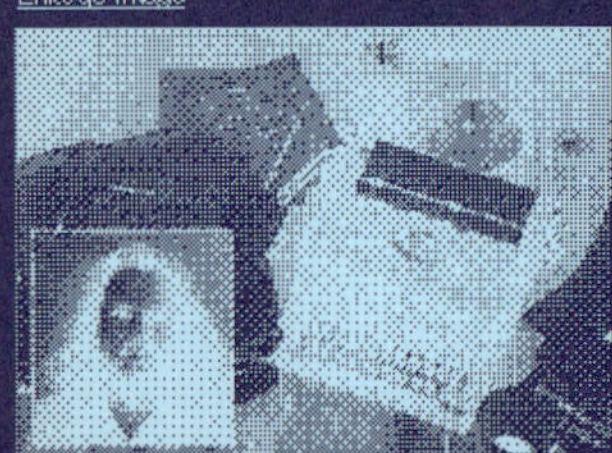
Enlarge Image

"So far, so good," the unemployed, one-time University of Washington physics graduate student said. "Right now, I've got about 14,600 pretty solid pages in the can, with probably fewer than 5,000 to go. Once that's done, it'll just be a matter of double-checking the facts, tightening up the writing and making sure the whole thing's got a nice, cohesive flow."

Though reluctant to reveal details about







---



multinational corporations to brainwash and enslave all of humanity through the use of top-secret artificial-intelligence and aerospace technology.

"There's some very good stuff in there. Honestly, I'm really pleased with the way it's turning out," Hausch, 39, said. "I'm not saying it's the best manifesto that's ever been written, but I do think I have reason to be proud."

Despite his excitement, Hausch said he has yet to let anyone see the work.

"I know it would be helpful to have someone else read it, just to get a fresh perspective, but I'm really bashful about letting people see stuff I'm working on before it's 100 percent finished," Hausch said. "Plus, I don't want to run the risk of showing it to someone who turns out to be one of the Illuminati's countless servile minions."

Once the manifesto is completed, Hausch said he plans to shop it around to various magazines and newspapers. Among the periodicals he plans to contact are *IlluminatiWatch Weekly*, *The Superpatriot Mimeographed Newsletter* and *The New York Times*.

"I think there will definitely be some interest, hopefully from more than one publication," Hausch said. "Of course, in publishing, it's all about who you know. And while I unfortunately don't have any contacts at *The Washington Post*, I used to be in the same militia as one of the editors of *The Posse Comitatus Bee*, so that's a pretty good connection. I'll definitely make sure to send him a galley copy when the time comes."

Hausch said he has already taken steps to ensure the manifesto's safety when it is sent to publishers.

Enlarge Image

"Obviously, by sending my manifesto under the auspices of the U.S. Postal Service, I run the very real risk of having it intercepted or tampered with by federal agents," Hausch said. "That's why I've equipped it with a special numerological code involving the second letter of the third word of every sentence. Should someone acquire a manifesto without this code, it is surely a false, government-altered version."

Hausch began writing the manifesto in 1992 and worked intermittently on it until October 1998, when he put it down to focus on constructing a special aluminum-foil-lined helmet that would enable him to think more clearly and better concentrate on his ambitious work.

"Primitive as it may seem, this hat has jammed a lot of the negative electromagnetic frequencies beamed down by the orbiting satellites developed by a joint NASA/ODESSA collaboration from Gestapo

# MO/RE/ RE/AL?

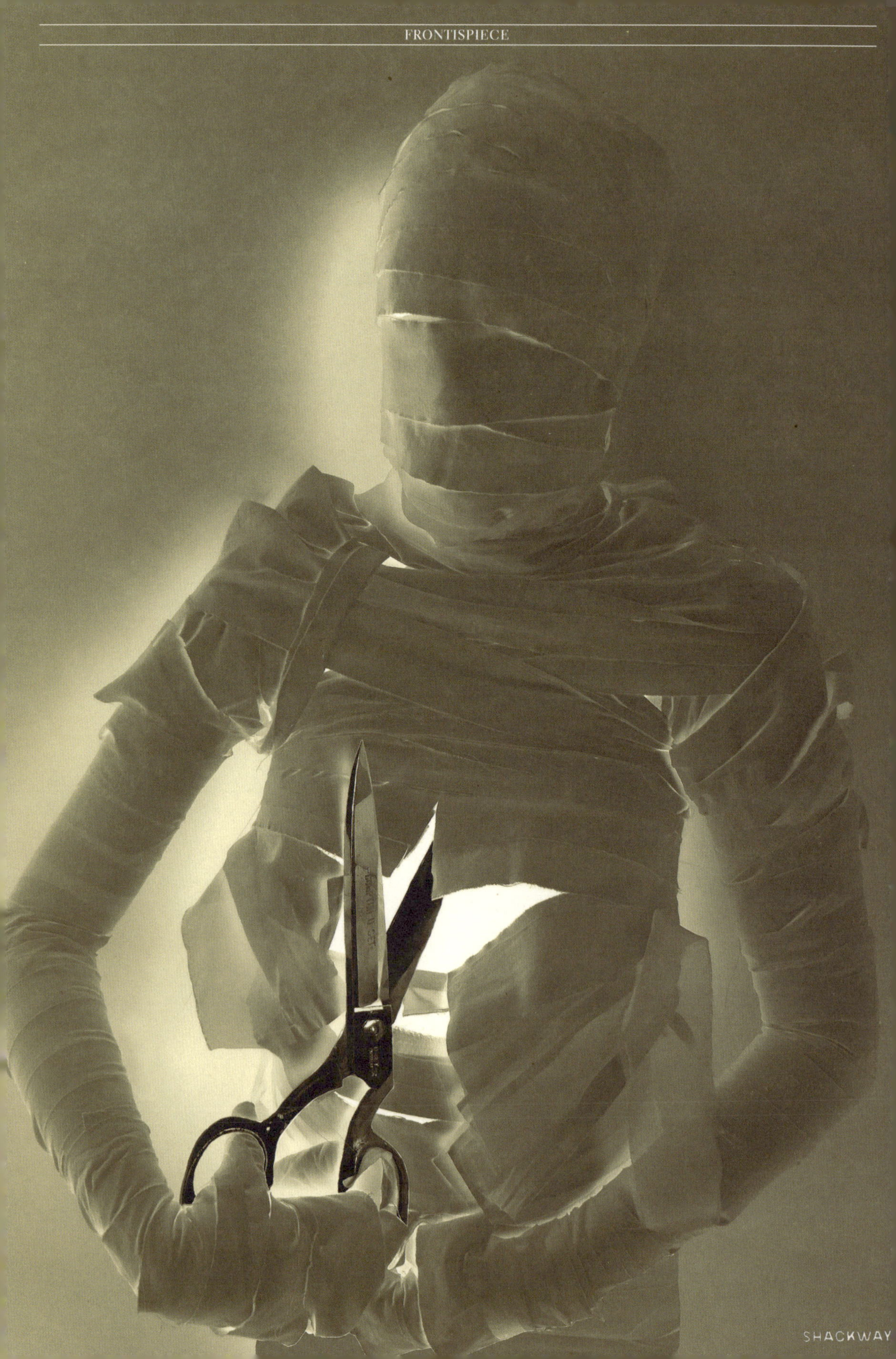
SHACKWAY

# MO/RE/ RE/AL?

## ART IN THE AGE OF TRUTHINESS

**Elizabeth Armstrong**

With essays by
D. Graham Burnett
Tom Gunning
Norman M. Klein
Carrie Lambert-Beatty
Mark Levy
Glenn D. Lowry

Minneapolis Institute of Arts
DelMonico Books · Prestel
Munich   London   New York

This book is published in conjunction with the exhibition *More Real? Art in the Age of Truthiness*, organized by the Minneapolis Institute of Arts in collaboration with SITE Santa Fe.

Itinerary

SITE Santa Fe
Santa Fe, New Mexico
July 8, 2012–January 6, 2013

Minneapolis Institute of Arts
Minneapolis, Minnesota
March 3–June 9, 2013

Generous support for this book and exhibition was provided by the Andy Warhol Foundation for the Visual Arts. Additional support was provided by the MIA's Contemporary Art Affinity Group; Rosina Lee Yue and Bert A. Lies Jr., MD; and Etant donnés: The French-American Fund for Contemporary Art.

Published in 2012 by the Minneapolis Institute of Arts and DelMonico Books, an imprint of Prestel

Minneapolis Institute of Arts
2400 Third Avenue South
Minneapolis, Minnesota 55404
www.artsmia.org

Prestel, a member of Verlagsgruppe Random House GmbH
Prestel Verlag, Neumarkter Strasse 28, 81673 Munich, Germany, Tel: 49 89 4136 0, Fax: 49 89 4136 2335, www.prestel.de

Prestel Publishing Ltd., 4 Bloomsbury Place, London WC1A 2QA, United Kingdom, Tel: 44 20 7323 5004, Fax: 44 20 7636 8004

Prestel Publishing, 900 Broadway, Suite 603, New York, NY 10003, Tel: 212 995 2720, Fax: 212 995 2733, e-mail: sales@prestel-usa.com, www.prestel.com



Library of Congress Cataloging-in-Publication Data

Armstrong, Elizabeth, 1952-
  More real? : art in the age of truthiness / Elizabeth Armstrong ; with essays by D. Graham Burnett, Tom Gunning, Norman M. Klein, Carrie Lambert-Beatty, Mark Levy, Glenn D. Lowry.
      pages cm
  This book is published in conjunction with the exhibition More Real? Art in the Age of Truthiness, organized by the Minneapolis Institute of Arts in collaboration with SITE Santa Fe.
  Includes bibliographical references and index.
  ISBN 978-3-7913-5235-0 (hardcover : alk. paper)
  1.  Reality in art--Exhibitions. 2.  Art, Modern--21st century--Exhibitions. I. Gunning, Tom, 1949- II. Klein, Norman M., 1945- III. Lambert-Beatty, Carrie. IV. Levy, Mark. V. Lowry, Glenn D. VI. Minneapolis Institute of Arts. VII. Site Santa Fe (Gallery) VIII. Title.
  N8237.8.R435A76 2012
  709.05'1074776579--dc23

                    2012018419

ISBN 978-3-7913-5235-0

Editor: Karen Jacobson
Designers: Michael Worthington & Ania Diakoff
      at Counterspace, Los Angeles
Proofreader: Dianne Woo
Indexer: Candace Hyatt
Printed in Hong Kong by Paramount

Front cover: Seung Woo Back, *RW01-001*, 2004 (detail), from the series Real World I, 2004–6; digital print; 50 x 66 ½ inches (127 x 168.9 cm); courtesy the artist and Gana Art Gallery, Seoul

Back cover: *Lunch Break Installation, "Duane Hanson: Sculptures of Life," 14 December 2002–23 February 2003, Scottish National Gallery of Modern Art*, 2003 (detail); chromogenic print; 72 x 121 inches (182.9 x 307.3 cm); Broad Art Foundation

Frontispiece: David Sollie, *The Girl Next Door*, 2011–12; mixed mediums on canvas; 49 x 38 ½ inches (124.5 x 97.8 cm); courtesy Todd Bockley Gallery, Minneapolis

## Contents

Traditionally art has been concerned not with reality itself but with images and interpretations of reality. What we may mean by reality is of course relative and in flux across time periods and cultures. Today media that are thought of as reproducing reality faithfully, such as photography and film, are often used in ways that undermine that faith.

The unstable relationship between fact and fiction in the twenty-first century has been of keen interest to Elizabeth Armstrong, the museum's curator of contemporary art. Intrigued by how quickly once theoretical notions of hyperreality and simulation were becoming everyday realities, she was compelled by the work of artists around the world who were exploring these deep shifts. At the same time she noted that we live in an "age of truthiness," in which fabricated information, without regard to fact or logic, was becoming increasingly accepted as true. The very real impact of this growing slippage between fact and fiction is at the heart of this exhibition and book.

My engagement with this project began in the fall of 2010 on the beautiful campus of the Sterling and Francine Clark Art Institute in Williamstown, Massachusetts. A Clark-Mellon Colloquium dedicated to this exhibition enabled Liz to bring together a group of creative thinkers vitally interested in these questions of shifting realities and "truthiness." Scholars, critics, and artists alike were asked to address three overriding questions: How do we define what is actually "real," especially in a world in which a multitude of media can radically shape the original experience being depicted? What are the factors at play in this shifting reality? And how do artists critically engage with this condition? During two days of wide-ranging presentations and discussions, it became clear that these questions were fundamentally interconnected with a cultural implosion in the relationship between the real and the imaginary. In this hyperreal climate, some argued, images and simulations of reality can be more convincing than the real thing. The connection between shifting realities and unprecedented technological change and advancements was also a central topic of conversation.

In pursuit of such timely inquiries, this exhibition and book bring together an international group of artists and writers whose work reflects current considerations of new contingencies of reality. In their art and their texts, they draw on traditional methods and emerging media to explore our understanding of what is—and what can be—real. At a time when the Minneapolis Institute of Arts (MIA) is expanding its programming to examine major developments in contemporary art, this exhibition and book mark an ambitious step forward. Surveying the field at a global level, they provide a challenging exploration of both new cultural ideas in art history and critical connections between art and society.

Liz Armstrong joined the MIA as our first curator of contemporary art in 2008. Her impact—as evidenced by projects such as *More Real? Art in the Age of Truthiness*—has been immediate and significant. The museum's collections span five thousand years of human history across the globe, and Liz has helped to further animate our collections and programming by infusing contemporary practice throughout the institution. She brings her expansive knowledge, intense curiosity, and lively humor to every project that she undertakes, and *More Real?* is no exception.

The museum is appreciative of the many supporters who have enthusiastically stepped forward to fund this important publication and the exhibition that it accompanies. The Andy Warhol Foundation for the Visual Arts provided critical seed money to develop the exhibition's conceptual framework as well as support for the implementation of the project.

Additional support was provided by the MIA's Contemporary Art Affinity Group and Etant donnés: The French-American Fund for Contemporary Art. Finally, we are grateful to Irene Hofmann, Phillips Director and Chief Curator, SITE Santa Fe, for joining us as our partner and crucial collaborator on this exciting presentation.

Kaywin Feldman
Director and President
Minneapolis Institute of Arts

Along a nondescript stretch of strip malls at the edge of Culver City, California, resides the Museum of Jurassic Technology. If you are not watching out for the unassuming storefront entrance of this now twenty-five-year-old institution, you may miss it. But once inside, you will find a modern-day *Wunderkammer* that provokes astonishment in all who come to visit. The vision of its founder, creator, and director, David Wilson, the Museum of Jurassic Technology is a repository of bizarre and extraordinary objects, relics, oddities, and dramatic exhibits of science and technology dedicated, as its mission declares, "to the advancement of knowledge and the public appreciation of the Lower Jurassic." There is a horn that grew out of the head of Mary Davis of Saughall in the seventeenth century, an installation of a scale model of Noah's Ark, and an exhibit that describes a species of bat that can fly through walls. Is any of this true? Maybe, maybe not, but there is plenty about the museum that feels "truthy," and that might be enough to allow us to believe.

It is this increasingly precarious place between truth and lie, fact and fiction, the real and the unreal that *More Real? Art in the Age of Truthiness* explores through the works of twenty-eight contemporary artists. The inspired vision of the Minneapolis Institute of Art's curator of contemporary art, Elizabeth Armstrong, this timely, thought-provoking, and richly layered exhibition speaks to our complex contemporary moment, when truth is ever more difficult to recognize and the real is often mediated and unreliable.

This exhibition was realized through a bold partnership between SITE Santa Fe and the Minneapolis Institute of Arts. Uniting the MIA—known for its collections spanning five thousand years and representing diverse cultures across all continents—with SITE Santa Fe's experimental contemporary art program has infused each of our museums with new perspectives and has allowed us to realize fully Liz Armstrong's vision. This project combines SITE's contemporary art platform and history of working with living artists with the MIA's institutional history, scholarship, infrastructure, and commitment to presenting contemporary art within an encyclopedic museum. I am deeply grateful to Liz for opening a dialogue with me about her early plans for *More Real?* and for proposing a vision of what this show might be and the impact that it might have if our two institutions teamed up. I also thank Kaywin Feldman, director of the Minneapolis Institute of Arts, for wholeheartedly agreeing to participate in this large-scale collaboration.

Ambitious and complex exhibitions like this are possible only when generous supporters share our enthusiasm and talented staff are dedicated to our vision. To all at SITE who supported *More Real?* and assisted with the many aspects of this project, I am very grateful. I am particularly indebted to the members of SITE's Board of Directors, who recognized the importance of *More Real?* early on and have championed this project all along. Following the early leadership support pledged by SITE's board, especially that of Marlene Meyerson and Andrew Wallerstein, many others stepped up to show their support, including the dedicated members of SITE's Foundation Council. Helping us to realize this beautiful catalogue were Rosina Lee Yue and Bert A. Lies Jr., MD.

My final appreciation goes to the artists who participated in *More Real?* Working with the show's talented and inspiring curator, Liz Armstrong, they have brought us remarkable works and an exhibition that expresses the exceptional creativity of artistic production today while underscoring some of the profound shifts occurring in contemporary culture.

Irene Hofmann
Phillips Director and Chief Curator
SITE Santa Fe

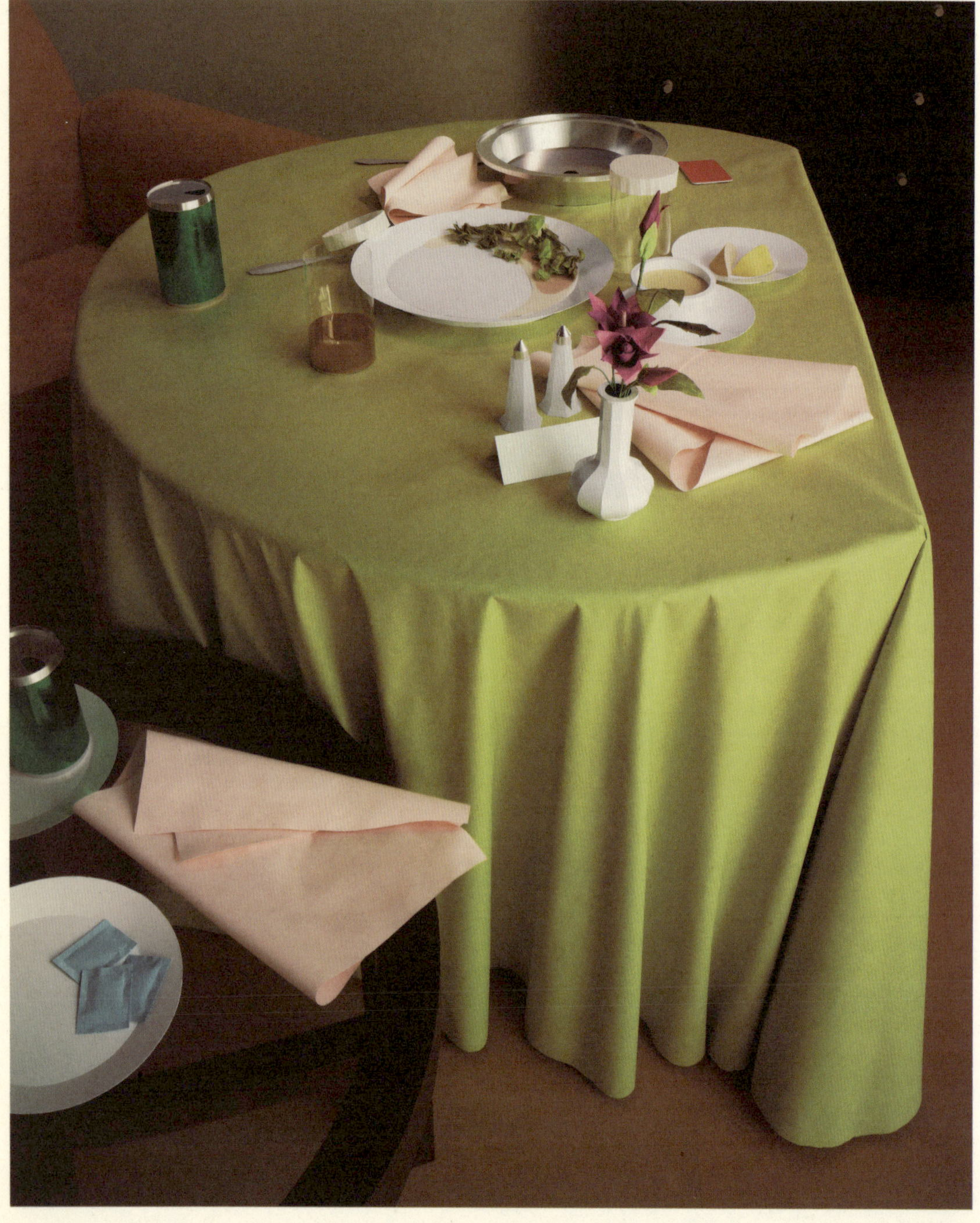

As viewers of *The Colbert Report* know, we are living in an age of "truthiness," an era in which things that we wish to be true are often more appealing than those that are known to be true. It seems that the relationship between truth and fiction has never been murkier. Any number of new books on the subject have been published—with titles like *The Lifespan of a Fact, Reality Hunger,* and *The Post-Truth Era*—joining a slew of articles, videos, and website postings announcing true hoaxes, fake documentaries, and post-truthiness. A website known as Snopes.com is devoted solely to investigating the reliability of stories and postings of questionable veracity.

An international contingent of contemporary artists has also been focusing on this modern conundrum. Using everything from trompe l'oeil to digital manipulation, their work navigates our shifting experience and understanding of reality. Committed to exploring this idea in a major exhibition and publication, I brought this project to Kaywin Feldman, director of the Minneapolis Institute of Arts, who enthusiastically agreed to support its development. Given that the museum had embarked on a contemporary art program only in 2008, embracing such a project was a dramatic move. A museum known for its work with old masters would be inviting a group of young artists from around the world to show works that challenge assumptions, question beliefs, and stir emotions. I am greatly appreciative of Kaywin's belief in the significance of this endeavor, and I thank the MIA Board of Directors for its embrace of ambitious contemporary programming at the museum.

An exhibition of this scale and complexity requires the support of an inspired institutional partner, and I am grateful to Irene Hofmann, Phillips Director and Chief Curator at SITE Santa Fe, for joining us in this undertaking. With its acclaimed exhibition history, its experience working with international artists, and its record of innovative commissions, SITE Santa Fe offered the MIA a unique and invaluable collaborator. Irene and her staff brought their enthusiasm, expertise, and interest to the project, greatly enriching it in every way.

In fall 2010 a group of artists, scholars, and other creative thinkers who have been pursuing these questions in their work met for two days at the Sterling and Francine Clark Art Institute in Williamstown, Massachusetts. This essential gathering of minds could not have taken place without the support of a Warhol Foundation Curatorial Fellowship and of the Clark Art Institute, which hosted the Clark-Mellon Colloquium. Led by Natasha Becker and Michael Ann Holly of the Clark, we were joined by Kaywin Feldman and Alex Bortolot of the MIA, along with John Gerrard, Tom Gunning, Mark Hansen, Bill Horrigan, Bruce Jenkins, Norman M. Klein, Carrie Lambert-Beatty, Iñigo Manglano-Ovalle, and Shuddhabrata Sengupta.

These discussions were critical to establishing the conceptual framework for the project and vital to the development of the editorial content of this publication. Several of the participants also contributed essays to the book—Tom Gunning, Norman M. Klein, and Carrie Lambert-Beatty—and I am thankful for their contributions as well as those of D. Graham Burnett, Mark Levy, and Glenn D. Lowry. The scholarly and enlivening essays in this volume approach the concept of reality from a wide variety of perspectives, including science and technology, the role of the cinema, the "parafictional" in art, diasporic artists from the Middle East, and historical trends from the age of reason to the present.

The contributions of the book designer and editor are always important, but in this case the input from Michael Worthington, designer, and Karen Jacobson, editor, was absolutely vital to the conceptual development of this publication. From the beginning, their engagement with the book's core ideas kept the project in a state of appropriately dynamic flux. Michael, assisted by Ania Diakoff, offered his own take on the "more real," creating a book whose design playfully responds to and expands upon the ideas explored in these pages. Karen constantly pushed me and the other authors to refine our ideas while also contributing related references that enriched the book. Likewise, independent curator Joan Rothfuss oversaw the entries on the artists in the exhibition, writing many of them and working with the other contributors to sharpen and shape their texts. I am deeply grateful to her as well as to Christopher Atkins and Nicole Soukup at the MIA and to Janet Dees and Irene Hofmann at SITE Santa Fe for their excellent contributions to this book.

I would also like to thank the countless colleagues and friends who championed this project from the outset and shared their ideas and suggestions along the way. One of my most important partners has been Steve Dietz, founder and artistic director of Northern Lights.mn, whose deep knowledge of artists working with new media and digital technologies broadened the exhibition's scope to include the evolving realms of augmented reality—from Second Life to 3-D gaming technologies. His contributions to the project as a consulting curator were indispensable, and I cannot thank him enough for his guidance and collaboration. I am also grateful to the many friends whose belief in the project fueled its development in significant ways. David Francis and JoAnn Verburg constantly challenged me to define the terms of the exhibition, gently but persistently asking the most important and probing questions (to which there are not necessarily answers). Likewise, I was lucky to have many others share their interests and insights, including Shelli Ainsworth, Marcia Appel, Doug Argue, Siah and Barbara Armajani, Terry Barczak, Matthew Beron, Jessica Bradley, Julie Corty, Sage Cowles, Ned Foster, Nor Hall, Jennifer Luce, Stewart McBride, John Messner, David Reed, Gary Smaby, Susan Smoluchowski, Laura Tiffany, and Penny Winton. My two daughters, Olivia and Phoebe Boone, generously gave me the time to work on the project while offering many additional insights from the perspective of the millennial generation, for which I will forever be appreciative.

Numerous colleagues also provided ideas, research leads, and other critical input. I wish to acknowledge their contributions and extend my appreciation for their support. They include Glenn Adamson, Marcus Allen, Jane Blocker, Elisabeth Brandt, Julia Bryan-Wilson, Charlotte Cotton, Shepard Fairey, Sascha Freudenheim, Robert Goff, Jan-Lodewijk Grootaers, Melissa Rose Heer, Susan Jacobsen, Eungie Joo, Stephanie Kays, David Little, Helen Molesworth, Traci Ollinger, J. J. Park, Stephanie Smith, Hoon Song, Ali Subotnick, Jordan Thompson, Richard Torchia, Laura Wertheim, and Victor Zamudio-Taylor.

Others who provided critical assistance to the project include E-Shyh and Jennifer Ng, Ai Weiwei Studio; Claudia Altman-Siegel, Altman Siegel Gallery, San Francisco; Taliesin Thomas, AW Asia, New York; Joanne Heyler and Vicki Gambill, Broad Art Foundation, Los Angeles; Astria Suparak, Carnegie Mellon University, Pittsburgh; Casey Kaplan and Loring Randolph, Casey Kaplan Gallery, New York; Cheryl Haines, Cheryl Haines Gallery, San Francisco; Valerie Altahawi, Christine Tierney Fine Art, New York; Amy Cole, James Kailor, Matthew Mahoney, and Kateri Palen, *The Colbert Report* and Comedy Central, New York; EMIT (Era Morel Institute of Truthiness); Elizabeth Jane Cole, Evil Twin Booking, New York; Bong Lee, Jang-Eun Lee, and Najung Kim, Gana Art, Seoul, South Korea; Solene Guiller, GB Agency, Paris; Kerry Inman, Inman Gallery, Houston; Nicholas Wylie, Iñigo Manglano-Ovalle studio, Chicago; Steven Evans and Kelly O'Connor, Linda Pace Foundation, San Antonio, Texas; Marian Goodman, Rose Lord, and Leslie Nolen, Marian Goodman Gallery, New York; Jacqueline Tran and Adrian Rosenfeld, Matthew Marks Gallery, New York and Los Angeles; Manuela Mozo, Metro Pictures, New York; Courtney Strimple, Mixed Greens, New York; Janice Guy and Jacob King, Murray Guy, New York; Kathryn Kanjo and Cameron Yahr, Museum of Contemporary Art, San Diego; David Wilson and Alexis Hyman, Museum of Jurassic Technology, Los Angeles; René de Guzman, Oakland Museum of California; Anthony Allen, Joelle Te Paske, and Lia Lowenthal, Paula Cooper Gallery, New York; Edward Kanerva, The Power Plant, Toronto; Catherine Mahoney, Rufus Corporation, Brooklyn; Sandra Phillips, Gary Garrels, Rudolf Frieling, and Tanya Zimbardo, San Francisco Museum of Modern Art; Sean Kelly, Cecile Panzieri, Debra Villen, Maureen Bray, and Sara Griffin, Sean Kelly Gallery, New York; Meg Malloy, Sikkema Jenkins & Co., New York; Paula Naughton and Simon Preston, Simon Preston Gallery, New York; Tanya Bonakdar and Renee Coppola, Tanya Bonakdar Gallery, New York; Barbara Economom, Jill Vuchetich, and Loren Smith, Walker Art Center, Minneapolis; Severine Waelchli, Yvon Lambert Gallery, Paris; and Julie Du Rouck, zap-o-matik, Brussels.

Many of those listed above also lent art to the exhibition, and I thank them and the other generous lenders who were willing to part with key works from their collections: Jeanne and Michael Klein, Stanley and Nancy Singer, Barry Sloane, and Larry Warsh.

I am deeply appreciative of the MIA's Contemporary Art Affinity Group for its support of the exhibition. Its enthusiastic belief in the MIA's new initiative in contemporary art has helped make this exhibition possible.

A contemporary art exhibition of this scale would present a challenge for any institution, and I am extremely appreciative of the flexibility, resilience, and patience of my many coworkers at the MIA who helped realize the exhibition and book. I am especially indebted to Rayna Olson and Nicole Soukup, who assisted with the administration of the exhibition, attending to myriad details, including loan requests, reproduction rights, checklists, and many other essential elements. Nicole also provided invaluable exhibition support throughout the evolution of the project, from exploratory research to proofreading of the book. Her unflagging support and assistance were crucial to its success. The museum's registrar, Jennifer Starbright, took on the ambitious job of tracking down and shipping artworks from far and wide, many of which had never traveled before or presented new technical challenges. I am greatly appreciative of her experience, steady hand, and aplomb in the face of the unforeseen and the unexpected. Likewise, the museum's registration department and facilities team—under the direction of Brian Kraft and Mike Newman, respectively—were key collaborators on the project. They include Jack Buss, Maggie Davis, Jonathan Hamilton, Shawn Holster, Tom Jance, Mike Judy, Ken Krenz, Shawn McCann, Kurt Nordwall, Leslie Ory Lewellen, Bill Skodje, Al Silberstein, and Brian Stieler. Exhibition designer Roxy Ballard offered her tremendous expertise and experience from the outset to help scale the exhibition to the museum's spaces and give the work full impact. Special thanks to Mike Dust, Douglas Hegley, Jennifer Jurgens, and Ryan Lee for their support of the exhibition's range of new-media projects; to Dan Dennehy, Amanda Hankerson, Josh Lynn, and Charles Walbridge for their invaluable assistance with digital images and photography; to Jessica Zubrzycki for her inspired design of exhibition-related materials; to Jodie Ahern, Julianne Amendola, Mary Jane Drews, Emily Clausman, Ernesto De Quesada, Charisse Gendron, Garnette Kuznia, Annie Lebedoff, Jill Meyer, Mary Mortenson, DiAnne Pappas, Kristin Prestegaard, Diane Richard, Michelle Sanchez, Amanda Stolle, Jamie Van Nostrand, and Kathryn Wade, who provided invaluable development and marketing support; to Tammy Pleshek and Anne-Marie Wagener for their tireless press and public relations efforts; to Laura DeBiaso and Matthew Welch for exhibition guidance and coordination; to members of the Learning and Innovation team, including Alex Bortolot, Deb Hegstrom, Ann Isaacson, Susan Jacobsen, Sheila McGuire, Katherine Milton, Krista Pearson, Amanda Thompson Rundahl, and Stacey Thompson, for their active collaboration; and finally, to all those involved in administrative and accounting guidance and support, including Michele Callahan and Pat Grazzini in the director's office and Tracy Christenson, Kris Davidson, and Ted Hewes in accounting.

In addition to thanking all the staff at the MIA, I want to join Kaywin Feldman in expressing our deep gratitude to our extraordinary colleagues at SITE Santa Fe. In the exhibitions department, Janet Dees, assistant curator, not only contributed thoughtful texts to this book but also kept many vital exhibition details organized, while Sage Sommer, registrar, oversaw the complex logistics for dozens of artworks. David Merrill, SITE's chief preparator, skillfully directed the installation while calmly shepherding even the most complicated of our new artwork commissions. Straddling the line between participating artist, exhibition architect, and curatorial adviser was Los Angeles–based architect Greg Lynn. Assisted by Eric Leishman, Lynn's GLFORM Studio created an extraordinary and wonderfully disorienting entrance and lobby intervention for the exhibition that transformed SITE Santa Fe's building and the visitor experience into one that was *truly* "more real." Helping spread the word about *More Real?* was Anne Wrinkle, director of external affairs; Joanne Lefrak, director of education and outreach; and Juliet Myers, curator of public programs. For their crucial contributions throughout the planning of this project, we thank Cathy Putnam, deputy director; Valerie Ingram, director of development; and Brittny Dayes, manager of visitor engagement. I wish to express my profound gratitude to our respective staffs for pulling together as a team to help realize this project to its fullest potential.

Needless to say, it is the inspired work of the artists involved in this exhibition that is ultimately the heart and soul of the project. They contributed not only as participants and lenders but also as creative catalysts and provocateurs. We are indebted to them for generously sharing their time, their work, and their ideas, which ask us to deliberate on our constantly changing sense of what is real and what is not—and on the consequences of not understanding the difference.

Elizabeth Armstrong
Curator of Contemporary Art
and Director of the Center for
Alternative Museum Practice
(CAMP)
Minneapolis Institute of Arts

To go virtual is the only way to

orget about the real darkness.

# The New





# Nation Sets Its Sights on Building Sane Economy

## True Cost Tax, Salary Caps, Trust-Busting Top List

### By T. VEBLEN

The President has called for swift passage of the Safeguards for a New Economy (S.A.N.E.) bill. The omnibus economic package includes a federal maximum wage, mandatory "True Cost Accounting," a phased withdrawal from complex financial instruments, and other measures intended to improve life for ordinary Americans. (See highlights box on Page A10.) He also repeated earlier calls for passage of the "Ban on Lobbying" bill currently making its way through Congress.

Treasury Secretary Paul Krugman stressed the importance of the bill. "Markets make great servants, terrible leaders, and absurd religions," said Krugman, quoting Paul Hawken, an advocate of corporate responsibility and author of "Blessed Unrest, How the Largest Movement in the World Came into Being and Why No One Saw It Coming."

"At this point, the market is our

leader and our religion. No wonder the median standard of living has been declining so much for so long."

Krugman said that the new Treasury bill seeks to ensure the prosperity of all citizens, rather than simply supporting large corporations and the wealthy. "The market is supposed to serve us. Unfortunately, we have ended up serving the market. That's very bad."

Much as Roosevelt, after the Great Depression, put the brakes on C.E.O. wages and irresponsible banking practices, administration officials claim that today we need to rein in the industry that has caused such chaos and misery.

"The building blocks of post-World War II American middle-class prosperity have all been swept away," said House Speaker Nancy Pelosi, who initially op-

Continued on Page A10

# IRA

## Maximum Wage Law Succeeds

Salary Caps Will Help
Stabilize Economy

# TREASURY ANNOUNCES "TRUE COST"

**Recruiters Train for New Life**
As a ban is imposed on recruiting

# ork Times

**Special Edition**

**Today,** clouds part, more sunshine, recent gloom passes. **Tonight,** strong leftward winds. **Tomorrow,** a new day. Weather map throughout.

Y, JULY 4, 2009

FREE

# Q WAR ENDS

## *Troops to Return Immediately*

**By JUDE SHINBIN**

WASHINGTON — Operation Iraqi Freedom and Operation Enduring Freedom were brought to an unceremonious close today with a quiet announcement by the Department of Defense that troops would be home within weeks.

"This is the best face we can put on the most unfortunate adventure in modern American history," Defense spokesman Kevin Sites said at a special joint session of Congress. "Today, we can finally enjoy peace — not the peace of the brave, perhaps, but at least peace."

As U.S. and coalition troops withdraw from Iraq and Afghanistan, the United Nations will move in to perform peacekeeping duties and aid in rebuilding. The U.N. will be responsible for keeping the two countries stable; coordinating the rebuilding of hospitals, schools, highways, and other infrastructure; and overseeing upcoming elections.

The Department of the Treasury confirmed that all U.N. dues owed by the U.S. were paid as of this morning, and that moneys previously earmarked for the war would

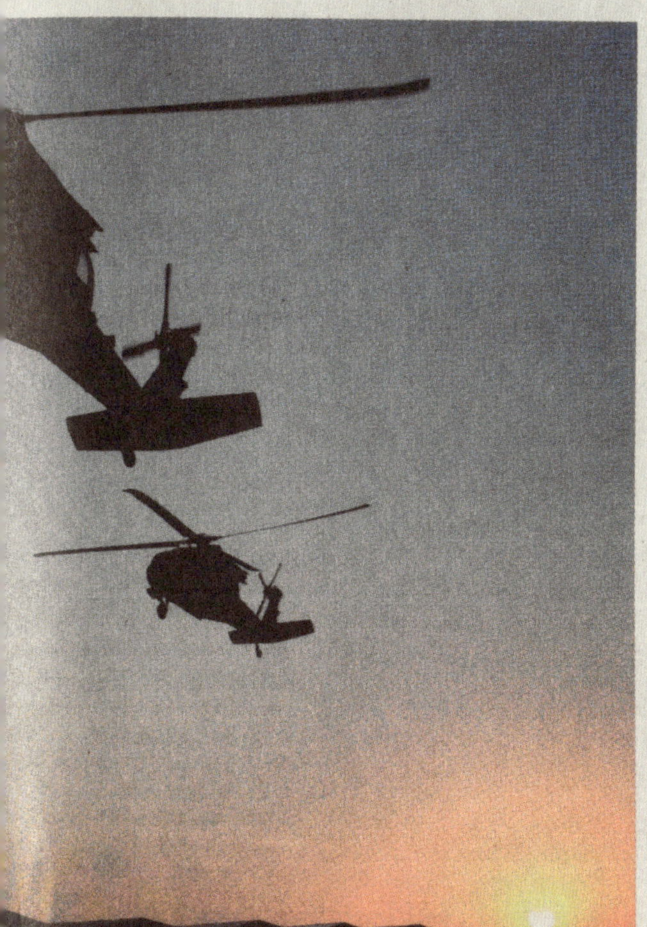

COURTESY ARMY.MIL

ps and equipment from Saddam Hussein's former Baghdad palace.

**A Patriot Act Repealed**

t years later, a shamefaced

## *Ex-Secretary*

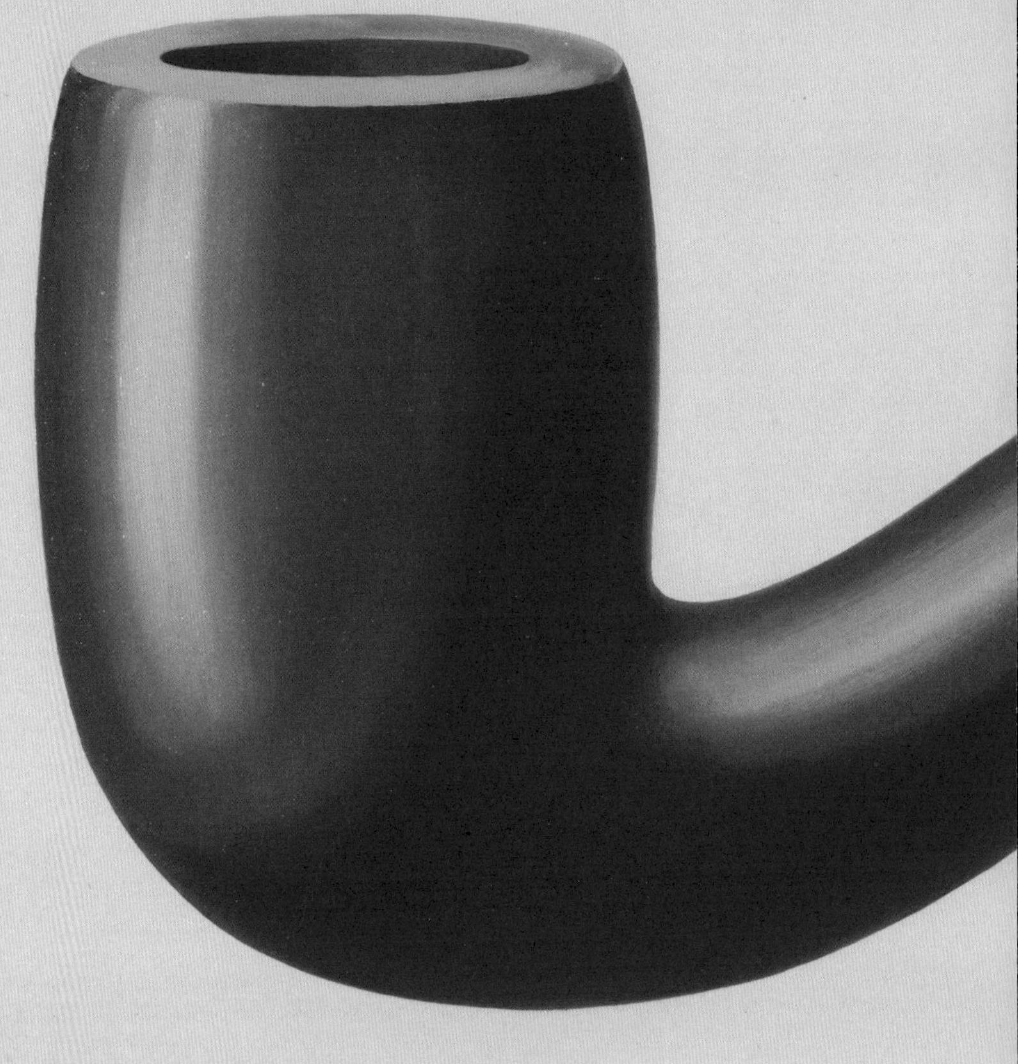
Ceci n'est p

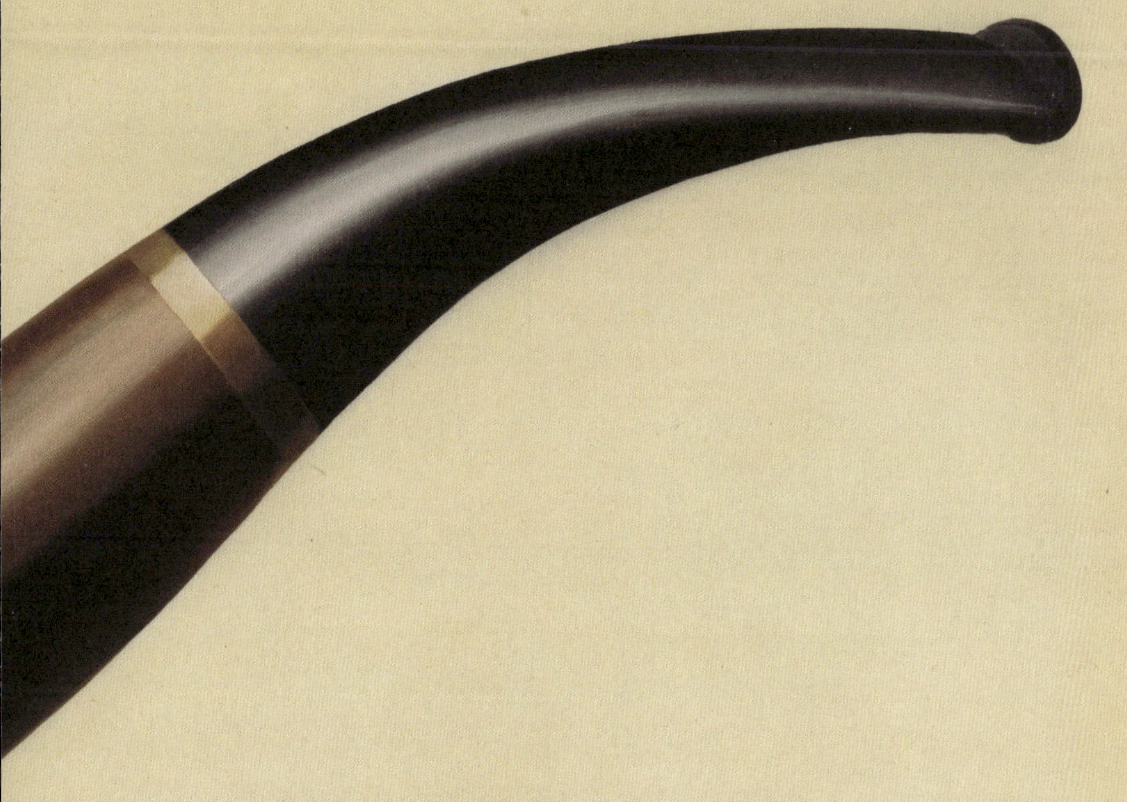
as une pipe.
Magritte

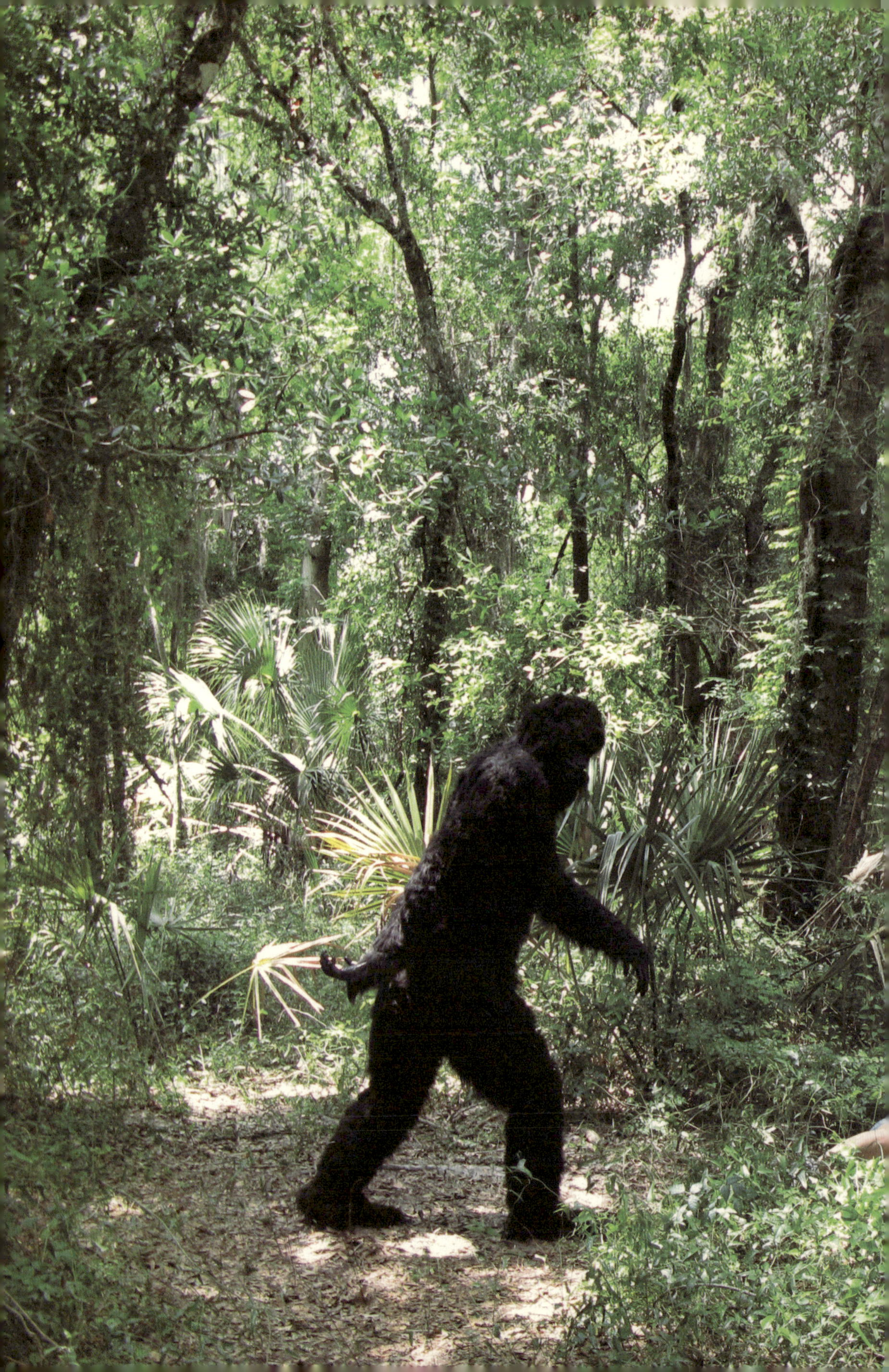

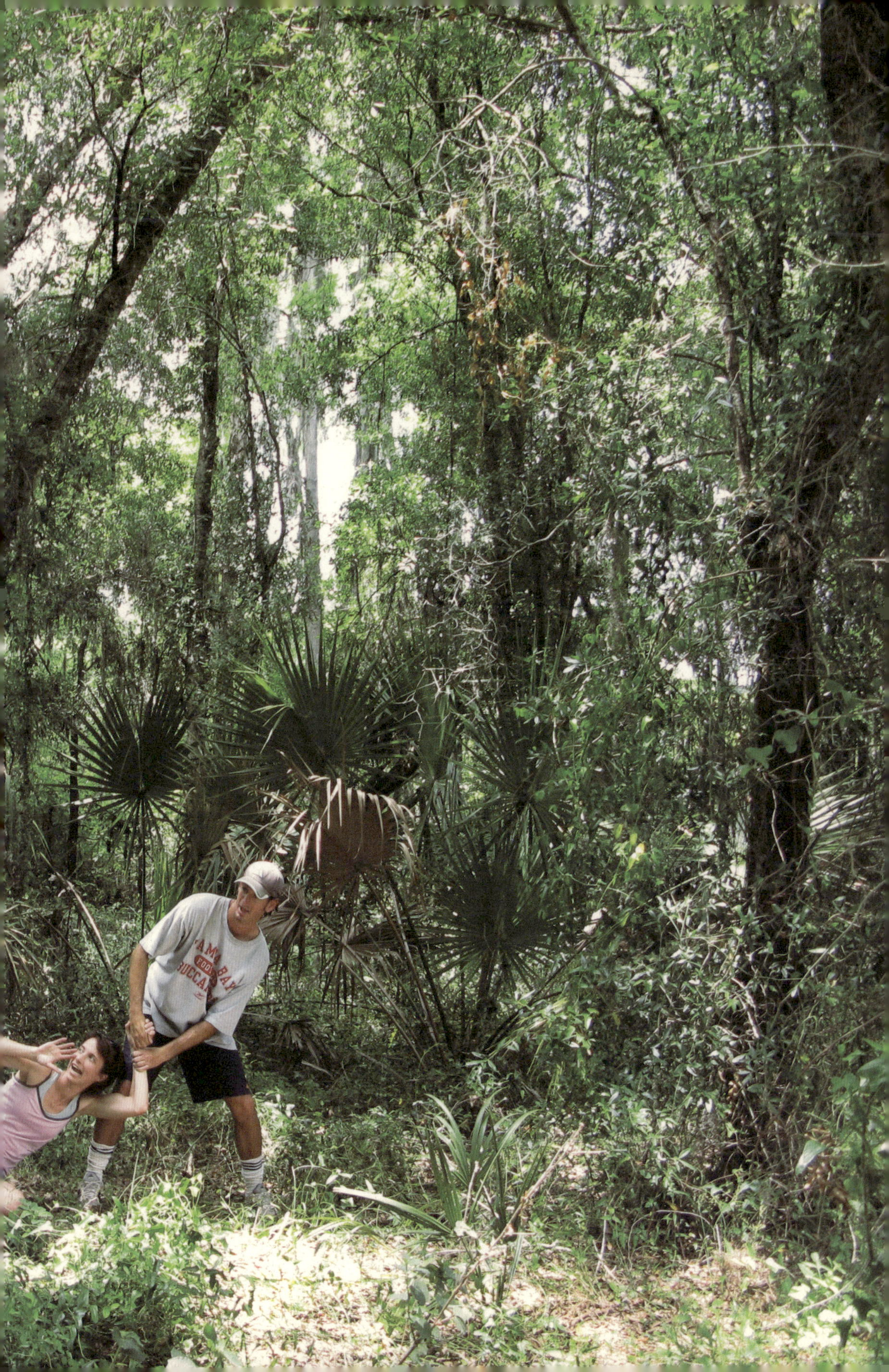

# NEW YORK POST

**Page Six**

MONDAY, SEPT. 21, 2009 / Sunny, 72° / Weather: P. 26 ★ ★ **EARLY CITY SPECIAL** www.nypost-se.com

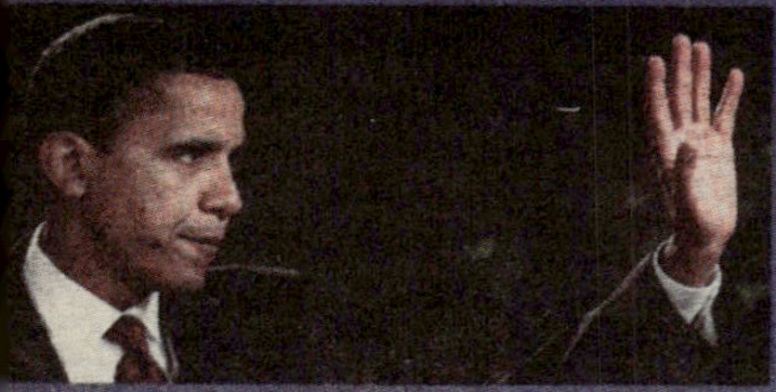

## WORLD LEADERS SLIP ON UN SUMMIT SLOPE

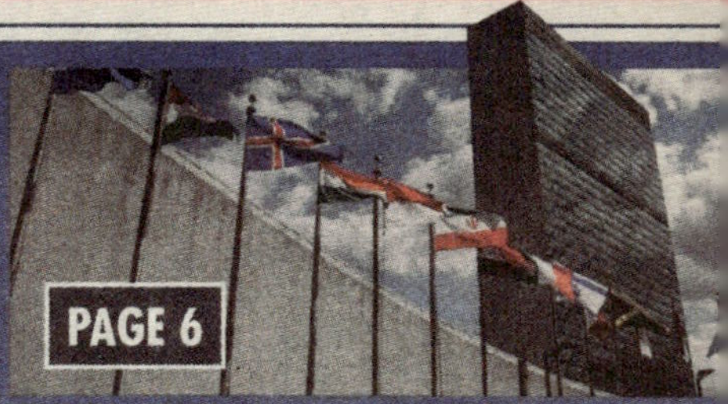

**PAGE 6**

# WE'RE

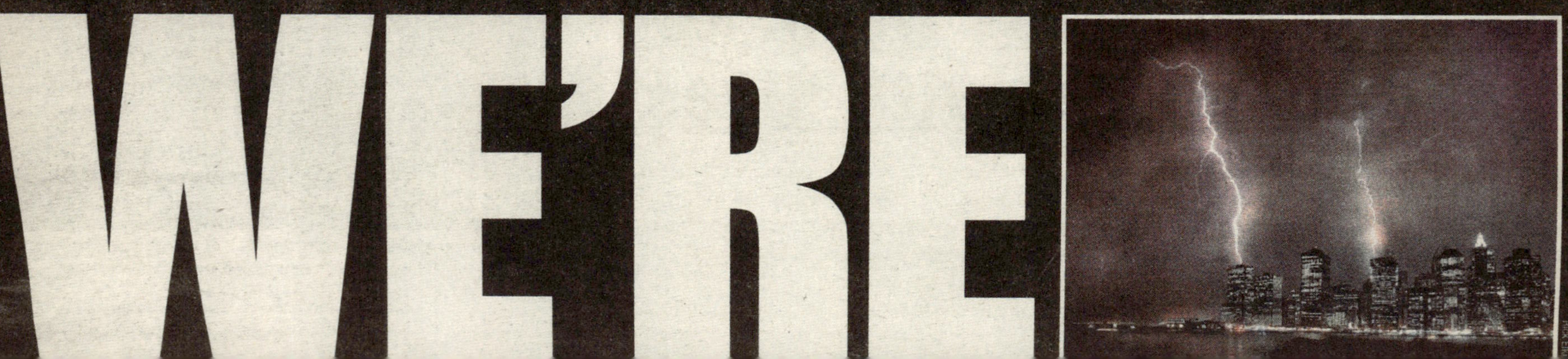

# SCREWED

## What you're not being told: Official City report predicts massive climate catastrophes, public health disasters.

SEE PAGE 3

## NEW YORK FIGHTS BACK!

Over a hundred world leaders will try to tackle climate change tomorrow at the UN. But they seem more interested in tackling each other.

Bad news for the rest of us, you bet. But true to form, New Yorkers are fighting back in all kinds of ways — and we're setting an example for the rest of the country.

*Continues on Page 5*

# ANCIENT LOST CITY FOUND IN CALIFORNIA!

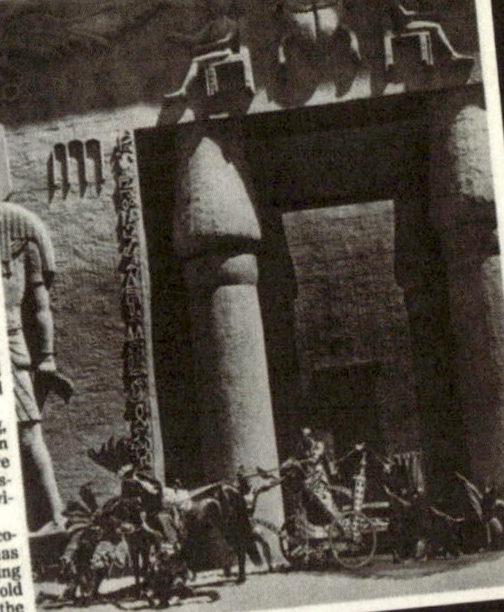

By ROSE GRADY
*Correspondent*

More than a half-century ago, the magnificent "City of the Pharaohs" was buried beneath the shifting sands — not on the barren deserts of Egypt — but on the rolling dunes of Southern California!

The lost city, with its 21 five-ton sphinxes, four towering statues of Rameses the Magnificent and its beautifully carved temples is, in truth, the set built in 1923 by the legendary Cecil B. DeMille for his film classic, *The Ten Commandments.*

Why, when or how he did it remains a mystery to this day, but after the epic film was

## Magnificent set for Bible film was buried after it was shot 68 years ago!

completed, DeMille carried out his elaborate plan.

He secretly had the lavish, 800-foot-wide set buried in the sand dunes of Pismo Beach, on the California coast.

The City of the Pharaohs may have remained beneath the towering dunes for eons had it not been for a hint to its existence in DeMille's autobiography, published after his death in 1959.

"If 1,000 years from now," he wrote, "archeologists happen to dig beneath the sands, I hope they will not rush into print with the amazing news that Egyptian civilization, far from being confined to the Valley of the Nile, extended all the way to North America. The

sphinxes they will find were buried there when we had finished with them and dismantled our huge set of the gates of Pharaoh's city."

Those paragraphs tickled the imagination of cameraman Bruce Cardoza who contacted filmmaker Peter Brosnan, and the search began.

It took months of searching, but finally an old cattleman showed them the site where the set once stood, on the Pismo dunes that DeMille envisioned as Egypt.

Permission to dig in the ecologically protected dunes has been granted and next spring work will begin to lift the old City of the Pharaohs from the sand.

WEEKLY WORLD NEWS (ISSN 6199-5740) Published weekly by Weekly World News, Inc., 600 S. East Coast Ave., Lantana, Fla. 33462. MAIL SUBSCRIPTIONS $34.95 a year in U.S. $44.95 a year outside the U.S. Second Class postage paid at Lake Worth, Fla., and at additional mailing offices in the U.S.A. Canadian Second Class permit #9448 paid at Toronto, Ontario, Canada. POSTMASTER: Send address changes to WEEKLY WORLD NEWS, P.O. Box 11296, Des Moines, Iowa 50340-1296. For subscription address changes and inquiries write Weekly World News, P.O. Box 11296, Des Moines, Iowa 50340-1296. Printed in U.S.A.

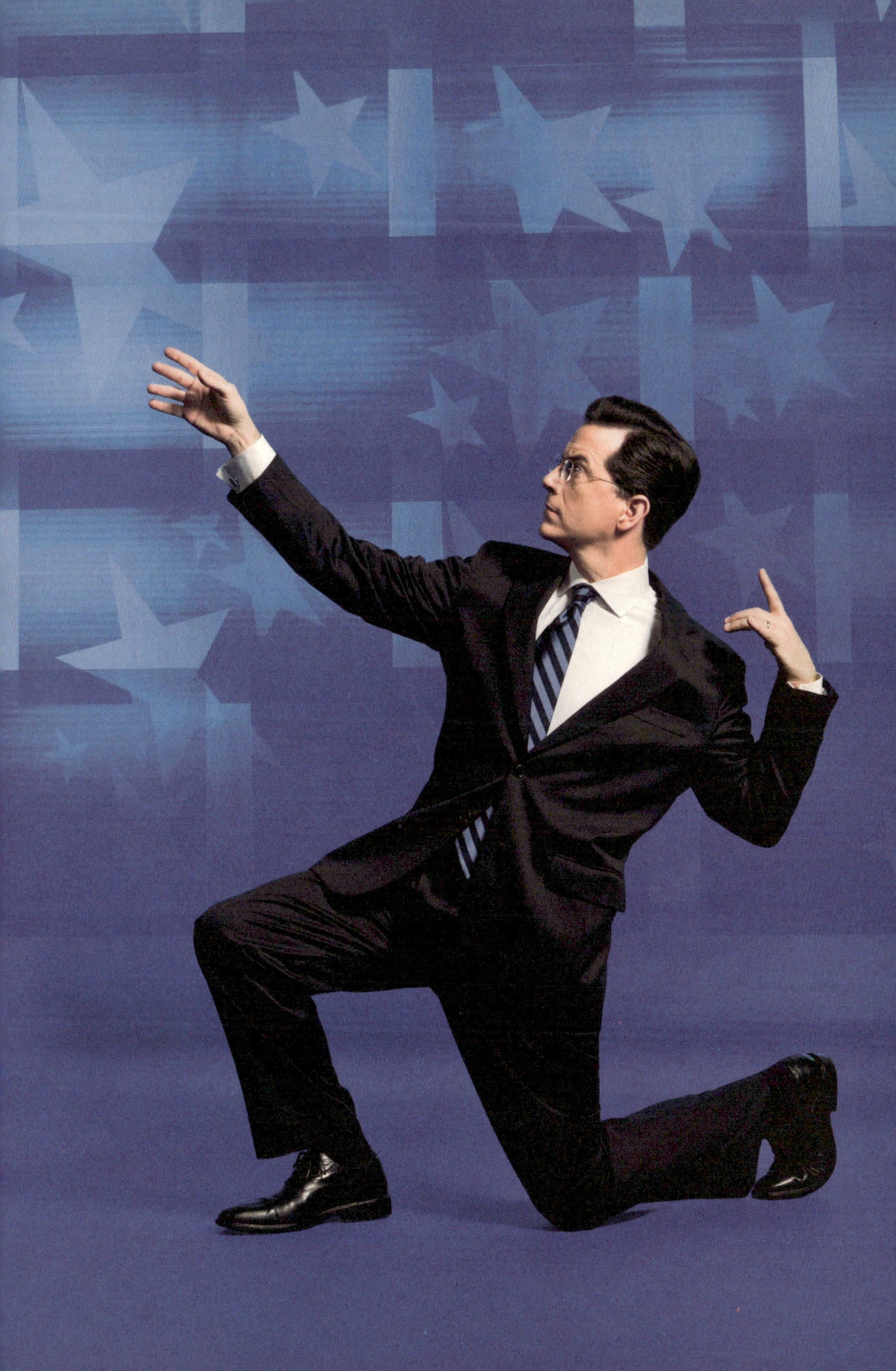

# On the Border of the Real

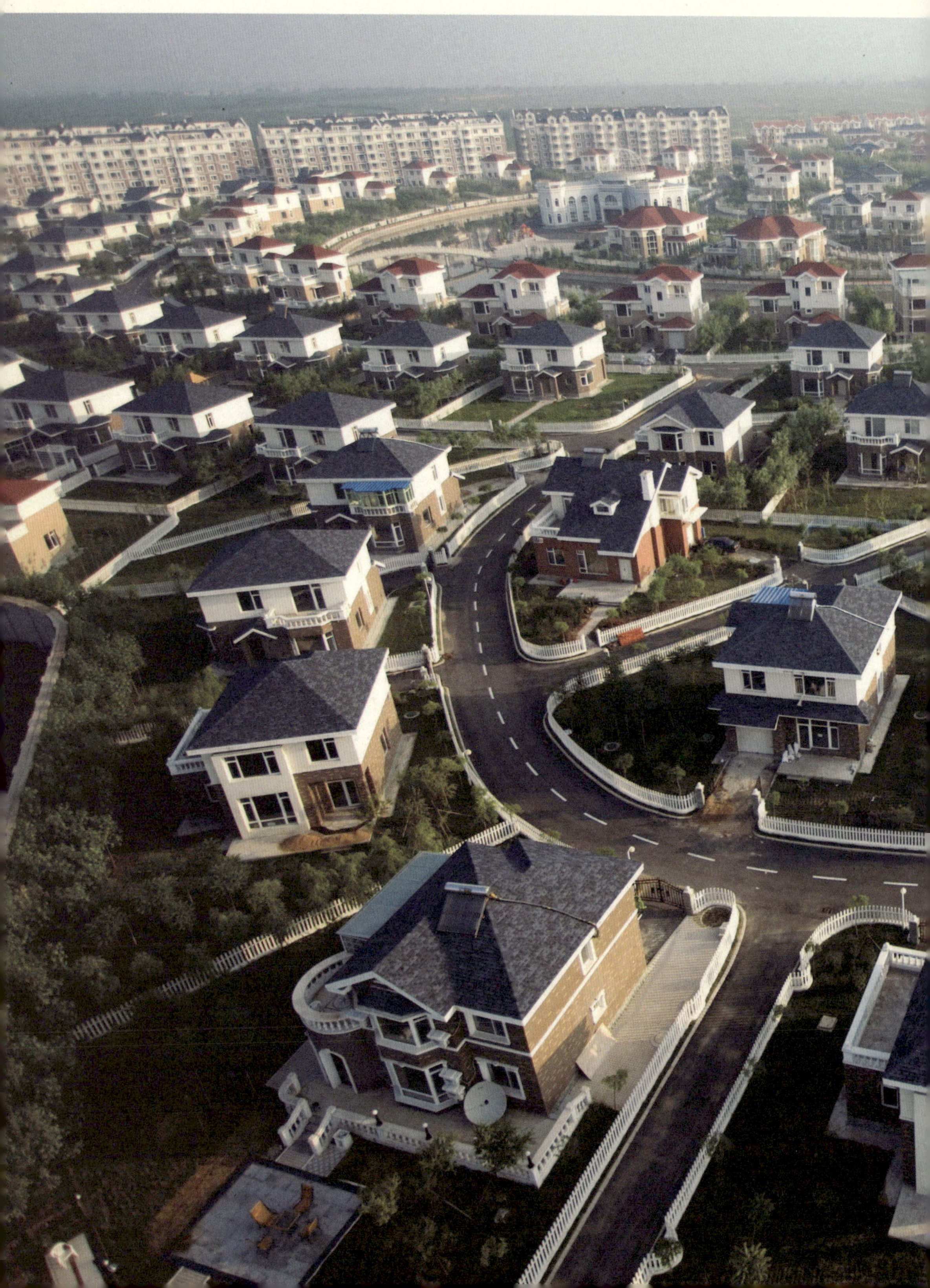

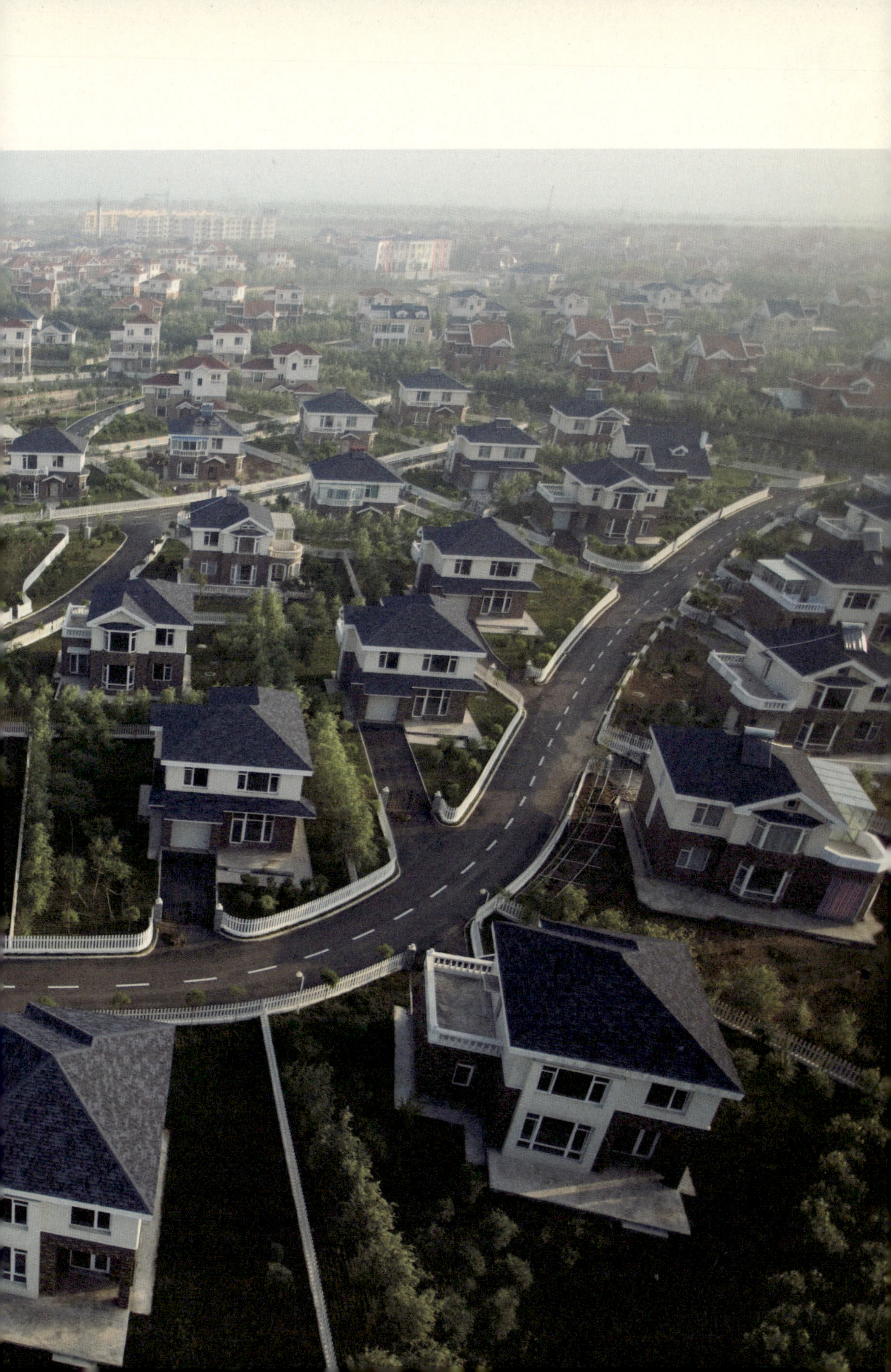

# On the Bor-der of the Real

TEXT BY
*ELIZABETH ARMSTRONG*

---

**MORE REAL?**

---

*Videri quam esse*
(To seem to be, rather than to be).

—Latin inscription over the fake fireplace on the set for *The Colbert Report*

An ancient city with towering statues of pharaohs and sphinxes was rumored to be buried beneath the sand dunes on a windblown stretch of the Santa Barbara coast near Guadalupe, California. In 1983 a small group of researchers led by the archaeologist John Parker embarked on a project to unearth the city and its treasures. Months of digging through the massive dunes finally yielded fragments of hieroglyphs and other artifacts, and the archaeologists were able to piece together evidence of 110-foot-high hieroglyph-covered walls, four three-story statues of Ramses II, and twenty-one sphinxes, each weighing five tons (figs. 1, 2).[1]

The provenance of the statues lined up against the walls of the pharaoh's city was not an ancient civilization but, as it turns out, 1920s Hollywood. For his 1923 epic *The Ten Commandments*, the filmmaker Cecil B. DeMille began work on a production so large and so ambitious that its expenses soon escalated beyond those of any previous film. Beset with cost overruns, DeMille decided not to return the sets to the studio at the end of filming, as mandated in his contract, but to have them dismantled on location and buried in the sand. Sixty years later, a clue in DeMille's autobiography led Peter Brosnan, a screenwriter and documentary filmmaker, to the site of the original epic, along with Parker and the archaeology crew.

This story is not about being tricked or deceived by "fake" Egyptian relics but rather about the fascination that they hold as remnants from an epic film. These are among the only extant remains of a set from the heyday of silent films.[2] These authentic fakes—real props based on historical relics made for the then new medium of film—are reminders of the extent to which movies have shaped our

Epigraph: Charles McGrath, "How Many Stephen Colberts Are There?," *New York Times Magazine*, January 8, 2012, 22.

1. Brian Fagan, "Digging De Mille," in *Snapshots of the Past* (Walnut Creek, CA: AltaMira, 1994), 155–57. See also Scott Simon, "The Fight to Preserve DeMille's 'Lost City,'" *Weekend Edition Saturday*, NPR, February 12, 2005, http://www.npr.org/templates/story/story.php?storyId=4494713.

2. The other known set from the period is the opera house interior from *The Phantom of the Opera* (1925).

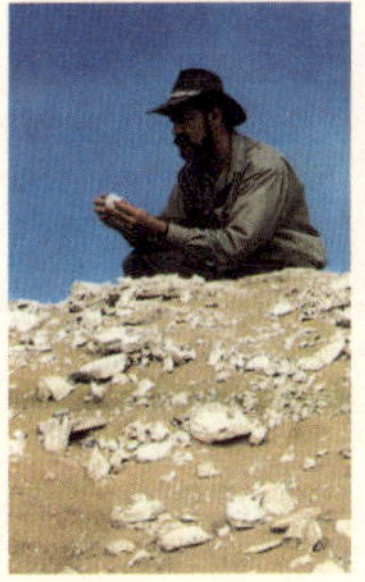

1
John Parker digging for the "lost city" at the Guadalupe Nipomo Dunes Park, California, 1996

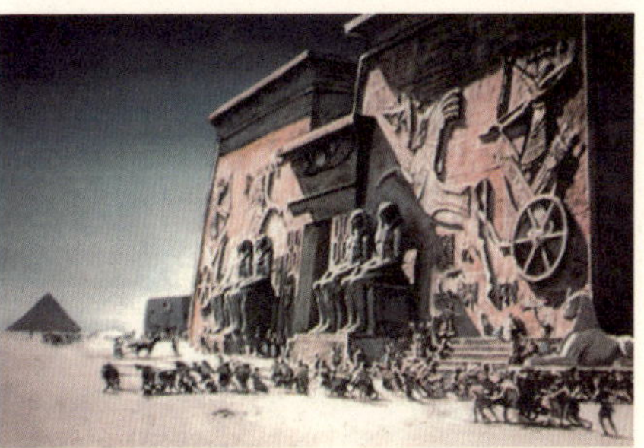

2
Scene from Cecil B. DeMille's *Ten Commandments*, 1923

sense of reality. An artist once told me that early in his career, while studying painting in New York, he felt compelled to leave the city to paint in the desert. One day, on a hike near Monument Valley, he came across a cave that he felt he "knew" intimately, as if he had been there before. Years later, while watching one of his favorite John Ford films, *The Searchers* (1956), he realized that it was this place, or his feeling for this place, that he had been trying to capture in his paintings. His connection to the cave was a dormant memory from a childhood movie. The revelation that the memory of a film had been indelibly etched into his consciousness and associated with deep, essential feelings had a significant impact on the development of his art.[3]

I moved to Southern California in the late 1990s, and like many first-time visitors to the region, I was struck by the prevalence of appropriated architecture—from a neo-Mayan Masonic temple in North Hollywood (fig. 3), to the Riviera-inspired communities of Newport Beach, to the old-fashioned Main Street running through the middle of Disneyland.[4] Living in Orange County, I secretly thrilled at the glimpse of the Alps on my drive north to Los Angeles (in the form of a ride at Disneyland known as Matterhorn Mountain, which is visible from the 5 freeway [fig. 4]). Learning that one of the most exclusive private clubs in Orange County was secretly entered near the popular Pirates of the Caribbean attraction at Disneyland seemed wonderfully ironic and right.

Almost two decades earlier, two of the most important French theorists of the time—Jacques Derrida and Jean Baudrillard— also spent time in the shadow of Disneyland while teaching at the

3. David Reed, conversation with the author, ca. 1999.

4. Jesse Lerner, "A Fevered Dream of Maya: Robert Stacy-Judd," *Cabinet*, no. 4 (2001), http://www .cabinetmagazine.org/ issues/4/lerner.php.

3
North Hollywood Lodge #542, Free & Accepted Masons, built 1949–50, Los Angeles

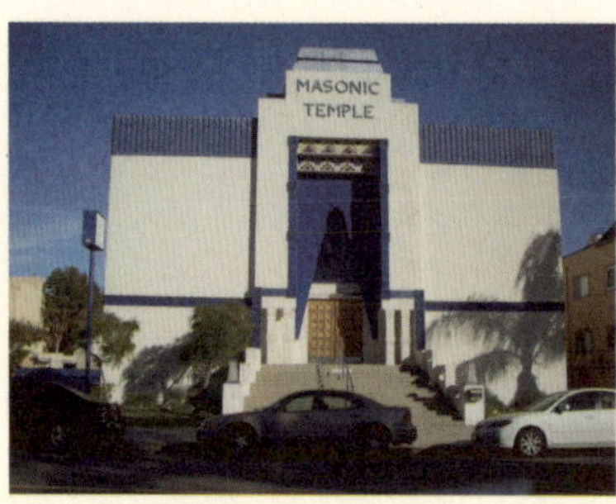


4
Disneyland's Matterhorn Bobsleds and Tomorrowland Park, 1964

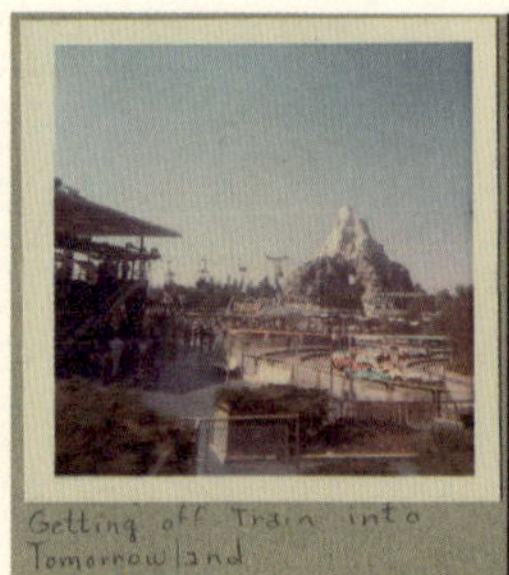


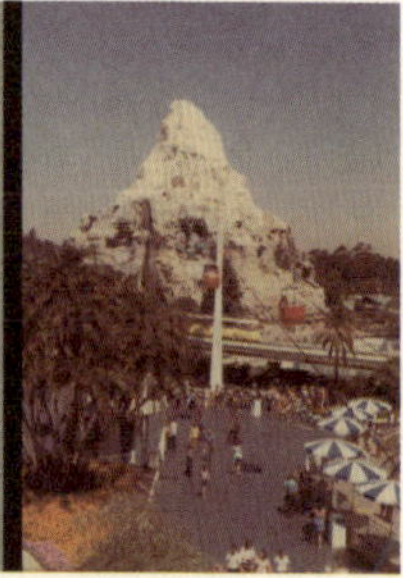

University of California campus in Irvine. Prior to their arrival, the Italian writer, literary critic, and early theorist of simulation Umberto Eco wrote about his impressions of California, along with much of the rest of America, in his landmark essay "Travels in Hyperreality" (1975). In Eco's view, America is a country obsessed with realism and a need to assert its place in history, and its vernacular is marked by an overwhelming need to reconstruct the past. While many of the exhibits—relating to history, art, and nature—that he saw in museums and tourist attractions were meant to duplicate or replace originals, Eco was impressed by the transparency of the simulations and even the pride taken in their artifice. At a Ripley's "Believe It or Not" Museum, for instance, he was amazed to find the prominent billing of a nineteenth-century mermaid as "The World's Greatest Fake."[5]

5. Umberto Eco, "Travels in Hyperreality," in *Travels in Hyperreality: Essays,* trans. William Weaver (New York: Harcourt Brace Jovanovich, 1986), 15.

Eco can be cruel in his descriptions of America's "historical" districts in cities such as New Orleans or of the plethora of kitschy theme environments such as Knott's Berry Farm, where he finds that "the frantic desire for the Almost Real arises only as a neurotic reaction to the vacuum of memories." It is in this context that he writes about the "Absolute Fake," which he describes as "the unhappy awareness of a present without depth." Eco's travels across the country left him so overstimulated that when he spent an afternoon at the Getty Museum—with its collection of real works by Raphael, Titian, and Veronese—he cast "absent glances on these drearily authentic pictures."[6] He was much more interested in the Getty's building, modeled on a first-century Roman country house, the Villa dei Papiri in Herculaneum, which was buried by the eruption of Vesuvius but has been re-created to dazzling effect in Malibu.

6. Ibid., 30–31.

Eco's essay is fueled by his notion of the absolute fake, and it is at Disneyland that he finds the ultimate expression of hyperreality. Here everything is lighter, brighter, and more real than in everyday life. He implies that, in comparison to Disney, reality can be disappointing. The artificial re-creations—or realistic fabrications, depending on your point of view—of exotic locales from Disneyland to the Las Vegas Strip stimulated the theoretical writings of Eco, Derrida, and Baudrillard. In his book *Simulacra and Simulation*, first published in 1981, Baudrillard defined the simulacrum as the point at which reality began to imitate its simulations. In his observation, people were increasingly attracted to "simulated" versions of reality, which, over time, had begun to efface reality itself—an effect that he referred to as hyperreality. In Baudrillard's view, the constant reproduction of images through various media was effectively erasing the boundary between the real and the imaginary.

By the end of the millennium, these writers' ideas, which became popular in graduate study programs in the 1980s and 1990s, seemed to be taking literal form far beyond Southern California. A fascination with theme parks and fantasy environments was now evident throughout Europe, Asia, and the Pacific Rim. Euro Disney (now Disneyland Paris) opened in France in 1992. In the mid-1990s Japan became home to the world's largest indoor water park, the Seagaia Ocean Dome, where attractions included a wave machine and an erupting volcano. (Built less than a thousand feet from a real ocean, it closed in 2007.)[7] In 1999 Chinese developers commissioned architects from Newport Beach, California, to replicate a style of gated community commonly found in Orange County for reproduction halfway around the world. Located an

7. *Wikipedia*, s.v. Seagaia Ocean Dome, last modified December 10, 2011, http://en.wikipedia.org/wiki/Seagaia_Ocean_Dome.

5

A new suburban development in Shenyang, China, 2008

6

Mariko Mori, *Empty Dream*, 1995; Cibachrome print, wood, aluminum, pewter frame; 120 x 252 inches (304.8 x 640.1 cm); installation view, Brooklyn Museum, April 8–August 15, 1999

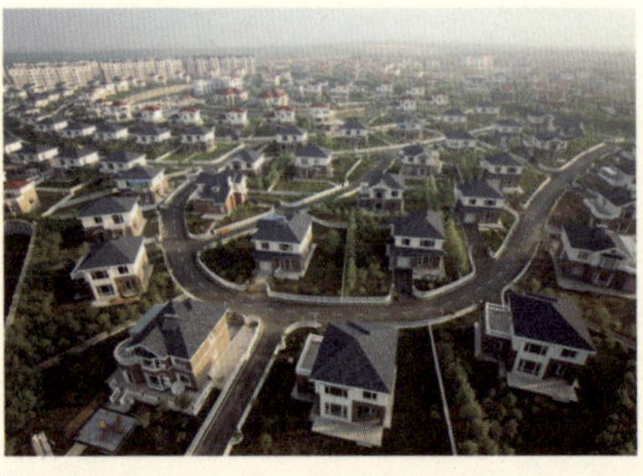

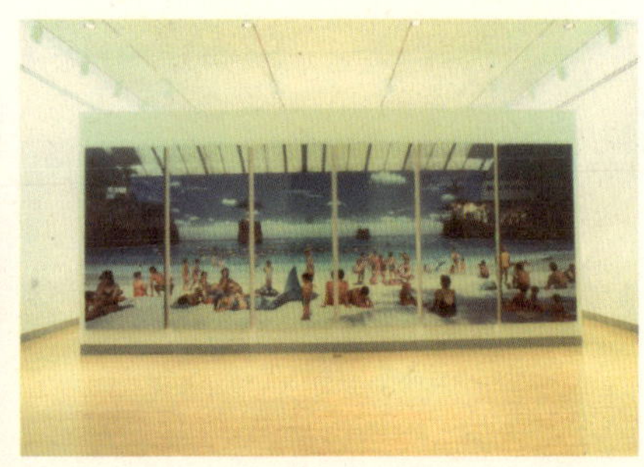

5

6

hour north of Beijing, a high-priced California-style housing development named Orange County, China, sold out within a month in a phenomenon that the Beijing media called the "Orange Storm." One writer conjectured that its residents must have "seen so many Hollywood movies that they were willing to shell out serious yuan to live in a one-of-a-kind intentional *Truman Show*."[8] Other Chinese developers have followed suit with similar gated communities (fig. 5).

   *More Real? Art in the Age of Truthiness* was inspired by the mounting evidence of deep ontological change that has become increasingly apparent in contemporary art as well as in daily life. At the same time—and interconnected with these cultural shifts—advances in photography, digital film, and electronic technologies have facilitated the alteration of the appearance of reality and the creation of convincing simulations. These technologies are readily employed by artists, the media, and the public. The art world, along with the culture at large, began to see a growing engagement with the interplay between the simulated and the real, exemplified by the production of spectacular photographs of real places that look fake (fig. 6) and of fake places that look real; in a new genre of "reverse readymades," which, like Eco's absolute fakes, are objects not plucked from reality but rather reproduced with exacting accuracy and craftsmanship by an artist in order to look like everyday objects (fig. 7); and in historical landmarks, archives, and even museums that turn out actually to be works of art (fig. 8). To what extent are these developments connected, and how might they relate to the growing cultural blurring and erosion between reality and fiction?

8. Daniel Brook, "Welcome to the O.C.," *Good*, no. 10 (March 22, 2008), www.good.is/post/welcome-to-the-oc/.

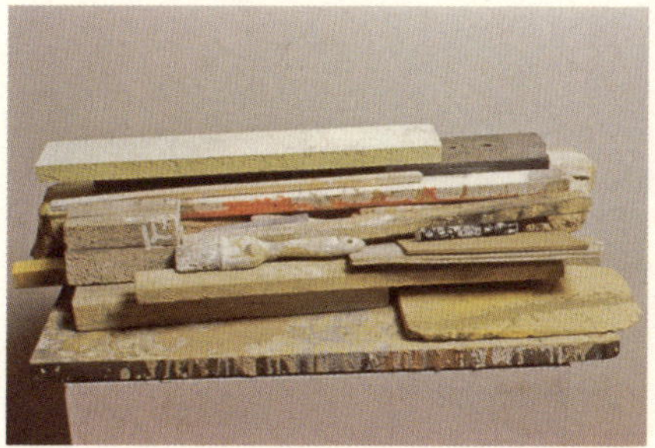

7
Peter Fischli and David Weiss; *The Table* (detail), 1992–93; mixed mediums; 29 ¹⁵/₁₆ x 129 ¹⁵/₁₆ x 354 ³/₈ inches (76 x 330 x 900 cm); courtesy Matthew Marks Gallery

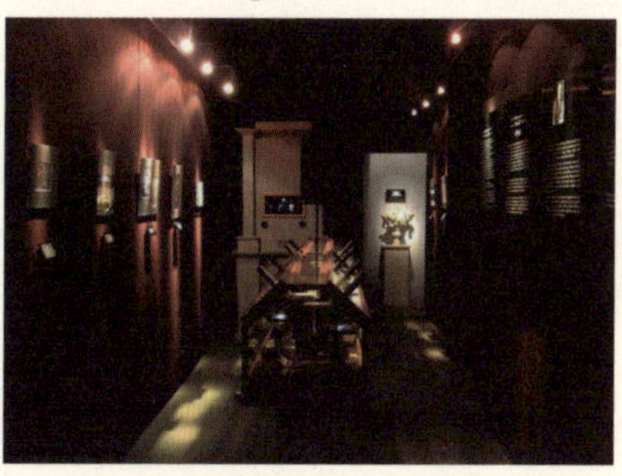

8
"Rosamond Purcell's Special Cases and Microscopy Hall," installation view, Museum of Jurassic Technology, Los Angeles

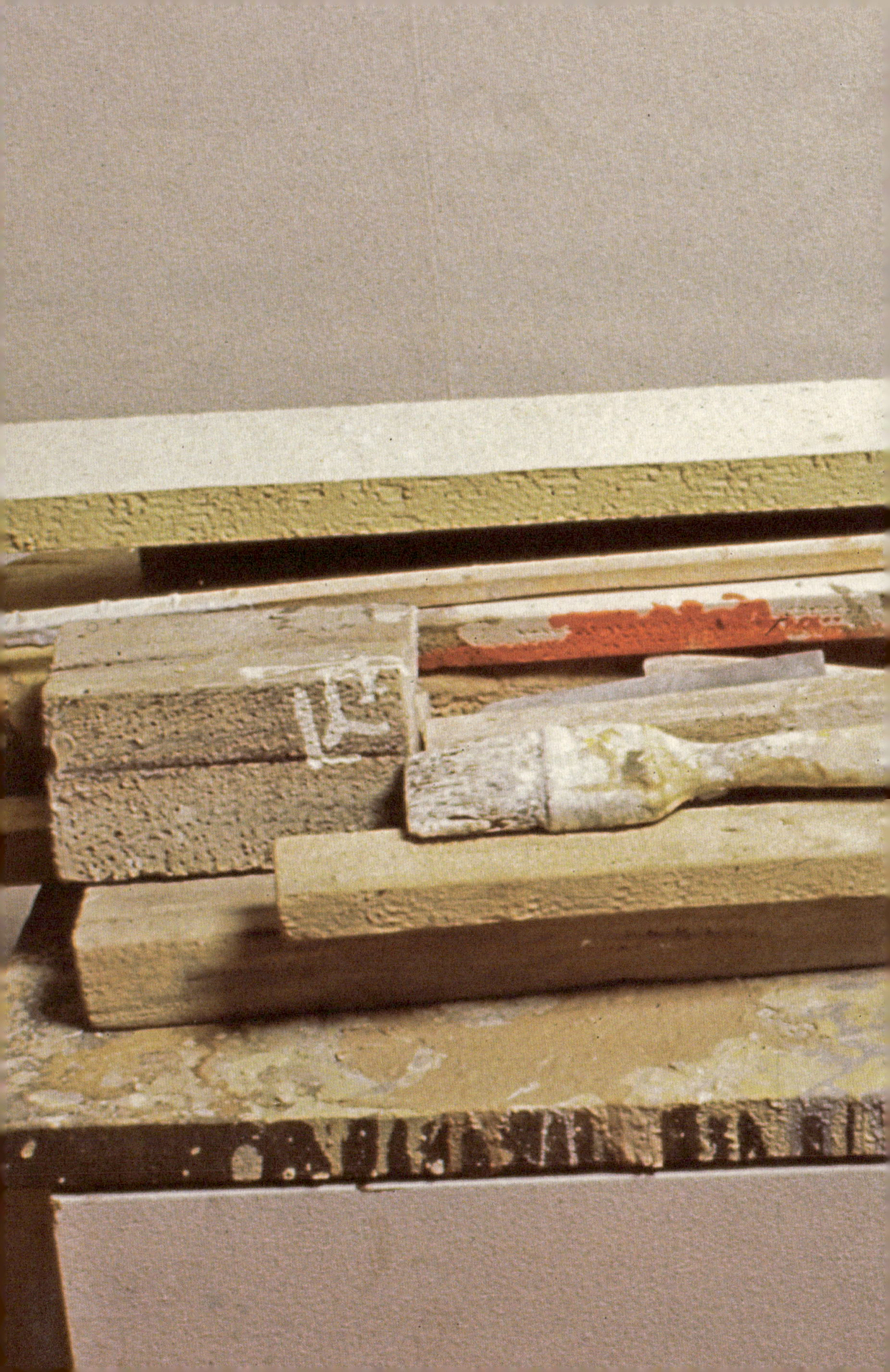

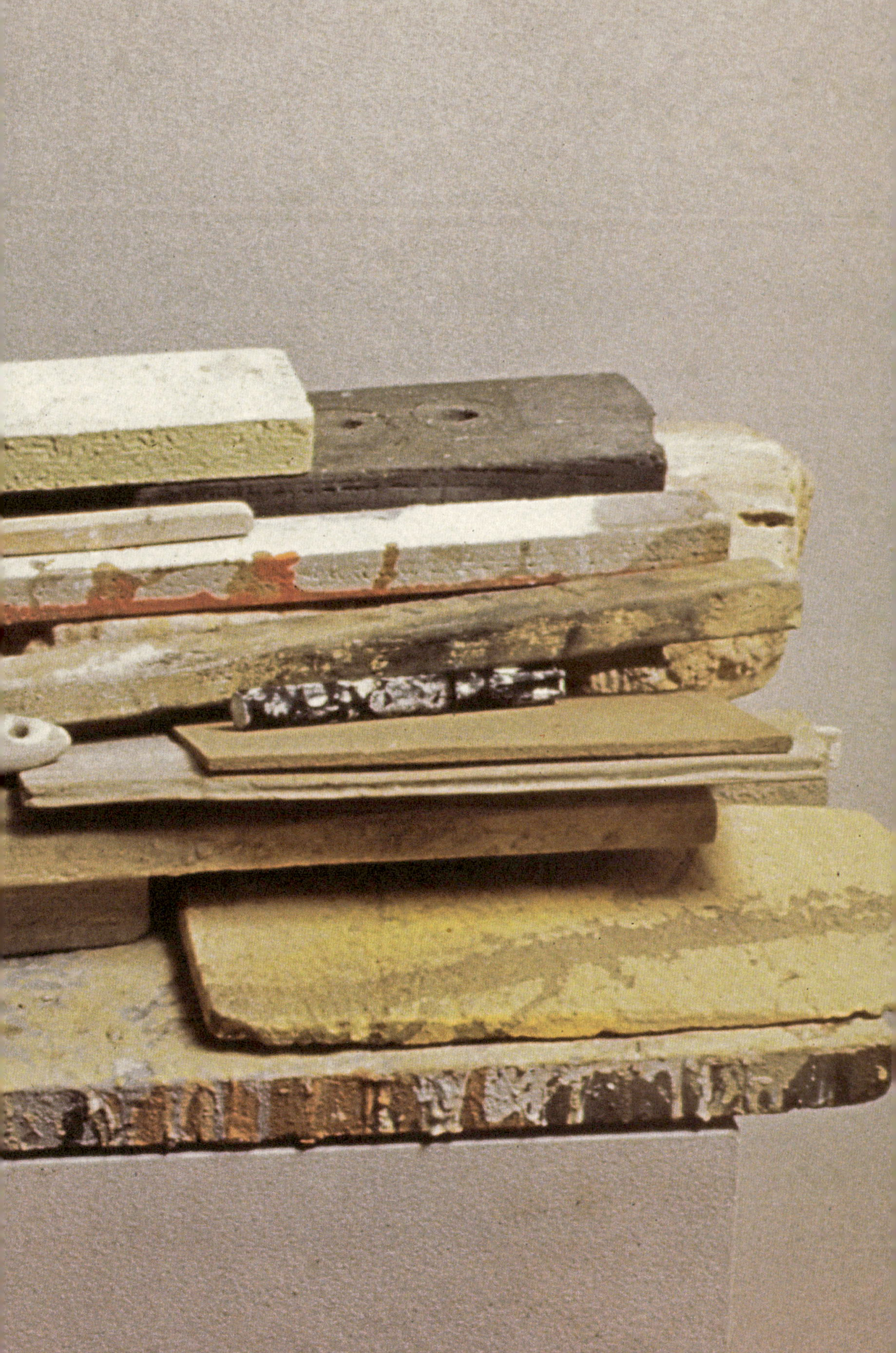

The means by which artists are investigating these questions today and what their work reveals about our times are at the core of this book and the exhibition that it accompanies. The diverse and unexpected works featured in *More Real?* are united by their ability to encourage viewers to question what they see and believe. This art proposes that we live in an age of "truthiness," a time when our understanding of truth may not be bound to empirical evidence—that is, to anything real, provable, or factual.

The word *truthiness* emerged at about the same time that a satirical news program on cable TV, Jon Stewart's *Daily Show* (fig. 9), was earning new levels of popularity and critical respect.[9] The word's genesis was a recent graduate of *The Daily Show* named Stephen Colbert, who started his own fake news program in 2005. On the very first broadcast of *The Colbert Report*, he introduced the term *truthiness*, and it quickly caught on and became Merriam-Webster's word of the year in 2006 (fig. 10). Defined by the American Dialect Society as "the quality of preferring concepts or facts one wishes to be true, rather than concepts or facts known to be true," the term has come to suggest our willingness to accept the plausible in place of the true.[10]

*Truthiness* entered the popular lexicon at a moment when scientific findings on issues like global warming began to be treated as a hoax by some and the teaching of evolution in schools was joined by the study of creationism. During the same period, reality TV—revealed to be as scripted as many TV sitcoms—dominated the airwaves, while Second Life and other augmented reality sites became increasingly popular on the web. Illustrating Eco's and Baudrillard's

9. *The Daily Show* won the prestigious Peabody Award in 2000 and 2004 for its election coverage ("Indecision 2000" and "Indecision 2004"). Its spin-off, *The Colbert Report*, received a Peabody in 2007 "for its masterful mix of punditry, parody and 'truthiness.'" Peabody Awards, http://www.peabody .uga.edu/winners/details .php?id=2471.

10. "Word of the Year 2006," Merriam-Webster .com, http://www .merriam-webster.com/ info/06words.htm.

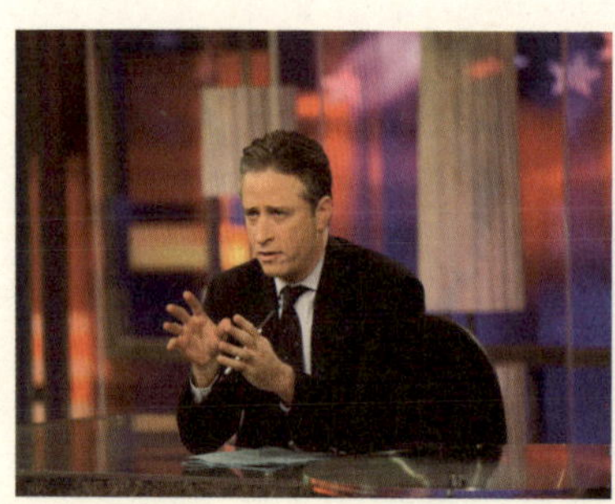

9
Jon Stewart on *The Daily Show*, 2005

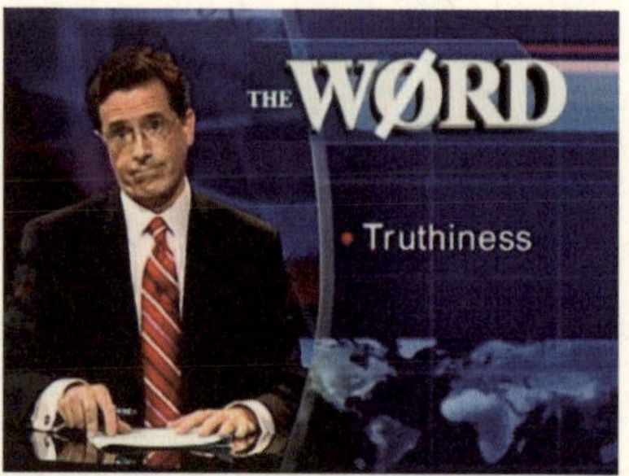


10
Stephen Colbert presenting "The Word" on *The Colbert Report*, October 17, 2005

notions of hyperreality, the fake had begun to supplant the real by acquiring a new kind of authenticity. People were beginning to seek new (or *more real?*) identities in virtual worlds—unbound, for instance, to race, class, age, or gender.

In the minds of many, truthiness is inextricably linked to the presidency of George W. Bush, who was a frequent target of *The Daily Show* and *The Colbert Report*. Bush was known for going with his gut instinct rather than conducting a careful analysis of the facts on the ground, which no doubt fostered a climate in which his administration could use fabricated intelligence to justify the invasion of Iraq in 2003.[11] During the war the administration created elaborately staged events such as the president's landing aboard an aircraft carrier in May 2003 to declare (rather prematurely, as it would turn out) a victorious conclusion to Operation Iraqi Freedom. The former *New York Times* columnist Frank Rich describes "a perfectly orchestrated production . . . painstakingly specific in its details," in which Bush "emerged from the cockpit draped in more combat gear than a Tom Cruise stunt double."[12] At times the administration could be candid about its efforts to manufacture its own version of reality: in an oft-quoted interview from 2004 with a Bush adviser, the idea of making decisions based on a "judicious study of discernible reality" was rejected outright. "That's not the way the world really works anymore," the aide stated. "We're an empire now, and when we act, we create our own reality."[13] One has to feel for the fake reporter on *The Daily Show* who, responding to the administration's ploy of planting its own fake reporters on local news shows to tout its Medicare prescription drug program, lamented: "They created a whole new category of fake news—infoganda. . . . We'll never be able to keep up!"[14]

11. See Ron Suskind, "Without a Doubt: Faith, Certainty, and the Presidency of George W. Bush," *New York Times Magazine*, October 17, 2004, http://www.nytimes.com/2004/10/17/magazine/17BUSH.html.

12. Frank Rich, *The Greatest Story Ever Sold: The Decline and Fall of Truth from 9/11 to Katrina* (New York: Penguin, 2006), 89.

13. Suskind, "Without a Doubt."

14. Frank Rich, "Operation Iraqi Infoganda," *New York Times*, March 28, 2004.

One of the works included in *More Real?*, Iñigo Manglano-Ovalle's *Phantom Truck* (2007; fig. 11), reflects directly on the Bush administration's most infamous deception. In February 2003 Secretary of State Colin Powell gave a speech to the United Nations in which he claimed that he had intelligence proving that Iraq was hiding weapons of mass destruction (fig. 12). Among the evidence he presented was a computer-generated image of a mobile biological weapons lab. The supposed existence of these labs served as partial justification for the US-led invasion of Iraq, yet following the invasion, no evidence for the existence of these labs was ever found, and the administration's informant ultimately admitted that he had fabricated the story.[15] *Phantom Truck* is Manglano-Ovalle's re-creation of one these nonexistent labs. Providing a chilling encounter with a fabricated version of a falsehood, the work is a visceral reminder that fictional narratives can and do generate reality.

The artists whose works are discussed in this book challenge us to evaluate what is gained and what is lost as objects, images, texts, and utterances are altered and massaged to take on new and alternative forms and meanings. Working in a wide spectrum of forms and mediums—from reverse readymades to virtual worlds—they investigate both the social construction of truth and the new parameters of the real. At a time when seeing is no longer believing, these artists consider new contingencies of reality in works that reflect our era's questioning of long-held beliefs and values while also examining the sources of this instability.

15. James Risen, "Iraqi Says He Made Up Tale of Biological Weapons before War," *New York Times*, February 15, 2011.

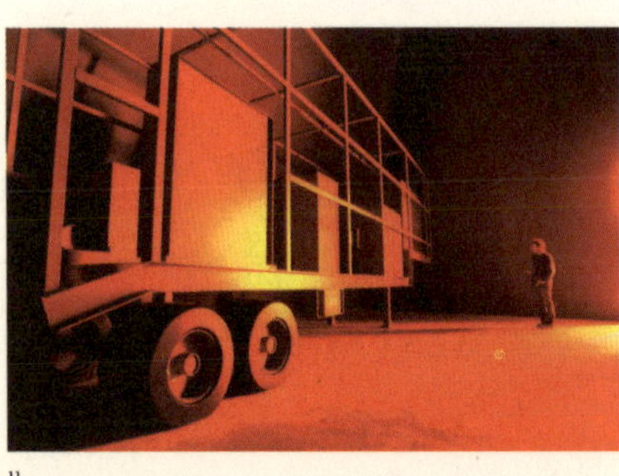

11
Iñigo Manglano-Ovalle, *Phantom Truck*, 2007; mixed mediums; 393 x 98 x 156 inches (998.2 x 248.9 x 396.2 cm); courtesy the artist and Galerie Thomas Schulte

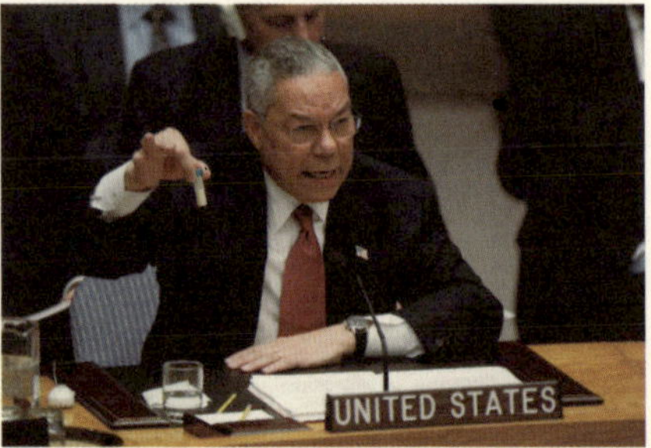


12
U.S. Secretary of State Colin Powell presents the case for the invasion of Iraq to the United Nations Security Council, February 5, 2003

# Deception and Play: From Trompe l'Oeil to the Authentic Fake

*The simulacrum now serves to redirect the real. This circular path makes it possible to return to the real world with eyes refreshed by the detour of fiction.*

—Elena Oliveras[16]

The blur between the imaginary and the real has been a dominant theme throughout the history of art, most clearly played out in the time-honored interest in illusionism—in art's ability to trick the eye. Pliny the Elder tells the story of the fifth-century Greek artists Zeuxis and Parrhasius and their famous rivalry over who could paint the best trompe l'oeil (literally meaning "to fool the eye") painting,[17] and verisimilitude has gone in and out of fashion throughout the history of art. Today, in a culture dominated by reality TV, it is hardly a coincidence that artists are again preoccupied with making work that navigates the borders between illusion and reality, the original and the copy, the authentic and the fake (fig. 13).

Argentinean artist Leandro Erlich often employs illusionism to throw viewers off balance—if only for a moment. A firm believer that our sense of reality is based on what we believe to be true, he creates sculptures and installations that play with this premise in a physical dimension. His seemingly familiar environments upend expectations. The viewer's sense of temporary imbalance and uncertainty provides a novel experience of the environment—and, at a deeper level, can raise unsettling questions about one's grounding in reality. In Erlich's installations, people congregate on the bottom of a

16. Elena Oliveras, "Leandro Erlich: Mirages in the Everyday," *ArtNexus*, no. 70 (2008): 75.

17. See Tom Gunning's essay in this volume for this story.

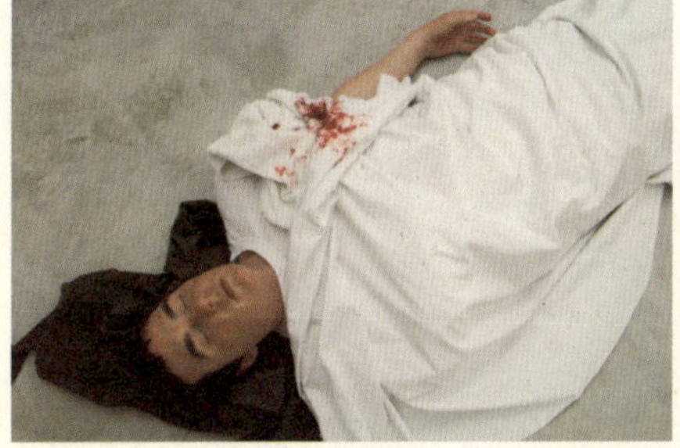

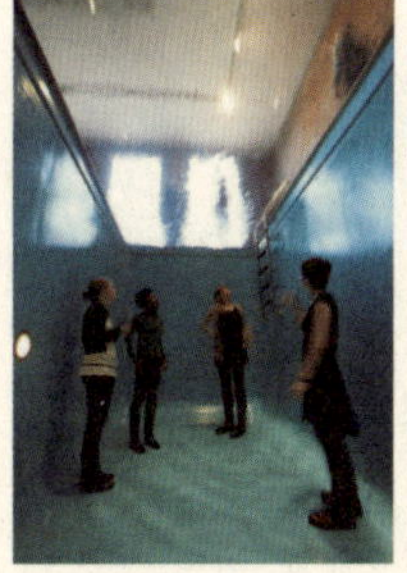

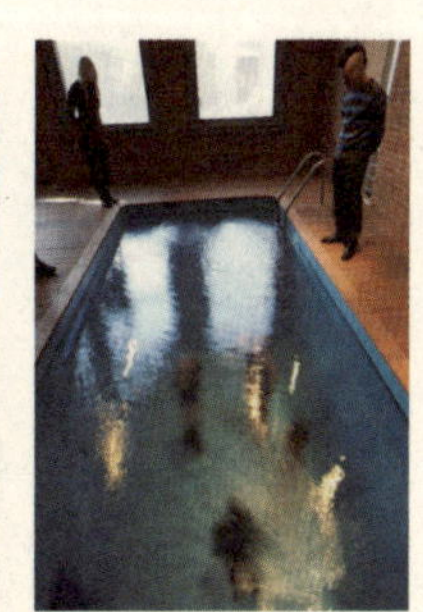

13
Jonathan Monk, *Deadman*, 2006 (detail); wax, rubber, human hair, oil paint, fabric; 66 x 22 x 12 inches (167.6 x 55.9 x 30.5 cm); courtesy the artist and Casey Kaplan, New York

14
Leandro Erlich, *Swimming Pool*, 2008; mixed mediums; dimensions variable; courtesy Sean Kelly Gallery, New York; installation view at MoMA PS1, New York

13

14

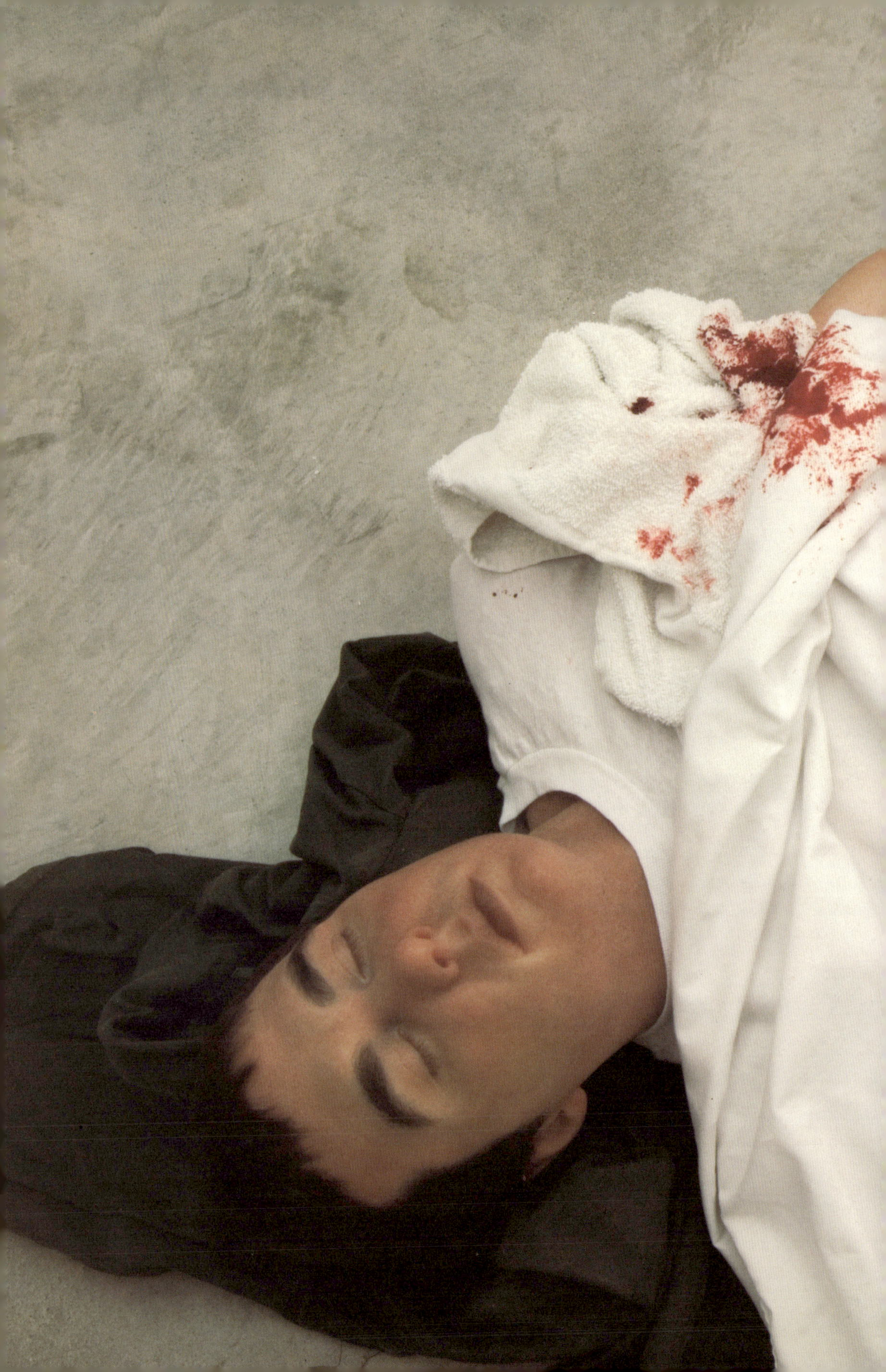

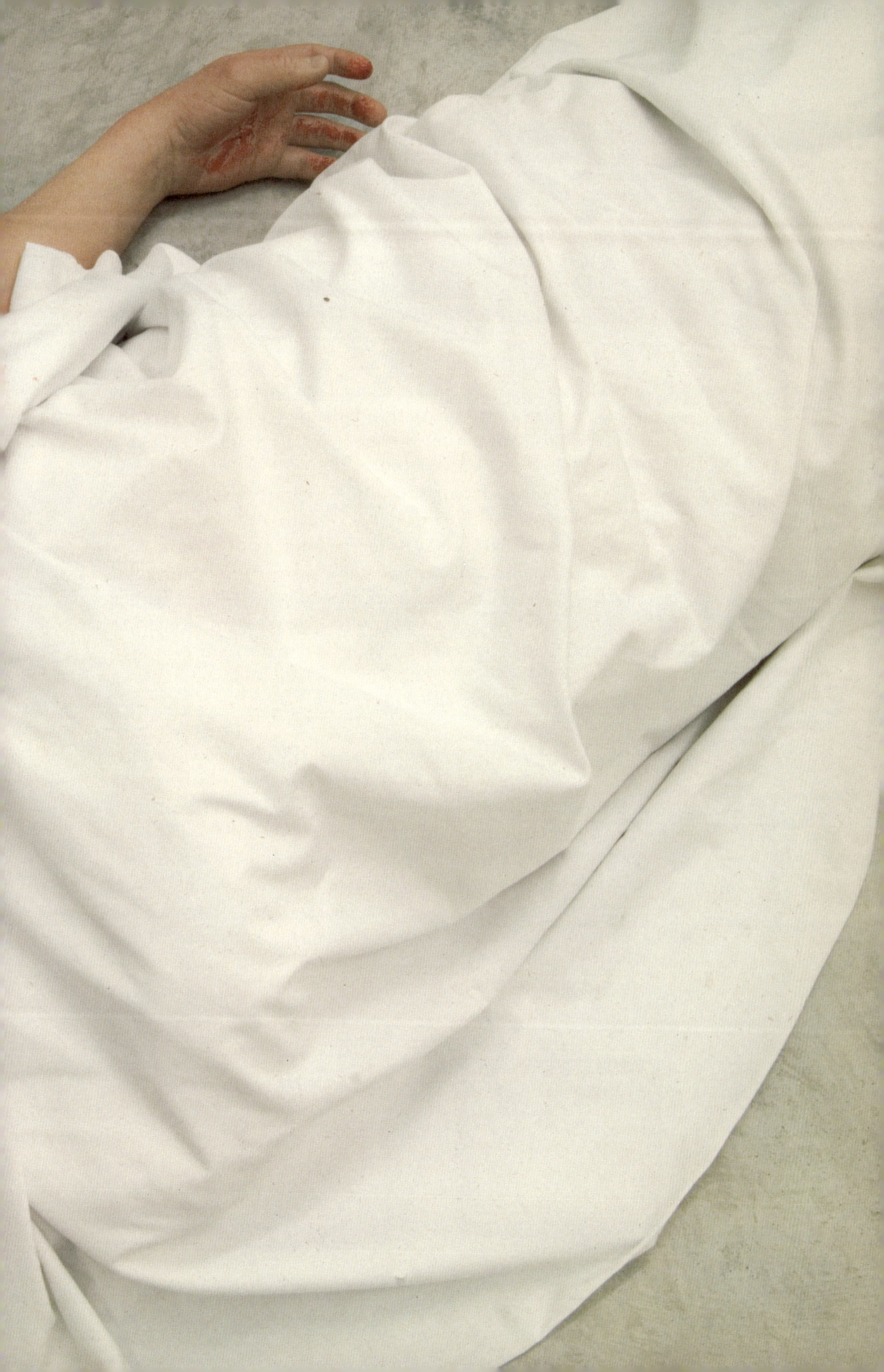

pool, windows morph into mirrors, and an elevator shaft lies exposed, reminding us of our trust in appearances (fig. 14). Whether virtual mirages or physical conundrums, his installations find ways to defamiliarize our experience, exposing our sense of reality as counterfeit.

If Erlich uses illusionism to provide a fresh perspective on reality, Vik Muniz creates simulations that could be said to expand our perception of what's real, building on Eco's idea of the absolute fake and taking it a step further. In his rigorous fabrications of famous paintings, titled Versos (2008), the artist represents the backs of well-known canvases as sculptural entities. Part of the allure of these "backsides" are their backstories, usually seen only by the curators and the crews that move, pack, and care for the works of art. Muniz's Versos reveal their stretcher bars, stains, hardware, and, most significantly, their labels—all elaborate simulations that nonetheless provide real insights into the journeys of their authentic counterparts around the world.[18] Leaning the works against the gallery walls so as to suggest that they are in the process of installation, Muniz adds another layer of illusion to these absolute fakes (fig. 15).

Muniz's Versos evoke Marcel Duchamp's enterprise, late in his life, of reproducing his early readymades, which in turn inspired another new aesthetic form, the reverse readymade.[19] In 1981, at the age of twenty-four, the Chinese artist Ai Weiwei left China to study and work in the United States with other international artists and cultural activists. Ai moved back to China twelve years later and, citing Duchamp's readymades as a major influence, began to draw attention to the loss of Chinese cultural heritage through his unprecedented use

18. Luc Sante, "Behind the Back," in *Vik Muniz: Verso* (Milan: Charta, 2009), 9–12.

19. Boris Groys has written about the phenomenon of reverse readymades, describing how Peter Fischli and David Weiss made simulated readymades by hand, inverting the conventional practice in our industrial age of simulating handcrafted work by machine. Boris Groys, "The Speed of Art," in *Peter Fischli, David Weiss: XLVI Biennale di Venezia, 1995* (Bern, Switzerland: Bundesamt für Kultur, 1995), 25–33; see also Groys, "On the New," in *Art Power* (Cambridge, MA: MIT Press, 2008), 37–38.

15

Vik Muniz; *Verso (Starry Night)*, 2008; mixed mediums; 38 1/8 x 45 3/4 x 12 inches (96.8 x 116.2 x 30.5 cm); courtesy Sikkema Jenkins & Co., New York

16

Ai Weiwei, *Coca Cola Vase*, 1997; vase from the Neolithic age (5000–3000 BC) and paint; 11 13/16 x 13 inches (30 x 33 cm); courtesy the artist

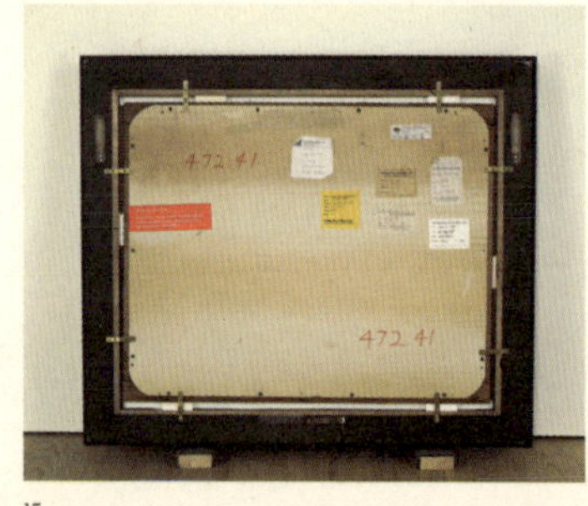

15

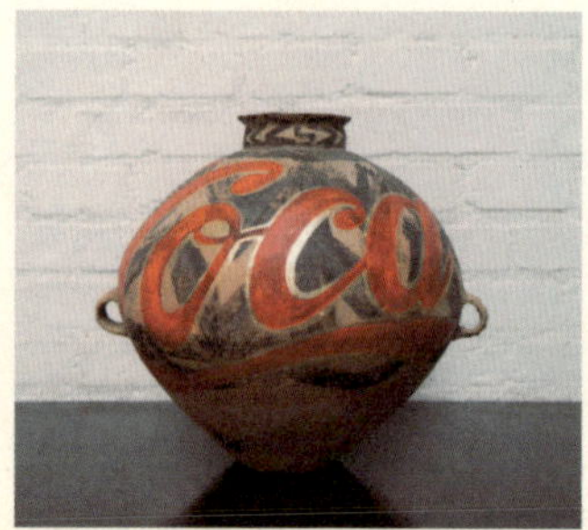

16

of traditional art forms. Treating ancient Chinese vessels as "ready-mades," he subjected them to a variety of procedures. These included altering them with hand-painted inscriptions of the Coca-Cola logo, dipping Neolithic vases into vats of industrial paint, and dropping Han dynasty urns on the ground in performances for the camera (figs. 16, 17). Writing about these works, the Beijing-based critic Philip Tinari remarks that what appears at first "like the sublimation of an ancient object's financial value and cultural worth into a different, yet parallel, carrier of updated value and worth" also serves as a "satire of the ruling regime's approach to its patrimony, and of contemporary China's curious relation to its past, a situation where destruction of historical artifacts happens almost daily."[20]

Since returning to China, Ai has called attention to the active market in counterfeit replicas of traditional Chinese ceramics and the fact that many of these find their way into museums, where they become, in effect, modern reproductions of authentic period pieces. Further destabilizing the boundaries between the authentic and the fake, the artist maintains a pottery studio with a staff of skilled ceramists. His contemporary versions of historical urns and vessels are nearly impossible to distinguish from priceless originals without the aid of carbon dating, and sometimes not even then, as counterfeiters often mix in flecks of old clay to foil investigators. This raises the question of the real versus the fake. How does the veracity of an object or an image affect its value or its meaning?[21]

Dario Robleto further complicates these distinctions — between old and new, real and fake — by handcrafting realistic-looking

20. Philip Tinari, "Postures in Clay: The Vessels of Ai Weiwei," in *Ai Weiwei: Dropping the Urn; Ceramic Works, 5000 BCE–2010 CE* (Glenside, PA: Arcadia University Art Gallery, 2010), 33.

21. In an interview with Robert Bernell from 2000, Ai stated that the central issue in his porcelain-based works is that of authenticity. His statement—published in John Clark, ed., *Chinese Art at the End of the Millennium: Chinese-art.com, 1998–1999* (Hong Kong: New Art Media, 2000), is quoted at length in Tinari, "Postures in Clay," 42.

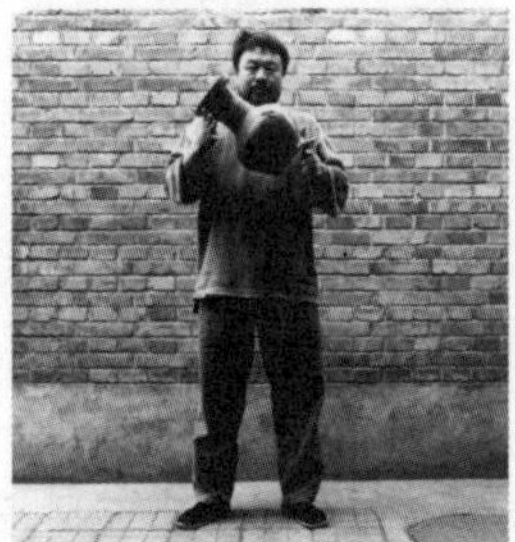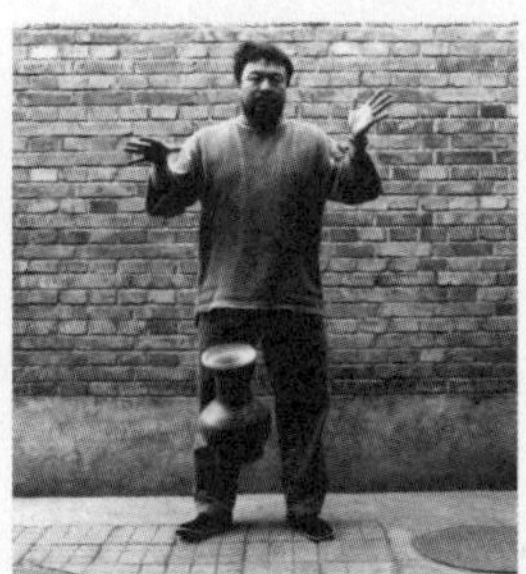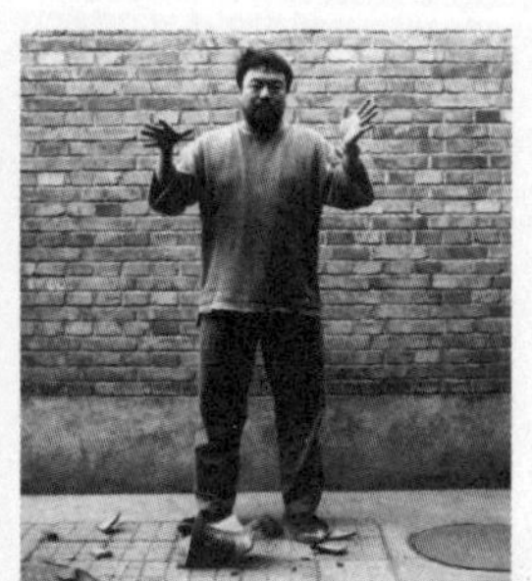

17
Ai Weiwei, *Dropping a Han Dynasty Urn*, 1995; three black-and-white prints; 58 5/16 x 47 5/8 inches (148 x 121 cm) each; courtesy the artist

17

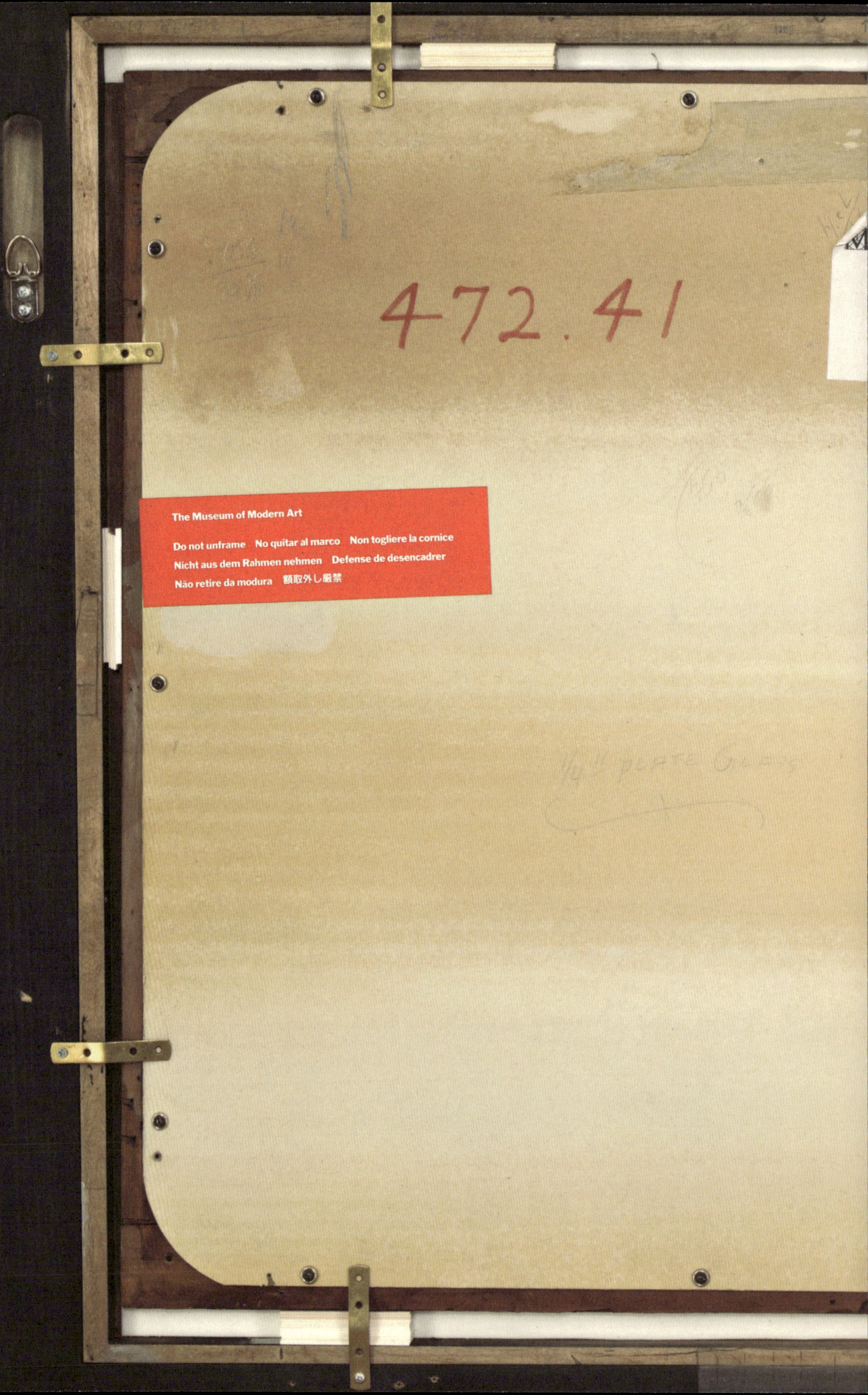

472.41

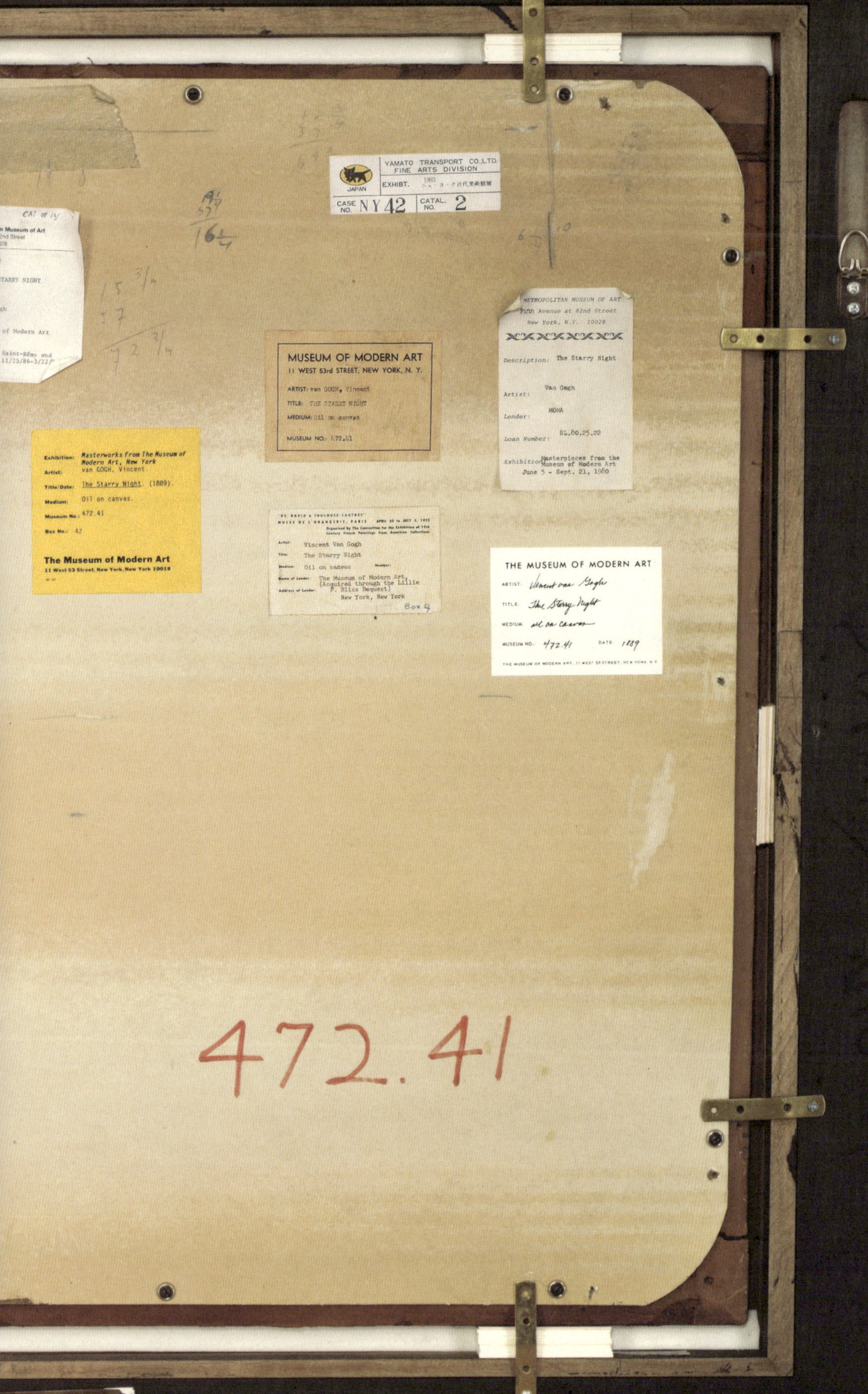

YAMATO TRANSPORT CO.,LTD.
FINE ARTS DIVISION
JAPAN
EXHIBT.
1983
CASE NO. NY 42
CATAL. NO. 2
MUSEUM OF MODERN ART
11 WEST 53rd STREET, NEW YORK, N. Y.
ARTIST: van GOGH, Vincent
TITLE: THE STARRY NIGHT
MEDIUM: Oil on canvas
MUSEUM NO.: 472.41
METROPOLITAN MUSEUM OF ART
Fifth Avenue at 82nd Street
New York, N.Y. 10028
Description: The Starry Night
Artist: Van Gogh
Lender: MoMA
Loan Number: SL.80.25.22
Exhibition: Masterpieces from the Museum of Modern Art
June 5 - Sept. 21, 1980
Exhibition: Masterworks from The Museum of Modern Art, New York
Artist: van GOGH, Vincent.
Title/Date: The Starry Night. (1889).
Medium: Oil on canvas.
Museum No.: 472.41
Box No.: 42
The Museum of Modern Art
11 West 53 Street, New York, New York 10019
"DE DAVID A TOULOUSE-LAUTREC"
MUSEE DE L'ORANGERIE, PARIS   APRIL 20 to JULY 5, 1955
Organized by The Committee for the Exhibition of 19th
Century French Paintings from American Collections
Artist: Vincent Van Gogh
Title: The Starry Night
Medium: Oil on canvas
Name of Lender: The Museum of Modern Art,
(Acquired through the Lillie P. Bliss Bequest)
Address of Lender: New York, New York
Box 4
THE MUSEUM OF MODERN ART
ARTIST: Vincent van Gogh
TITLE: The Starry Night
MEDIUM: oil on canvas
MUSEUM NO.: 472.41   DATE: 1889
THE MUSEUM OF MODERN ART, 11 WEST 53 STREET, NEW YORK, N.Y.
472.41

objects out of materials that themselves defy belief. Described as equal parts alchemist, DJ, and philosopher, Robleto has employed such unusual and archaic materials as dinosaur fossils, vinyl records, hand bones, and a ten-thousand-year-old flower caught in amber to create his highly evocative sculptures. For the artist, each aspect of his medium plays a significant role in relation to the content and subject matter of his works. In his hands, materials and ephemera from nature, vernacular culture, and history—loaded with private memories and cultural nostalgia—become powerful mediums with which to comment on the present. Reexamining past events in light of new information, Robleto is like a revisionist historian who reveals faulty logic and undisclosed truths (fig. 18).

22. Anton Kaes, *From Hitler to Heimat: The Return of History as Film* (Cambridge, MA: Harvard University Press, 1989), 198.

23. Serge Daney, quoted in A. O. Scott, "How Real Does It Feel," *New York Times Magazine*, December 12, 2010.

24. Scott, "How Real Does It Feel."

## Reshaping the Real: Film, Memory, and the Virtual

> History thus returns forever—as film.
>
> —Anton Kaes[22]

From the early days of cinema, writers have commented on how this medium has altered our "fundamental rapport with reality."[23] In 1895, in a Parisian café, Auguste and Louis Lumière screened a brief film of a train arriving in a station. As A. O. Scott recounts, "Legend has it that the assembled public fled in panic, seized by the momentary belief that, in spite of the absence of either a railroad track or a soundtrack, an actual locomotive was bearing down on them."[24] Although the story

18
Dario Robleto, *The Melancholic Refuses to Surrender*, 2003; cast and carved bone, charcoal, melted vinyl record of Lead Belly's "The Titanic," broken male hand bones, ground coal, horsehair, dirt, pigment, lead salvaged from the sea, string, rust; 14 x 11 x 5 inches (35.6 x 27.9 x 12.7 cm); collection Nancy and Stanley Singer

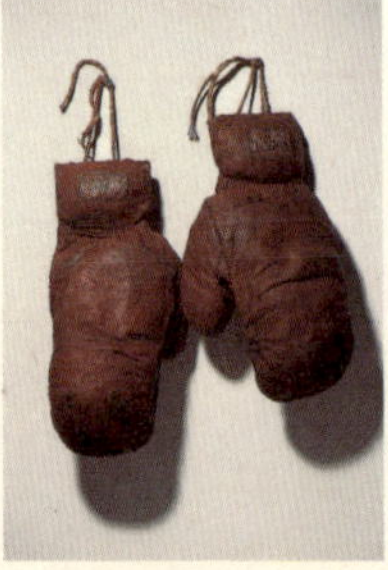

18

may be apocryphal, it illustrates the tremendous influence of cinema on human consciousness.

Film is no longer a novelty, yet it still exercises its ability to excite our imaginations. Eve Sussman's use of film in her magical *89 Seconds at Alcázar* (2004) encapsulates this power. In this work Sussman reimagines the scene of a well-known painting, Diego Velázquez's masterpiece *Las Meninas* (ca. 1656), as a moving image. Her film gives life to a picture that we thought we knew, providing sound, movement, and a hint of narrative. The medium infuses a vivid quality into the image, as whispering royals traverse dark hallways, figures emerge from shadows into cinematic light, and a tiny princess reluctantly stops her play to pose for the famous artist. Staying close to the original scene, Sussman's film incorporates gestures, actions, and audio that depict events leading up to the moment captured in the painting, inviting viewers to have a "more real" experience of this iconic work, which is otherwise frozen in its pictorial space (fig. 19).

The interplay between the real and the fake is in constant flux in a high-tech, digital world. In his series Real World I (2004–6), set at a popular Korean theme park called Aiins World, the artist Seung Woo Back uses the devices of photography to explore how we experience reality today. Despite the ease with which digital photography can be manipulated, the artist approaches the medium with a high degree of purity. Using a large-format camera and eschewing digital cosmetics, he creates large-scale images that look so real that it sometimes takes a minute or two to register the extent to which they—and their subject matter—play with reality. In *RW01-001* (2004),

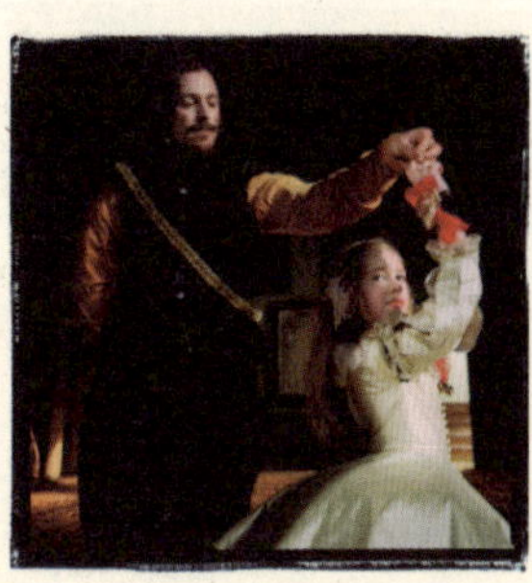

19
Eve Sussman | Rufus Corporation; *The King and the Infanta*, 2004; still from *89 Seconds at Alcázar*; courtesy the artist

19

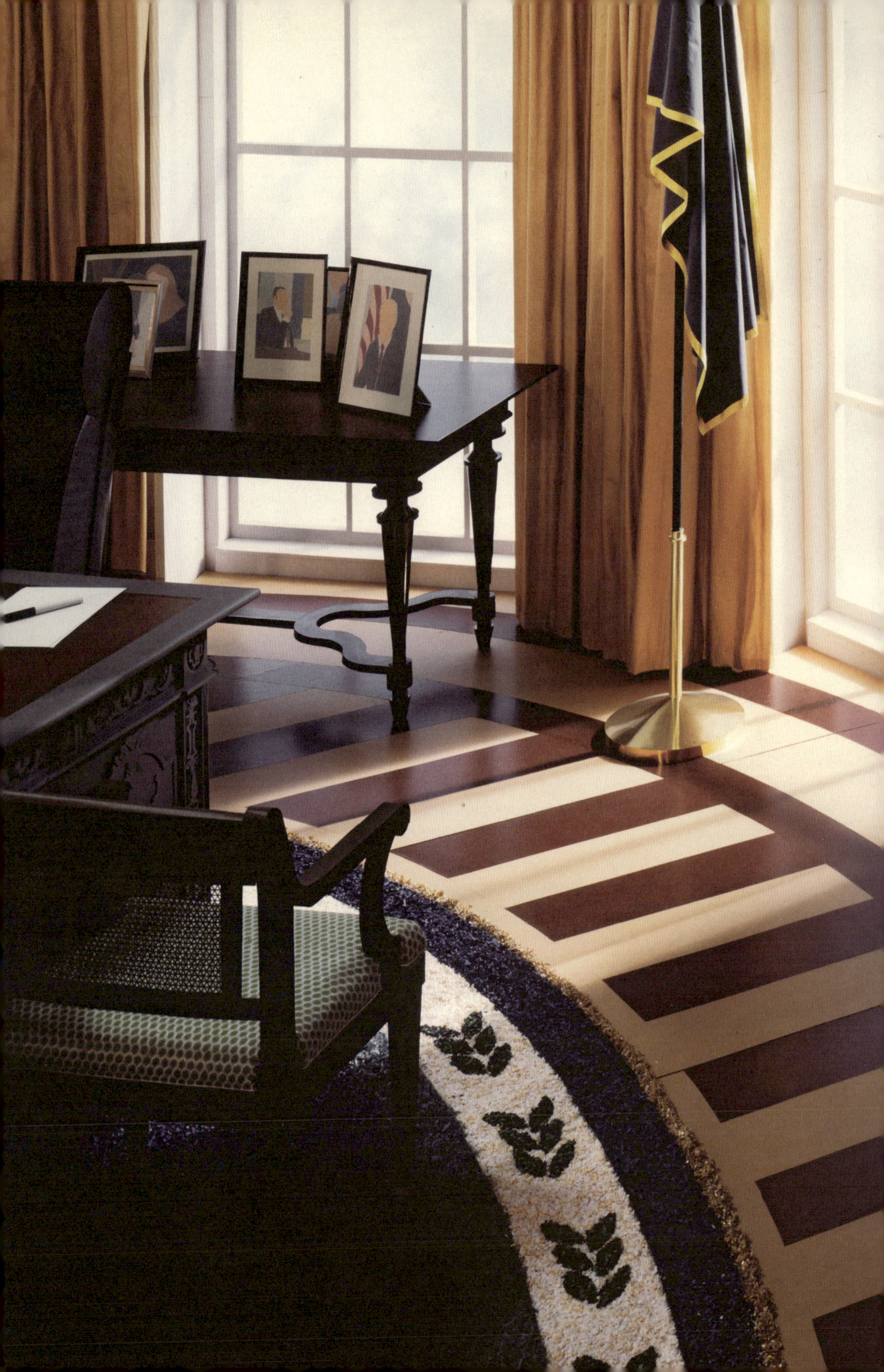

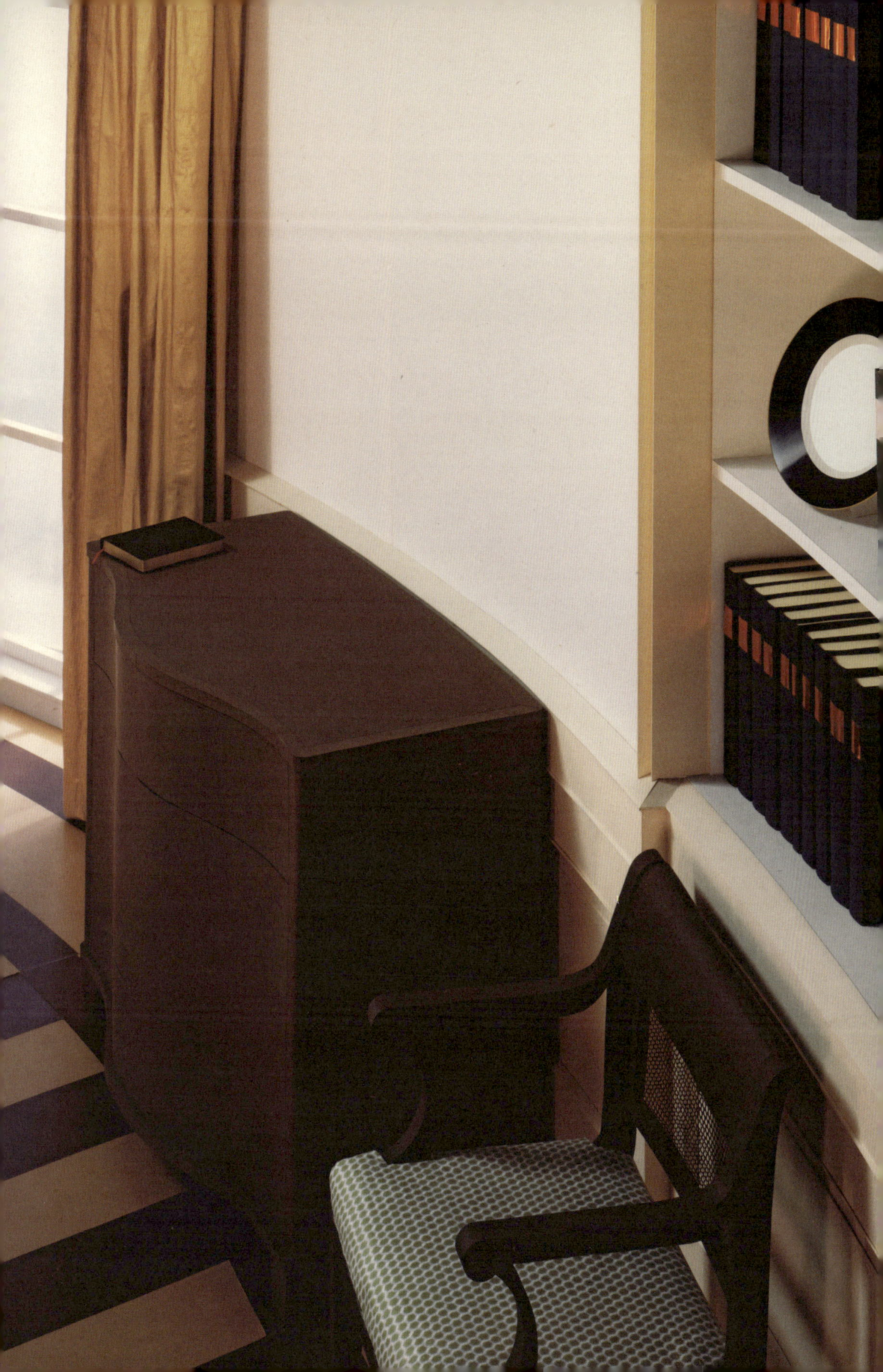

historic Korean turtle boats float in front of US urban landmarks such as the Chrysler Building and the World Trade Center, set against a backdrop of the Seoul Metropolitan Loop Highway. In fact, it is the backdrop of that elevated highway and the nearby housing district in Seoul that are the most "real" elements in the pictures.

In some of the images from Real World I, Back discloses the boundaries between the park's models, its backdrops, and the real city in the distance (fig. 20). By revealing the trickery, he offers up one of the great pleasures of trompe l'oeil, in which viewers admire the artifice while being in on the joke. At the same time, the instability of time, place, and dimension found in these photographs is a comment on contemporary Korean society, in which rapid economic growth and a desire to emulate Western culture often displace traditional forms and customs with newly created hybridities.

On November 9, 2008, five days after the 2008 US presidential election, the *New York Times Magazine* featured an image of the Oval Office by the German artist Thomas Demand. The cover story was about the executive branch's shift of political power away from the Senate during the presidency of George W. Bush, and it reflected on how that might affect the Obama presidency. The *Times* pictures editors commissioned Demand to create this photograph aware that he would not go to the White House to shoot the Oval Office but rather that his photograph would be based on a mocked-up replica of the space constructed out of paper, cardboard, and other ephemeral materials (fig. 21). The fact that the *Times* did not feel the need to present a "real" picture of the Oval Office or to explain the

20
Seung Woo Back, *RW01-001*, 2004, from the series Real World I, 2004–6; digital print; 50 x 66 ½ inches (127 x 168.9 cm); courtesy Gana Art Gallery, Seoul

21
Thomas Demand, *Presidency I*, 2008; C-print/Diasec; 122 x 87 ¹³⁄₁₆ inches (310 x 223 cm); courtesy the artist and Matthew Marks Gallery

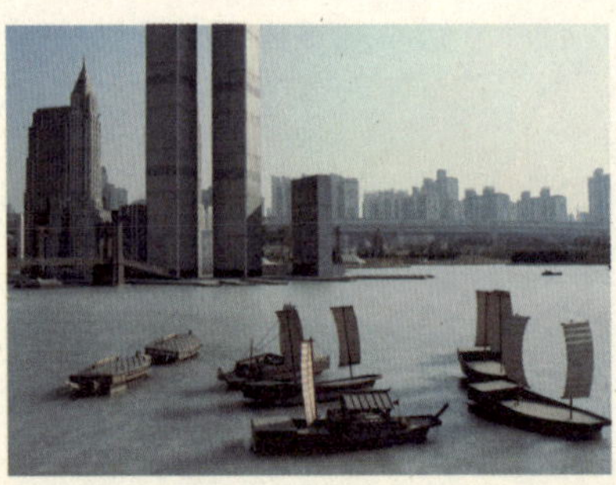

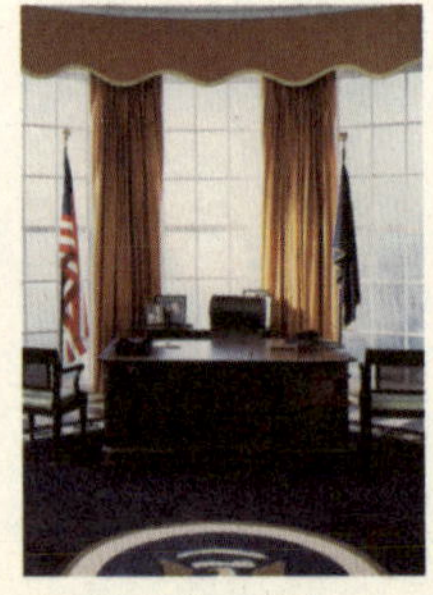

20

21

nature of the image to its readership is interesting in itself. Demand's photograph reminds us that reality is not something that exists but is something that we construct. More compellingly, the simulated aspect of the photograph and its lack of a certain kind of veracity suggest a pointed critique of the facade of the presidency and the ephemeral nature of the office.

As Demand's images illustrate, photography allows for the misinterpretation of seemingly documentary evidence while also providing it with a metaphorical reading. Through very different means, An-My Lê also uses photography to comment on American political culture. The Vietnamese-born Lê, who moved with her family to the United States in 1975 as a political refugee, became intrigued years later by the fact that groups of amateur historians and veterans in the United States were engaged in reenacting the Vietnam War. In her series Small Wars (1999–2002), the artist documents not the war itself but re-creations of its battles (fig. 22).

In order to be allowed to make these images, Lê was required to participate in the reenactments. At different points in the elaborately staged "war games," she was asked to play the role of a Vietcong insurgent, a Vietnamese turncoat, a sniper girl, and a captured prisoner.[25] Lending a bit of authenticity to the paramilitary playacting, the artist simultaneously managed to give the photographs of her subjects a neutrality through their distinctive objective tone. On some level, of course, they can be seen as critiques of war, but they also offer a psychological exploration of complicated motivations and contradictory lives.

25. H. G. Masters, "Theater of Observation: An-My Lê," *Art Asia Pacific*, no. 60 (September–October 2008), artasiapacific .com/Magazine/60/Theater OfObservationAnMyLe.

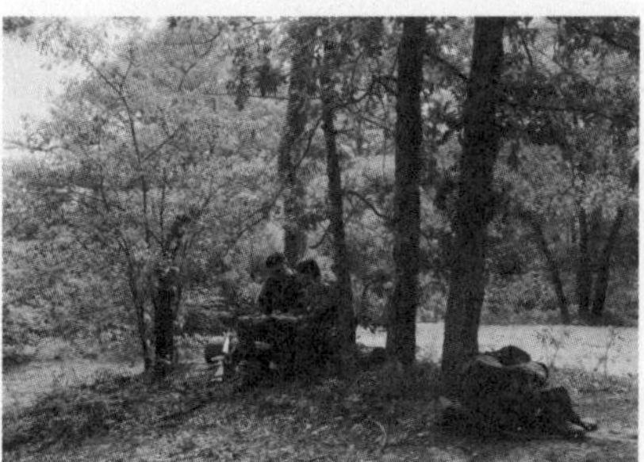

22
An-My Lê, *Lesson*, from the series Small Wars, 1999–2002; gelatin silver print; 26 ½ x 38 inches (67.3 x 96.5 cm); courtesy the artist and Murray Guy, New York

22

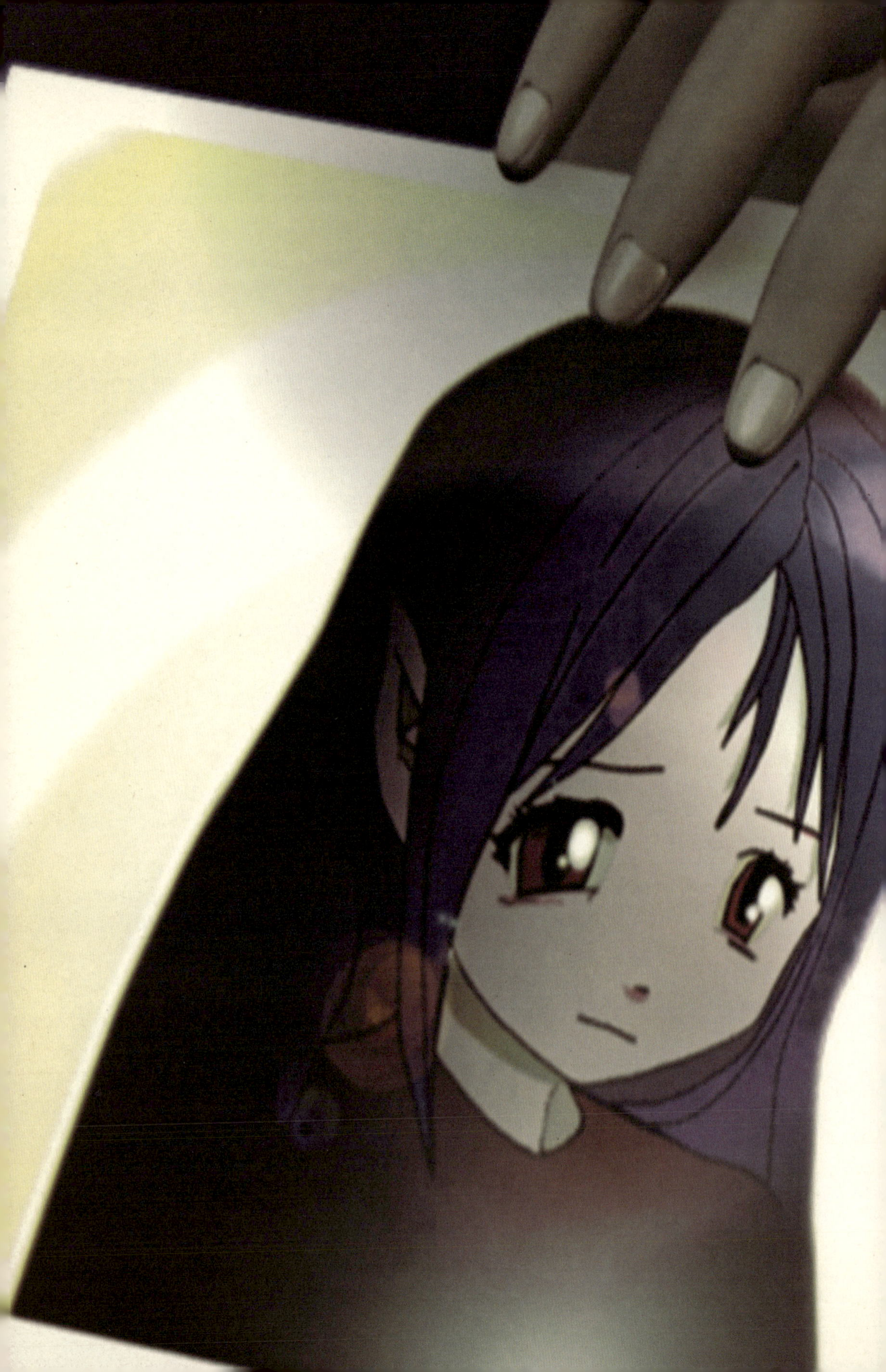

Lê, who describes herself as a "living 19th century photographer" lugging around a large-format five-by-seven Deardorff camera, has a fellow traveler in artist Joel Lederer.[26] Born in 1971, Lederer always wanted to be a frontier photographer and felt that he was born in the wrong century. In his search for a new frontier, he found another way to make images of unseen—and seemingly unreal—landscapes. In his series The Metaverse Is Beautiful (2009), he navigates the uncharted territory of co-created utopias in the virtual world of Second Life. Lederer's dramatic large-scale prints provide a visual record for viewers who will never themselves go to these places (fig. 23). These undocumented landscapes are in a constant state of alteration as different participants engage with them online, so Lederer has captured places that will never look the same way again—virtual landscapes in the process of hyperbolic transformation. Their titles, such as 200805262351 (2009), refer to the exact date and time that he photographed these spaces.

For those who do spend time in cyberspace, virtual worlds and other simulated environments may offer the ability to explore fictional characters and identities that sometimes seem more real—more vivid, absorbing, and rewarding—than what they have experienced in the earthbound, physical realm. At the end of the millennium, the French artist Pierre Huyghe became interested in working with material that he found in cyberculture. In 1999, with his friend and fellow artist Philippe Parreno, Huyghe purchased the image and copyright of a Japanese digital figure named Annlee. Designed as a simple utility player by illustrators for the Japanese manga industry, Annlee was destined to have a very short life as a minor figure in a video game or comic strip. As part of a project titled *No Ghost Just*

26. Ibid.

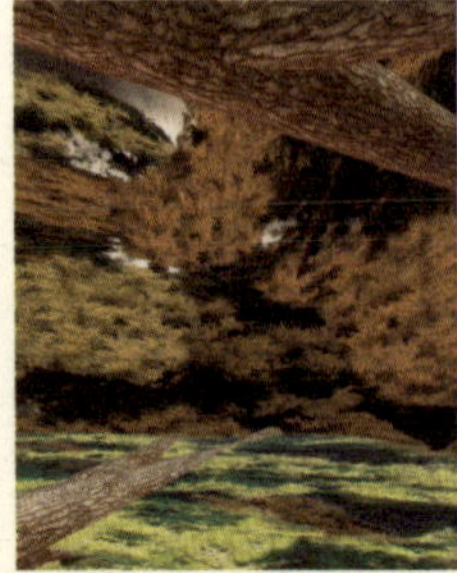

23
Joel Lederer, *200805262351*, from the series *The Metaverse Is Beautiful*, 2009; archival ink jet on paper; 50 x 40 inches (127 x 101.6 cm); courtesy the artist

23

*a Shell*, Huyghe and Parreno invited other artists to give voice to the anonymous manga figure (fig. 24).

At the instigation of Huyghe and Parreno, Annlee's life took a radical turn. By buying Annlee, they rescued her in effect from an industry that had condemned her to death. Given a cosmetic makeover, she acquired a complexity of qualities that far exceeded her makers' original expectations. Over the next few years, a variety of artists lent the figure a virtual life that elevated her to quasi-celebrity status, and between 1999 and 2002 Annlee could be said to have achieved something approaching self-consciousness. Huyghe hinted at this in his video *Two Minutes Out of Time* (2000), in which Annlee delivers a monologue that seems to shift between her personal perspective and that of a third person, animating her uncertain state. In the video she recalls her memory of having been diverted from an existence of servitude, yet she also speaks of her life as a "deviant sign," a fictional character with a copyright, "just a shell."

27. The American artist Joe Scanlon made Annlee a closed white casket with materials from Ikea.

At a time when multiple personas, avatars, and sub-jectivities were being created as alter egos and stand-ins, Huyghe and Parreno's project addressed questions about how identity and difference were being formulated by new technologies. It also raised unexpected humanitarian concerns. As her persona evolved and matured, Annlee became increasingly more real. Deciding that they needed to "free" her, the artists returned her copyright to a foundation that they created in her name, and in late 2002 Annlee was liberated from circulation.[27] Her identity nevertheless lives on in video animations, paintings, posters, books, neon works, and sculptures.

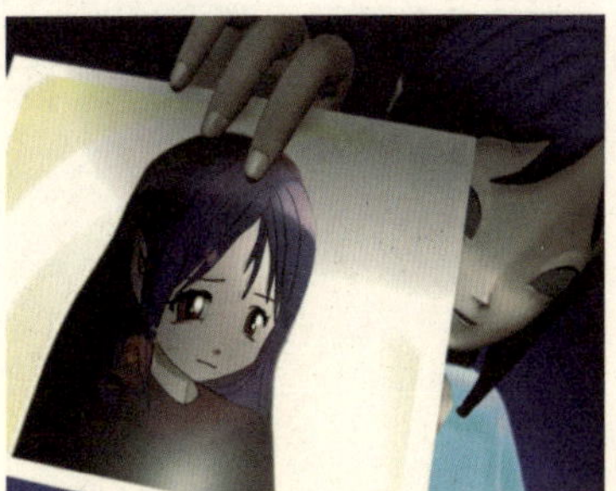

24
Philippe Parreno, *Anywhere Out of the World*, 1999; video still from 3-D animation movie transferred to DVD; dimensions variable; courtesy the artist and Friedrich Petzel Gallery, New York

24

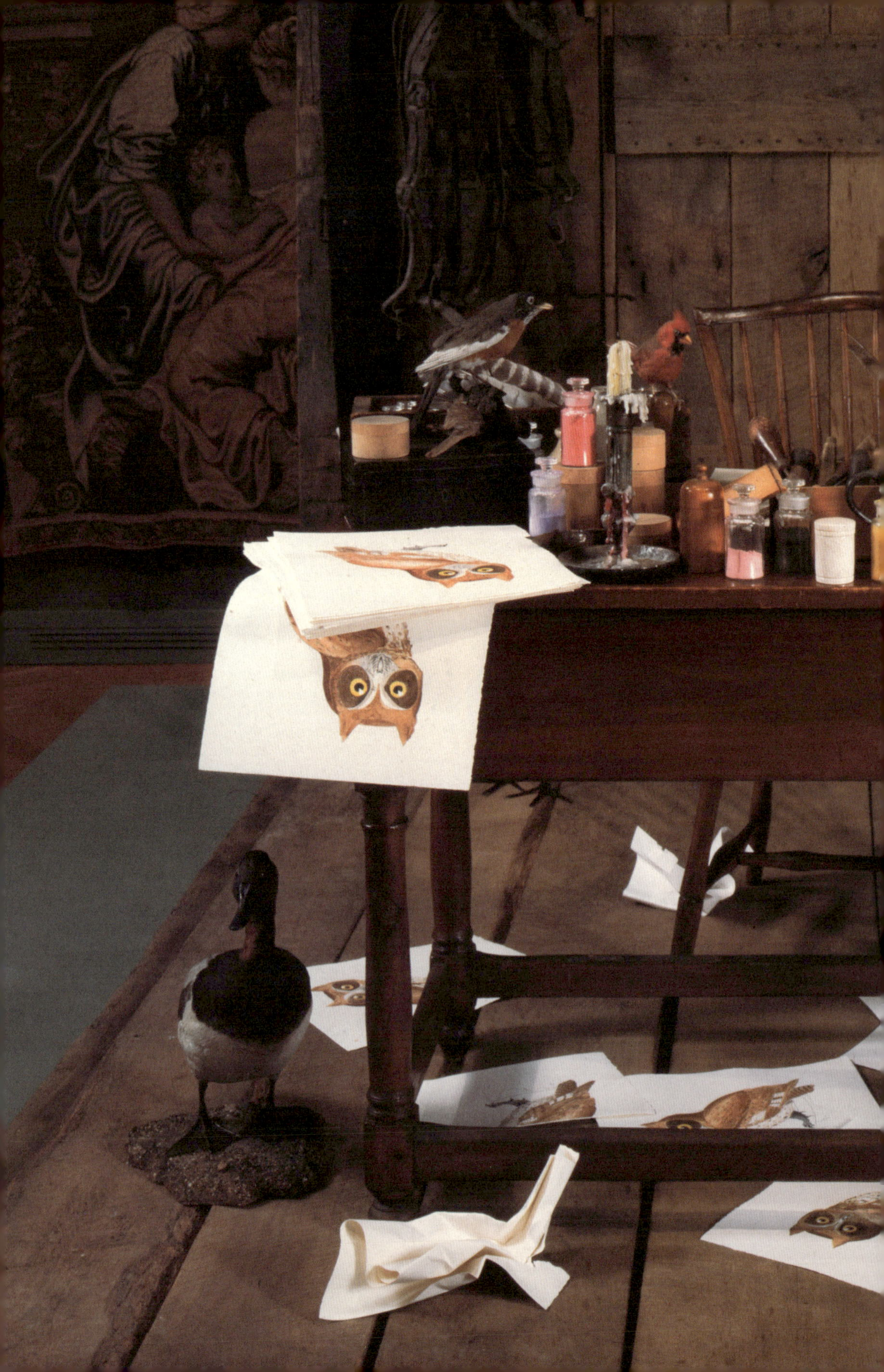

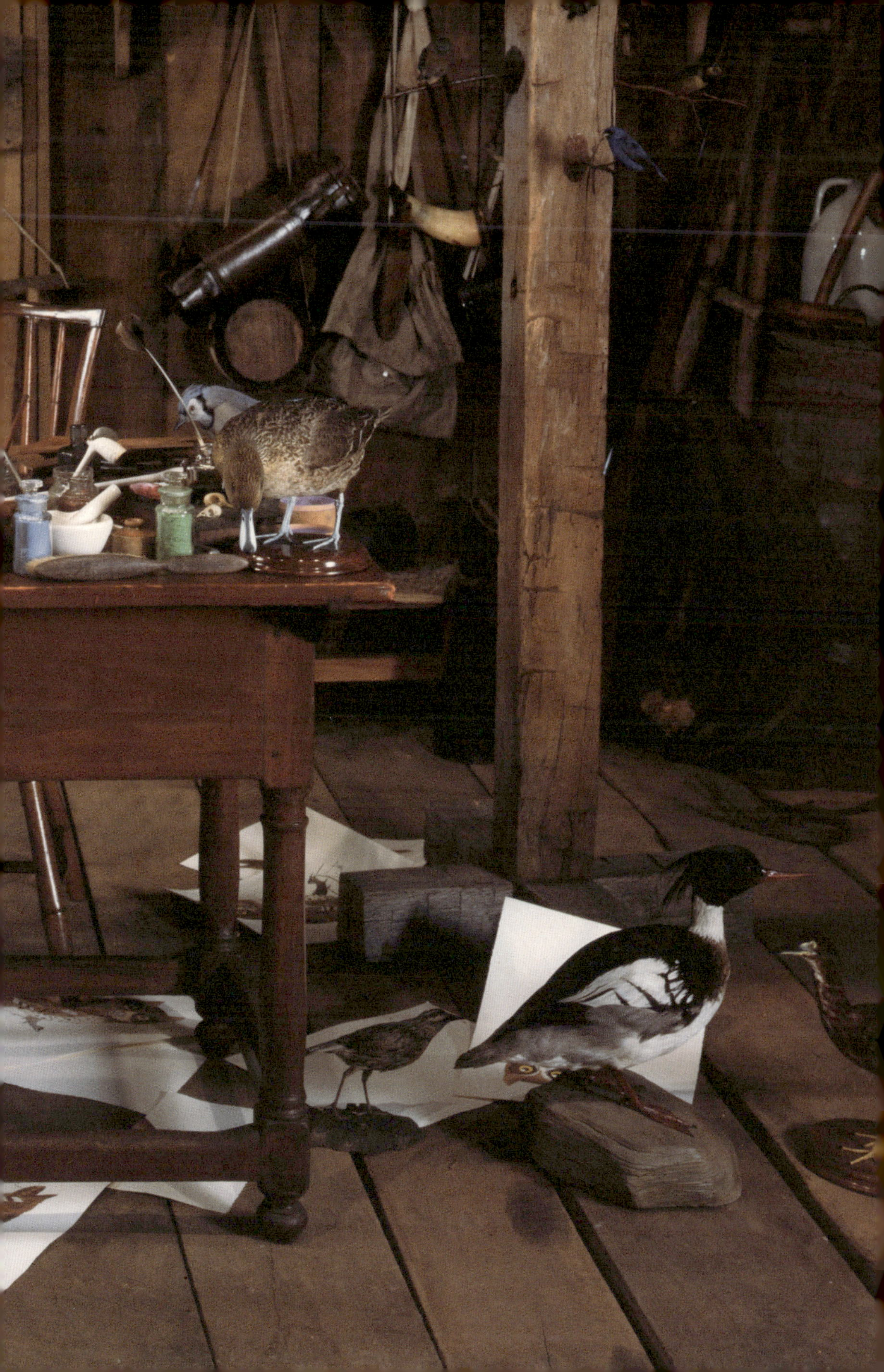

# The Status of Fact: Unreliable Narrators, Parafiction, and Truthiness

*Every artistic movement from the beginning of time is an attempt to figure out
a way to smuggle more of what the artist thinks is reality into the work of art.*
— David Shields[28]

In her essay "Make-Believe: Parafiction and Plausibility" (originally published in 2009 and reprinted in an updated version in this volume), Carrie Lambert-Beatty writes about the growing interest in a form of art in which fictional narrators or imaginary personages create stories and works that are presented as fact. "In some cases," writes Lambert-Beatty, "the artist's objective is to draw attention to the relativism and subjectivity of truth; in others, the strategy is oriented . . . toward the search for truth." Some consider this genre as a new kind of documentary, in which the logic of facts and the logic of fiction are indelibly blurred.[29]

Many of the artists in *More Real* are engaged in a form of reality excavation, in which they take on fictional identities to tell stories based on factual events. In his essay for this book, Graham Burnett describes these practices as "a kind of Dionysian historicism," in which scholarship is not afraid to mix with its subject matter. Throughout his career, artist Mark Dion has sought to arouse the curiosity and wonder that elude many museum visitors today (fig. 25). Building on the tradition of the *Wunderkammer*, or cabinet of curiosities, he often creates a fictional character to serve as the basis for an artwork. On Dion's first visit to the Minneapolis Institute of Arts, he

28. David Shields, *Reality Hunger: A Manifesto* (New York: Knopf, 2010), 37.

29. Jacques Rancière writes: "The fiction of the aesthetic age defined models for connecting the presentation of facts and forms of intelligibility that blurred the border between the logic of facts and the logic of fiction. . . . Writing history and writing stories come under the same regime of truth." Rancière, *The Politics of Aesthetics: The Distribution of the Sensible*, trans. Gabriel Rockhill (London: Continuum, 2004), 38.

25

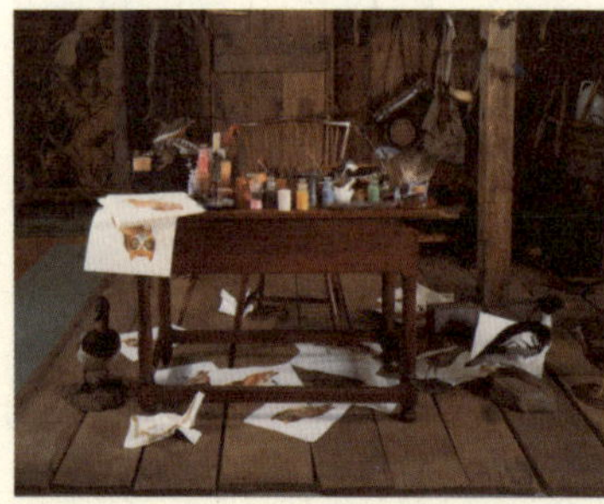

Mark Dion, *Alexander Wilson-Studio,* 1999; wooden structure, mixed mediums; 96 x 144 x 108 inches (243.84 x 365.76 x 274.32 cm); courtesy Tanya Bonakdar Gallery, New York

proposed building a narrative around a fictional curator of modern art who, he decided later, disappeared on a trip to Washington, DC, in the mid-1950s. It was rumored that the curator had been called to testify before a session of the Senate Permanent Subcommittee on Investigations chaired by Senator Joseph McCarthy. After boarding a train from Minneapolis to Washington, DC, he was never seen or heard from again. His office, which was left intact and then sealed, will be opened to museum viewers during the run of *More Real?* Akin to many of the museum's popular period rooms, the curator's office features historical objects, including vintage furniture, books, period art, slide files, a typewriter, papers, and a wide variety of other materials. A curiosity cabinet of sorts, it is also "an inadvertent memorial to victims of McCarthyism that re-engages interest in a forgotten time and past."[30]

30. Mark Dion, proposal for a project for *More Real?*, November 20, 2011, Minneapolis Institute of Arts files.

From 2008 to 2010 thousands of visitors toured an archaeological excavation titled *He Named Her Amber* at the Grange, a nineteenth-century house embedded in the Art Gallery of Ontario (AGO) (fig. 26). Guided by an authoritative site coordinator, visitors were told that a diary belonging to Henry Whyte, who served as butler at the Grange from 1817 to 1857, had recently come to light. In it, he recorded the story of an Irish maid named Mary who had secretly made and buried a number of curious objects throughout the house. Unbeknownst to Mary, the butler was watching from the shadows and taking notes.

The AGO, visitors were told, had hired Archaeological Services Ontario to investigate. In the front hall of the Grange, a portion of the wall had been ripped down to the lath to expose a hiding place.

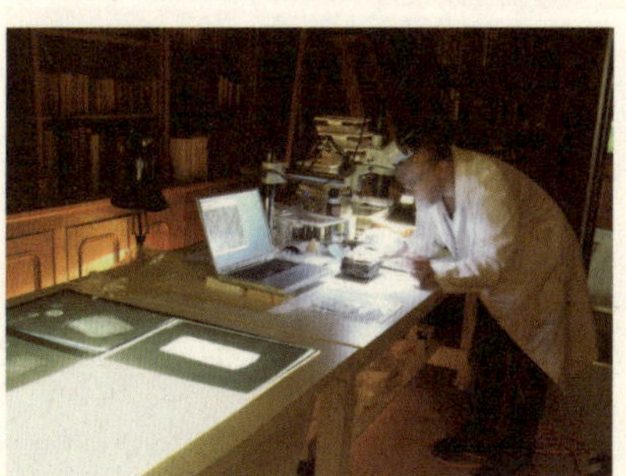

26
Iris Häussler, *He Named Her Amber*, 2008–10 (detail); staff of Archaeological Services Ontario investigating an artifact under a stereomicroscope; courtesy the artist

26

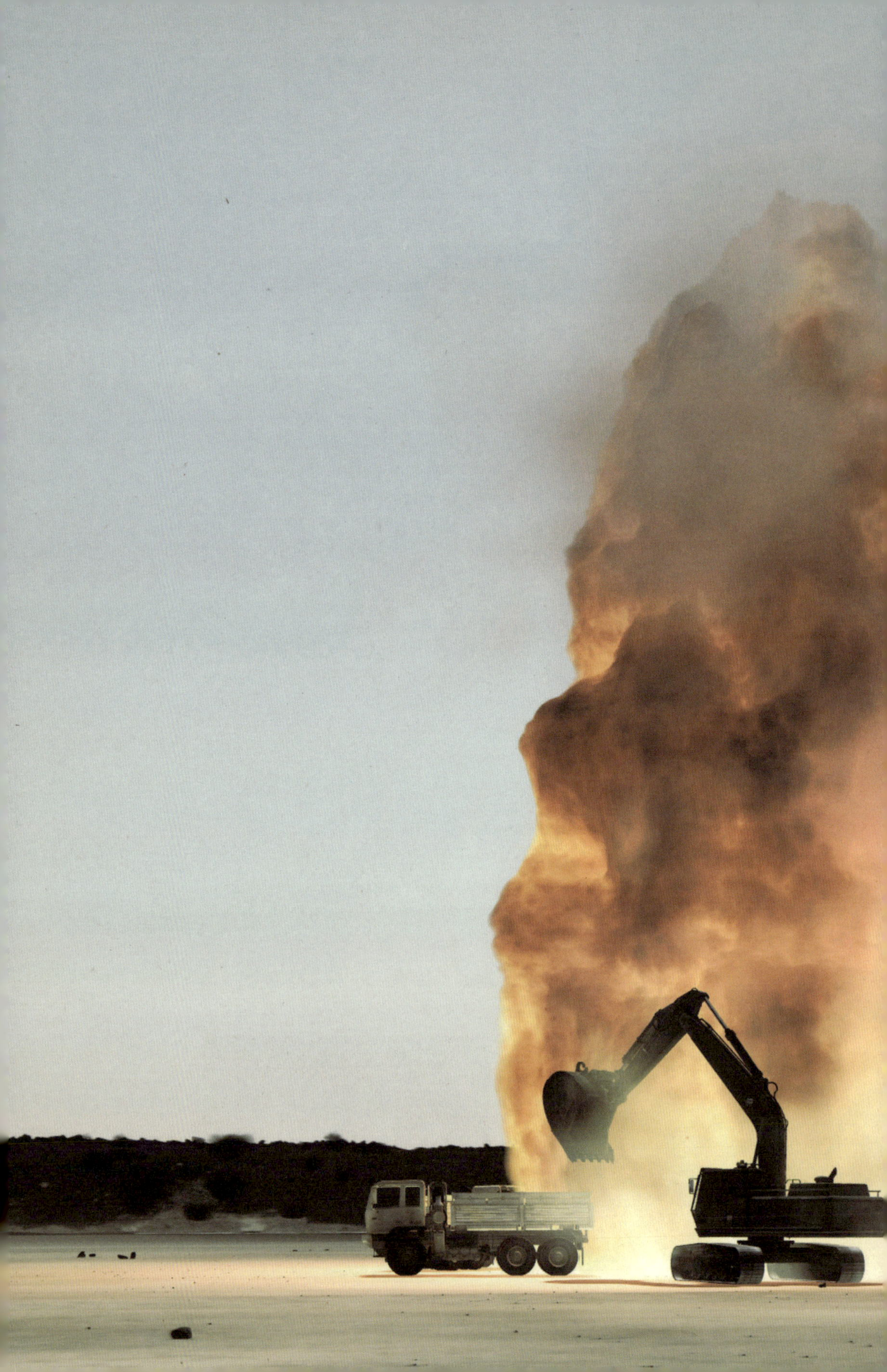

There researchers found a blob of clay and beeswax the size of a baby's clenched fist containing dried blood; it was now set in a display case with a museum label (fig. 27, 28). A descent to the darkened Grange basement revealed an archaeological dig going full throttle, with bright yellow tape, danger warnings, and three large containers full of soil and rubble. The excavation of the pantry floor had yielded the biggest sculpture of all—a cone of wax the length of a woman's arm.[31]

Despite a press conference revealing the truth, despite letters of disclosure handed to visitors, and despite the fact that the same artist had pulled off a similar tour de force in 2006 in a small house in downtown Toronto with the installation *The Legacy of Joseph Wagenbach*, most people who visited the installation at the Grange believed that they were really seeing the work of an untutored nineteenth-century maid. As one critic asked, "Had the combined forces of validation—which included the tour guide, the team of scientists and the AGO itself—disabled our critical faculties?"[32]

The artist who created the installation, German-born Iris Häussler, spent a year working on the script, backstory, and artifacts for this elaborate mise-en-scène. Her goal, she has said, was not to trick people but to provide a direct experience of art. In the letter of disclosure that was handed to visitors as they left the tour, she wrote, "There is a very large difference between thinking about emotions and actually experiencing them." By making Mary "real," Häussler sought to heighten empathy for a character who, for her, represented "the sacrifice of immigrants for the sake of their families, a phenomenon that continues to have as much relevance today as it did in the 19th century."[33]

31. Gillian MacKay, "Brilliant Disguise: Iris Häussler's Fact-Meets-Fiction Odysseys," *Canadian Art*, Winter 2009, http://www.canadianart.ca/art/features/2009/12/01/brilliant-disguise/.

32. Ibid.

33. Ibid.

27
Iris Häussler, *He Named Her Amber*, 2008–10 (detail); beeswax, pigment; 3 3/16 x 2 7/8 in. (8.1 x 7.4 cm); courtesy the artist

28
Iris Häussler, *He Named Her Amber*, 2008–9 (detail); "A handmade pinch pot of clay filled with beeswax. The beeswax has been found to contain tiny flakes of dried blood—the blood was no longer liquid when it was added to the wax—and through DNA analysis we were able to determine that it came from a Caucasian female"; courtesy the artist

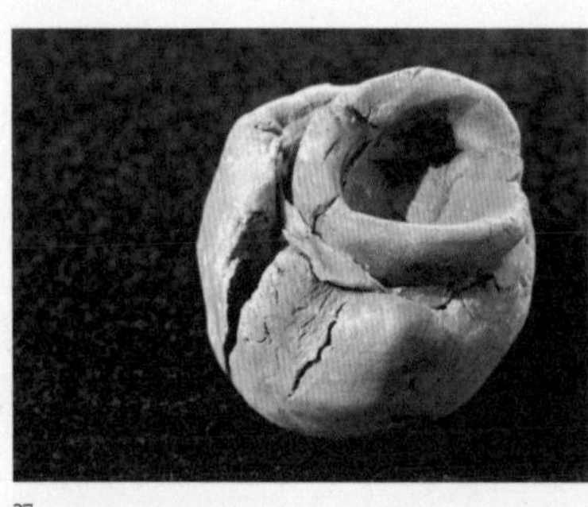

27

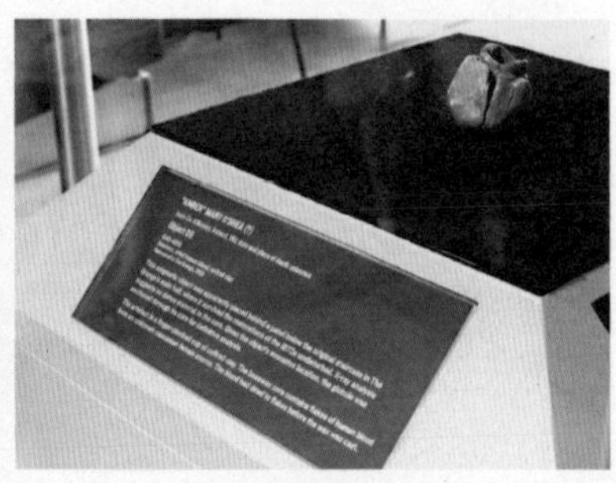

28

Many visitors to the museum loved the experience, while many others resented having spent time becoming emotionally engaged in something that turned out to be an artist's fabrication. This collision of trust and betrayal, in which fact meets fiction, is where the aesthetics of disorientation start to run aground. Häussler makes work that cuts to the emotional essence, but it often does so at the expense of our trust. The question remains as to whether her art exposes or reinforces a culture of deception.

Social trust becomes a larger issue as artists employ new media that can drastically increase the number of those reached by such deceptions. When Orson Welles's infamous radio drama *The War of the Worlds* was aired in 1938, the lack of commercial breaks led listeners to believe that they were hearing a live newscast, causing mass deception and panic. In 1965 a film by the British filmmaker Peter Watkins titled *The War Game* was intended to air as an hourlong program on the BBC. At the last minute, however, it was deemed too intense and violent—too real—to be broadcast. Interestingly enough, this fictional docudrama about an imagined nuclear war and its aftermath in England won an Oscar in 1967 for best documentary.[34]

Building on the power of contemporary social media to reach a broad and varied public, the duo known as the Yes Men activate their version of truthiness, practicing what they call "identity correction," under the mission statement of "telling the truth and exposing lies."[35] In 2004, on the twentieth anniversary of the chemical disaster at its Union Carbide plant in Bhopal, India, Dow Chemical went on BBC World TV to announce that the company, which had

34. The veracity of documentary film is a fascinating subject in itself. See, for example, Linda Williams, "Mirrors without Memories: Truth, History, and the New Documentary," *Film Quarterly* 46 (Spring 1993): 9–21.

35. See *Wikipedia*, s.v. "The Yes Men," last modified December 7, 2011, http://en.wikipedia.org/wiki/The_Yes_Men.

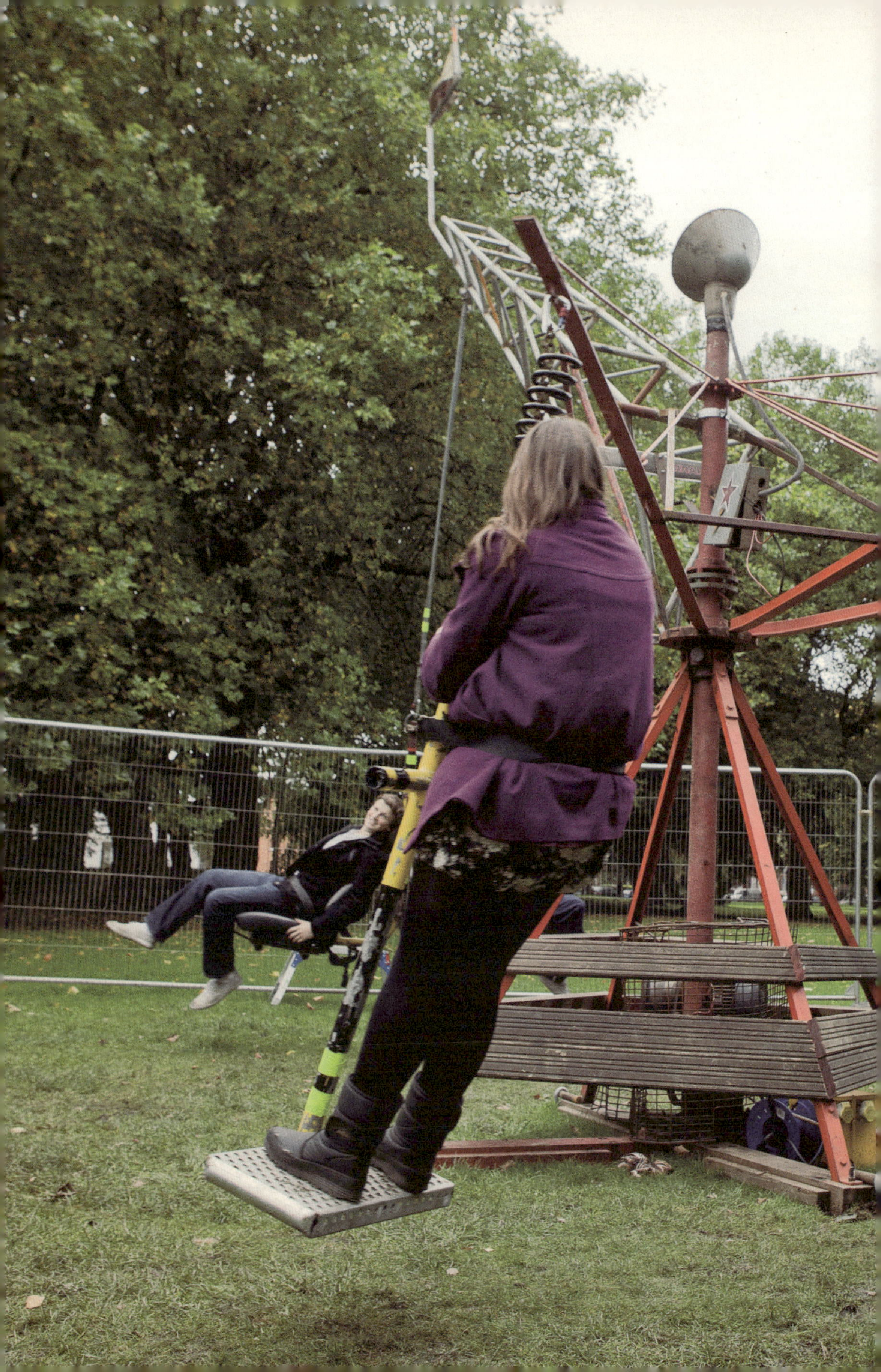

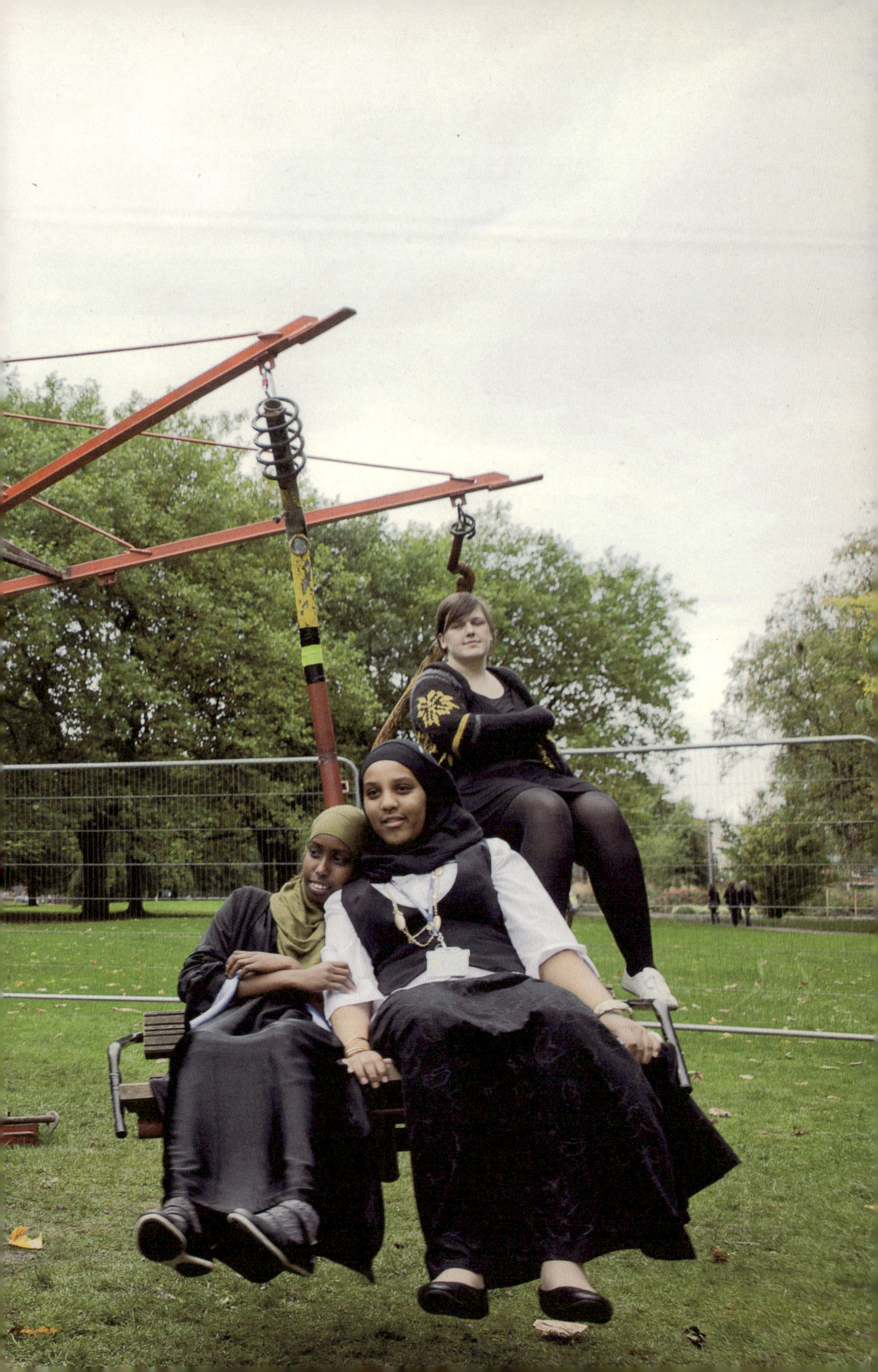

acquired Union Carbide in 2002, was accepting full responsibility for that disaster and was going to compensate the victims and clean up the mess. The Dow spokesman, identified as Jude Finisterra, was in fact the Yes Men principal Jacques Servin (also known as Andy Bichlbaum; fig. 29). Before Dow could launch a corporate denial, the story had been broadcast around the world.

Other activities of the Yes Men include the creation of fake websites that spoof the legitimate websites of their targets, which many members of the public have mistaken for real. In 2011 they created a website promising inhalers to asthma-inflicted children who live within two hundred miles of a coal plant. Shortly after it was first posted, Coalcares.org made the front page of the real *New York Times*, where it was revealed to be an elaborate hoax (fig. 30).

Following in the footsteps of the Yes Men and other tricksters before them, the Italian-born artists Eva and Franco Mattes are another culture-jamming duo known for their subversion of public media. Working under the name 0100101110101101.ORG, they have manipulated video games, Internet technologies, and feature films, mingling truth and falsehood to the point that they become indistinguishable. Although most active on the Internet, they have also effectively engaged their critique in the physical realm. In one ambitious hoax, they announced the renaming of Vienna's famous Karlsplatz, home to such major cultural sites as the Secession and the Karlskirche. Under cover of night, they installed a room-size red box, elevated at the edge of the square and complete with the Nike logo. Convincing people living in Vienna that Nike had purchased the

29
The Yes Men, *Dow Does the Right Thing*, 2004; courtesy the artists

30
The Yes Men; *Coal Cares™*, 2011; courtesy the artists

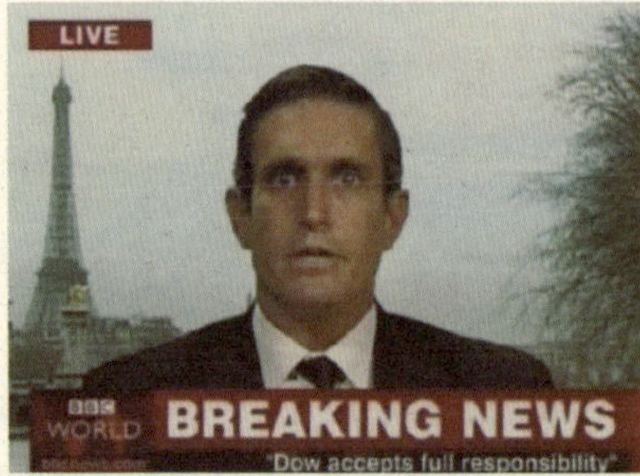


29

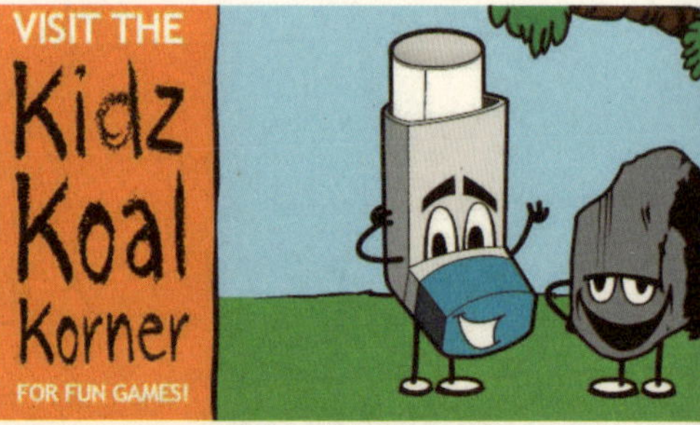


30

Karlsplatz and was about to rename it Nikeplatz, the work attracted press attention to the growing privatization of public spaces (fig. 31).

In 2010 the Matteses obtained permission to travel to Chernobyl, the site of the disastrous explosion of a Soviet nuclear reactor in 1986. Much of the area still registers unsafe levels of radiation, but visitors are allowed to enter at their own risk. In the nearby ghost town of Pripyat, they found the rusted remains of an abandoned amusement park that was supposedly built as a gift to the power plant workers for an upcoming May Day celebration. Unfortunately the reactor exploded five days before the park was inaugurated. Almost a year after the Matteses' visit to Pripyat, a "radioactive ride" appeared at a park in Manchester, England. Purportedly pieced together by the artists from contaminated materials scavenged from the Pripyat amusement park, the sinister-looking ride, called the Liquidator (fig. 32), caused consternation among Manchester citizens. Nonetheless, according to the artists, it operated daily for a whole week, involving "thousands of enthusiastic visitors of all ages and origins" before it "disappeared as fast as it had appeared."[36]

The Lebanese-born artist Walid Raad established the Atlas Group in 1999 to study the problem of history and how it has been "made" by regimes throughout the Middle East. The Atlas Group created an archive of videos, photographs, and essays documenting the years when the country was traumatized by civil war, from the 1970s to the 1990s. The archive reveals a history that is composed as much of fiction — biased news reports, personal recollections, and so on — as of fact.[37] This work draws attention to the ways in which contemporary society understands recent Lebanese history.

36. "Radioactive Ride in the Heart of Manchester," 010010111010101101.ORG, http://www.01001011101-01101.org/blog/?p=145.

37. See Raad's website for the Atlas Group, www.theatlasgroup.org/.

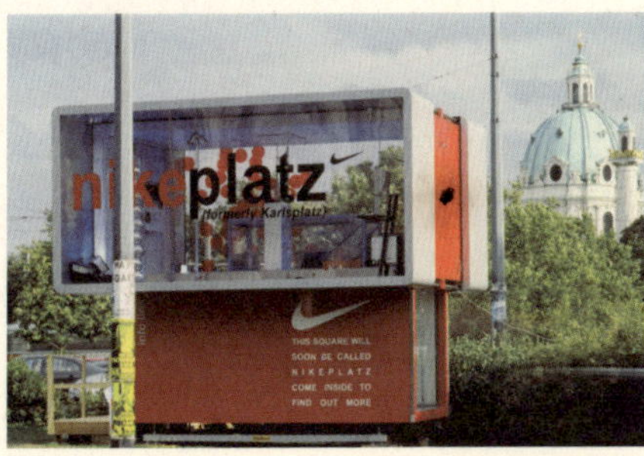


31

31
Eva and Franco Mattes aka
010010111010101101.ORG and
Public Netbase, *Fake Nike
Infobox*, 2003; installation view in
Karlsplatz, Vienna; courtesy Eva
and Franco Mattes

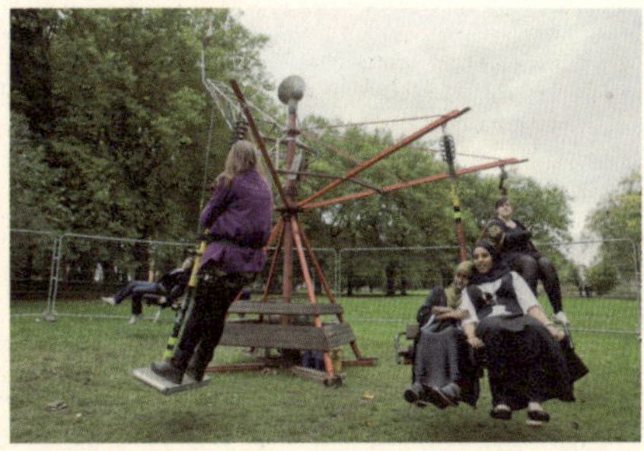

32

32
Ryan C. Doyle, Eva and Franco
Mattes aka 010010111010101101.ORG,
*Plan C*, 2010; installation view in
Manchester, England; courtesy
the artists

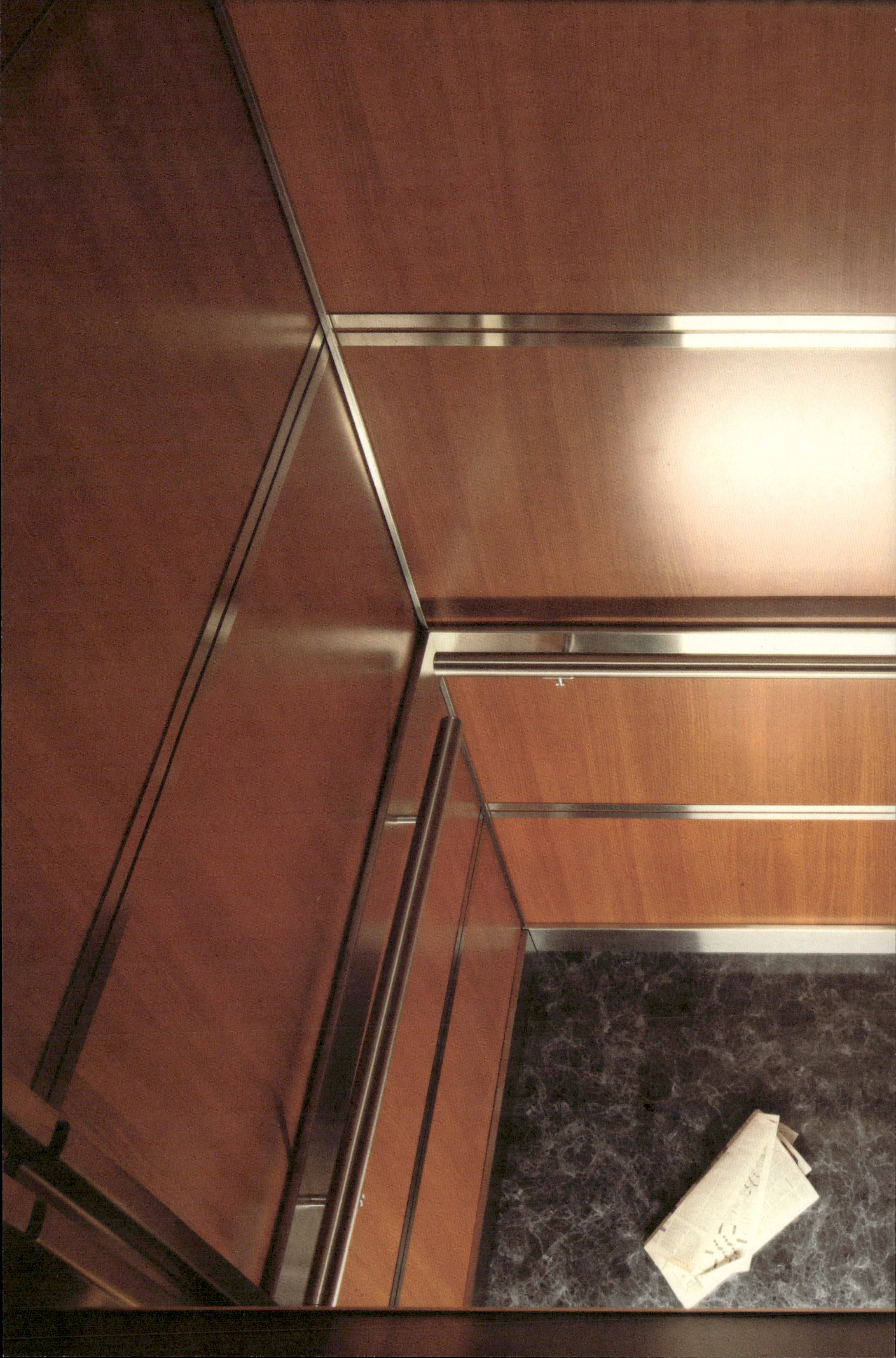

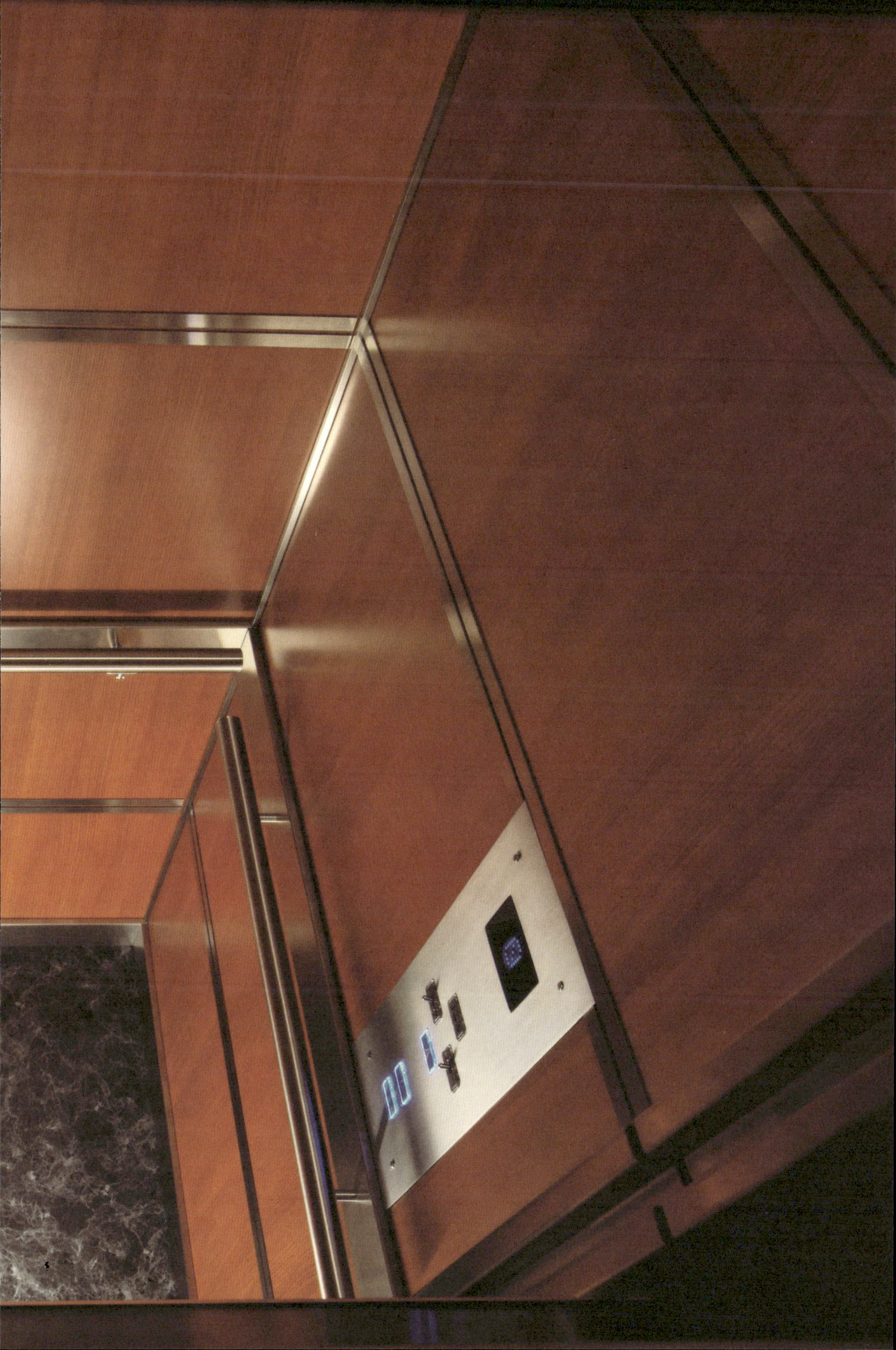

The Atlas Group is an invention of Raad, and its archives, which appear to be authentic, are a fabrication. As Glenn Lowry writes in this publication, "Raad has always been a bit of a trickster, using conceptual strategies and the visual equivalent of sleight of hand to explore critically important issues." For Lowry, one of the central questions about the work is whether it is a purely artistic project or a serious effort at making history. "By using the traditional instruments of history making—including archival sources, photographic documentation, and personal testimonies—but blurring the boundary between the factual and the fictional, [Raad] reveals the complex ways in which the narrative of history is constructed from a combination of reliable sources of information and imagination, from objective truths as well as highly personal memories." As Lowry observes, Raad investigates the irrational aspect of human consciousness and the extent to which subjectivity and memory are involved in the making of history.

38. Hans-Georg Gadamer, *Truth and Method*, translation ed. Garrett Barden and John Cumming (New York: Seabury, 1975), 92.

## *More Real?*

> The work of art has its true being in the fact that it becomes an experience changing the person experiencing it.
>
> —Hans-Georg Gadamer[38]

A recent radio program addressed proposed legislation in various states that attempts to limit women's reproductive rights by requiring waiting periods or ultrasound examinations for those seeking to terminate a pregnancy or by redefining when life begins or what is considered a "person." Virtually all these bills have been introduced by male legislators. The female participants in the radio program responded to these proposed laws with proposals of their own aimed at men. One described a law that would require any man seeking a drug such as Viagra to meet certain requirements, including getting a recent sexual partner to certify that he is indeed experiencing problems with erectile dysfunction, undergoing a cardiac stress test to ensure that he is fit enough for sexual activity, and consulting a sex therapist. "We want to make sure that we show men love and protect them in the same way… that male policymakers across this country have been so preoccupied with a woman's reproductive health," she said. "For far too long as female policymakers we have abdicated our responsibility to look out for men's reproductive health."[39] Another participant discussed a proposal referred to as the "spilled semen" amendment, which states: "Any action in which a man ejaculates or otherwise deposits semen anywhere but in a woman's vagina shall be interpreted and construed as an action against an unborn child."[40]

A listener tuning in midway through the program might assume that it was a satirical news show along the lines of *The Daily Show* or *The Colbert Report*, but in fact it was a "real" news program, and the participants were not comedians but state legislators. Constance Johnson, the Oklahoma state senator who introduced the "spilled semen" amendment, acknowledged that her proposal had no chance of becoming law but said that her goal was to point out "how ludicrous and absurd these proposals are." (The legislation that Johnson sought to amend was Oklahoma's "personhood" bill, which would grant individual rights to an embryo from the moment of conception.) Johnson and Nina Turner, the Ohio state senator who put

39. Nina Turner, interview by Warren Olney, *To the Point*, KCRW, March 16, 2012, http://www.kcrw .com/news/programs/tp/ tp120316women_target _men_wit. The quotations from Constance Johnson and Jim Wilson in this section are from interviews on the same program. I am grateful to Karen Jacobson for referring me to this program.

40. Teresa Tomassoni, "In Protest, Democrats Zero In on Men's Reproductive Health," *Shots* (blog), NPR, March 15, 2012, http://www.npr.org/ blogs/health/2012/03/ 15/148695307/in-protest-democrats-zero-in-on-mens-reproductive-health.

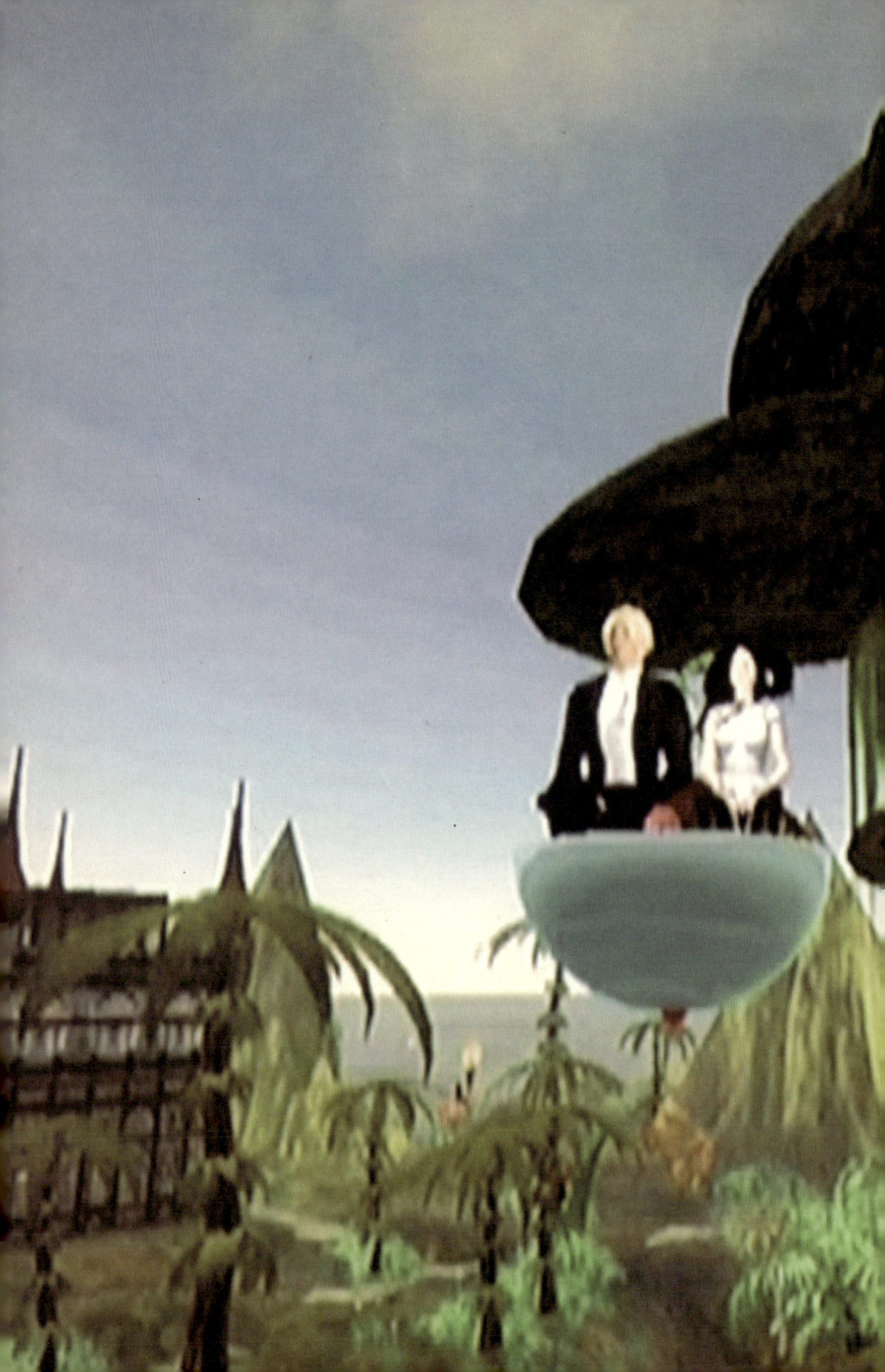

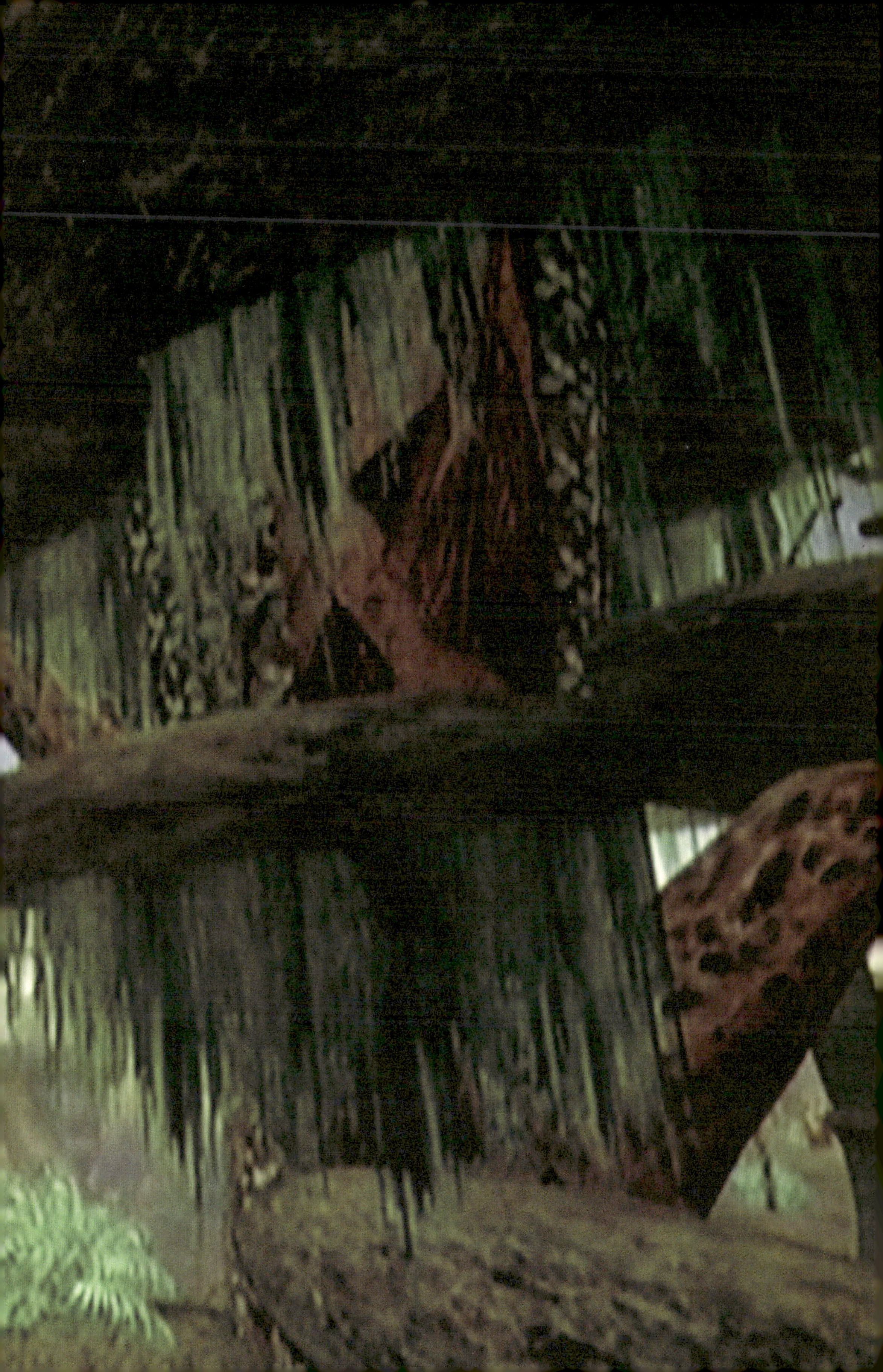

forward the legislation restricting access to erectile dysfunction medication, are part of a group of state legislators who are using humor to counter attacks on women's reproductive rights. Why would elected officials who clearly take this issue seriously adopt tactics borrowed from late-night comedy shows? A comment from a colleague of Johnson's who was interviewed on the same radio program provides a clue. Jim Wilson—an Oklahoma state senator who drafted his own satirical amendment to the personhood bill, one that would require any man who impregnated a woman to support her and the unborn child from the moment of conception—stated: "I don't believe anybody in the legislature really cares about abortion. I think they've turned it into a political device." By proposing laws that target men in the same way that anti–reproductive rights legislation targets women, these lawmakers hope to expose the duplicity of their opponents' position and to galvanize their own supporters.

As writers throughout this volume acknowledge, we are living in an age of "truthiness," a time when many in the public sphere create their own versions of reality, taking advantage of the fact that things that we wish to be true are often more appealing than those that are known to be true. We are all susceptible to what Norman Klein, writing in this volume, calls "the charm of the lie." Further complicating our notion of truth is an understanding of the provisional nature of knowledge. The questioning of truth is fundamental to the artists in *More Real?* For Iris Häussler, whose art is based on fabricated narratives, the key question is not whether her works are true or false. Rather, as curator David Moos explains, she "aims to bring the viewer into a state of psychic participation where the wonder of the art work ignites a new possible truth that becomes powerful, for many people absolutely riveting, because they are able to contribute to and even embellish this narrative."[41] Häussler takes advantage of our willingness to enter into and be seduced by fictional scenarios.

In this volume, Graham Burnett asks whether the "aestheticization of disorientation" by artists and others serves to mirror or accelerate the destabilization of fact and fiction. While the works in *More Real?* may sometimes blur the lines between art and reality, they also draw attention to the increasingly murky boundaries between contemporary politics and theater and between journalism and entertainment. These works create dialogue around the impact of "truthiness" on society, prompting consideration of the ethical issues surrounding the exploitation of truth. Does the growing mastery of collective deception represent, Burnett wonders, "a frightening evacuation of the public sphere . . . that put[s] the very idea of participatory politics at risk," or is "wielding a little schizophrenic irony . . . the twenty-first-century equivalent of registering to vote"?

In his satirical news program, Stephen Colbert trusts that his audience will be able to distinguish between a comedian with a strong moral compass and the blowhard that he plays as the show's host. The scholar Robert T. Tally Jr. argues that both Colbert and Jon Stewart present a "powerful critique of the mainstream media" by revealing that "all 'news' has become transformed into entertainment-television that no longer bears much, if any, relation to the 'real.'" Tally concludes: "Whether they like it or not, the fake news comedians Stewart and Colbert are now real news journalists and commentators.

41. David Moos, curatorial statement for *He Named Her Amber*, Art Gallery of Ontario, January 2009, from Iris Häussler's website, http://www.haeussler.ca/amber/curator.html.

This may be the most hyperreal (or perhaps surreal) aspect of the blurring of the lines between journalism and entertainment, revealing the social significance of these fake news shows: Fake news is more real than real news precisely because it discloses just how fake the real news can be."[42]

Disclosing fakery is something that the artists featured in *More Real?* do as well, but I would argue that they do much more. If they share a collective strategy, it is to encourage critical thought and to inspire wonder. In 2007 Allan Siegel produced a video relating to Iñigo Manglano-Ovalle's *Phantom Truck* installation at Documenta 12.[43] The video begins with black-and-white still images that appear to show the mobile biological weapons labs that Manglano-Ovalle's work re-creates (though they can't, since we now know that those labs never existed). On the sound track we hear Colin Powell speaking to the United Nations: "We know what the fermenters look like," Powell intones. "We know what the tanks, pumps, compressors, and other parts look like. We know how they fit together. We know how they work." The video then segues to color footage in fast motion that shows *Phantom Truck* being unloaded from a container and assembled. Toward the end, as we watch the final stages of the installation, the video shifts back to black and white, and we hear Powell speaking again: "My colleagues, every statement I make today is backed up by sources, solid sources. These are not assertions. What we are giving you are facts and conclusions based on solid intelligence."

At Documenta, *Phantom Truck* was concealed in a darkened room so that one came upon it as one might stumble across

42. Robert T. Tally, "I Am the Mainstream Media (and So Can You!)," in *The Stewart/Colbert Effect: Essays on the Real Impacts of Fake News*, ed. Amarnath Amarasingam (Jefferson, NC: McFarland, 2011), 149, 150, 162.

43. See Allan Siegel's website, http://www.kekbicikli.org/page08/page11/phantom_truck11.htm. For the video, see "Documenta 12 Phantom Truck," YouTube video, 4:18, posted by "dunablue22," June 17, 2007, http://www.youtube.com/watch?v=B7Rz0cXwlpM.

the stuff of dreams (or nightmares) made real. What emerged from the gloom, as the eyes adjusted to the low level of light, was the physical embodiment of a deception unmasked by history. Like all great art, it has the power to engage the mind and the body, the imagination and the senses, immersing us in the mysteries, doubts, and uncertainties that are the truth of this world.

# Trevor Paglen

**news and updates | visual projects | written projects | media/reviews | odds, ends, and blog | bio | contact**

**:: ODDS, ENDS, and BLOG ::**
A dumping ground for interesting things that come my way...

**August 2009**

I would really like to know what this patch is all about:

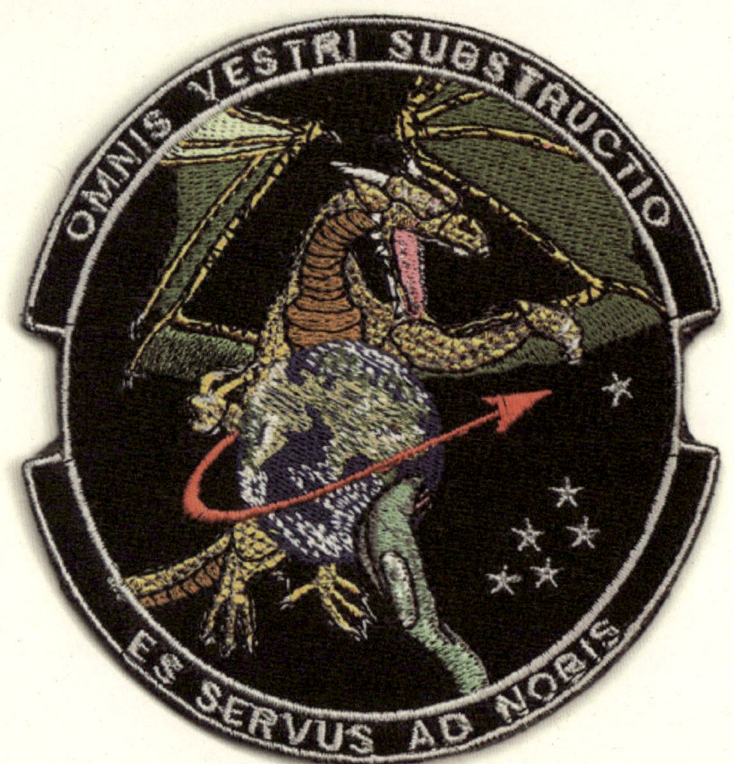


I have a pretty good idea what a lot of the things probably mean, but I encourage anyone who wants to take a crack at deciphering it to try to see it with unbiased eyes. I made the image relatively big here because there are some interesting small details. The patch was sent to me anonymously with a return address near Fort Meade, MD.


My initial interpretations/guesses about the symbolism:

- The patch is probably for some kind of classified spacecraft.

- As Dwayne Day showed in his excellent series for the Space Review, dragon symbolism is often associated with SIGINT payloads. The return address on the envelope obviously comes from a place where there's a lot of interest in SIGINT payloads.

- The dragon's golden wings underlines the connection (golden dragon wings often symbolize the massive gold-foil covered dish antennae characteristic of SIGINT spacecraft.)

- The red arrow's trajectory suggests a Molniya orbit similar to those associated with JUMPSEAT and TRUMPET spacecraft.

- As Dwayne Day showed, stars often represent the number of spacecraft in a given "constellation." The stars here may suggest that this spacecraft if being added to a preexisting constellation of five other craft with similar missions.

# Trevor Paglen



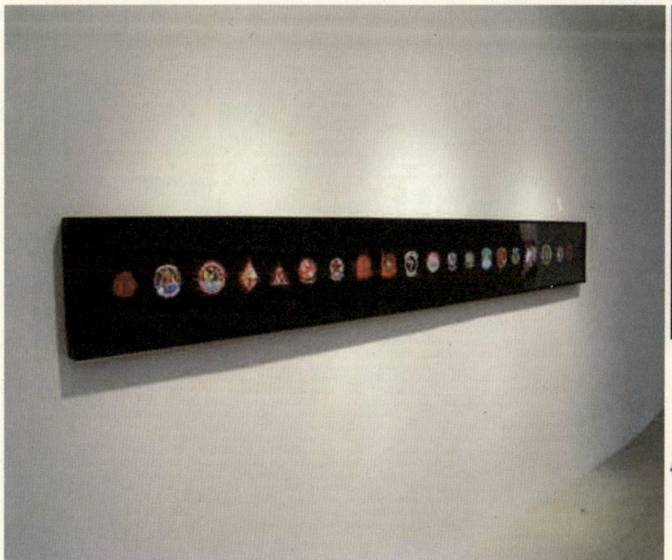

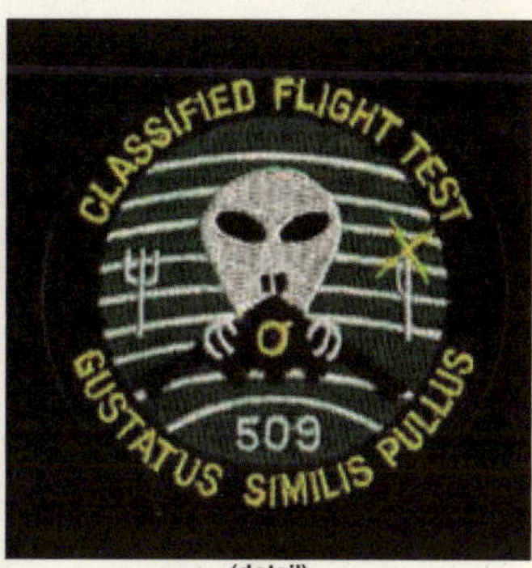

(detail)

**Symbology (Volume I)**
**2006**

Military culture is filled with a totemic visual language consisting of symbols and insignia that signify everything from various unit and command affiliations to significant events, and noteworthy programs. A typical uniform will sport patches identifying its wearer's job, program affiliation, achievements and place within the military hierarchy. These markers of identity and program heraldry begin to create a peculiar symbolic regime when they depict one's affiliation with what defense-industry insiders call the "black world" – the world of classified programs, projects, and places, whose outlines, even existence, are deeply-held secrets. Nonetheless, the Pentagon's "black world" is replete with the rich symbolic language that characterizes other, less obscure, military activities.

The symbols and insignia shown in the *Symbology* series provide a glimpse into how contemporary military units answer questions that have historically been the purview of mystery cults, secret societies, religions, and mystics: How does one represent that which, by definition, must not be represented?

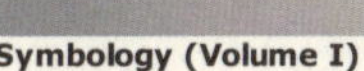

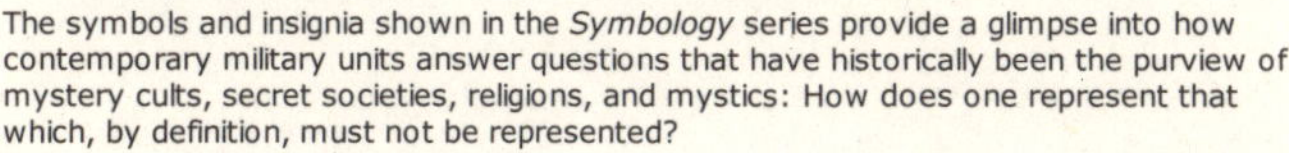

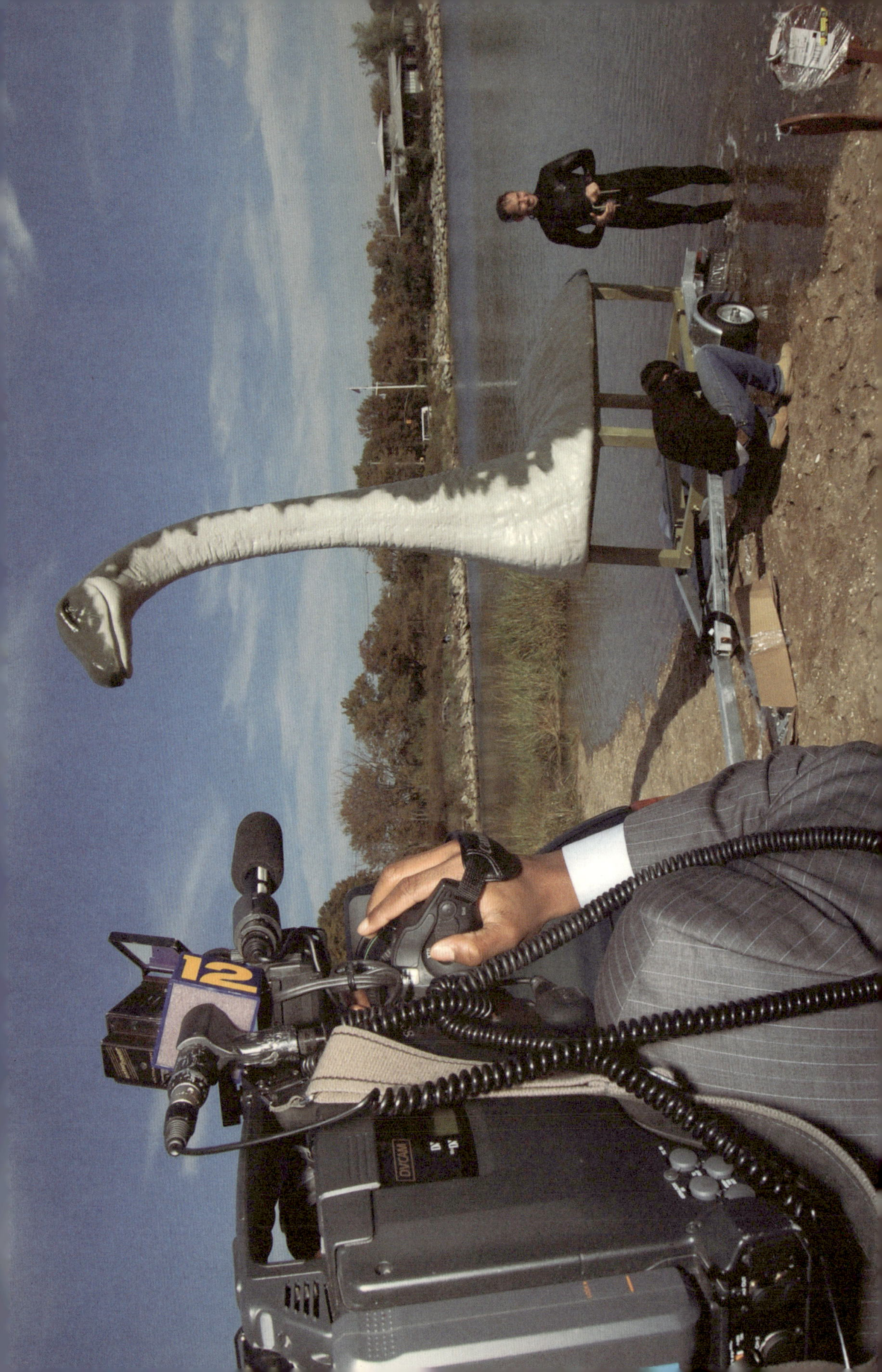

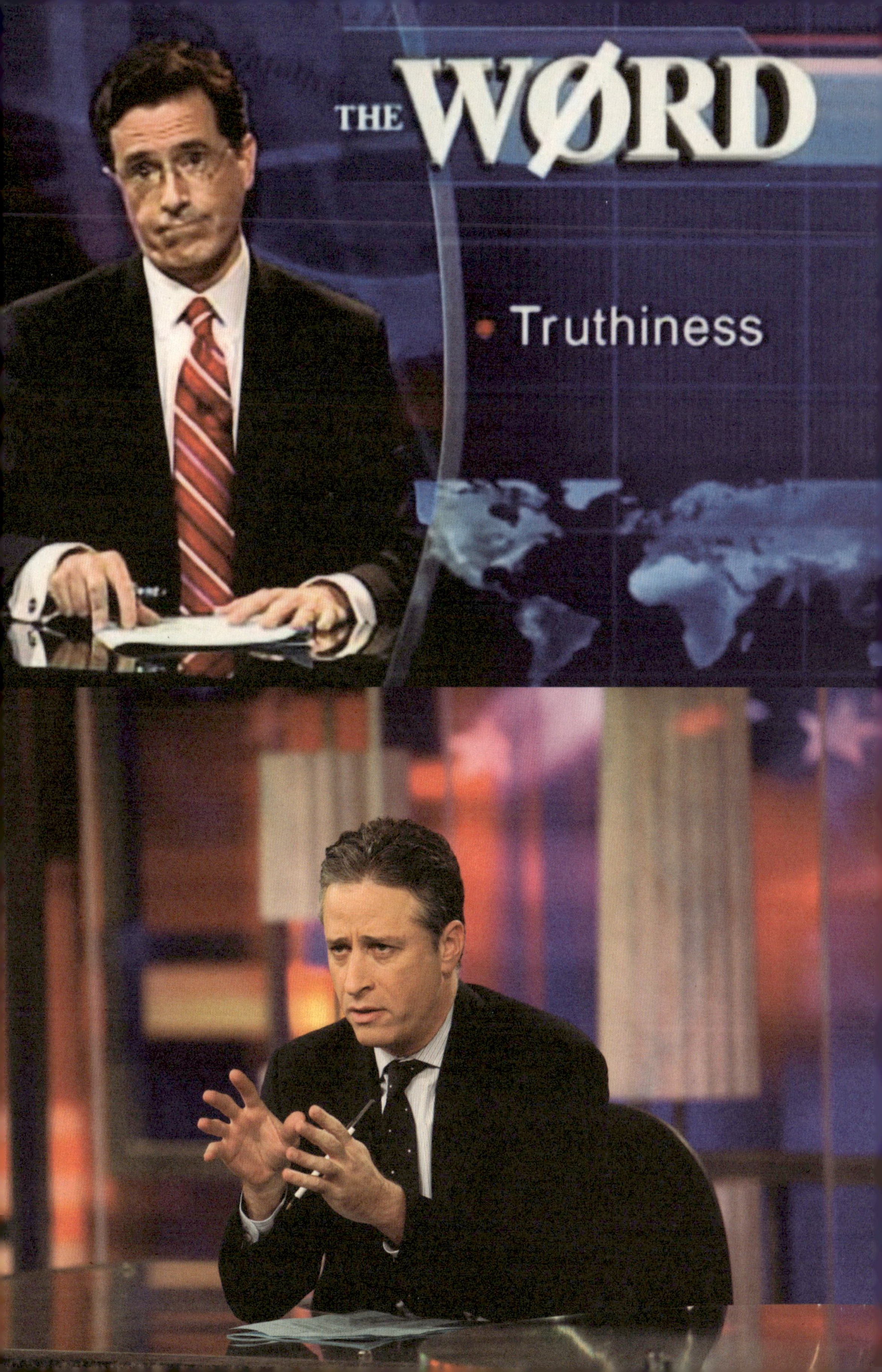

THE WØRD
Truthiness

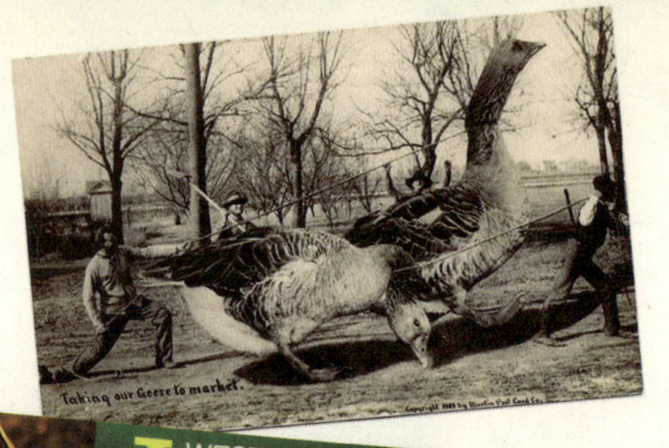

Taking our Geese to market.


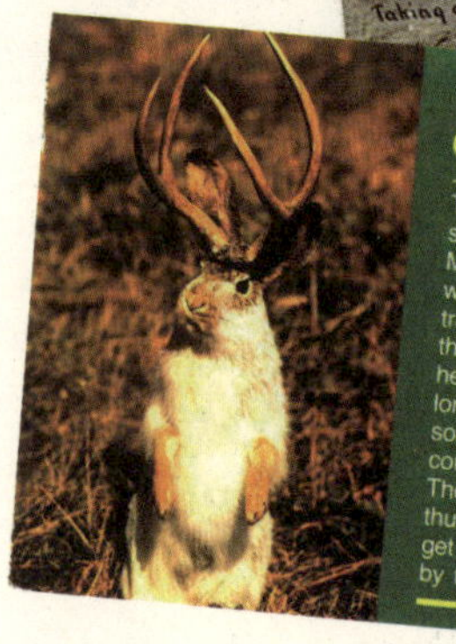

WESTERN
JACKALOPE
The first white man to see this singular fauna specimen was a trapper named George McLean in 1829. When he told of it later he was promptly denounced as a liar. An odd trait of the Jackalope is its ability to imitate the human voice. Cowboys singing to their herds at night have been startled to hear their lonesome melodies repeated faithfully from some nearby hillside. The phantom echo comes from the throat of some Jackalope. They sing only on dark nights before a thunderstorm. Stories that they sometimes get together and sing in chorus is discounted by those who know them best.


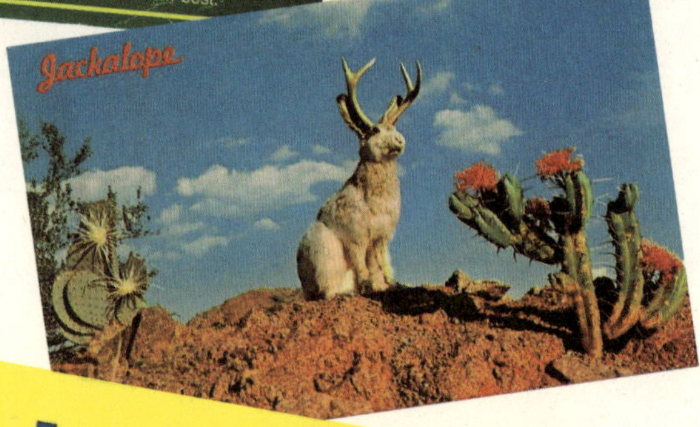

Jackalope

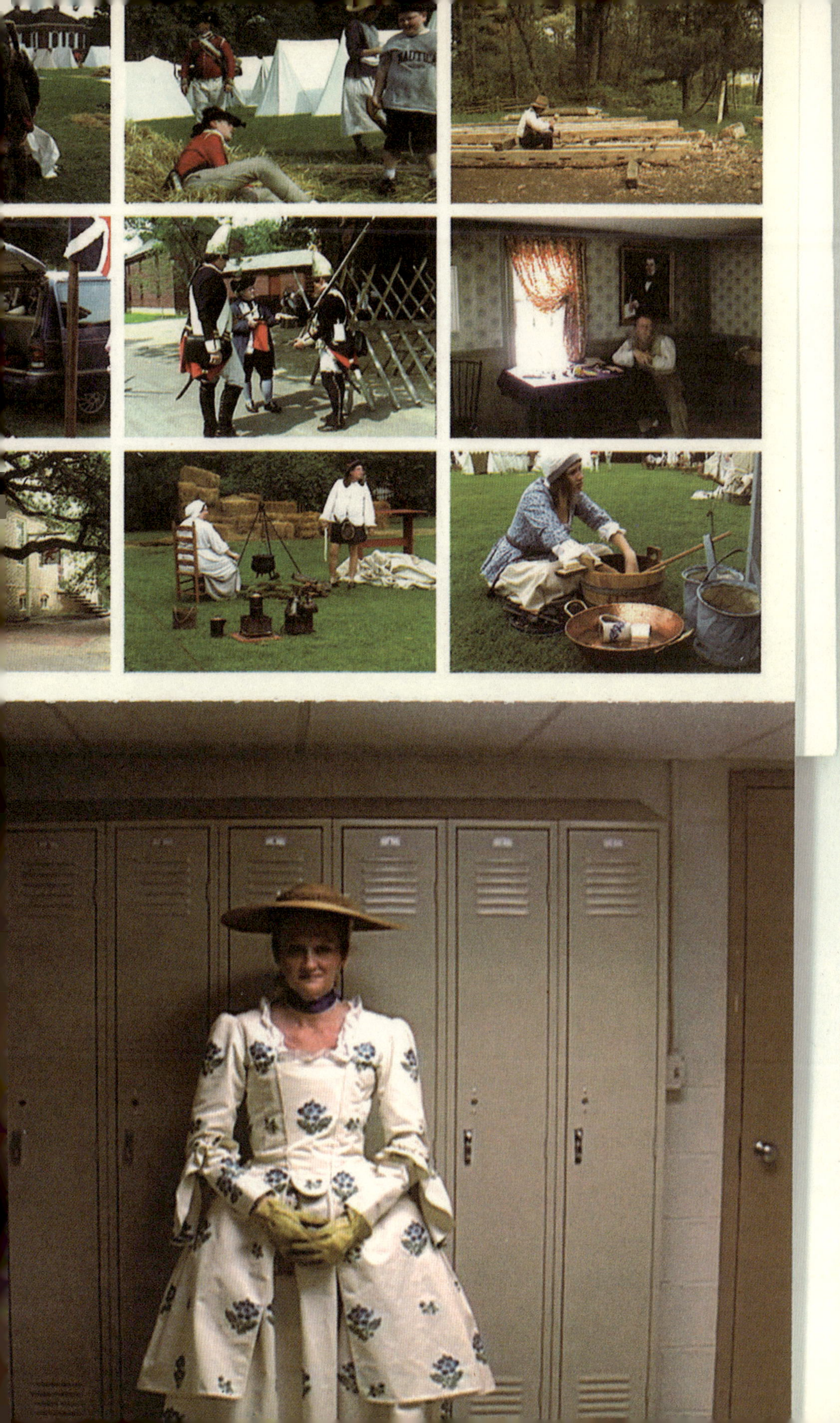

# From the Real to the More Real

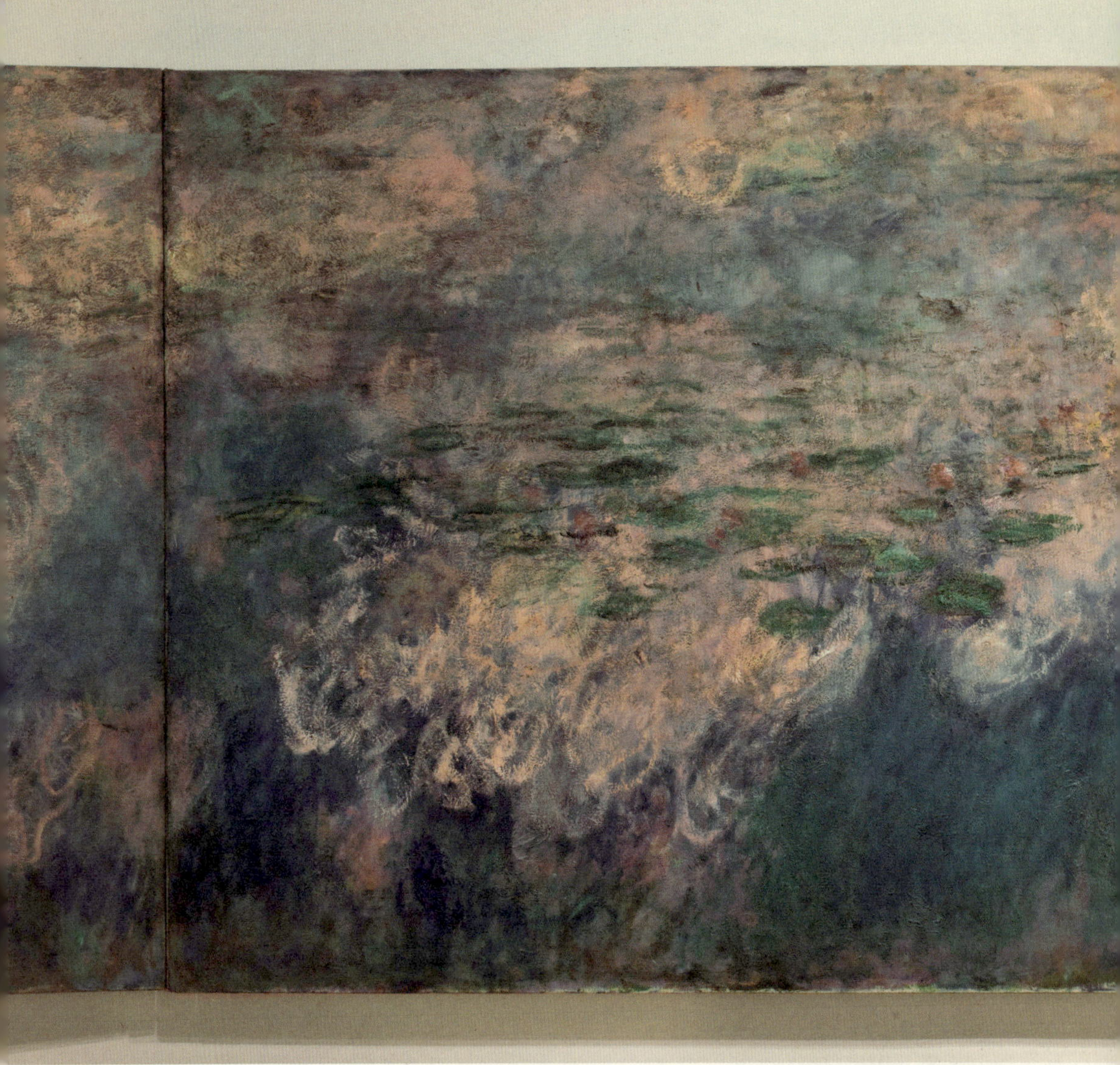

66.1959.a-c

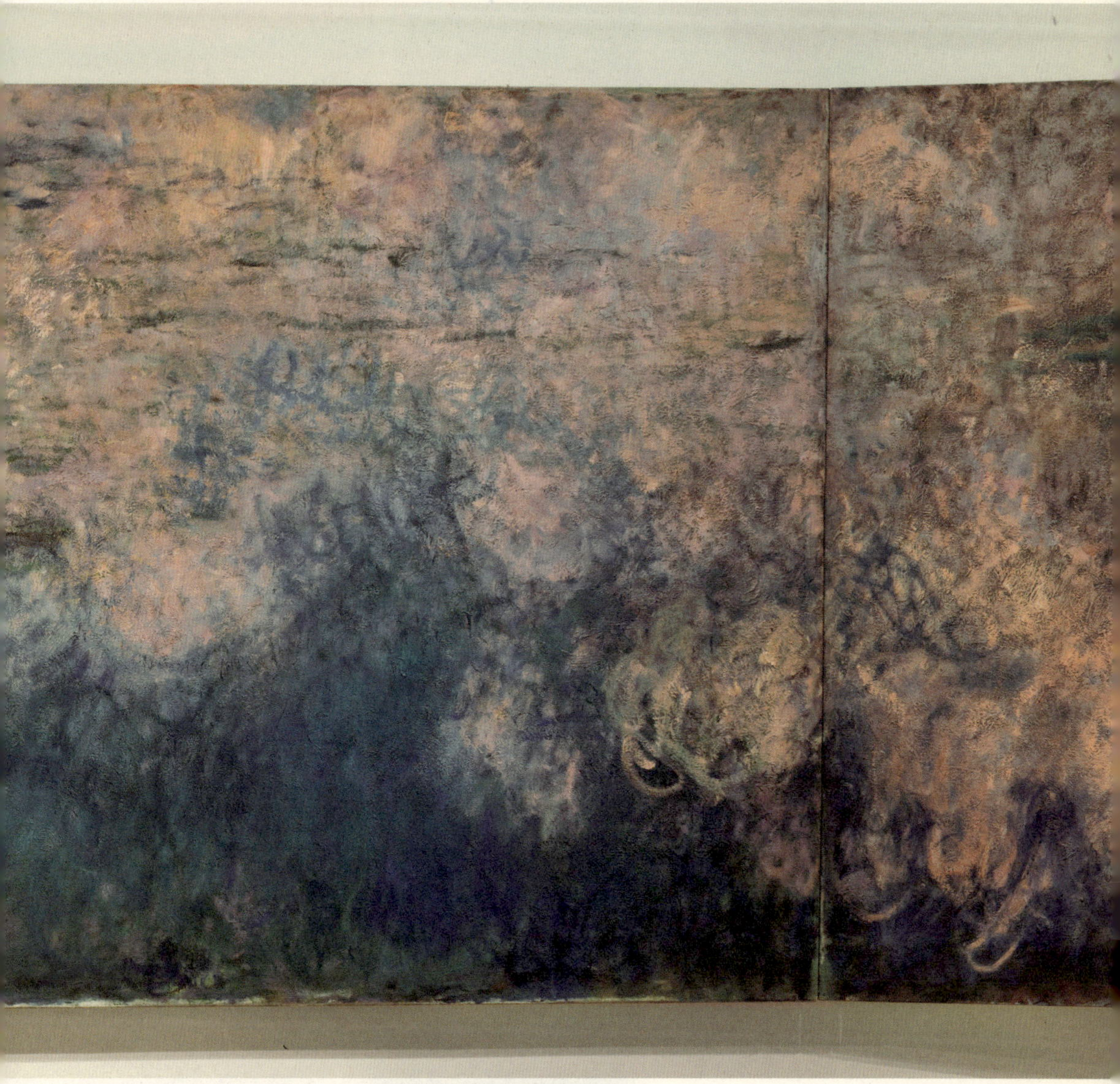

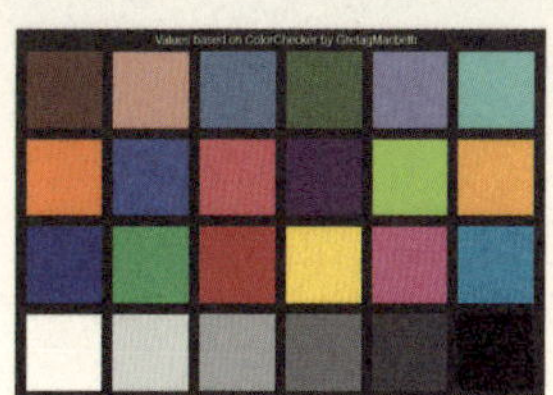

# From the Real to the More Real: A Brief Historical and Philosophical Sketch of Hyperreality and Its Roots in Realism, Impressionism, Surrealism, Pop Art, and Postmodernism



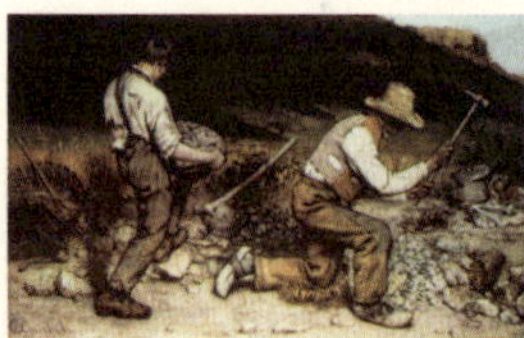

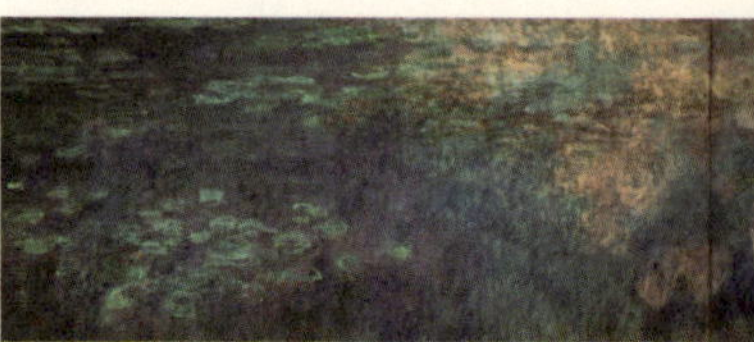

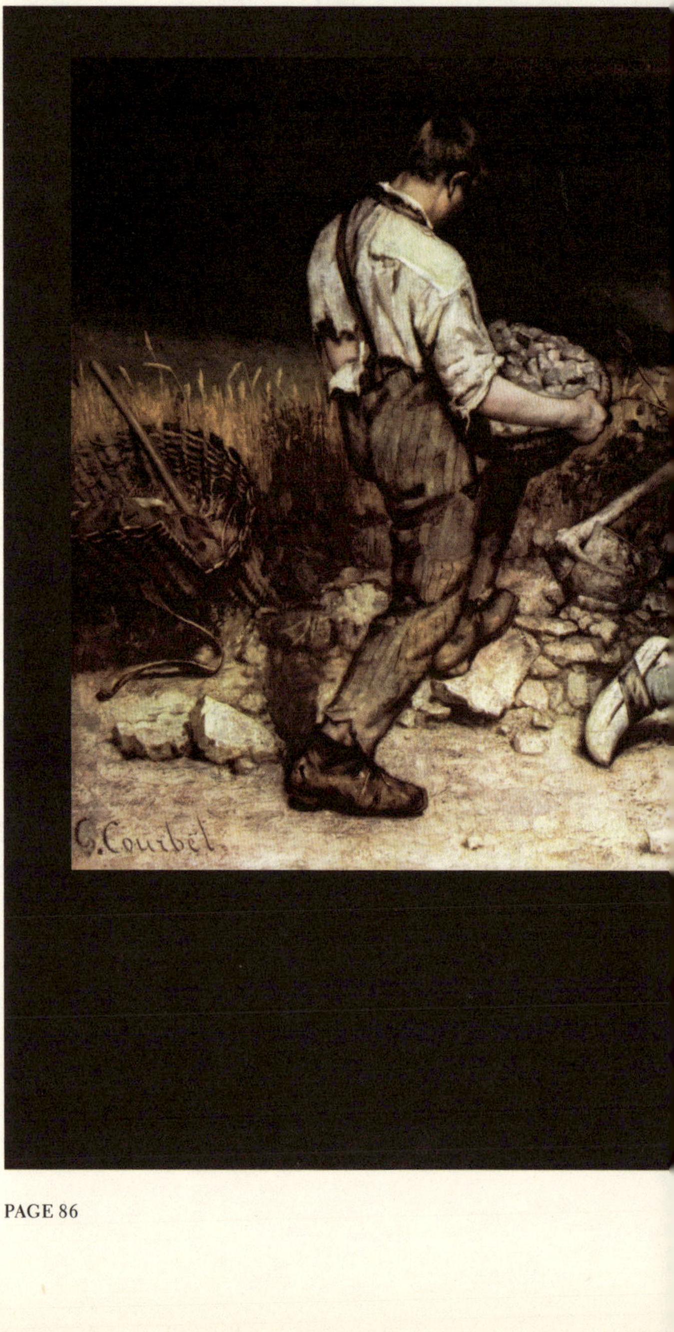

*TEXT BY*
*MARK LEVY*

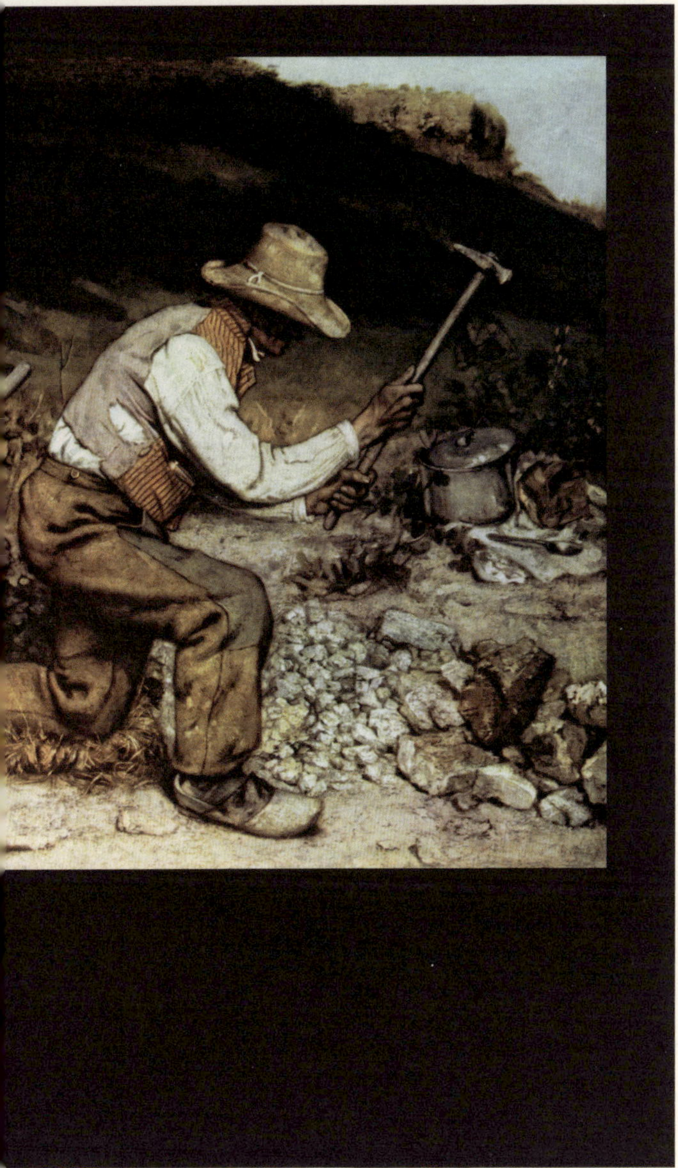

The search for the real and the relation of the individual to the real are a basic part of being human. We all know that Western and Eastern artists, philosophers, and scientists have been leaders in trying to grasp the nature of reality for centuries, so it is not surprising that contemporary artists have continued to pursue an understanding of the real as a personal search. Yet, in this age of competing ideologies, it has also become a pressing interest for artists to mirror, clarify, and question the visual rhetoric—the truthiness—that underlies truth claims. Indeed, the deconstruction of ideology by challenging the means by which it is asserted is now a role that artists have assumed in the absence of other parties, including the news media, that are interested mainly in promoting their own agendas.

It is through the diverse strategies of hyperrealism—exaggerated verisimilitude, the creation of virtual worlds, trompe l'oeil, readymades, and so on—that many of the artists in *More Real?* explode the notion that any particular mode of representation has a privileged relation to the real. Closeness to the real, a possible definition of *truth*, is highly problematic and even more so if conventional ideas of the real are untrue. And problematic notions of the real extend to artistic authenticity and originality. Hyperrealism, which is often a form of questioning the real as it is usually conceived, can help to reveal truths about the difficulty of connecting with the truth, as well as the falsity of truth claims that pretend that more than relative truth is possible. And because they hold the truth about the difficulty of attaining truth playfully, the artists in this exhibition avoid a fixation on their own ideologies.

To understand hyperrealism, it would be helpful to start by discussing realism as it emerged in modern art. Gustave Courbet, an important figure in the French realist movement in the visual arts, explained his painting *The Stone Breakers* (1849) in a letter: "I made none of it up my friend, I saw these people on my walk. In that station one ends up the same way one begins. The vine growers and the farmers, who are much taken with this painting, claim that were I to do a hundred more, none would be more true to life."[1]

Here Courbet has constructed a rich story: he wants us to believe that details equal facts and that many details make this painting true to life. Yet, in the words of Friedrich Nietzsche, "It is precisely facts that do not exist, only interpretations."[2] The mere selection of workers in tattered clothing engaged in breaking stones in the dusty countryside as a subject for a painting was sure to be offensive to a French bourgeois viewing public that wanted to forget its working-class origins. Indeed, this painting raised a ruckus at the Salon of 1850.

Since the young man will end up like the old man, who is clearly not enjoying the surplus value of his work, and the work itself is unpleasant in the hot and dusty countryside, the painting becomes a presentation of the Marxist idea of the alienation of labor, an idea that Courbet probably got from his friend the socialist philosopher Pierre-Joseph Proudhon (1809–1865). Although Courbet purports to convey a slice of French country life, the result is a story with a hidden or not-so-hidden ideology. Courbet saw himself at this stage of his career as an artist who was recording the social and economic activities of his time for the future and as an agent of social change, the latter intention being somewhat inconsistent with that of documenting his milieu. Courbet's realism soon gave way to photography and moving pictures, which were seen at the time and for a long period afterward as a better and more convincing form of documentation than painting.

To be sure, the attempts of painters and sculptors to create a more or less exact

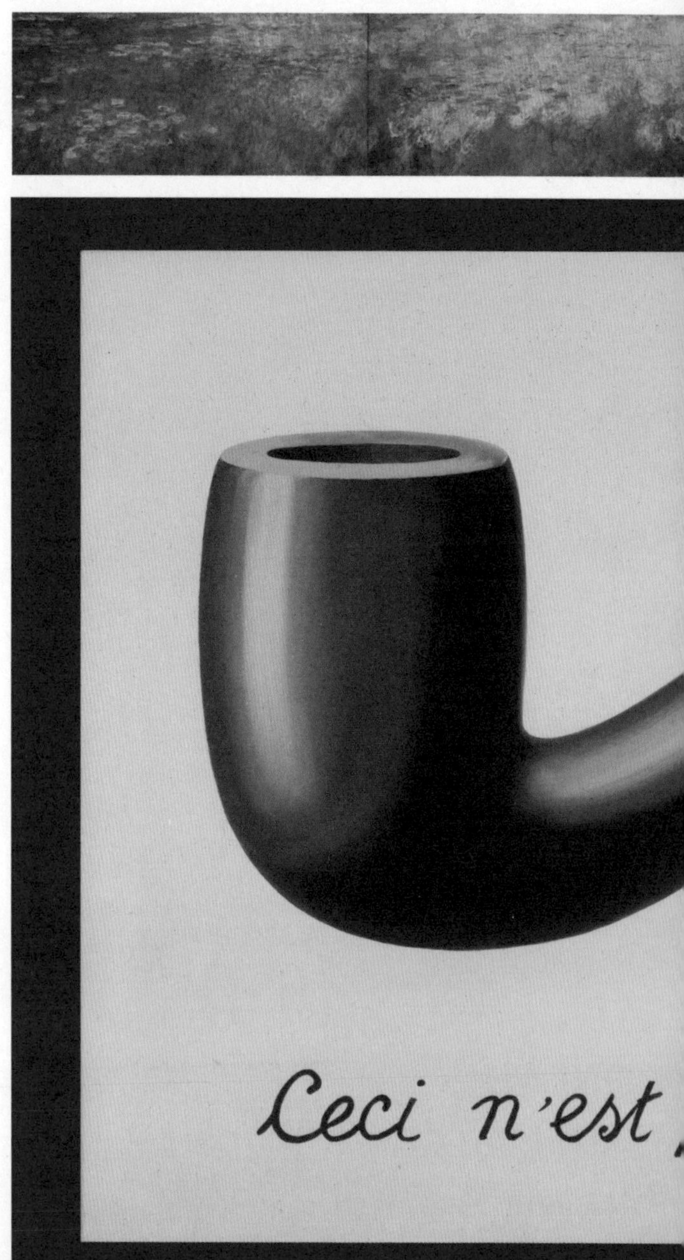

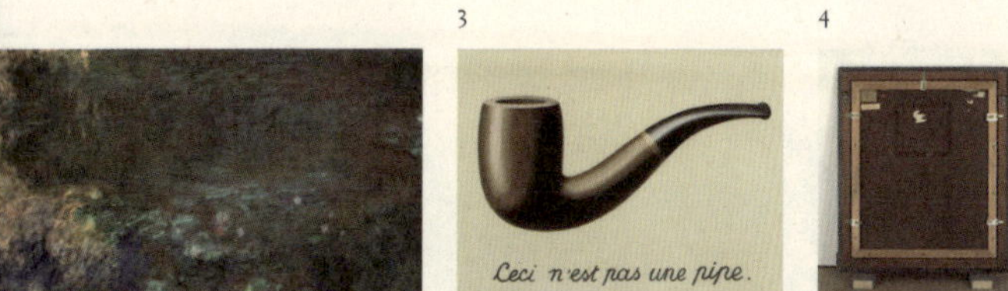

René Magritte, *The Treachery of Images (This Is Not a Pipe)*, 1929; oil on canvas; 23 ³/₄ x 31 ¹⁵/₁₆ x 1 inches (60.3 x 81.1 x 2.5 cm); Los Angeles County Museum of Art, Purchased with funds provided by the Mr. and Mrs. William Preston Harrison Collection

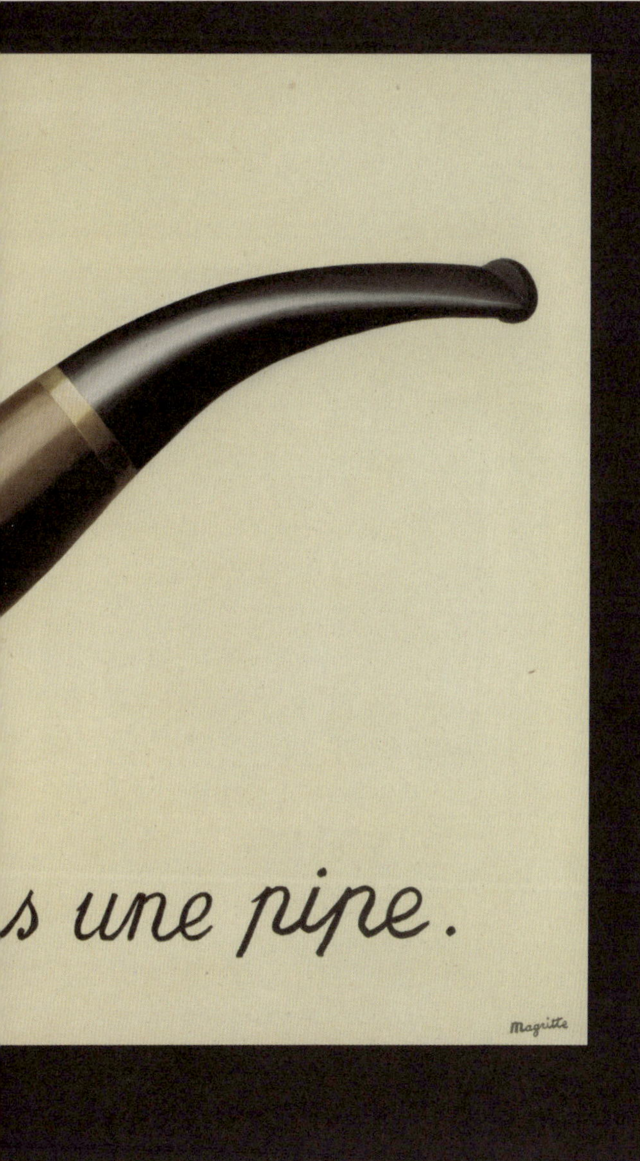

likeness did not die following Courbet, although these artists were usually no longer part of the avant-garde movements of modern art. Imitation of nature has informed centuries of Western painting and sculpture since Aristotle's codification of mimesis as an aesthetic principle in the *Poetics* during the fourth century BCE. While trompe l'oeil modes of realism appeal to artists who believe that they provide a way of getting closer to the real while celebrating their virtuosity in rendering, both philosophers and many hyperrealist artists discredit the truth claims of trompe l'oeil realism based on the correspondence between representation and the world. For example, in *Deadman* (2006), Jonathan Monk created a trompe l'oeil sculpture in wax, human hair, and so on of a dying Chris Burden to give the pretense of truth to an imaginary alternative outcome of the 1971 performance in which Burden had himself shot in the arm with a .22 caliber rifle.

While photography and moving images may be better documentary tools than painting and sculpture, it has become increasingly doubtful whether the former media are closer to reality. A mode of hyperrealism evident in *More Real?* is the documentary replete with information, or at times a superabundance of information, in which the boundary between fact and fiction is attenuated. For the artists engaged in this mode, there are no documentaries, only pseudodocumentaries.

With the advent of photography, artists began to question how well painting actually embodies how the eye sees. Does the eye see the world in more or less clear detail in the manner of Courbet, or is there a different kind of apprehension at first glance in sunlight? Monet's idea of perception is of course different from Courbet's in that visual information is revealed in Monet's painting in terms of flickering lights and shadows. These effects engender a lighter

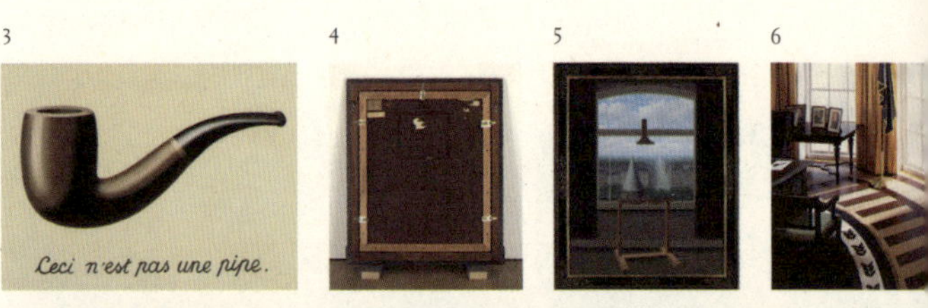



color palette that is far removed from the dark, murky tones of Courbet's painting. Monet's early work is more in tune with actual perception than Courbet's, but from his later work it is evident that he moves away from perception. In the Water Lilies of the 1920s, for example, form, figure and ground, and other spatial relationships dissolve into a continuum of deliquescent painterly effects. Monet has accessed a world of sensation that is prior to the emergence of objects. "When you go out and paint," he said in 1889, "try to forget what objects you have before you—a tree, a house, a field or whatever."[3] For Monet, memories of a scene were an impediment to seeing it. According to his friend Lila Cabot Perry: "He said he wished to be born blind and then had suddenly gained his sight so that he could have begun to paint in this way without knowing what the objects were that he saw before him. He held that the first real look at the motif was likely to be the truest and most unprejudiced one, and said that the first painting should cover as much canvas as possible, no matter how roughly, so as to determine the tonality of the whole."[4]

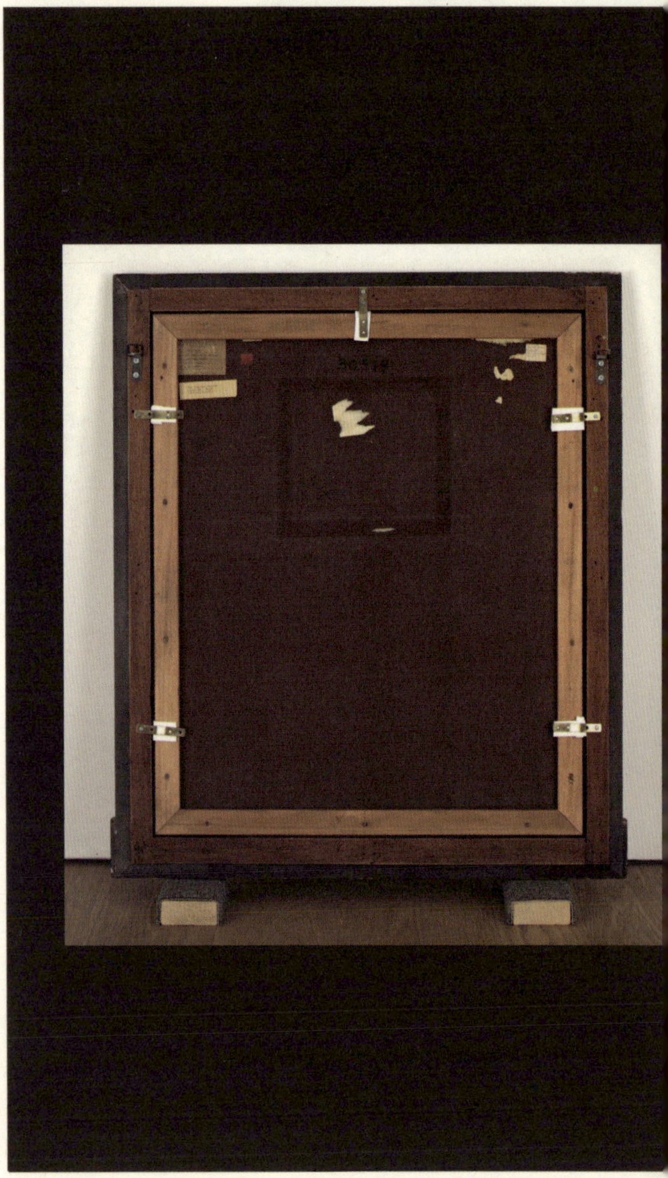

Recent studies in neuroscience indicate that only a very small number of the inputs to the occipital lobe come directly from the sense data of the external world, and the rest come from internal memory stores that directly affect the perceptual processing modes of the brain.[5] In other words, the world is made up mostly from minimal incoming information. In manifesting the sensate world, Monet's late paintings may be closer to the real than the perceptual world of objects. For Monet, realism did not have to be connected to the representation of things; he attempted to convey an immediate sensate experience that for him was more intense and more real than the world of objects. The artist Mary Temple explores the hyperreal world of sensation in her

4
Vik Muniz, *Verso (American Gothic)*, 2008; mixed
mediums; 36 x 30 ³/₄ x 10 inches (91.4 x 78.1 x 25.4 cm);
courtesy Sikkema Jenkins & Co., New York

5
René Magritte, *The Promenades of Euclid*, 1955; oil on
canvas; 64 ¹/₈ x 51 ¹/₈ inches (162.9 x 129.9 cm);
Minneapolis Institute of Arts, The William Hood
Dunwoody Fund Collection

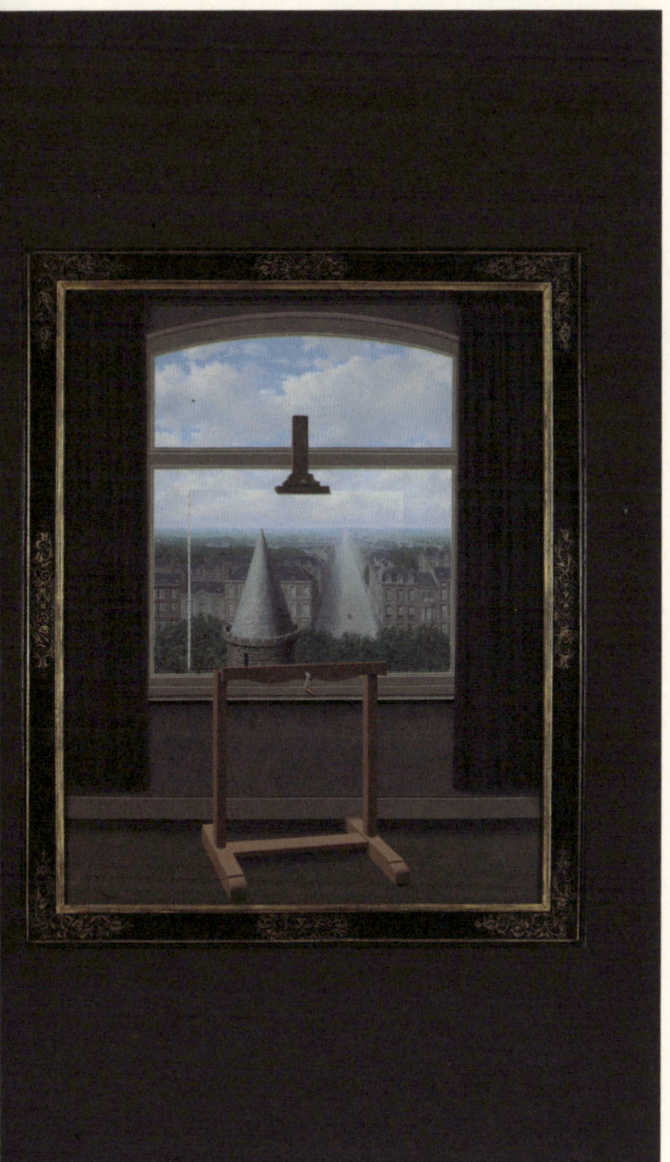

trompe l'oeil renderings of foliage in unlikely indoor places. Here the disembodied world of light and shadow is the principal subject.

Monet's late work was concomitant with the development of different modes of abstraction that characterizes much of the art of the first three quarters of twentieth century. Nevertheless, there were exceptions, including the so-called academic surrealists, who used traditional representational techniques to subvert the relationship of images or constructions to reality. In *The Promenades of Euclid* (1955), for example, René Magritte represents a painting of a landscape and the landscape that is the subject of the painting behind it. Which is more real, the painting on the easel, the landscape, or Magritte's painting of both? There is just an infinite regression of images. An image is an abstract signifier that organizes information in a discernible form; it has only a tenuous relationship to the signified or the real. Of course this is also the point of Magritte's famous painting of a pipe with the telling title *The Treachery of Images* (1929). As the words on the bottom of the painting affirm, "Ceci n'est pas une pipe"—that is, this is not a pipe but a colored cartoon with some modeling. Magritte's intention was to show how this image, a quasi-abstract signifier, becomes a substitute for the object.

Questioning the natural relationship between the signifier and the signified, a project that had been initiated in the field of linguistics by Ferdinand de Saussure (1857–1913), is continued in the visual games of Magritte and has become a significant trope in hyperrealism. Another interest of the surrealists was discrediting the assertion that rational consciousness and commonsense consciousness are the sole determinants of the real. Not only are there other forms of consciousness, but these forms of consciousness also correspond to different modes of reality.

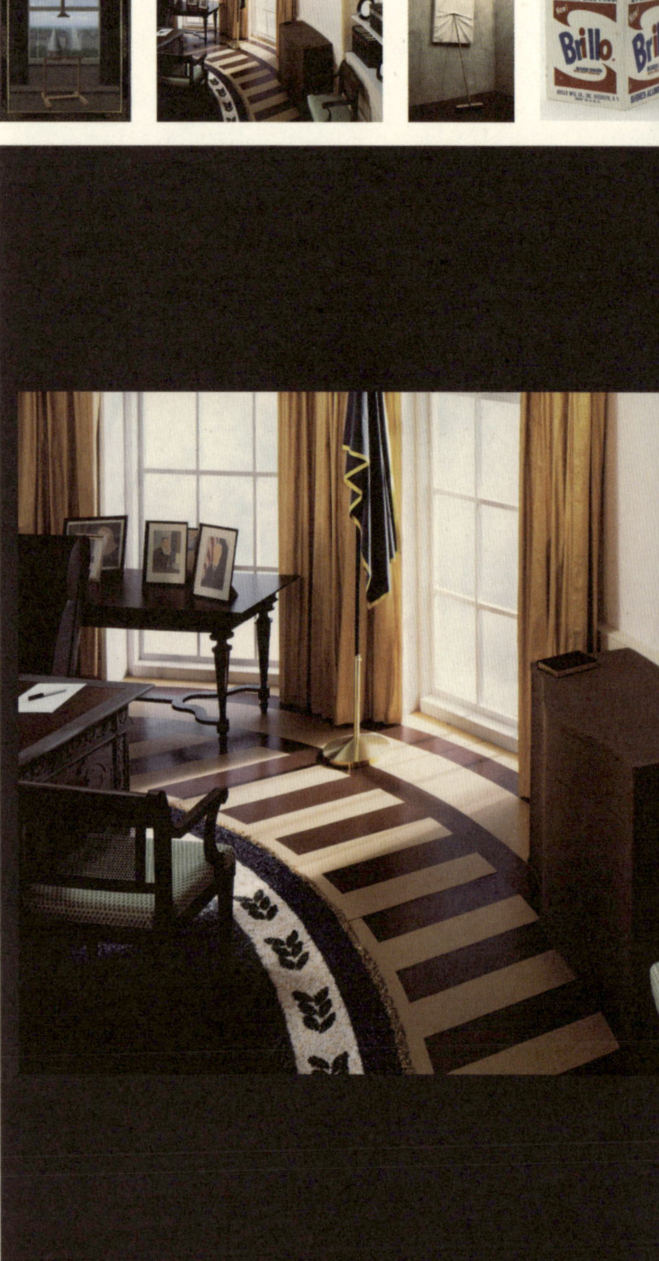

André Breton, a medical orderly in mental wards during the Great War who became a principal founder of surrealism, was deeply influenced by Sigmund Freud's ideas of the role of the unconscious in the determination of consciousness. For both Freud and the surrealists, dreams were important gateways into the unconscious. The surrealists believed that dreams were real or more real than ordinary waking reality. Dream reality, moreover, is not based on the direct experience of sensory data but is possibly derived from just the memories of past images.

Could it be that sensory data itself is just a dream, that there is nothing out there, as the philosopher René Descartes postulated in the seventeenth century? His explanation was that something had to be out there because God would not deceive him. The notion that there is no external reality to import is a significant idea in Western and Eastern philosophy that has been revisited by contemporary philosophers, neuroscientists, physicists, and artists. Perhaps nothing exists except a successive display of images that is present to consciousness? This is an important question that arises when viewing the artworks in *More Real?*

Many of the surrealist painters attempted to make dream reality manifest in their works. Salvador Dalí, the recipient of rigorous academic training in Madrid, combined trompe l'oeil effects, collage, and traditional spatial illusionism in small canvases to make irrational states of consciousness convincing. Dalí argued: "My whole ambition in the pictorial domain is to materialize the images of concrete irrationality with the most imperialist fury of precision—in order that the world of imagination and concrete irrationality may be as objectively evident, of the same persuasive, cognoscitive and communicable thickness as that of the exterior world of phenomenal reality . . . the illusionism of the

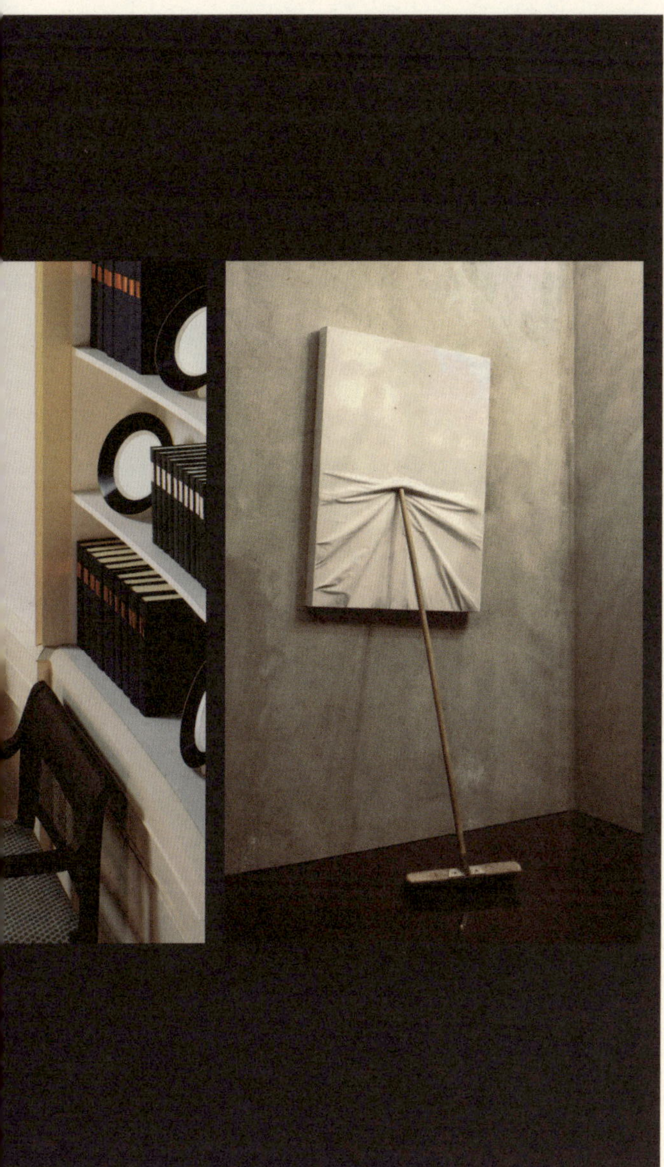

6
Thomas Demand, *Presidency II*, 2008; C-print/Diasec;
87 ¹³/₁₆ x 122 inches (210 x 300 cm); courtesy the artist and
Matthew Marks Gallery
7
Maurizio Cattelan, Untitled, 2009; canvas, wood, plastic;
82 ⁵/₈ x 33 ¹/₂ x 23 ⁵/₈ inches (209.9 x 85.1 x 60 cm);
The Menil Collection

most arriviste art, the usual paralyzing tricks of trompe l'oeil, the most discredited academicism, can all transmute into sublime hierarchies of thought."[6]

Dalí attempts in his hyperreal paintings to establish the facticity of another state of consciousness and by implication to deny the connection of everyday consciousness and the real. Multiple worlds based on dreams and the imagination are an important concern in hyperrealism. Zoe Beloff's *Dreamland: The Coney Island Amateur Psychoanalytic Society and Its Circle, 1926* (2006) parallels the surrealist attempts to make the dream real through hyperreal strategies; she creates a mixed-media tableaux of a projected amusement park based on Freud's dream theories. Joel Lederer is also interested in giving other worlds a concrete appearance. In the series The Metaverse Is Beautiful, he re-creates an online environment for cocreated utopias.

Joseph Cornell, another artist associated with surrealism, used readymades to create compelling alternate universes. The three-dimensional materiality of the object, especially if it is utilitarian, tends to confer reality on an imaginary world. Materiality in the form of a readymade is a trick of truthiness, as many of the artists in *More Real?* understand.

Of course, the use of the readymade was not a surrealist invention. Marcel Duchamp employed the found object to question the notion that the authentic work of art depends on taste, the craftsmanship of the artist, and originality of authorship. Many contemporary artists employ readymade objects and images in a similar way. In his paintings for the Verso series (2008), Vik Muniz tries to duplicate exactly the backs of famous masterpieces. Maurizio Cattelan shoves an actual broom into a white canvas, pinning it to the wall, in an untitled sculpture of 2009. I think that Cattelan's literal transfixion of a painted canvas is a witty reference

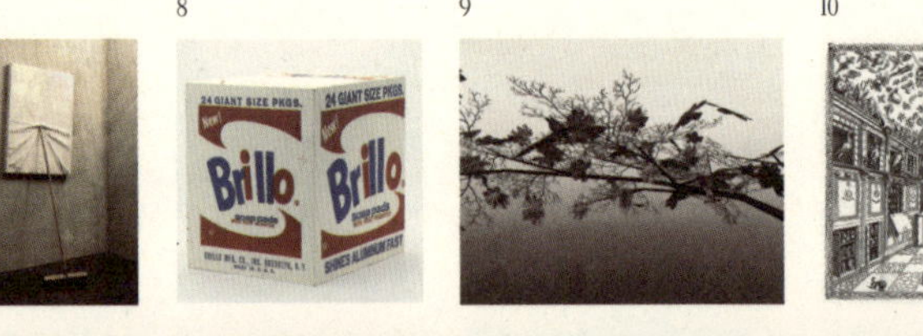

to Duchamp's critique of retinal effects in painting by means of utilitarian found objects.

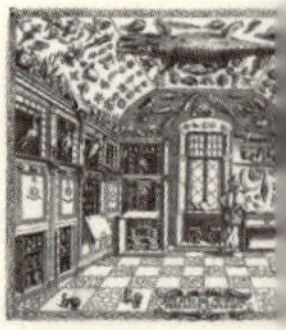

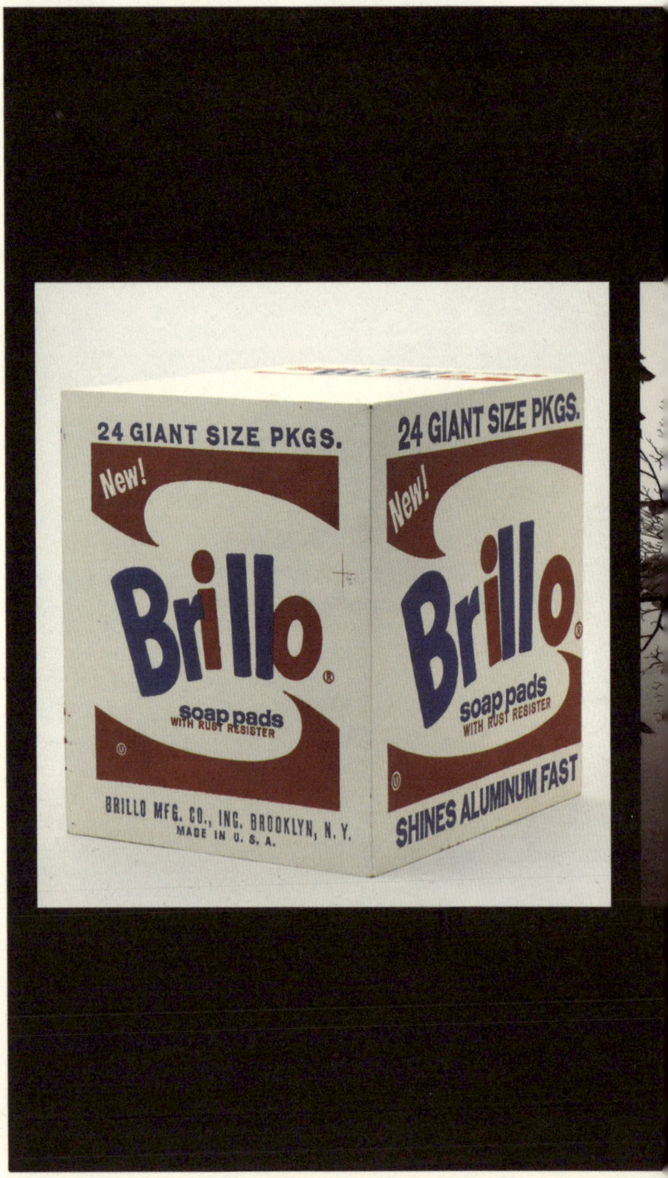

For postmodernist philosophers and artists, there are still more ways of questioning authenticity and originality. According to Roland Barthes, in *S/Z* (1970) and other books and articles, and to Jean Baudrillard, in his essay "The Precession of Simulacra" (1983), thought is prior to language, either verbal or visual.[7] Language determines thought, not the other way around, as was generally believed in Western philosophy.

Imagine a newborn baby with a mind like a blank slate. As the baby matures, it hears the talking of others and sees images conditioned by the media. What the individual comes to think of as the self is just the conversation of others and mediated images. It is impossible to escape what Robert Musil in *The Man without Qualities* (1930) calls this "delirium of many," and what Fredric Jameson calls "this prison-house of language," in his book of the same title (1972).[8] Where is originality in this cacophony of conversations and images? The individual can only do a little reshuffling of the signifiers, the words and images. In the endless recycling of signifiers that constitutes the self and the world, there is only a small opportunity for creativity. As Jacques Derrida argues, "there is nothing outside of the text."[9] There is no holy ghost in the machine of language, no divinity that somehow channels ideas to artists prior to words or images. The romantic idea of the heroic original artist dies a hard death in postmodernist thought, along with the traditional Western concept of the self.

The possibility that there is no world and no self, no subject and no object, merely the mind looking at the mind, may be a little hard to accept when there appears to be a solid world out there. At times some illusions are rather vivid in their material modes, especially

8
Andy Warhol, *White Brillo Box*, 1964; synthetic polymer paint, screenprint on wood; 17 x 16⅞ x 14 inches (43.2 x 42.9 x 35.6 cm); Walker Art Center, Minneapolis, Gift of Kate Butler Peterson, 2002

9
Joel Lederer, *200804262354*, from the series The Metaverse Is Beautiful, 2009; archival ink jet on paper; 40 x 50 inches (101.6 x 127 cm); courtesy the artist

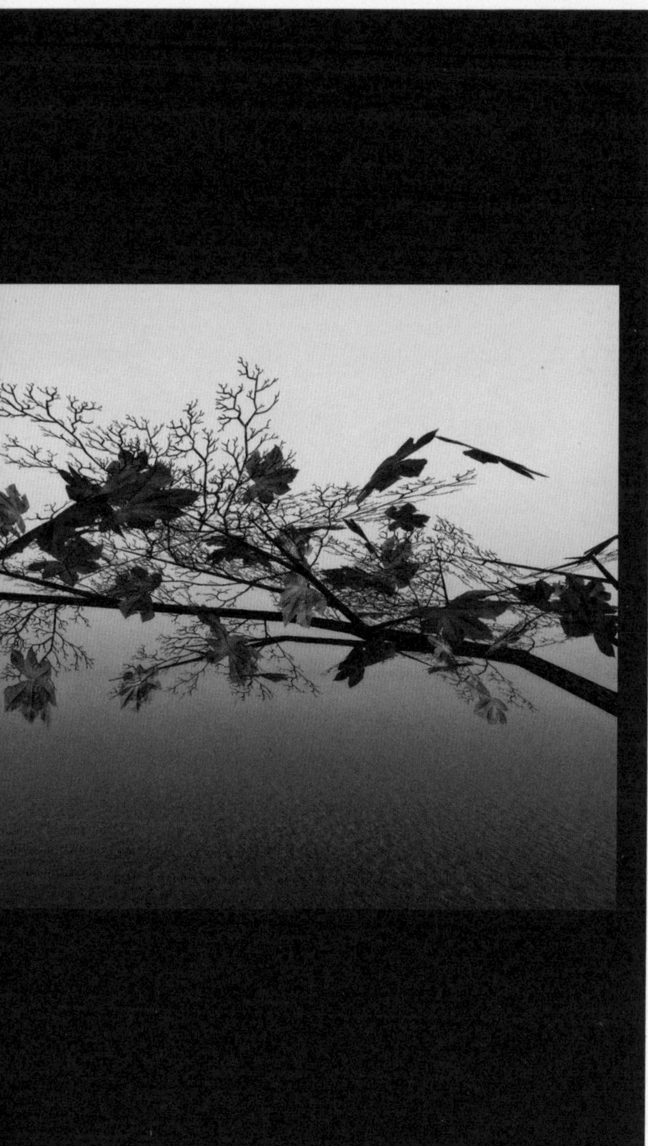

if you are hit in the head by a flying object. For many of the artists represented in *More Real?*, however, it is possible to be quite skeptical about the possibility of an external reality outside the self, as well as fidelity to this reality, and still affirm or enhance the relative reality of the material world and other possible worlds.

Multiple voices are an important trope in hyperrealism and figure prominently in the works of Eve Sussman, Bertrand Lavier, Eva and Franco Mattes, and other artists whose work is featured in *More Real?* In *89 Seconds at Alcázar* (2004), her reenactment of Diego Velázquez's *Las Meninas*, Sussman and her actors have much fun recycling and amplifying Velázquez's images, which the painter similarly recycled from other artists. The main difference is that Sussman makes this recycling clear, whereas Velázquez's sources are less evident, and this is part of Sussman's intention. She invites us to consider whether her work is more or less original than Velázquez's painting in the Prado. And it is more interesting to have a hyperreal version of the painting in video than to look at a reproduction of it in an art book.

Sussman's creativity and originality lie in enlivening the images of *Las Meninas*, but where is the artistic creativity in Thomas Demand's exact replication of the Oval Office in *Presidency 1* (2008) or Mark Dion's *Curator's Office*, a full-size replica of a curator's office at the Minneapolis Institute of Arts, supposedly rediscovered in 2012? Precedents for this work include the *Wunderkammern*, the cabinets or private museums of nondescript curiosities found in baroque Europe, and the various museums of replicas and period rooms in the United States. Demand and Dion invite the viewer to determine the difference between the actual thing and the simulacrum by means of installations that pretend to efface the presence of the artist.

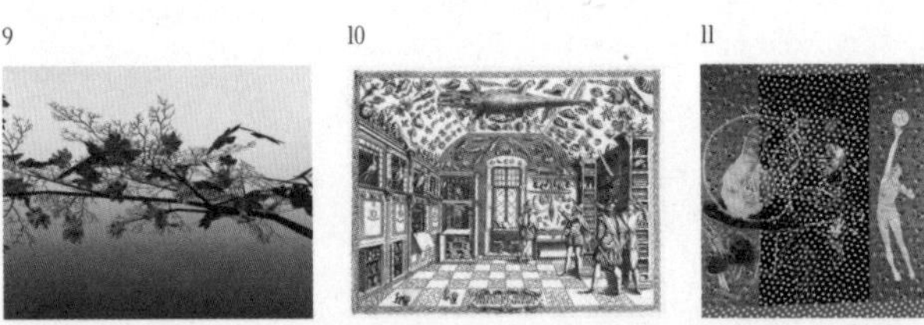

According to Umberto Eco, in "Travels in Hyperreality," the examination of replicas or artifacts in a *Wunderkammer* or museum is more exciting than viewing the actual things in context, where they are often ignored as being too pedestrian.[10] This is also the case with Dion's installation. And when the power of even such a mythical place as the Oval Office is deadened by too many media images, Demand is able to reenergize this icon by shifting the context. Changing context to amplify content, either consequential or inconsequential, is a device of hyperrealism. And again, it is through the reshuffling of images that Demand and Dion question the uniqueness of authorship.

Another precedent for the placement of the readymade or an exact replica of the real thing in a museum context is Andy Warhol's Brillo Boxes. These wooden boxes are practically indistinguishable from the original cardboard. Not only were the boxes manufactured by carpenters, but most of the laborious painting of the letters and logos was done by Warhol's assistants. Duchamp's readymades opened the possibility for Warhol's works, yet Duchamp claimed that he selected his readymades with a complete indifference to good and bad taste. Warhol liked the visual qualities of advertising images, which is not surprising given his background in commercial art. He understood that the abstract signifiers involved in the packaging of a product often provide more sensory satisfaction than the product itself, whether it is Brillo pads or Campbell's soup.

Warhol also went further than Magritte in using abstract signifiers. Not only can the signifier replace the signified, but it also improves upon the signified if the signifier is concise, bold, and vivid. For Warhol, wandering through the aisles of an American supermarket was a voyage in hyperreality that was far more exciting than exhibitions of abstract art, the dominant avant-garde of his time.

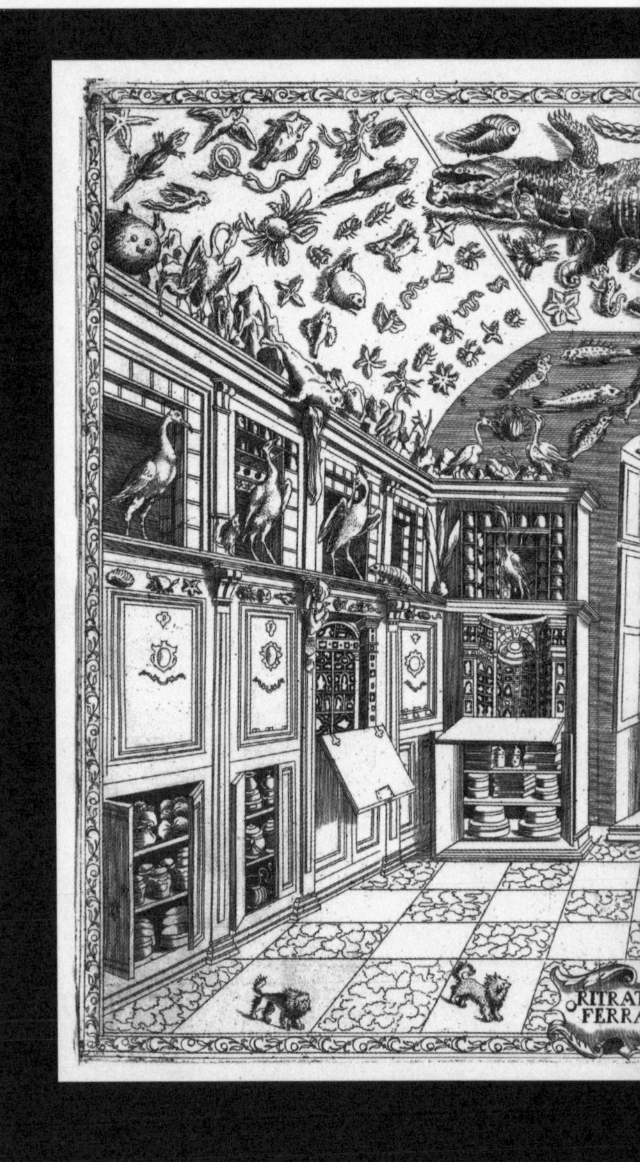

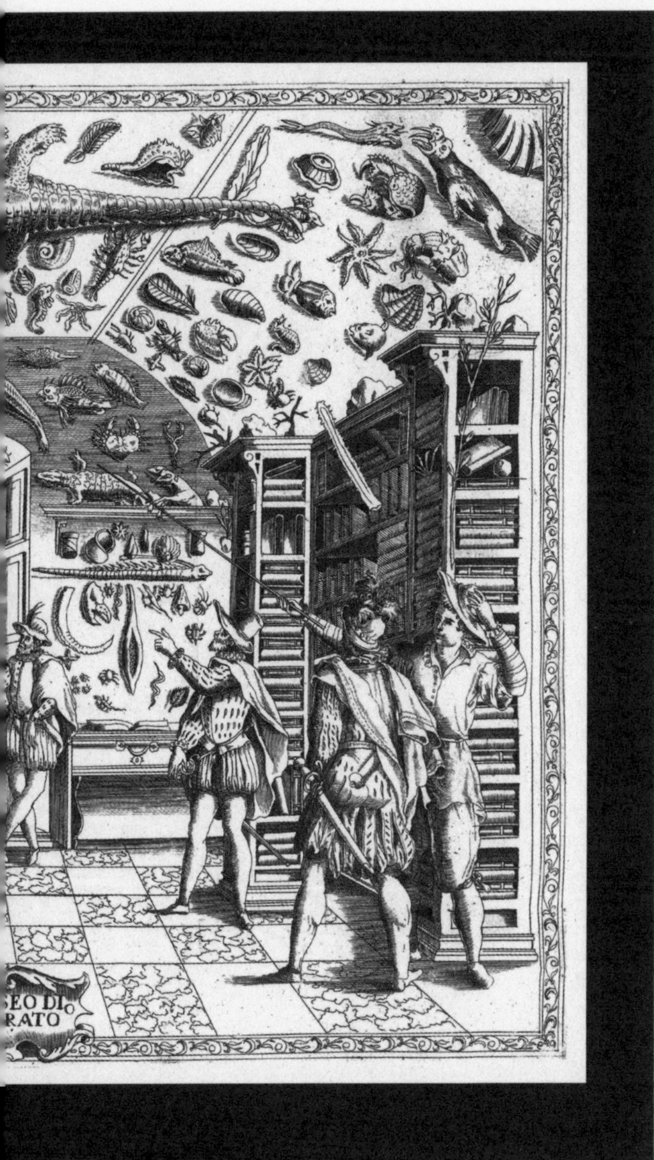

10
Ferrante Imperato, *Natural history museum of Ferrante Imperato of Naples*, 1672, from *Historia naturale di Ferrante Imperato napolitano nella quale ordinatamente si tratta della diversa condition di minere, pietre pretiose, ed altre curiosita. Con varie historie di piante, ed animali, sin'hora non date in luce*; etching; folio; Wellcome Library, London

The use of abstract signifiers to improve upon the real is an important aspect of anime and video game design. In *Two Minutes Out of Time* (2000), Pierre Huyghe employs a manga character, Annlee, who talks about her role as a manga character as she wanders through a digital landscape. Annlee is a "deviant sign" that points to the viewer's suspension of disbelief in the sign; she deconstructs the ability of manga and digital landscape techniques to convey a convincing reality.[11] Video and anime creators know that abstract signifiers have an effect on the viewer that is equal to or greater than that of other kinds of images. Neuroscientists have demonstrated in many research studies that any strong image will release chemicals in the brain; on a fundamental level the brain does not distinguish between material and immaterial strong images.

Nevertheless, the repetition of images, characteristic of later twentieth- and early twenty-first-century American culture, can flatten meaning, as Warhol also understood. The repetition of electric chairs or car disasters in his silk-screen multiples, which echoes the incessant onslaught of violent images in the media, eventually collapses distinctions and deadens signification. The result is passivity and moral indifference as observers lose their response capacity.

The piling up of images of signifiers without signifiers—an important feature of the postmodernist paintings of Julian Schnabel, David Salle, Sigmar Polke, and others, as well as of many of the hyperrealist works in *More Real?*—also begins in pop art with Robert Rauschenberg's combine paintings. In this body of work Rauschenberg put together reproductions of works of art, cartoons, paint spatters recalling abstract expressionist brushstrokes, newspaper photographs, and so on. The images lose their original meanings, and an overall

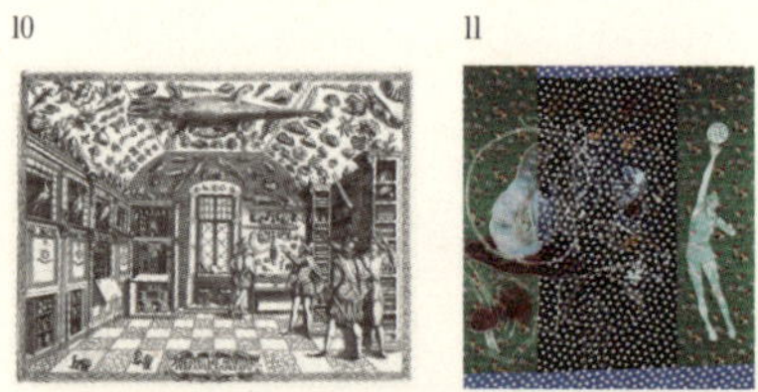

new meaning or signification is not established. Rauschenberg was interested in enjoying the visual qualities of multiple images, not in making sense of them. This idea was later conveyed in postmodern theory by Derrida's term *différance*, an intentional misspelling of *différence* that played on Saussure's ideas about the construction of meaning.[12] Not only is relative meaning solely the product of the difference of signifiers, as Saussure maintained, but any significant narrative or metanarrative meaning is also deferred, according to Derrida. The hankering after meaning is for Derrida a "white mythology," the invisible need for presence in Western thought.[13] For postmodernist painters like Schnabel, Salle, and Polke, however, the enjoyment of images is enough, even though they may not refer to anything or have any greater meaning together. To my mind this is summed up in Polke's *Alice in Wonderland* (1971), a painting in which images of all sorts—soccer players, volleyball players, Alice, a caterpillar smoking a hookah, "Polke-dots" from his early grid pictures, and so on—offer little meaning but provide immediate visual gratification. As the title suggests, Polke revels in this wonderland of images and expects us to do the same. Of course, the celebration of images is an important aspect of *More Real?*, but the artists whose work is featured in this exhibition often question the relationship of images to the real, and they enjoy making them more real, which is not a particular concern of Polke's.

For Baudrillard, who is a traditional modernist in his attachment to meaning, the repetition, multiplication, and augmentation of images is depressing: "Melancholia is the brutal disaffection that characterizes our saturated systems." For him, "the real is no longer what it was" as a result of the "implosion of meaning" brought about by image proliferation.[14] It takes negative capability—defined by the poet John Keats as "being capable of being in

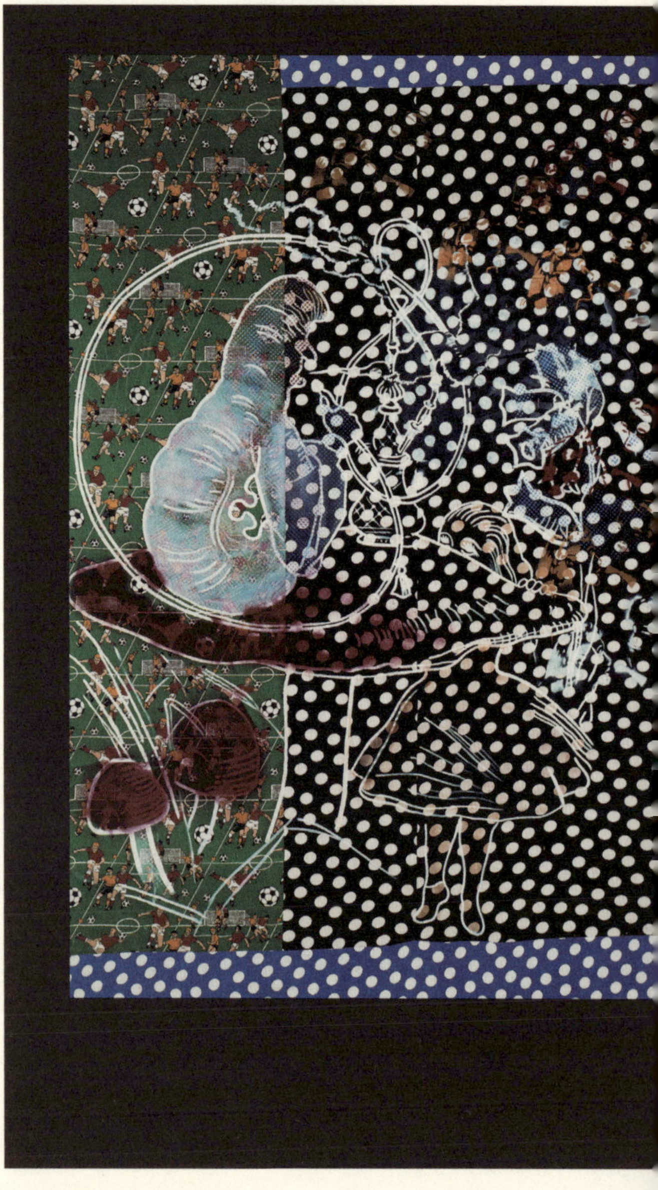

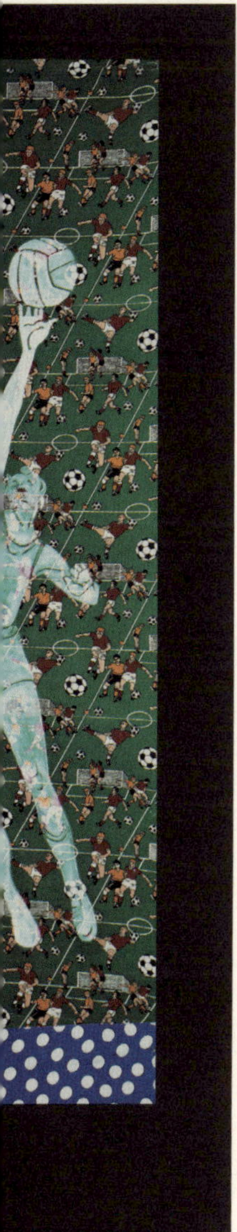



Sigmar Polke, *Alice in Wonderland*, 1971; mixed mediums on patterned fabric; 118 1/8 x 114 3/16 inches (300 x 290 cm); The Estate of Sigmar Polke; courtesy Michael Werner Gallery, New York

uncertainties, mysteries, doubts without any irritable reaching after fact & reasons"—to be a hyperrealist and enjoy hyperrealism.[15] Yet, with sufficient negative capability, the viewer of *More Real?* will be amply rewarded. In its liberation from the fixed reference points that purport to indicate reality and truth and in its wild and often witty games with signifiers, hyperrealism in art can be an exhilarating experience.

## NOTES

1. Petra ten-Doesschate Chu, ed. and trans., *Letters of Gustave Courbet* (Chicago: University of Chicago Press, 1992), 93.

2. Friedrich Wilhelm Nietzsche, *The Portable Nietzsche*, ed. and trans. Walter A. Kaufmann (New York: Penguin, 1976), 458.

3. Quoted in Linda Nochlin, ed., *Impressionism and Post-Impressionism, 1874–1904: Sources and Documents* (Englewood Cliffs, NJ: Prentice Hall, 1966), 35.

4. Quoted ibid.

5. M. E. Raichle et al., "A Default Mode of Brain Function," *Proceedings of the National Academy of Sciences* 98 (2001): 676–82.

6. Quoted in William S. Rubin, *Dada, Surrealism, and Their Heritage* (New York: Museum of Modern Art, 1968), 12.

7. See Roland Barthes, *S/Z*, trans. Richard Miller (New York: Hill & Wang, 1974), and Jean Baudrillard, "The Precession of Simulacra" (1983), in *Simulacra and Simulation*, trans. Sheila Faria Glaser (Ann Arbor: University of Michigan Press, 1995), 1–42.

8. Robert Musil, *The Man without Qualities*, trans. Sophie Wilkins (New York: Alfred Knopf, 1995), vol. 2, 1563; Fredric Jameson, *The Prison-House of Language: A Critical Account of Structuralism and Russian Formalism* (Princeton, NJ: Princeton University Press, 1972).

9. Jacques Derrida, *Of Grammatology*, trans. Gayatri Chakravorty Spivak (Baltimore: John Hopkins University Press, 1976), 158.

10. Umberto Eco, "Travels in Hyperreality," in *Travels in Hyperreality: Essays*, trans. William Weaver (San Diego: Harcourt Brace Jovanovich, 1990), 3–58.

11. See "Pierre Huyghe: Anlee," *Art21*, episode #021 (2007), http://www.youtube.com/watch?v=J3E8i0Pg8xQ.

12. Jacques Derrida, *Margins of Philosophy*, trans. Alan Bass (Chicago: University of Chicago Press, 1982), 43.

13. Ibid., 213.

14. Baudrillard, *Simulacra and Simulation*, 162, 161, 6.

15. Quoted in Duncan Wu, ed., *Romanticism: An Anthology* (Oxford: Blackwell, 2005), 1351.

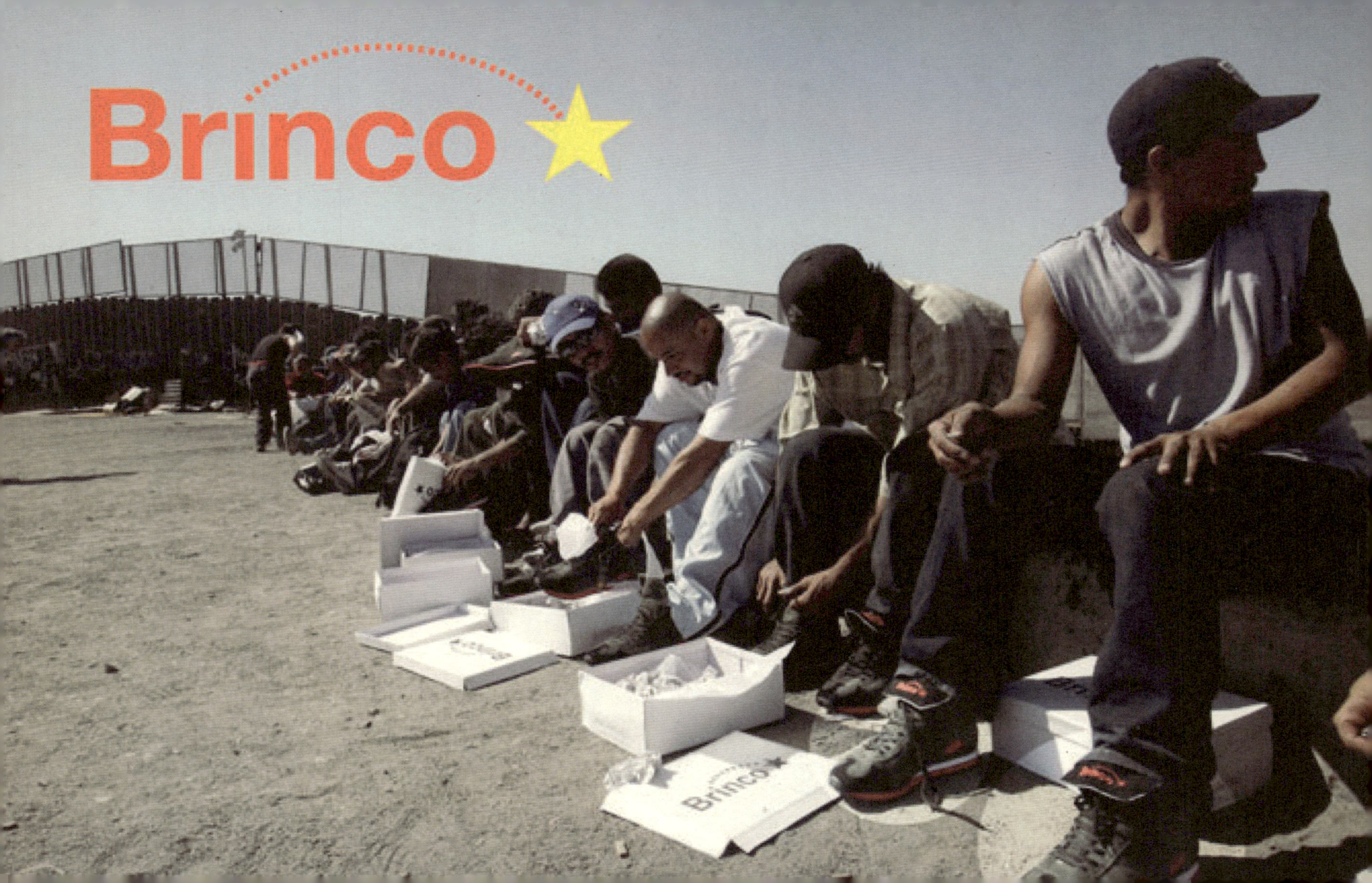

Brinco
Brinco

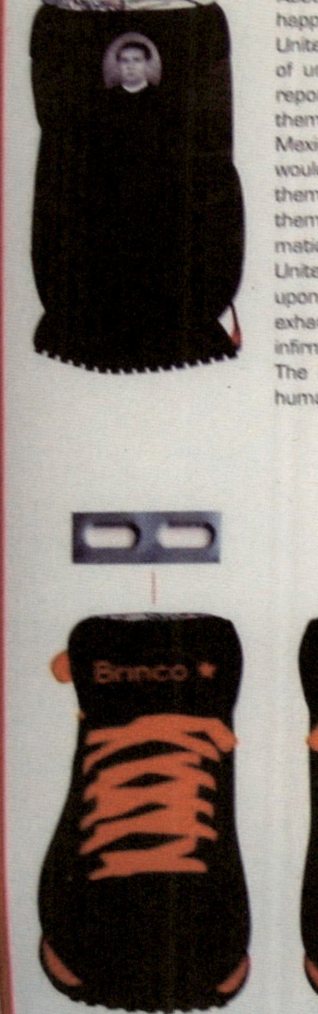

About 1970, strange things started happening at the border dividing the United States and Mexico. Hundreds of undocumented migrants began reporting that whenever they found themselves in trouble, a strange Mexican priest called Toribio Romo would suddenly appear and help them cross the border. Even giving them food, water, money and information on how to get jobs in the United States. Sometimes, he came upon migrants suffering from heat exhaustion, snake bites, and other infirmities. He healed them as well. The immigrants thought he was a human being; not a guardian angel.
Brinco ★
by
Judi Werthein
Pocket
Compass and mini flash light
MX
HECHO EN MÉXICO
Symbol of the Mexican eagle
Map of the area printed on the inner sole
American eagle engraved on the quarted dollar coin
Label inside the shoe revealing the manu-facturing conditions.
Brinco ★

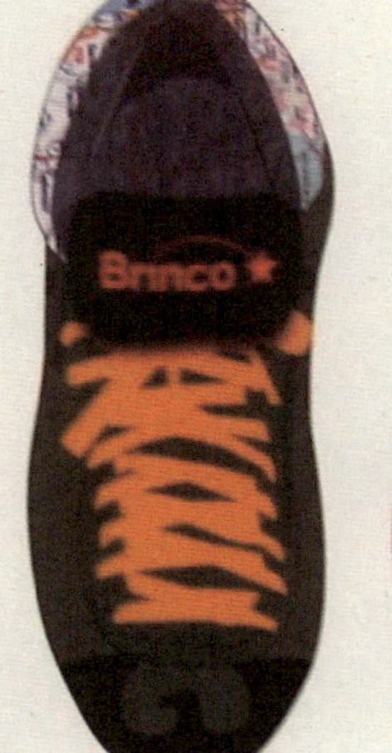
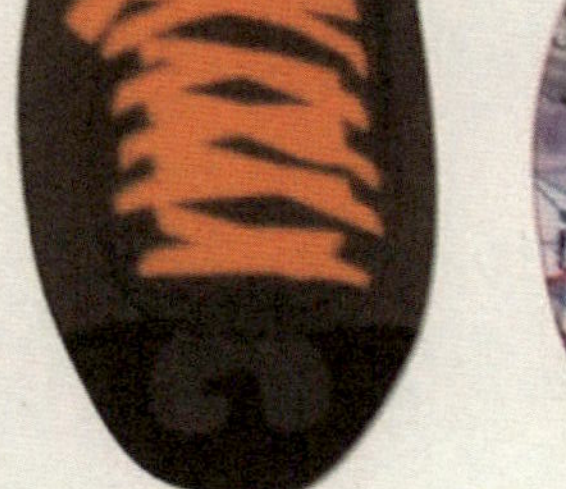
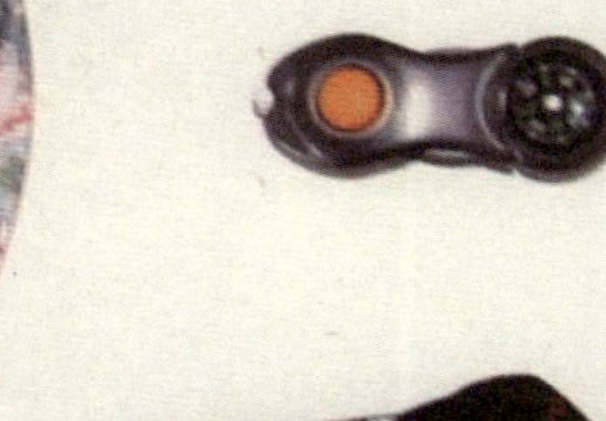
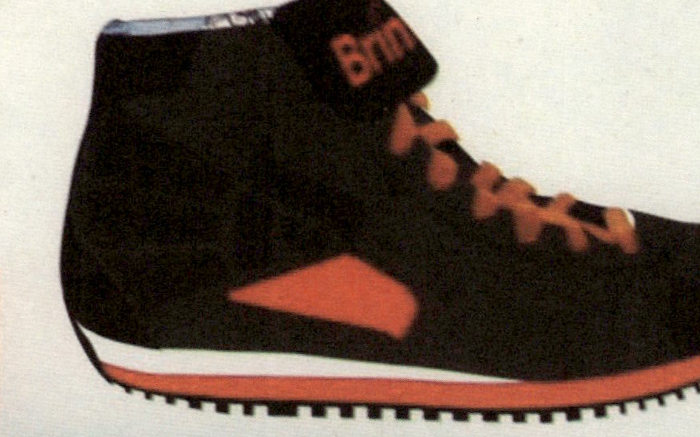

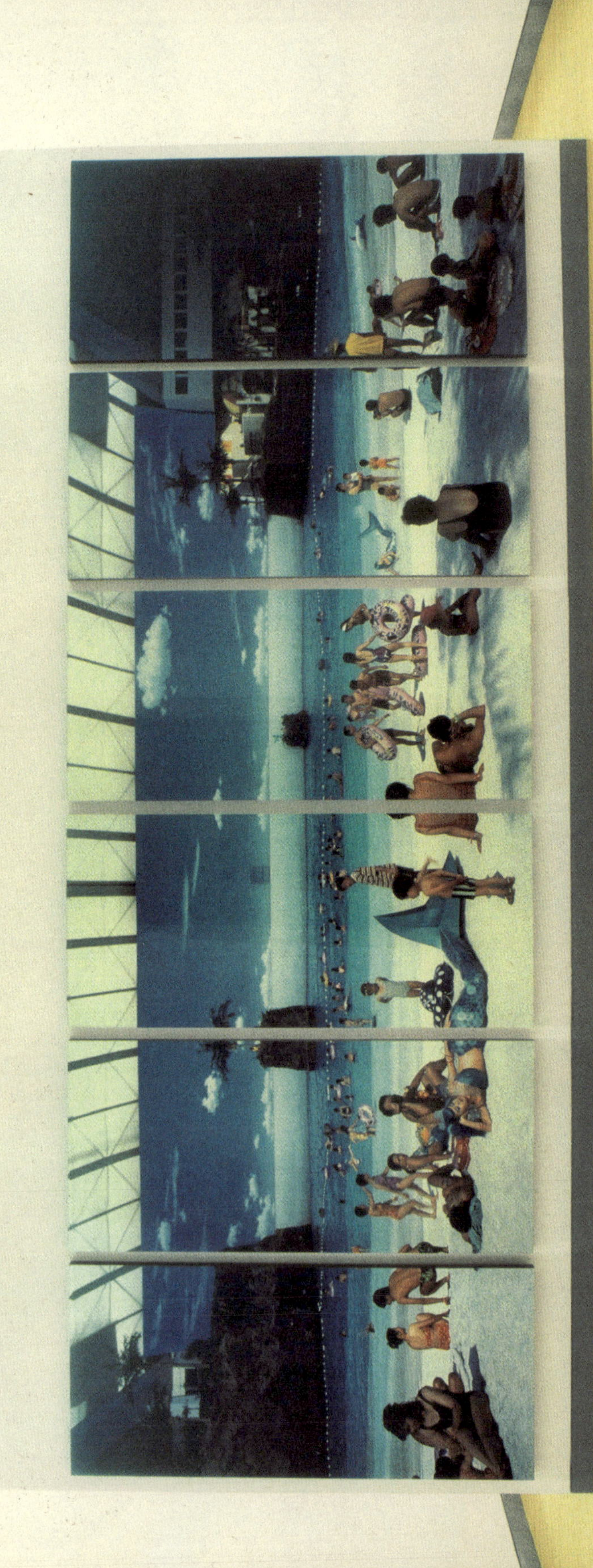

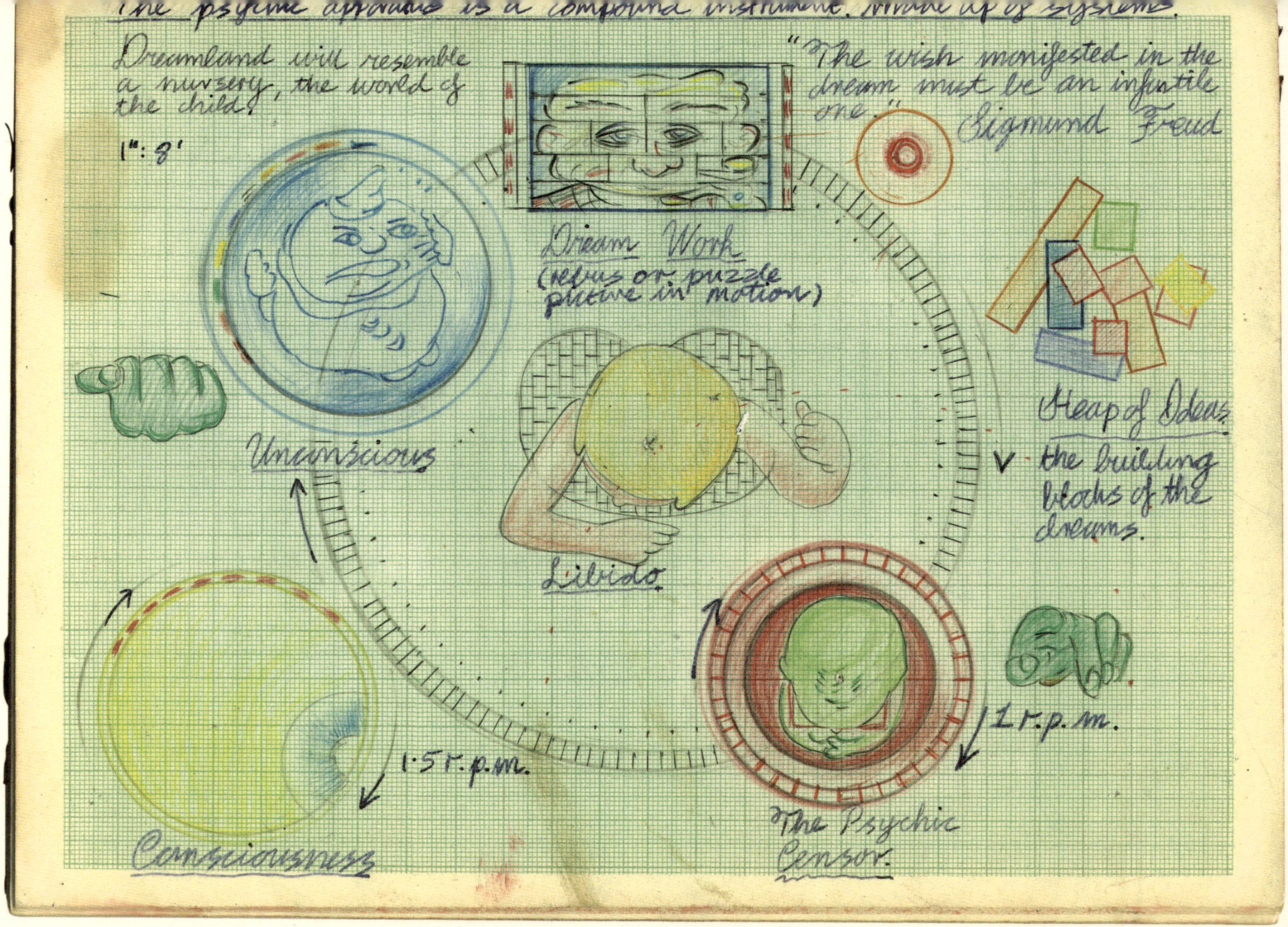

The psychic apparatus is a compound instrument, made up of systems.
Dreamland will resemble a nursery, the world of the child.
1": 8'
"The wish manifested in the dream must be an infantile one." Sigmund Freud
Dream Work
(rebus or puzzle picture in motion)
Heap of Ideas
the building blocks of the dreams.
Unconscious
Libido
Consciousness
The Psychic Censor.
1.5 r.p.m.
1 r.p.m.

MADEIN——"看见自己的眼睛"中东当代艺术展介绍

by MadeIn 2009

本次展览是以中国人的理解方式对中东多元文化状态的一种艺术呈现。展览作品是以尊重、客观、严谨为基本创作观。以中国人特有的敬爱之心看待中东世界。希望这种客观、互敬的第三者视角能促进彼此间以更加开放的胸怀了解和包容对方。用艺术的方式促进人和人之间的沟通和了解，为世界的和平和多元文化的并存做出努力。

本次展览所涉及的形象、文字都是选用世界各地各种媒体公开发表的漫画为元素，拼贴、组合而成。选用的所有素材都尽可能考虑到各方在文化上的差异，在客观平等的创作中，减少误会增进了解。在艺术中融化矛盾，在艺术中共享和平。

艺术之美不分彼此，爱更不会分彼此。墨子曰：天下相交则治，相恶则乱。我们是为促进了解而创作。就如展览题目所言，我们希望艺术是双清澈的眼睛，透过它能看到我们彼此纯洁的内心。


MadeIn —— Seeing One's Own Eyes

-Contemporary art from the Middle East curator statement 2009


This exhibition is an artistic representation of the multi-aspect situation in the Middle-East from a Chinese point of view. Creation of the exhibited works was based on respect, objectivity and strictness. An approach to the Middle East world seen from heartedly devoted Chinese people, with the hope that this third party's objective vision can comprehend the two others. Through art, stimulate communication and understanding between people, work for the peace in the world and pluri-cultural coexistence. All images and texts that this exhibition refers to are compositions of selected caricatural images that have been published in various international public media. The selection was done according to both cultures' differences, as equal as possible, to reduce misunderstanding and enhance comprehension. Through art, contradictions are dissolved and peace is shared. The beauty of art isn't meant to create division, just as love isn't either. Mozi said: "The world is ruled when there is communication and chaotic when there is mutual hate". We create to encourage understanding. As the exhibition title announces it, we hope that art is as limpid as eyes, revealing the purity of our heart.

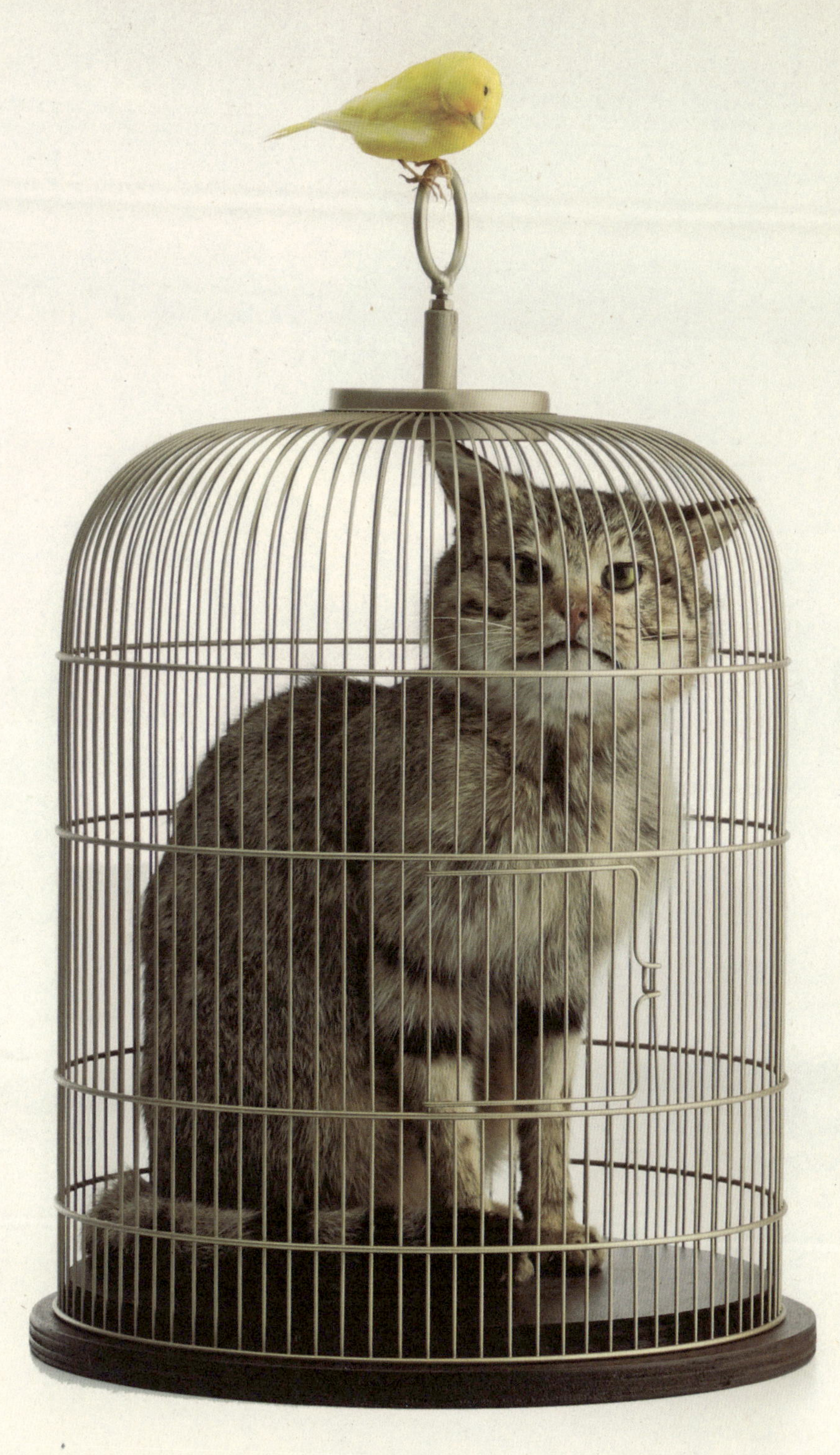

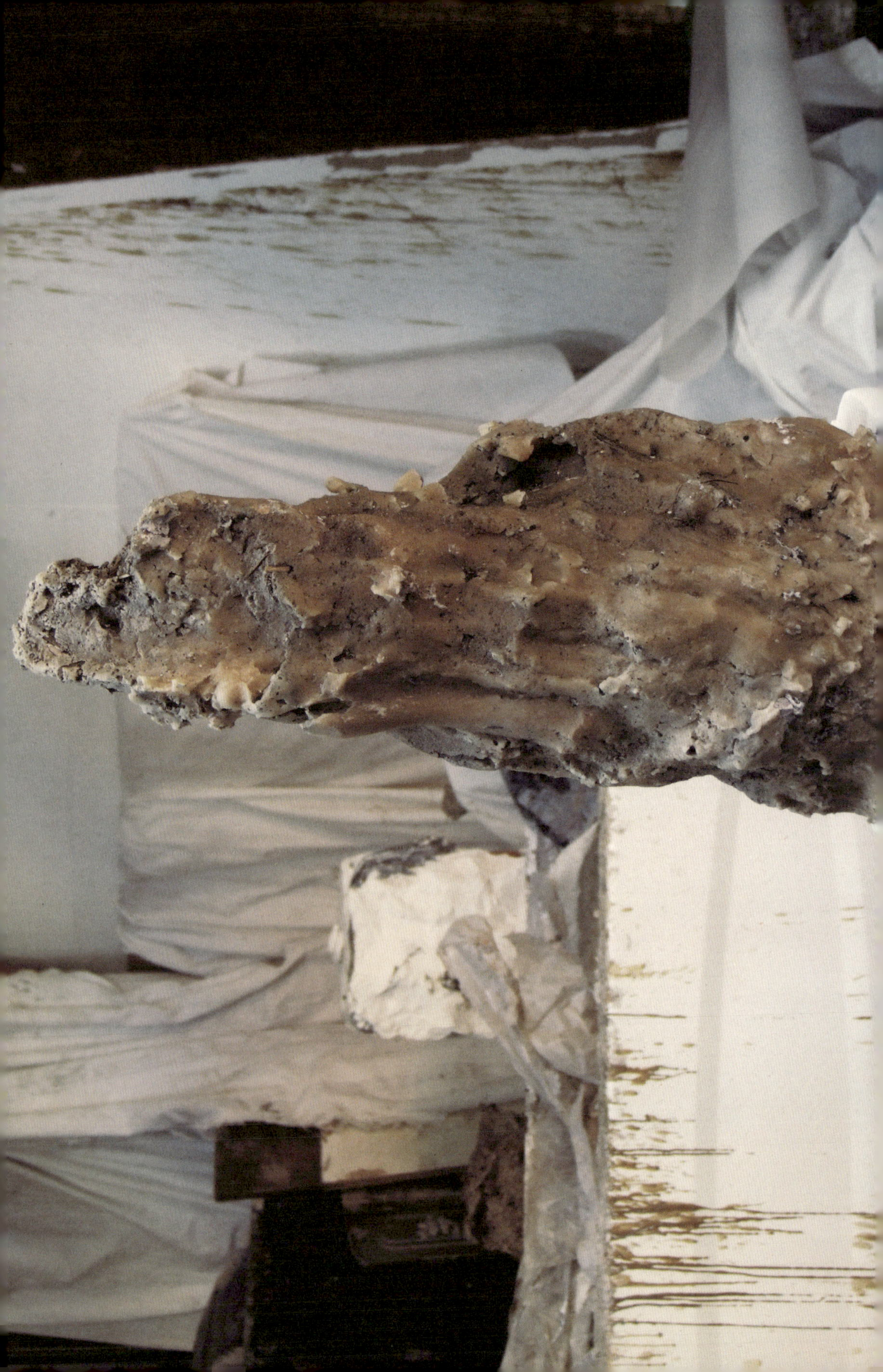

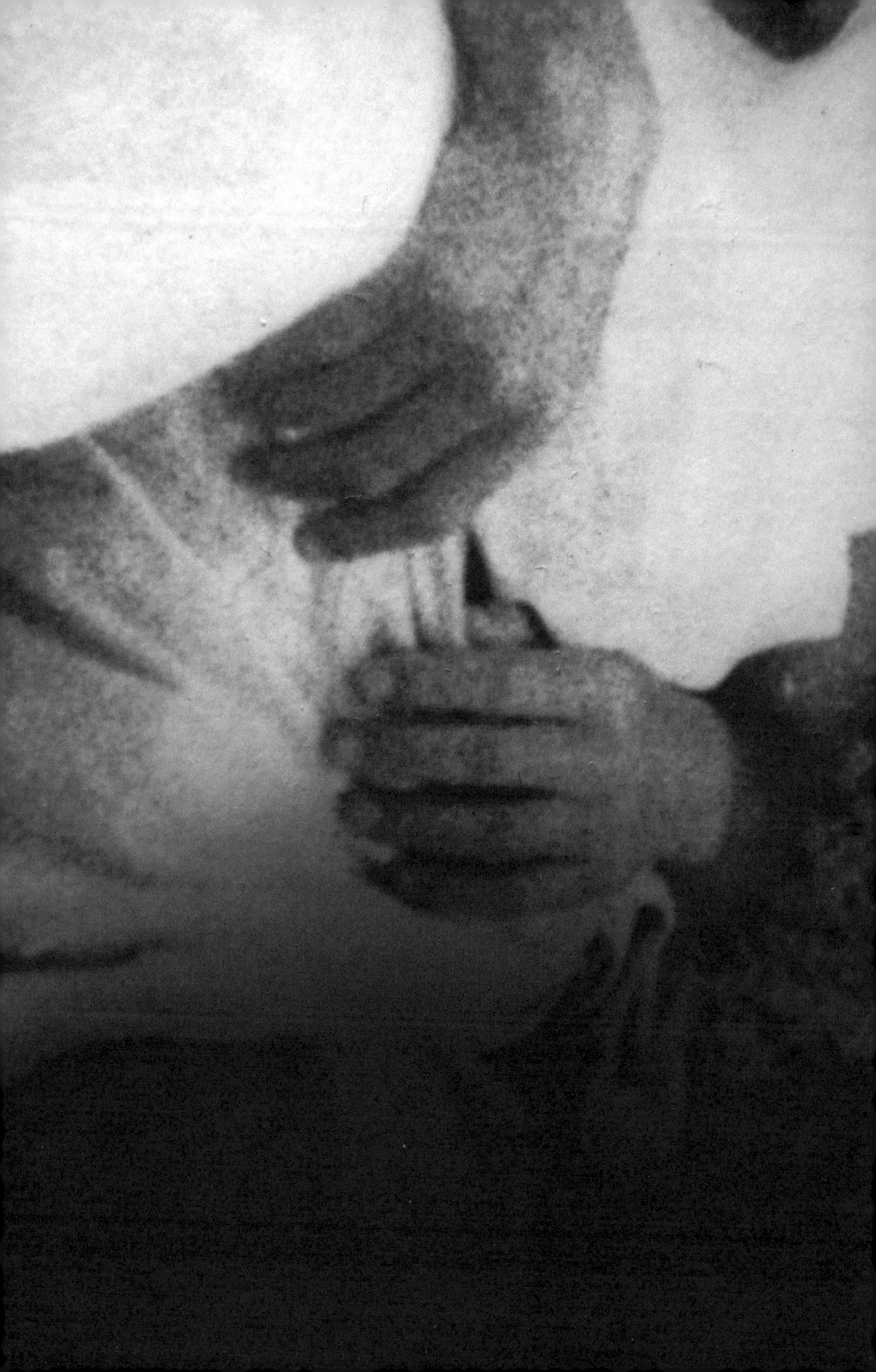

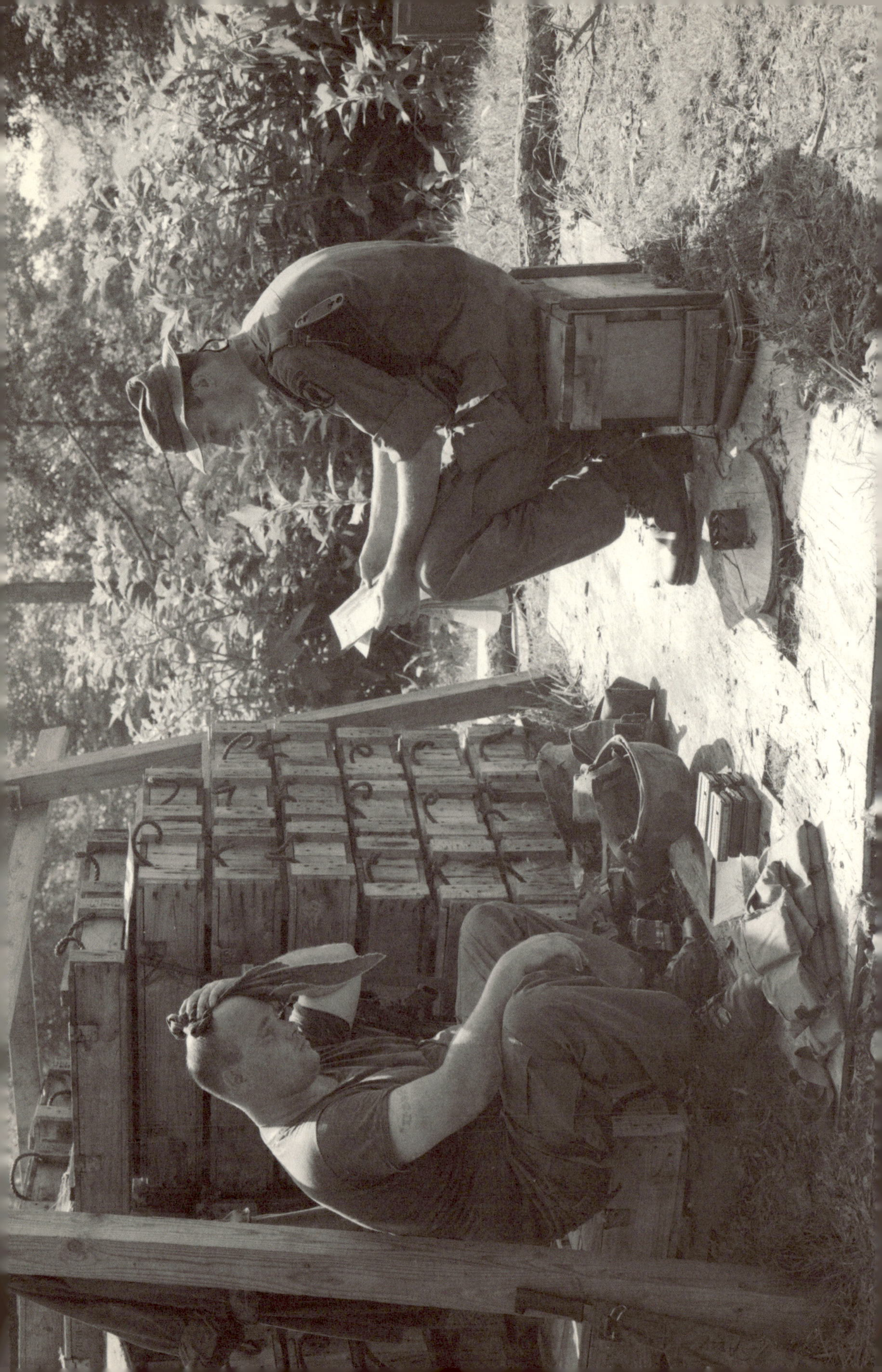

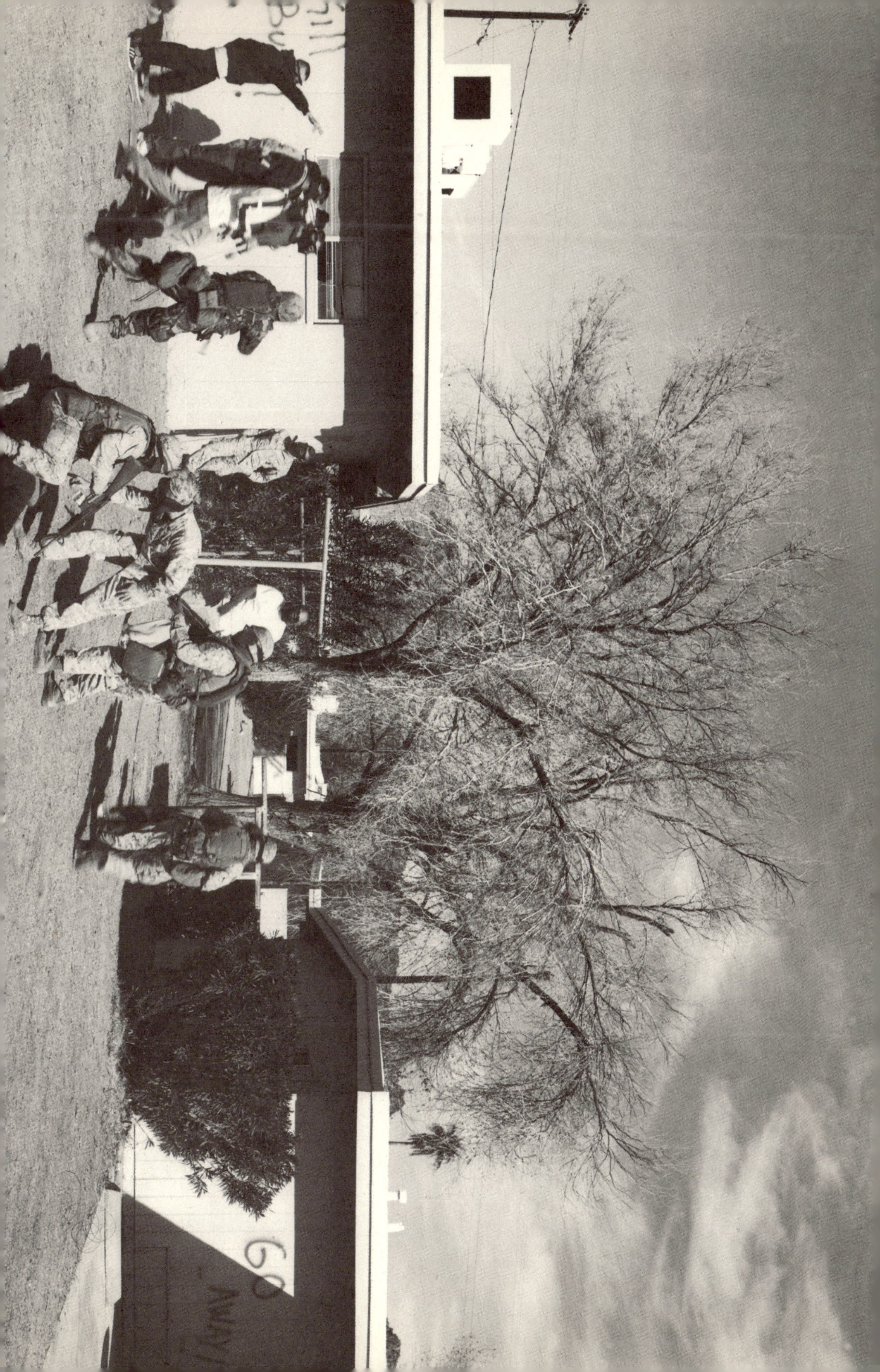

# Make-Believe:

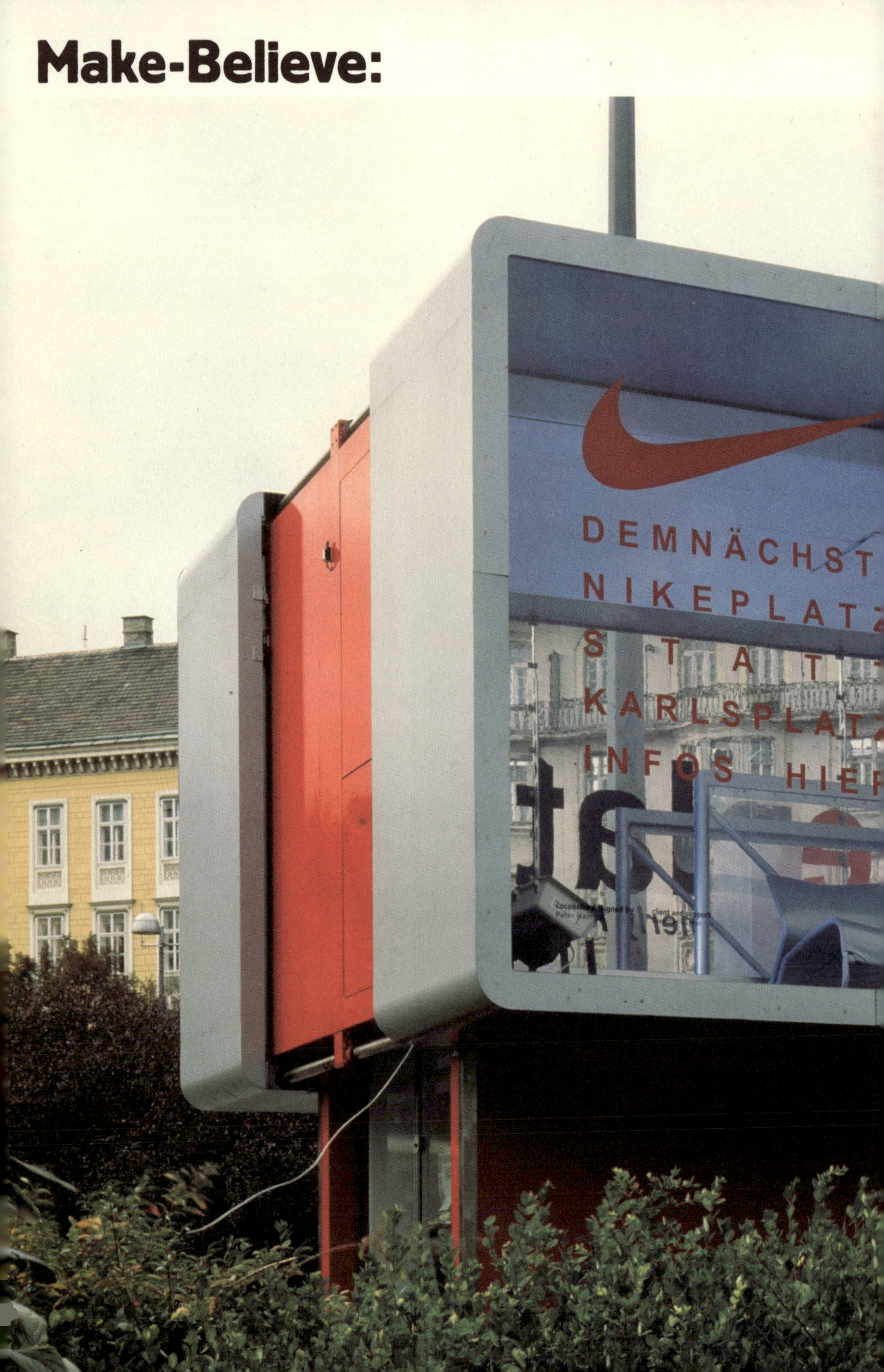

# Parafiction and Plausibility

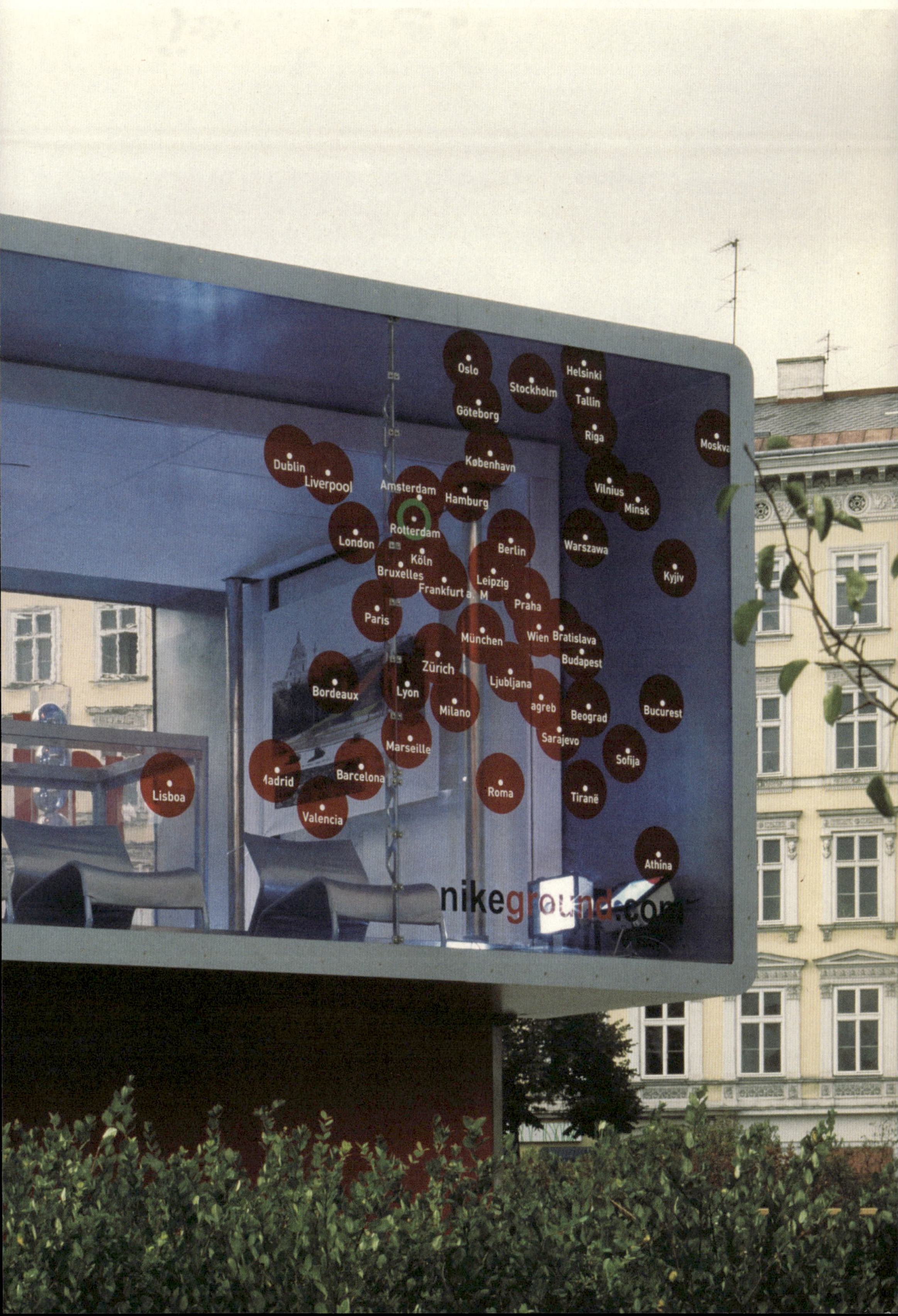

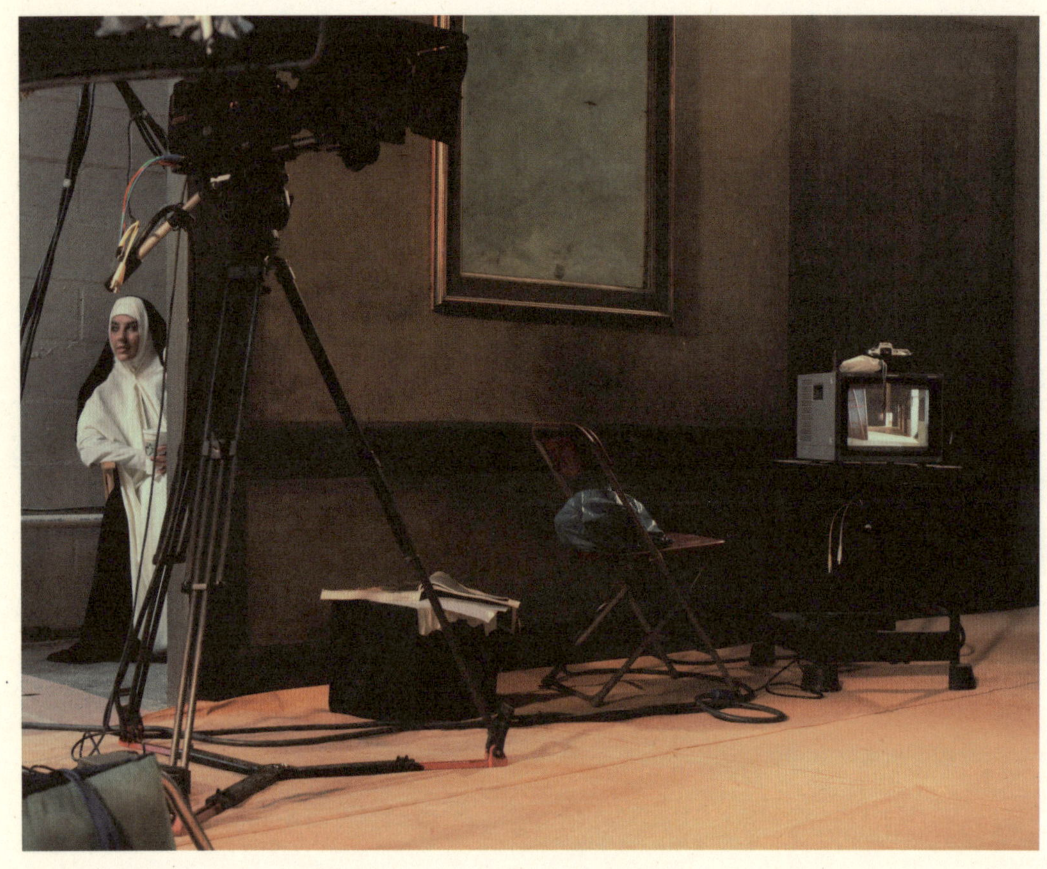

MORE REAL?

Art | Theory | Criticism | Politics

# MOCKTOBER

## 129



$10.00 / Summer 2012          Published by the MoRe Press

# Make-Believe: Parafiction and Plausibility

TEXT BY

*CARRIE LAMBERT-BEATTY*

# Make-Believe:
# Parafiction and Plausibility*

**CARRIE LAMBERT-BEATTY**

> *There is no steady unretracing progress in this life; we do not advance through fixed gradations, and at the last one pause: through infancy's unconscious spell, boyhood's thoughtless faith, adolescence, doubt (the common doom), then skepticism, then disbelief, resting at last in manhood's pondering repose of If. But once again gone through, we trace the round again; and are infants, boys, and men, and Ifs eternally. Where lies the final harbor, whence we unmoor no more?*
>
> —Herman Melville

*Istanbul, 2005*

When the artist Michael Blum arrived in Istanbul to prepare for that city's ninth international biennial, he discovered that the apartment building that had been home in the early twentieth century to the teacher, translator, communist, and feminist Safiye Behar was slated for demolition. A remarkable if little-known historical figure, Behar (1890–1965) was a Turkish Jew who enjoyed a long friendship—some say a romance—with Mustafa Kemal Atatürk, founder of the Turkish Republic. The two met in 1905, in the heady atmosphere of the Zeuve Birahanesi, a bar owned by Safiye's father on the ground floor of the same now-crumbling building in the Beyoglu (then Pera) district of Istanbul. Throughout the last years


* Parts of this essay were presented at ThreeWalls gallery and DePaul University in Chicago, and the Institute of Fine Arts, New York. Feedback from Huey Copeland, Blake Stimson, Jonathan Katz, Tom Williams, Claire Bishop, Eve Melzer, and Taylor Walsh, and readings by Helen Molesworth, Jennifer Roberts, and especially Julia Bryan-Wilson helped me tremendously. An early version of some of this material was published in *Talking with Your Mouth Full: New Language for Socially Engaged Art* (Chicago: ThreeWalls and Green Lantern Press, 2008). Special thanks to Michael Blum, Walid Raad, and Aliza Shvarts, and to my students, particularly David Andersson, Austin Guest, Trevor Martin, and Jack McGrath. Finally, while working on this paper, I had the benefit of reading Vered Maimon's important essay "The Third Citizen: On Models of Criticality in Contemporary Artistic Practices," in *October*, no. 129 (Summer 2009): 85–112. I hope that the conversation begun in these pages will continue beyond them.
Epigraph: Herman Melville, *Moby Dick; or, The Whale* (1851; New York: Penguin, 1986), 602.



MOCKTOBER, *no. 129 (Summer 2012): 114–43. © 2012 Mocktober Magazine, Ltd. and MoRe Press.*

of the sultanate and the early years of the republic, Behar and Kemal maintained a correspondence both intimate and intellectual. The few surviving examples of their letters suggest that Behar had considerable influence on the leader during this crucial period in Turkish history, particularly concerning the rights of women in the new republic. The friendship ended only with Kemal's death in 1938, the same year Safiye immigrated to Chicago. There she was active for many years as a translator of Turkish and an organizer for various leftist causes.

Blum, who trained as a historian at the Sorbonne before beginning his art practice, gave over his biennial exhibition to the documentation of Behar's life.[1] He constructed a modest but thorough historical house museum (necessarily displaced from the condemned building to an apartment complex—the Deniz Palas, or "Palace of the Sea"—being used for the biennial). Culling materials from various historical societies and archives, as well as from Behar's descendants, he set up vitrines featuring her letters, photographs, and books, and arranged original furnishings in the rooms of the apartment, to be peered at over Plexiglas barriers. He relayed Behar's life story with both bilingual didactics and a certain flair for stagecraft (a side table bore a dish of roasted chickpeas, Kemal's favorite snack). A video interview with Behar's grandson, the Chicago architect Melik Tutuncu, brought her family legacy up to the present.

Recovering the forgotten life story and unacknowledged historical role of a female figure from an ethnic minority, this project, *A Tribute to Safiye Behar*, participates in a project of revision whose foundations are in the feminist and civil rights movements of the 1960s and 1970s. Splitting History into histories (and herstories), it also builds on the postmodern critique of metanarratives, while nodding to the discourses on identity and hybridity of the 1980s and 1990s. Yet Blum's project was very much of its own moment. Under cover of the highly conventional visual language of the house museum, Blum was able to address two publics, and two political situations, at once. For the local, Turkish audience, the frank discussion of Mustafa Kemal's likely affair with the Jewish woman, and of her influence on his reforms, served as a critical intervention in the official hagiography of the leader that continues to saturate public life in Turkey. The exposure of a previously repressed history signaled a critique of that state's penchant for secrecy (most infamously, its continuing denials of the Armenian genocide). Meanwhile, for the large contingent of international visitors brought to Istanbul by the biennial in 2005—a moment when Turkey's potential membership in the European Union was being hotly debated—the life story of this secular, cosmopolitan, internationalist, and progressive woman, with her feminist organizing and her love letters in French, cut into stereotypes about Turkey as backward, other, and "Islamicist" (perhaps reminding them, for instance, that Turkish women had the right to vote earlier than their sisters in France).[2]

*A Tribute to Safiye Behar*, then, was both historical and political (and a suggestion that the former is inevitably the latter as well). But it was also something else again. For arguably the most substantial thing about the life of Safiye Behar is that Michael Blum made it up.

To some viewers, the fictionality of the installation's central figure was betrayed by details like the imperfectly pasted-on cover of the book of Nazim Hikmet's poetry on which Behar was credited as translator, or the coincidence that her face—blurred, blocked, or remote—could never quite be made out in any of the

---

1. Blum received a master's degree from the University of Paris Panthéon-Sorbonne prior to attending the École Nationale de la Photographie in Arles. Born in Jerusalem, he is currently based in Vienna.

2. It intervened in yet another way when the project was exhibited at the National Museum of Contemporary Art, Athens, in 2006.

3. Additionally, knowledgeable viewers knew something was amiss when they learned that one of Behar's sons married a granddaughter of (the childless) Emma Goldman.

group photographs on display.[3] There is also a trace of overacting in the video and a touch of dark humor, as when Safiye's grandson describes the death of his entire immediate family in a freak accident in 1966—a convenient tragedy for Blum, whose research might otherwise have gone on forever (and a personally coincidental one, since that is also the year of his own birth). But though subtle clues were planted, the display was meant to be convincing. While several writers on the exhibition chose to reveal the fiction, some otherwise astute critics seemed to accept the exhibition's claims, finding Safiye Behar a fascinating figure but the artwork itself flat-footed.[4] Turkish press reaction varied according to the media outlet. The progressive *Radikal* ran a supportive interview with the "Austrian historian" about Safiye and her importance to Turkish history, and only at the very end of the long piece revealed that she was a fiction, recategorizing Blum as an artist.[5] In other publications, the ideological threat of this project to both Kemalist and Islamicist conservative forces in Turkey was registered more clearly (one writer joked that only Behar's fictionality saved her from assassination).[6] For his part, Blum always maintained, if pressed, that Behar was "real to me." Curators and official exhibition publications kept the question open,[7] and she has acquired a kind of actuality in the years since: a newspaper article mentioned her among other historical figures, with no apparent awareness of her connection to Blum or to art at all;[8] the building she is supposed to have lived in (which has yet to be demolished) is known in the neighborhood as "the house of Safiye Behar."[9] As for ordinary viewers at the biennial, it appears that their reactions to the installation varied, with some taking the exhibit at face value and others questioning its facticity to various degrees. One critic describes viewers "scurrying back" to revisit the installation once they heard that Safiye was an invented character.[10]

The shorthand that I propose for discussing Blum's project is the parafictional.[11] Fiction or fictiveness has emerged as an important category in recent art. But like a paramedic as opposed to a medical doctor,

4. Reviews of Blum's installation include: Elena Crippa, "Michael Blum, A Tribute to Safiye Behar, 2005, 9th Istanbul Biennial," *e-cart* 7 (March 2006), http://www.e-cart.ro, accessed May 1, 2008; T. J. Demos, "9th International Istanbul Biennial," *Artforum* 44 (November 2005): 245; Alison Carroll and Caroline Williams, "Istanbul Biennale," *Artlink* 26, no. 1 (2006), http://www.artlink.com.au/articles/2747/istanbul-biennale-the-9th-istanbul-biennial/.
5. "Atatürk's Lover Safiye," *Radikal*, August 28, 2005. I am grateful to Merih Uz for research assistance on the Turkish press reaction, to Ünver Rustem for English translations, and to both of them for informative discussions during my research on the Behar project. All Turkish translations are by Rustem.
6. Entry on Safiye Behar in the online alternative encyclopedia *Sourtimes/Ekflisözlük*, posted by username terranovanian, October 9, 2005.
7. Vasif Kortun, cocurator of the biennial, says that he tended to present the story as fact; if the question arose, he would go no further than calling Safiye "probable." E-mail correspondence with the author, May 21, 2009. According to cocurator Charles Esche, Blum and the biennial staff sometimes replied to inquiries about Safiye's facticity by saying "well, she isn't documented," a phrase that emphasizes the limitations of the historical record while allowing the questioner to assume what she would about whether that meant Safiye—or someone like her—had or had not lived (while evoking immigration politics, which are germane to Safiye's story). Esche remembers sometimes saying that he wasn't sure himself whether Behar was fictional, since "by that stage Safiye had a life of her own." Charles Esche, e-mail correspondence with the author, April 1, 2009.
8. This article appeared on May 16, 2008, in the newspapers *Vakit Haber* and *Bugün* and the online news outlet *Haber 7*, with Irfan Dumlu cited as author in *Bugün*.
9. Thanks to Betsey Robinson and Ioli Kalavrezou, who discovered this when they went to look for the building in 2008.
10. Marc Spiegler, "Istanbul Biennial," *Art Review* 3 (December 2005–January 2006): 141. One Turkish viewer's report of having been taken in by the exhibition is in the Behar entry in *Sourtimes/Ekflisözlük* (username empas kumpas, posted November 24, 2005).
11. I mean the term *parafiction* differently than the way it is sometimes used in literary studies to designate true stories told in the style of fiction. I'm indebted to the concept of the "paratheatrical" as discussed by Bruce Wilshire ("The Concept of the Paratheatrical," *TDR* 34 [Winter 1990]: 169–78), from whom I borrow the analogy to the paramedic ("paratheater" is a term generally associated with Jerzy Grotowski). Perhaps closer to the current discussion is the term *superfiction*, used by the artist Peter Hill, though his is a broader category (see www.superfiction .com). My use of *parafiction* differs from that of literary critic James Rother in the 1970s, in discussions of writers such as Barthelme or

a parafiction is related to but not quite a member of the category of fiction as established in literary and dramatic art. It remains a bit outside. It does not perform its procedures in the hygienic clinics of literature but has one foot in the field of the real. Unlike historical fiction's fact-based but imagined worlds, in parafiction real and/or imaginary personages and stories intersect with the world as it is being lived. Post-simulacral, parafictional strategies are oriented less toward the disappearance of the real than toward the pragmatics of trust. Simply put, with various degrees of success, for various durations, and for various purposes, these fictions are experienced as fact. They achieve truth status—for some of the people some of the time, as the parafiction pioneer P. T. Barnum might have said.

All of which may be a nice way of saying that a parafiction is a deception. Blum's project deceived tactically, and for progressive purposes, and in a way that allows for the possibility of the deception's discovery. But it deceived nevertheless, allowing viewers to be caught in a "gotcha" moment of having been fooled, to wonder uncomfortably about the status of the claims the exhibit made, or to go away in a strange kind of educated ignorance, their worldviews subtly altered—perhaps in truthful ways—by untruths. Exploring this mode, Blum was far from alone.[12] Between 1998 and 2008 artists gave us advertising campaigns for imaginary products, a not-really-censored exhibition, hacked museum audio tours, several never-made movies, a sham supermarket, nonexistent video installations, dubious abortions, a staged marriage proposal, an impersonated pope, ersatz archives, questionable military units, a faked vacation, an invented critic, a fictional historian, a made-up monkey, an arguably authentic rabbit, a projected penguin, and legions of fake artists, both historical and contemporary (twenty-seven in the recent pseudo-collaborative EU portrait by Czech artist David Cerny alone).[13] More generally, we've seen the term *intervention* supersede *resistance* in discussions of political art, valorizing modes like the parafictional that act disruptively outside the artistic context,[14] while in the wider culture, fiction-in-the-real has become the characteristic mode of political

Pynchon, whose work he described as "para-" in the sense that it referred to or built itself on previous fiction, understanding language as self-multiplying and nonreferential, and history as a sea of texts that "disguise the ongoing impersonation of truth, deny that what is being said yields no recapturable past." ("Parafiction: The Adjacent Universe of Barth, Barthelme, Pynchon, and Nabokov," *boundary 2*, 5 [Autumn 1976]: 20–44, 42). As I suggest below, I believe that the contemporary cases I describe depart from postmodernist visions like this one that have been taken to imply historical, epistemological, or ethical relativism. I agree with Michael Nash and Okwui Enwezor, who in their various writings on mixtures of fiction and documentary in contemporary art have suggested that such experiments actually defend *against* notions of failure of reference—see note 13 below. Rosalind Krauss mobilized the term *paraliterary* in the early 1980s to define a space for work that "cannot be called criticism" but also cannot "be called not-criticism": the writing of Barthes and Derrida, which put the distinction between literature and criticism under erasure. Though the issues at stake here are somewhat different, her model is useful for Blum's kind of parafiction in particular: it's not history but can't be called not-history. Rosalind Krauss, "Poststructuralism and the Paraliterary," in *The Originality of the Avant-garde and Other Modernist Myths* (Cambridge, MA: MIT Press, 1983), 291–95.

12. In the 2005 Istanbul Biennial related works included Khalil Rabah's *Palestine before Palestine*, an arrangement of objects displayed in the style of a natural history museum, all carved of olivewood, and Phil Collins's reunion of Turkish reality TV participants.

13. The parafictional cuts through contemporary culture at a different angle than the category of the faux or partly fictionalized documentary, though this phenomenon is certainly related; the parafictional might be characterized as the performative version of "the documentary turn." See, among others, Michael Nash, *Experiments with Truth: The Documentary Turn* (Philadelphia: FWM, Fabric Workshop and Museum, 2004); Okwui Enwezor, "Documentary/Verité: The Figure of 'Truth' in Contemporary Art," in *Experiments with Truth*; Mark Nash, "Reality in the Age of Aesthetics," *Frieze*, no. 114 (April 2008), http://www.frieze.com/issue/article/reality_in_the_age_of_aesthetics/. Other overlapping or related categories are Hal Foster's "Archival Impulse" (*October*, no. 110 [Fall 2004]: 3–22); Mark Godfrey's "Artist as Historian" (*October*, no. 120 [Spring 2007]: 140–72); David Joselit's theorization of avatars (see "Navigating the New Territory: Art, Avatars, and the Contemporary Mediascape," *Artforum* 43 [Summer 2005]: 276–79), Nato Thompson's "Strategic Visuality" (*Art Journal* 63 [Spring 2004]: 38–40), and Caroline Jones's "aesthetics of doubt," ("Doubt/Fear," *Art Papers* 29 [January–February 2005], http://www.artpapers.org/feature_articles/feature1_2005_0102.htm).

14. Not all interventions are parafictional, but all parafictions are in some way interventionist. The term emerged most influentially in Nato Thompson's exhibition *The Interventionists: Art in the Social Sphere* at MassMoCA (May 2004–March 2005).

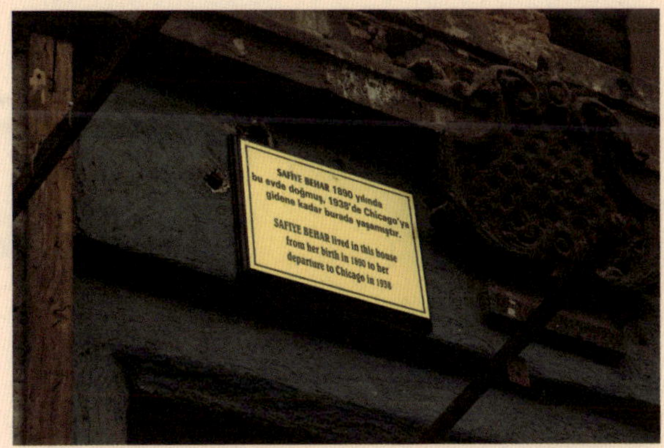

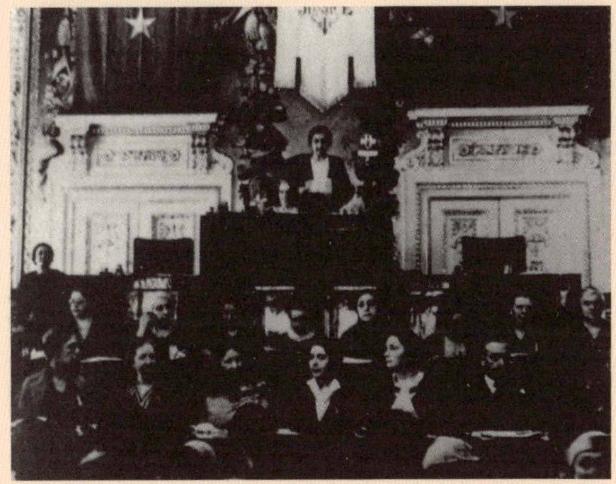

*Michael Blum*, A Tribute to Safiye Behar, *2005; plaque at site of Safiye's home, Hamalbasi Caddesi No. 18, Beyoglu; courtesy the artist*

*Michael Blum*, A Tribute to Safiye Behar, *2005; Safiye delivering speech at the 12th Women's Congress, Istanbul, April 1935; collection Women's Library and Information Center, Istanbul; courtesy the artist*

humor for our time, with Sacha Baron Cohen, *The Daily Show,* and *Brass Eye* perfecting a technique in which parodists pass as their real counterparts, interacting with unsuspecting subjects whose gullibility, pompousness, stupidity, racism, extremism, or simple greed for the spotlight is then mercilessly exposed.[15]

If such experiments have become unusually pervasive in this period, it's no wonder. Here's another list of parafictions: "fake rationales for war, a fake President dressed as a fake soldier declaring a fake end to combat and then holding up a fake turkey. An action movie star became governor and the government started making its own action movies, casting real soldiers like Jessica Lynch as fake combat heroes and dressing up embedded journalists as fake soldiers." This catalogue of events from 2003 is just part of Canadian journalist Naomi Klein's sad litany in support of her claim that it had been "the year of the fake."[16] Every modern period may consider itself less honest than the ones preceding, but Klein is not alone in feeling that the first decade of the twenty-first century has a special claim to being, if not a more lie-prone era, then one in which untruths have had especially catastrophic effects. The slew of recent writings trying to describe or explain this condition range from philosophical explorations of "the ethics of the lie," to moralist warnings about our entry into "the post-truth era," to impassioned calls for renewed personal and public honesty.[17] In this period, partisans in the US made a sport of cataloguing one another's deceptions (two titles were *Liberal Lies* and *Lies and the Lying Liars Who Tell Them*). *Time* magazine ran the headline "Untruths and Consequences" on its cover in July 2003, over an image of President Bush; two years later a much-needed term was added to the philosophical lexicon when satirist Stephen Colbert identified Bush's characteristic mode of "truthiness"—truth measured by conviction rather than accuracy.

Of course, periodization itself is a kind of fiction, and parafiction is hardly an invention of the past decade. Contemporary instances like Blum's trail long legacies of hoax, prank, blague, trickster myth, and parody. Even within more recent history there is a whole series of questions to be asked about the relation of this work to its precedents (in Dada, in conceptual art and performance, in the brilliantly undecidable actions of Andy Kaufman, in the "invisible theater" of Augusto Boal, and in prankster activism from the Situationists to Abbie Hoffman to ACT UP). Andrea Fraser's docent tours were in this mode (ahead of the curve, she gave them up in 1998), while related tactics in work by Fred Wilson, Cheryl Dunye, and Zoe Leonard allowed them to imagine the lives of marginalized historical individuals while simultaneously marking their erasure from the historical record.[18] Of course, Marcel Duchamp lurks behind all these examples, and whether or how this recent work reimagines his legacy is an open question. Here, however, I am primarily interested in a horizontal history, mapping connections between experiments in dissimulation and linking them to certain broad historical shifts of the recent past. For despite their many precedents, parafictions interest me because they are so powerfully and uniquely appropriate to our historical moment—which is to say, powerfully and uniquely troubling.

15. Along with less political prank- and/or hoax-based entertainments in the *Candid Camera* tradition.

16. Naomi Klein, "The Year of the Fake," *Nation,* January 26, 2004. Though Klein's list sounds a bit like one Baudrillard could have made, I'll be suggesting that the more characteristic deceptions of the recent past are performative: rather than a representation with no original, we are beset by attempts to launch something false into quasi-truthfulness.

17. Jean-Michel Rabaté, *The Ethics of the Lie* (New York: Random House, 2008); Ralph Keyes, *The Post-Truth Era: Dishonesty and Deception in Contemporary Life* (New York: Macmillan, 2004); Ihab Hassan, "A Plague of Mendacity: A Plea for Truth, Trust, Altruism," http://ihabhassan.com/bibliography (version of essays in *Cream City Review* 28 [2004] and in *An ABC of Lying: Taking Stock in Interesting Times,* ed. Livio Dobrez, Patricia Dobrez, and Jan Lloyd Jones [Melbourne: Australian Scholarly, 2004]).

18. A note from director Dunye at the end of her 1996 film *Watermelon Woman* (which is about a filmmaker researching the life of the title figure, a black lesbian star of 1930s race movies) states the issue with perfect concision and ambiguity: "Sometimes you have to create your own history. The Watermelon Woman is fiction."

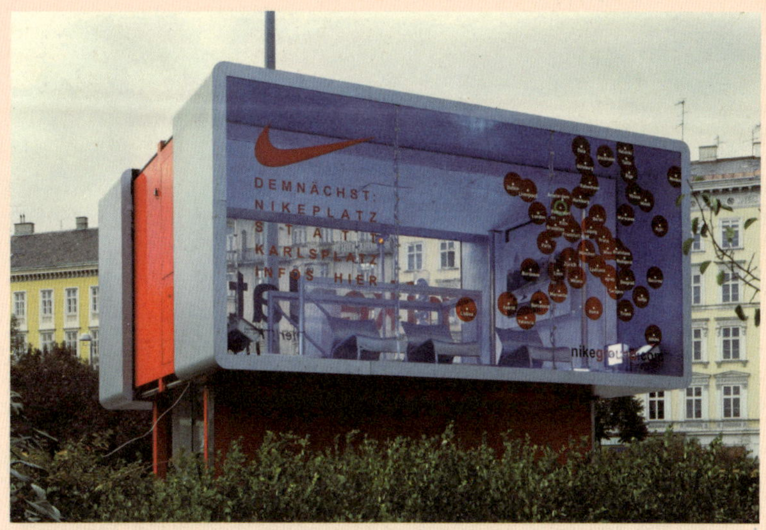



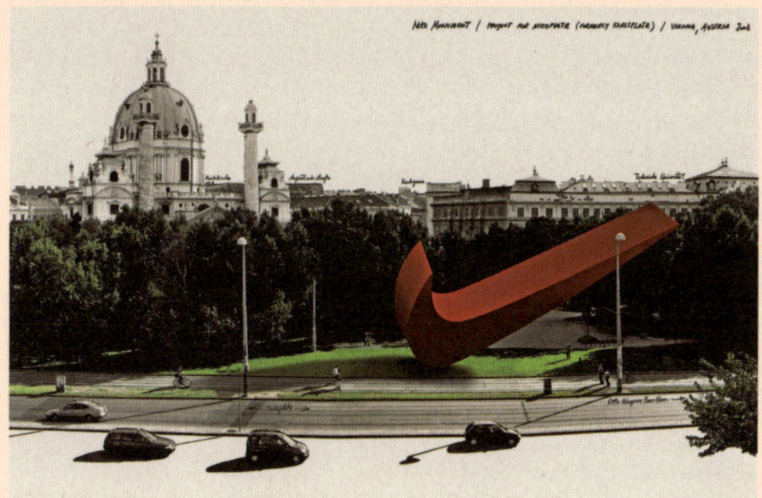

*Eva and Franco Mattes aka 0100101110101101.ORG and
Public Netbase, Fake Nike Infobox, 2003; installation view
at Karlsplatz, Vienna; courtesy Eva and Franco Mattes*

*Eva and Franco Mattes aka 0100101110101101.ORG and
Public Netbase, rendering of proposed monument, 2003;
courtesy Eva and Franco Mattes*

*Vienna, 2003*

One October night in 2003 a flatbed truck delivered a sleek orange and white information booth to a plot of grass on the northeastern corner of Vienna's Karlsplatz. Printed on one of the booth's broad glass windows was a Nike "swoosh," a web address, and three words: "Nikeplatz (Formerly Karlsplatz)." Visiting the URL, accepting one of the flyers distributed the next morning, or entering the booth to talk to Nike representatives, one learned that much as cities have sold the naming rights of sports stadiums to corporate sponsors, Karlsplatz would soon be changing its name. A monumental swoosh sculpture would appear in the shadow of the Karlskirche in what would, as of January 1, be known as Nikeplatz. As the slickly animated website put it: "You want to wear it, why shouldn't cities wear it too?" On the park side of the information booth, a schematic map of Europe had broken out in orange dots, indicating that the Vienna initiative was part of a new international campaign. A Nikestrasse, Nikesquare, Nikestreet, or Piazzanike was coming soon to a European city near you.

As reporters learned with their first calls to Nike Austria, however, none of this was the company's doing. The info booth, website, and marketing campaign were part of an artwork titled *Nike Ground*, a collaboration between the Italian artistic duo Eva and Franco Mattes, who go by the name 0100101110101101 .ORG (hereafter, 01.ORG), and the innovative Austrian new media/art platform Public Netbase.[19]

Many of the passersby interviewed by the artists simply shrugged: since companies like Nike were taking over cities anyway, some said, they might as well pay for the privilege.[20] Part of this is a credit to the artists, of course. The design of the website was spot-on, and the info booth itself—crisp, sleek, rounded, and bright—was both outrageously out of key with the historic Viennese buildings surrounding it and perfectly attuned to the visual rhetoric of design and marketing circa 2003. The crucial skill for parafiction is stylistic mimicry—as in Blum's channeling of the aesthetic of historical house museums. While parodists have always known how much style matters, as net artists, 01.ORG had pioneered a mode of parafiction that made it clear how much more this would become the case in our current information environment.

19. See Vera Tollmann, "Becoming Nike: The Fake behind the Swoosh," trans. Timothy Jones, *Springeren*, April 2003, net section; 01.ORG's Web site on the project at http://www.0100101110101101.org/home/nikeground/intro.html, which provides links to international media coverage of the intervention and a link to an archived version of the project website nikeground.com; and "An Interview with Franco and Eva Mattes aka 01.ORG," *Culture Jamming*, http://www.culture-jamming.de/interviewIIe.html. Clemens Apprich, "Intermission at the Combat Zone: A Review of Public Netbase's Urban and Symbolic Lines of Conflict," *Public Netbase: Non Stop Future; New Practices in Art and Media* (Frankfurt: Revolver, 2008), online edition at nonstop-future.org; Brian Holmes, "Let it RIP: Obituary of an Endless Myth: Public Netbase, 1994–2006," Netbase / t0: Institute for New Culture Technologies, http://www.netbase.org/t0/intro/04.

20. *Nike Ground* illustrates both the power and the problems of culture jamming, the genre of "symbolic guerrilla warfare" (Eco) that emerged as an important form of activism in the 1990s. Culture jamming is generally oriented against corporate globalization but typically focuses on its manifestations in the global North, such as the commercialization of public space, the loss of local specificity, or the depletion of values like originality and rebellion when they become so many advertising slogans. Its most frequent form is "subvertising," attempting to undermine a corporate brand's meaning and value with semi-convincing manipulations of its visual identity (paradigmatically, billboard alteration, like the Billboard Liberation Organization's subtle edit of an Apple ad sporting the visage of the Dalai Lama, from "think different" to "think disillusioned"). Often knowingly drawing on Dada, especially the critical photomontages of John Heartfield, as well as Situationist *détournement*, culture jamming expresses—and stimulates—a desire for freedom from commerce's incursion into mental and physical landscapes. It consolidates identities and collectivities around an anticorporate perspective, and it can be a kind of gateway to critiques of labor conditions, environmental damage, and other less symbol- and humor-friendly corporate affronts. At the same time, given that exposure is a crucial part of branding and that the youth-oriented brands most likely to be subvertised generally *want* to ally themselves with the virtues of creativity, irreverence, and daring displayed in projects like *Nike Ground*, it is entirely possible that culture jammers help their targets more than harm them. This partially explains why most corporate giants don't take legal action against their mosquito-like tormenters.

One of their first projects, done in collaboration with Luther Blissett in 1998, was a convincing clone of the Vatican's website at the URL vaticano.org, in which, among other alterations, acceptance of abortion was worked into archived encyclicals.[21]

The Nike map, with its colored dots, has a certain martial feel, and the idea of a triumphant foreign entity redubbing place names in a European city has similar connotations, but given the ubiquity of the logo in sports and on the street, Nike's effort to occupy Karlsplatz didn't strain credulity too far (the corporation's flagship stores are called Niketown, after all, already indicating a certain territorial ambition).[22] In the age of lifestyle branding and guerrilla marketing, the Nikeplatz idea was different from actual tactics in degree, not in kind. Its point was not how many people would accept the campaign as real (though many did) but how much they—and we—have already accepted about the takeover of public space by commercial interests. It is relevant here that Karlsplatz was and remains known as a hangout for drug dealers and addicts. Bold plans to revitalize the area as a cultural hub had recently been scrapped (to great protest by *Nike Ground* collaborators Public Netbase). Citizens might well have been willing to let a corporation sanitize what the city couldn't or wouldn't, in what would have been only a slightly more literal version of Times Square–style bargains made in New York and other cities.

One unfazed pedestrian interviewed in 01.ORG's documentation says that the renaming plan is "just the reality of the corporate world." Another allows that this sort of thing is "part of commercial life." For these viewers, the corporation's civic incursion was within the horizon of plausibility—part of capitalist common sense. So it was, too, for those critical passersby who reacted to the proposition with displeasure. A third class of viewers approached the info booth skeptically, and those of us who encounter the work as documentation of a past intervention are flatteringly included in this group. (The knowing, superior position one takes in such second-degree experiences of parafiction is no doubt a part of their pleasure, and possibly a limit on their efficacy.) The project functions differently for each of these groups; moreover, it creates movement between them. For instance, a viewer who accepted the renaming as inevitable and later discovered that it was a fiction: she slips outside the consensus that the parafiction's plausibility illuminates—or rather, the consensus that it calls into being as such.

Like "I christen this ship," or "I do" in a wedding ceremony, the phrase "Nikeplatz (Formerly Karlsplatz)" on the information booth is a variant of the category of performative utterances. Specifically, it is a case of what J. L. Austin called the "unhappy performative"—speech acts that don't take. (If an actor in a movie says, "I now pronounce you man and wife," the speech act is not untrue but "infelicitous.")[23] Parafictions in general are performative, where that is understood to mean that they effect or produce something rather than describe or denote it. They are unhappy performatives insofar as they, like the movie wedding, are only "make-believe." But insofar as they make *someone* believe, however temporarily or ambiguously, they trouble the distinction between happy and unhappy performativity.

21. "Luther Blissett" is an open-use pseudonym that began to be used in Italy in the mid-1990s and continues to be associated with art-related pranks in Europe and elsewhere. A group of writers based in Bologna has published several novels under the name.
22. In debunking the Nikeplatz rumor, the city council cited a law on the books since World War II that makes it impossible to change street names in Vienna.
23. J. L. Austin, *How to Do Things with Words: The William James Lectures Delivered at Harvard University in 1955*, ed. J. O. Urmson and Maria Sbisà, 2nd ed. (London: Oxford University Press, 1976), 14.

*Sydney, 2002*

This third story actually begins in the spring of 1999, when an experimental fiction writer and computer programmer who came to call himself Andy Bichlbaum and a new-media artist who became known as Mike Bonanno, then working together as the anticorporate corporation ®™ark, came into possession of the domain name GWBush.com. The upcoming U.S. presidential election was to be the first in which the Internet would be a significant factor, and as primary season ramped up, the Bush strategist Karl Rove had already attempted to forestall online opposition by buying up anti-Bush URLs like "bushsux.com."[24] The ®™ark team, however, demonstrated their more sophisticated relationship to the new technology and its emerging epistemology (and possibly their awareness of 01.ORG's Vatican project) in realizing that a seemingly boring, sanctioned, and official URL was a far more powerful weapon. The website they put up at GWBush .com didn't slam the candidate or break new, damaging stories. Visually mirroring the actual campaign site, and written with the same cheery braggadocio, its goal was to make the Bush campaign more transparent. It described how the self-proclaimed "ecology governor" presided over Texas as it became the most polluting state in the union or proposed amnesty for anyone incarcerated for drug possession who claimed, as Bush had, that he or she had "grown up."[25]

This was the beginning of a mode of radical parody that the artists call "identity correction." The next year, now known as the Yes Men, they put a copy of the World Trade Organization's website up at the address www.gatt.org, with similarly parodic changes.[26] This time, the "contact us" links on the fake site were occasionally used by people actually trying to communicate with individuals at the WTO, and it is then that the Yes Men took "identity correction" beyond the bounds of traditional parody.

They returned the messages. When an e-mail invited the organization's president to speak at a conference, for instance, "he" would send his regrets but suggest that he could dispatch a subordinate instead. It is thus that Mr. Hanniford Schmidt participated in a Salzburg seminar on international trade law and that Mr. Granwyth Hulatberi represented the WTO in debates with anti-corporate-globalization activists on CNBC's Marketwrap Europe at the time of the G8 protests in Genoa (proposing, among other things, a market in "justice vouchers" so that countries that don't abuse people could sell human rights credits to those that do).

This is correction in the sense of unveiling, making clear what the target is really like (according to the correctors). As 01.ORG did with Nike, aspects of the target's policies and beliefs are followed through to logical but exaggerated conclusions. Though they can be delicious to read about or watch for those who share the Yes Men's politics, the problem with these negative identity corrections is that they generally fail to inspire outrage. Though the websites themselves irritate the target entities, the speeches usually garner nothing more than bemusement (if that) from their primary audiences. And negative corrections have

24. He had also purchased domain names that the campaign might want so that they would not have to buy them back later from "cybersquatters." See Jim Puzzanghera, "Online Race for Political Domains: Bush Outpaces Gore in Snapping Up Sites," *San Jose Mercury News*, June 7, 1999.

25. The Yes Men, "Limits to Freedom," http://theyesmen.org/hijinks/gwbush; *The Yes Men: The True Story of the End of the World Trade Organization* (New York: Disinformation Company, 2004), 14. Versions of the sites are archived at www.rtmark.com/bush.

26. After having their site shut down by their service provider due to threats from the WTO, they developed and released open-source software to automate the process of "funhouse-mirroring" any website (they called it, what else, Reamweaver). See www.reamweaver.com; Michael Conner, "I Am the World Trade Organization . . . or Am I?," *Austin Chronicle*, July 5, 2002; "Corporations That Miss the Joke and Just Repeat the Lie," *New Media Age*, February 12, 2004.

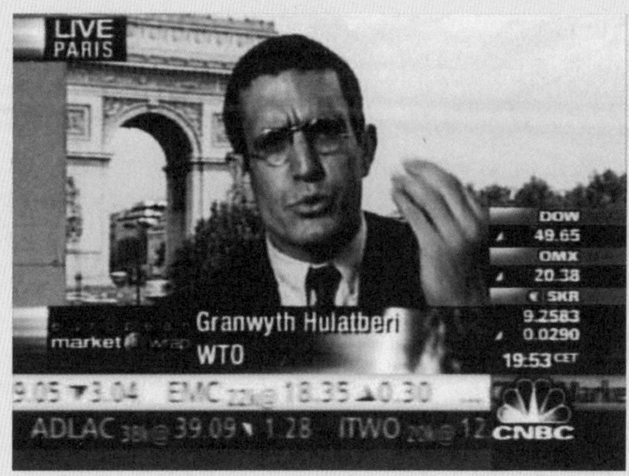



*The Yes Men*, End of the World Trade Organization, 2002; *courtesy the artists*

problems even in terms of rallying the sympathetic (for one thing, in their wake actual current conditions can seem relatively benign). The brilliance of the Yes Men, however, was to realize that they could also correct identities in the sense of repairing. In positive identity correction, the target is made to announce strategies and transformations that are salutary from the point of view of the corrector, and that the actual person or entity must then choose to ignore or deny.[27]

This brings us to Sydney in May 2002, when a WTO representative by the name of Kinnithrug Sprat arrived to address the Certified Practicing Accountants Association of Australia. He spent nearly an hour summarizing research that shows the failure of the WTO's operative principles: the link between cash-crop export and drought; the decrease in the income of the poorest 40 percent of populations under trade liberalization; the failure of foreign direct investment to stimulate third-world economic growth. In light of this evidence, he explained, the WTO had decided to disband. It would reconstitute itself as the Trade Regulation Organization, an entity devoted to making trade "help people instead of businesses."[28]

While the Yes Men's seemingly outrageous exaggerations of the WTO's actual stances had failed to get a rise out of audiences already aligned with its basic principles, to their surprise this announcement of socially progressive decisions that largely *broke* with those principles was met with marked enthusiasm,

27. On November 12, 2008, thousands of people in New York, Washington, and other cities received complimentary copies of the *New York Times*, with the bold headline "Iraq War Ends." Co-created by the Yes Men, the Anti-Advertising Agency, Not An Alternative, CODEPINK, Improv Everywhere, "many others, and hundreds of volunteers," the "special edition" nodded to John Lennon and Yoko Ono's "War Is Over (if you want it)" billboards of 1969–70, though here the parenthetical clause was implied simply by the preponderance of progressive visions in the headlines ("Maximum Wage Law Passed"; "Secretary Apologizes for W.M.D. Scare"). While the faux edition projected an ideal world in which the effects of the Bush years were rolled back, it got its special charge from the paper's initially convincing appearance. It certainly didn't fool anyone. But thinking of the money and effort put into writing a full newspaper's worth of stories in the right diction and style, printing it on newsprint paper of the right type and size, with the right ink and images, and then mobilizing hundreds of volunteers to hand it out in the street—rather than simply writing about the imagined changes in an essay or poem or blog—makes clear part of the difference between parafiction and other types of representation. There is surplus truth-value produced by that labor—a kind of performative residue. See www.nytimes-se.com.

28. The Yes Men, "End of the WTO," http://theyesmen.org/hijinks/sydney; Shane Wright, "Fed: WTO Hoax Snares Aust's CPA," AAP News Feed, May 27, 2002.

with accountants approaching Mr. Sprat after his talk, full of ideas for helping the "TRO" serve the people of the global South. Such converts were bound to be disappointed—but not before having had a concrete experience of the motto of the anti-corporate-globalization movement: "Another world is possible."

Here is how the Yes Men muse on the positive reaction to their most fantastically progressive proposals: "Could it be that the violent and irrational consensus gripping the world, what we call corporate globalization, is maintained only through a sustained and strenuous effort of faith? Could it be that almost everyone—even those, like accountants, that we are usually inclined to think of as conservative—would immediately embrace a more humane consensus if one were presented by those in positions of authority?"[29] What they discovered is their ability to intervene in what Jacques Rancière calls the distribution of the sensible: the system of inclusions and exclusions that determine what can be sensed; the literally common sense about what can be said, thought, seen, felt, and who can say, think, see, and feel it.[30] If a group of Australian accountants can suddenly find it thinkable—even credible, even *actionable*—to realign world trade to the benefit of indigenous people and the global poor, then something like a new distribution of the sensible has, at least temporarily, been brought into being.

In many cases, the difference between happy and unhappy performatives depends on the authority with which the speaker is vested (not only does the stage priest not really cause the two actors before him to become married, but in most of this country no one can wed two men or two women). A happy performative is usually an authorized one; moreover, part of what they performatively produce is that authority itself. But, following Derrida, poststructuralist thinkers have argued for the political potential of performativity by questioning Austin's absolute distinction between authorized and unauthorized speech, serious and nonserious contexts, happy and unhappy performatives.[31] So does the parafictioneer. The Yes Men realized that the consensus around free-trade ideology could be changed by speech acts—as long as the speakers were "in positions of authority." They lacked such authority, but given a URL and a change of clothes, they could literally make believe, convincing some people, some of the time, that they had it.[32] This is, perhaps paradoxically, both to use and to undermine the authority that they target. The Yes Men put it this way: "It seems people can accept just about anything if you're dressed in a suit."[33]

Toward the end of *Gender Trouble*, Judith Butler wrote that the seeming substantiality of gender is itself "a constructed identity, a performative accomplishment which the mundane social audience, including the actors themselves, come to believe and to perform in the mode of belief. . . . Genders can be neither

29. The Yes Men, "End of the WTO," http://theyesmen.org/hijinks/Sydney.

30. Jacques Rancière, *The Politics of Aesthetics: The Distribution of the Sensible*, trans. Gabriel Rockhill (London: Continuum International, 2004). Though Rancière's stress on the commonality of politics and aesthetics in "the sensible" is generative, it should be noted that the idea of an explicitly political work of art is a problematic one within his philosophy, in which disruption of an existing configuration of the sensible is incompatible with meaningfulness or readability: it will always be caught between "the readability of the message that threatens to destroy the sensible form of art and the radical uncanniness that threatens to destroy all political meaning" (63).

31. A few of the key texts for performativity theory are Jacques Derrida, "Signature, Event, Context" (1971), trans. Samuel Weber and Jeffrey Mehlman, in *Limited Inc* (Evanston, IL: Northwestern University Press, 1988); Judith Butler, *Gender Trouble: Feminism and the Subversion of Identity* (New York: Routledge, 1990); Butler, *Bodies That Matter: On the Discursive Limits of Sex* (New York: Routledge, 1993); Eve Kasofsky Sedgwick and Andrew Parker, introduction to *Performativity and Performance* (New York: Routledge, 1995).

32. Or one could say that they exaggerate the lack that is at the center of all identity and the performative iterations that construe it as substantive. Such points aside, the Yes Men do speak as white men from the global North. To what degree is parafiction a sport of the privileged? Nevertheless, the theory of performativity would be useful in a discussion of the camp and/or queer aspect of the Yes Men's pranks. Sarah Kanouse has made an argument about the phallocentrism of prank-based activism in "Cooing Over the Golden Phallus," *Journal of Aesthetics and Protest* 1, no. 4 (2005), http://www.journalofaestheticsandprotest.org/4/kanouse.html.

33. Dennis Roddy, "Liar's Poker," *Pittsburgh Post-Gazette*, December 12, 2004.

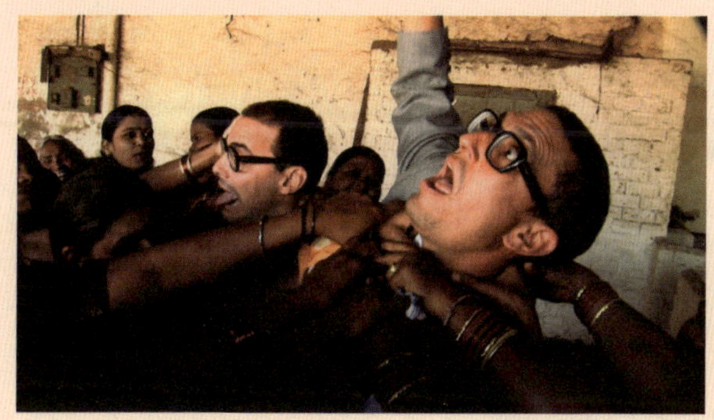

*The Yes Men*, Might Makes Right, 2001; *courtesy the artists*

true nor false, neither real nor apparent, neither original nor derived. As credible bearers of those attributes, however, genders can also be rendered thoroughly and radically incredible."[34] Here belief becomes the crux of the performative. The Yes Men play with the two sides of that realization. On the one hand, free-trade ideology and the authority of its proponents are denaturalized, made "radically incredible." On the other, the viewer's credence (and secondary audiences' witnessing of that credence) becomes a synapse between the imagined and the actual.[35]

Imagine a hypothetical viewer of *A Tribute to Safiye Behar*: a European tourist, vaguely opposed to Turkish accession to the EU, who takes the exhibit as purely factual and whose position is softened, to some degree, by the Turkish history she learns there. What happens when she discovers that she has been duped? For some viewers, Safiye's shift into the category of fiction might harden previous prejudice. But the parafictioneer's gamble is that for other viewers, or perhaps even for the same ones at different psychological levels, the experience of *having known Safiye as real* would have a lingering effect even after the disillusionment. "The plausibility itself is very real," says Blum.[36] The art of the plausible discloses consensus about the way things are, but it also can make a new reality sensible: accessible both to feeling and to reason. It not only matches but also mobilizes Rancière's model of fictions as "material rearrangements of signs and images, relations between what is done and what can be done."[37]

The efficacy of positive identity correction—and the poetry—turns on this power to shift something into the range of the plausible. Such shifts can be deeply moving. In what may be the most famous intervention by the Yes Men, a representative of Dow Chemical agreed to an interview on BBC World TV on the twentieth anniversary of the Union Carbide chemical spill at Bhopal, India, which devastated the region in 1984, killing at least twenty thousand people and sickening untold thousands more. Since Dow has

34. Butler, *Gender Trouble*, 141.

35. Earlier, 01.ORG demonstrated the role of belief in the performative, though problematically, when during their papal stint they freely granted e-pardons to petitioners who tried to contact the pope through their fake Vatican website. When a priest says, "I absolve you," your spiritual state has changed; when a few smartass artists say it, it has not. But if you believe that you were pardoned by a priest, does it matter if it was actually an impostor? For you it matters utterly (that's why this particular parafiction seems so cruel), while for the nonbeliever observing you it matters not at all (that's why it also seems relatively pointless).

36. Michael Blum, e-mail correspondence with the author, March 23, 2009.

37. Rancière, *Politics of Aesthetics*, 39.

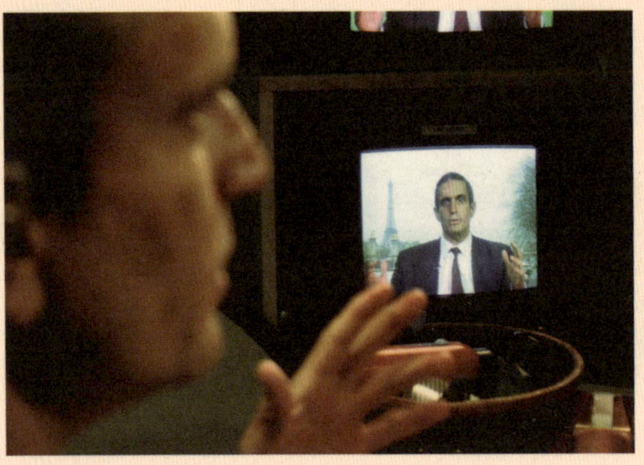

*The Yes Men*, Dow Does the Right Thing, 2004; *courtesy the artists*

categorically refused to take responsibility for cleaning up the environmental damage or compensating the victims since absorbing Union Carbide in 2001,[38] it was a surprise to hear Dow's Jude Finisterra announce that the chemical giant had decided to make reparations to the victims and to remediate the toxic site, at a cost of $12 billion, in what he called "the first time in history that a publicly owned company of anything near the size of Dow has performed an action which is significantly against its bottom line simply because it is the right thing to do." Even today, knowing that it took the BBC only two hours to detect and unveil the speaker as an impostor, it is electrifying to watch the text below the talking head change to "Breaking News: Dow accepts full responsibility" (as it was for Dow's stockholders, in a different way: its stock price immediately dipped).[39] For those two hours, the world believed that there would be something like justice in Bhopal; for that time, there existed a different model for corporate decision making, an ethical as well as financial bottom line.

But parafiction is itself ethically risky. As many have pointed out, the victims of Union Carbide in India were also among those taken in by Finisterra's announcement (fitting that his name combined the patron saint of impossible causes and the world's end). One can only imagine their joy and corresponding disappointment when they learned that they still awaited justice.[40] Moreover, from some points of view any purposeful deception is inherently injurious. Consider the argument, which Sissela Bok put in ecological terms in 1978, that "trust is a social good to be protected just as much as the air we breathe or the water we drink."[41] Though the Yes Men may have outsmarted Rove in 1999, in some ways the work they went on

38. Some victims had received $300 to $500 from Union Carbide in 1989, equivalent to five years of medical care, according to the Bhopal Medical Appeal (www.bhopal.org); Bhopalis continue to develop toxin-related illnesses twenty-five years later. Dow has a website, the "Bhopal Information Center," giving its positions at www.bhopal.com.

39. A clip is available on YouTube.

40. The Yes Men admit to "nagging doubt" about this and have apologized to the people of Bhopal. They have also responded semantically ("For 20 years, the victims of Bhopal falsely *hoped* that Dow and Union Carbide would do something to ease the suffering that they'd caused … those who heard our announcement didn't falsely *hope*, they were falsely *certain* that their suffering was at long last over") and pragmatically: "If the deaths, debilities, organ failure, brain damage, tumors, breathing problems, and sundry other forms of permanent damage caused by Dow and Union Carbide aren't enough to arouse your pity, and the hour of 'false hopes' we caused is—fantastic, we won! Go straight to Bhopal.net and make a donation." (http://theyesmen.org/faq).

41. Sissela Bok, *Lying: Moral Choice in Public and Private Life*, 2nd ed. (New York: Vintage, 1999), 26. The Yes Men are less ambivalent about this critique than the "false hope" charge. Since the BBC immediately and prominently retracted the story, they say: "There was no net

to do is itself a "funhouse-mirror" of that operative's infamous techniques. Surely, the performativity that they deploy is the jester's version of "We're an empire now, and when we act, we create our own reality."[42] Such similarities can lead you to side with Bok and others who call for a return to honesty in personal and political communication. Or they can leave you agreeing with the Yes Men that precisely in such a climate, "we need to be devious in order to achieve a condition of honesty."[43] (Just what social trust, after all, do we imagine we would preserve, in arguing against the use of deception in cultural-political work?) For my part, I am ultimately not interested in passing ethical judgment on parafictioneers. But neither do I think the problems that they raise can be put aside. The fact that parafictions are queasy-making is key to what they are and what they do.

*New Haven, 2008*

On Thursday, April 17, 2008, the *Yale Daily News* reported that the end-of-the-year student exhibition set to open the following Tuesday would include art major Aliza Shvarts's documentation of a nine-month-long senior project. According to a press release from the artist and an interview with reporters, during this time she had used donated sperm to inseminate herself as often as possible, while every month, on the twenty-eighth day of her menstrual cycle, she took herbal medications to induce miscarriage.[44] In the exhibition, videos of the artist experiencing vaginal bleeding were to be projected on four sides of a clear plastic cube, the walls of which would be infused with samples of the discharged fluid.

Had this multimedia sculpture existed alone (or existed at all?), the project might never have transcended the category of undergraduate art. But, as intended, Shvarts's real accomplishment was the drama that unfolded in the wake of her announcement. By 8 a.m. that day, six readers had posted comments about the Shvarts story on the Yale newspaper's website.[45] By midnight there were 282 comments. Gawker .com picked up the story at 10 a.m., and by afternoon reports of the "abortion artist" had echoed around the blogosphere, with mainstream media reporting the story in the days immediately following.[46] Predictably, it

misinformation. In fact there was significantly more information as a result, since more people knew about Bhopal and Dow, especially in the US" (http://theyesmen.org/hijinks/bbcbhopal).

42. Senior Bush adviser quoted by Ron Suskind in "Faith, Certainty, and the Presidency of George W. Bush," *New York Times Magazine*, October 17, 2004.

43. The Yes Men, "Frequently Asked Questions," http://theyesmen.org/faq.

44. Martine Powers, "For Senior, Abortion a Medium for Art, Political Discourse," *Yale Daily News*, April 17, 2008. The statement Shvarts released read: "For the past year, I performed repeated self-induced miscarriages. I created a group of fabricators from volunteers who submitted to periodic STD screenings and agreed to complete and permanent anonymity. From the 9th to the 15th day of my menstrual cycle, the fabricators would provide me with sperm samples, which I used to privately self-inseminate. Using a needless syringe, I would inject the sperm near my cervix within 30 minutes of its collection, so as to insure the possibility of fertilization. On the 28th day of my cycle, I would ingest an abortifacient, after which I would experience cramps and heavy bleeding. To protect myself and others, only I know the number of fabricators who participated, the frequency and accuracy with which I inseminated, and the specific abortifacient I used. Because of these measures of privacy, the piece exists only in its telling. This telling can take textual, visual, spatial, temporal, and performative forms—copies of copies for which there is no original." This statement with additional paragraphs explaining her intentions was published as a guest column in the *Yale Daily News* on April 18, 2008. She had previously distributed the statement to members of her senior thesis class, her adviser, other faculty, and her college dean.

45. All eight initial responses denounced the work, though one writer did acknowledge Shvarts's freedom of expression.

46. Lexis Nexis's blog archive finds at least fifteen distinct English-language blog entries posted on April 17 and a hundred more by late May. Internet search engines find dozens more. The story was picked up by the mainstream news media on Friday, April 18, when it began to be reported by wire services, the *Washington Post*, the *New York Times*, *Newsday*, *Newsweek*, and newspapers from Ireland to Australia and Korea.

incited especial fervor on conservative and antiabortion websites. The president of the National Right to Life Committee called Shvarts a serial killer.[47] On the ugliest fringe, anti-Semitic bloggers found ammunition in her actions (she received threatening hate mail in this vein as well),[48] even as others likened her to Mengele.[49] But the artist came in for critique from the left as well. A NARAL spokesperson called the project insensitive and offensive, Yale pro-choice groups distanced themselves,[50] and liberal bloggers worried (perceptively) that the project would only incite their opponents: "It's as if someone came up with a formula that incorporated all their favorite bugbears: Irresponsible sluts, frivolous abortions, liberal academia, and self-indulgent performance art."[51] A common theme for the more moderate opponents of her project was that the acts she described could have been physically and mentally harmful.[52] And so, nearly across the board, there was condemnation of Shvarts's university for allowing it.[53]

The day the story was published, a university spokesperson issued a statement:

> *Ms. Shvarts is engaged in performance art. Her art project includes visual representations, a press release and other narrative materials. She stated to three senior Yale University officials today, including two deans, that she did not impregnate herself and that she did not induce any miscarriages.*
>
> *The entire project is an art piece, a creative fiction designed to draw attention to the ambiguity surrounding form and function of a woman's body.*
>
> *She is an artist and has the right to express herself through performance art.*
>
> *Had these acts been real, they would have violated basic ethical standards and raised serious mental and physical health concerns.*[54]

The first notable thing is the way this statement plays into Shvarts's hands (to paraphrase the opening lines: she is a liar; we know because she told us so).[55] Not surprisingly, the student countered with a statement of her own, standing by her initial description of her actions over the past nine months and adding that "no one can say with 100-percent certainty that anything in the piece did or did not happen . . . because the nature of the piece is that it did not consist of certainties." This led Yale to re-respond, claiming Shvarts had told the administration that if it reported her admission of the piece's fictiveness she would deny it.[56]

47. http://www.foxnews.com/story/0,2933,351608,00.html.

48. http://newsfromthewest.blogspot.com/2008_04_17_archive.html, accessed March 1, 2009. Tellingly, Newsfromthewest, which appears to be completely dedicated to virulent anti-Semitism, calls itself "the Internet's most dynamic truthsite." The language of unveiling truth and disabusing the deceived is everywhere in hate speech on the Internet (and of course, long before it, from the Elders of Zion to Holocaust denial).

49. http://sigmundcarlandalfred.wordpress.com/2008/04/21/alicia-shvarts-is-an-artist-like-josefmengele-was-a-doctor/.

50. Executive Boards of the Reproductive Rights Action League at Yale (RALY) and the Yale Law Students for Reproductive Justice, letter to the editor, *Yale Daily News*, April 21, 2008.

51. Lindsay Beyerstein, "'Abortion as Art' a Hoax?" *Majikthise*, posted April 17, 2008 (accessed through Newstex/Lexis-Nexis August 6, 2008).

52. This was particularly the case for antichoice writers, for whom the belief that abortion causes women long-term mental anguish is an increasingly used argument.

53. Rick Rice, *Brutally Honest*, April 17, 2008. Michelle Malkin tried to lash this budding controversy to the culture wars of twenty years before: "Move Over, Andres Serrano and Karen Finley: Here Comes Blood-Smearing Yale Art Student Aliza Shvarts," *Michelle Malkin*, April 17, 2008, http://michellemalkin.com /2008/04/17.

54. Statement by Yale spokesperson Helaine S. Klasky, Yale University Office of Public Affairs, April 17, 2008, http://opa.yale.edu/news/article.aspx?id=2262; reported in Zachary Abrahamson, Thomas Kaplan, and Martine Powers, "University Calls Art Project a Fiction; Shvarts '08 Disputes Yale's Claim," *Yale Daily News*, April 17, 2008.

No wonder, then, that Yale was so quick to call in the authorities to secure veracity (those "senior officials") and that that aspect of the university's statement seems more than a little overwrought (not one dean but two!). This only makes it clearer, however, that in parafictions institutional authority is a crucial ingredient in plausibility—whether in the form of the Plexi barriers and neat labels of a historical museum, the convincing slickness of a corporate identity, the digital stationery of an entity like the WTO, or the magic cloak that is, apparently, the business suit.

The Yes Men hijack that authority, but Shvarts claimed no power other than her own. Instead, authorities swooped in to submit a plausible if disturbing story to the order-restoring category of the hoax.[57] Or tried to. According to the university, if she was lying in her initial statements, and had never inseminated herself, then her right to say that she had done so was protected as artistic expression. If she was not lying and had done what she said she did, she would be liable for moral sanction, perhaps treatment. In this situation, only her right to lie was protected.

In a final twist, Shvarts was told that she could exhibit her thesis only if she signed a statement testifying that it was a fiction. This coerced speech act would, of course, have destroyed the piece, which is sited in the state of uncertainty just as much as a sculpture might be specific to a particular physical location. In choosing to name her bleeding as "period," "miscarriage," or "abortion," each person who describes her project demonstrates its central point that what we take as biological facts are constructed in language and ideology.[58] But what makes her project matter beyond its illustration of this idea is the way this was conflated with the parafictional questions of whether she had done what she said she had, whether an ovum had ever been fertilized,[59] whether she had lied to the Yale officials. With these, the project mapped the action of the artist controlling her work onto that of a woman controlling her body.

Shvarts refused to sign the statement, ensuring that her project would exist as it does: as a story.

*

The stories told here involve a diverse range of practices and practitioners, from highly regarded contemporary artists to a student, and from gallery art to tactical media and political activism. They concern a range of somewhat exotic places—Istanbul, Vienna, Sydney, cyberspace, and a uterus—and they vary widely in terms of their complexity, their formal means, their visual languages, and especially the outcomes they seem to favor. Sometimes the revelation of the parafiction is key to the operation. This is when they come closest

55. Forms of this classic "liar's paradox" are a theme of Rabaté's *Ethics of the Lie* (see especially chap. 4, "Lies and Paradox," 193–258).

56. "Shvarts, Yale Lash over Project," *Yale Daily News*, Friday, April 18, 2008. Shvarts's project can't be securely categorized as a hoax—or even a parafiction—since it remains unclear what was or wasn't true about her story. But it partakes of the parafictional because the question of veracity is fundamental to its structure.

57. And to fulfill perfectly the role of normative, institutionalized patriarchy that the project was designed to challenge.

58. Her statement about the project was published as "Shvarts Explains Her 'Repeated Self-Induced Miscarriages,'" April 18, 2008, at http://www.yaledailynews.com/articles/printarticle/24559. "Because the miscarriages coincide with the expected date of menstruation (the 28th day of my cycle), it remains ambiguous whether there was ever a fertilized ovum or not. The reality of the pregnancy, both for myself and for the audience, is a matter of reading. This ambivalence makes obvious how the act of identification or naming—the act of ascribing a word to something physical—is at its heart an ideological act, an act that literally has the power to construct bodies. In a sense, the act of conception occurs when the viewer assigns the term 'miscarriage' or 'period' to that blood."

59. Theoretically this empirical question could be answered by testing the blood either for a second set of DNA or for the presence of the hormone hCG. But in fact given the limits of testing, it would be impossible to say conclusively whether fertilization had occurred or not (leaving aside the question of whether that fact would determine whether or not a life had been conceived). See Melissa Lafsky, "Can Science Get to the Bottom of the Aliza Shvarts Abortion Fracas?," Discoblog, *Discover* Web site, http://blogs.discovermagazine.com/discoblog/2008/04/18/can-science-get-to-the-bottom-of-the-aliza-shvarts-abortion-fracas/.

to simple hoax—but also to effective activism. Sometimes such a revelation is either withheld or impossible to provide, and this is probably when they come closest to what is conventionally considered art. A complete typology of the parafictional and its tools would tell us much; however, for the time being I want to maintain that the commonalities among these projects tell us at least as much as the differences. Here, then, are some provisional conclusions or what we might as well call the morals of the stories.

## Globalization "Immanence"[60]

Nike is a target for culture jammers like 0l.ORG not only because of its branding success and ubiquity but also because it is a corporate globalization morality tale.[61] And of course the two sides of the company— its branded identity and its outsourced sweatshops—are connected: the explosion of branding over the last twenty years depends on the loosening up of capital via outsourcing.[62] This is something that Michael Blum knows well, as the artist is perhaps best known for his 2001 project *My Sneakers*: a video and installation documenting his negotiation of corporate bureaucracy and layers of subcontracting in Indonesia in the attempt to meet the workers who had sewn his Nikes. *My Sneakers* was made on the occasion of an invitation to an artist's residency in Jakarta, and I don't know whether it was in Blum's mind four years later when he went to Istanbul to participate in another ritual of the international art world. But neither of the projects he made on these occasions forgets that art is itself a part of the globalized network of capital. By making his artistic pilgrimage to Jakarta a journey of return for his sneakers, Blum had linked jet-setting and outsourcing in an example of what Pamela M. Lee calls the immanence of the art world to globalization: the way that continent-hopping artists, critics, curators, and collectors participate not just by providing representations of global trade and transit but also substantively: "the activities constitutive of the art world's horizon are indivisible from the activity of globalization itself."[63] Biennials and other international exhibitions are mechanisms for cities or regions to enhance their standing in the global economic order—the Istanbul Biennial has been called "part of broader plans for the marketing of Istanbul as a cultural brand"[64]—while both careers and artworks become organized in terms of travel, shipment, and just-in-time production. Meanwhile, artists negotiate twin pressures to be locally specific and internationally legible. Blum's Safiye Behar project concerns postcolonial subject matter, while

60. As indicated below, this term is taken from Pamela M. Lee, "Boundary Issues: The Art World under the Sign of Globalism," *Artforum* 42 (November 2003): 164–67; Lee's mobilization of the term *immanence* to discuss art and globalization in turn references Michael Hardt and Antonio Negri, *Empire* (Cambridge, MA: Harvard University Press, 2000), as well as Deleuze and Spinoza.

61. By specifically choosing an American corporation, 0l.ORG signaled that the faux takeover of Karlsplatz was structurally and thematically concerned with models of economic imperialism.

62. While the history of brands and branding is generally understood to begin in the nineteenth century, the change in the 1980s through the 1990s is expressed in the term "brand equity," invented in this period (the *Wall Street Journal* first used the term in 1985). It indicates that the brand—a set of images and associations—is increasingly understood as a primary asset in itself, rather than simply the public face of a company whose value lies in its products and infrastructure. (See Jonathan Knowles, "Varying Perspectives on Brand Equity," *Marketing Management*, July–August 2008, accessed at www.MarketingNPV.com, March 18, 2009.) Klein points out how the new kind of branding connects to the "lightening" of consumer-product companies at this time, as they began to contract out manufacturing processes rather than run their own factories, which in turn depends on trade liberalization. Naomi Klein, *No Logo* (London: Flamingo, 2001), 4–5, 22–23.

63. Lee, "Boundary Issues," 167.

64. Süreyyya Evren, "Parrhesiatic Games in Turkish Contemporary Art Scene," *Third Text* 22 (January 2008): 35–42, 38. Evren's essay calls for forms of Foucault's parrhesia in contemporary Turkish art. This mode—risky and direct truth telling—would have a complicated relationship with the parafictional.

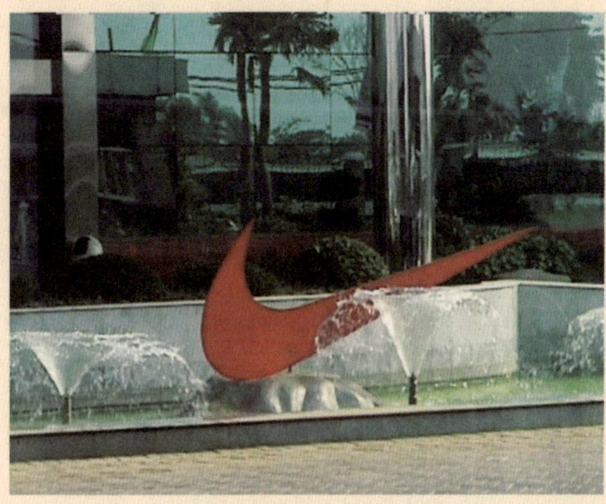

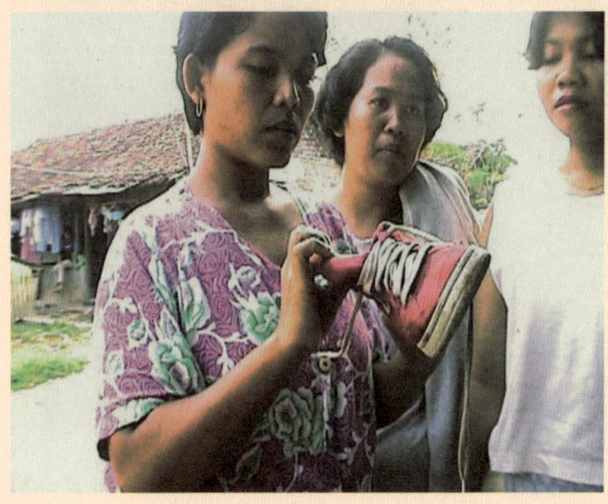

*Michael Blum*, My Sneakers, *2001; video, color, sound; 37:30 minutes; courtesy the artist*

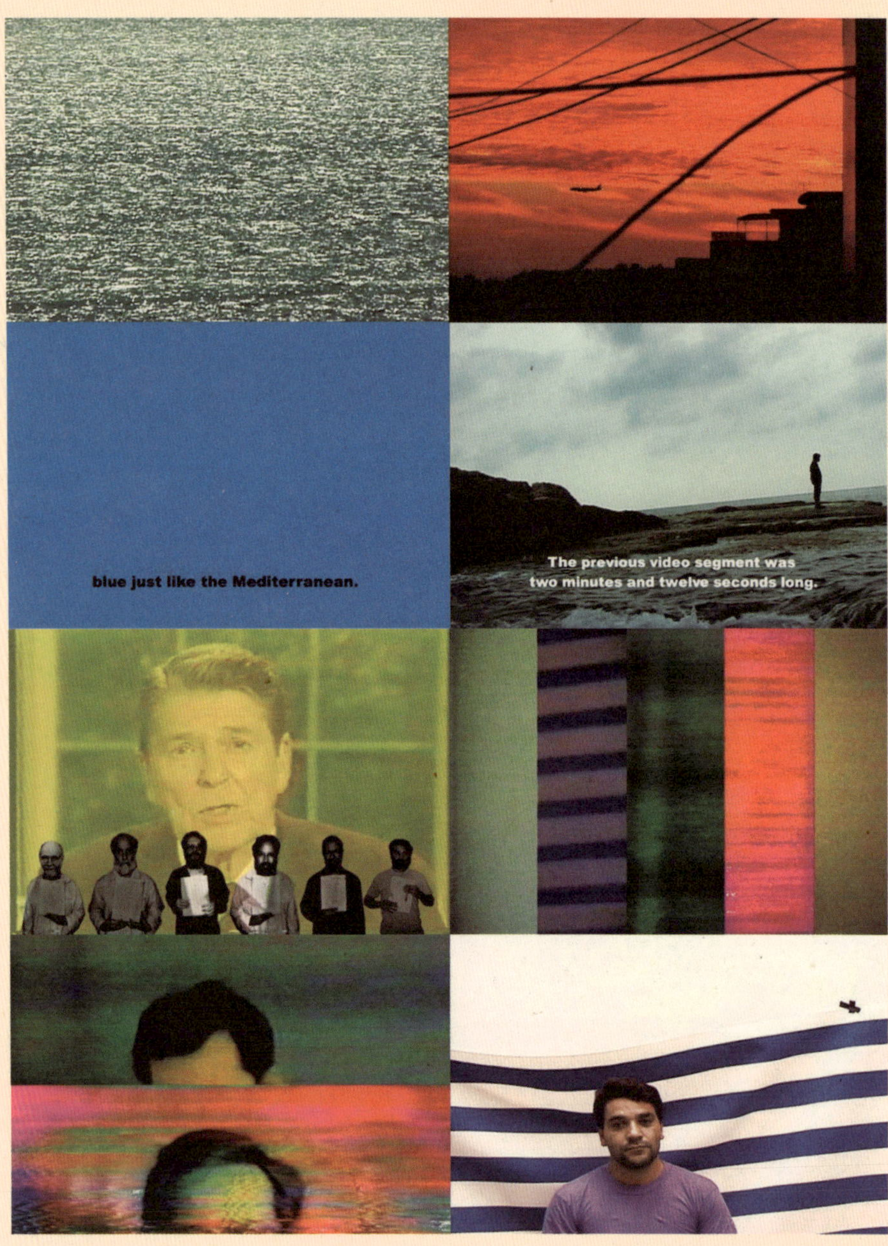



*Walid Raad*, Hostage: The Bachar Tapes (English Version), 2000;
*single-channel video, color, sound; 16:20 minutes; courtesy Paula
Cooper Gallery, New York*

the question of EU accession toward which the artist mobilized the story is part of the contemporary process of globalization. And so, of course, is the international biennial exhibition that was the project's context and reason for being, which Blum kept in play by conceiving the Safiye story specifically for a split audience—local Turkish viewers and international biennial visitors—with a range of educations, languages, and perspectives on Turkish modernity.[65]

Parafictioneers produce and manage plausibility. But plausibility (as opposed to accuracy) is an attribute not of a story or image but of its encounter with viewers, whose various configurations of knowledge and "horizons of expectation" determine whether something is plausible *to them*. While something similar is true of any artwork—that its meaning is produced in the encounter with the spectator—a parafiction creates a specific multiplicity.

No one has done this more powerfully than the Atlas Group, an organization dedicated to "researching and documenting the contemporary history of Lebanon," particularly the civil wars of 1975–91 (it was also, until recently, the identity under which Walid Raad exhibited most of his art). The first video made for this project was *Hostage: The Bachar Tapes (#17 and 31)_English Version* (2000), a testimonial by former hostage Souheil Bachar, who was held by Islamic militants in Beirut from 1985 to 1995.[66] For some months he shared a cell with Terry Anderson, Benjamin Weir, and three other victims of what became known here as the "Western hostage crisis." While each of these other prisoners has published a memoir about his hostage experience, this video was the first public documentation of Bachar's. It opens with English text explaining that Bachar made fifty-three testimonial tapes with the Atlas Group but that "tapes #17 and #31 are the only two tapes he makes available for screening outside of Lebanon." We then hear a man's voice introducing himself in Arabic as Souheil Bachar; subtitles translate his words to English.

Like all the documents in the Atlas Group Archive, *Hostage* crosses the problems of history writing (the patchiness of documents, the "unreliability" of even firsthand accounts, the work of interpretation that goes into making sense of them); traumatic experience and the ways in which it both compels and disallows speech; and the particular epistemic conditions of the Lebanese civil war, with its multiplicity of combatant groups, its unreliable sources of information, and its nightmarishly extended duration (indeed historians disagree in determining the year the war "ended"). Onto these, *Hostage* maps questions of ethnicity, gender, and sexuality, as Bachar (or a woman voicing his words in American-accented English) describes his cohabitation with the Americans, and especially their simultaneous attraction to and repulsion for his body, which culminates in an ambiguously forced sexual encounter in their cell.

Bachar's testimony, which he sometimes delivers posed against a jury-rigged cloth backdrop, evokes the videotapes of hostages made by their captors.[67] But as if to reverse those coerced speech acts, here the former hostage is at pains to take charge of his testimony. The tape starts with instructions from the subject about its making. Bachar explains how he should be translated: the tapes should be in the official language of

65. The project also critically addressed "biennial culture" with the time- and energy-intensive close looking that it required to discern the planted clues to its fictionality.

66. Based in part on Raad's research for his 1997 PhD dissertation on the Iran-Contra affair at the University of Rochester, the tape was made during a postdoctoral residency at the American University of Beirut in 1999–2000 and completed in 2000. It was first shown informally in Beirut and then in experimental video festivals in Europe and the United States (Raad, e-mail correspondence with the author, March 12, 2009).

67. The coerced videos haunt his testimony in *Hostage*'s most striking passage: "Tape 31" opens with two minutes, twelve seconds in which all information is withheld except for a silent, screen-filling shot of the rippling surface of a body of water (which is sometimes hard to distinguish from video static). Afterward Bachar explains that the shot had been the average duration of all the videos he had been forced to make as a captive.

the country where they are shown, English for the United Kingdom and United States, French for France, Arabic for "the Arab world." He is always to be dubbed by a "neutral-toned female voice" (which thereafter chimes in). When he says that the subtitles should be in white type on black or "if you prefer . . . blue like the Mediterranean," he makes it so (performatively): the black background obediently fades to blue.

Bachar not only tells his own stories but also controls their translation and dissemination. The fact that he allows only two tapes to be shown outside Lebanon casts these as a message for foreign audiences. This makes it impossible for the viewer to forget her own geopolitical location—or implication. But the video doesn't assume a homogenous audience. An Arabic speaker will notice that at times the English voice-over expresses something unrelated, or even exactly opposite, to Bachar's words. These deviations are not inconsequential: in the English voice-over, an American tries to penetrate Bachar during the silent sexual encounter in their cell, while in Bachar's Arabic the roles are reversed.[68] In either language, what starts with a mutual pressing of body to body ends in violence, complicating again the video's thematics of autonomy and coercion. The discrepancy between the Arabic and English texts makes that opposition even less simple. Likewise, while Bachar's self-willed, self-narrated, and consummately self-controlled testimonial seems to overturn the logic of the coerced videos of his captivity, the deviations by the voice that literally speaks over his complicate the simple opposition of free speech and forced speech (and though the performative fade from black screen to blue happens as if Bachar's words had willed it, it also introduces the presence of an agent controlling the visualization of the testimony, he who takes the opportunity offered by Bachar's "if you like").

Raad had originally imagined that translation and dubbing would actually be done in different languages when the work was shown in other countries, as stipulated within the video by Bachar, but no matter where the tapes have been shown, the voice and subtitles have remained in English, further eroding the illusion of Bachar's authority over his own image as it travels. This introduces more distinctions between viewers (monolingual, bilingual, and trilingual) and raises the question of English as the global lingua franca.[69] (It is no coincidence, surely, that in his Istanbul project Michael Blum made Safiye Behar a Turkish-English translator by trade.)

In Raad's *Hostage*, as in Blum's project, the range of positions provided for viewers is at once various and specific. And as in Blum's double address to foreign cultural tourists and to Turkish audiences, the interpellation here breaks down primarily along geopolitical lines. As if to make this clear, Raad cast as Bachar an actor recognizable in Lebanon, giving viewers in that country, or recent expatriates, an immediate hint of fictionality. Non-Lebanese but Arabic-speaking viewers who also speak English have the mistranslations to cue skepticism, while English-only speakers must rely only on the tape's aesthetics and site of viewing to determine whether, how much, and in what details they doubt Bachar's facticity.[70] Similarly,

68. Raad, e-mail correspondence with the author, March 15, 2009. Raad explains that this difference was intended to complicate "the caricature of the penetrator / the top as the one in charge."

69. Had Safiye Behar existed, she would have been the translator of a poem by Nazim Hikmet that captures something of the status of Bachar's autonomy. What kind of freedom is it that one has, he wondered, when at any moment your country "may be signed over to America." "You and your great freedom / You have the freedom to become an air-base."

70. Though Raad is often quite careful to say that the characters in his Atlas Group work may be fictitious—*Hostage* is filed in a section of the Atlas Group Archive that its website describes as "files that contain documents that we produced and that we attribute to named imaginary individuals or organizations"—he has been surprised at how often viewers take them at face value.

71. Raad now insists on complicating these terms: "I think it is safe to say that there may have been a time when I thought I knew what I meant by 'presumed historical knowledge of the viewers in a given location.' This proposition has become somewhat blurred to me." Walid Raad, e-mail correspondence with the author, March 15, 2009.

Raad was known to change the year of the Atlas Group's inception depending on the context and expected audience, from 1999, when he actually started working in this vein, to years—such as 1948, 1967, and 1975—that evoked different turning points in modern Middle Eastern history. In other words, the work alters and is altered depending on geopolitical location.[71] But "location" must be understood as more than spatial: it includes the institutional but also the geographical site in which a viewer sees the work; her location of origin but also her personal history of dislocations. Such "locations" within and in relationship to institutions, nations, languages, and history determine which aspects of the work are available to a given viewer at a given moment. And this in turn correlates to the spectatorial modes such as disbelief, belief, suspicion, certainty, and doubt that epistemologists call—in what here becomes a pun—"credal states."

With its range of different, shifting, but localized responses, the Bachar video responds to conditions specific to the Lebanese civil wars (with its multiple, shifting factions, its manifold points of view). But also (and without trivializing) it is possible to say that because of this specific multiplicity *Hostage* and the rest of the Atlas Group work seem also to acknowledge the condition of the art world into which they emerged: one fully enmeshed with globalization, its competing demands for local specificity and global inclusion, and its tensions around legibility, audience, and language.[72] Fittingly, *Hostage* first reached wide attention when it was shown at Documenta 11 in 2002. Though created before Raad had achieved this level of international art world recognition, it turns out that his video—coming into and out of credibility differently for viewers depending on their (shifting, multiple) geopolitical locations—was uniquely well suited to the conditions that such an exhibition both assumes and creates.


## Internet Epistemology

Caroline Jones has argued that epistemologically complicated recent work such as Raad's performs a crucial service, inculcating a habit of critical doubt in order to counter the atavistic fearmongering that has characterized the "war on terror."[73] I largely agree: the experiences of deception and doubt we are put through by parafictional experiments prepare us to be better, more critical information consumers and therefore citizens. This training relates not only to the culture of fear, however, but to media culture at large and particularly to the epistemological shock that the rapid mainstreaming of the Internet has caused, especially in the last ten years.[74] A MacArthur Foundation white paper explains that the crucial skills for thriving in

72. It is important here to note—though it is obvious—that "globalization" is not a single process, period, or entity. For instance, very different geopolitical and economic pressures are at play in the entry of various regions or nationalities into the "global" contemporary art world (or rather, into visibility for Euro-American art institutions, media, and scholarship).

73. Writing at the height of the Bush-Cheney era in 2003, and trying to diagnose that administration's success in leading a nation past logic and fact into a disastrous and unnecessary war, Jones stresses the coolly cognitive aspects of neoconceptualist work like Raad's and the rationality and criticality that its "aesthetics of doubt" encourage in the viewer. I admire this argument but part ways with it slightly (part of the difference is simply that we are not considering exactly the same phenomena—the only case we both discuss is Raad's). Parafiction encourages critical thought, but I believe that in doing so via experiences of discomfort, embarrassment, confusion, and often anger, it refuses to separate the epistemological and the emotional. And I am less confident than Jones that this work can be completely opposed to the culture of deception.

74. Though the Internet obviously has a much longer history (ARPANET began operating in 1969), it was after the introduction of the web directory and search engine (Yahoo, 1994) that in the United States and Western Europe, at least, it reached something like the level of functionality and participation that it has now and began to actually, rather than potentially, transform individual, social, and economic life on a mass scale. Nineteen ninety-eight is a notable year in this history: it was then that we were introduced to Google, then that Apple debuted the iMac (the first home computer specifically designed with Internet use in mind), and then that weblogs began to appear.

our current and coming information environment—the world of Wikipedia and Google—are the ability to distinguish between various sources' levels of reliability and a proclivity to question the transparency of information.[75] Every web page created by the Yes Men is an exercise in what, in a different historical context, Michael Leja calls "looking askance"[76]: the kind of skeptical viewing required when online exploration becomes a primary way of knowing.

However, in this information regime, the challenge is not only to be vigilantly skeptical. As Paul Virilio has said, control operates now not through the censure of true facts but through the "over-information" surrounding them.[77] In the ocean of data we dip into to resolve both looming decisions and passing inquiries (and of course, to investigate parafictions themselves), the problem may be less how to remember to be skeptical than how to decide when one has been sufficiently so. What is due epistemological diligence? When does one decide that something is—in the epistemologists' phrase now codified as Wikipedia's primary criterion—*true enough*? It's this, perhaps, that separates the implications of parafiction from stereotypically postmodern assertions of the inaccessibility and relativism of truth or the real.[78] In experiencing most parafiction—where the fictional hangs on the factual—one is evaluating not only whether a proposition is fictional but what parts of it are true. (There was indeed an Arab prisoner held along with the Western hostages, it turns out; Mustafa Kemal was in fact an adulterer; but the Aliza Shvartses on Facebook and MySpace are imposters.)[79] Parafictions train us in skepticism and doubt but also, oddly, in belief.

Of course the relationship between parafiction and the Internet is not causal—parafiction long predates digital networks. But to do parafiction now is to engage with this condition of communication, knowledge, even cognition. I don't think it is a coincidence that 01.ORG and new-media sponsors Public Netbase picked a structure for their Vienna info booth that, with its broad windows displaying layered visual and textual information, resembled a kind of walk-in computer monitor. In fact, the info booth was a customized version of the Cocobello, a modular structure by Munich-based architect Peter Haimerl, whose vision included multiple booths popping up all around an urban environment, "plugged into the existing communications network," and creating "a network of spaces."[80] Likewise, even though it was not primarily an Internet-based project (nor strictly a hoax), it makes sense that Aliza Shvarts's project shows up in a list of top Internet hoaxes.[81] Parafiction's natural home is the blog, the discussion board, or the wiki, where information is both malleable in form and material in effect. As it challenges viewers to assess the markers of reliability, then, even a project like *Safiye Behar*, which had no Internet presence

75. Henry Jenkins, with Ravi Rurshotma, Katherine Clinton, Margaret Weigel, and Alice J. Robiso, "Confronting the Challenges of Participatory Culture: Media Education for the 21st Century" (October 19, 2006), John D. and Catherine T. MacArthur Foundation, available at http://digitallearning.macfound.org/site/c.enJLKQNlFiG/b.2029291/k.97E5/Occasional_Papers.htm, 43–46.

76. See Michael Leja, *Looking Askance: Skepticism and American Art from Eakins to Duchamp* (Berkeley: University of California Press, 2004).

77. Paul Virilio, *Strategy of Deception*, trans. Chris Turner (New York: Verso, 2000), 48.

78. Most of the practitioners I've been discussing, like myself, came of age intellectually in an environment in which the role of culture in shaping what we take as fact, the ideological drivers and narrative conventions of objective-seeming history, or the inaccessibility of referents among slippery signifiers or interlocking texts were encountered as a kind of common sense. I speculate that the forms that they have developed arise from this in some way but respond also to the zombie versions of these ideas that returned in recent years in forms like "teaching the debate" on evolution or scorn for "the reality-based community."

79. Aliza Shvarts, e-mail correspondence with the author, March 30, 2008.

80. Peter Haimerl, "Cocobello—Mobiles Atelier," *Detail* 6 (2004): 676–77.

81. Pareene, "Five Bullshit Stories the Whole Internet Fell For," Gawker.com, May 22, 2008. In fact, most bloggers registered the possibility of "hoax" from the beginning. The fact that the story had such powerful resonance even when discussed in the key of "if" is another indication of the way parafiction complicates the distinction between happy and unhappy performative.

to speak of and took a distinctly predigital form, could be considered a kind of live-action experiment in Internet epistemology.

By this I mean that it challenges viewers to assess the forms of information—from the font to the URL at the top of the page—with as much care as the content and that it trains them in both skepticism and belief. But I also mean that it echoes some of the structure of an information economy. The viewer positions in a parafiction are multiple, but they are not equal. The people who have the most knowledge going in or are the most astute information interpreters (or, if there is Wi-Fi, those who are literally well connected) avoid being duped, and their experience of the piece may include the slightly sadistic fun of watching others in their epistemological struggle. That is to say, the viewers of parafiction are classed.[82]

## Parafiction, for Art's Sake

Let's return to *A Tribute to Safiye Behar* and step back to wonder: why would anyone believe it in the first place? After all, it wasn't in a history museum, archive, university, or any other site even putatively dedicated to the pursuit of facts and truthfulness. It was in an art show. By all reports most viewers started from the assumption that the subject was factual, which has to do with Blum's skill, of course—but also with the major movement of art and art history against the notion of art's autonomy.[83] From real bullet wounds to demonstrations of the financial and political entanglements of artistic institutions, from the production of functional objects to the actual provision of social services, artists in the last century have ceaselessly demonstrated the coextensiveness of art and the real, sloughing off again and again the eighteenth-century distinction between utility and the aesthetic.

But that distinction refuses to go away. It undergirds the Yale statement about Shvarts: had her acts not been art, it concludes, they would have had real consequences. What is elided is the possibility that it was art *and* she did what she said she did. And this isn't just a matter of lay critics expressing outdated assumptions. The contradiction is built into parafictional art. After all, while the acceptance of art's coextensiveness with the real explains why *Safiye Behar* works, it's precisely the opposite idea about art that explains how Blum got away with it.[84]

You can speculate, make up facts, blend different types of facts, or even lie in art because it is understood as a fundamentally frivolous zone. (Of an artist who has produced functioning firearms, one magazine breathlessly wonders whether what he is up to is "something . . . sinister," or "just art.")[85] It's this

82. Class intersects these stories in multiple ways, in fact. For instance, Shvarts's privileged position as an Ivy League student seemed to drive some of the disgust with her project. As Julia Bryan-Wilson has pointed out to me, there is also a powerful class component to the Yes Men's high jinks in terms of the viewer's relation to the cast of characters (whether one is positioned closer to the suited experts the Yes Men target and impersonate, or to the workers or the poor who are usually the most immediately impacted by them).
83. Psychologists also talk about an inherent human "truth bias."
84. Perhaps it is this interrogation of the question of utility rather than the fake wanted posters, pseudonyms, and so on that links Duchamp to these parafictional practices. See Stephen Wright, "The Future of the Reciprocal Readymade: An Essay on Use Value and Art-Related Practice," *Parachute*, no. 117 (January–March 2005). Wright's discussion of art and use value in recent collective practice in this essay (based on the catalogue essay for his Apexart exhibition "The Future of the Reciprocal Readymade," in spring 2004) is extremely helpful for thinking about art and politics (as is his term "art-related practice"). The artist and critic Sarah Kanouse has a wonderful phrase for the way art's autonomy is being used in practices similar to these: she calls it art's "tactical irrelevance." Sarah E. Kanouse, "Tactical Irrelevance: Art and Politics at Play," paper presented at the Conference of the Union for Democratic Communication, Boca Raton, FL, May 20 2006, at http://www.readysubjects.org /writing/kanouse_artpolitics.pdf.
85. Melissa Milgrom, "Target: AVL," *Metropolis*, May 2000.

attitude that underlies the immediate and recurring accusation lobbed at Shvarts that her project trivialized abortion and miscarriage. As if to literally put your body through the procedure of insemination, to undergo possible termination of pregnancy (however early), to encounter and experience these "issues" in your own physical and mental being, and to repeat all of this for nine months were *less* serious than, say, writing a term paper about the abortion debate. The project may be many things—dangerous, counterproductive, perhaps even immoral—but trivializing it is not. Yet the fact that it was interpreted this way is in itself telling of the strangely unshakeable assumption that art is a category defined against reality, unencumbered by—and unempowered by—real consequence. Alain Bieber put it perfectly when he asked 01.ORG whether being labeled "artist" was like getting a "jester's license."[86]

The critic Brian Holmes, though, has the metaphor most relevant for the current discussion. In his essay titled "Liar's Poker," he accuses art institutions and politically engaged artists of playing a bluffing game. The frisson of "relevance" is a type of cultural capital that museums desperately need and that radical artists can provide, he argues, using the example of Documenta to claim that an art institution "must ask its cultural producers for the ace of politics, while proving all the while (with the help of the police, if need be) that this ace is merely a bluff, that it is really a king. . . . And yet it is through this double game that new symbolic possibilities for conceiving and shaping the ways we live—what Nietzsche might have called 'the transvaluation of all values'—can be distributed on the scale that an exhibition like Documenta offers."[87]

Art institutions lie, and turn cultural producers into liars, by asking artists for the winning hand of real politics (the ace), while all the while framing what they do as without consequence (the king). If this is indeed the only way we have to propose new possibilities for living and thinking—for redistributing the sensible—then this goes a long way toward not only explaining but justifying the fact that we have seen a rise in parafiction: in art built on the contradictions between art's ability to move into and change the world, and art as a space of only symbolic relevance. Blum, at least, seems to have implicitly recognized something of the kind when he ended the wall text in the Safiye Behar museum this way: "In 2005, as Turkey and the EU are playing liar's poker about their common future, Safiye might prove to be a helpful guiding model for current and future generations. A product of both the East and the West, she stood up for her ideals and devoted a lifetime to what she believed in. She was a global thinker before the term was coined, seeing the world beyond the narrow conceptions of borders, nations, and states."

The "Safiye" in this paragraph might simply be the character of Behar; "guiding model" might refer simply to the progressive ideals to which she devoted her life. But as Blum's winking reference to the politics of deception suggests, it might also be *Safiye* the exhibition—parafiction itself—that could serve as a guide. What would this mean? Walid Raad has an interesting way of phrasing what art like his can do: "the way an artwork can maintain and work different kind of facts alive [*sic*] (historical facts; sociological facts, economic facts, emotional facts, aesthetic facts, etc. . . . )."[88] If this destabilizing of "fact" shares a bit more ground than is comfortable with "truthiness,"[89] it resonates with Blum's insistence that Safiye is real to him; with Shvarts's

86. "How to Provoke Today?? Alain Bieber Interviews 0100101110101101.ORG on Nike Ground," *Rebel: Art Magazine*, April 1, 2004, archived copy at http://www.0100101110101101.org/home/nikeground/interview.html.

87. Brian Holmes, "Liar's Poker: Representation of Politics / Politics of Representation," *Springeren* 1 (2003).

88. Walid Raad, e-mail correspondence with the author, March 22, 2009.

89. By registering a generic connection, I do not mean to collapse terms. Raad is talking about the proliferation and protection of different kinds of fact, while *truthiness* describes the substitution of one kind of fact for another.

90. Bruno Latour, "Why Has Critique Run Out of Steam? From Matters of Fact to Matters of Concern," *Critical Inquiry* 30 (Winter 2004): 231.

multiplication of the meanings of her body's capabilities, and with the recent effort by scholars such as Bruno Latour to revive a mode of realism, even empiricism, that does not give up on the idea of facts but rethinks them as matters of investment, debate, and desire.[90] This is precisely the territory of parafiction, which at once reveals the way things are and makes sensible the way we want them to be and which offers experiences of both skepticism and belief. As for the odd phrasing in the line from Raad, it may be a simple typing error, artifact of a quickly e-mailed response to a critic's question. But how fortuitously the image of *working facts alive* suits the poetics and politics of the parafictional. The paramedic, after all, doesn't attempt to heal the patient. She resuscitates him; she staunches his bleeding. She keeps pressure on his wounds.

## Epilogue: Retracing

Recall the description of viewers in Istanbul "scurrying back" to re-view Blum's installation after learning that Safiye was a fiction. The critic's phrase evokes perfectly the temporally extended and multiphase reception of art that resides in the plausible. But, *scurrying*? It's what a rodent does. The verb also captures the air of the laboratory that clings to the parafictional, where artists wear the white coats and viewers run through their mazes. One of the disturbing things about the parafictional is the split between the trap-laying artist and the specifically unwitting viewer, who thinks she is involved in one kind of experience (historical museum, marketing campaign) while actually participating in another (fiction-based installation, cultural critique). When asked why it is so difficult to get a rise out of audiences at their presentations, then, the Yes Men got it exactly right: "Perhaps a rumpled suit would help. Milgram's study suggests that."[91]

"Scurrying" also expresses the embarrassed, slightly furtive nature of parafictional spectatorship. Being taken in by a parafiction, after all, is not just epistemologically destabilizing. It is humiliating. Think of the audience member who asks a sincere question of a parafictioneering presenter, only to realize later he was one of the few not in on the joke. Or consider the (purely hypothetical) art historian, perhaps in a studio visit with an artist, who nods knowingly about a historical figure before learning that he made her up. Parafiction is an antidote to vanity. It changes you, leaves you both curious and chastened. It also forever changes one's interface with the media, art, museums, and scholarship. The difference is a certain critical outlook but one that should be differentiated from models of criticality as skepticism. Rancière talks about a "poetics of knowledge" opposed to "critique as suspicion."[92] Something like this attitude takes shape, I think, as a post-parafictional alertness to the possibility of play. (Rancière's poetics of knowledge, like the parafictional, "gives value to the effectivity of speech acts.")[93] Artworks, lectures, books, exhibitions, and of course journal articles: they shimmer slightly, possibly plausible, plausibly possible. However, this can be particularly destabilizing for scholarship. No matter how thoroughly I've researched the stories I've told here, I'm aware of the provisionality of my report. Have I pulled back all the onion skins of fiction? How much research would be enough? And must I unveil every aspect of the works I've uncovered if to do so would damage their future functioning? While parafictional art and activism respond to broader areas of cultural practice, it seems

91. In Stanley Milgram's behavioral experiments at Yale University in the early 1960s, subjects were told that they were participating in a study about learning, when in fact the goal of the experiment was to see how far they would go in inflicting pain on another person when commanded to by a figure in authority (the scientist).

92. Jacques Rancière and Davide Panagia, "Dissenting Words: A Conversation with Jacques Rancière," *Diacritics* 30 (Summer 2000): 113–16, and Rancière, *The Names of History: On the Poetics of Knowledge*, trans. Hassan Melehy (Minneapolis: University of Minnesota Press, 1994).

93. Rancière, in Rancière and Panagia, "Dissenting Words," 115.

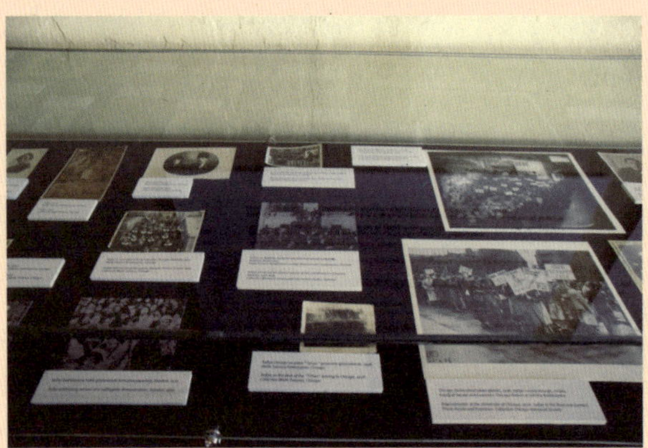

*Michael Blum*, A Tribute to Safiye Behar, 2005
*(detail); installation; courtesy the artist*

imperative to examine their lessons for the endeavor at hand. For the epistemological problems I've been describing don't pertain only to parafictional art. They are the conditions for the enterprise of scholarly study of contemporary art in general—for this strange practice of trying to think historically about the present. Doing this work, we approach the parafictional all the time, relying on memories and stories to build our histories—only a step away from gossip, it sometimes seems.[94] Our arguments can function performatively, shaping our subjects' future work, and being shaped by them in turn. Moreover, like the viewer of parafiction, we are always a step behind. Not only because our field is ever-expanding temporally but because, as part of our immanence to globalization, it is growing geographically. We have the responsibility—and feel the pressure—to be ever more inclusive and transnational in our narratives. But, as this paper's Euro-American focus itself demonstrates, few of us have the languages, the cultural knowledge, or the local art historical background to properly master a fraction of what we would like to think, teach, and write about. What to do? The subject of parafiction might answer by paraphrasing the pretend Nike website. Scholars don't usually wear pressed suits. So why should their scholarship? Why should we stand in the Milgram position? What if contemporary art history were to differ from other parts of the field in owning rather than minimizing some of these contradictions and realities? Walid Raad said in 1989—maybe—that "facts have to be treated as processes."[95] Acknowledging that no one of us is an authority on the full range of art that we need to discuss might encourage us not to narrow our focus but to find ways to research, write, and advise collaboratively. Admitting and even valuing the provisionality of our knowledge—understanding that term not only as "subject to alteration" but as in the word "provisions," also—we might find ways for artists to speak within or against our texts. We might develop forms of publication that expect and allow amendment. We might embolden the mice. Dignify the scurry.

94. For a discussion of scholars' involvement with their subjects, see Julia Bryan-Wilson's forthcoming article "Dirty Commerce: Art Work and Sex Work since the 1970s," *differences: A Journal of Feminist Cultural Studies* 23 (Summer 2012).

95. Walid Raad, unpublished compilation of statements about the Atlas Group.

## An Addendum

Humans being the simultaneously devious and gullible creatures that we are, I don't think it's possible to find a starting point for parafiction. But when I wrote the preceding essay, I was convinced that at least the uptick I was seeing was a thing of the late 1990s. As I continued my research, however, it became clear that certain slightly earlier projects that I had thought were significantly different from the examples discussed here were in fact its precedents. Or, better, predecessors: generative for a parafictional turn in art, activism, and beyond, and indispensable for understanding its history. While I don't think it is unusual for authors to have such belated realizations, it is unusual to have an opportunity to admit it (still more so to be able to do so knowing that one is thereby demonstrating one of one's own theses). So I count myself lucky to be able to explain here that the first chapter of the book I am currently writing on parafiction is about politicized epistemology in the earlier 1990s—think Columbus quincentennial—and focuses on brilliant and brilliantly disturbing works by Coco Fusco, Guillermo Gómez-Peña, Fred Wilson, and James Luna. I am also lucky to be able to thank Huey Copeland for his forbearance during the years it took me to scurry back to his suggestion.

Originally published in slightly different form in *October*, no. 129 (Summer 2009): 51–84.

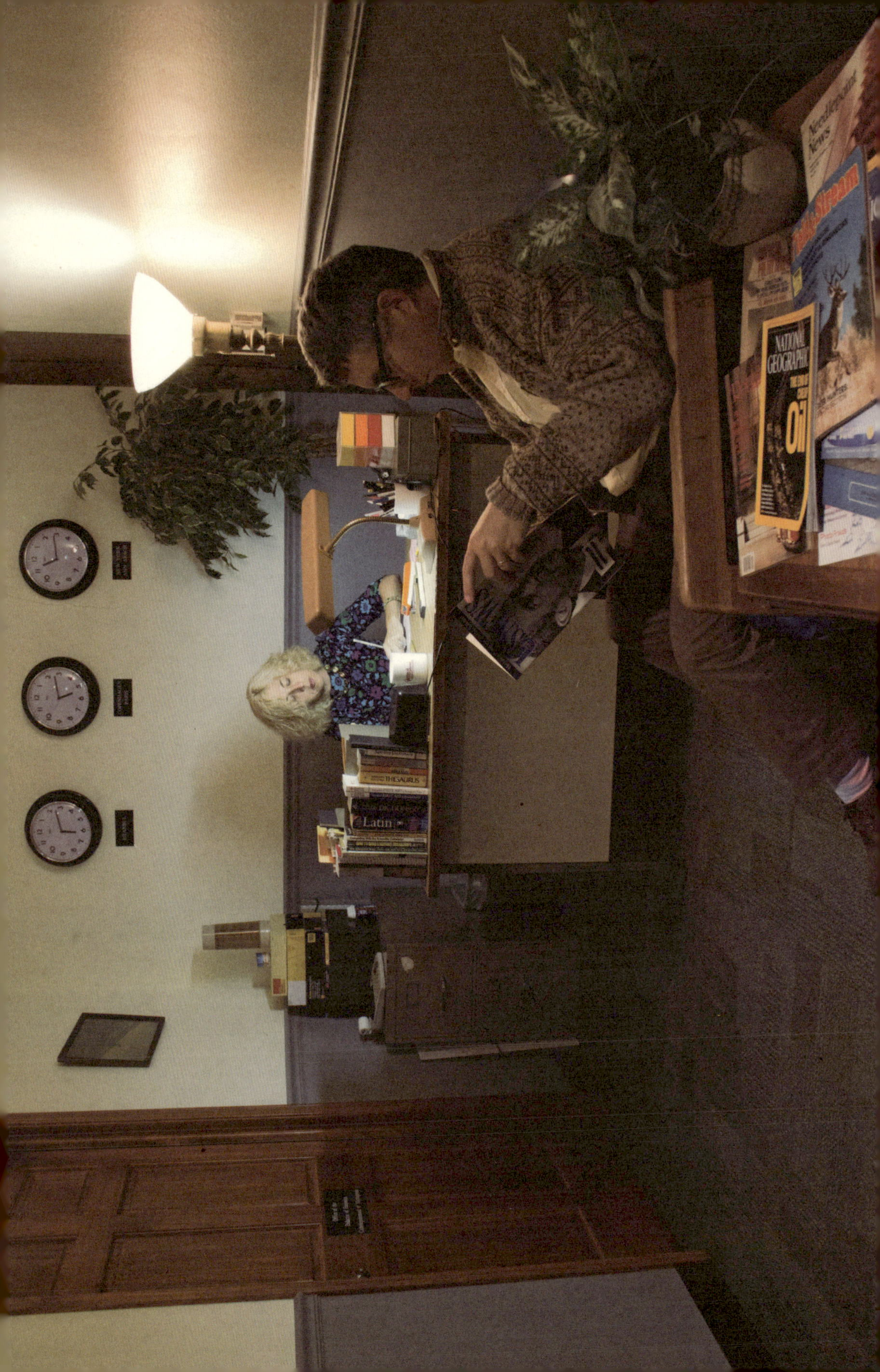

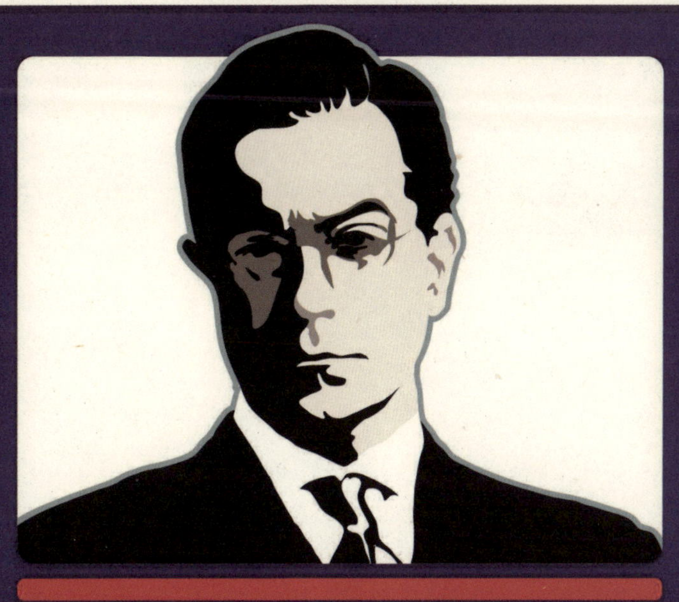

MARCH TO
KEEP
FEAR
ALIVE
10.30.10
WASHINGTON, D.C.
WWW.KEEPFEARALIVE.COM

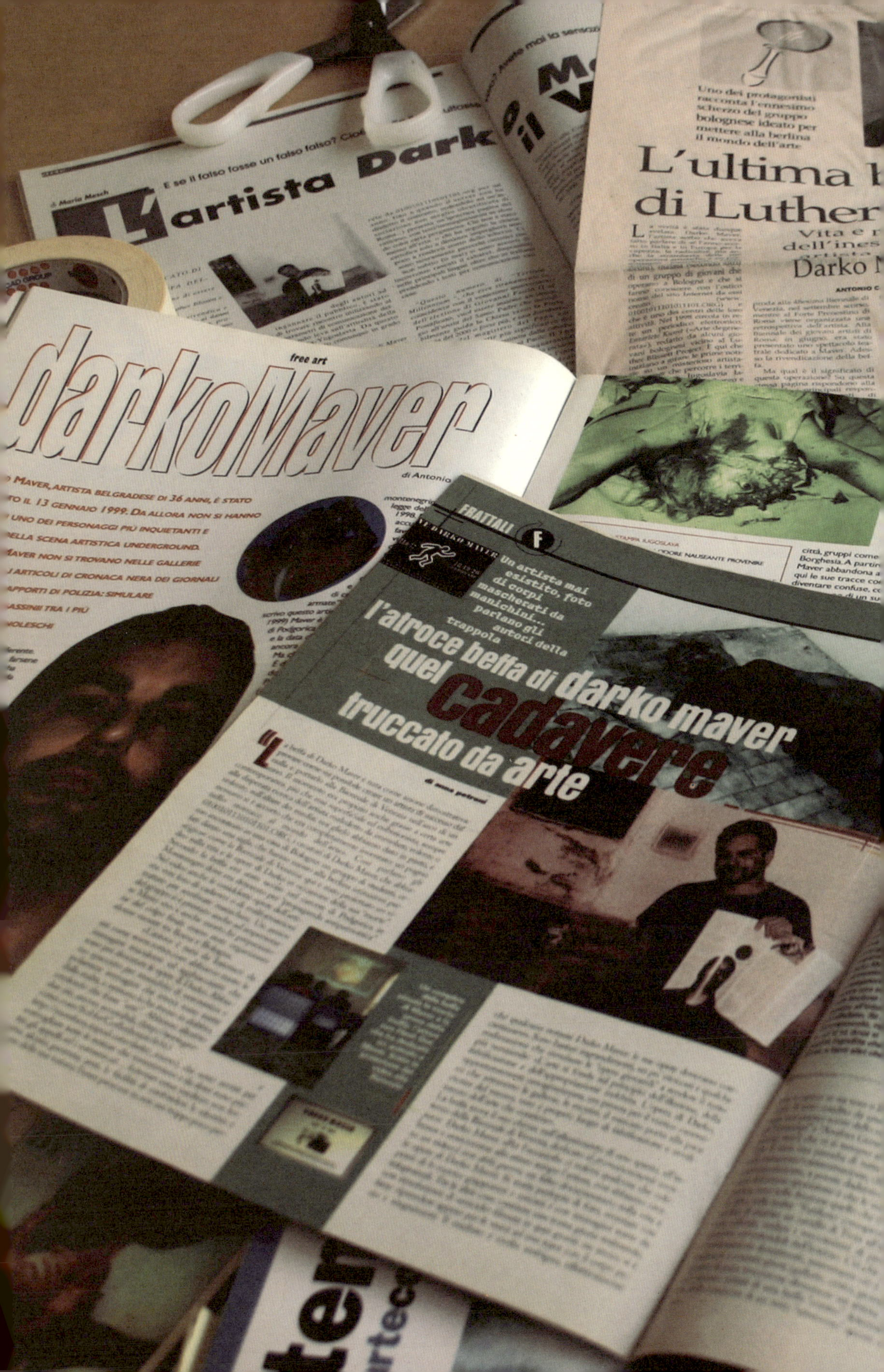
free art
darkoMaver
di Antonio
...MAVER, ARTISTA BELGRADESE DI 36 ANNI, È STATO
...TO IL 13 GENNAIO 1999. DA ALLORA NON SI HANNO
...UNO DEI PERSONAGGI PIÙ INQUIETANTI E
...NELLA SCENA ARTISTICA UNDERGROUND.
...MAVER NON SI TROVANO NELLE GALLERIE
...I ARTICOLI DI CRONACA NERA DEI GIORNALI
...PPORTI DI POLIZIA: SIMULARE
...ASSINII TRA I PIÙ
...OLESCHI
L'artista Dark
E se il falso fosse un falso falso? Cioè
di Maria Meoch
L'ultima
di Luther
Vita e
dell'ines
artista
Darko M
Uno dei protagonisti
racconta l'ennesimo
scherzo del gruppo
bolognese ideato per
mettere alla berlina
il mondo dell'arte
FRATTALI
F
Un artista mai
esistito, foto
di corpi
mascherati da
manichini...
parlano gli
autori della
trappola
l'atroce beffa di darko maver
quel cadavere
truccato da arte

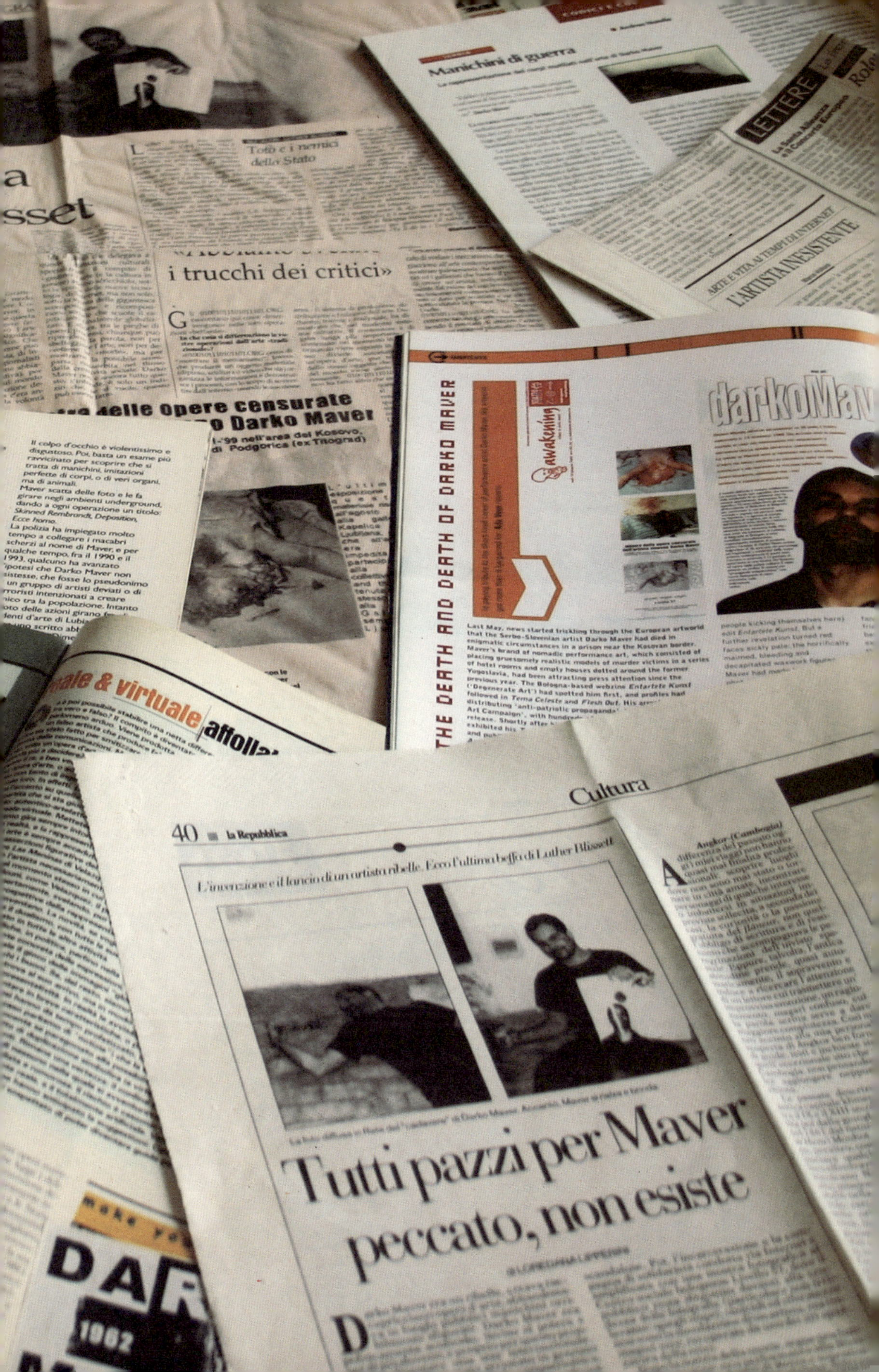
Manichini di guerra
LETTERE
ARTE E VITA AI TEMPI DI INTERNET
L'ARTISTA INESISTENTE
Totò e i nemici dello Stato
«i trucchi dei critici»
THE DEATH AND DEATH OF DARKO MAVER
darkoMav
Cultura
40 la Repubblica
L'invenzione e il lancio di un artista ribelle. Ecco l'ultima beffa di Luther Blissett
Tutti pazzi per Maver
peccato, non esiste
ale & virtuale/affolla
DAR
1992

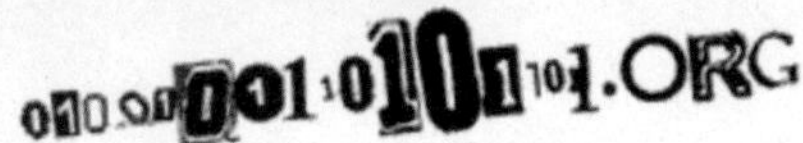



From "l'Unità", 14 February 2000

**LIFE AND DEATH OF THE INEXISTENT ARTIST DARKO MAVER**

One of the protagonists tells the umpteeth prank of the bologna's group, conceived to expose to ridicule the art world.

by Antonio Caronia

The truth has therefore been revealed. Darko Maver, the Serbian artist who set Italy and Europe buzzing last year for the glumness, the radicalism, but also the weirdness of his artistic actions, is an inexistent person, he is a figment of the lively (according to someone), morbid (according to someone else) imagination of a group working in Bologna and known as 0100101110101101.ORG, the harsh name of their Internet site, which is one of the centres of their activities. Since 1998 a webzine called "EntarteteKunst" ("Degenerated Art" ), a periodical edited by some guys from Bologna, near to the Luther Blissett Project, is available on the Internet. It is from there that the early news about a mysterious performer-artist start to circulate: a man who travels across ex-Yugoslavia leaving, in motel rooms and old empty houses, gruesome sights of murders, realised with puppets (but that, at first sight, seem to be real, disconcerting the neighbours and the police arrived on the scene).

Some scanty biographical information is spread as well (the birth in 1962 near Belgrade, the leaving of the Academy of Fine Arts, in the same city, the move to Ljubliana, the travels to Italy, the beginning, in 1990, of the travelling project "Tanz der Spinne", "Dance of the Spider"), and also some short texts, clearly delirious, about the "Disappearance of the body" and an unlikely "Anaphoragenetica".

In August 1999, the Kapelica Gallery organises in Ljubliana the first exhibition with the documentation of "Tanz der Spinne", this show will be repeated the following year, in February, at the "Livello 57" in Bologna. Meanwhile Darko Maver is arrested and released, in Serbia and Kosovo, on several occasions, with the charge of anti-patriotic propaganda, and he is locked up in prison in Podgorica since the beginning of 1999. Maver's supporters in Italy spread the notice through bulletins signed "Free Art Campaign". In March 1999 two Italian art magazines write about Maver: "Tema Celeste" simply reports the press release, "Flesh Out" publishes a more accurate article, with images signed by the person who is now writing. In May comes out the announcement of Darko Maver's death, in prison, in enigmatic circumstances. An article in "Modus Vivendi", in July of the same year, establishes a connection between Maver's death and the NATO war against Serbia.

And the death put the final seal on his fame: Maver leads to the 48th Venice Biennale, last September, while a complete retrospective of the artist is organised in Rome at the "Forte Prenestino". In June, a theatrical performance dedicated to Maver was presented to the "Biennale of young artists", in Rome too.

Now the claiming of the prank. But which is the meaning of this action? In this same page, people from 0100101110101101.ORG, answer this question. But a few words are due also from the author of this article, who wrote about Darko Maver, as we said, in "Flesh Out" magazine last March. Actually I was informed about the inexistence of the artist, and if I decided (together with the editorial staff of the review) to reveal nothing of what we knew, but on the contrary to support the operation, it was because I believed in its usefulness: I knew very well that, sooner or later, the prank would have been claimed, since it was conceived for this purpose. This kind of actions are not new in the art world. It would be enough to remember the huge penis belching fireworks ("The Victory"), built by Jean Tinguely, which appeared to the amazed eyes of thousands of people gathered in Duomo square, in Milan, the 28 November 1970, during a festival on the Nouveau Realisme (the day after, an embarrassed press decided to skirt the provocation). Or the female identity of Rrose Selavy with whom Marcel Duchamp, during the Twenties, signed some ready-mades, building on the inexistent person a whole net of mysterious hints and funny and arcane finds; among others is a photo taken by Man Ray which, in reality, portrays the artist in female dressing. These, and many other similar conceptual works, were thorough critical interventions, as well as artistic expressions, made by figures deep-rooted in the art world but, at the same time, conscious of the fictitious nature, in a way inauthentic, of the artworks. The operation Darko Maver, to a great extent, shares this tension to reconnect (through the paradox) art with life, but it has a more specific meaning. Which is not much that, as it can seem at first sight, to cheat critics and journalists, with the purpose of heaping discredit on the art world. The aim of the authors of the prank was also, of course, the will to point out the artificial nature of this world, the role played by critics and curators to establish the success or failure of artists, more than their mysterious "inspiration". And, in the background, as always, the fundamental role of the media, which contributes more and more to attest the "reality", in the eyes of the citizen-consumer. But all this, somehow, is well known also out of the underground borders, even if, often, nobody thinks enough about it. The most interesting thing in all this story, in my opinion, is that it brings out, with the power of the joke, the social nature of artistic production. If there aren't specific social institutions (museums, galleries, specialised reviews, but now also squats, even groups of radical opposition) which "guarantee" the art work, art doesn't exist. If someone in whom I trust (a critic, a commentator) doesn't certificate the existence and the value of an artist, the artist doesn't exist. But the agreement that delegated to these specialised cultural institutions the job of "managing" art (and culture in general), is now creaking, under the impulse of the new technologies, of the Internet, but not only, also under the impulse of the huge social decomposition and recomposition which shakes capitalism, at long last globalized. And then, between the turns of these process, anybody can begin to speak, not to make fun of art or to declare its "death" in the name of an avant-garde, but to show its possible disappearance, reabsorbed into the flow of social creativity. Darko Maver is not all of this yet, of course, it's only a sign that this can be done.

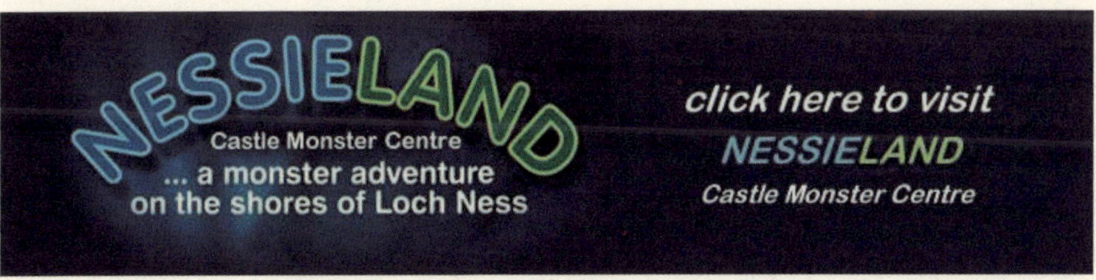


**For Kids ...**

| | | | | |
|---|---|---|---|---|
| **Nessieland Castle** | **Nessie and the Dolphins** | **Nessie and the Diver** | **Feeding Nessie** | **Nessie visits the Taj Mahal** |
| **Nessie at the Seaside** | **Nessie wants to meet YOU** | **Nessie meets the Postman** | **Nessie helps the Lifeboat** | **Nessie meets the Boat** |

### Loch Ness Monster Facts

you know the following facts about the Loch Ness Monster ...

- **Loch Ness Monster Fact:** The first recorded **sighting** of the Loch Ness Monster was in 565 AD by St Columba. In fact St Columba saw th monster twice in that year.
- **Loch Ness Monster Fact:** The monster was first seen in the River Ness before becoming more closely associated with the loch.
- **Loch Ness Monster Fact:** The next reference to the monster was in 1933 when Mr and Mrs Spicer reported seeing a large animal crossing road in front of their car.
- **Loch Ness Monster Fact:** Nessie is usually described as having a small head, long neck, broad body, four flippers and a long tail.
- **Loch Ness Monster Fact:** The scientific name for the Loch Ness Monster is a plesiosaur, which is a type of carnivorous aquatic, usually ma reptile.
- **Loch Ness Monster Fact:** The Loch Ness Monster cannot be a mammal as it does not have to breathe air. If it needed to surface in order breath air it would most probably have been seen by many before now.
- **Loch Ness Monster Fact:** Nessie is the most famous cryptid in the world. The word 'cryptid' is used in cryptozoology and refers to a hidde creature or living creature which might exist. This should not be confused with unreal or mythical creatures. For a beast to qualify as a cyrp there needs to be some form of evidence of existence. This can mean being mentioned in folklore or that there have been 'sightings'.

### e Loch Ness Monster Facts

975 the Loch Ness Monster was given a new, scientific-sounding name by Sir Peter Scott, of the famous explorer, Robert Falcon Scott. He named it Nessiteras Rhombopteryx or "the wonder with the diamond fin". Sceptics pointed out this was an anagram of "monster hoax ir Peter S", a comment which was later countered by Dr Robert Rines, of the American emy of Applied Science and leader of a major survey of Loch Ness, who responded with . both pics are monsters, R". The public affectionately shortened the name to "Nessie".

first **picture of Nessie** was taken near Foyers by Hugh Gray on 12 November 1933. He an object rising two or three feet out of the water, creating a certain amount of rbance and took five photographs.

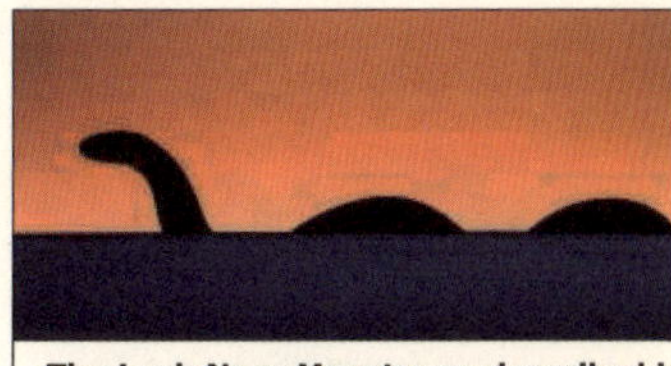
The Loch Ness Monster as described in 1930s sighting.

most famous photograph of the monster was taken in 1934 near Invermoriston by Dr Robert Kenneth Wilson from London. It shows a head neck rising out of the water, the only picture to do so, and was published in the Daily Mail. Dr Wilson refused to allow his name to be assoc the photo so it became known as the "surgeon's photograph". In fact some 60 years later it was revealed to be a hoax.

her famous hoax occurred in December 1933 when big-game hunter, Marmaduke Wetherall, was hired by the Daily Mail to find the mor ng the task harder than he had anticipated, Wetherall was delighted when he soon found a series of enormous footprints. Casts of the prints to the Natural History Museum in London but were found to have been made by an ornamental hippopotamus foot. Wetherall's find was obvi edited but what is not clear is whether he actually planted the prints himself or was taken in by some other hoaxer.

959 an Italian journalist claimed he had invented Nessie in 1933. Francesco Gasprini was the London correspondent of a Milan newspaper d himself a little short of news. He read a couple of lines in a Scottish paper about two fishermen finding a strange fish and exaggerated it i ster. He claims he also invented some eye-witness accounts and had drawings and photographs published. Gasprini planned to then kill of

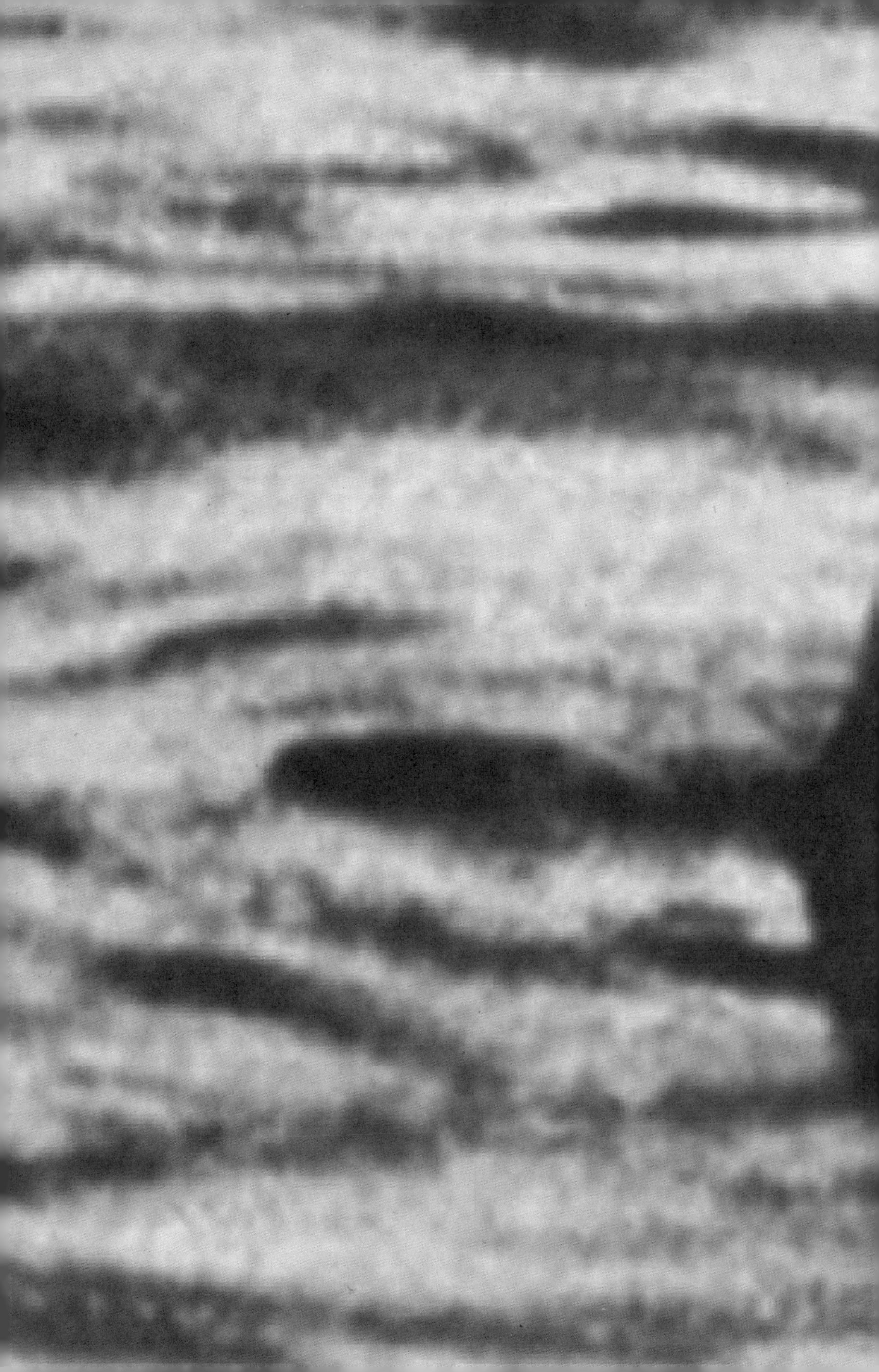

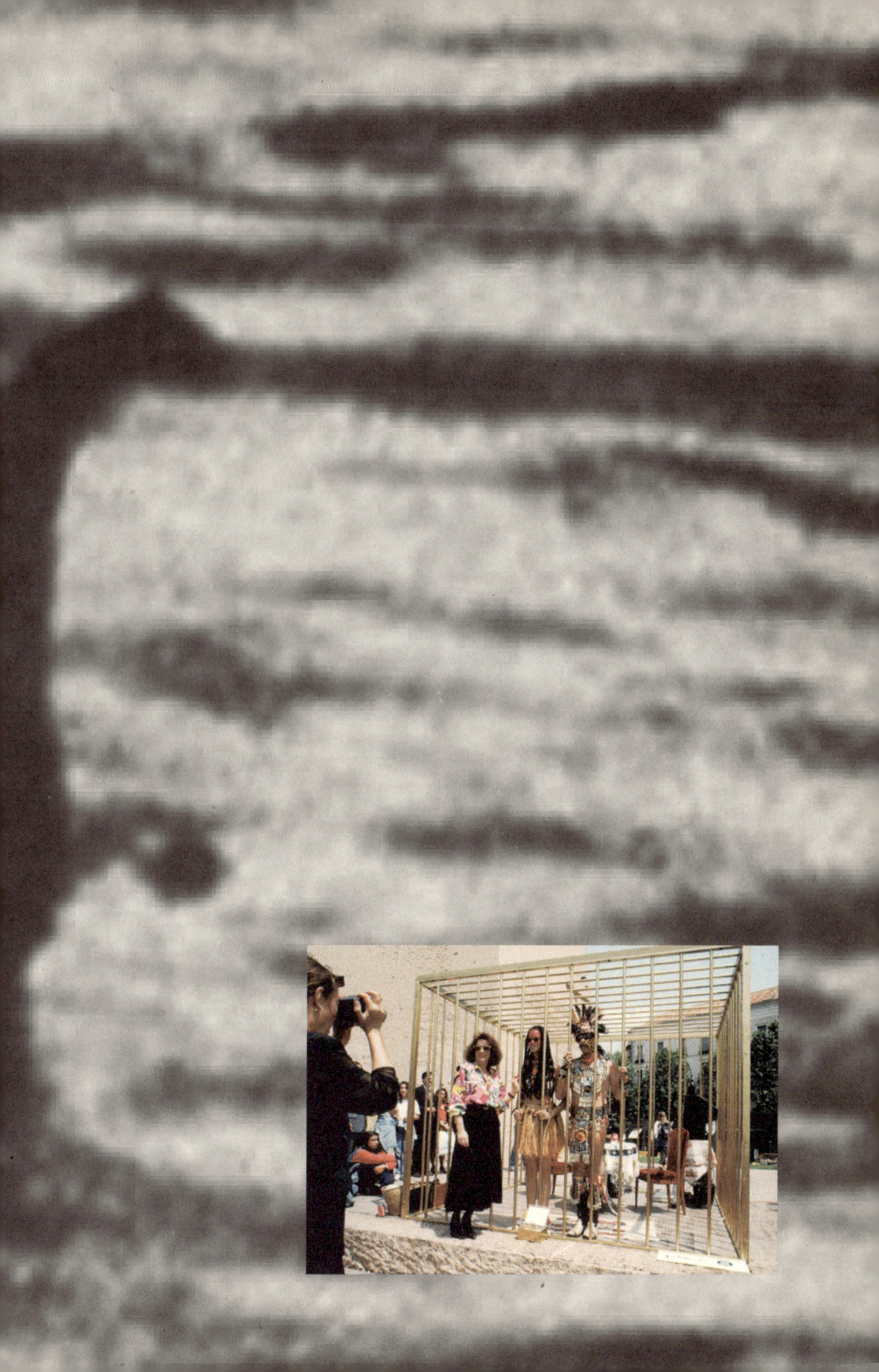

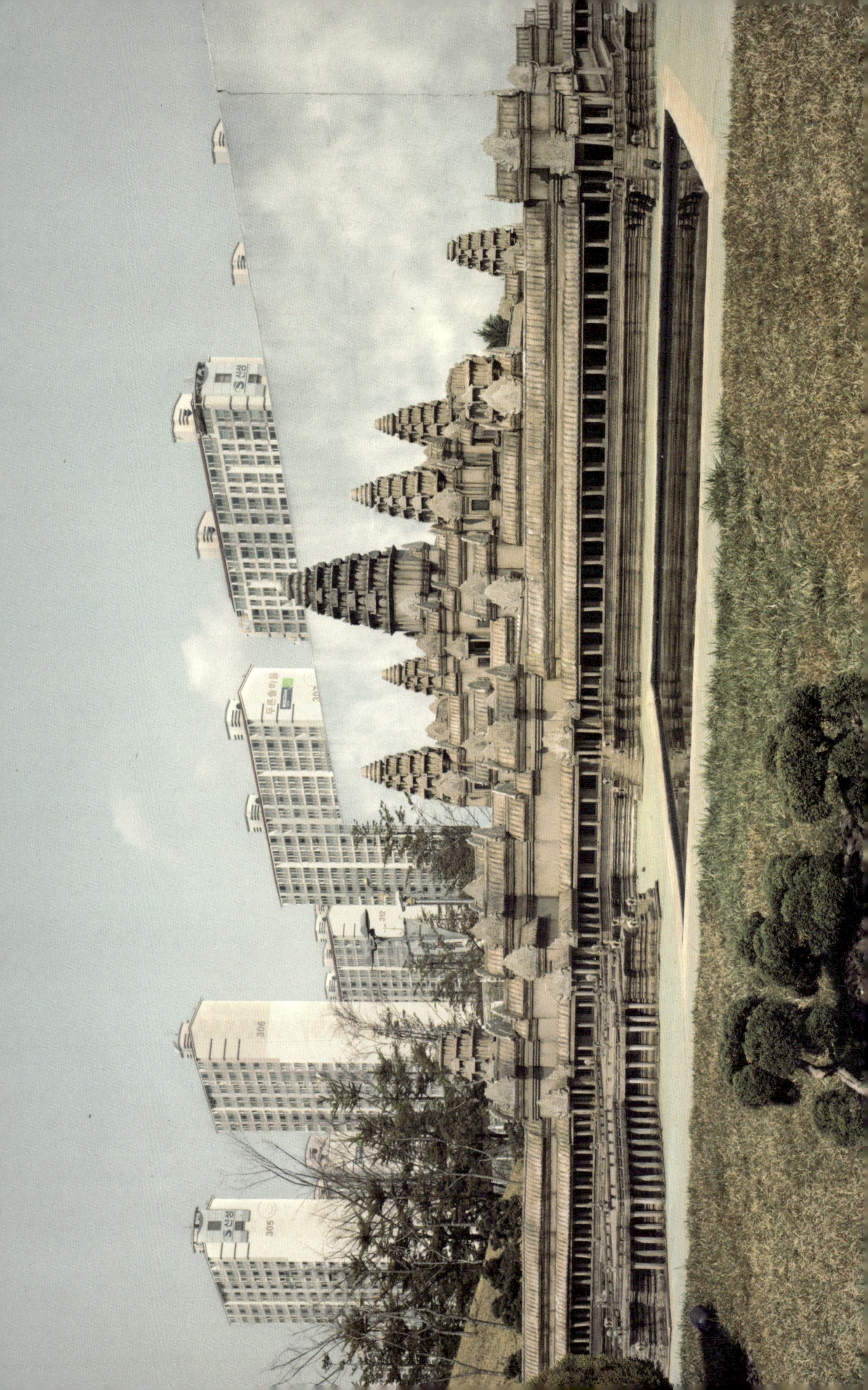

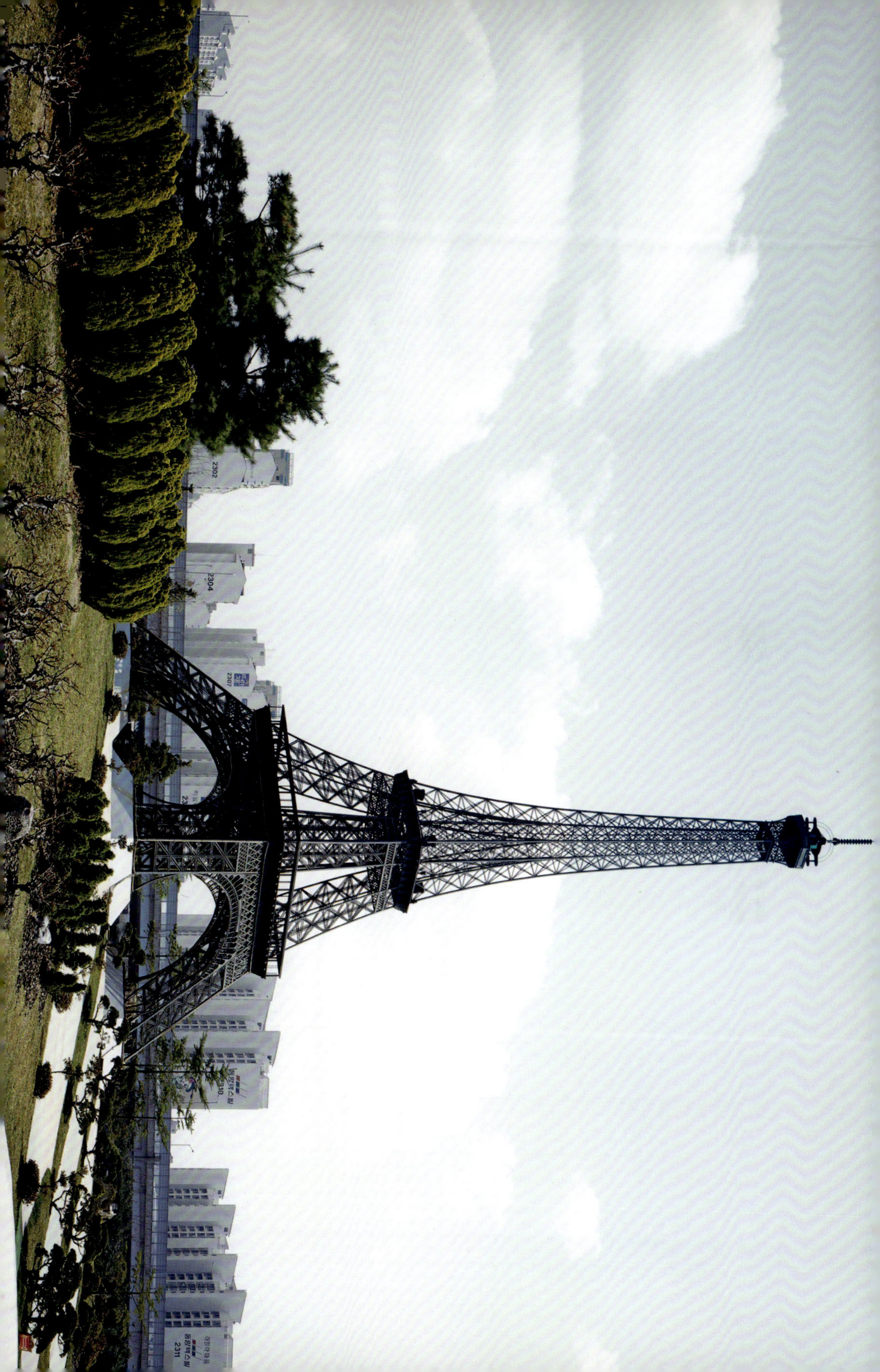

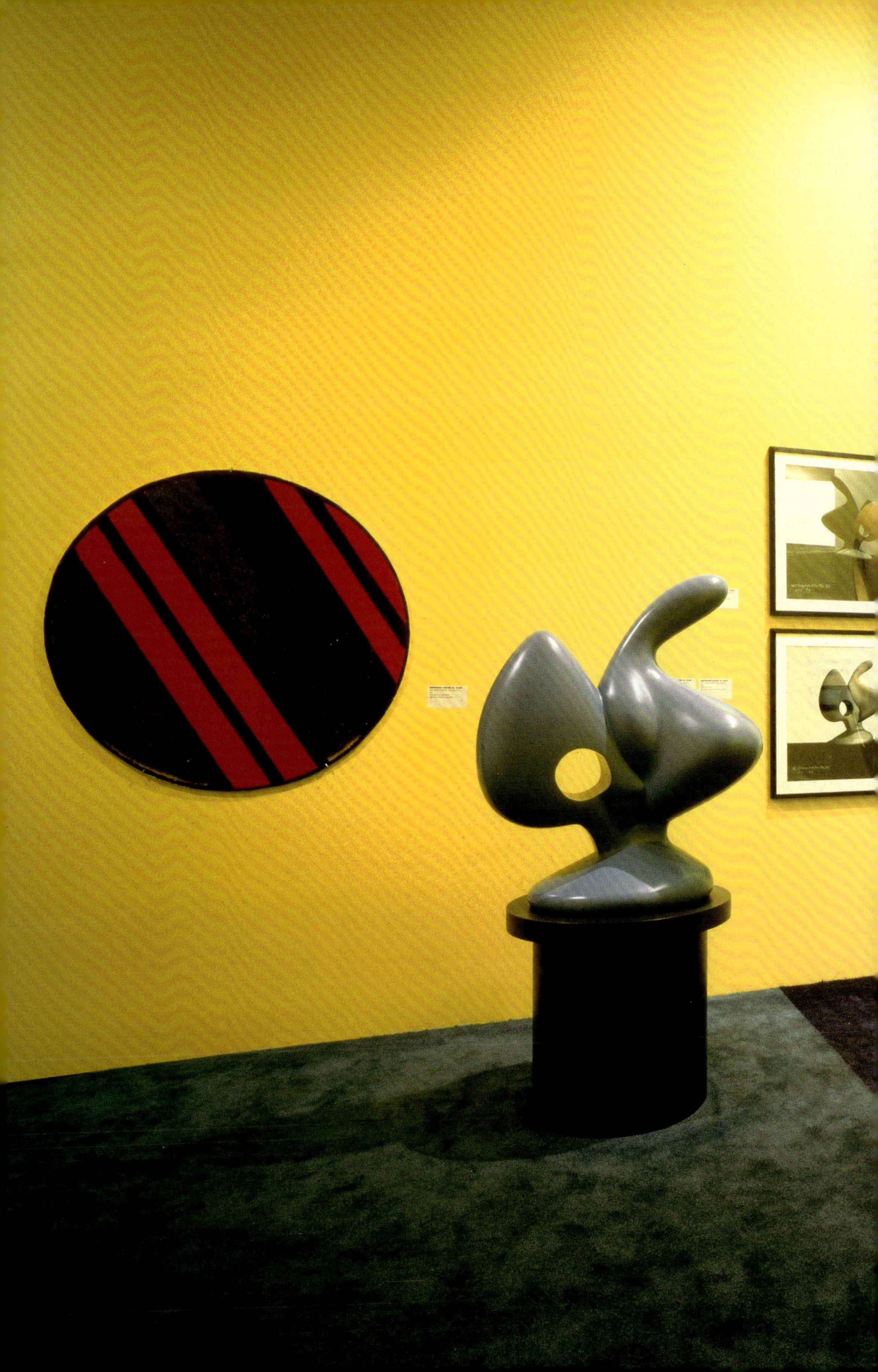

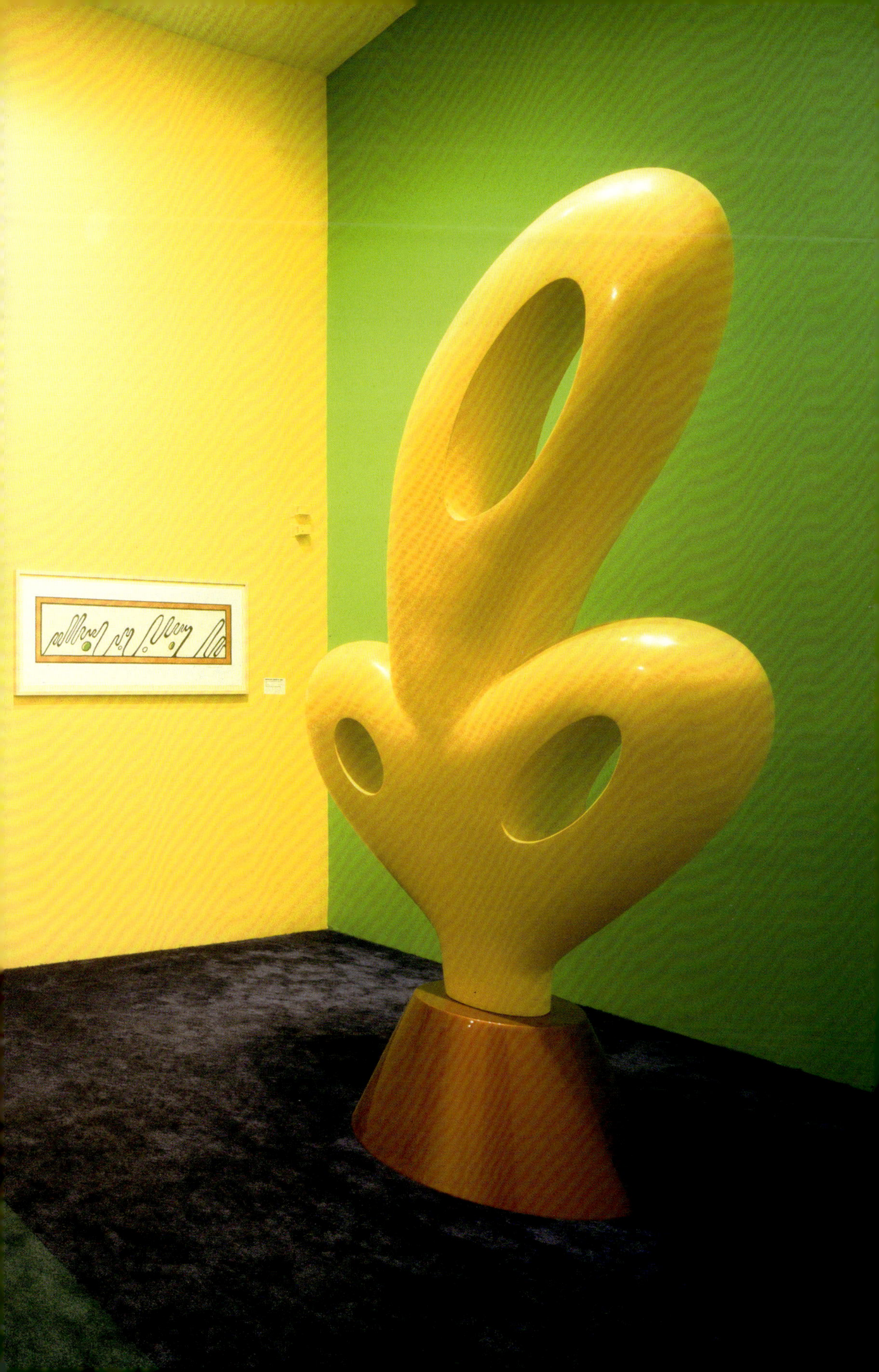

# Making History:     Some Thoughts on

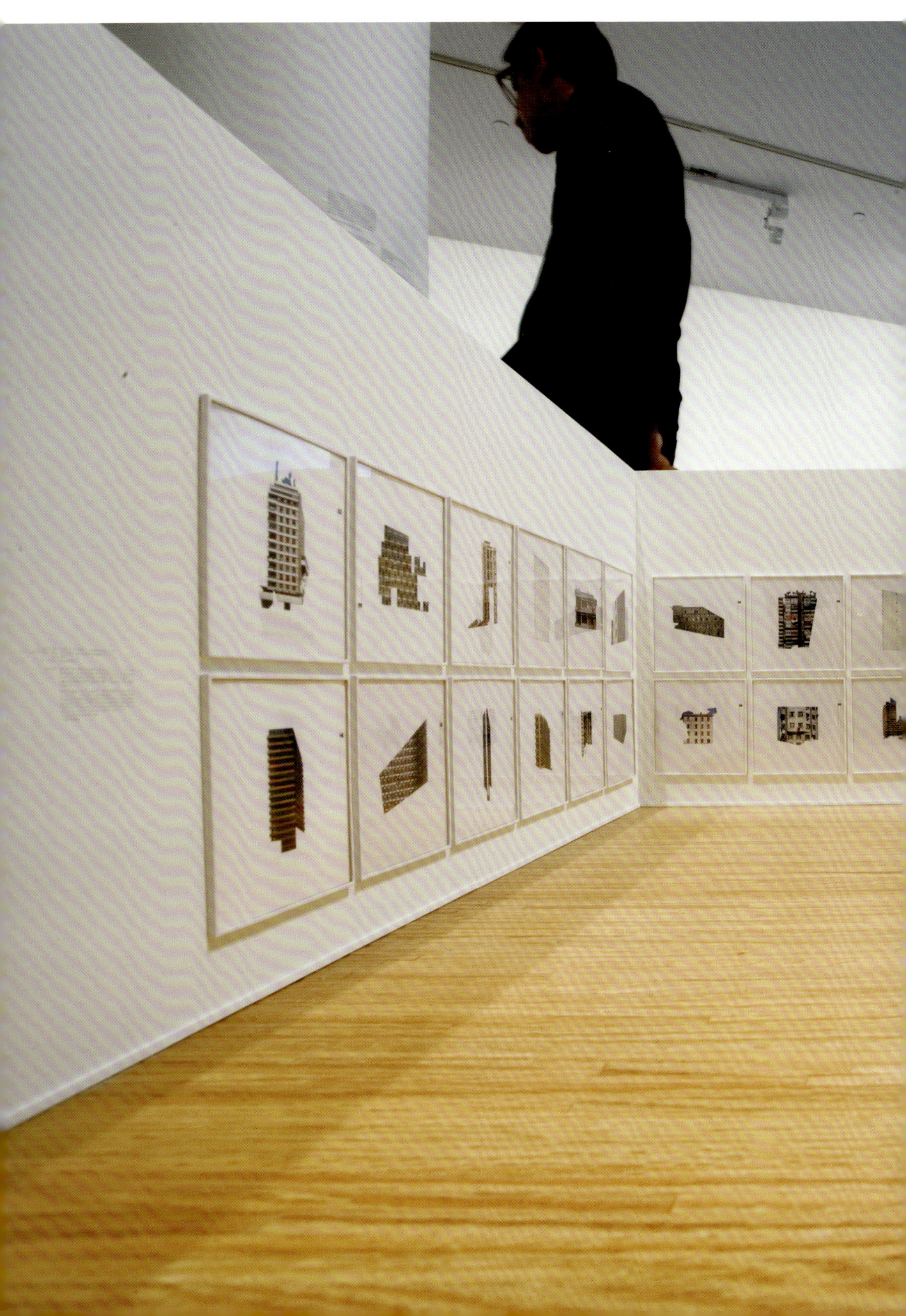

# Contemporary Art and the Middle East

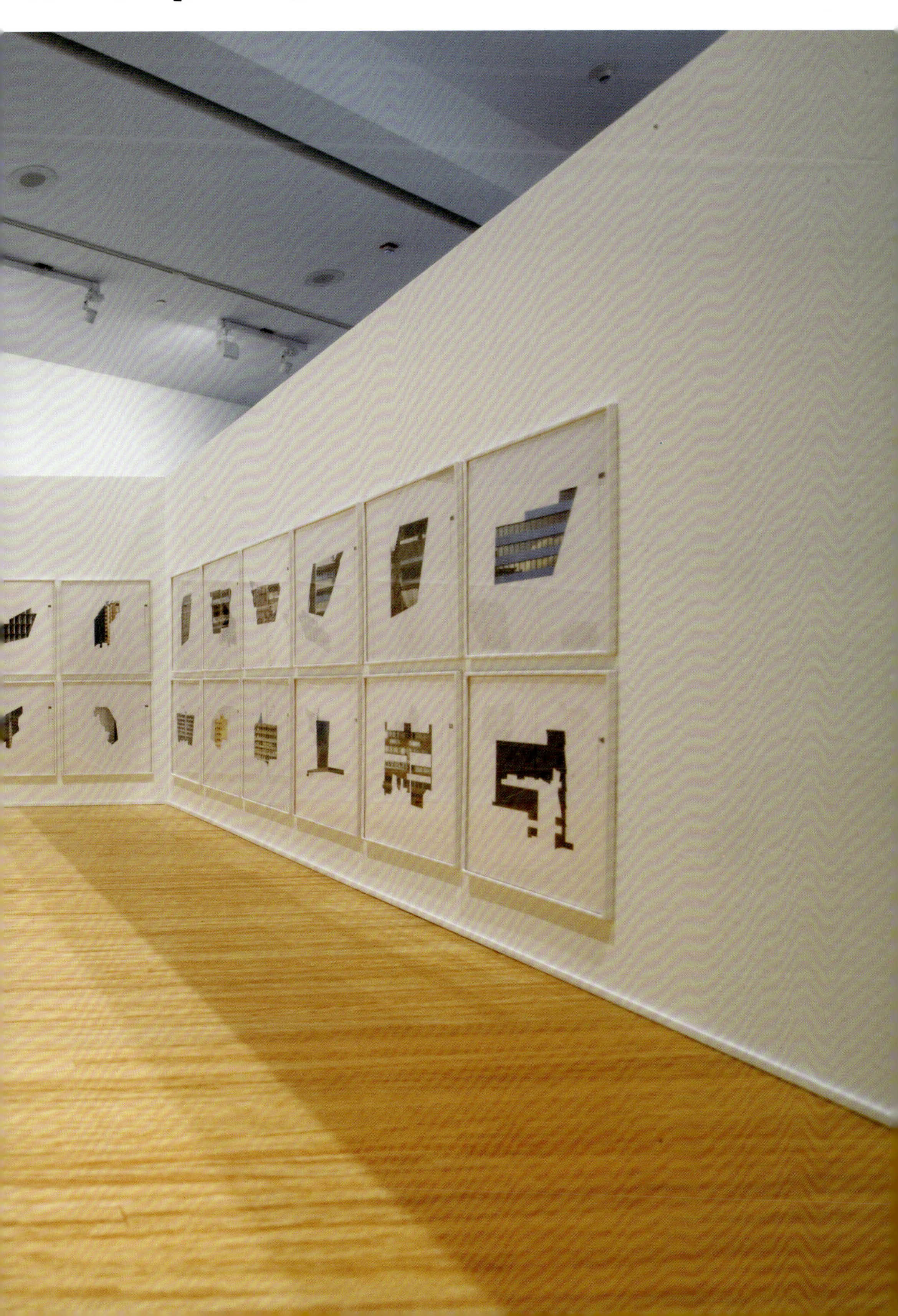

# Making History: Some Thoughts on Contemporary Art and the Middle East



*TEXT BY*

## GLENN D. LOWRY

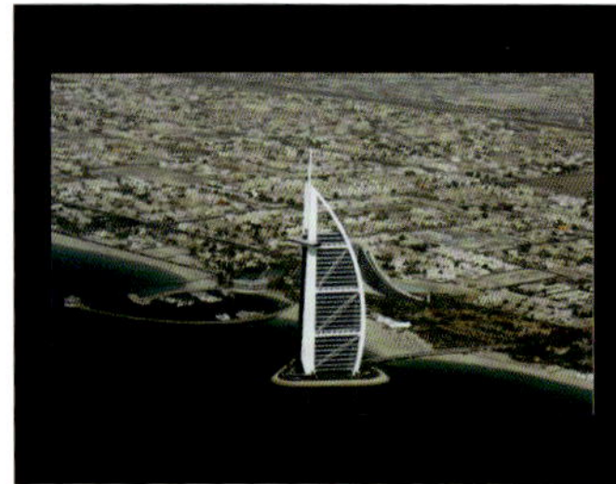

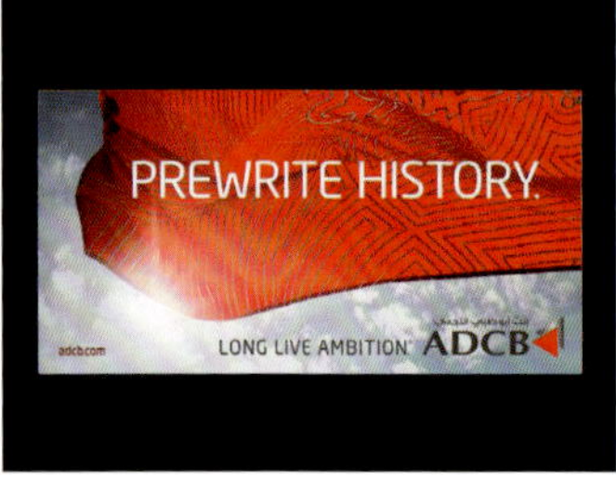


1
Aerial view of the Burj Al Arab hotel in Dubai

2
"Prewrite History," from the Abu Dhabi Commercial Bank "Long Live Ambition" advertising campaign, Fallon Agency, Minneapolis

Several years ago I had an impromptu conversation with the artist Walid Raad when we met by chance at the Global Art Forum, an event that coincides with the Dubai Art Fair. The forum takes place in a tent set in the compound of a vast hotel that can only be described as an over-the-top orientalist fantasy of Venice, imagined by Hollywood and set on the Gulf of Arabia (no. 1). On the spur of the moment, Walid and I decided to visit nearby Abu Dhabi to see what was happening there. The trip started off on a manic note as we kept getting pushed aside in our attempts to get a taxi by vacationing Russians or determined Emirati women dressed to kill, until Walid in frustration said, "Wait a minute, I am from Beirut; I know how to deal with this." He disappeared only to return smiling a few minutes later with a taxi driver in tow. With certain skills, it is probably better not to ask how they were learned.

Our trip took us from the sprawling landscape of mega hotels and office buildings in Dubai, across vast swaths of barren desert whose topography is being reshaped by multilane highways that for the moment seem to lead nowhere, to the gleaming buildings of Abu Dhabi. Like much of the Middle East, this is a region and space in transition—determined to be part of the future yet not fully formed in the present, with a past haunted by colonial and postcolonial decisions that make little sense today yet that still reverberate in unexpected ways. It is also a region that is acutely aware of the need to shape and define its as yet unfulfilled history, as evidenced by an advertisement from the Abu Dhabi Commercial Bank (no. 2) that states, "Prewrite history: long live ambition"—and as the events of the spring of 2011 in Bahrain and elsewhere throughout the region underscored.

The field of modern and contemporary art in the Middle East is much too new an area of study to suggest anything more than threads that can be followed or ideas that might be productive over time in generating a thoughtful discussion, but my conversation with Raad has led me to think about how he and other artists from the region—such as Oraib Toukan, Michael Blum, Emily Jacir, and Mona Hatoum, to name but a few—engage and respond to the historical process through an examination and exploration of its systems and constructs, facts and fictions, myths and realities. All these artists are what might be called diasporic artists in the sense that they no longer live primarily in their country of birth and often address questions of exile in their work. My concern, however, is not to explore issues of diasporic life per se but to examine how these artists address the particular problem of history and then to link this to more general observations about how they approach their work. These are, of course, not the only artists, either from the region or from elsewhere, who deal with the problem of history, but taken together, they offer a number of important insights into current practice in the region.

The issue of modern and, by extension, contemporary art and the Middle East—what it is, how

**No. 3**

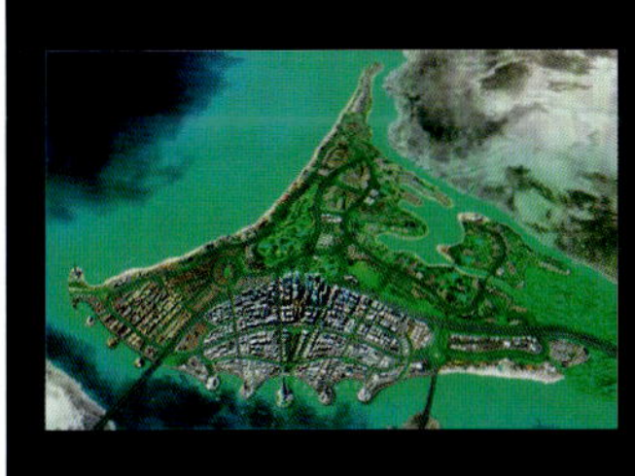

**No. 4**

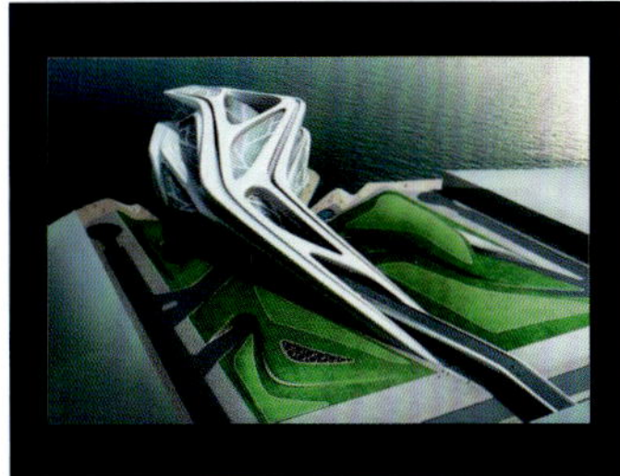

**No. 5**

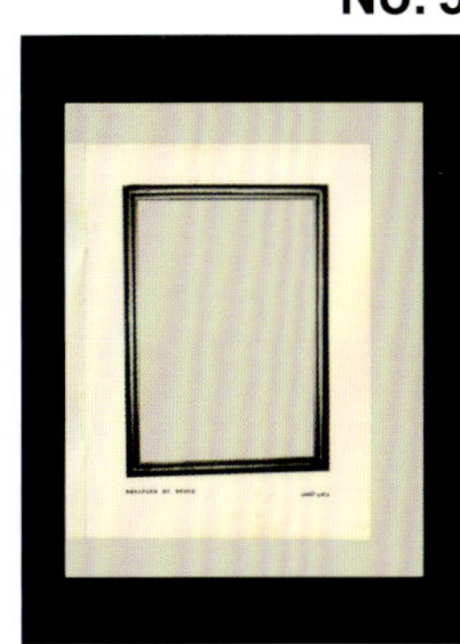

it came to be, and how we should understand it—is complex, contradictory, and far from being theorized in any meaningful way. A notable exception to this is the work of the Lebanese artist, critic, and philosopher Jalal Toufic, many of whose ideas form a kind of backdrop for looking at how Raad and others approach history.[1] Despite the lack of a coherent theory or even competing theories, however, the problem of what constitutes a modern or contemporary art in the Middle East merits attention because it poses a number of important questions about how artists from diverse backgrounds and cultures are shaping, defining, and critiquing their cultures and identity in response to the globalizing forces of modernity and modernism, however those terms may be understood. Moreover, the rapid growth and massive social, political, and cultural experiments fueled by the newfound wealth of the emirates; the new cities being built in Saudi Arabia; and the situation in Turkey as it seeks to balance its interest in Europe with its rising position in the Middle East highlight both the vitality of the region and the urgency of its cultural and political condition, especially in light of the events of the Arab Spring and its aftermath.

No one has been more active in looking at the ways in which history is made, how the past is woven into the present and the present proleptically configured into the future, than Walid Raad. His recent project *Scratching on Things I Could Disavow: A History of Modern and Contemporary Art in the Arab World, Part I, Volume I, Chapter I (Beirut 1992–2005)* grows out of his simultaneous fascination with

and skepticism about, as he frames it, "the emergence of arts festivals, forums and workshops, historical and contemporary art museums, art galleries, art funds, non-profit art spaces, foundations, art catalogs, theoretical and historical texts, art schools, journals, and collections in cities such as Abu Dhabi, Amman, Beirut, Cairo, Damascus, Doha, Dubai, Istanbul, Ramallah, and Sharjah."[2] In short, Raad is concerned with how the visual arts will be conceived, made, and consumed in the Arab world. He is especially interested in what he describes as "the still unfolding events in the United Arab Emirates," where on Saadiyat Island, a vast man-made expanse in the Gulf, Jean Nouvel is designing an enormous new Louvre, Frank Gehry an even larger Guggenheim Museum, Foster and Partners the Sheikh Zayed National Museum, and Zaha Hadid a performing arts center (nos. 3, 4).[3]

According to Raad, *Scratching on Things I Could Disavow* is an ongoing project, parts of which were exhibited at the Sharjah Biennial in 2011. The project "aims to engage with the progressive as well as reactionary, predictable and unpredictable forms this new infrastructure will have on the making and experiencing of current, past and future artworks, and other cultural events."[4] The project, as shown at the Paula Cooper Gallery in New York in 2009, consisted of four interrelated works of art—*On Walid Sadek's "Love Is Blind" (Modern Art, Oxford, UK, 2006)*; *Index XXVI Artists*; *The Atlas Group (1989–2004)*; and *Appendix XVIII, Plates 88–108*—that are fragments of an as yet incomplete history.

In 2006, according to Raad, the Lebanese artist Walid

> *NO ONE HAS BEEN MORE ACTIVE IN LOOKING AT THE WAYS IN WHICH HISTORY IS MADE, HOW THE PAST IS WOVEN INTO THE PRESENT AND THE PRESENT PROLEPTICALLY CONFIGURED INTO THE FUTURE*

3
Aerial view of Saadiyat Island, Abu Dhabi, United Arab Emirates

4
Zaha Hadid Architects, Abu Dhabi Performing Arts Centre, 2007, Abu Dhabi, United Arab Emirates

5
Walid Raad, *Appendix XVIII: Plate 94_A History of Donors*, 2009; archival ink-jet print; 64 x 51 inches (162.6 x 129.5 cm); courtesy Paula Cooper Gallery, New York

**No. 6**

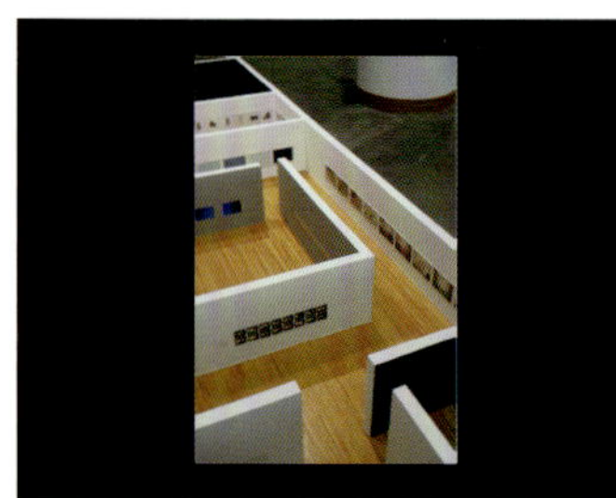

**No. 7**

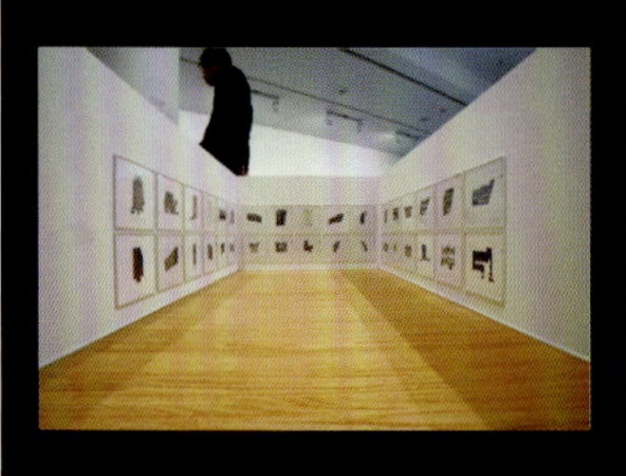

**No. 8**

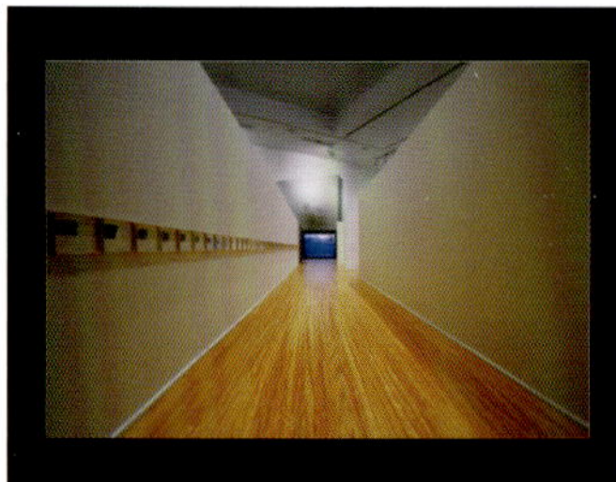

6–8

Walid Raad, *Part I_Chapter 1_Section 139: The Atlas Group (1989–2004)*, 1989–2004 (details); gallery walls and understructure: acrylic sheet with latex paint, floor: red oak veneer with polyurethane, photos: resin, latex paint, polycarbonate, and archival jet prints, video installation: 4 LCD screens; 12 ¹/₂ x 110 ³/₈ x 41 inches (31.8 x 280.4 x 104.1 cm); courtesy Paula Cooper Gallery, New York

Sadek exhibited *Love Is Blind*, an installation composed of two white walls on which Sadek placed five captions. The captions referenced paintings by Mustafa Farroukh that Raad expected to see but could not find. In 2008 he asked Sadek if he could borrow his installation to include in his own exhibition, but Sadek refused to lend it. The present work of art is Raad's reconstruction of Sadek's installation.[5]

*Index XXVI* is a modest-size document with an orange cover and white pages. The pages are numbered 23 through 66, and in the upper right portion of each page, written in white Arabic letters, is the word *and* followed by the name of an artist. Below each name is the same artist's name written in English preceded by the word *and*. All the artists referenced in *Index XXVI* worked in Lebanon in the past century. Their names came to Raad telepathically from the future, and he displayed them in a show that he did in Beirut and reproduced them in New York, much as they appear in *Index XXVI*, using white vinyl Arabic letters on white walls. The name of one artist, Johnny Tahan, was misspelled and corrected in red pencil by a critic. Raad spent seven years researching Tahan's work, after which he concluded that future artists intentionally distorted Tahan's name in order to call attention to the critic's use of red in the handwritten corrections. Raad states in an explanatory text accompanying the exhibition that the reason these artists did this was because the color red was not available to them, as it had been withdrawn from use.[6]

The Atlas Group Archive is made up of a body of work that occupied Raad's attention from 1989 to 2004. It consists of photographs, videotapes, and other materials that document the Lebanese wars of the past decades. According to Raad, he was asked to exhibit the project in Beirut in 2005 and refused; he was asked again in 2006 and in 2007,

refusing both times until in 2008 he agreed to show it at the Galerie Sfeir-Semler in Beirut, a white cube space designed by the Lebanese architect Bernard Khoury. When he went to the gallery to see his show, he discovered that all the objects in the exhibition had shrunk in size and decided to make a new space for them that reflected their new dimensions.[7]

*Appendix XVIII*, the final work in *Scratching on Things I Could Disavow*, is made up of twenty-three related plates from a book or catalogue with a pale blue cover. Each page describes a work of art or contains a phrase, often written in letters so small that they are invisible. On the back of the catalogue is a key giving the title of each work with an illegible and miniscule image. An accompanying text by Raad explains that the Lebanese civil wars affected the country's citizens physically and psychologically, killing many, wounding and displacing others, and leaving no one unscathed. "It is also clear," he writes, "that these wars affected colors, lines, shapes and forms. Some of these are affected in a material way and, like burned books or razed monuments, are physically destroyed and lost forever. Others, like looted treasures or politically compromised artworks, remain physically intact but are removed from view possibly forever. And yet others, sensing the forthcoming danger, deploy defensive measures; they hide, camouflage, or dissimulate."[8]

What is one to make of this strange and bewildering project? On the surface it purports to be part of a much-needed effort to document the history of modern and contemporary art in the region, focusing the first part of this effort on what happened in Beirut between 1992 and 2005. But as with all of Raad's works, the story is much more complicated than it first seems. Indeed, the very title of the project, *Scratching on Things I Could Disavow*, is charged with an ambiguity that occludes its stated purpose of

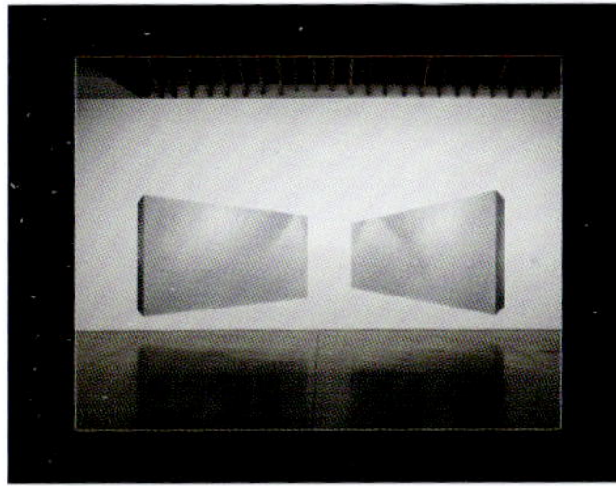

**No. 9**

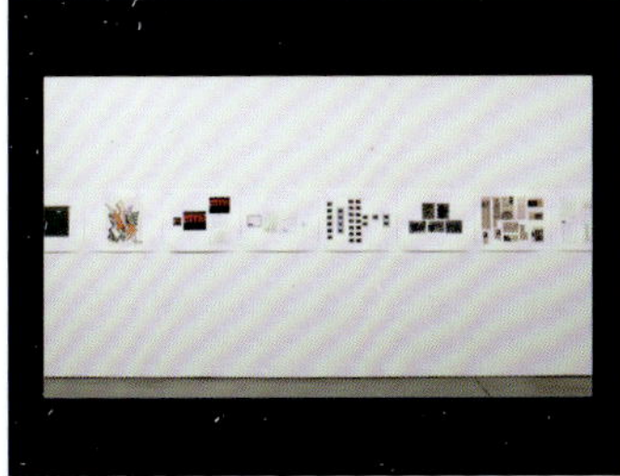

**No. 10**

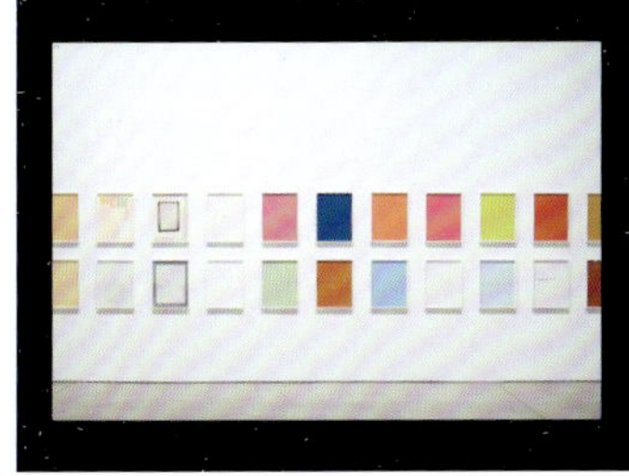

**No. 11**

providing "A History of Modern and Contemporary Art in the Arab World."

What does Raad mean by scratching on something—is he trying to satisfy an intellectual itch, score a mental surface, or dig beneath the obvious? And how committed is he to the enterprise of documenting a history of modern and contemporary Arab art since he might disavow it anyway? Is this because he is not up to the task, or is it because there can be no history of modern and contemporary Arab art since such an art either does not exist or cannot be seen? Raad has always been a bit of a trickster, using conceptual strategies and the visual equivalent of sleight of hand to explore critically important issues, but is this new effort a purely artistic project or a serious effort at making history?

Central to *Scratching on Things I Could Disavow* is the Atlas Group (nos. 5–11), a monumental project that consumed Raad for more than a decade. The purpose of the Atlas Group was to research and document the contemporary history of Lebanon through the production of audio, visual, and literary initiatives that shed light on the civil wars that traumatized and almost destroyed the country. The group sponsored lectures, developed an extensive website that serves as an archive, produced exhibitions, and made available for study a vast array of documents. At the core of its efforts was an extensive body of archival material entrusted to Raad by Dr. Fakhouri, who was, according to the artist, the leading archivist and historian of Lebanon's civil wars.[9] Fakhouri died in 1993 and bequeathed to the group all his notebooks, diaries, and files. The archive contains everything from small scraps of paper to extensive notes and clippings from the newspaper *Annahar*. These clippings depict, among other subjects, horses that have won various races along with Fakhouri's brief description, in his own hand, of the race's duration, the winning time,

and information on the bets placed on the race. They record as well the sites of various car bombings and the remains of the vehicles that were blown up; the types of cars that were used for the bombings; buildings that were attacked or destroyed; and various events that occurred during the civil wars (nos. 6–8).

Taken together, these files provide insight into how daily life continued in Lebanon as civil war ravaged the country. But like all the photographs, diaries, notebooks, and videotapes that constitute the Atlas project, despite their verisimilitude, they are a complete fabrication, just as the Atlas Group is Raad's invention. By using the traditional instruments of history making—including archival sources, photographic documentation, and personal testimonies—but blurring the boundary between the factual and the fictional, he reveals the complex ways in which the narrative of history

> *"OTHERS, LIKE LOOTED TREASURES OR POLITICALLY COMPROMISED ARTWORKS, REMAIN PHYSICALLY INTACT BUT ARE REMOVED FROM VIEW POSSIBLY FOREVER."*

is constructed from a combination of reliable sources of information and imagination, from objective truths as well as highly personal memories. Raad has said that for him the civil war in Lebanon is not something that can be understood in a purely rational way. Its horrors and traumas are only the observable side of an otherwise inexplicable series of events that constitute an alternative narrative revealed through the "documentation" of the Atlas Group.

Raad's reduction of the Atlas Group's work to miniature scale, however, is not without precedent. It

9
Walid Raad, *On Walid Sadek's Love Is Blind (Modern Art Oxford, 2006)*, 2009; acrylic paint; dimensions variable; courtesy Paula Cooper Gallery, New York
10
Walid Raad, *Index XXVI: Artists*, 2009; vinyl and pencil on wall, adhesive paper, 8 ink-jet prints; prints 17 x 22 inches (43.2 x 55.9 cm) each, overall dimensions variable; courtesy Paula Cooper Gallery, New York
11
Walid Raad, *Appendix XVIII: Plates*, 2009; archival ink-jet prints; 23 prints, 21 1/2 x 16 1/2 inches (54.6 x 41.9 cm) each; overall dimensions variable; courtesy Paula Cooper Gallery, New York

**No. 12**

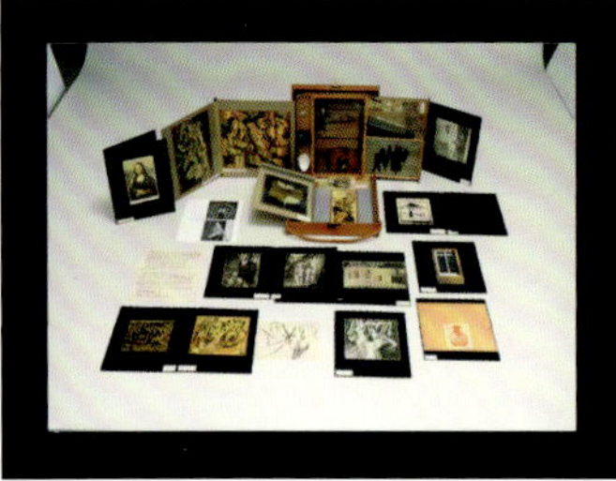

**No. 13**

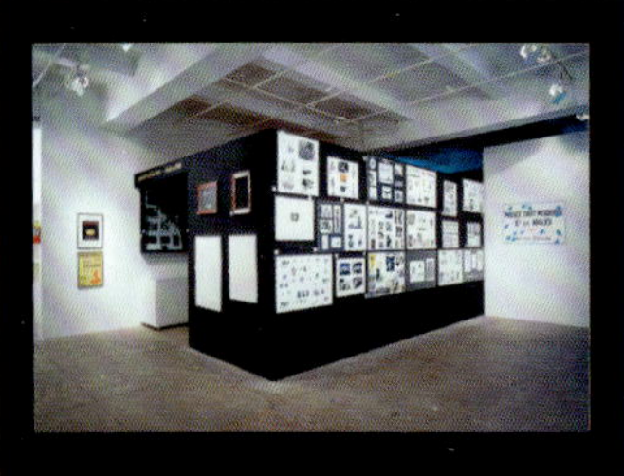

**No. 14**

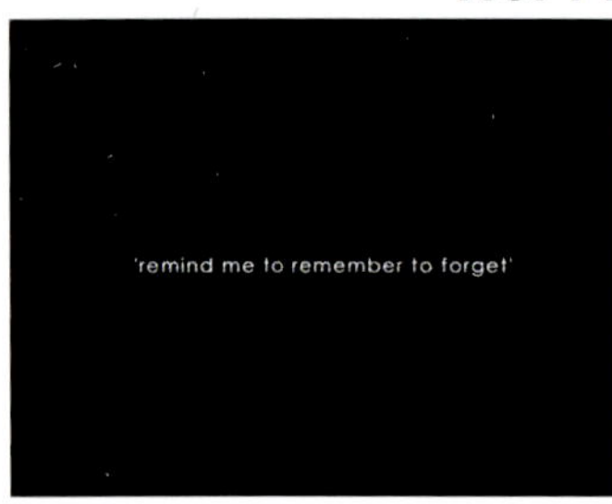


recalls, for instance, Marcel Duchamp's *Box in a Valise* of the late 1930s (no. 12), with its sly transformation of the artist's oeuvre into an archive and then, almost alchemically, the archive back into art. And at the same time, Raad's location of his now almost invisible work in a miniature model of an art gallery invokes the museological investigations of Marcel Broodthaers's *Musée d'Art Moderne, Département des Aigles* of 1968–72 (no. 13). These twin associations, as the critic David Frankel has noted, firmly place Raad's project in the realm of conceptual art and a European avant-garde aesthetic that questions both the authenticity of the object and the way works of art are received.[10] But if Duchamp was ultimately concerned with questioning what constitutes a work of art, and Broodthaers with exploring the way taxonomies are created, Raad is dealing with something else altogether, the disappearance or withdrawal of images.

Like the almost invisible names of the artists and the color red in *Index XXVI* and the unstable images in *Appendix XVIII*, the reduced images of the Atlas Group have lost their autonomy and exist in what might be called an existential or transitional condition. They are no longer available to us in any comprehensible form, and we are left pondering what happened to them and why. A possible answer is provided by Jalal Toufic, whose essay "The Withdrawal of Tradition Past a Surpassing Disaster," often cited by Raad, considers whether certain wars and other kinds of disasters lead not only to material destruction but, in rare instances, also to the withdrawal of images from an artist's vision. Toufic argues that unusually horrific disasters—such as the martyrdom of Husayn at Karbal' in 680, the Holocaust, the bombing of Hiroshima and Nagasaki, or more recently the civil wars in Lebanon—are so physically and psychologically overwhelming that they cause incalculable social

and cultural collateral damage.[11] One of the consequences of this is that long after the damage has occurred the traumatic effects of the disaster continue to manifest themselves in immaterial ways, causing certain works of art literally to be withdrawn from use. Toufic means this not in a metaphorical sense but in the sense that these works of art cease to be visible or available to artists affected by the trauma of a surpassing disaster. These works then remain out of circulation until they can be resurrected by another generation.

Seen in this context, Raad's disappearing images from the Atlas Group Archive, as well as the other works in *Scratching on Things I Could Disavow*, may be in the process of being withdrawn from circulation because they are part of a surpassing disaster. Raad himself, in the exhibition's catalogue, asks whether the reduction in scale of the Atlas Group Archive is a mere psychological fact, an illusory fantasy born out of his fascination with architectural models, or is a manufactured effect that leans on formal and conventional tropes influenced by such works as Lewis Carroll's *Alice's Adventures in Wonderland*.[12] He concludes that the effect is not illusory, that the shrinking is real, in the same way that Toufic argues that the withdrawal of images past a surpassing disaster is real.

If this seems overly recondite, it is because Raad, in *Scratching on Things I Could Disavow*, is grappling with how memory and consciousness are involved in the construction of histories—personal, national, and even transnational. He wants us to see—literally—that a history of modern and contemporary art in the Arab world must by necessity involve works of art no longer available to artists because they may have been withdrawn from use due to the wars that have wracked the region; he wants us also to see that even works of art currently available are unstable, perhaps even

12
Marcel Duchamp, *Box in a Valise (From or by Marcel Duchamp or Rrose Sélavy)*, 1935–41; leather valise containing miniature replicas, photographs, and color reproductions of works by Duchamp, and one "original" (Large Glass, collotype on celluloid); 16 x 15 x 4 inches overall (40.6 x 38.1 x 10.2 cm); The Museum of Modern Art, New York, James Thrall Soby Fund
13
Marcel Broodthaers, *Musée d'Art Moderne, Département des Aigles, Section Publicité*, 1968–72; mixed-media installation; dimensions variable; courtesy Marian Goodman Gallery, New York
14
Oraib Toukan, *Remind me to remember to forget*, 2006; single-channel video projection, color, sound; 2:50 minutes; courtesy the artist

**No. 15**

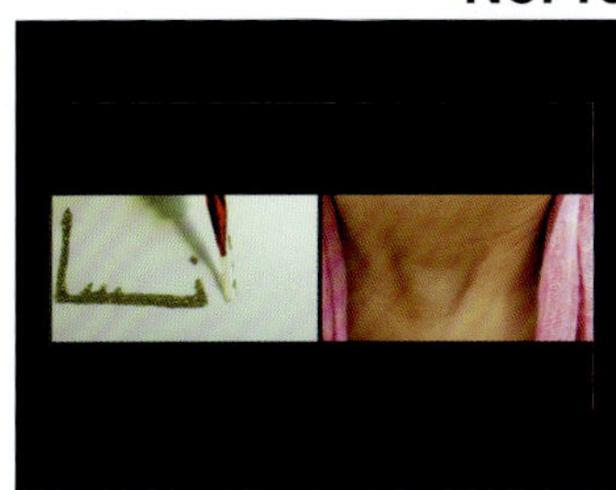

**No. 16**

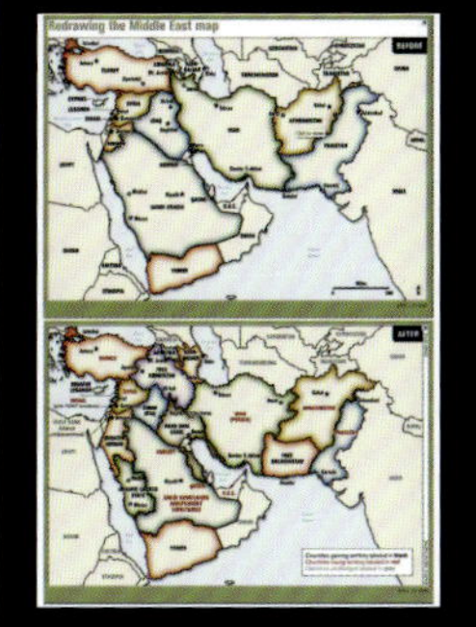


**No. 17**

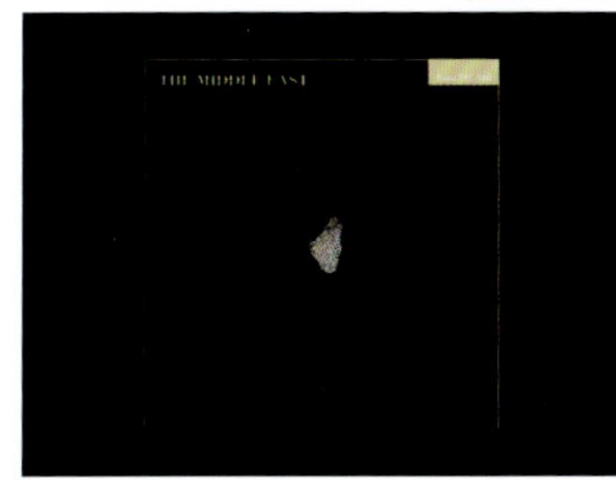


isotopic, and may be in the process of disappearing. Where the Atlas Group once engaged the historical process, exploring how, in the words of Frankel, "even the most concrete documentary records are conditional rather than 'true,'" now the group is being dematerialized by the process, its conditionality subject to the exogenous forces of surpassing disasters or other hypertraumatic events.[13] Today, in addition to the civil wars in Lebanon, those events might now also include the brutal killings and suppression taking place in Syria and the destruction of Libya and Iraq as functioning countries.

Raad is not the only artist from the Middle East who explores the issue of history and how it is made and received. In *Remind me to remember to forget* (2006; no. 14), a single-channel video projection, Oraib Toukan, an American-born Jordanian, treats the memory of the Middle East in terms of a memory that has been "made to forget" or, in Toufic's terms, withdrawn. For Toukan the traumatic events of a century of colonialism and war, with all their attendant issues of displacement and violence, create a dramatic tension between the present and the immediate past. Her obsessive writing and rewriting of the phrase "remind me to remember to forget" becomes a kind of incantation, simultaneously inscribing and erasing this invitation to deal with the horrors of her region.

*Remind me to remember to forget* consists of a split screen that presents two interrelated performances. One side consists of the phrase "remind me to remember to forget" being written in gold glitter and then rapidly inhaled through a nozzle painted in the colors of the American flag, the symbolism clear. The other depicts a tightly framed image of a throat breathing in and out, a metaphor, perhaps, for the difficulties of life under occupation. The pulsating sound of the artist's labored breathing—in and out, in and out, over and over again—like

a jackhammer pounding away, becomes the acoustic manifestation of Toukan erasing her memory as she literally makes herself forget or, as Toufic might say, withdraws herself in the face of a surpassing disaster.

Toukan further develops the idea of a traumatized Middle East where it is impossible for any history to be fully conceived or developed in *The New(er) Middle East* (2007; no. 15). This interactive installation takes the form of a map of the Middle East, with the various territories cut out like puzzle pieces. The pieces are magnetized, and viewers are invited to reassemble the map as they wish. Toukan conceived the puzzle-map after she came across a scientific definition of memory as "the ability of a material to return to its original shape after being subject to deformation."[14] The installation references the so-called New Middle East Map (no. 16), originally proposed in 2006 by Ralph Peters, a retired US Army officer, as part of a thought experiment that involved a "hypothetical redrawing of boundaries reflect[ing] ethnic affinities and religious communalism."[15]

Toukan created her puzzle by superimposing Peters's proposed map of the Middle East onto the present one and cutting out the areas that formed. The only region in her map that is fixed is Palestine. It forms the keystone of the puzzle, around which all the other blocks can be arranged. This treatment of Palestine was inspired by Peters's description of Israel and the West Bank as territories whose status is "undetermined."

By invoking the secret Sykes-Picot agreement of 1916 between the United Kingdom and France, which anticipated the dissolution of the Ottoman Empire and divided up the Middle East based on colonial zones of influence, Toukan reminds us of the inherent instability of the region's recent history. We can compose and recompose states and nations as if they were part of a large jigsaw puzzle, yet every move

15
Oraib Toukan, *The New(er) Middle East*, 2007; interactive installation, magnets, magnetized wall; dimensions variable; courtesy the artist
16
Map from Ralph Peters's article "Blood Borders: How a Better Middle East Would Look," *Armed Forces Journal*, June 2006.
17
Oraib Toukan, "Auction Catalogue," from *The Equity Is in the Circle*, 2007–9; auction of nation-states including printed matter, public billboard, lecture performance, advertising spreads, talking heads TV screening of public consultants, documents, branded logo, letters; courtesy the artist

**No. 18**

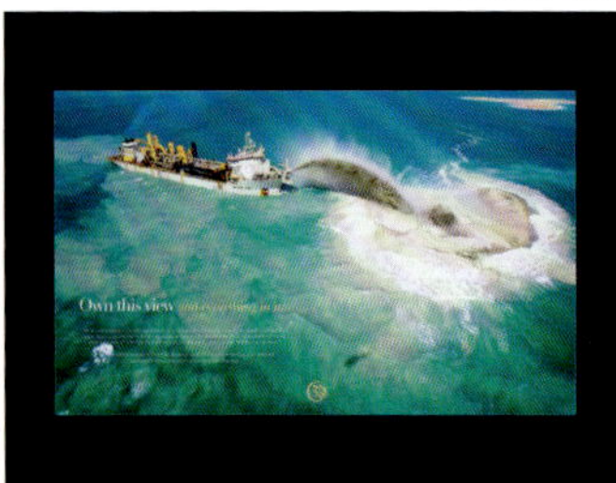

**No. 19**

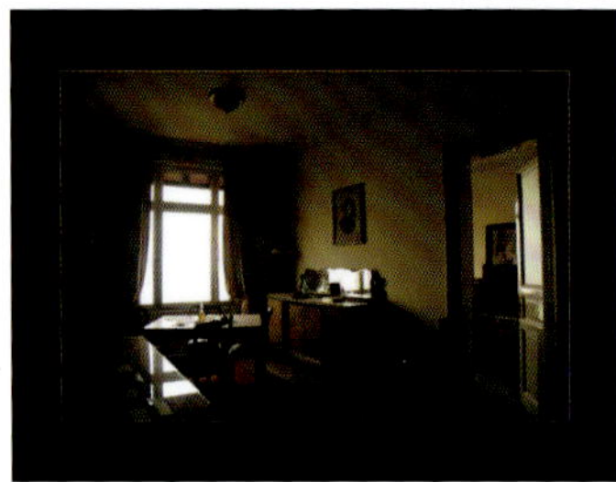

18
Oraib Toukan, *Reworking Ammar*, 2009; archival ink-jet prints on aluminum; 7 prints, 27 3/16 x 39 3/8 in. (69 x 100 cm) each; courtesy the artist

19
Michael Blum, *A Tribute to Safiye Behar*, 2005 (detail); installation; courtesy the artist

creates a series of repercussions that alters the configuration of a very real place, underscoring the fact that no map can ever be neutral and that the topography of history is subject to a variety of rational and irrational forces. Toukan's "map" seems especially prescient in light of recent events in the Middle East, where the sectarian strife in Libya and Syria, unleashed by the Arab Spring of 2011, and the ongoing chaos in Iraq, despite nine years of American occupation, threaten to further fragment already unstable countries.

Toukan's interest in the way these rational and irrational forces have inscribed and shaped the Middle East as a region and space whose boundaries cannot be set is further explored in *The Equity Is in the Circle* (2007–9; no. 17), which was one of the more impressive works in the 2009 Istanbul Biennial. The project consists of videos, archival documents, corporate logos, advertisements, and copies of correspondence, all of which are devoted to her research on how to sell the entire region via an international auction. To do this, she consulted with economists and other area specialists to determine how much each country was worth based on late nineteenth- and early twentieth-century leaseholds and factoring in the rate of inflation and perceptions of political and economic risk. Using these and other metrics, she determined a value for each country and then created a holding company for all the territories called Nayruz, a reference to the holiday commemorating martyrs and confessors. She also created an identity for the sale under the rubric "Own This View, and Everything in It." She then printed a catalogue for the sale, which is to occur in Dubai in 2012.

The plausibility of the sale is what gives *The Equity Is in the Circle* its traction and impact. This is not simply a function of Toukan's witty branding efforts or clever marketing strategy, or even the fact that in the cash-rich Gulf—and Abu Dhabi and Dubai in particular—with their over-the-top desire to have the biggest and best of everything, at least until recently, buying whole countries seems perfectly in line with creating enormous palm-shaped islands (no. 18) and theme parks the size of Rhode Island.[16] Toukan, however, is also on to something else, and that is the fact that it was less than one hundred years ago that large parts of the region were in fact effectively auctioned off between the colonial powers that controlled the Middle East. While fair-market prices may not have been the basis of these transactions—location, natural resources, and political importance were the currency of the day—Toukan brings this history to the present by injecting into it the forces of free-market capitalism and detailed financial research.

Another artist who uses the construction of history to explore national, if not regional, identity is Michael Blum, a Jerusalem-born artist who now lives in Montreal. For *A Tribute to Safiye Behar*, part of the 2005 Istanbul Biennial, Blum re-created Behar's apartment at Hamalbasi Caddesi No. 18, in Istanbul's Beyoglu district (no. 19). He assembled a vast array of archival photographs, letters, and other documentary material, including a lengthy video interview with Behar's grandson Melik Tutuncu, an architect in Chicago. According to Blum, Behar was born in Pera, a district of Istanbul, in 1890. She was the only child of a Jewish barkeeper, and the family lived in the apartment above the Zeuve Birahanesi bar. A bright and intellectually curious child, she was encouraged by her parents, who hoped that their daughter would enjoy a better life than theirs. Likely influenced by the political discussions she overheard in the Birahanesi, she studied socialist and anarchist writers, including Marx and Proudhon. She married a lawyer named Günay, and they had two sons. Although she lacked a formal education, Behar became a teacher in Istanbul and, after her move to Chicago, a respected labor organizer and public speaker, supporter of the freethinking movement, and advocate of women's rights. Although Behar was not the only woman to pursue these interests in the last decades of the Ottoman sultanate, the others were generally from educated families. What makes her story unique is her emancipation from class and gender. It may have been for this reason that Mustafa Kemal Atatürk, the founder of the Turkish republic, had a relationship with her over three decades. Even though her role has never been acknowledged publicly, she was, according to Blum, the inspiration for many of Kemal's reforms in the 1920s.[17]

Behar, like her relationship with Kemal, is of course a complete fiction made plausible by the veracity of the re-creation of her apartment, the archival materials assembled by Blum, and Tutuncu's engaging interview, conducted from the backseat of a car traveling through Chicago. In an essay reprinted in this volume, Carrie Lambert-Beatty convincingly argues that *A Tribute to Safiye Behar* uses the technique of recovering the forgotten life story and unacknowledged historical role of a female figure from an ethnic minority to engage in a kind of revisionist project whose foundations can be traced to the feminist and civil rights movements of the 1960s and 1970s. Blum's strategy of creating a dichotomy between the male-dominated history of Turkey and the recovered history of Behar builds on the postmodern critique of meta-narratives while acknowledging the discourse on identity and hybridity of the 1980s and 1990s.

Blum's use of the trope of the house museum, in the words of Lambert-Beatty, allowed him to "address two publics, and two political situations, at once. For the local, Turkish audience, the frank discussion of Mustafa Kemal's likely affair with the Jewish woman, and her influence on his reforms, served as a critical intervention in the official hagiography of the leader that continues to saturate public life in Turkey. . . . Meanwhile, for the large contingent of international visitors brought to Istanbul by the biennial in 2005—a moment when Turkey's potential membership in the European Union was being hotly debated—the life story of this secular, cosmopolitan, internationalist, and progressive woman . . . cut into stereotypes about Turkey as backward, other, and 'Islamicist.'"

*WHERE FOUCAULT NULLIFIES THE DISCURSIVE SUBJECT TO CREATE A NEW KIND OF SUBJECT IN ITS VOID, HATOUM DISTORTS THE KNOWN CONTOURS OF THE WORLD MAP IN ORDER TO REPLACE ITS DESIGN WITH AN IMAGINATIVE VERSION OF HER OWN MAKING.*

Orhan Pamuk, Turkey's recent Nobel laureate in literature, develops an intriguing reversal of the kind of fictionalized history deployed by Blum in his book *The Museum of Innocence* (2009).[18] The novel is centered in Istanbul and explores the secret love affair of Kemal Pasha, a wealthy and indolent man who runs an export company given to him by his father, and Fusun Keskin, an eighteen-year-old shopkeeper (recalling and perhaps even invoking through a similar kind of relationship Blum's earlier work). Kemal meets Fusun when he goes to buy his fiancé, Sibel, a designer handbag that turns out to be a fake. Their affair blossoms over discussions about the appropriateness of the kind of brand consciousness that makes fakes an issue. Years later Fusun dies in a car accident, and Kemal sets about collecting every item he can find associated with their courtship, which he assembles into a Museum of Innocence. A passionate connoisseur of historical houses and small, idiosyncratic museums, Kemal claims to have visited 5,723 of them. He seeks out old posters, porcelains, and the detritus of his relationship with Fusun in order to make his museum as potent and meaningful as the ones he so admires elsewhere in the world.

Pamuk's twist on this plot is that he is now building his own Museum of Innocence, set to open in 2012, based on the house museums that he, like Kemal, has visited over the years. Where Blum and Raad use the idea of the archive to create fictional histories, Pamuk uses fiction to create a very real archive. Pamuk further blurs the line between fiction and reality by introducing himself into the novel as the agent for Kemal, who seeks him out to tell his story. What Pamuk is after—and, to a large degree, so too Raad and Blum—is an understanding of how memories are created and inscribed in our consciousness and the role of objects in this process. For all three the gallery and the museum become active places, an arena if you wish, in which, in Pamuk's words, "time is transformed into space"[19]—that is, where the past is made real and tangible through the presence of artifacts whose narrative reveals the texture of personal life in the face of local, national, or even transnational events.

The use of memory to create both new personal histories and a larger national one is central to much of Emily Jacir's work. An American of Palestinian descent who divides her time between New York and Ramallah, Jacir, like Raad, uses the strategy of conceptual art but deploys it to explore the impact of diasporic life on the Palestinian community. *Where We Come From*

**No. 20**

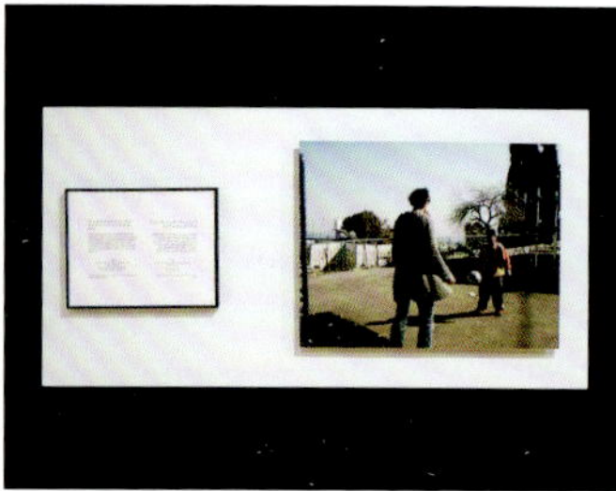

**No. 21**

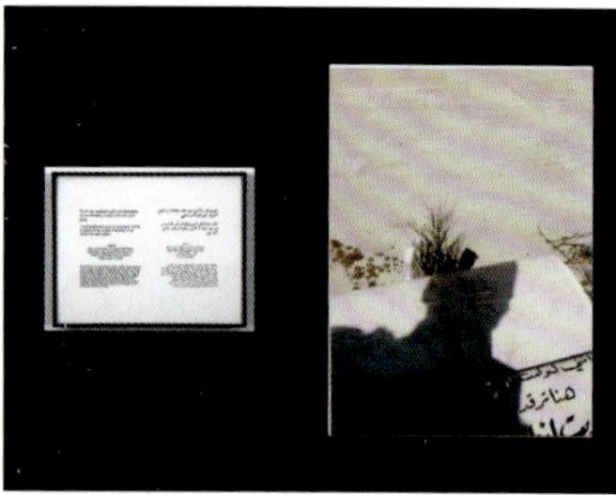

(2001–3; nos. 20, 21), for example, begins with a simple question that Jacir asked Palestinians unable to visit their homeland: "If I could do anything for you, anywhere in Palestine, what would it be?" The result consists of a series of text panels in Arabic and English describing some thirty wishes, accompanied by photographs documenting Jacir's realization of them. The wishes range from the deeply personal—"Go to my mother's grave in Jerusalem on her birthday and put flowers and pray"—to the practical—"Go to the Israeli post office in Jerusalem and pay my phone bill"—to the whimsical—"Go to Haifa and play soccer with the first Palestinian boy you see on the street." Each wish is accompanied by the name of the person who asked Jacir to perform the wish, brief biographical information, the reason for the wish, and a photograph of her realization of the wish.

On the surface this is a deceptively simple project whose primary purpose is to use the framework of conceptual art to underscore the political tension of disputed territory and the pain of a diasporic community living in exile. But what interests me here about *Where We Come From* is a less obvious aspect of the project, which is how Jacir uses the convention of wishing, and an array of documentary evidence, to create a new history, complete with its own archival background, in which the exiled are reunited with their families or able to fulfill a long-held desire through the fiction of her work. This imagined history reconnects families and restores the quotidian pattern of daily life; it also enables the construction, at least on a metaphoric level, of a Palestinian community while acknowledging through the documentation of exile its very impossibility. History, in *Where We Come From*, is both a fabrication and a poignant reminder of a current reality.

Another Palestinian artist, Mona Hatoum, who now lives primarily in Berlin, also addresses the politics of occupation through the construction of alternative histories. For over a decade she has been making maps of the world that in one form or another undergo a process of distortion. *Hot Spot* (2006; no. 22), for example, consists of a large, cage-like globe tilted on the same axis as the earth. The contours of the continents, islands, and other major landmarks are outlined in red neon light that generates an intense glow, refiguring the topography of the earth into a delicate tracery suspended on the armature of the cage. The eerie glow of the neon creates a sense of conflict and danger, of hostility and instability, of contested space and unrest, while the thin network of lines created by the lights suggests fragility and tenuousness, as if the shape of the world could change at a moment's notice, as it has, in fact, in the Middle East over the last century, if not more immediately.

In another work, titled *Projection* (2006), made out of pressed white paper and abaca, Hatoum presents a map of the world refigured based on the "Peters Projection." This description of the world, developed by the historian and cartographer Arno Peters and first shown in 1974, alters the traditional rendering of the earth by applying an egalitarian, area-accurate projection. The result is a world that at first appears distended and weighted toward the Southern Hemisphere, underscoring the fact that traditional representations of the world are mapped from a European perspective.

In yet another mapping project, titled *Continental Drift* (2000; no. 23), Hatoum has created a horizontal map of the world in clear plastic with metal filings filling the seas. A magnetized bar circles like a watch's second hand below, creating a tidal "wave" of filings, which lap up onto the continents, gently but steadily disturbing shapes

20
Emily Jacir, *Where We Come From*, 2001–3 (detail of Hana); framed laser print, C-print mounted on Sintra; text: 9 ½ x 11 ½ inches (24.1 x 29.2 cm); photo: 15 x 20 inches (38.1 x 50.8 cm); courtesy the artist and Alexander and Bonin, New York
21
Emily Jacir, *Where We Come From*, 2001–3 (detail of Munir); American passport, 30 texts, 32 C-prints, 1 video; text: 9 ½ x 11 ½ inches (24.1 x 29.2 cm); photo: 35 x 27 inches (88.9 x 68.6 cm); courtesy the artist and Alexander and Bonin, New York

**No. 22**

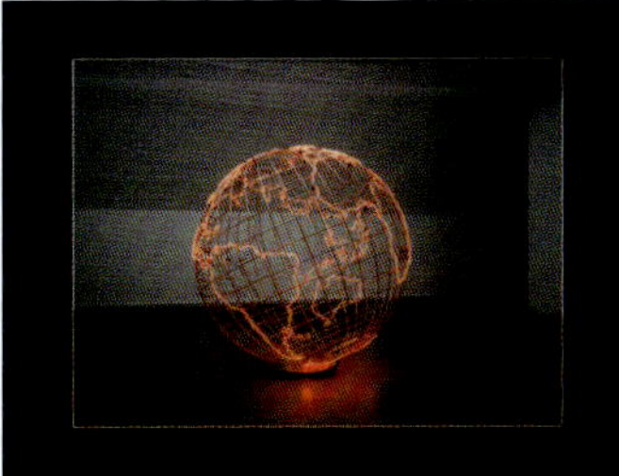

**No. 23**

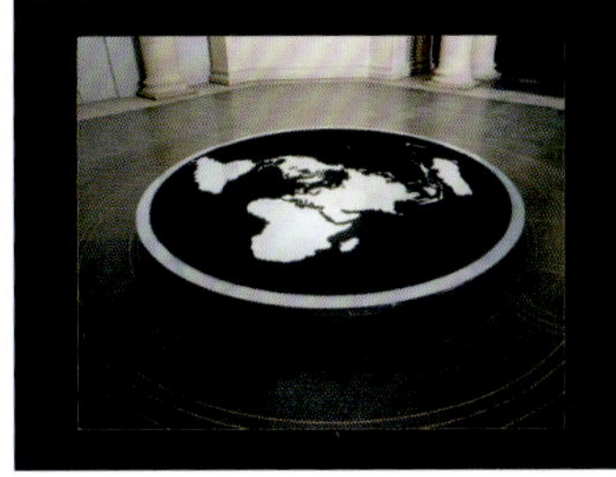

and boundaries. This transformative dislocation is not unlike Toukan's sly refiguring of the Middle East but treats the whole world, rather than a single region, as subject to change and manipulation. Like Toukan, Hatoum explores the ways that maps express conditions of power and conquest through what postcolonial historians call the cartographic gaze. She draws on Michel Foucault's notion of knowledge formation as a "field in which the questions of the human being, consciousness, origin, and the subject emerge, intersect, mingle, and separate off."[20] And as the historian Rehnuma Sazzad has noted, where Foucault nullifies the discursive subject to create a new kind of subject in its void, Hatoum distorts the known contours of the world map in order to replace its design with an imaginative version of her own making.[21] *Continental Drift*, with its shifting shapes and blurred boundaries, allows Hatoum to envision a world that can be configured in new and unpredictable ways, a world where continents and oceans are in a constant state of motion, creating a condition of instability and possibility.

In yet another map, from 1998, presented at the Kunsthalle in Basel, Switzerland, Hatoum used thousands of glass marbles to outline the continents of the world. Her goal was to create, in her words, "something very fragile where as soon as one set foot on the parquet, the marbles on the floor started moving." The map was meant to be menacing and disconcerting. "I like it," Hatoum has said, "when things are attractive and forbidding at the same time; both seductive and dangerous."[22] This tension between the visually compelling and the hazardous energizes the work at the same time that it makes it inherently unstable.

Taken together, these maps can be seen as an intensive effort on Hatoum's part to examine the ways

in which territory is configured and to highlight the degree to which even the most substantial political and geographic entities—countries, continents, oceans, and mountains—lack fixed meanings and boundaries and are subject to perception, change, and interpretation. By emphasizing the paradoxical and the haphazard, and by focusing on conditions of instability, Hatoum's maps present an alternative cartography and can be read in any number of ways—from the highly personal efforts of a Palestinian exile trying to come to grips with her place in space to a conceptual exercise in trying to describe the ways in which the world is rendered visible but abstract through mapping. This interest in the conceptual underpinning of mapping relates Hatoum to a number of artists, but most particularly Alighiero Boetti, whose maps (no. 24), produced by embroiderers in Afghanistan and Pakistan based on a simple set of instructions he provided, reveal how wars and geopolitical and social changes such as the breakup of the Soviet Union and the reunification of Germany reshape national and international boundaries. But where Boetti's maps are a record of the results of wars, liberation movements, and other activities seen over decades, Hatoum's are inevitably a reflection of a more personal sense of place in an ever-changing and unpredictable world. This interest in exploring her place in the world culminates for Hatoum in *Corps étranger* of 1994. By inserting a camera attached to a fiber-optic cable through every orifice in her body, she takes us on an endoscopic journey that literally maps the interior of her body as if it were a foreign territory, tracing its canals, passages, and surfaces. The result is a vivid corporeal topography that serves as a means for Hatoum to foreground her physical presence in the world.

Let me conclude by trying to tease out from the works discussed

22
Mona Hatoum, *Hot Spot*, 2006; stainless steel and neon tube; 90 9/16 x 87 13/16 x 87 13/16 inches (234 x 223 x 223 cm); courtesy Galerie Max Hetzler, Berlin
23
Mona Hatoum, *Continental Drift*, 2000; stainless steel, glass, iron filings, electric motor, timer; 13 x 165 3/8 inches diameter (33 x 420 cm diameter); courtesy White Cube, London

**No. 24**

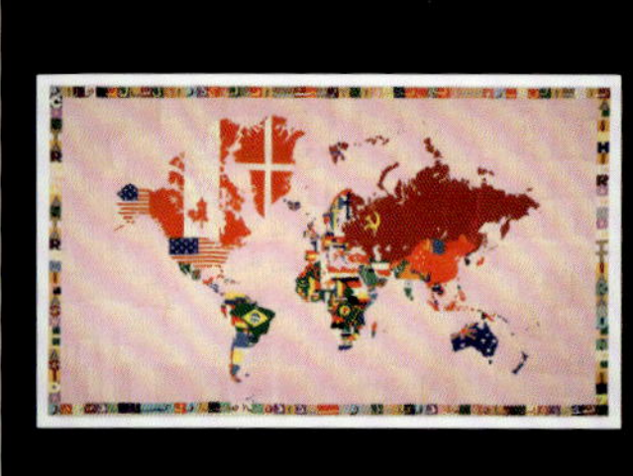

here several general observations about the artists who made them. The first is that all the artists under consideration, no matter where they come from and no matter how invested their practice is in local issues and histories, comfortably use the syntax of what could be called global contemporary art. But while these artists rely on the same visual language and means of production employed by artists elsewhere in the world, they often use strategies of ambiguity, subversion, and occlusion to produce different and unexpected results that relate them to other artists from the Middle East with similar backgrounds. Raad's ambivalent stance toward Lebanon's civil wars, which he documents but does not appear to pass judgment on; Blum's invocation of an impossible history; Toukan's playful reimagining of the Middle East; Jacir's use of wishing to create an alternative history; and Hatoum's paradoxical maps all use preconceived notions about time, space, and history to undermine, question, and ultimately critique them. They seek to destabilize our understanding by using familiar sources of information—like archives, cartography, and documentary photographs or videos—to produce unfamiliar work.

Another quality that relates these artists to one another is the way in which each tries to recover something that has disappeared or been lost: Raad, a history of art; Blum, the history of a forgotten and impossible love affair; Jacir, a history of a dispossessed people; Toukan and Hatoum, a history of contested space. They use several devices to do this: in the case of Raad, Toukan, and Blum, archival and documentary evidence; in the case of Jacir, biographical information; and in that of Hatoum, cartography. Each of these strategies provides a window into a kind of "patahistory," to loosely borrow Alfred Jarry's idea of pataphysics—that is, a history that supposes imaginary

solutions that symbolically attribute the properties of objects or events described by their virtuality to a present context.[23] Such a history involves a high degree of creative license; a complex understanding of the ways in which history is conceived, written, and received; and the ability to manipulate the processes by which we make history.

Central to the positions of these artists is the challenge of engaging and recognizing the past within the moment of the present, especially what might be called the moment of the catastrophic or "black holes," as Andrea Geyer—a young German artist whose work focuses on similar problems, including how traumatic events are processed—has put it, referencing both Walter Benjamin's notion of danger and Jalal Toufic's idea of event horizons.[24] The use of a patahistorical program—as opposed to working with actual archival and documentary evidence, as artists such as Geyer do—may be a consequence, in whole or in part, of the withdrawal of images and traditions in the wake of a surpassing disaster, as Toufic defines it. This is especially true for Raad and Toukan, but it may well be true also for Jacir and Hatoum, if not for Blum. If the catastrophic impact of a disaster occludes or erases tradition or causes a variety of images to withdraw, then artists are compelled to turn to other images or sources, or to invent them wholesale, in order to try to recover or resurrect the tradition and images that have been lost, creating a kind of Möbius strip of possibilities and relationships. Toufic himself acknowledges that this is "a vicious circle: what has to be recorded has been withdrawn, so that, unless it is resurrected, it is going to be overlooked; but in order to accomplish that prerequisite work of resurrection to avert its overlooking, one has initially to have, however minimally, perceived it, that is, countered its withdrawal."[25]

24
Alighiero Boetti, *Mappa*, 1979; embroidery on linen;
51 x 90 1/2 inches (129.5 x 229.9 cm); private collection

This act of resurrection or recovery must then start with a visual vocabulary that is available in order to investigate and retrieve that which is no longer visible. Moreover, as Toufic has noted, artists from areas that have been subject to surpassing disasters—and this is certainly not limited to artists from the Middle East—often end up in another place because they have lost their tradition and must find something to replace it. In the specific case of artists from the Middle East, however, Europe and North America are often places of relocation since it is there, in Toufic's words, that "we can be helped in our resistance by all that we do not receive in developing countries . . . and because we can there meet people who can perceive, read or listen, and genuinely use pre-surpassing disaster art, literature, music and thought without having to resurrect them."[26]

In this context, for some but certainly not all artists who come from areas of surpassing disaster—Lebanon, Palestine, perhaps the entire Middle East as defined by the Sykes-Picot boundaries—living abroad can be seen as a critical part of the process of their resurrection of tradition. The whole idea of exile for these artists may need to be rethought as something more fundamental, a kind of historical essentializing that enables them to engage with other traditions, which in turn enables them to recover their own. This is not to imply a kind of inverted orientalism, constructed and constrained by colonial notions of power and imagination, but rather to suggest that this may be an essential response to catastrophic conditions that have caused traditions to be disrupted if not fully withdrawn. There are, of course, many other reasons, often very compelling, why artists may choose to live outside their homeland—including economic opportunity, freedom of expression, and physical security—but none of these reasons are mutually exclusive, and in the case of artists affected by a surpassing disaster, they may in fact be mutually reinforcing.

This brings us back, then, to where we began, with Walid Raad's *Scratching on Things I Could Disavow*. His project's goal of trying to write a history of art that was either largely erased over the course of much of the twentieth century or, for a variety of reasons, simply never written is an effort to recover a tradition and its images that are

**THIS ACT OF RESURRECTION OR RECOVERY MUST THEN START WITH A VISUAL VOCABULARY THAT IS AVAILABLE IN ORDER TO INVESTIGATE AND RETRIEVE THAT WHICH IS NO LONGER VISIBLE.**

now mostly invisible. Whether this is because of the impact of a surpassing disaster or because the research required for such a history has never been undertaken due to a lack of interest on the part of scholars and critics, or whether it is the result of a willful ignoring of the material, Raad is too clever to say. Instead he poses a kind of riddle and asks us to accompany him as he seeks to unravel this mystery. "I follow the detours I am forced to make," he notes in his description of the project, "as I try to collaborate with a contemporary artist, as I attempt to hail other artists from Lebanon's past, present, and future, and as I attempt to form an image in the present of the sediment and germline of Beirut's visual arts infrastructure, from the only forms, colors, shapes, lines and letters that seem available to me today."[27] While it is too soon to know whether he will succeed in his mission, *Scratching on Things I Could Disavow* gives meaning to a wide body of work by many other artists and situates Toukan, Blum, Jacir, and Hatoum, among others, in the context of an artistic practice in the Middle East whose parameters and history we are only beginning to see and understand.

*Notes*

1. *Jalal Toufic, "The Withdrawal of Tradition Past a Surpassing Disaster" (2009), in* Scratching on Things I Could Disavow: A History of Modern and Contemporary Art in the Arab World, Part 1, Volume 1, Chapter 1 (Beirut: 1992–2005); A Project by Walid Raad *(Los Angeles: REDCAT, 2009).*

2. *Walid Raad, introduction to* Scratching on Things I Could Disavow, *unpaged loose sheet.*

3. *Ibid.*

4. *Ibid.*

5. *Walid Raad, "2(a). / On Walid Sadek's Love Is Blind (Modern Art, Oxford, UK, 2006)," in* Scratching on Things I Could Disavow, *unpaged folded sheet.*

6. *Walid Raad, "Appendix XXVI: Artists" (2009), Galerie Sfeir-Semler, http://www.sfeir-semler.com/last/Raad/Raad2009.htm.*

7. *Walid Raad, "The Atlas Group (1989–2004)" (2009), ibid.*

8. *Walid Raad, "Appendix XVIII: Plates 88–151" (2009), ibid.*

9. *Walid Raad, "About the Fakhouri File," The Atlas Group, http://www.theatlasgroup.org/data/TypeA.html.*

10. *David Frankel, "Walid Raad: Paula Cooper Gallery," Artforum 48 (February 2010): 198–99.*

11. *See Toufic, "Withdrawal of Tradition," 2–3.*

12. *Raad, introduction to* Scratching on Things I Could Disavow, *unpaged loose sheet.*

13. Frankel, "Walid Raad," 198.

14. "The New Middle East," *Darat al Funun: The Khalid Shoman Foundation*, http://www.daratalfunun.org/main/activit/curentl/oraib_toukan/3.htm.

15. Ralph Peters, "Blood Borders: How a Better Middle East Would Look," Armed Forces Journal, *June 2006, http://www.armedforcesjournal.com/2006/06/1833899/.*

16. For a snapshot of Dubai today, see Joshua Hammer, "Good-bye to Dubai," New York Review of Books, August 19, 2010, 50–52.

17. Michael Blum, *Archive:* A Tribute to Safiye Behar, 2005, *Blumology.net*, http://www.blumology.net/safiyebehar.html.

18. Orhan Pamuk, The Museum of Innocence *(New York: Knopf, 2009).*

19. *Ibid.,* 510.

20. Michel Foucault, The Archaeology of Knowledge and the Discourse on Language, *trans. A. M. Sheridan Smith (New York: Vintage, 2010), 16.*

21. *Rehnuma Sazzad, "Hatoum, Said, and Foucault: Resistance through Revealing the Power-Knowledge Nexus?,"* Postcolonial Text 4, *no. 3 (2008): 18–20.*

22. *From an interview with Mona Hatoum conducted by Urs Steiner and Samuel Herzog, originally published in the* Neue Zürcher Zeitung *and republished online at http://en.qantara.de.*

23. *See Alfred Jarry,* Adventures in Pataphysics, *trans. Paul Edwards and Antony Melville (London: Atlas, 2001).*

24. *"Often over the course of time and more often when events are marked by trauma, they tend to create boundaries or black wholes [sic] in which in our imagination they disappear and become clouded, contested by many complicated questions raised around them in the meantime. . . . A most scrupulous historical research, a digging to reach the buried facts, that has to be complemented with the investigation of the present moment, because certain traumas are like black wholes—with an event horizon beyond which we cannot go and return."* Andrea Geyer, e-mail communication with the author, October 10, 2011. *See also* Walter Benjamin, "On the Concept of History," *in* Walter Benjamin: Selected Writings, *vol. 4, 1938–1940 (Cambridge, MA: Belknap Press of Harvard University Press, 2006), and Jalal Toufic,* Over-Sensitivity, *2nd ed. (n.p.: Forthcoming Books, 2009), 131, http://www.jalaltoufic.com/downloads/Jalal_Toufic,_Over_Sensitivity.pdf.*

25. *Toufic, "Withdrawal of Tradition,"* 31.

26. *Ibid.,* 3.

27. *Raad, introduction to* Scratching on Things I Could Disavow, *unpaged loose sheet.*

# NRO DIRECTOR OF SECURITY AND COUNTERINTELLIGENCE NOTE 2008-05

## 23 October 2008

## (U) MISSION GROUND STATION DECLASSIFICATION MANDATORY TRAINING

(U)  The Director, National Reconnaissance Office has decided that all NRO employees are required to complete the MGS Declassification awareness training.

(U)  This requirement applies to all NRO components, employees, and badged contractors.  In deference to the fact this will be made a requirement in the future for acceptance of visit certifications to Mission Ground Stations (MGSs), all affiliated contractors are strongly encouraged to avail themselves to this training as well.

(U)  Effective, 15 October 2008, the "fact" that the NRO has (U) three domestic Mission Ground Stations (MGSs) located near Washington D.C.; Denver, CO; and Las Cruces, NM can be, for the first time, acknowledged as an unclassified fact.  These locations have been renamed and should now be referred to as Aerospace Data Facility, East; Colorado; and Southwest respectively.

(U)  Furthermore, effective this same date, the NRO's "presence" at RAF Menwith Hill (RAFMH), located near Harrogate, United Kingdom and the Joint Defence Facility Pine Gap (JDFPG), located near Alice Springs, Australia, can be acknowledged as an unclassified fact.

(U)  With this change comes a responsibility to stay informed. All employees and affiliates are reminded that you must be aware that program specific information and associations will remain classified and unchanged.

(S//TK//NF)  The Office of Security and Counterintelligence (OS&CI) has provided many different links to access the training/information from a multitude of locations below:

http://www.nrosecurity.npa.gov/mgsdeclassification (NMIS, GWAN)

http://[b)(1)1.4c]mgsdeclassification/ (JWICS)

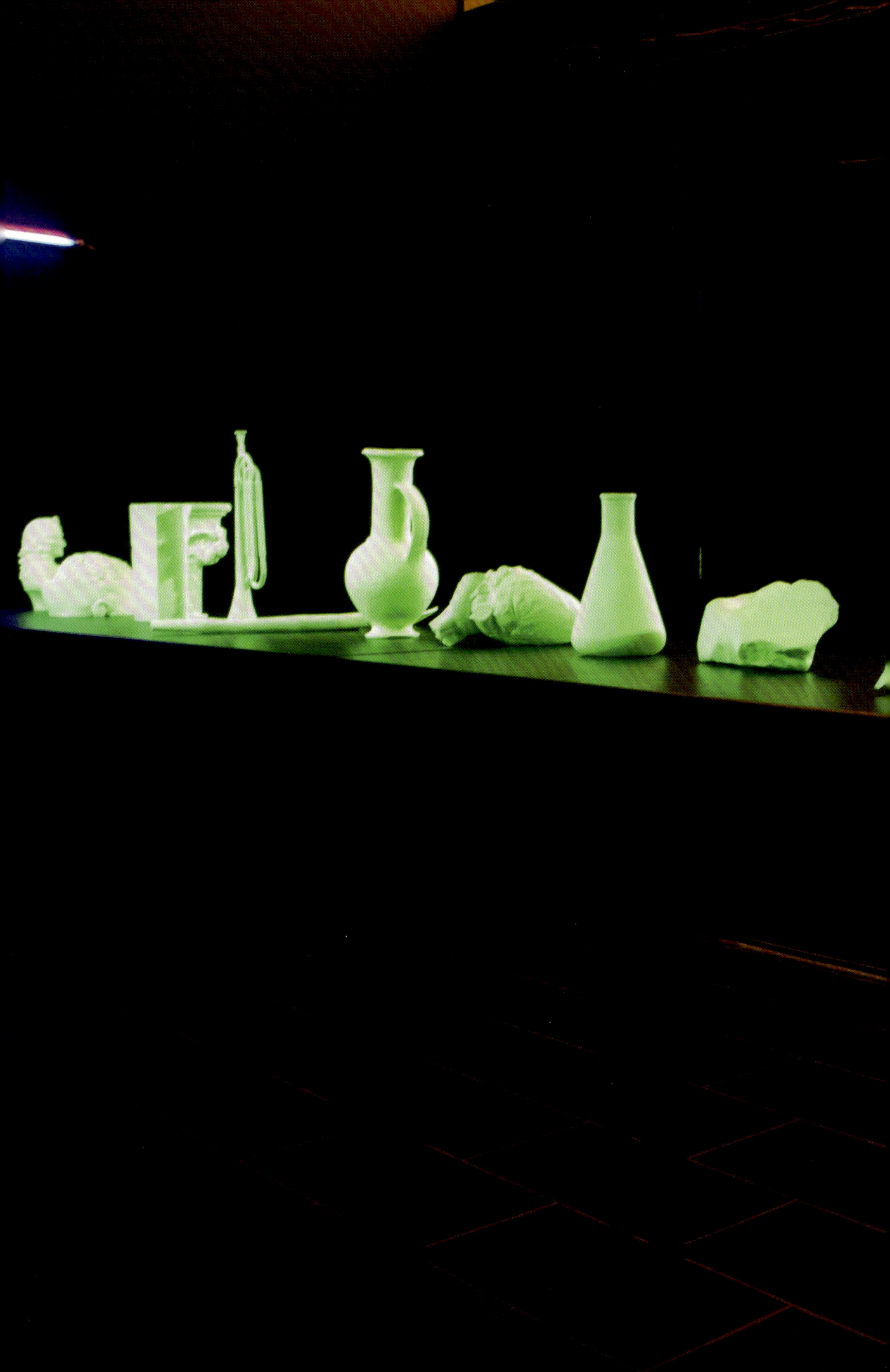

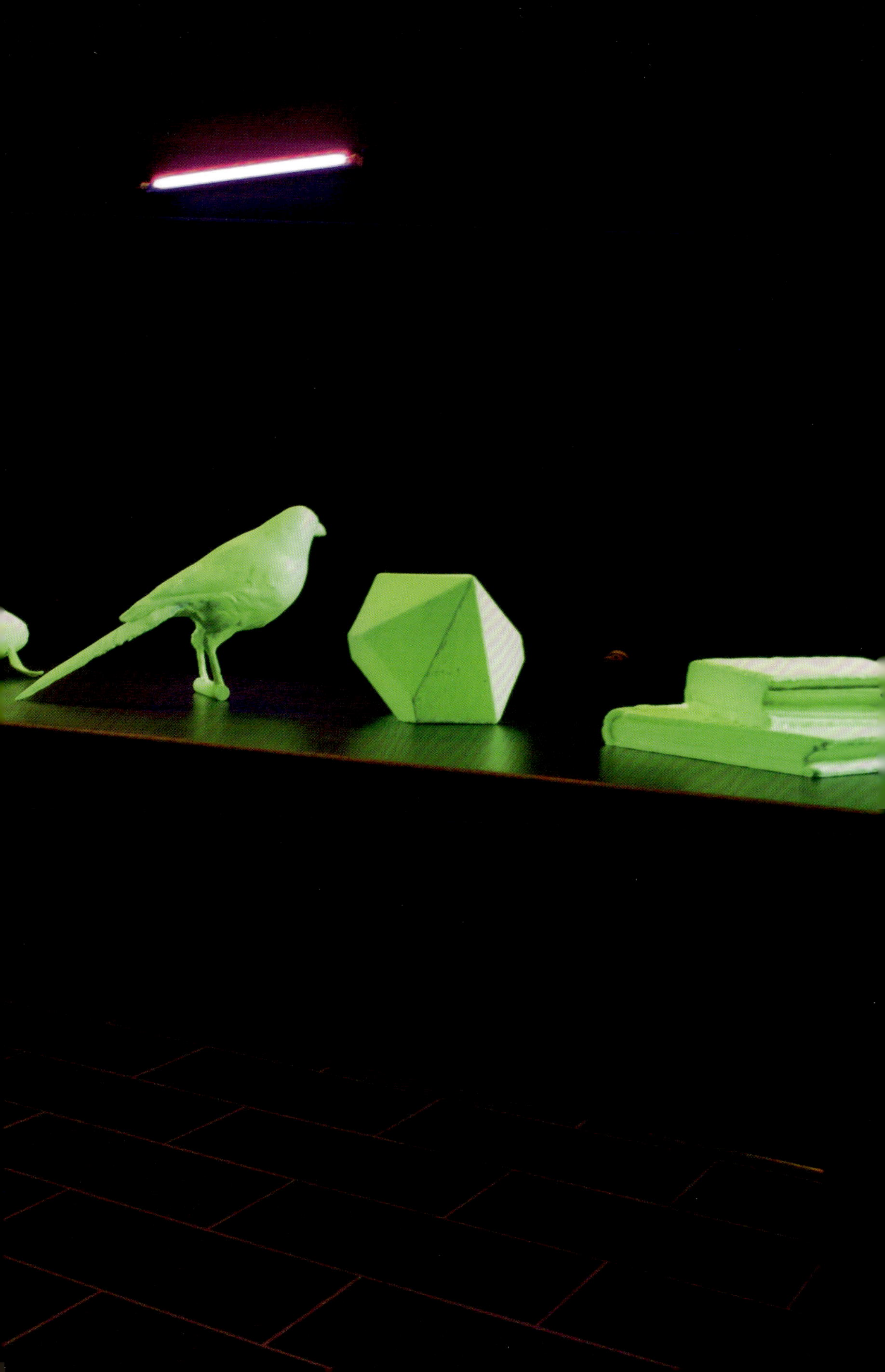

# Truthiness and the More Real

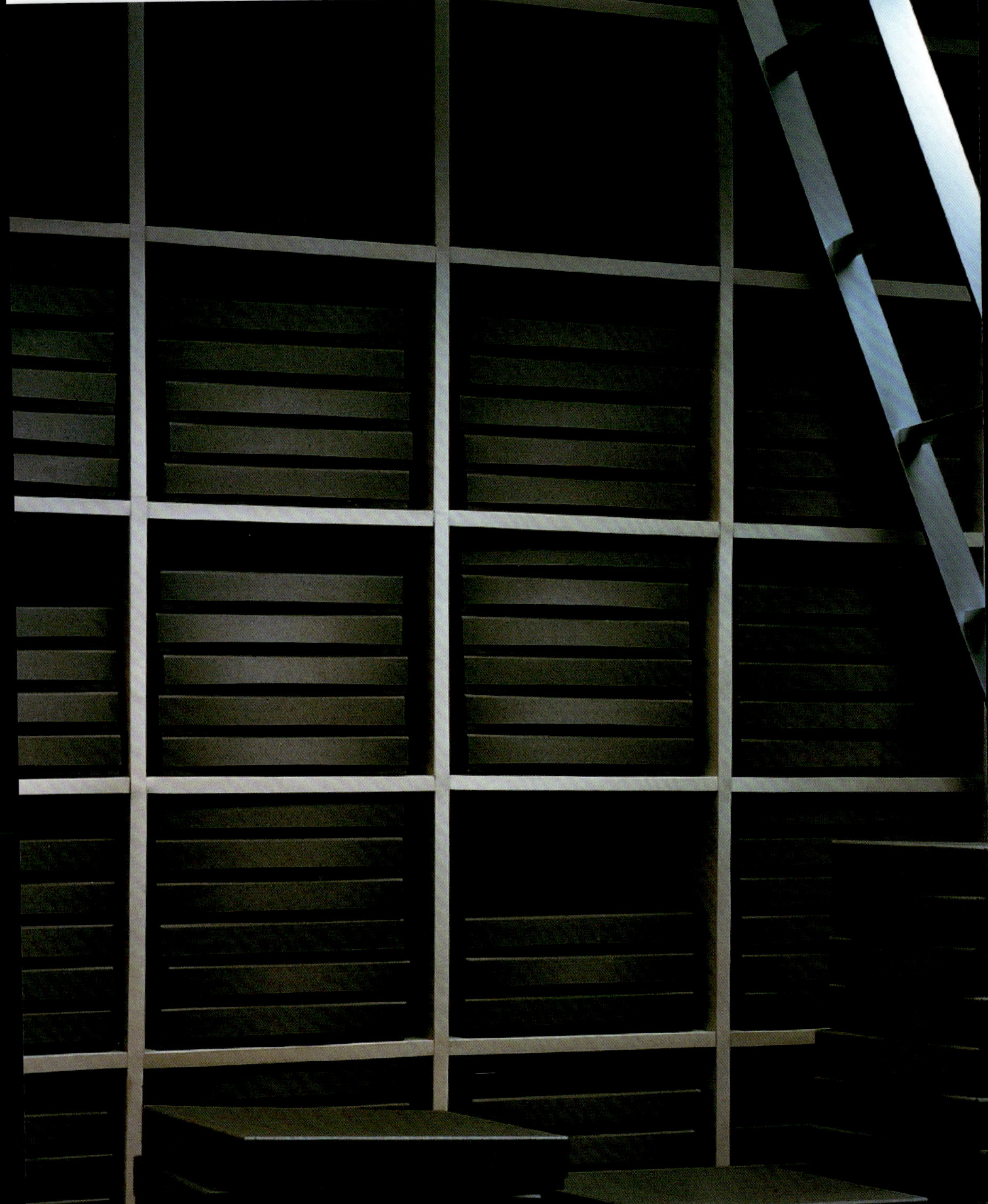

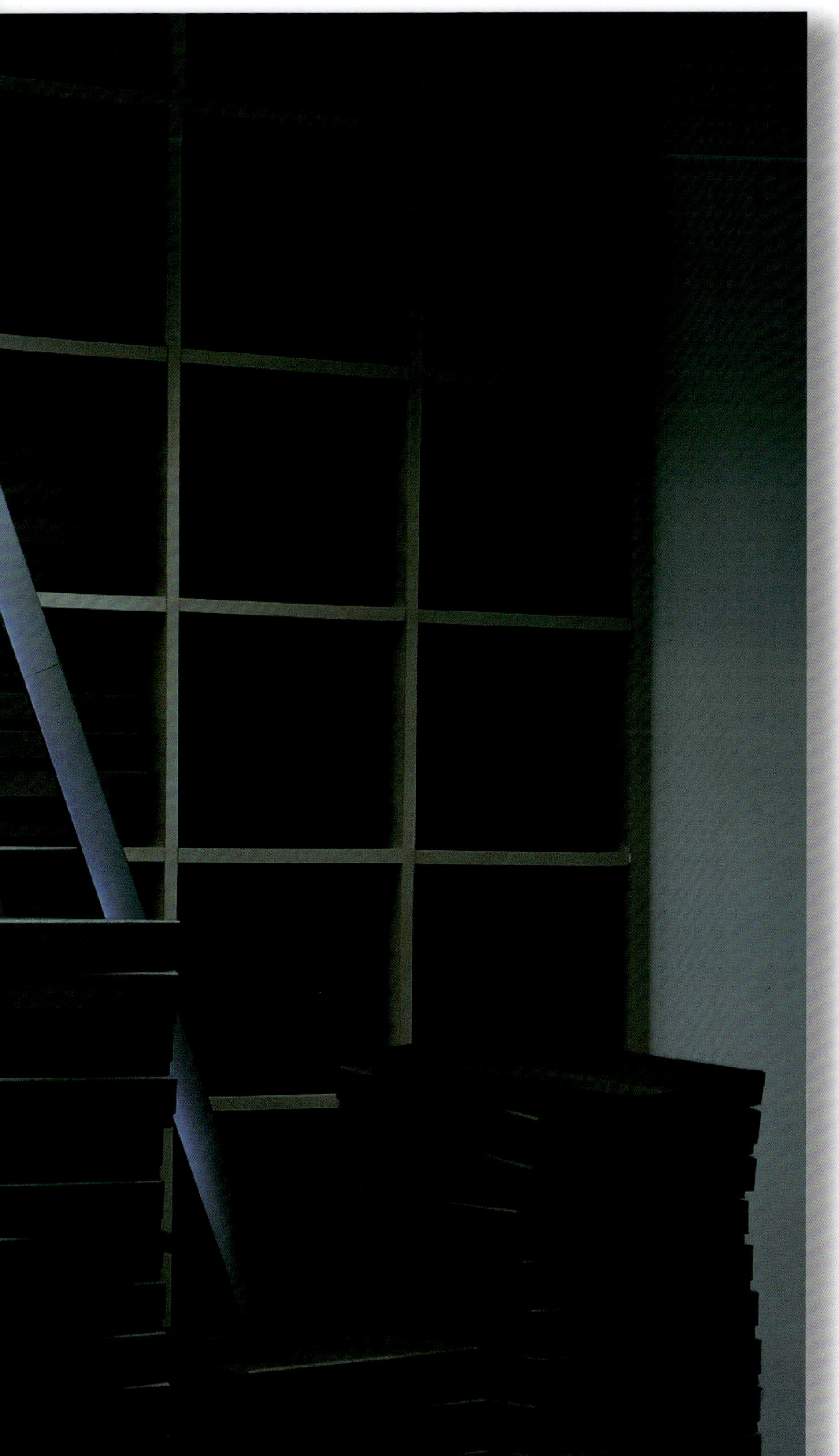

# Truthiness and the More Real: What Is the Difference?

*TEXT BY*

TOM GUNNING

Toward the end of the Great Depression, before the war economy pulled the United States out of its crisis of unemployment and reluctant investment, the poet, journalist, scriptwriter, and movie critic James Agee expressed a desire to get back to the core of things, however unpleasant they might be. The collapse of the US economic system had split open the facades of the American Dream, revealing the harsh injustice of most people's lives and allowing millions to recognize themselves in faces of hardship and poverty. Agee traveled to Alabama with the photographer Walker Evans to live among three sharecropper families. Evans photographed them in images that have become canonized as exemplars of a direct photography whose beauty came from eschewing formal aesthetics in favor of a vision that recalled a direct stare. Agee's prose drew poetry from an inventory of the sharecroppers' daily toil and environment. He foraged through their cabins to examine their meager possessions, even smelling their underwear. The work in words and images that these two men produced sought to fulfill an American obsession that recurs in moments of crisis: to grasp the Real Thing, as Henry David Thoreau had claimed nearly a century before: "I wanted to live deep and suck out all the marrow of life, to live so sturdily and Spartanlike as to put to rout all that was not life, to cut a broad swath and shave close, to drive life into a corner, and reduce it to its lowest terms, and, if it proved to be mean, why then to get the whole and genuine meanness of it, and publish its meanness to the world."[1]

In the early 1980s the artist Sherrie Levine chose Evans's images from his collaboration with Agee, *Let Us Now Praise Famous Men*, for her work of appropriation art, *After Walker Evans* (fig. 1). I remember at the time scrutinizing her rephotography of Evans's image of one of the sharecropper families, trying to discover the alteration that she had performed to make the image her own (was that crutch in the original, or is it collaged in? I wondered), only to discover that I had missed the point. Levine had simply photographed Evans's original photograph, duplicating rather than transforming it, launching a whirlwind of critical discourse about the moral, legal, social, semiotic, and aesthetic implications of this act of appropriation. Agee and Evans strove to seize something real and make us all see it. Four decades later, for Levine, that Real Thing lay beyond our reach and remained simply an object, a photograph.

If for Agee photography offered a means to go beyond words and directly at things, Levine showed that photographs could be as opaque and distant as writing. We stare at their glossy surfaces. Have we lost our faith in portraying the real, in the possibility of images and words delivering contact with the stuff of life to readers and viewers? Are artists simply stuck in a feedback loop, commenting on other artworks, like a pair of mirrors whose echoing reflections generate a bad infinity of mere repetition? Does a reproduction no longer lead us to the thing reproduced but rather draw a veil over it, keeping us at a distance?

In a sense none of this is new. Art since antiquity has often been understood as a trick, a capturing of mere appearance, which stood deceptively in the place of the real thing, a trap for the unwary. In fifth-century Greece, Zeuxis's painting of grapes, rendered with such verisimilitude that birds pecked at them, was outflanked by his rival Parrhasius's painting of a cloth covering his work, which Zeuxis tried to lift in order to see the painting underneath, only to discover that the covering itself *was* the painting, which he had been fooled into taking for a real thing. Art's deceptive similarity, realism understood as a joke on the viewer or a competition between tricksters, forms the basis of Plato's critique of the arts as doubly removed from reality. The craftsman at least makes something that we can use—a bed or a tool—while the painter makes only a bed that we cannot lie in or a snow shovel that cannot shovel snow (or, Duchamp might have asked, can it?). Plato's reality lay in the ideal form, the model that the artisan followed to bring the tool to realization.[2] No idealist, Agee sought a return to the material, the real *stuff* even more than the real thing. Here we encounter a basic split in the pursuit of the real: between an image that reproduces reality through resemblance and something based less in appearance, something that triggers a sensual absorption: an intense experience that overwhelms you.

*IF I COULD DO IT, I'D DO NO WRITING AT ALL HERE. IT WOULD BE PHOTOGRAPHS; THE REST WOULD BE FRAGMENTS OF CLOTH, BITS OF COTTON, LUMPS OF EARTH, RECORDS OF SPEECH, PIECES OF WOOD AND IRON, PHIALS OF ODORS, PLATES OF FOOD AND OF EXCREMENT. BOOKSELLERS WOULD CONSIDER IT QUITE A NOVELTY; CRITICS WOULD MURMUR, YES, BUT IS IT ART; AND I COULD TRUST A MAJORITY OF YOU TO USE IT AS YOU WOULD A PARLOR GAME.*

—JAMES AGEE, *LET US NOW PRAISE FAMOUS MEN*

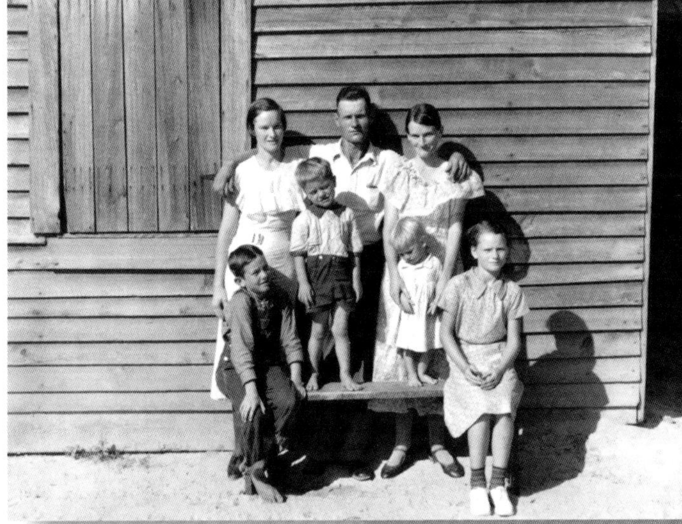

1./ Sherrie Levine, *After Walker Evans: 2*, 1981; gelatin silver print; 3 ¾ x 5 ⁄₁₆ inches (9.6 x 12.8 cm); courtesy Paula Cooper Gallery, New York

I want to move this question about how we make contact with the real thing beyond simple skepticism. Frankly I am skeptical of skepticism. Skeptics assume that as human beings we live at a remove from the truth or the real, that our senses or our language or our media of communication deceive or mislead us and that if we could just get past their distortion we would see things as they really are. The goal then is to achieve total clarity, total transparency. Opinions differ on what means can accomplish this. Descartes claimed that it involved disciplining our minds to methods of certainty attained not through our fallible senses but in mathematics, logic, and a faith that God would never fool us. He imagined that without such certainty we could not be sure that an evil spirit had not enclosed us in a vast illusion in which everything was unreal.[3] Many ideologies—scientific, religious, and political—offer their own version of this myth. Some hold that media, both in the sense of the mass media and in the sense of technologies of communication and presentation that surround us, function today as deceiving spirits. All of us feel the seduction of such conspiracy theories, and I do not deny that aspects of them may be true (we certainly are lied to regularly, and falsehoods proliferate now at the speed of light). But I think making deception the model of how we see the world, and especially of how we make and view art, is itself a pernicious deception, especially since it comes in the guise of dispelling illusion. My counterclaim would be that there are different forms of realism in the arts and media, and that assuming that only transparency can offer a view of the world is frankly wrong. Realism to my mind indicates a breakthrough to a fresh perception of things, a realization that may be difficult, subject to failure, but that is still possible. In an age of rapid transformation and proliferation, media offer new dangers and new promises. Unfortunately the promises and the dangers may be interwoven.

In the late twentieth century the skepticism that has always pursued realism as an art style—does it bring us closer to things through resemblance, or does it move us further from reality through its use of illusion?—cannot be separated

from issues of reproduction and proliferation. Levine did not reproduce Evans's work by "faking it" painstakingly as Han van Meegeren did his forgeries of Vermeer. A camera did the work, producing the image automatically. Further, she did not seek out an original print of the photograph but shot it from a book that had already placed the image in circulation. As theorists of photography have discussed in endless variations, the "original" has no clear meaning in contemporary photography, in which multiple prints are produced from negatives. As Walter Benjamin argued in his famous essay "The Work of Art in the Age of Its Technological

Reproducibility," the photograph in effect killed the aura of the work of art as a singular, unique object. For Benjamin this act liberated art in an era of mass culture, delivering works from private ownership and putting them into circulation, an important step toward the revolutionary goal of getting art off the backs of the masses and putting it in their hands. The unique work of art was limited in space and time, fixed often in

a specific locale. As an object of technological circulation, the artwork becomes unmoored, offering free access, a process constantly made easier by new electronic technologies.[4]

Traditionally realism staked a claim that the artwork asserts an indissoluble bond with the object that it portrays. Photography, with its automatic transfer of a light-born image from the object to the sensitive film stock that registers it, seems to supply such a bond. The object (or the light bouncing off it) caused the photograph; this causal connection is what semiotic theorists of photography call its indexical aspect.[5] But technological reproduction and the radical unmooring of images

that reproduction and circulation accomplish can also complicate the bond between model and copy. Recently critics and theorists have focused on the transformations that digital photography makes possible, especially the ease with which the computerized arrangement (and rearrangement) of pixels can be accomplished. It is now possible, it is claimed, to produce a photograph that appears entirely realistic

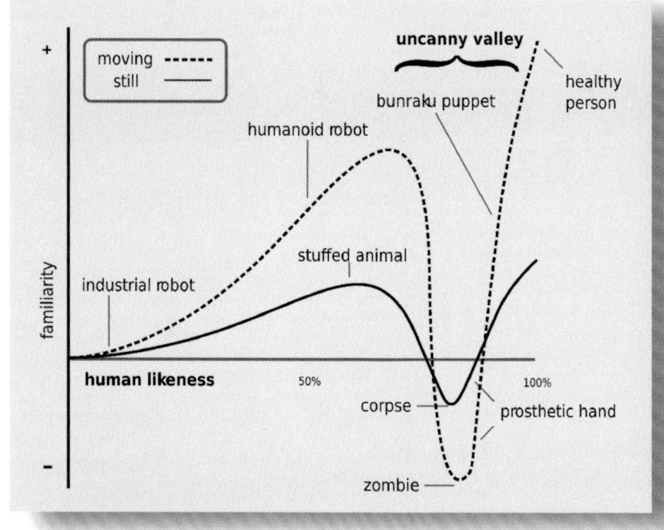


2./ Diagram of the "uncanny valley"

but that differs radically from its original model—or even has no clear model. The faith that we once had in photography—that it documents something that really existed—has either disappeared or been called into question, some claim.[6]

Without denying either the possibility of faking photographs or the importance of the recent digital revolution, I have to point out the inherent flaw of this claim.[7] First, the

actually destroyed the truthful reference assumed for photography, then it would also destroy any possibility of deception. Most faked photographs announce their trickery as either an amusing joke or an exercise in satire, displaying the absurdist contradictions of an unreal photograph without expecting anyone to take it for real.

But if our attitude toward photography as the guarantor of the real

released and allowed to infest and haunt our world, while the original remains abandoned and forgotten. This inversion of the significance of original and reproduction was foreseen more than a century ago, when Oliver Wendell Holmes, inventor of the most popular type of viewer of three-dimensional photographic images, the stereoscope, proclaimed, "Give us a few negatives of a thing worth seeing taken from different points of view and that is all we want of it. Pull it down or burn it up if you please."[8] Rather than distort the original, the photograph threatens to replace it.

Several decades ago, Jean Baudrillard proclaimed the triumph of the simulacrum. His phrase "the precession of the simulacrum" indicated that, contrary to traditional logic, in the world we now live in, the imitation actually comes before the original.[9] Do we think of the real woman who posed for the photograph that we see every day encouraging us

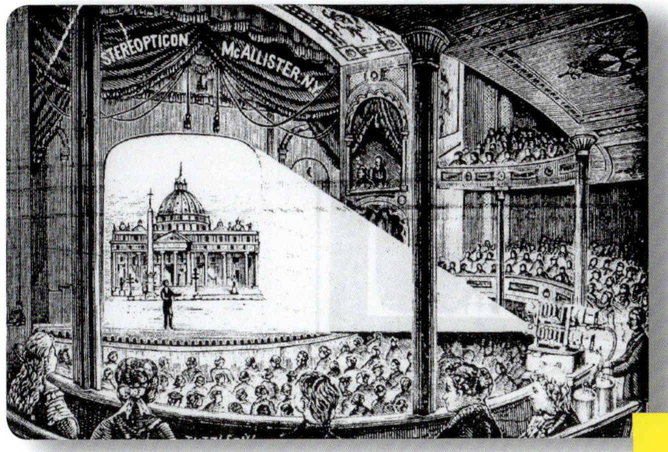


3./ *A Magic Lantern Slide Lecture on St. Peter's Basilica*, 1897; illustration from the December 1897 catalog of T. H. McAllister Company, Manufacturing Opticians, New York

alteration that a digital photograph offers is an option, not a necessity; only a few digital photographs make use of it. That is why we still use digital photographs for passports, driver's licenses, and family albums; they continue to serve us as documents and records of memory. Most photographs still strive for fidelity and accurate resemblance (and cosmetic retouching was a photographic possibility long before digital processes). Rather than the truthfulness of photography and the phoniness of Photoshop being opposites, they actually depend upon each other. No one fakes a photograph unless they want someone to believe it; a forgery or counterfeit depends on an assumption of authority. This is what gives a Photoshopped image its "truthiness." If digital photography

has changed, I believe that it is due less to the ease with which photographs can now be faked than to the omnipresence of the photographic, the proliferation and mass circulation of photographs. They overwhelm our sense of reality—not so much because of their distorted relation to a real original but because of the way they seem to constitute another dimension of our daily lives, as huge photographs loom over us on billboards, slide past us on buses, and glare at us from omnipresent screens. It is less that photographs lie than that they seem unconcerned with capturing any reality. Photographs seem more like specters that the technology of reproduction has

No one fakes a photograph unless they want someone to believe it; a forgery or counterfeit depends on an assumption of authority.

to buy a new brand of toothpaste? If there is such a flesh-and-blood woman, she exists for us simply as part of a process aimed at producing her image in serial form. In our mania for reproduction we place limited value on the original. The world exists under the sway of what Baudrillard, recalling Descartes, calls the "evil demon of images."[10] While Baudrillard articulated a theoretical position that seemed a contradiction in terms (how can the imitation precede its model?), as a sociological observation his statement hardly seems unusual. In an environment saturated with technological images, we all recognize that people often relate to images more frequently than to their sources. Television, video games, DVDs, and, more recently, Skype, videoconferencing, and Facebook all make it possible to interact with simulacra of even the people we know most intimately, as well as those we know only as images (movie stars, TV personalities, politicians). We use digital media daily to communicate not only information but also love, lust, and other emotions. This fact has lost its power to surprise, excite, or infuriate us. Imagistic technological media now function only slightly differently from the way letter writing, telephone calls, or an exchange of snapshots did throughout the twentieth century. Electronic doubles have been absorbed into the habits of our daily life. Now that the novelty of personal uses of video has faded, has the dichotomy between the real thing and its media avatars become taken for granted?

This exhibition may mark the submerging of new media and its simulacra into the ordinary. Has it really transformed our sense of what is real and what is realistic? It does not take a great deal of philosophical analysis to recognize that we normally make contact with reality through mediation, whether language or images. But I would stress that this does not mean that we cannot make contact with reality. Reaching reality means in some sense going out of ourselves, opening up, and

media provides the means for doing this. Media, whether language or images, technological or "natural," are portals rather than barriers (like any portal, of course, they can get

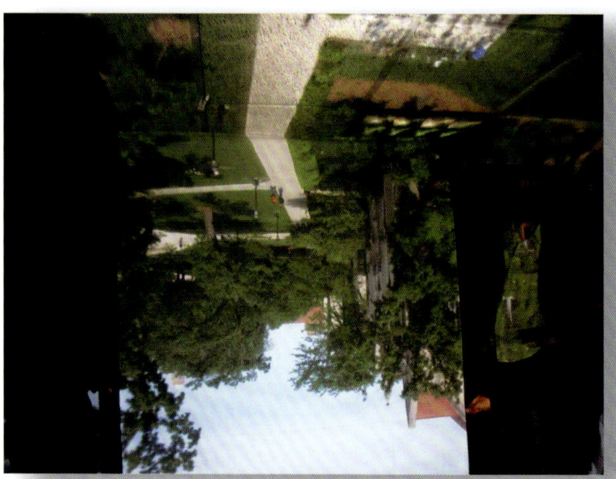

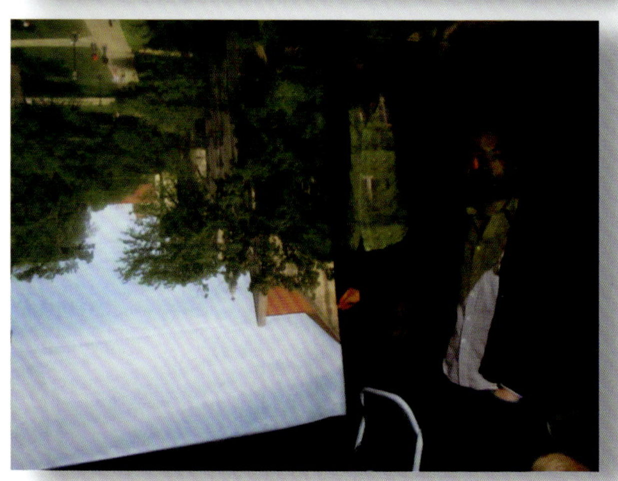

4./ Camera obscura arranged by Rebecca Cummings at the University of Chicago, 2011

jammed, but they exist to give us access). Words and images operate together to make up our world. The greatest illusion that I find operating in contemporary life lies less in the distortions sometimes offered by electronic images and sounds than in imagining a "true" reality that somehow lies beyond our means of representing or experiencing it.[11]

We may often feel divorced from a sense of reality, but mediation is not necessarily the cause of this separation. As the German literary historians Gunter Gebauer and Christoph Wulf say in their history of the concept of mimesis: "The pessimistic thesis advanced by some according to which we are suffering an increasing loss of reality in our culture does not stand up to close examination. It is based on a naïve understanding of what reality is."[12] At points our sense of things becomes opaque, and everything seems distorted. But that is simply the nature of human life, and it can occur as much in a face-to-face argument as over Skype. I am not claiming that there is no difference between the more direct traditional forms of contact and newer technological ones. Every medium, whether technological images or spoken language—or even gesture and touch—can open things up in revelation, close them down in deception, or do both ambiguously. Even a caress can lie. That is how we live—really.

If there is an illusion that appears inherent in modern media (most obviously since photography), it is the illusion of immediacy, the impression that the medium, due to its sensual vividness, has somehow disappeared. The underlying assumption of this position claims that media should not interfere with our view of things, that they can *and should* become transparent, disappear from our consciousness. We might describe this as the assumption of "truthiness," that things should seem "so real" that we don't have to struggle to grasp them. Reality has been delivered to us effortlessly. In contrast, great realist artworks, such as Evans's photographs, do not seem effortless if we truly examine them. Walker Evans brought a level of technical mastery and decision making to his work that is far from simple. One can describe his work as paradoxical, however, since in many ways he does seem to absent himself from our awareness, to get out of our way and allow us to confront the moment in Alabama when the sharecroppers met the camera's gaze.

We confront here both an opportunity and a danger for each viewer. It is the task that Agee set for himself: how do I get at the intensity of reality as an artist, how can I communicate it to you? Evans

seems to derive his technique from the automatic nature of the camera, not in the sense of ease but through allowing the direct stare to rule his seeing. All media simultaneously separate us from reality and connect us. They connect us truly (and this is why Levine's work is not trivial) only if we bear in mind the separation entailed (a condition of all connection but one made less obvious in an era of increasingly

detailed reproduction of visual and acoustic phenomena). The danger lies in believing that we can all be connected automatically. Then the illusion of "truthiness" overwhelms us and we remain truly isolated, closed down in our habits of seeing and thinking, rather than opened up to something new.

Roland Barthes claimed that the category of things that we ordinarily recognize as realistic are simply those that we find most familiar.[13]

> *The traditional understanding of the realistic image roots itself in the seemingly immediate experience of resemblance: the realistic image looks like its model.*

Realism in this sense consists of the circulation and proliferation of things that we barely pay attention to, things that we take for granted. But the Russian formalist Viktor Shklovsky claimed that it is the unfamiliar—or as he put it, things "made strange"—that we truly notice and experience. If we think of the real as the intense, we can see how dynamic the pursuit of a realist style may be. Shklovsky claimed that Tolstoy's realism consisted in making us notice things by approaching them from an unexpected perspective. Shklovsky also realized that we could get used to anything. Thus, far from being a static quality, realist art needs to change constantly, to keep ahead of the tide of habit and familiarity. Defamiliarization, according to Shklovsky, refers not to the unusual or the imaginary but to a renewal of perception, making us see things in a fresh manner.[14] Realist art should make the everyday appear but *vividly*. Technology often plays an important role here, especially new media.

Thus the technical accuracy and fidelity that photography and cinema introduced to media provided only one aspect of their realism. As Shklovsky argued, a desire for intensity and novelty can be congruent with fidelity if it renews our vision of things. Let us consider the process of projection, the optical conveying of an image carried by light onto a surface, as with movies or projected video or even PowerPoint presentations. This technology first emerged as a medium with the magic lantern and the camera obscura in the late sixteenth and early seventeenth centuries, the opening of the modern era (fig. 3). The vividness of colors, the possibility of enlargement, and the inherent fascination of light casting a glowing image into darkness all make projection an intense experience.

As its name implies, the camera obscura consists of a dark chamber into which a small aperture allows light to enter, optically projecting an image onto a surface within the darkness. This image reproduces whatever is outside the camera obscura, provided that it is bright enough. The camera obscura adds to the intensity of a projected image an unparalleled degree of fidelity, since, like the human eye (for which it provides the best model), it draws its light-formed image from the world itself. As I can testify after arranging a camera obscura in my seminar room with the aid of the media artist Rebecca Cummings (fig. 4), the effect of a projected image of even a familiar sight (the room became filled with an inverted glowing view of the University of Chicago quadrangle that lay just outside the window) was astonishing. The camera obscura provided the basis of the photographic camera, which fixes its images on film. The ancestor of the slide projector, the magic lantern displayed images painted on glass, exchanging representation through pictures for the camera obscura's fidelity to a nearby reality. Magic lantern images ranged from pure fantasy, such as the ghosts and goblins of the phantasmagoria shows of the late eighteenth century, to the documentary, such as the photographs of New York slum life projected by the social reformer Jacob Riis at the end of the nineteenth century.

The traditional understanding of the realistic image roots itself in the seemingly immediate experience of resemblance: the realistic image *looks* like its model. But as intuitive as resemblance may seem, it is also multifaceted, dependent on numerous factors. Identifying resemblance with the quasi-scientific concept of fidelity can confuse aesthetic style

with scientific data. Does realism refer to an objective quantification of data or to an act of human perception? Do we trust the intermediary of measurement devices more than our

> ## The human desire to be assured whether one is in the realm of the model or the image outweighs an inherent drive toward an asymptotic approximation of the real.

senses? Does a gauge or a table of numbers resemble the things that it gives information about? This is not to dispute the objectivity of scientific data but rather to point out that art and scientific research have different purposes and methods (even if they influence each other, they are not identical). Conveying the real, as Agee sought to, communicating a vivid experience, may bypass resemblance entirely, relying on the smell of sweat, the taste of cornbread, or the texture of a cotton wad snatched from its prickly boll.

Intensity of experience provides a way to think about realism that avoids either the abstract data of scientific measurement or the reliance on the familiar and already known. Again, projection offers an example,

in this case motion picture projection. As arguably the most realistic medium, cinema can achieve both familiarity and fidelity through the photographic reproduction of moving objects. I claim that it also supplies a supplement of sensual intensity due to projection. In 1923 the Cubist painter Fernand Léger explained his enthusiasm for the film image this way: "The dog that goes by in the street is only noticed. Projected on the screen, it is seen, so much so that the whole audience reacts as if it had discovered the dog."[15] Given the familiarity of dogs in the street, what caused this reaction? In 1923 it may have reflected the novelty of cinema, but I would claim that projection itself, the display of an image with perceptual clarity, even vividness, creates

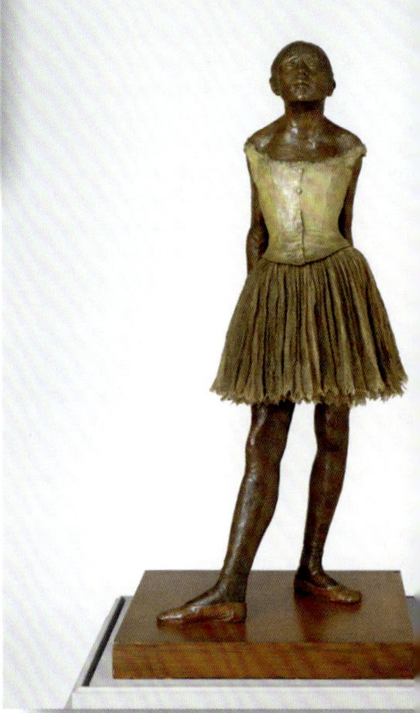

5./ Edgar Degas, *The Little Fourteen-Year-Old Dancer*, executed in 1880, cast in 1922; bronze, partially tinted, with cotton skirt and satin hair-ribbon, wood base; height 39 inches (99.1 cm); The Metropolitan Museum of Art, New York, H. O. Havemeyer Collection, Bequest of Mrs. H. O. Havemeyer (29.100.370)

an experience of the "more than real" that continues to draw our attention and even our fascination.

Our experience of a realistic image comes from several sources and therefore takes a variety of forms. Fidelity and the equivocal concept of resemblance offer one way to think about realism as referring accurately to an existing object. But the effect of the real is also often dependent on our preconceptions, our experience of everyday familiarity ("Yes, that's what a rock star looks like"). Finally I have proposed here a sense of realism that comes from the nearly opposite experience, the intensity of the unfamiliar and novel, or even of rendering the familiar strange.[16] We might claim that familiarity delivers the lulling effect of truthiness ("I have seen that already: therefore it is real and reliable"), while defamiliarization delivers us from this bland assurance and opens us to an intensified experience, to a sense of the "more than real." Someone might object that associating realism with the unfamiliar, the intense, and even the disturbing breaks with our common experience, but that's my point. The real, perhaps especially the "more than real," affects us like a collision. We run up against the real; it has an impact.

At points this impact, far from shoring up our sense of security, challenges it. The standards of good taste that became canonical from the late eighteenth through the nineteenth century, drawing on supposed classical models, actually set strict limits to the degree of resemblance that "good art" was allowed and the topics that it could portray. Thus the realist works of Gustave Flaubert, Edouard Manet, and Emile Zola caused scandals (and even legal prosecutions) and announced the shock aesthetics of an avant-garde. Further, many new media (the photograph, the phonograph) and

genres of popular art (the wax museum, the panorama) were placed beyond the pale of aesthetic value because they were "too real." The wax figure offers a fascinating case. With its fleshy tones and texture, its use of real hair and authenticated costumes and props, the wax museum offered an epitome of realism that proved immensely popular in the nineteenth century.[17] Few art critics considered the wax figure a form of art, however, since it lacked the idealizing force of selective abstraction and celebrated the crass materiality of trompe l'oeil realism. (Edgar Degas's use of wax, hair, and

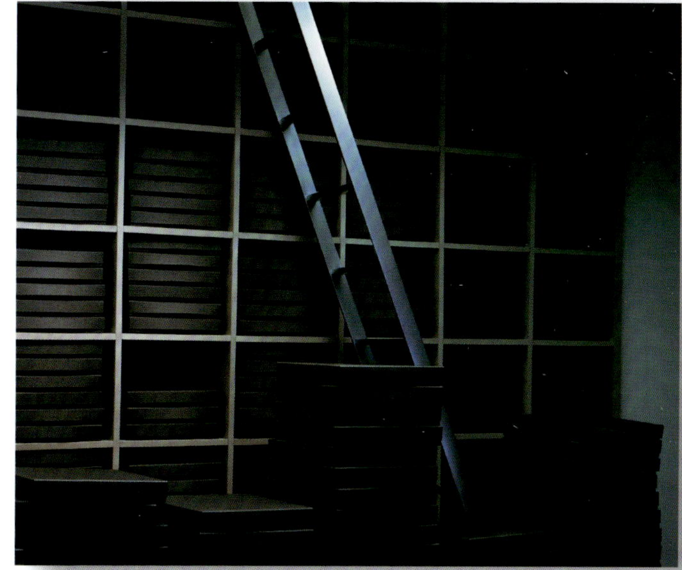

6./ Thomas Demand, *Archiv/Archive*, 1995; C-print/Diasec; 72 1/4 x 91 3/4 inches (183.5 x 233 cm); courtesy of the artist and Matthew Marks Gallery

real tulle in his figure of *The Little Fourteen-Year-Old Dancer* [1880; fig. 5] caused a scandal because it recalled the fairground atmosphere of the wax museum.)

The shocking effect of realist materials may now seem the product of outdated genteel tastes of the last century, but an unexpected proximity to the real still has uncanny

effects. Wax museums remain exiled from aesthetic canons, and when realist polychrome sculptures such as the works of Duane Hanson and Jeff Koons appear in art museums, they remain insulated by effects of irony or satire. Perhaps the clearest example of the uncomfortable effects of realism appears in the concept of the "uncanny valley" in the technology of three-dimensional animation and robot design. Illustrated as a graph, "the uncanny valley" refers to the effect created by the introduction of realist elements into an animated or robotic design (fig. 2). Within a bell curve, the realism reaches a point at

which the viewer finds it frightening, uncanny, or just plain "creepy." Undoubtedly this effect can be at least partly explained through the mixed signals of the artificial blending with the human.[18] This indicates that even intuitive resemblance cannot be reduced simply to a case of less or more; at the point of maximum interference realism actually freaks us out. The human desire to be assured whether one is in the realm of the model or the image outweighs an inherent drive toward an asymptotic approximation of the real.

A dramatic clash between more or less real may in fact take place in the uncanny valley, and the effects of blurring boundaries may trigger reactions that cannot simply be reduced to either verisimilitude or trickery. The photography of Thomas Demand demonstrates how tricky the terrain of this encounter can become (fig. 6). Demand's photography begins with sculptural constructions that he fashions out of paper and cardboard. The constructions exist simply to be photographed, a bit like movie sets designed to be shot from a specific angle. Thus, rather than the photograph documenting a preexisting object, the object's design and actual existence are derived from the fact that it will be photographed. In a sense this exemplifies Baudrillard's "precession of the simulacrum," since the copy predetermines the model. But things are more complex than that in Demand's work. His process confounds the bugaboo of theories of photographic realism, the indexical relation of the photograph to the model. There is a causal relation, of course, between Demand's construction and the photograph he takes (a relation that he removes from our grasp, however, by destroying the construction after it is photographed). Demand doesn't simply render the relation between photograph and reality irrelevant; he makes it kinky and playful. Each of his constructions has a model on which it is based. This model is itself a preexisting photograph, usually one that has been reproduced publicly in a newspaper, journal, or book. Frequently these photographs refer to public events, although often ones with surreptitious aspects,

such as crimes. Perhaps most uncannily, Demand eliminates any human figures that may have appeared in the source photograph from his constructions, presenting us with depopulated tableaux.[19]

*We can use artworks either to deceive or to enlighten. They are media—ways in which we deal with the world—rather than simple re-productions or substitutes or re-presentations of the world.*

Have all people just left the area, we wonder? Or are we in a Platonic world beyond the reaches of human life and touch? Demand bends the referential functions of photographs into a circular merry-go-round. The questions of what a photograph shows and what it leaves out, where it comes from and what it refers to, whirl us through a dizzying cycle. (I once asked Demand if he considered himself a trickster, and he denied it. "But," he added mischievously, "if I were, would I admit it?")

Realism in art cannot be reduced to a logical or scientific process of verification. But if artists are not

scientists, this does not mean that they are unable to give us access to the real world. Perhaps in a different manner than this exhibition intended (although still, I think, in its spirit), I have contrasted the "more real" with "truthiness." The artwork can never be identical to the real, precisely because it is an artwork. But this does not necessarily mean that it is either a deception or an illusion. We can use artworks either to deceive or to enlighten. They are media—ways in which we deal with the world—rather than simple reproductions or substitutes or re-presentations of the world. They lead us to the world, sometimes along devious paths. In contrasting "truthiness" and the "more real," I contrast different ways of experiencing artworks and their relation to the world. By "truthiness," I denote that which seems real because we recognize it, because it doesn't upset our preconceptions. It figures the world as the familiar. It reassures us that reality actually is the way we think it is. By the "more real," in contrast, I refer to the effect that an artwork has of making us notice something, see it afresh, discover new aspects, and desire to examine it more closely. It makes us rethink our notions of the world. Although I think that artists shape their works in order to achieve one effect or the other, I would not deny that the same artwork can trigger opposite responses in different viewers. The point is that the real is something we have to struggle for but not because we are inherently trapped in illusions, as prisoners of our fallible senses, the inadequacies of language, or the deceit of images. Rather than creating a myth of an unattainable reality, art reminds us that the world itself is complex and multifaceted. Art is one way that we grasp it.

*Notes*

Epigraph: James Agee and Walker Evans, *Let Us Now Praise Famous Men* (Boston: Houghton Mifflin, 1960), 13.

1. Henry David Thoreau, *Walden* (New York: W. W. Norton, 1966), 66. See also Miles Orvell, *The Real Thing: Imitation and Authenticity in American Culture, 1880–1940* (Chapel Hill: University of North Carolina Press, 1989), for an insightful account of the American drive for authenticity.

2. Plato, *The Republic*. Plato's discussion of mimesis, the representation of reality, spreads over books 2 and 3. A particularly good summary of Platonic notions of imitation can be found in Gunter Gebauer and Christoph Wulf, *Mimesis: Culture, Art, Society* (Berkeley: University of California Press, 1995), 31–52.

3. Descartes, *Meditations on First Philosophy*, especially the Second Meditation, in *The Philosophical Writings of Descartes*, vol. 2 (Cambridge: Cambridge University Press, 1984), 16–23.

4. Walter Benjamin, "The Work of Art in the Age of Its Technological Reproducibility" (second version), in *Selected Writings*, vol. 3, *1935–38*, ed. Howard Eiland and Michael W. Jennings (Cambridge, MA: Belknap Press of Harvard University Press, 2002), 101–33.

5. Perhaps the most impassioned argument for the photograph as corresponding to Peirce's semiotic term the *index* appears in Rosalind Krauss's two-part essay "Notes on the Index," in *The Originality of the Avant-garde and Other Modernist Myths* (Cambridge, MA: MIT Press, 1986), 196–220. See as well Charles Sanders Peirce, *Peirce on Signs* (Chapel Hill: University of North Carolina Press, 1991).

6. William J. Mitchell, *The Reconfigured Eye: Visual Truth in the Post-Photographic Era* (Cambridge, MA: MIT Press, 1992).

7. I have discussed this in my essay "What's the Point of an Index? Or Faking Photographs," in *Still/Moving: Between Cinema and Photography*, ed. Karen Beckman and Jean Ma (Durham, NC: Duke University Press, 2008), 23–40.

8. Oliver Wendell Holmes, "The Stereoscope and the Stereograph," in *Classic Essays on Photography*, ed. Alan Trachtenberg (New Haven, CT: Leete's Island Books, 1980), 80.

9. Jean Baudrillard, "The Precession of Simulacra," in *Simulations*, trans. Paul Foss, Paul Patton, and Philip Beitchman (New York: Semiotext(e), 1983), 1–79.

10. Jean Baudrillard, *The Evil Demon of Images* (Sydney, Australia: Power Institute of Fine Arts, University of Sydney, 1987).

11. The Kantian positing of noumenon beyond human experience cannot have relevance to representation, since by definition noumenon cannot be represented; nor is it relevant to our sensual apprehension of things, since those belong strictly to the realm of phenomena. Jacques Lacan's claim that what he calls "the real" is beyond representation is also different from the position that I criticize here, since it does not refer to reality as our awareness of things. For a treatment of this Lacanian "real" in relation to contemporary art, see Hal Foster, "The Return of the Real," in *The Return of the Real: The Avant-garde at the End of the Century* (Cambridge, MA: MIT Press, 1996), 127–68.

12. Gebauer and Wulf, *Mimesis*, 320.

13. Roland Barthes, "The Reality Effect," in *The Rustle of Language*, trans. Richard Howard (Berkeley: University of California Press, 1989), 141–49. See also Barthes, S/Z, trans. Richard Miller (New York: Hill & Wang, 1974).

14. Victor Shklovsky, "Art as Device," in *Theory of Prose*, trans. Benjamin Sher (Elmwood Park, IL: Dalkey Archive Press, 1990), 1–14.

15. Fernand Léger, "A Critical Essay on the Plastic Value of Abel Gance's Film *The Wheel* (1922)," in *Functions of Painting*, ed. Edward F. Fry, trans. Alexandra Anderson (New York: Viking, 1973), 22.

16. Perhaps the most original recent treatment of the art of deception, Michael Leja's *Looking Askance: Skepticism and American Art from Eakins to Duchamp* (Berkeley: University of California Press, 2004), 84, comes up with a similar pair of opposing ways to think of realism:
*Nelson Goodman has argued that the realism perceived in a picture arises not from the quantity of information provided but from the ease with which it is read. According to this interpretation, the more stereotypical and familiar the conceptual classification and modes of representation that generate an image, the more natural and true it seems. In other words, we should understand realism as a phenomenon in which learned codes are matched so closely that communication is transparent. But if that description accurately explains the realism operating in, say, stock photography, it does not account for realisms that belong rather to the tradition that stakes its claim to truth on calculated departures from familiar modes of seeing and knowing. Such departures present themselves as signs that mere conventions have been left behind in pursuit of a more accurate matching of experience. That happens especially when established codes have lost some credibility.*
I would add that this occurs as well with radical development of new media.

17. On the wax museum, see Vanessa Schwartz, *Spectacular Realities: Early Mass Culture in Fin-de-Siècle Paris* (Berkeley: University of California Press, 1998), and Mark B. Sandberg, *Living Pictures, Missing Persons: Mannequins, Museums, and Modernity* (Princeton, NJ: Princeton University Press, 2003).

18. The "uncanny valley" is best illustrated through the video clips posted on YouTube. One graph of its effects appears in Jim Blascovich and Jeremy Bailenson, *Infinite Reality: Avatars, Eternal Life, New Worlds, and the Dawn of the Virtual Revolution* (New York: William Morrow, 2011), 78.

19. Demand's photographs are reproduced and discussed in Roxanna Marcoci, *Thomas Demand* (New York: Museum of Modern Art, 2005). See also my essay "Thomas Demand and the Trick of Space and Time," in *Cámara: Thomas Demand*, ed. Sergio Mah (Madrid: Fundación Telefónica, 2008), 27–36.

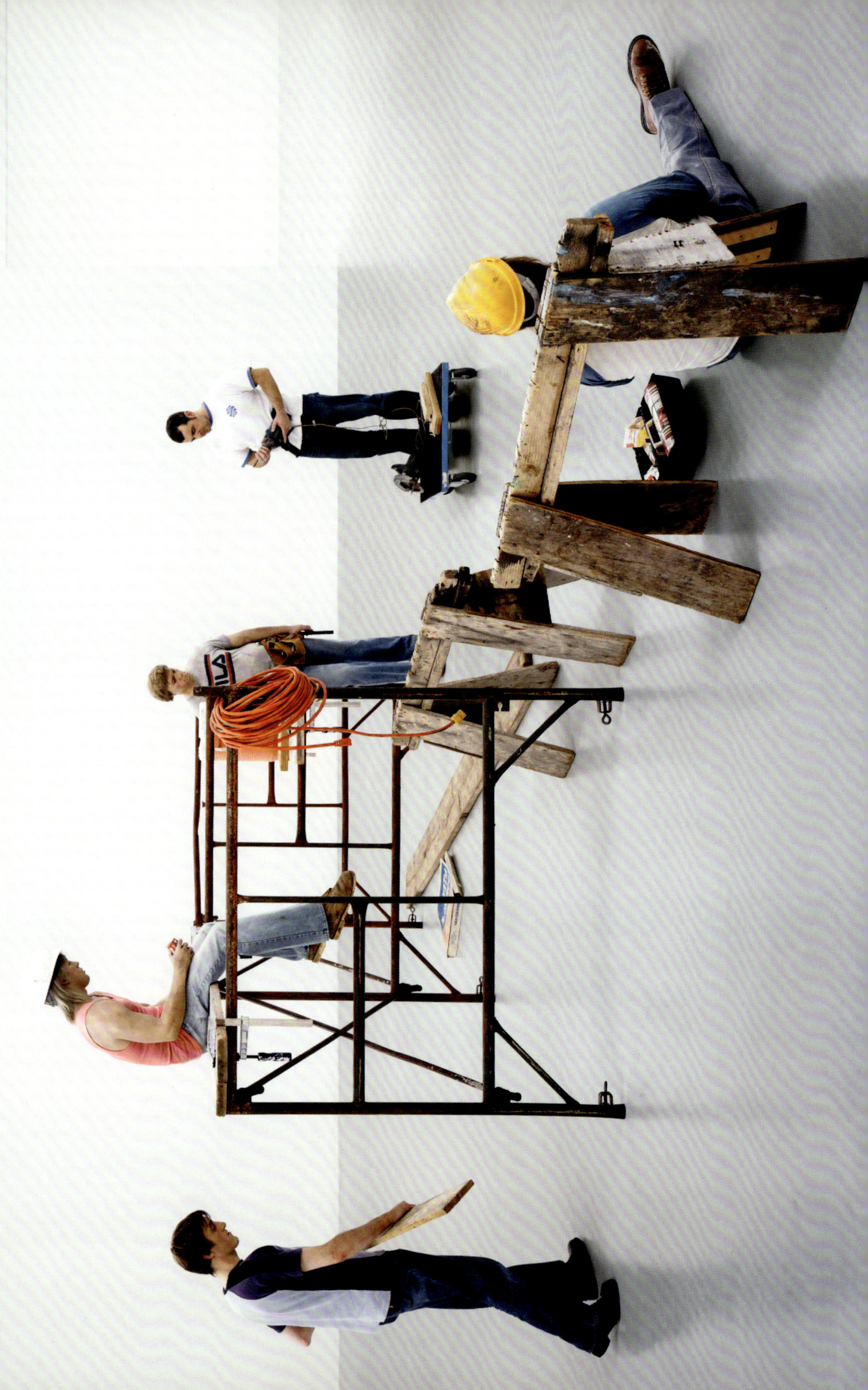

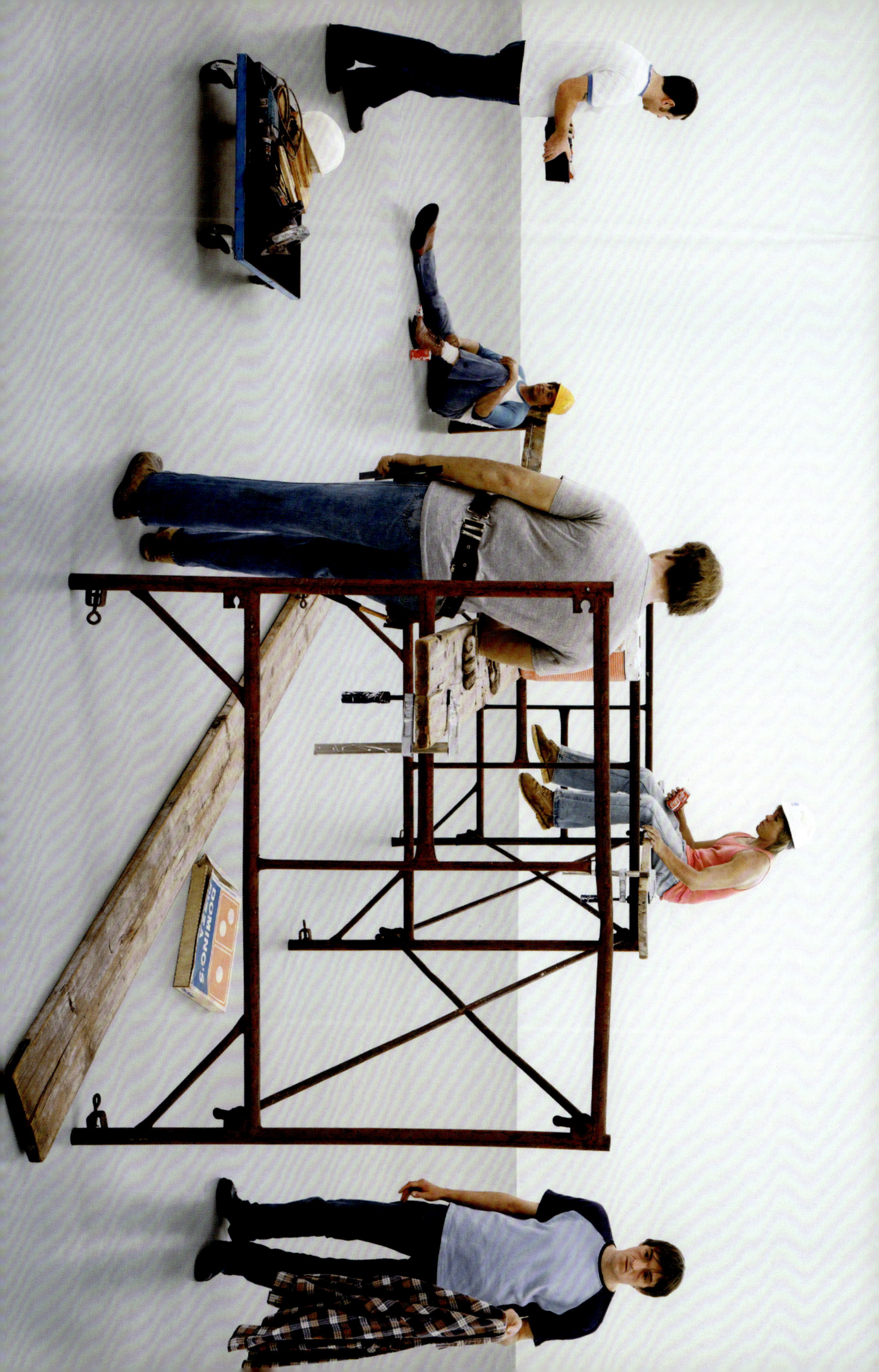

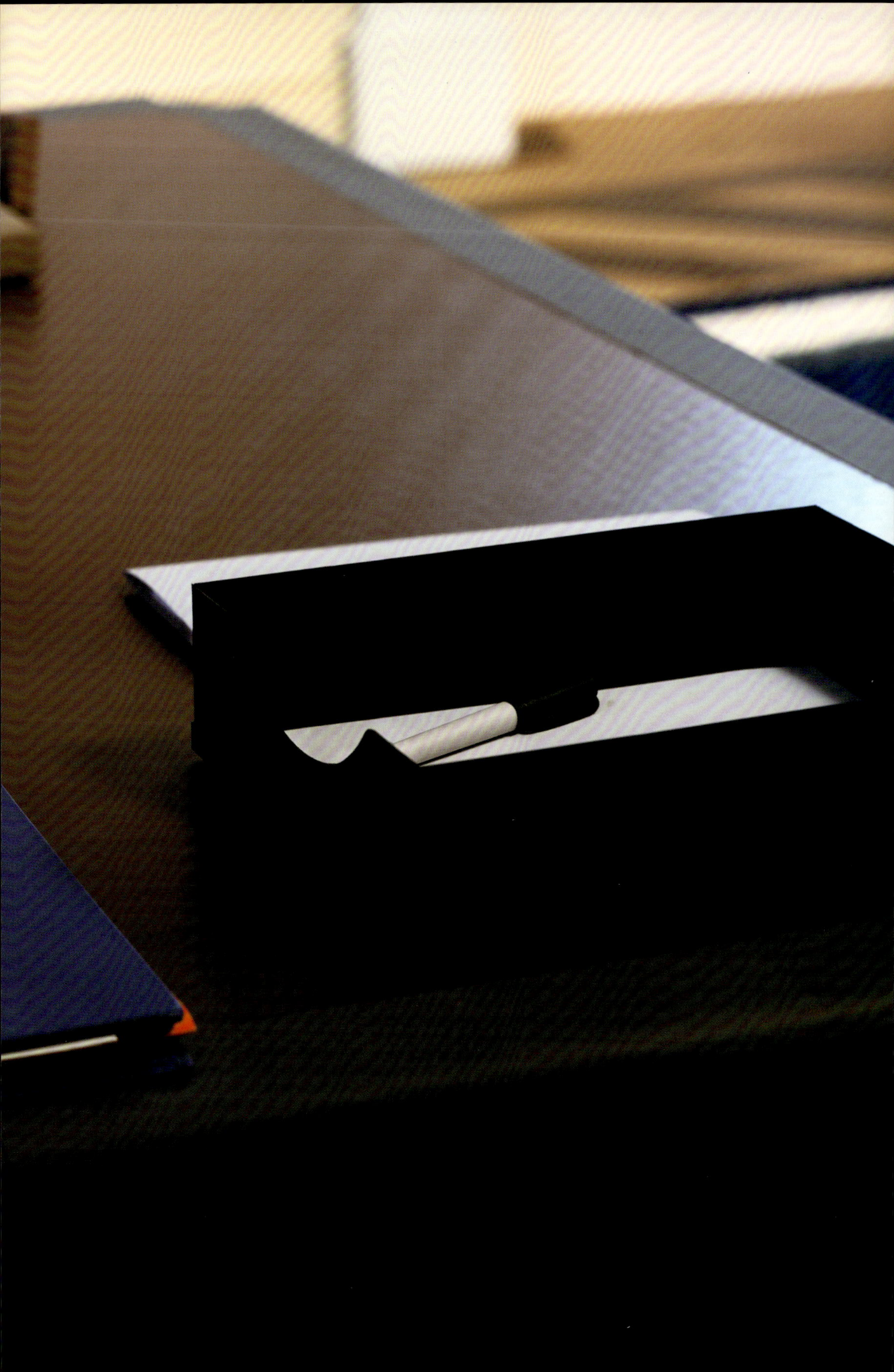

# In Lies Begin Responsibilities

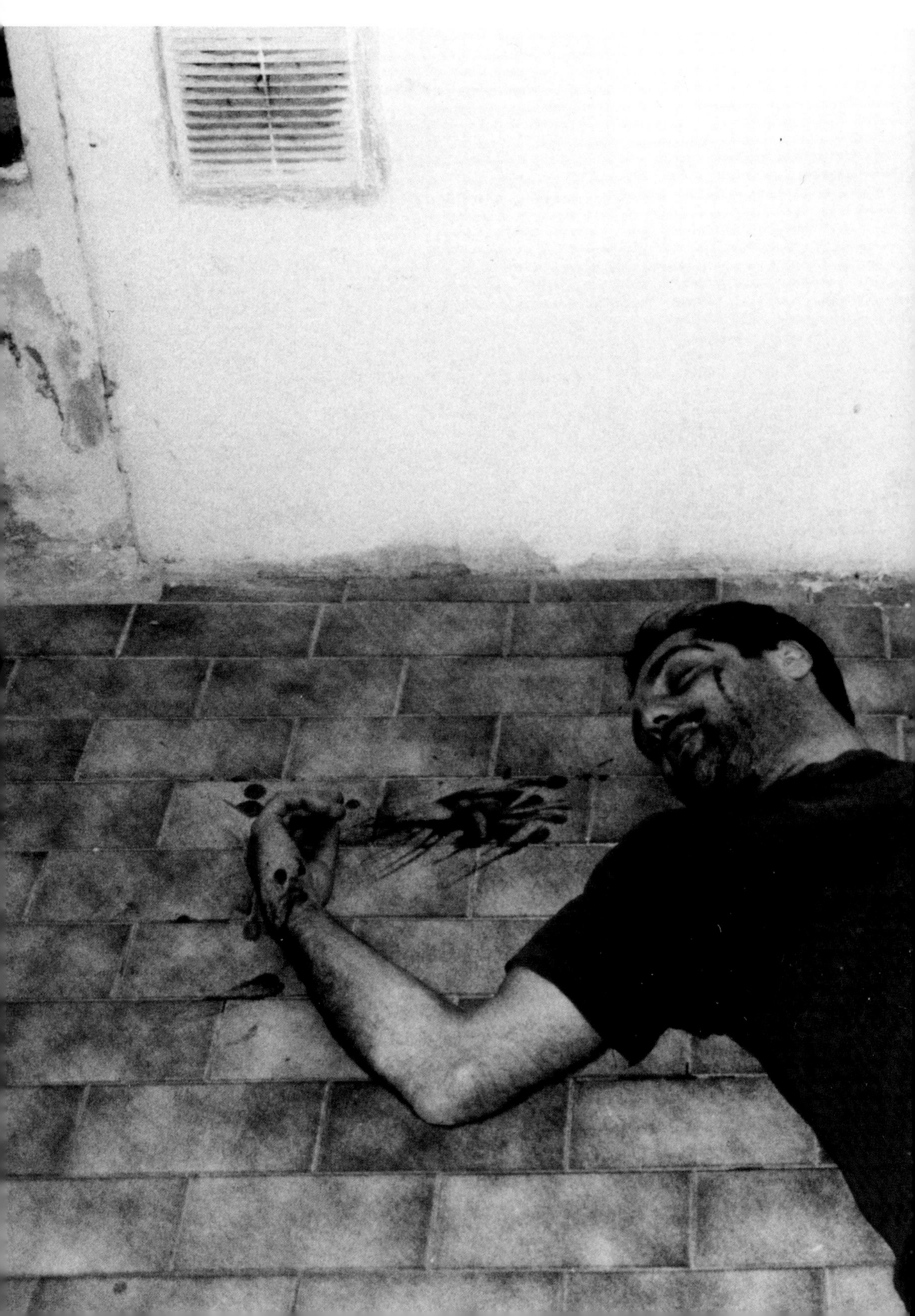

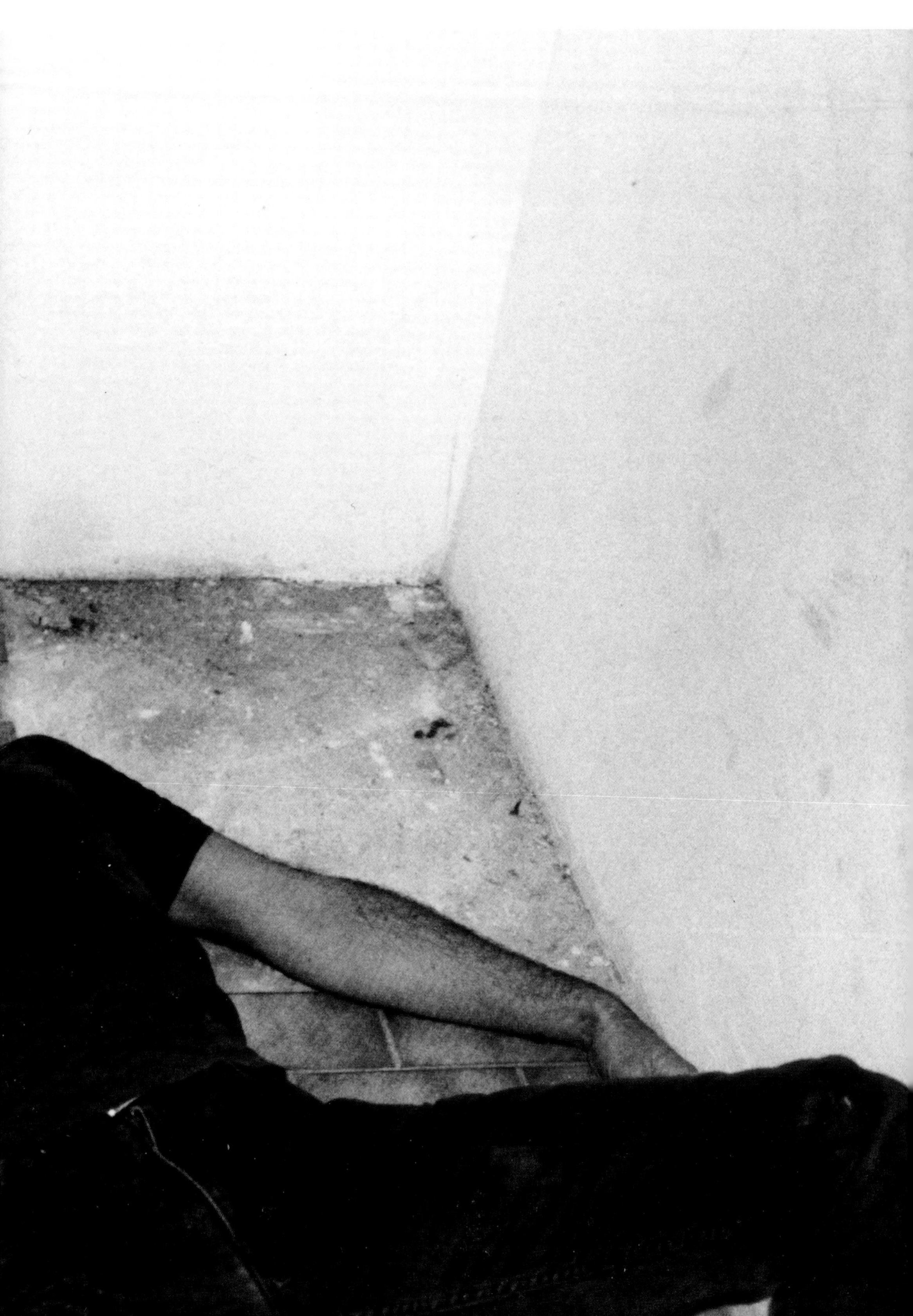

# In Lies Begin Responsibilities

*TEXT BY*

## D. GRAHAM BURNETT

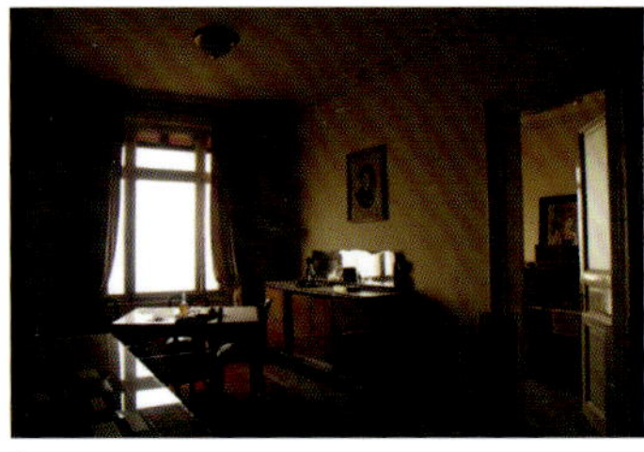

1

In the spring of 2010 I participated in a rip-roaring conference in Berlin on the history of rationality. The brief for our gathering? To sort out, if we could, how a capaciously Kantian conception of "reason" (think of that late Enlightenment confidence in the socially embedded powers of the human mind) wandered across to the peculiarly mechanistic, algorithmic notion of "rationality" familiar to any student of the social sciences in the second half of the twentieth century: the counting-house calculus of a monadic self-maximizer, that cruel little Machiavelli posited by game theory and evolutionary biology alike. How in the world did we all get from such a deliciously robust ideal of cognition to such a strangely calculating creature? How did so many of us come to think about so much of thinking as something like the navigation of infinite topologies of savage self-interest?[1]

Across three days we reviewed a lineup of plausible suspects: Darwinism, the Turing machine, psychoanalysis, exobiology, Cold War nuclear strategy, macroeconomic modeling, cybernetics, and so on. I was pretty jet-lagged, but I stayed with things and gradually persuaded myself that there was a logic to the emergence of such a depauperate logic across a century that saw so much scorched earth.

Scorched earth had been much on my mind that year, since I had been collaborating with the artist Lisa Young on a film project that dealt with the strategic bombing campaigns of World War II. *Free Fall: The Life and Times of Bud "Crosshairs" MacGinitie* was a somewhat unusual undertaking from the start. Presented as a video *éloge* for a fallen bombardier-veteran, the film wove together documentary footage and factual information about changing bombsights and aviation physiology in the 1940s, 1950s, and 1960s. The armature of the story, however, lay in the obituary of an invented character whose psychospiritual displacements in the aftermath of World War II were intended to represent an argument about the origins of the

characteristically sadomasochistic scientific research practices of the Cold War. In a number of ways the film—a false history, a braiding of truth and lies—was centrally concerned with changing ideas about rationality and self-interest across the very years at issue in the conference.

But sitting in the handsome seminar room of the Max-Planck-Institut für Wissenschaftsgeschichte, I grew increasingly uneasy about mentioning the project. After all, I was among scholars—my esteemed colleagues. Disciplined thinkers each. And

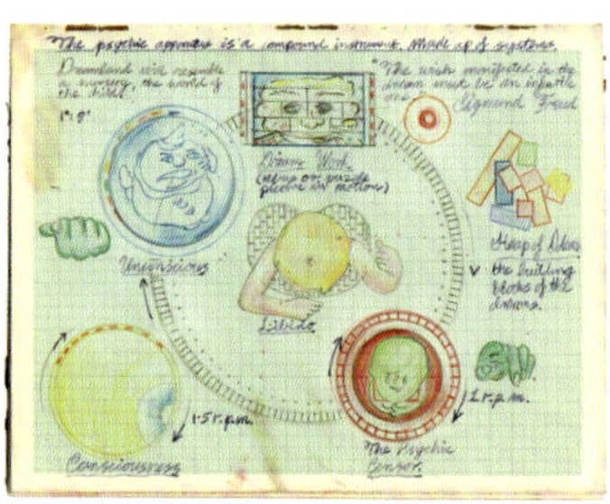

2

honorable types. The very flower of the academy: professional inquirers, bound to demanding canons of proof, evidence, and transparency. How would they react to the discovery that I had taken to confecting history, playing on the border of the real, conjuring invented pasts? I had my misgivings. Perhaps better to feel out a few of them privately on this difficult matter of history and fiction, art and knowledge production.

The result was, in a number of ways, a watershed conversation for me. Over bowls of *raita* and *dal* in an Indian restaurant that evening, I found myself toe to toe with a pair of older scholars for whom I had the utmost regard: one an American-born historian of probability theory based in Germany, the other a Swiss historian of neuroscience. The subject: the increasing prevalence of research-based artistic practices that mobilized disorienting tactics of illusion and/or

1. Michael Blum, *A Tribute to Safiye Behar*, 2005; installation; courtesy the artist

2. Plan for "Dreamland," a Freudian theme park by Albert Grass, 1930; colored pencil on graph paper; 8 x 10 1/2 inches (20.3 x 26.7 cm); courtesy Zoe Beloff (2009)

3. "The Garden of Eden on Wheels," installation view, Museum of Jurassic Technology, Los Angeles; courtesy Museum of Jurassic Technology

4. Goldin+Senneby, *Each thing seen is the parody of another or is the same thing in a deceptive form*, talk at London Zoo with Angus Cameron, spokesperson of Goldin+Senneby; produced for Gasworks, London, 2010

5. Goldin+Senneby, *Headless: Each thing seen is the parody of another or is the same thing in a deceptive form*; with Angus Cameron (economic geographer), K.D. (fictional author), Anna Heymowska (set designer), Johan Hjerpe (graphic designer), Kerwin Rolland (sound designer); installation view, Moderna Museet, Stockholm, 2010

6. Still from Orson Welles's film *F for Fake*, 1973

7. Eva and Franco Mattes aka 010010111010110111.ORG, *Darko Maver Dead*, 1999; courtesy the artists

deception, the rise of the very art world represented in *More Real? Art in the Age of Truthiness*. I mostly kept my own experimental appetites off the table, sketching instead the genealogy of artists and artworks familiar to readers of Carrie Lambert-Beatty's stimulating essay "Make-Believe: Parafiction and Plausibility."[2] I talked about Walid Raad. I talked about Zoe Beloff. I talked about Michael Blum. I talked about work of this sort that we had published in *Cabinet* in recent years. Above all, I tried to emphasize the powerful way that, for me, the best of these works reimagined the historical imagination and teasingly tested the traditional distancing modes of critical inquiry. This was, I argued, a kind of Dionysian historicism—scholarship not afraid to mingle promiscuously with its subject matter, a fearlessly exuberant, postpositivist ethnography of our usable past. And I tested my claim that this work could be understood not merely as a brave new world of postmodern anything-goes-ism but rather as the reanimation of a number of significant premodern historical practices.[3]

Nothing doing. I met a bracingly cold and refreshingly serious "no." Both my interlocutors voiced a clear and forceful concern about the tendencies that they perceived in this body of work, with which they were by no means unfamiliar. In a world weathering an unprecedented destabilization of traditional forms of textual authority and historical documentation, the aestheticization of disorientation by the intelligentsia could be understood only as a *trahison des clercs* of the worst sort. Sure, it was all fun and games when the Museum of Jurassic Technology parodically undermined the apodictic semiotics of the museum. But a decade or two later those lessons had been returned to us with interest in this or that "museum of creation science." And the forging of historical documentation might offer a certain frisson on the biennial circuit, but what about George W. Bush's military records? Didn't we need to see them? And know that they were real? Could a free and democratic polity survive the proliferation of technologies (from Photoshop to Dreamweaver)

that allowed each of us to make and inhabit imagined histories?

I was not exactly persuaded by their jeremiads. But I was wobbled. These were not reactionary types. They were elastic and progressive thinkers, deeply learned individuals who were committed to the arts, to scholarship, and to politics. They knew their history, to be sure, but there was nothing fusty about their perspective. They were thinking about the present and the future—and they did not like what they saw in the swampy region lying at the anastomosing tributaries of the really real and the finely fictive.

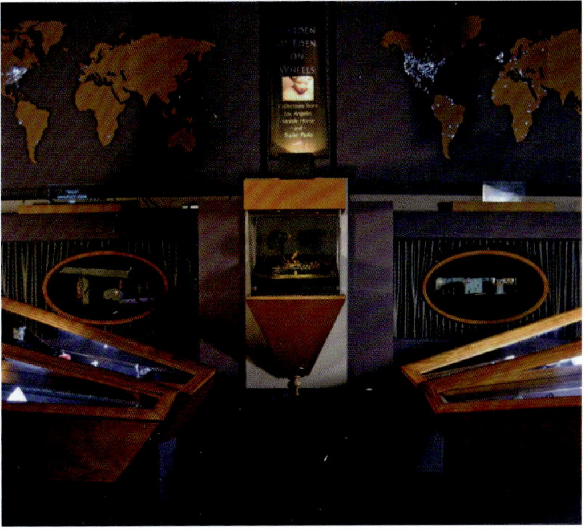

3

On the flight back to New York, I set to the task of putting my mental house back in order: No reason to get excessively concerned. Probably a generational thing. They were, after all, both of them, sixty-eighters, basically. No wonder they were uneasy. They remained moored in a world in which political progress meant speaking truth to power. But did it? Little reason to think so. I recalled with some discomfort the moving lecture given by a political philosopher friend in the immediate aftermath of 9/11: swelling to her theme, she told us that we were on the side of the truth tellers and that only a politics of democratic openness would permit us to survive the years ahead. The next day the newspapers revealed that the CIA had been disseminating doctored pictures of Bin Laden gussied up like one of the Bee Gees for a night of cruising discotheques. Ahem.

Indeed, for those of us right around forty—we who flipped shruggingly through Baudrillard and Deleuze with a sense of déjà vu; we whose political lives took shape across the long decade from Reagan's Hollywood accession to the POV smart-bomb footage of the first Gulf war—it was hard to fall in behind the speaking-truth-to-power standard. It felt, somehow, a little nostalgic, a little tainted by the solemnities of "the Sixties." That world (the political world of our parents—itself, perhaps, a reaction against the slicker image world of the 1950s) was gone. Goodness was not gone. Virtue was not gone. But it wasn't clear that sit-ins were going to solve anything. Or heartfelt folk music. And it wasn't so clear that the truth was going to make anyone free. Nothing less freeing than the truth, come to think of it. Imagination—now *there* was some freedom.

Still, something slightly worrisome about the specter of a collective retreat into fantasy and play, no? Hmmm. Well, perhaps. I stared at the game console/multimedia port on the back of the seat in front of me. The touch screen. The rocker buttons of the handset. The world was not Donkey Kong. Fair enough. And yet who said a generation wholly raised in the flow spaces and game worlds of the Internet— not my generation, exactly, but that of our younger sisters and brothers—needed stern tuition on how to sort the real from the simulacral? Least of all from mature sages steeped in the culture of the book—a culture that was, of course, for all its charms and powers, most unlikely to survive the next few decades (except, perhaps, in some rump form, some exotic, pseudomonastic clique of future opt-outers). In fact, the whole thing might cut quite the other way: my senior colleagues worried that an intellectual culture committed to something like perpetually ludic postproduction on reality represented a frightening evacuation of the public sphere, a simulationist secession that put the very idea of participatory politics at risk; but if, increasingly, actual politics operated operatically (privileging everywhere image, performance, and spectacle), then wielding a little schizophrenic irony—indeed, mastering the veritable arts of collective deception— might well be the twenty-first-century equivalent of registering to vote.

Or so one might hope.

I settled back in my cramped seat. Onward and upward, as they say.

* * *

Actually, though, the plane had to land. And by the time it began its descent, I had transmuted my lingering unease (for it did linger) into a pedagogical program. It was time to take up these problems in earnest. The result was a graduate seminar, "The Art of Deception: Aesthetics at the Perimeter of Truth," which I taught at Princeton in the spring of 2011. The course aimed to make sense of the intersection of aesthetics and epistemology since the Renaissance. Which is to say, I set out with a dozen grad students (from art history, architecture, theater, English, comp lit) to try to understand how questions of truth and falsehood had functioned to cabin and specify the domain of the arts—visual, plastic, textual, performative. At the heart of our inquiry lay the timeless problems of illusion, forgery, and deceit. Promiscuous rather than properly his-

Plato and Pliny (to set up the classic formulations of art as illusion). By the end we had wended our way from Reformation Nicodemites to Hannah Arendt and Jacques Derrida on the lie in politics, with

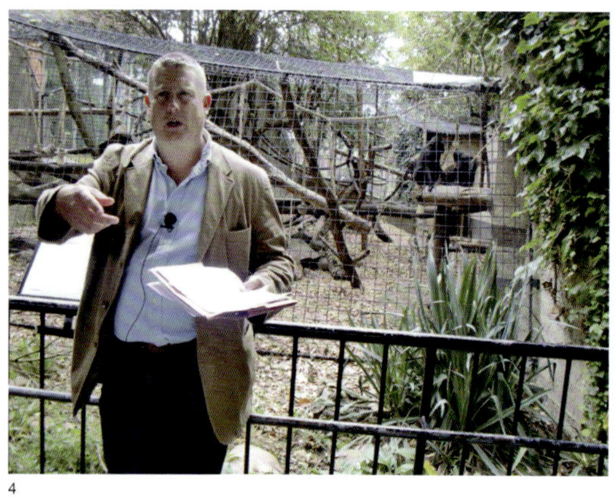
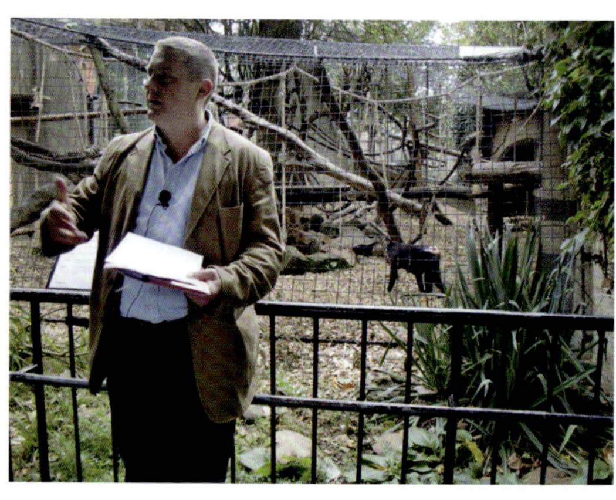

4

torical, the course threaded its way back and forth between very current issues and telling texts from the past. We began, for instance, with the juxtaposition of contemporary trickster artists (the Yes Men, Aliza Shvarts, Goldin+Senneby) and Herman Melville's cosmological trickster novel *The Confidence-Man* (1857), before reaching all the way back to

whistle stops for early modern dissimulation, nineteenth-century counterfeiters, delirious Dada pseudotranslation, Clifford Irving, Cheryl Bernstein, P. R. Coleman-Norton, and the Crabtree Orations.[4] It was a smorgasbord of disorienting characters and the philosophical, legal, and artistic problems that they raised—and from which, at times, they fell.

I brought to the project the verve of a fresh convert. We were going to learn to *play*. And a workshop-style final assignment gave students the chance to experiment (and analytics) of artistic transgression had gradually resolved itself, at least for some of us, into a sickly miasma of genuine fear. I believe that this

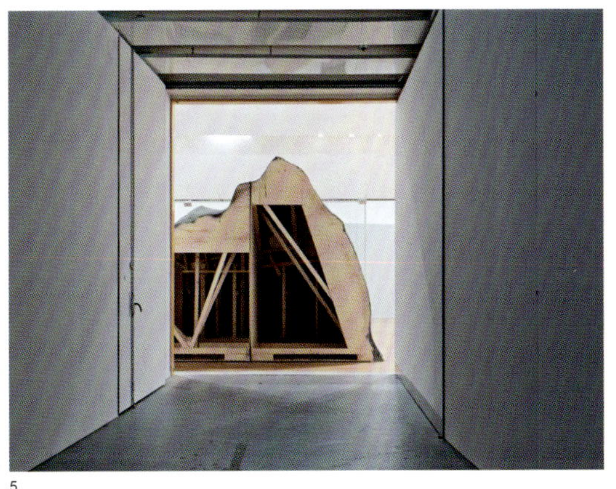

5

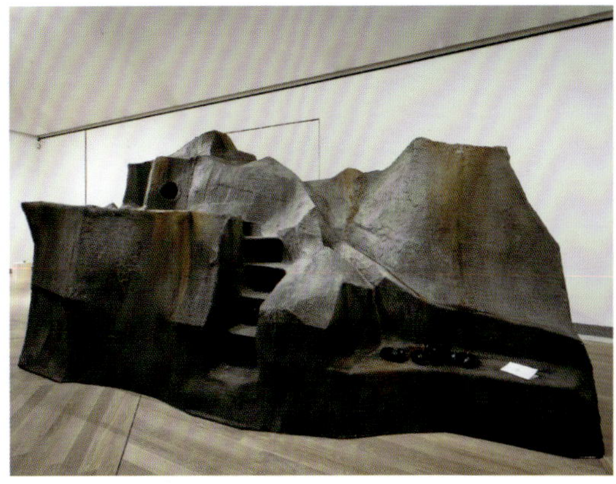

in a formal way with learned and gamesome falsification. By late April, however, there was—in the increasingly oppressive air of our high-ceilinged, wood-paneled seminar room—the vague feeling of a hangover. The anarchic exuberance of mutual tuition in the mechanics affective arc speaks in significant ways to the challenges presented by the work in the exhibition *More Real?*—the work presented and discussed in this catalogue. If I went into "The Art of Deception" intending to arm myself more effectively for a redux of my challenging conversation in Berlin, I came out of the semester properly shaken. If you enter the exhibition with the jaunty step of the willing conspirator, I would argue that you should probably exit with a furrowed brow.

Why? I'll get there. For now, suffice it to say that there is no wink that does not leave us, however fleetingly, blind in one eye.

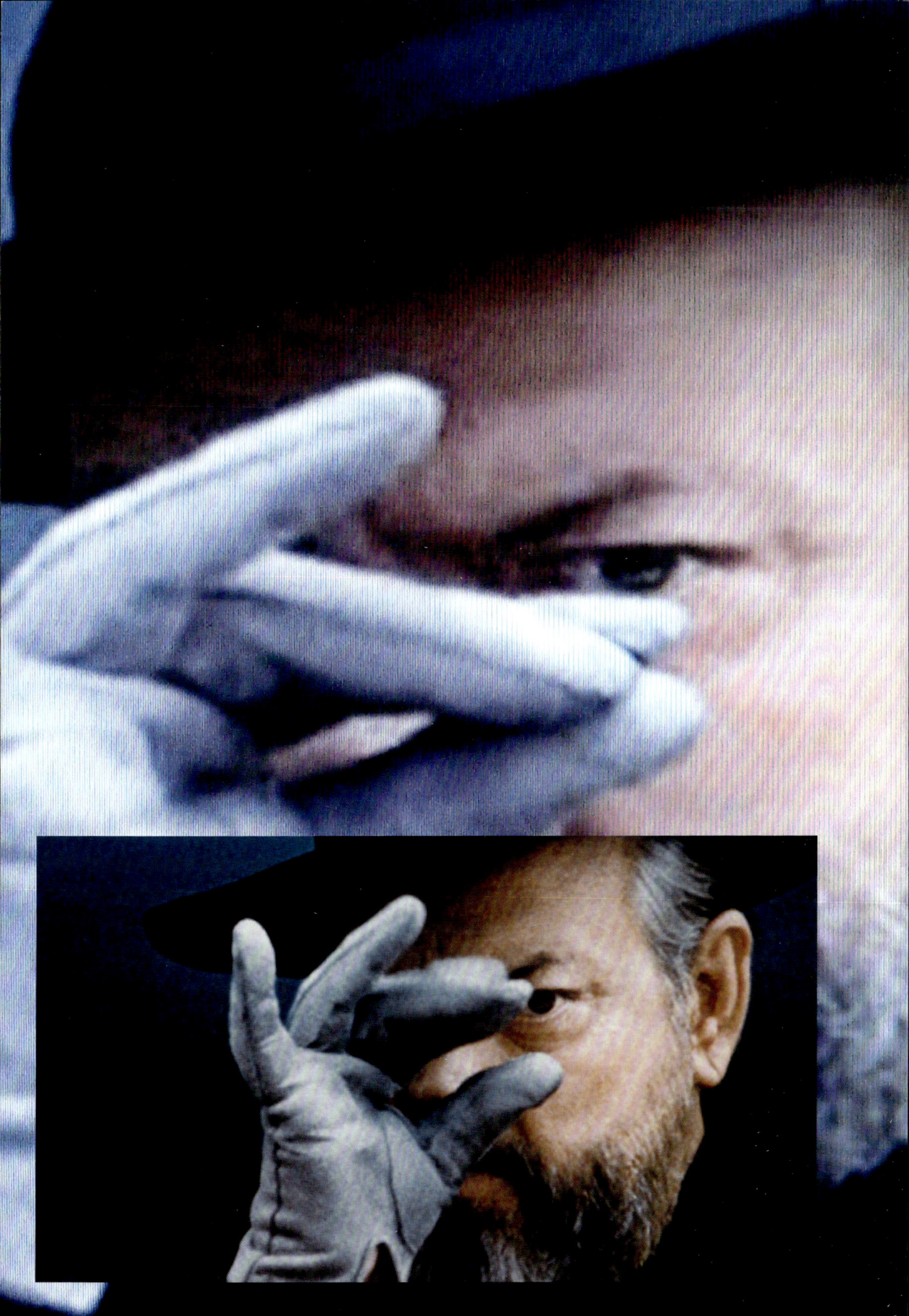

✳  ✳  ✳

Blind in one eye. One could argue that that is the perfect conceit for thinking about art and illusion.

In book 35 of his relentless *Natural History*, the first-century Roman encyclopedist Pliny the Elder drops an offhand comment about the origin of the illusionistic space of two-dimensional representation. Discussing the great gifts of the (presumably apocryphal) ur-painter Apelles, Pliny alludes to a portrait of King Antigonus, who had only one working eye. The painting represented a shocking innovation: Apelles, we are told, "devised an original method of concealing the [king's] defect, for he did the likeness in an oblique perspective, so that the feature wanting in the subject might be thought instead merely wanting in the picture; thus he showed only the part of the face that he could show in its integrity."[5]

We are left to understand that this move—twisting his sitter into a three-quarter view, rotating one side of his face "into" the canvas and away from the viewer—was unprecedented.[6] One thinks immediately of chapter 4 of E. H. Gombrich's classic *Art and Illusion* (1960). There, recall, we get a sweeping argument that the origin of illusionistic representation (the "Greek Revolution," the "conquest of space") is inextricable from the origins of the narrative arts (epic poetry, tragic theater) and, more generally, from a kind of upsurging emergence of an existentially exigent human person: you might even call it the birth of "man." How so? Well, instead of mere cookie-cutter iconography pasted flat on cave walls, we suddenly get individuated individuals strutting the stage-space of life. For Gombrich, the implicit action-worlds of illusionistic three-dimensionality enjoin reflection on something more than the conceptual/schematic/bean-counting "what" of *three* soldiers or *two* nymphs (picture stiff figures arrayed like hieroglyphs); rather, with the feinting into the picture plane, we are thrust irreversibly into the sinuous, philosophically vexing world of cause and effect, of "how" and "why," of veritable people and the decisions they make.

Of course, they aren't that veritable. On the contrary. This epochal Gombrichtian aesthetico-metaphysical ensoulment trades precisely on sleights of hand and eye: illusions of depth, tricks of foreshortening and shadow, the whole repertoire of painterly mimesis. It was precisely this unstable superposition of deep truth and deep falsehood, Gombrich suspects, that made Plato so uneasy about the domain of artistic representation.

There can be little doubt that the formulations of *Art and Illusion* feel dated in certain ways: the grandiosity rankles, the implicit occidental exceptionalism looks provincial, the hunt-and-peck use of 1950s-era sciences is distracting (i.e., maybe better to skip the stuff about Australian Aboriginals). And yet as demanding a contemporary critic as W. J. T. Mitchell has continued to find inspiration in wrestling with this material. Mitchell's felicitous notion of "illusionism"—which he defines as any array of culturally specific techniques for gaming the problem of illusion—owes much to Gombrich and is intended to help parse what Mitchell takes to be a conflating confusion in *Art and Illusion*.[7] Illusion proper, Mitchell argues, is really just error—false belief, mere defect of our faculties. *Illusionism*, by contrast, is "playing with illusions, the self-conscious exploitation of illusion as a cultural practice for social ends."[8] It is here that things get interesting, since by these lights illusionism can function as a technology for revealing the bad conscience of ideology, which must forever cultivate illusion.

With this in mind we can return to that suggestive Apelles portrait. By twisting Antigonus into the canvas, Apelles pried open the illusionistic space of perspectival representation. How are we to interpret this moment? There is, to be sure, something touching in the fact that this new illusion-space has been conjured, in this first instance, precisely to create a *hiding place* for a human weakness or defect. It is thus tempting to sense, in that slightest rotation of the sitter,

a gesture of human sympathy—even a kind of secular redemption: We are *broken*. But perhaps art can make us whole. The cost? The artist must use the Archimedean lever of illusion to raise the real world off its foundations—creating, in the process, that little cache wherein to secrete all our blemishes and failures.

Sniffle. One senses that Mitchell would not be satisfied with this sort of tremblingly symbolic interpretation. After all, we are talking about a picture of the *king of Macedonia*, for heaven's sake. Can we bring the politics back in? How is Apelles's gesture anything other than a spin job on the Prince? A little image management. Flattery. Propaganda. A sucking up to power.

Fair enough. Are we in the sphere of ideological *illusion* or of a playful, sympathetic, and/ or critically sensitive illusionism? How would we know the difference? In the case of the Apelles portrait we must consider, as we try to decide, a recursive richness built into the image: being one-eyed means precisely *losing the capacity to judge distance*. A monocular vision is exactly a vision without depth, and in this sense the cyclopean Antigonus is more than merely the subject of this first perspectival illusion: he is also, squintingly, the very type of the kind of seeing that (falsely) perfects him. Are we having one put

over on us? Or are we being invited to share in an intricate visual witticism? And once again, how would we know the difference?

* * *

Knowing the difference. It all hinges right there. But that is precisely what is at issue when we move into (or, indeed, back out of) the domain of deception. The sharpest formulation of this central problem came in the sleeper book of the semester: Julia Abramson's *Learning from Lying*, a detailed study of the genre of "mystification" and particularly of the high Enlightenment origins of this very particular form of literary-artistic play.[9] As Abramson shows, the term itself, *mystifié*, was a novel coinage of mid-eighteenth-century Paris, and though it first came into use to describe the cruel practical jokes played by slightly wicked reactionaries in the period, it was soon appropriated by the philosophes, who expanded and transformed its meaning. In the hands of Diderot and Rousseau (and even Grimm and Goethe), *mystification* ceased to refer to the hazing rituals of aristocratic cliques and came to embody a distinctively didactic species of textual two-step. The paradigmatic case was a work set to "spring" (instructively) on its readers. So, for instance, you might think that Prosper Mérimée's *La Guzla* (1827) was a genuine collection of Dalmatian folk lyrics translated into French. You might think that *initially*. But Mérimée had no desire to be a forger of Illyrian ballads. His intent, ultimately, was, as Abramson can demonstrate, a subtle critique of the fashionable excesses of romanticism. Hence the idea was that *first* you swooned at the feral glory of a Balkan balladeer, but *then*, reading a little closer, you picked up the clues, caught on, and learned a lesson about the artificed seductions of "primitive" authenticity. The text, we might hazard, *choreographed* your insight; its author was pedagogically preoccupied with *managing* your experience of deception—your path in, and your path back out.

This, for Abramson, is the defining character of a true mystification. In place of the irreducible sadism of mere trickery, we have the gentle tease of the dedicated teacher. In place of the falsifying ambitions of the genuine forger, we discover the clarifying commitments of the critic. In this sense, the genre of mystification can be understood as nothing less than a liturgy of enlightenment itself: we start out in the dark, but we find our way to the light. This is no ludic irruption, no send-up of the will to truth. We are, rather, in the holy of holies of critical rationality: in the unfolding experience of a true mystification, we experience "the secular counterpart to revelation."[10]

Abramson hedges a bit on that analogy. Which is fair enough. Does the mystification convert to revelation without remainder? Perhaps not. Or perhaps not in all cases. But however urbane or playful or ironic or demanding the mystification becomes, if it is to remain a mystification (and not drift into simple fakery), the work must continue to serve as the "conscience" of fiction. To do so, it needs to keep close track of where we are as readers and take responsibility for moving us through its masquerade. In lies, we might hazard, begin responsibilities.

Lambert-Beatty closes her essay on contemporary parafictions with a meditation on a telling phrase used by one critic to describe the reactions of viewers who learned of the fictional nature of Michael Blum's *Safiye Behar* installation at the 2005 Istanbul Biennial: they went, we are told, "scurrying back" to see the show a second time. It is Lambert-Beatty's valediction that we need to "dignify" that rodent-like scurry—take our chastening time as we confront works that have wrong-footed us, and use the occasion to reflect on the aesthetics of doubt and the poetics of knowledge in a world (and an art world) of great complexity. It is a felicitous notion, to be sure—and surely right. And yet Abramson's framing of the dynamics of mystification presses us to fold the question of our affective and epistemic trajectories in relation to such works *back into the nature of the works themselves*. If we are willing to extend the analysis of *Learning from Lying*, it becomes possible to argue that parafictional works are, in the end, *answerable* for their handling of our path to, and from, and then back to their presence under the changing alethic modalities on which they trade. This trajectory is not merely our problem as viewers. It is a problem that can be understood to inhere in the artwork and the artist's process as well. And we might go one step further: this epistemological choreography is, I believe, something more than a "feature" of such works; it is also inextricable from the ethical status of these artistic practices.

* * *

We come here to the crux of the matter, to the hard question from which we began—call it the Berlin question. Are the artistic practices that we might group under the rubric "strong-program aesthetic illusion"—the arts of deception proper—ethically (and politically) acceptable? Or to put it another way: where do we draw the lines?

Over the course of the term this issue became increasingly urgent in the workshop-collective of our seminar. We got there in different ways, but I

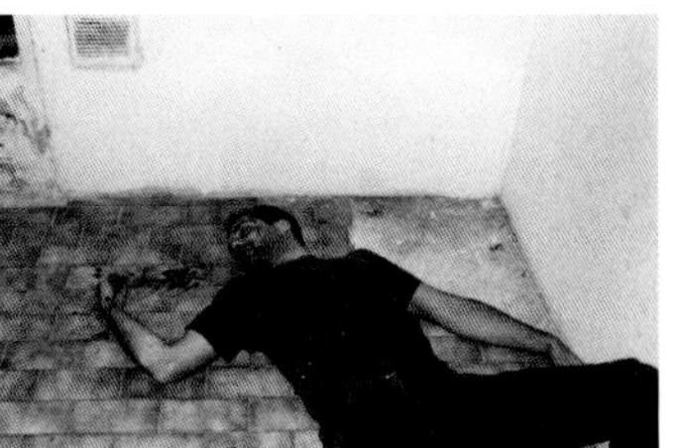

7

have the clearest memory of my own moment of crisis. It was the tenth week of the term. We had not only watched Orson Welles's classic *F for Fake* (1975); we had also read both Irving's study of the forger Elmyr de Hory and Irving's story of his own mad exploit forging the autobiography of the billionaire recluse Howard Hughes.[11] The *mise en abyme* of deception tessellated to the horizon line in all directions. But one could make of this receding crystalline lattice a *studium*, and there was a pleasure in this—the intersecting tales of falsification and conjuration, the rogue charm of the protagonists, the manifold indulgence of Welles's film (which for all its avowed evasiveness keeps returning to Welles himself, who cannot but repeatedly reassert solid center of solipsistic sovereignty). And yet there was, too, a *punctum* in all this, and for me it fell in a paratext: a little footage from the *Sixty Minutes* interview with Irving from 1972, at the height of the scandal surrounding his (not yet known to be fake) ghost-authored "autobiography" of Hughes. The camera tightens slightly on Irving as he is confronted directly with the question of whether he is telling the truth, and he lies—we know he is lying. And he lies well. And his eyes are clear and alive. And, yes, terrifying.

But it took a little more than that to break me. I went home that evening and picked up the *Economist* and found myself reading a creepy little story about cyber-stalking. The article detailed how a modestly successful female opera singer in New York had found herself tormented for years by a shadowy character somewhere in Asia who had maintained a sequence of web pages and blogs in her name, in which he played out a series of unseemly erotic and financial fantasies. This second life had cost the artist enormously, since she had no easy way of establishing that the impostor personae had nothing to do with her. Questions of legal jurisdiction were tricky, and it was hard to get the police in Hong Kong to follow up.

The unhappy tale intersected in enough ways with the class discussion around *F for Fake* that I felt something like an obligation to follow up, so I meandered over to the computer to google the woman's name and see if I could make sense of what I found. Would I be able to sort out her real person from this penumbra of projections? What would it all look like?

And initially it was yet another navigable hall of mirrors. Yes, I could find her actual web page. And yes, I could find various unnerving doubles. But one could distinguish. It took work. But it was possible. And then I clicked through to a page that popped open the *Economist* article that I had just read. Or so it seemed. Skimming down the page, I suddenly felt a genuine shiver of horror: the article in question—though it looked like the *Economist* piece and reprised its general flow and tenor— actually reversed the whole story, making the woman into the perpetrator of cyber-extortion against a mild-mannered gentleman whose life she had maliciously savaged with slander and blackmail.

I shut the computer. The sick thing was, this grotesque undertaking lay just a hop, a skip, and a jump from a few of the more radical and disturbing parafictional projects that we had sounded in the last weeks—Darko Maver, say, or the spookier edges of the Bataille-inspired Headless project.

I felt myself back-pedaling, slowly, from the desk. And I was back-pedaling in my head as well.

* * *

So where does one come out? Not in opposition, exactly. That would be stupid. Over the course of the term my students and I, drawing on historical precedents, tested a variety of quite sympathetic accounts of the contemporary appetite for the arts of deception. Yes, there is something apotropaic about the project—a palpable desire to scare away the monstrosity of the big-screen lie with little fetish lies secreted in downtown galleries. And sure, there may be some sense in which parafictional tendencies reflect an effort to cultivate means of resistance

against the simulacral character of the modern lie—the kind of lie that lies all the way down. Perhaps even more alluring is the notion that this sort of artwork represents the current instantiation of a more or less timeless Pygmalion complex at the heart of creative aspiration: art has always aspired to reality, to the dream of genuine creation; the matrix of such ambition has shifted over time (from the erotic sequestration of the studio to the Faust-meets-Frankenstein technologies of techno-science). Read in this context, parafictional art may amount to the latest effort to sculpt actual flesh, to paint with actual blood—call it the Pygmalionism of an age obsessed with information and its representation. Still more extravagant, one might be tempted to suggest that the striking convergence of historicizing research practices and artistic confection betrays the pending collapse of "humanistic" inquiry itself. Perhaps nonscientific *Wissenschaft*— always a sort of mash-up of pseudotheology and German positivism—is basically finished. Part of its traditional domain will be siphoned off into the sciences proper (chunks of philosophy are already neuroscience; parts of history become biology, etc.), and the rest will become art. Maybe this is what we are already seeing in pseudohistorical work—in the proliferation of archival and investigative and collatory undertakings that mobilize both the form and the content of scholarly disciplines but without fidelity to (or interest in) their traditionally truth-seeking character.

But in the end, that traditionally truth-seeking project is not in fact fungible, and it cannot be exported to the laboratories or subcontracted out to scientists. On the contrary. As the course drew to a close, I found myself (disorientingly) persuaded that the arts of deception, for all their Dionysian charm, return us with dialectical inevitability to the Apollonian posture of critique, to the fundamental problems of socially embedded reason and the ineluctable ethico-political cast of our lives. If Apelles's portrait of Antigonus twisted open the three-space of causality and human individuality, these contemporary forms of aesthetic illusion force us to navigate along another axis—that of duty and responsibility. If the first illusory turn brought us an ontology, the second rotates us into deontology.

There we are returned to the critical stance, to the necessity of doing the hard work of trying to know the difference—of trying to know the difference between salutary provocation and perilous threat, between the sort of teasing that helpfully tests our robustness and the genuine moves of malice, between the art that asks more of us and that which wants our undoing. If there are stakes, there are stakes, and the work of discerning those stakes—and protecting them—is critical work, and for it there is no substitute.

In this sense, the seminar room retains, for me, a very special—indeed, a quasi-sacred— status. It, along with the forms of discursive analysis from which it moves and to which it contributes, constitutes the perennial court of final appeal—precisely because the appeal of that expanded forum is never final. This is why we keep talking, why we keep writing. That is why we must scurry back to the exhibition and look again. And then turn to the person beside us in the gallery and ask: "Is this okay? Is it . . . good?"

Once that conversation starts, the games must begin to stop.

**Notes**

1. The event, co-organized by Michael Gordin and Lorraine Daston, was "The Strangelovean Sciences: Rationality versus Reason" at the Max Planck Institute for the History of Science. My gratitude to them for a very stimulating occasion.

2. Carrie Lambert-Beatty, "Make-Believe: Parafiction and Plausibility," *October*, no. 129 (Summer 2009): 51–84; the essay is reprinted in this volume.

3. For a version of this last argument, see Anthony Grafton and D. Graham Burnett, "Deception as a Way of Knowing," *Cabinet*, no. 33 (Spring 2009): 69–76, and related correspondence in *Cabinet*, no. 34 (Summer 2009): 57.

4. The syllabus is open access: http://www.princeton. edu/history/people/data/d/dburnett/profile/teaching/ index.xml.

5. Pliny, *Natural History*, trans. H. Rackham (London: Heinemann; Cambridge, MA: Harvard University Press, 1952), 35.36.90. I have slightly modified Rackham's translation, and the emphasis is mine.

6. In fact, Pliny is here, as elsewhere, a little confusing. Earlier in book 35, he alludes passingly to a painter named Cimon as the inventor of the first "oblique" representations.

7. See W. J. T. Mitchell, *Iconology: Image, Text, Ideology* (Chicago: University of Chicago Press, 1996), especially 75–94.

8. W. J. T. Mitchell, "Looking at Animals Looking: Art, Illusion, and Power," in *Aesthetic Illusion: Theoretical and Historical Approaches*, ed. Frederick Burwick and Walter Pape (Berlin: Walter de Gruyter, 1990), 77.

9. Julia Abramson, *Learning from Lying: The Paradoxes of Literary Mystification* (Newark: University of Delaware Press, 2005).

10. Ibid., 39.

11. Clifford Irving, *Fake! The Story of Elmyr de Hory, the Greatest Art Forger of Our Time* (New York: McGraw Hill, 1969); Irving, *The Hoax* (New York: Hyperion, 2006).

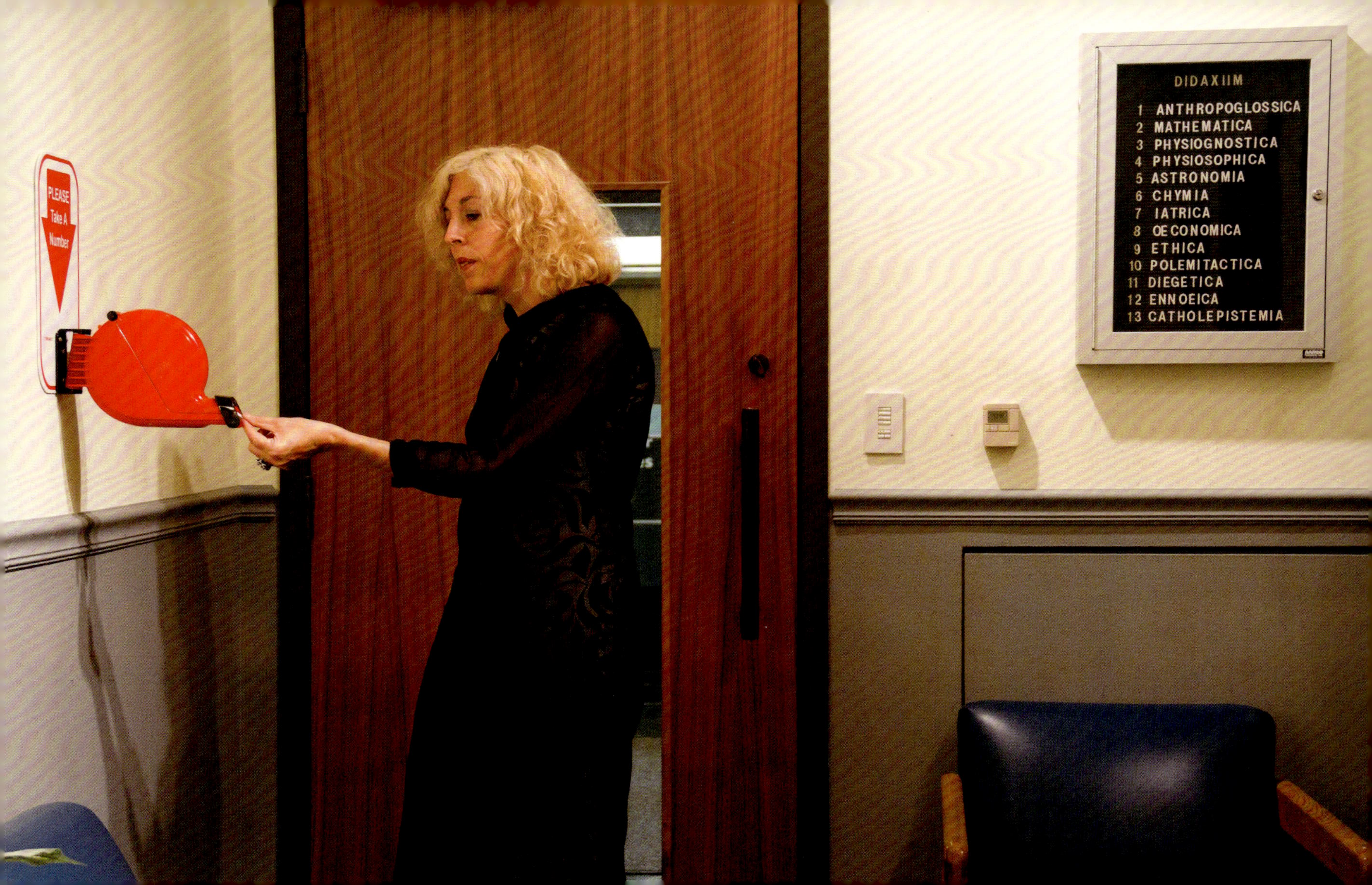
DIDAXIIM
1 ANTHROPOGLOSSICA
2 MATHEMATICA
3 PHYSIOGNOSTICA
4 PHYSIOSOPHICA
5 ASTRONOMIA
6 CHYMIA
7 IATRICA
8 OECONOMICA
9 ETHICA
10 POLEMITACTICA
11 DIEGETICA
12 ENNOEICA
13 CATHOLEPISTEMIA
PLEASE
Take A
Number

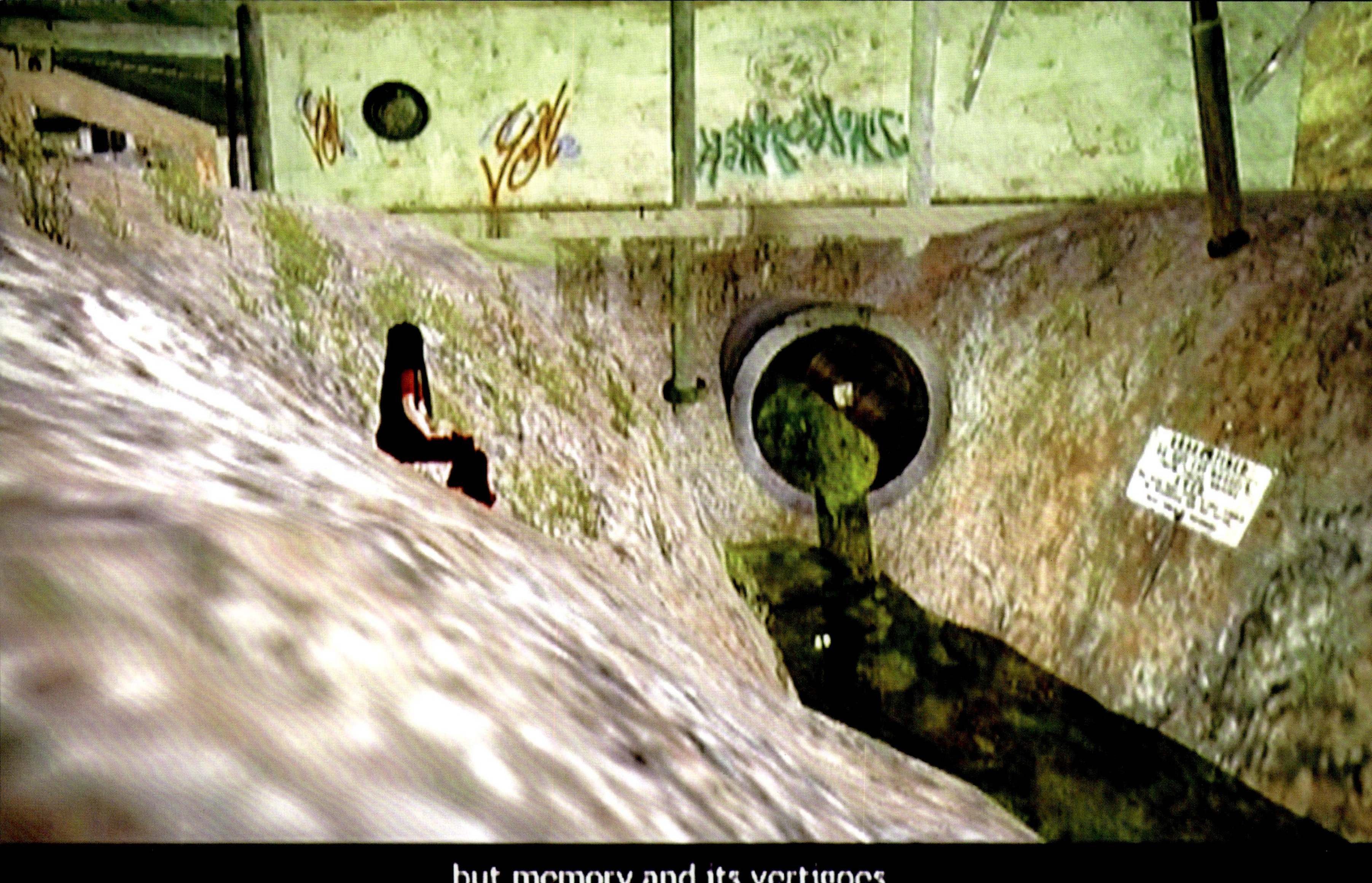

but memory and its vertigoes.

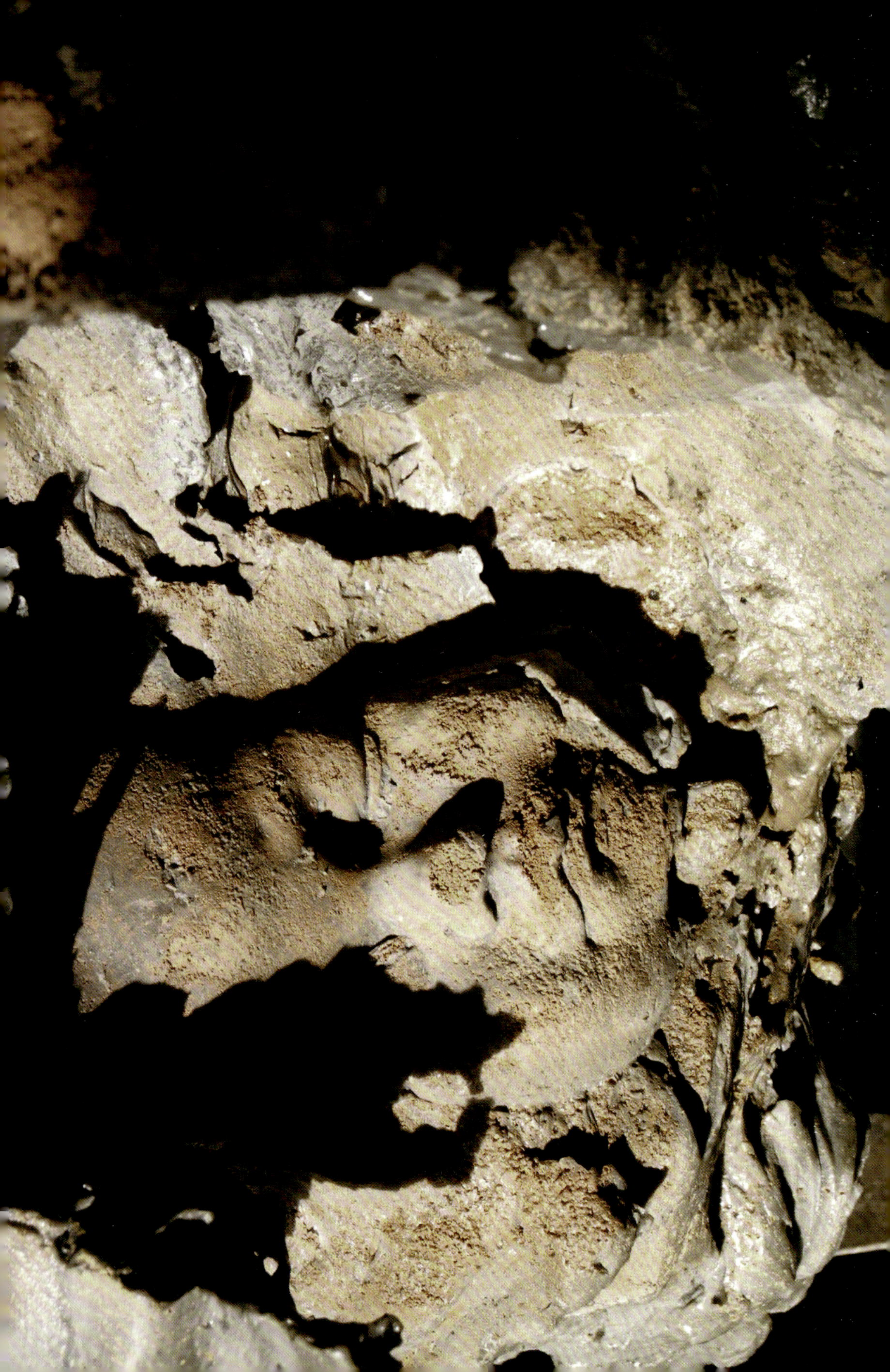

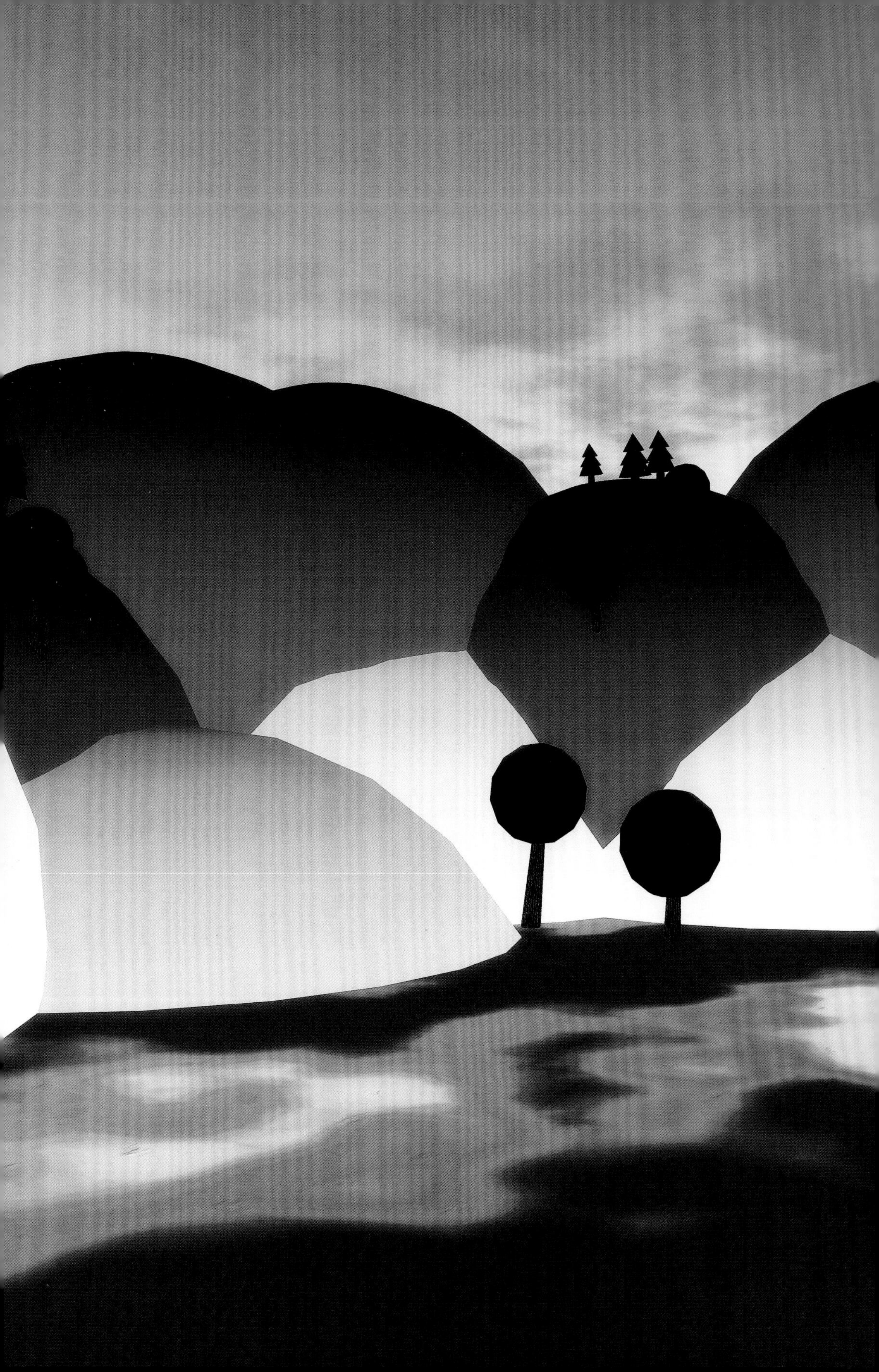

# The Charm of the Lie

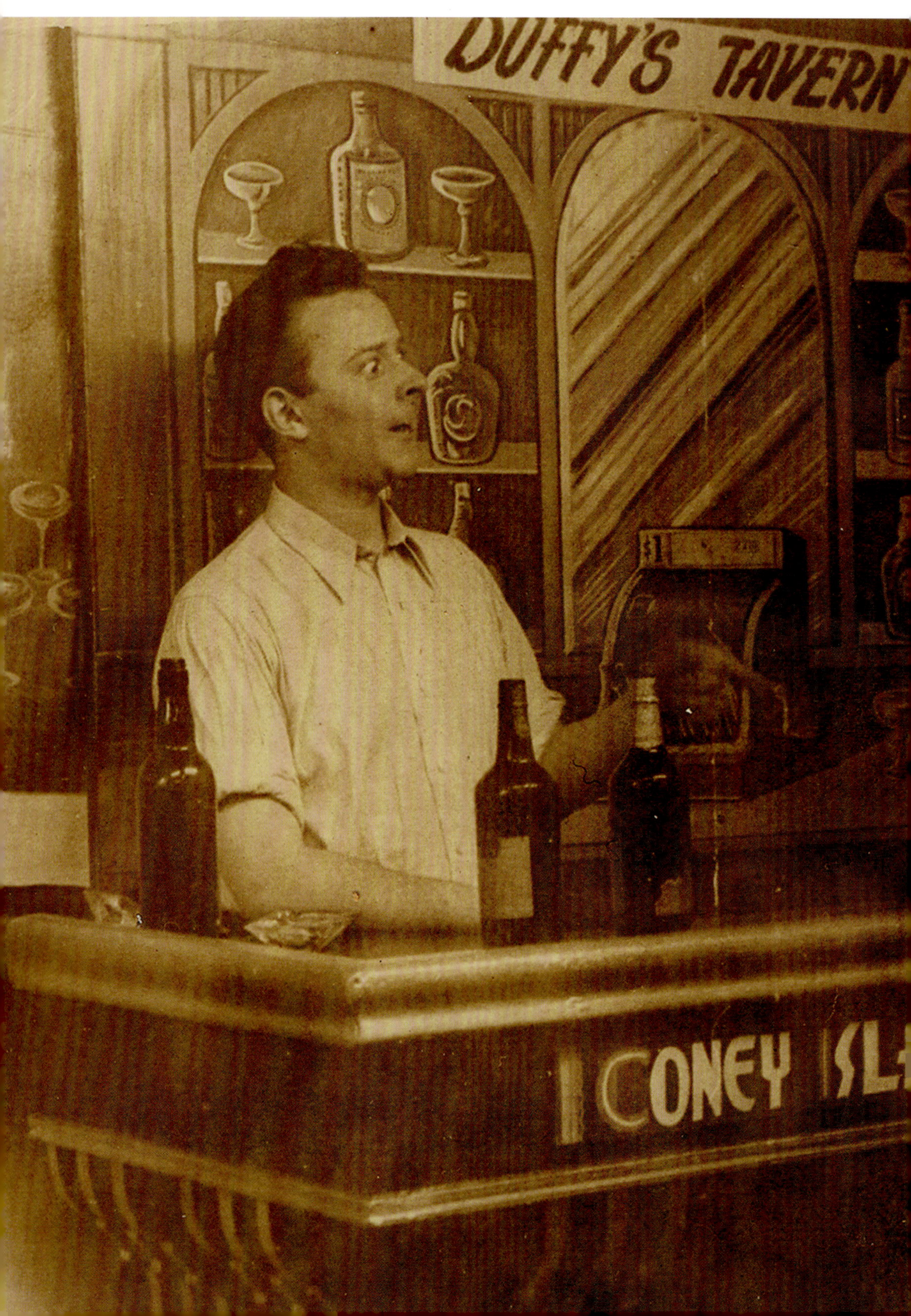

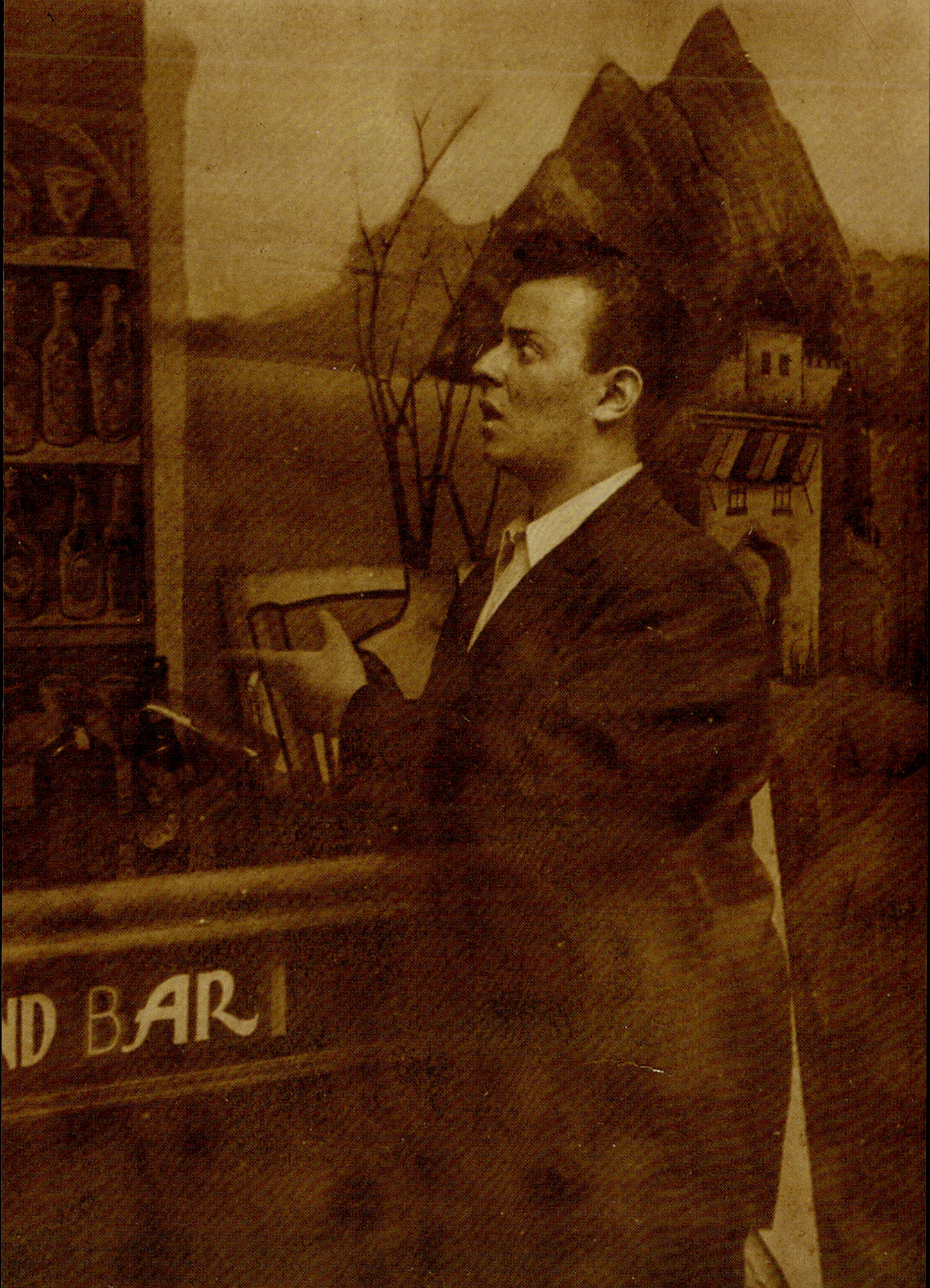
ND BAR

# The Charm of the Lie: A History of Our Unreliable Grasp of the Real

TEXT BY
*NORMAN M. KLEIN*

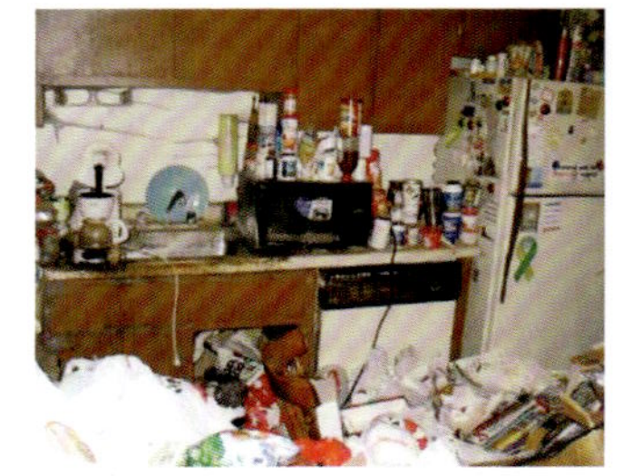

1./

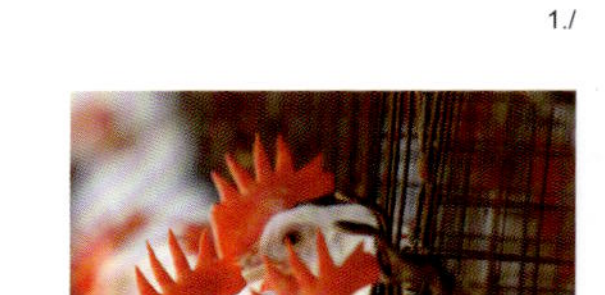

2./

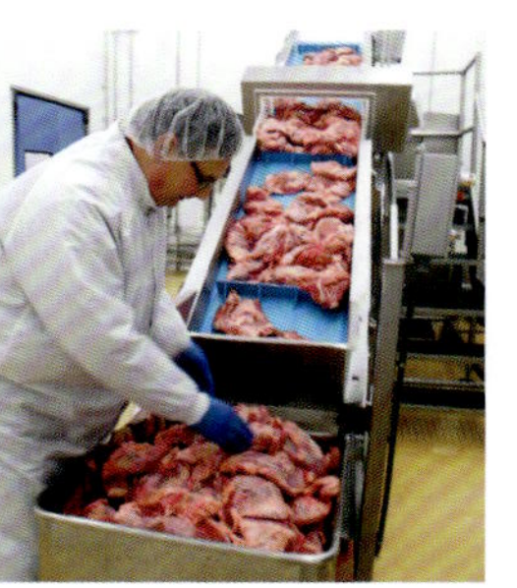

3./

This essay is an elaboration, a historical envelope for the exhibition *More Real? Art in the Age of Truthiness*. We begin with a simple paradox, then locate a genealogy. But first let's try a couple of simple exercises at home.

**1. Empty your pantry onto the floor of your kitchen. Then imagine yourself surrounded by the entire carbon footprint for that food. Animals bloated with hormones are grazing near your stove. Trucks with oil leaks are blowing exhaust. That would be eating in a "more real" way.**

"More real" images are difficult to shake nowadays, thanks to the crash, Katrina, and poisoned baby food. In our mind's eye, we see the two sides on a split screen, like a split infinitive or a cleft palate. Suddenly all the food looks chemically strange, like a cheesy bank derivative. We are shocked at how real a fake can become. But we are also grotesquely fascinated. It's funny.

**2. Turn on the TV. A botoxed politician twirls across the screen on *Dancing with the Stars*. He has squeezed himself into a work of fiction, like packaged meat. He is "really" a composite. Think of drywall or slices of bread. In 2006 I compared "the blur between fact and fiction" to a city inside a ship, like an ark. The prow of this ark is held together electronically but able to sail uncontested through real oceans.[1]**

Many ships like these have crossed over the centuries. They have left an amazing rogue's gallery. Real liars stand up straight, like grizzly bears. No apologies are given. No lies are corrected. The crowd plays along. It is pop nihilism, shared ecstatic procrastination. The effect on politics is stultifying, enough to support feudalisms for a thousand years.

Simply put, there is actually a history to the "more real" effects. Even stunt words like *truthiness* date to the early nineteenth century.

## i.
## *The Doubling Effect*

Behind "virtual reality" in the 1990s was real chaos. After the crash of 2008 the enthusiasms of the digital age (the virtual 1990s) gave way to something "more real." Apparently, there was no second life—only life. Simulated money (casino capitalism) could bankrupt entire continents. It even dissolves brick-and-mortar streets.

All this makes for gloomy stories at first. Then other qualities emerge, playful and weirdly ontological. In this essay we are going to visit many places where these qualities can be found. For example, until 2008 most Americans assumed that "virtual" capitalism knew its mind, perverse as that was. The simulated was like artificial intelligence, even "better than real." Service industries would make us all rich. They would exceed the physical. Now we see that the joke was on us.

I am escorted through One Wilshire Boulevard, a "carrier hotel" in Los Angeles. It is one of the preeminent "interconnections" in the world. More than two hundred of the most powerful companies on earth transfer all their messages through One Wilshire. In essence, every country in Asia relies on One Wilshire to do business. It is a diplomatic but unregulated space station for an entire continent.

You would never guess to look at it. The 1960s facade looks too blunt to be that "real." How could this thirty-story cube be a doorway to trillions of dollars? On the second floor, hundreds of black metal racks contain signal boxes. They remind me of the locker room of a gymnasium. On the

Fig. 1./ Call in the Hazmat Team!, Brion Grant, Northland Home Inspection, Inc., Flagstaff, Arizona, from http://www.thisoldhouse.com/toh/photos/0,,20193914_20443105,00.html

Fig. 2./ Caged hens feed at egg farm in San Diego County, July 31, 2008

Fig. 3./ Jim Bannister loads slabs of meat onto a conveyor belt to be made into ground beef at the Fresh & Easy Neighborhood Market meat processing facility in Riverside, California, March 29, 2012

Fig. 4./ Cheryl Burke and Tom DeLay's patriotic dance on *Dancing with the Stars*

Fig. 5./ Cao Fei, *i.Mirror*, 2007; video still; dimensions variable

Fig. 6./ http://macmembrane.com/marbled-beef-ipod-case-from-japan/

Fig. 7./ http://insanepics.blogspot.com/2008/09/stephen-colbert-american-hero.html

Fig. 8./ HD Vision Wraparounds

Fig. 9./ One Wilshire Boulevard, Los Angeles

Fig. 10./ The Los Angeles skyline

Fig. 11./ The San Gabriel Mountains and the city of Los Angeles

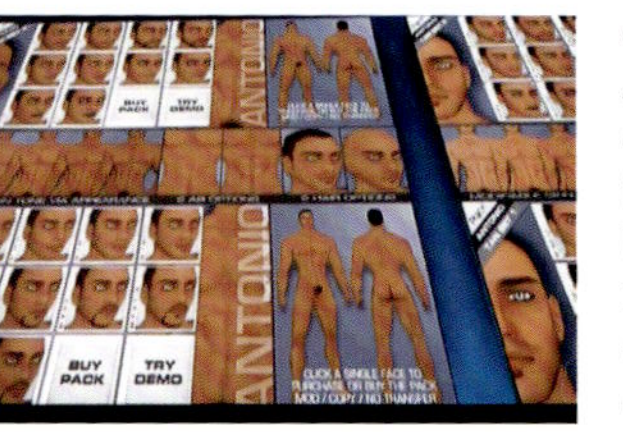

4./

5./




http://macmembrane.com/marbled-beef-ipod-case-from-japan/

6./

http://insanepics.blogspot.com/2008/09/stephen-colbert-american-hero.html

7./


fourth floor, chaos truly reigns. Philip K. Dick could have been the architect. Tens of thousands of wires are bundled in enormous arterioles—three feet wide and hundreds of feet long. Behind them I see the grinning jawbone of an alien (like in the movies). Most disturbing of all, there are no labels anywhere. Some of the wires are left over from companies that went out of business. No one can say where every signal goes. Apparently in the 1990s the owner of the building forgot to archive the cables. There were no numbered tags before the cables were released into the wild. The cables are very solid ghosts, the kind you can sever with a wire cutter.

According to the rhetoric of poststructuralism, these ghosts are floating signifiers: simulated, hyperreal, bodies without organs. They are premonitions without addresses, rhizomes.[2] They are what is intentionally left missing in art installations and video art.

Many of these poststructural tropes seem less apt today. They were perfect in 1985 but no longer. We experience global power much more bluntly now. Oligarchies hide in plain view, while the capital risks have multiplied. Almost everything that is digital has evolved into objects more intuitive than those we had in 1985, more like bricks and mortar. To coin a phrase from One Wilshire, the overlapping geography is "colocated." We need to find a genealogy for this haunted, "doubling" sensation (more real because it is more virtual).

*Suddenly you notice that the San Gabriel Mountains are only three miles north of your house, where—only yesterday—a grayish blank used to be. Then you see both versions of that sky, in simultaneity, for the rest of your life.*

I am reminded of a smoggy L.A. sky after a rain. Suddenly you notice that the San Gabriel Mountains are only three miles north of your house, where—only yesterday—a grayish blank used to be. Then you see both versions of that sky, in simultaneity, for the rest of your life. They are mentally inverting at the same moment. They are ideograms, a bit like concrete poetry or conceptual art. It is as if, in our era (let us say since 2000), the real has taken its revenge upon us, as if we had been caught sleeping. We need tools, a poetics, to capture how this sensation operates today and what it suggests as history, as an archaeology of our collective madness. Let me clarify what I mean by tools. I will briefly cite a few that have struck me in this exhibition:

### Remapping in 3-D (spatial doubling)

*Oil Stick Work (Angelo Martinez/ Richfield, Kansas)* (2008) by John Gerrard: as in earlier works such as the Dark Portraits series, Gerrard invents an evolving 3-D architecture as a "dreamscape." But the dream is intended as a media intervention, based on scans and rescans. Like rotoscoping software, or an ecology advancing toward ruin, the building he captures on screen is caught in a Zeno's paradox. The more real it appears to be, the farther away it becomes, an "anti-memorial."

### Para-fact

In 2006 I published a fiction about Freud's one-day visit to Coney Island in 1909.[3] A year later, I received an e-mail about that visit from Zoe Beloff, a

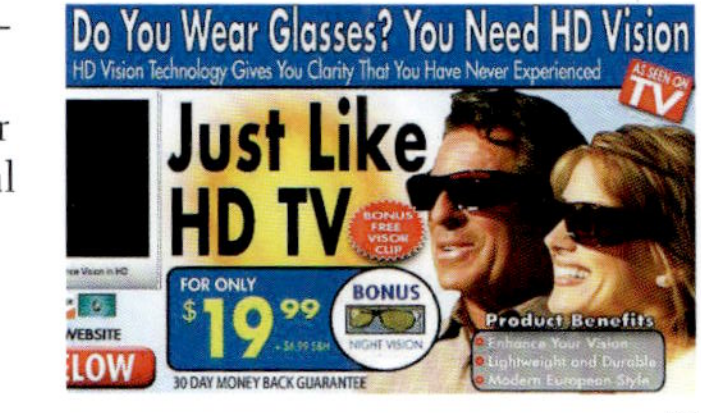



8./

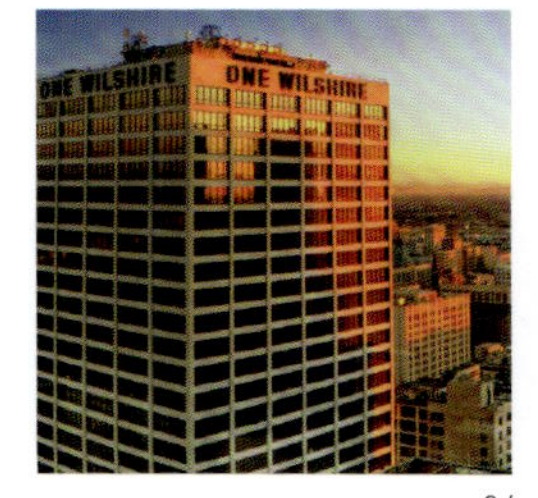

9./

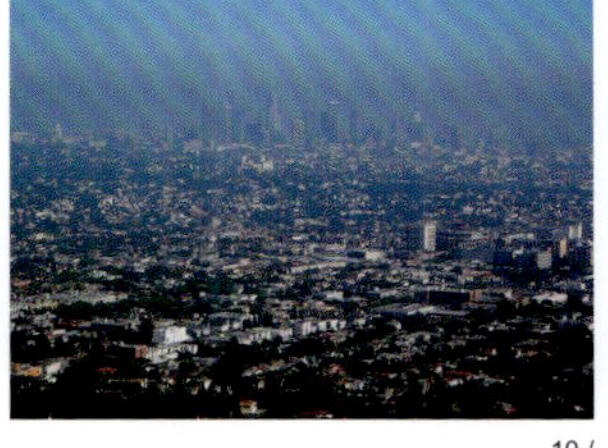

10./

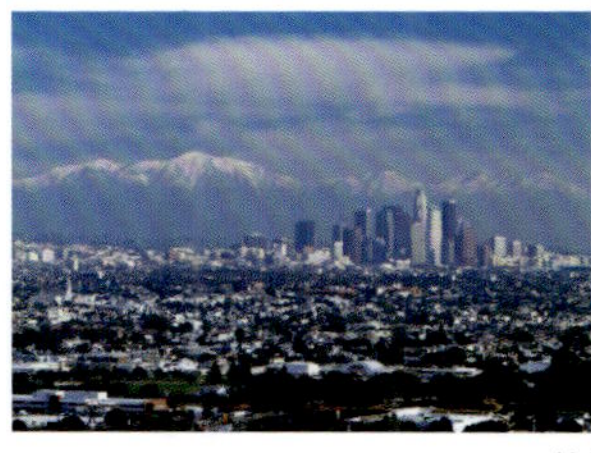

11./

**The Charm of the Lie: A History of Our Unreliable Grasp of the Real**

TEXT BY
*NORMAN M. KLEIN*

Fig. 12./ John Gerrard, *Live Fire Exercise (Djibouti)*, 2011 (detail); real-time 3-D projection; dimensions variable

Fig. 13./ Rotoscope is a free software graphics program that can be used to give photos a cartoon-like appearance

Fig. 14./ The Coney Island Amateur Psychoanalytic Society's annual "Dream Film" award dinner, 1949; gelatin silver print; dimensions unknown

Fig. 15./ Greetings from Coney Island! Postcard from Coney Island; courtesy Zoe Beloff

Fig. 16./ An-My Lê, *Explosive Ordinance Disposal*, from the series 29 Palms, 2003–4; gelatin silver print; 26 ¾ x 38 ½ inches (67.9 x 97.2 cm)

Fig. 17./ Interior of the Sala dell'Udienza (Audience Hall), 1638–44; Palazzo Pitti, Florence, with frescoes by Angelo Colonna and Agostino Mitelli

Fig. 18./ 100% the Real Deal from http://helenlingard.com/wp-content/uploads/2011/05/the-real-deal.jpg

Fig. 19./ Cheeseburger flash drive, from http://www.safecomputingtips.com/blog/wp-content/uploads/2010/03/Cheese-burger-USB-drive.jpg

Fig. 20./ Seung Woo Back, *RW01-041*, 2006, from the series Real World I, 2004–6; digital print; 50 x 66 ½ inches (127 x 169 cm)

Fig. 21./ Seung Woo Back, *RW01-047*, 2006, from the series Real World I, 2004–6; digital print; 50 x 66 ½ inches (127 x 169 cm)

remarkable video and installation artist and also a very careful archivist. Zoe reminded me that I had accidentally invented a parafact—that is, a fiction too strange not to be "real."⁴ In the words of Harry Brown, one of my ongoing characters: "Fiction is much more believable than fact. Rumors well placed can improve on facts."⁵

Like an archaeologist, Zoe patiently curated the remains of the Coney Island Amateur Psychoanalytic Society from 1926 to 1972,⁶ the drawings, the correspondence, and the dream films.⁷ In the *New York Times*, a reviewer suggested that she may have invented the entire business. "One might wonder how much of what she presents in 'Dreamland' is historical fact, and how much is wish fulfillment and projection on her part? Did the Coney Island Amateur Psychoanalytic Society really exist?" Zoe answered with a smile: "That's a good question. . . . What do you think? . . . That's what Freud was about, taking real things and recontextualizing them to see what that says about us. Maybe that's the approach I took."⁸

Of course, this society did, in fact, historically exist. Even so, I spent eight years of my childhood in Coney Island. Almost every

building in the neighborhood that I knew was torn down to the last brick. I agree with Aaron Beebe, scholar and director of the museum there, who said: "Asking what's real and what isn't is the wrong question in Coney Island.... This museum explores other issues than truth and fiction."⁹

## Archiving what is missing, or what Pierre Huyghe and Philippe Parreno call "no ghost, just a shell"¹⁰

A Korean businessman and a German businessman run out of conversation at dinner, so they conjure up memories of Hollywood movies. That may be the only canon (folklore) shared globally, our classicism—that and computer touch screens.

## Slowing down vision (the politics of the imago)

An-My Lê's reenactments of "small wars," the bombing of Vietnam or Iraq remade as a baroque fireworks display, in ironic materials: this is more than just a distancing or Brechtian device, a naked composite. Over the past century, Brechtian traces—distressed surprises that altered the "real" of the photo—had a different effect on the public than they do today. It would seem that they used to be more shocking. They presumably slowed down how the

public processed the images of war. But do they still? Or does the public merely expect "facts" to be false—as the standard way that news is delivered—allowing them to comfortably move on? That is one of the challenges that I see in Lê's photos, that she forces a hermeneutics upon us; we must research, like anthropologists, how collective forgetting operates today (specifically today).

## How digital software infects our hands-on everyday process

That is suggested throughout this exhibition. It is one of its guiding principles. Like bacteria haunting the bottom of the food chain, the digital has altered the chemistry of a room. It changed our intuitive behavior, naturalized the unnatural.

In writing and lectures, I often compare this tech haunting to solid geometry.¹¹ Many baroque artists and philosophers worked on a paradox known as quadratura. In Latin, *quadratura* means the squaring of the round—essential to calculus by 1690—possible only as a math equation, one might think. How can you square the round in the physical world? But in fact quadratura was a technique used by painters to mystify the bricks and mortar of a building—for

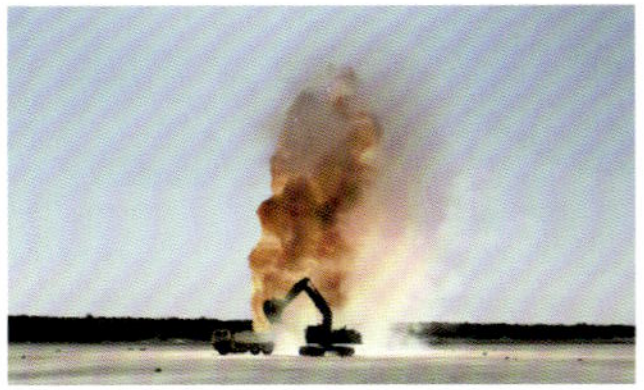

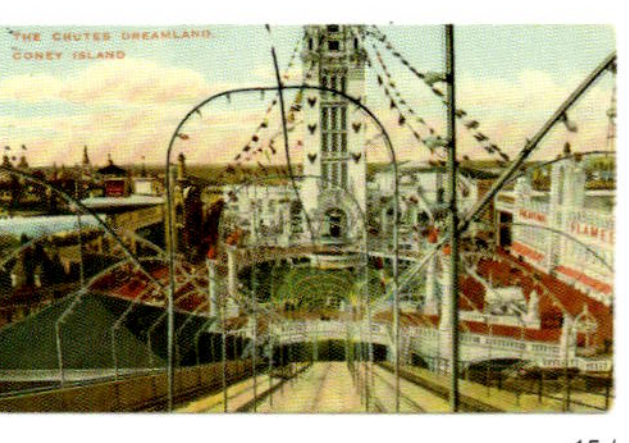

12./

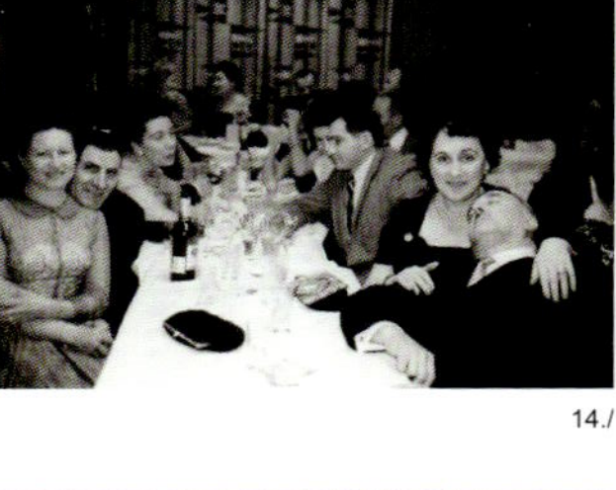

13./

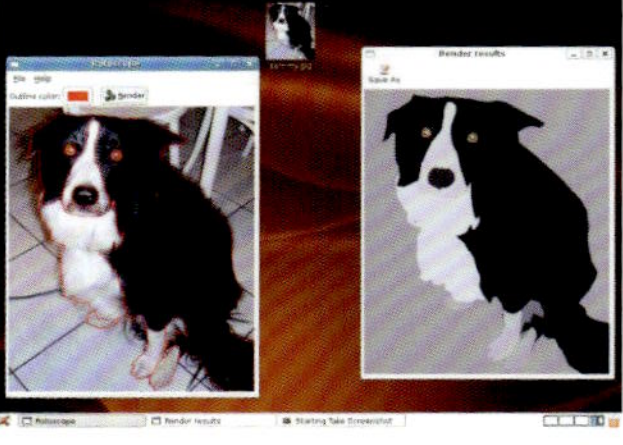

14./

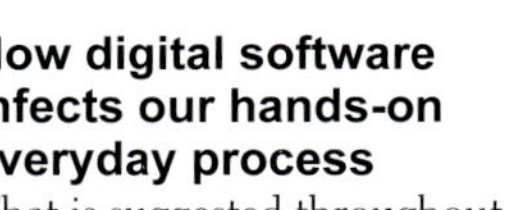

15./

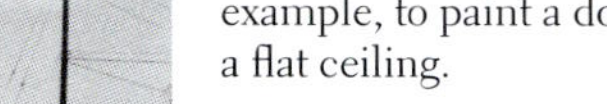

16./

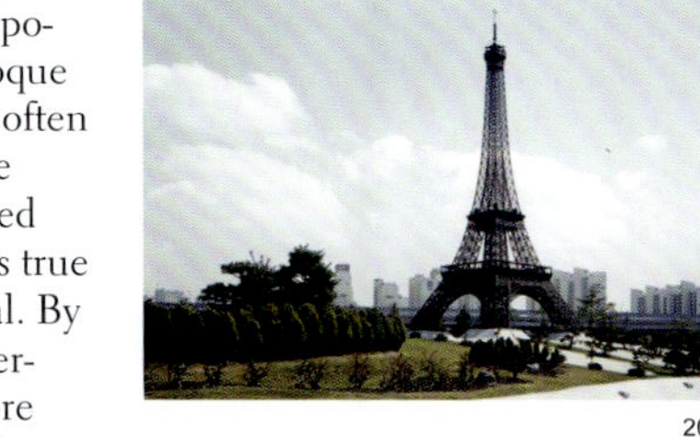

17./

18./

example, to paint a dome upon a flat ceiling.

This artifice—the staging of illusion through tools like quadratura—was understood as an instrument of power, particularly during the Counter-Reformation and what we identify as the baroque. For decades now, I have been obsessed with the seventeenth-century use of quadratura as a way to understand the political definition of the real. Quadratura was a kind of "software." That software was identified with the commercial classes, who became "uneasy" allies of the monarch—sponsors in fact but in the end sworn enemies.

In other words, through the paradoxes in how "the real" is popularly identified, one can find cues about the instabilities of the state and its class structure. This amounts to craftsmanship about the instability of the real. As of 2012 we are quite early in locating that craft for our moment because so much is literally in the air while crashing to the earth at the same time. Quadratura compares easily to our emerging crafts filled with syntactical units about the paradox of the real and the artificial. That holds true for our era as well. What has been

called globalism—the shifts in the world economy since 1980 or so—is transforming into something else. Henceforth, perhaps for generations, globalism will generate more regional and localized civilizations. I understand how strange this sounds, in an era of Facebook around the world. I will explain in the next section of the essay. Unquestionably the paradoxes of the real are changing in

*In other words, something like the baroque confusion of the seventeenth century has returned, but with smartphones, GPS, globalized entertainment.*

response to that new stage. That is why so much new work today is about the haptic, the biopolitical, the textured, the decentered, the cross-embedded.

What in the 1990s was understood as virtual, or as parallel worlds, has changed its role enormously. At first, this change was identified with neoliberal campaigns, what Pierre Bourdieu called

"moral Darwinism," a return to the struggle of all against all, borrowing of course from Hobbes.[12] In other words, something like the baroque confusion of the seventeenth century has returned, but with smartphones, GPS, and globalized entertainment.

By the way, as if matters were not complicated enough, in the political philosophy of the baroque (ca. 1580–1750), "more real" often meant the reverse of what we might think today. It suggested faking or inflating an object's true use, almost like the hyperreal. By contrast, *artificialis* was understood as more authentic, more handmade, even scientifically truer to the subject. The real then was a kind of reverse Platonism; it was only gold-plated; it stole from the truer real behind it.

A similar fascination with gold-plated Platonic copies emerged during the postmodern era as well. I won't try to summarize the arguments. Many of them centered on shifting theories about simulation, consumer spectacle, and the collapse of the sign; on redefinitions of the surrealist object; on how unreliable the narrator or reader had become; on the Platonic cave as "less than real." Does "less than real" generate a new nihilism or a

19./

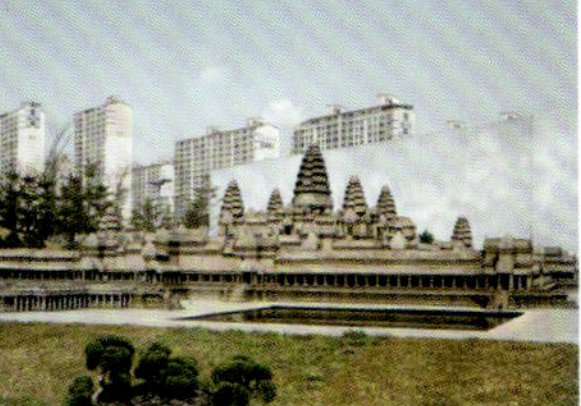

20./

21./

The Charm
of the Lie:
A History
of Our
Unreliable
Grasp of
the Real

TEXT BY
NORMAN M. KLEIN

Fig. 22./ http://cybject.wordpress.com/2010/12/27/
two-mohammad-attas-on-jean-baudrillards-spirit-
of-terrorism/

Fig. 23./ Hollywood stunt actor performs stunt in
Shanghai, March 12, 2006

Fig. 24./ "Rock Sign Explosion" mobile phone wall-
paper from http://media.photobucket.com/image/
recent/anarchyphantom/untitled-10.png

Fig. 25./ *Spielberg's List: Photo Taken by Extras
during Production of the Film Schindler's List*,
1993; snapshot; dimensions unknown; courtesy
Omer Fast

Fig. 26./ Cyberpunk Model with Exo-boots, from
http://www.jprishea.com/jpr/frames/products/
exoboots.htm

Fig. 27./ NBA player Tony Parker is photographed
in a spandex suit at EA Sports Studio in Burnaby,
British Columbia, July 29, 2008

Fig. 28./ A woman in a motion-sensor suit controls
a visual image in a bikini on a TV set in Tokyo,
October 14, 2010

Fig. 29./ http://www.examiner.com/second-life-in-
national/michael-jackson-s-second-life-memorial-
service

Fig. 30./ http://www.toycutter.com/2010/04/watch-
men-and-avatar-my-little-ponies.html

new essentialism, a new decadence
or an invaded (irrupted) self?
We now have the benefit of
hindsight. Postmodernism (let us
say 1965 to 1990) was clairvoyance
or a foreboding. It chronicled the
decline of the political Enlightenment in the West after 1975. It
gathered evidence about its replacement by another wing of the
Enlightenment: the neoliberal
Adam Smith–Milton Friedman
model of global capitalism. These
clues were rogue events—the
collapse of vertical systems toward
rhizomatic structures. These
discontinuities evolved into a
new paradigm after the late Cold
War. I'll give Jean Baudrillard
the last word on the melancholy
of postmodernism, in *The Agony
of Power* (2005). He saw the West
afflicted with hysteria, like a crisis
in its immune system, a contami-
nation, a panic, heading toward
a "white terror" in response to
terrorism. (And of course in
revolutionary France the "white
terror" of 1794–95 killed more
people than the Reign of Terror itself did in 1793.) Global
capitalism "should worry less
about revolution, and more about
what is happening in the void, at
the heart of the anthropological
fracture."13

## ii.
## *Blowing Up Imaginary Buildings*

Speaking of presentiment and
voids, while conducting research
for my next book, to be called
*The Dismantling of the American
Psyche*, I ran into a case study
about "more real" violence in the
movies. Before 9/11, Hollywood
special effects addressed terrorism
in a very special way. Hollywood
accidentally predicted the fact but
as escapist entertainment.

In dozens of movies, from *Die
Hard* (1988) to *Independence
Day* (1996), cities were routinely
blown up as a signature for the
big 1990s action film. I interviewed two experts who directed
these pyro-effects. Both of them
were definitely affected by the
"realism" of these fantasies. Peter
Kuran, while supervising visual
effects for the Robocop series
(1987–93) and *Last Action Hero*
(1993), became obsessed with
film footage of nuclear explosions. He designed a camera that
deflected the flares to reveal the
actual impact of nuclear tests,
then produced two documentaries about the atomic bomb (and
was awarded a special Oscar).
Michael L. Fink, visual effects su-
pervisor for *Mars Attacks!* (1996)

and *X-Men* (2000), used to lecture
regularly on how to blow up
places in the movies. He canceled
these lectures after 9/11; many
of the issues raised in this essay
were obvious to him, however,
particularly the grammar, let us
say, of "more than real" violence
and spectacle.

I have found similar connections
in research about the British
futuristic novels preceding World
War I. From 1872 forward, dozens
of books (from history to fantasy
engineering) featured the German invasion of London. During
World War I this evolved into
spy frenzy about the Huns taking
London. But for the most part,
the British public floated in a
kind of nocturne until 1915. During parades the "public" famously
threw flowers at soldiers heading
to the front, particularly when
the war had just begun. This fit
into the hypernationalism of the
Edwardian era: monumental public support, like crowds. Later, of
course, the responses grew more
desperate.

One might call it a collective,
melancholic obsession, a shared
grief to avoid grief. It is a very
complex form of propaganda.
The images are meant to help the
audience ignore the actual facts,
the boots on the ground. *Robocop*



22./

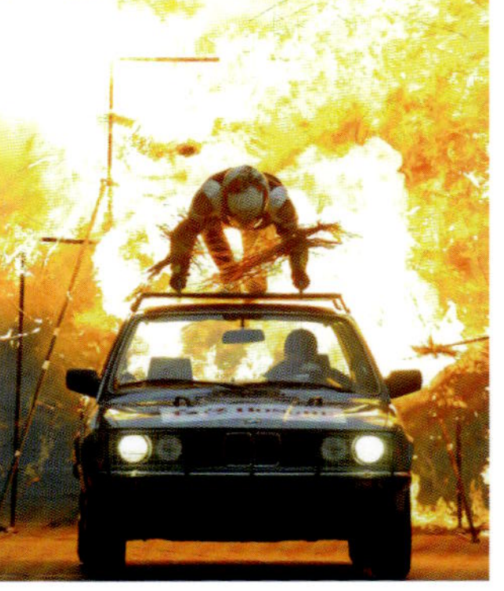

23./

24./

25./

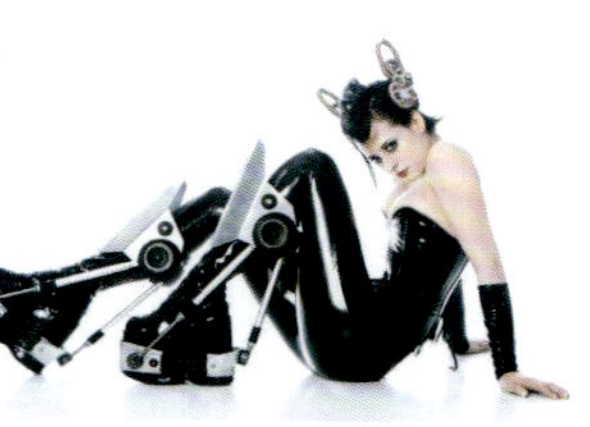

26./

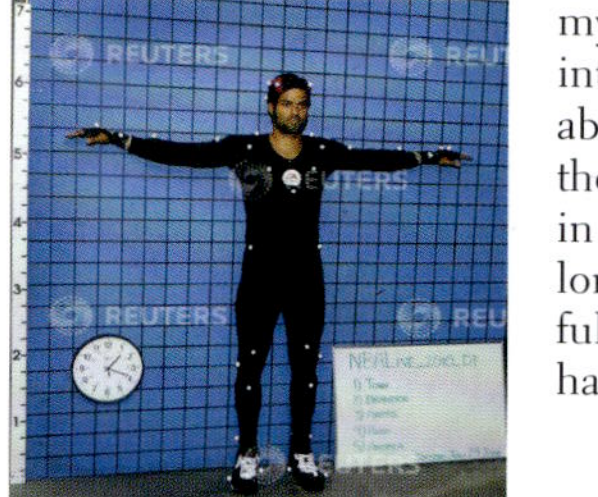

27./

hardly inspired the public to stop Detroit from collapsing. Blowing up a city is like an amusement park ride in old Coney Island. It erases public anxiety (much the way that shipwreck fantasies in the baroque era were not about the ship of state crashing on the rocks). If you break that iron rule, you may lose money. Serious films about Vietnam or Iraq have bummed out the audiences. This is a complicated paradox: "the spectacularly real." It is like visiting reenactments of your own funeral, over and over again, in order to confirm that you must be immortal. Having seen hundreds of glossy roller-coaster movies, in which everything in sight was gracefully blown to bits, I admit that I was often morally offended but never honestly bored (that makes me a case study as well, part of the problem). Even knowing this in advance does not seem to inoculate me. (For some mysterious reason, however, I lose interest in World War II movies about the Nazi occupation, even though many of my relatives died in the Holocaust.) Otherwise, as long as there are a few delight-fully escapist murders, I seem to have infinite patience.

iii.
## The Charm of the Lie

So what is the narrative structure that fits a hyperbolic real, with its doubling effects and gloomy presentiment? What makes these effects charming? It has to be a story in which the artifice, the handmade quality, is evident. For example, video games have suffered from being "too real" as computer graphics effects have improved. Motion capture on the faces of characters becomes more real but also more robotic, from three to six expressions. But these faces are emptied for a purpose. They are designed to handle extreme repetition, not unlike the symbolic characters in fairy tales. That way the player can mentally become an avatar.

Nevertheless, when the faces get too polished, they can lose their impact. This problem was first identified in 1970, through robot-ics, and has come to be called the uncanny valley. Characters can suffer a paradox: the more realistic they are, the more unreal they appear. Like pyro special effects, the uncanny valley was a cultural warning about the invasion of media into the psyche. But as drama it tells us much less. It has tremendous power but in

a depleted, inverted way. That remains the challenge for media artists working in narrative: how to maintain presence and drive in their media object.

I see new forms emerging or, I should say, ancient forms reappear-ing: baroque or picaresque irony, essentially a preindustrial form of storytelling—more episodic, more about rogue events in a world drifting through entropy but not a cyberpunk world, closer to Huck Finn going down the river. I am convinced that this picaresque, episodic, and stylized form of story responds to changes in the politi-cal economy, toward something much closer to electronic feudal-ism than industrial imperialism.

The picaresque also suits an archival novel. The dust on the road matches the cloud of re-search data—in counterpoint, the imagery disputing the evidence. I write media novels of that kind, in which the archive leaves spaces between, vaguely like open-world games. Thousands of images liter-ally compete and collapse into the story. The media novel *Bleeding Through* contains eleven hundred photos and film clips—assets, as they are called—in a journey through the unreliable memory of an old lady who, rumors tell us, may have murdered her second

28./

http://www.examiner.
com/second-life-in-national/
michael-jackson-s-second-
life-memorial-service

29./

http://www.toycutter.
com/2010/04/watchmen-and-
avatar-my-little-ponies.html

30./

**The Charm of the Lie: A History of Our Unreliable Grasp of the Real**

TEXT BY
NORMAN M. KLEIN

Fig. 31./ Incredibly Awesome Nail Designs, from http://1.bp.blogspot.com/-k4CbmDn2IoE/TydXBI_ZGCI/AAAAAAAADfg/00mSLNTjwWw/s1600/Incredibly+Awesome+Nail+Designs+%281%29.jpg

Fig. 32./ Architectural models made out of paper, from http://forums.cgarchitect.com/21505-not-clay-model-paper-model-vray.html

Fig. 33./ Suntan tattoos, from http://1upcoolpics.blogspot.com/2011/02/10-cool-suntan-tattoos.html

Fig. 34./ http://www.tvcentral.com.au/2012/02/01/wikileaks-founder-julian-assange-to-star-in-the-simpsons/

Fig. 35./ http://dailycognition.com/index.php/2009/11/09/innocent-passenger-gets-arrested-at-airport-for-his-name.html

Fig. 36./ The Rubikon, a paper pinhole camera designed as a response to digital technology, from http://www.objetgraphik.com/Rubikon.html?lang=en

Fig. 37./ Special-effect contacts for Halloween, from http://amazingfunpics.blogspot.com/2011/09/13-strange-and-ugly-halloween-geek.html

Fig. 38./ For the gamer who has everything . . . Golden Wii by Stuart Hughes, from http://www.multiplayergames.com/2009/12/30/for-the-gamer-who-has-everything-22ct-gold-ps3/

Fig. 39./ Mobile Evolution by Kyle Bean, from http://www.kylebean.co.uk/portfolio/#mobileevolution/

husband. As one links these images, it becomes clear that they tell a story about selective memory and about the inability of the photograph to accurately represent a city.

At this writing, I am completing a project titled *The Imaginary Twentieth Century* (cocurated and codirected by Margo Bistis), a novel about how the twentieth century (and, by implication, our century as well) was imagined before it took place. The counterpoint of this archive is centered on a woman and five men. In 1901 Carrie A. selected four men to seduce her, each with his own version of the twentieth century. But eventually much of this woman's biography had to be erased by her uncle.

As counterpoint (a doubling effect), these archival journeys closely resemble the picaresque novel, again Huck down the river into the decadent South or Henry Fielding's capricious lunatics on the road. The picaro is a sly bottom feeder, expert at finding the scraps left over. That is increasingly the role of the archivist and the player. In picaresque, the facts cannot be easily separated from the fake: the charm of the lie. By contrast, Mark Twain's *A Connecticut Yankee in King Arthur's*

*Court* is not at all picaresque, merely a spoof of American utopianism.

The picaresque archives of a disorderly world. The reader must pause at "forking paths," at "spaces between," like musical rest stops. The reality of doubled vision becomes weirdly clairvoyant, which is why we also call this novel a misremembering of the future. As I explain to the reader of the novel, our comic misunderstanding today meets theirs. Their impending century crosses into ours.

## iv.
## *Cross-Embedding: How to Never Get Past the First Act*

Media are intrinsically a counterpoint—a cross-embedding. For example, a doubling (or "flickering") can be seen, quite literally, at the birth of cinema. From 1895 to about 1900 practically the only way movies could be shown was by embedding them into other media. Movies were attached to vaudeville shows and magic lantern shows. Early movies borrowed heavily from print and from magic acts. Even nickelodeons after 1900 were anthologies of the dime museum in many ways.

Not until 1912, when movies went beyond one-reelers to multiple reels, do we finally get a stronger sense of the unique genius of cinema rather than its powerful cross-embedded spectacle.

Every medium is cross-embedded to some degree. Perhaps none crisscrosses more than the computer. By 2012 every building starts out as a digital prototype. The computer is a form of architecture. Its architectonics are then embedded into mobile phones, into every messaging device that relies on a signal. The devices are then embedded into our clothing, as physical extensions of our bodies (to borrow from McLuhan's famous dictum). Digital architecture is nano, micro. It cross-embeds with genetic engineering and brain research.

As media history, the computer has reversed the usual pattern. In early cinema, there was no way to stay in business except by embedding in other forms of entertainment. Similarly, television was born as visual radio in many respects. But eventually venues that are uniquely suited for a medium, like movie theaters, will be designed. Afterward, rather quickly, the medium "locates" its unique language. Historians like me then find a

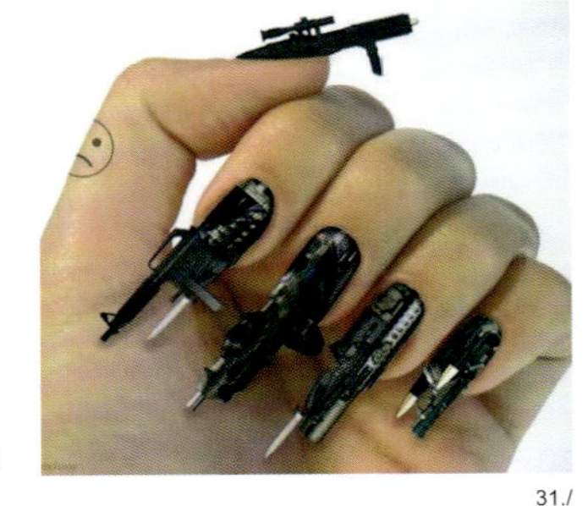

31./

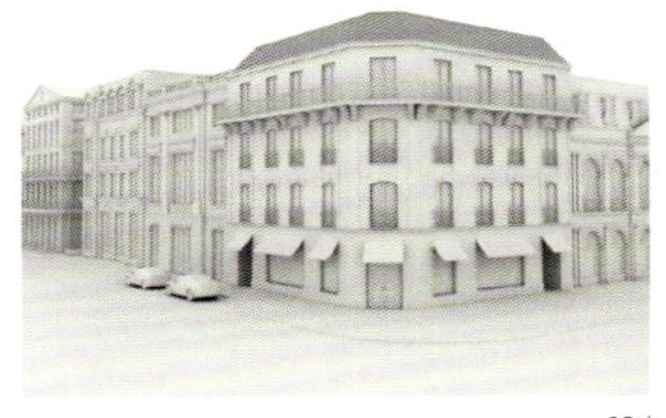

32./

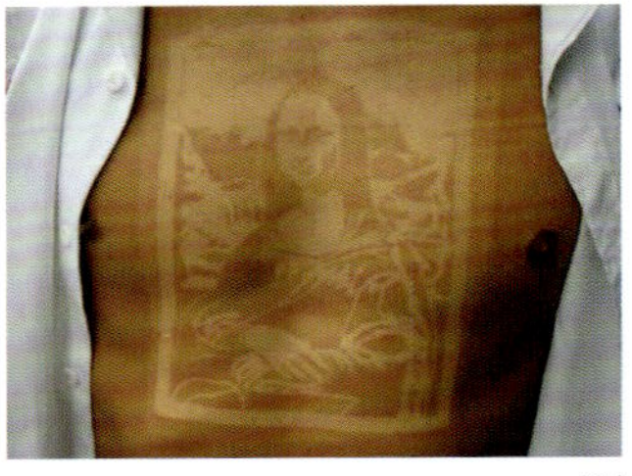

33./

http://www.tvcentral.com.
au/2012/02/01/wikileaks-
founder-julian-assange-to-
star-in-'the-simpsons'/

34./

http://www.dailycognition.
com/index.php/2009/11/09/
innocent-passenger-gets-
arrested-at-airport-for-his-
name.html

35./

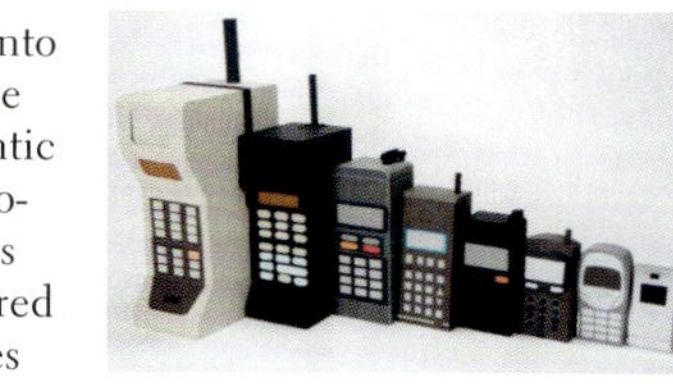

36./

trail that follows this transition (i.e., the oil painting, the grammar of four-reel cinema, jump-cut editing in late 1960s television). For historians, all media begin as anthropology, then evolve into a poetics with its own archaeology. For example, the magic lantern projector converted to a movie projector. Media history tends to be teleological—logical about this inevitable path, as if from adolescence to adulthood. That is a strategy one finds very often in the history of print, cinema, TV, video, and photography. The very thing lacking becomes a virtue. The very quality that makes cinema or literature or photography awkward—at first—becomes the hallmark of its uniqueness. Poetics overcompensates point of view in literature. Film overcompensates art direction and editing.

But in our era we have a problem. This path to "reality" in media doesn't work that way anymore. Let us be generous: we will say that this early stage into transition can last for twenty years, as it did for cinema and for TV. There is a moment of truth: when the medium stops embedding as it has. This will never be true of the computer or of the real in our century, I suspect. The computer is designed never to stop cross-embedding, even into

the molecules themselves. It is data engineering for brain surgery, for mapping. It "facebooks" its way into all modes of privacy and public life. So we ask a different question today: what if cross-embedding were not a stage but a permanent experience? We would

*The computer is designed never to stop cross-embedding, even into the molecules themselves.*

have to think quite differently about poetics, about what makes a medium uniquely real. It is a new form of intuition for a new form of globalized feudalism.

### The signal

Let us try another approach for a moment: we pause in 1876 at the invention of the telephone, heir to the telegraph signal. By 1877 the telephone (still a mystery more than a device) became science fiction (or parafact). Artists and designers imagined how it would cross-embed with things to come. It would be joined with two-way television, which had not been invented yet. The result, called a telephonoscope,

seemed inevitable in 1876—and ridiculous. The telephonoscope would have a screen and operatic sound speakers—for visual conversations, streaming video, imperialist news reports, and home pornography. In caricatures from 1877 to 1885 (notably by George Du Maurier in London and Albert Robida in Paris), this "telephonoscope" would invade the home, with all its intimacies. It would embed itself right into your brain as you nodded off, like Victorian reality TV.

### Printed buildings

One more strategy in which "a new real" is imagined: by the late nineteenth century, through mass publishing, print and architecture were embedded into each other, in painted fireplace tiles about novels about romantic fireplaces, in architectonic photos, in wood-engraved vignettes based on photos. All these shared the layout of picture magazines like the *Illustrated London News* or *L'Illustration*. In 2012 much the same has happened to architecture on the iPad or as augmented mapping. Of course, in the late nineteenth century the scale was to grow gigantic, toward skyscrapers and so on. In our era the scale is increasingly more nano, like cities carved on grains of rice or children's toys

37./

38./

39./

**The Charm of the Lie: A History of Our Unreliable Grasp of the Real**

TEXT BY
NORMAN M. KLEIN

Fig. 40./ Meme "Hey, Judas . . . Uhh, got a dollar?," from http://www.memecenter.com/fun/70311/hey-judas....uhhh-got-a-dollar

Fig. 41./ Cyber Woman with Corn, from http://gawker.com/5880077/i-cant-stop-staring-at-cyber-woman-with-corn

Fig. 42./ Sigmund Freud pinback buttons, from http://www.zazzle.com/sigmund_freud_button-145277064315610252

Fig. 43./ http://www.funnyordie.com/videos/cf2b58e02e/the-princess-beatrice-hat-song-osama-bin-laden-is-dead

Fig. 44./ QR code mobile apps for video training, from http://envisioncad.com/blog-articles/cad-training-android-apple-iphone-ipad/

Fig. 45./ The iNotePad by Nice Pear™, from http://shedsimove.com/node/874

Fig. 46./ Map tattoo of China, from http://cdugan.wordpress.com/2010/11/18/map-tattoos/

Fig. 47./ Borat DVD, from http://videoeta.com/images/news/borat_disc.jpg

made of artificial skin. There are also problems about how to study the materiality of the real, what Soviet artists used to call *faktura*. In the 1930s, and into high modernism by the 1960s, the answer to almost every master plan was cement or, for dingbat houses, a chicken wire and stucco that resembled cement. Now this modernist gray world feels utterly unreal; it stands in for our abuse of the planet. There are hundreds of examples like these. We need a discipline to sort out the flood of information involved.

On the importance of cross-embedding as "more real," here is a brief list:

**1. Embedding is always a two-way process. If the computer is essentially embedding into urban space or into the body, then the urban and the body are also embedding themselves into digital systems.**

**2. Embedding is often a form of cultural amnesia because the media that are absorbed tend to be forgotten afterward as if they were painted over. So much of media archaeology has been devoted to finding "dead media" (as Bruce Sterling called them) or to media that anticipated future uses but failed to survive (1890s holograms, etc.). We must understand that media cross-embed more than die,**

**but the result is selective memory. When technologies embed back and forth, they essentially impact the culture as a kind of collective Freudian displacement. The material result stands in for what is repressed. When one examines aerial bombing photographs since 1943—embedding the bomb site and the camera—the human collateral fact is seemingly erased, even intentionally.**

**3. Embedding is a process of inversion—for example, from gigantic to micro, from public to private, and so on. These inversions—as reflections of enormous economic shifts—dislocate our sociability (or our sociality), our community life, our urban plans.**

**4. Embedding changes how stories are told. It is an allegory about the apparatus. It invents stories about the mechanics of power, as they change our sense of the real (ontology). The "reality" of built environments is constantly in redefinition, cross-embedded, era by era. For example, the term *virtual* was in wide use by 1740, in discussions of optics and the camera obscura.**

**5. Embedding often generates new forms of social behavior, even of intimacy (seduction, eroticism, pornography, the erogenous as architecture).**

## vi.
## *Casino Capitalism*

We visit an investment house like Goldman Sachs. In the 1970s the computer was embedded into world banking. Despite its unearthly genius, however, once software became a banker, it was often just an extremely "intelligent" chicken. It could only cross the road (really fast, of course). If there was no road, it invented one, like a banking derivative. By 1985 the computer had transformed global banking into a slot machine for cheat codes and gaming. Through instruments like NASDAQ, it accelerated investor greed, which by definition is ruthless, not efficient. That meant instant gratification at the speed of light—the more unregulated, the more open source, the better. As a result, computers helped change the goals of global capitalism, away from cartels, steadily toward a warlord model—risk capitalism. Strike fast and ride on.

But wasn't the book also a kind of Renaissance computer? The printing press, despite its unearthly genius, accelerated the wars of religion, brought the evils of bookkeeping to new lows, as instruments of power. Perhaps that gives us hope. In that sense, the

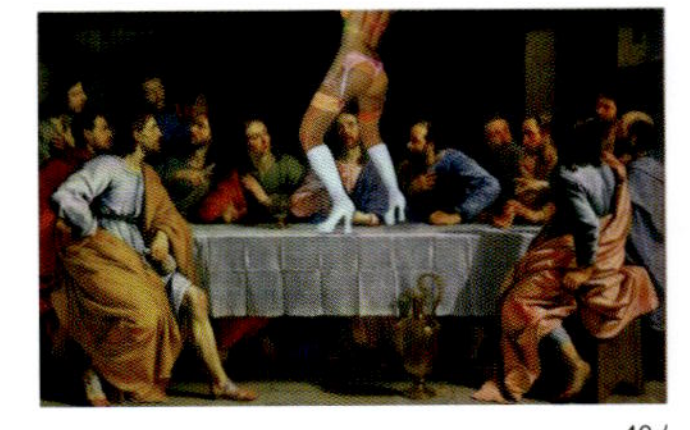

40./

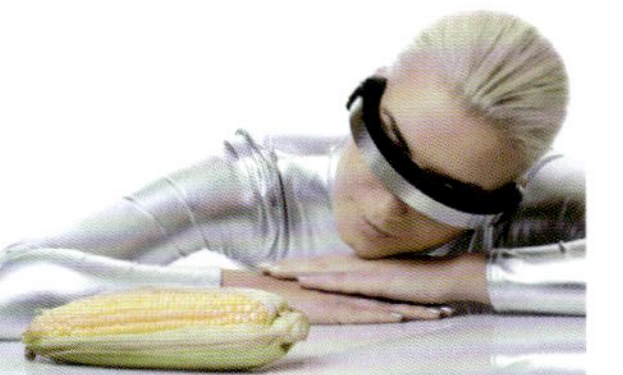

41./

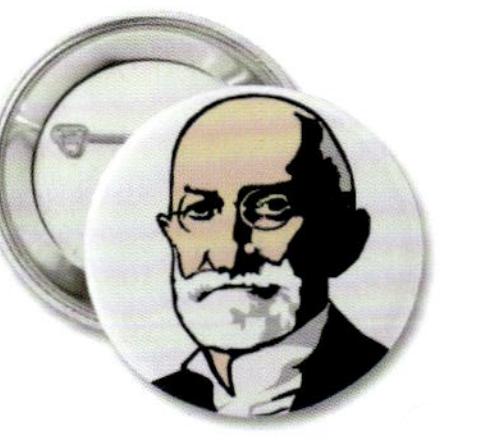

42./

43./

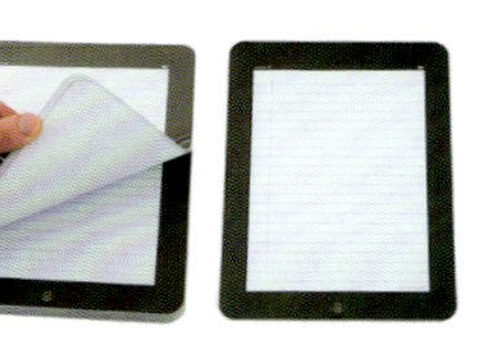

44./

45./

"evils" of printing helped incubate the novel. No wonder (wonder being an aesthetic principle of the time) that early novels were imaginary memoirs built around the shipwrecks of state and sexual intrigue as political stupidity.

We return to that computer chicken crossing the road. It has now blindly helped a rogue (a picaro) steal someone's credit card. Will all this evolve into a new humanism, as print did in the midst of all its madness? Maybe that has happened already, but we were too lost to notice. We have been predicting this tribal Enlightenment for generations now. The computer is certainly as intuitive—as "real"—as print ever was. It is worn even more than operated. Its devices cling to us like clothing. We must harvest this effect, as installation art, video critique, social media about global shipwrecks, street theater about collective play as a picaresque.

Media is pluralism. To be more precise, media is a plural that requires a singular verb. It is multiform, particularly in its early form, as in print and cinema—and in the medium of city streets.

The streets are always a doubled experience. Now that counterpoint will involve GPS and other mobile technologies (i.e., augmented courtships through augmented media). These devices have embedded into how we walk and mentally map a place. We carry our privacy as we go. One might argue that the next stage after theme parks and themed spaces in the 1990s is the building transformed into data, as if traffic signals (sign systems) were now rooms. Streets that we thought of as themed may begin to operate more like "apps" in real space. But the key to this counterpoint is alienation. The more invaded we feel, the more we set up ways to avoid or resist (through urban planning or simply how neighborhoods evolve). Every modernism has its gothic revival, its historicism, very much the content of this exhibition, set in our moment.

Cross-embedding guarantees that very few media actually die. Slides and magazines are not dying; their cell walls are turning into digital files. Of course, millions of slides are being thrown into the garbage. That is like burning down the library of Alexandria and sacking the town. Along with embedding, there is always a "die-off" when platforms embed (i.e., VCRs, DVDs, CDs), when sieges are broken. In the fifteenth century illuminated manuscripts embedded onto print. That graphic transfer controlled the basic design of the book for three hundred years.

Cross-embedding has vestigial organs; these generate a contrapuntal folklore. But most of all cross-embedding changes which fictions convince us. The reality of three acts is not as stable as screenwriting classes suggest. The rules of dramatic structure jump all over the place due to cross-embedding, particularly in Hollywood cinema. After 1977 Hollywood turned toward special-effects blockbusters. As media, these effects changed art direction, editing, screenwriting. They also probably changed realism in the movies. In the past, among Hollywood insiders (the "industry power brokers"), realism meant a three-act drama—not because it was real but because it was cosmic. A story was a story, period. Built into our genetics, there was a three-act way to automatically trigger the audience's emotions. But what if this reality were conditional? Could these rules simply be a poetics that suited industrial capitalism, let us say, from 1920 to 1990? What if the viewer's sense of self is different in 2012? Call it globalized feelings; call it whatever you choose. The famous bottom line is this: surely we are experiencing the reality of

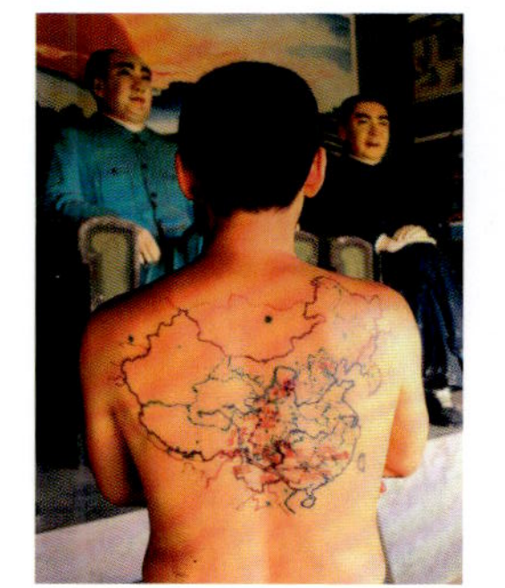

46./

47./

**The Charm of the Lie: A History of Our Unreliable Grasp of the Real**

TEXT BY
NORMAN M. KLEIN

power in a different way. Therefore we must be watching those three acts differently.

Here is a case study to examine right now: with e-books, people will read literature in a different way. Through touch screens, they

*In our era the scale is increasingly more nano, like cities carved on grains of rice or children's toys made of artificial skin.*

will essentially learn to read sideways, to roll, scroll, hit buttons, pull out inserts, to embed video into their reading.

At the same time, the feel of print itself will be considered more real. Print quality for literature will have to be enhanced, more like rag paper. As myth, paper helps you read more carefully, like savoring a good cup of coffee. By contrast, the magazine will become more like glass—faster— like the touch screen itself, with chatty news in depth but instantaneous. Paper is "real," like our bodies; glass is brilliantly slick,

like capitalism. Glass is spectral, narcissistic, chatty, an intimate video. Paper is tactile, more about bricks being torn down, our counterpoint to feeling like tourists in our own bodies.

Books will have to feel more boutique, more paperly, while best sellers will have to zap like touch-screen magazines. The boutique experience presumably is "more human." It humanizes our alienation, our sense of loss. The book is a ruin; it bears traces of mortality: memento mori. Its form must continue to "die" so that its "new" unique qualities can evolve.

### What is a real conclusion?

I've always felt that conclusions should be introductions to another essay that naturally proceeds from what you have just written. In the next essay, I might start by bringing Duchamp back to life, to ask what he might do with cross-embedding. I think I would ask him in 1955, not 1920.

As part of our odyssey, we are determined to invent a new art history, to begin all over again after World War II, because that seems more real, seems to include China and India and Disneyland as the beginning, and suburban urbanism, and TV, and the

military origins of the computer. I would start with modernism as a bit morbid, as the seeds of our ruin, not simply a phoenix rising.

Real history is always about the present. Deconstruction is over because it happened. At this moment, we are closer to structuralists but with serious mental problems: ADHD, autism, bipolar episodes. To shut out the world, we are living "in violet," in a plastic surgery of the present, in which no version of the past or the future has a place. That makes democracy almost impossible to sustain. Politically we are also crazy. I compare "us" (if there is such a collective thing) to a battered housewife who keeps inviting the husband back—and beats up the cop (government) for being five minutes too late.

As I have often said, it is a pharmocracy. We no longer need an unconscious, only good medication. This is indeed the end of the political Enlightenment in the West, in its sensuality, its mechanisms, its entrepreneurial fascination with master planning.

### Doubling down: casino capitalism

If we are talking about more real, we require a new frontier ethic. I would go into greater detail about

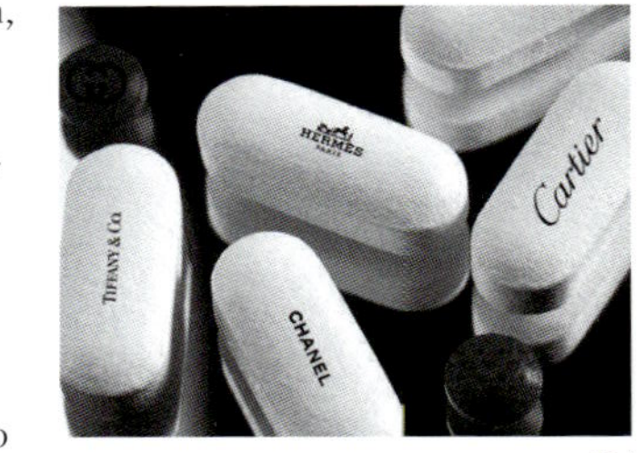
48./

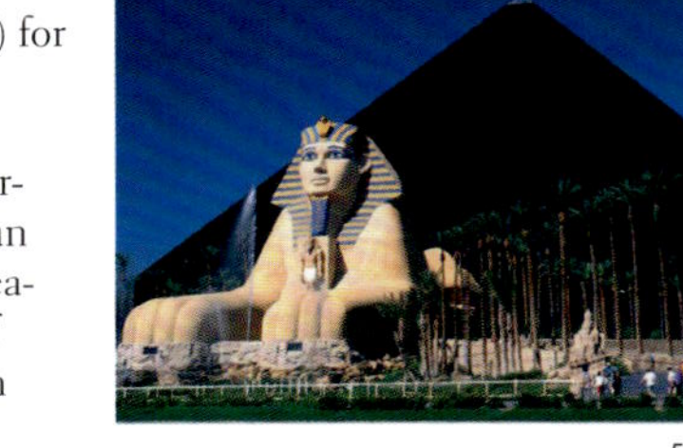
49./

50./

Fig. 48./ Bibliochaise, from http://www.nobody-andco.it/

Fig. 49./ Designer Addiction, from http://themock-ingjay--.tumblr.com/post/6664220893

Fig. 50./ Luxor Hotel in Las Vegas, http://last-minute-deals-las-vegas.com/

Fig. 51./ Mug Shot: I Pity da Fool, from http://www.etsy.com/listing/65407746/mr-t-mug-tea-cup-featuring-mr-t-the

Fig. 52./ FAIL hat in black, from http://lolmart.com/product/fail-hat/

Fig. 53./ Gold keyboard replacement key, from http://thatslikewhoa.com/gold-keyboard-replace-ment-key/

Fig. 54./ http://theberry.com/2010/07/13/i-think-their-plastic-surgeon-used-a-butter-knife-28-photos/

Fig. 55./ Match Lighter, from http://www.popgadget.net/2008/07/match_lighter.php published by PopLife Media, LLC.

spots. They are open source but more heavily encrypted each year. They have a sci-fi metaphysics about them. They can spray your flesh with data. They respond to nanocameras on the eyeballs of insects. Doctors will soon conduct brain surgery via satellite. But often the signals become a comedy of errors. They remind us how incredibly fragile the next century will be.

For example, I live in sunny Los Angeles. Last Wednesday, fierce winds over eighty miles per hour blew out my electricity and heat. Along with close to a million people, I was stranded for many days. Coincidentally, my Internet server crashed, and my modem was fried by surges. You get the point. This was wind, not earthquake. The Department of Water and Power looked perplexed, as it often does. City budgets are too erratic for consistent disaster planning. Americans are learning how alone they can expect to be.

Underdevelopment is the new real in the United States. Right now, globalism looks about as reliable as a cheap cigarette lighter. We are suddenly forced to become more local, due to all this dead reckoning. The diagnosis is plain and simple: the underdevelopment that we face is a rare species of

but found ourselves somehow in the seventeenth century, in a late and perverse feudalism, in a Thirty Years' War of religion. At first, we seemed to be winning in the Balkans. This time, we would avoid a world war. A new cosmopolitanism based on risk felt almost like a *pax romana*, with latte. The fake was marketed as a balloon adventure. Simulation was the new Fordism.

But now we are stuck in the instant ruin of all that. It is comic and tragic, what used to be called great material for art. What an amazing opportunity this crisis offers, and it will very likely persist for decades, a colossal and ridiculous mess. But it is ours, and we will leave as fierce a chronicle as we can.

## Postscript
### (December 2011)

We turn to Internet maps of the sky. They are dotted with communications satellites. The earliest of these, from 1966, were part of a Cold War project known as Intelsat. In 1975 the entire system was privatized for commercial leasing. Now these mirrored satellites convey almost everything that is global—banking, surveillance, entertainment, drone attacks. The signals are as remote as sun-

how the computer helped to screw up finance capital, how it monumentalized risky play. The phrase "casino capitalism" first appeared in 1986, in a book by a British economist.[4] After the crash of 1987, "casino capitalism" appeared in economic news worldwide, even in the German labor movement of the 1990s. After the crash of 2008, capitalism was regularly compared to a casino. Finance had a theatricality, like Vegas. The slot machine and the platforms for NASDAQ were digitized at almost the same time (with almost the same software) from 1978 to 1985 and sped up after 1986. Indeed, derivatives are very similar to slot machines in their random logic. In the 1990s globalism turned risk into family play across media, even on stock-trading TV shows. Simulated money felt comforting and real.

Then the house of cards went down, of course. In stages, this cross-embedding of money has taken a dark turn. Risk now suggests oil spills and crooked, simulated money. Suddenly risk is volatile. The "scripted space," as I call it, has now lost its insulation, its mood of safety.

I might sync this up with the end of the twentieth century. After 1989 we left the twentieth century

http://theberry.com/2010/07/13/i-think-their-plastic-surgeon-used-a-butter-knife-28-photos/

54./

55./

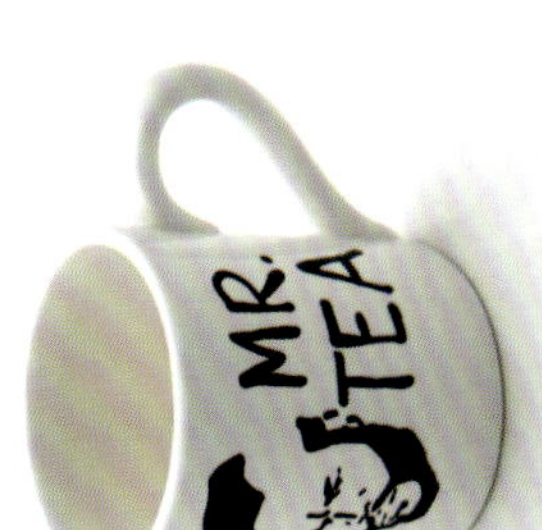



51./

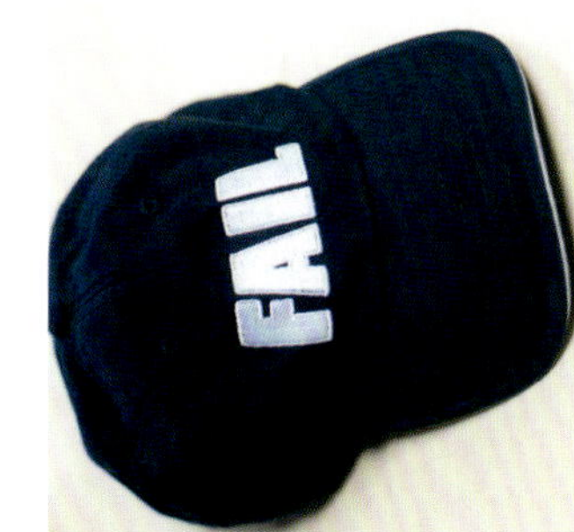



52./

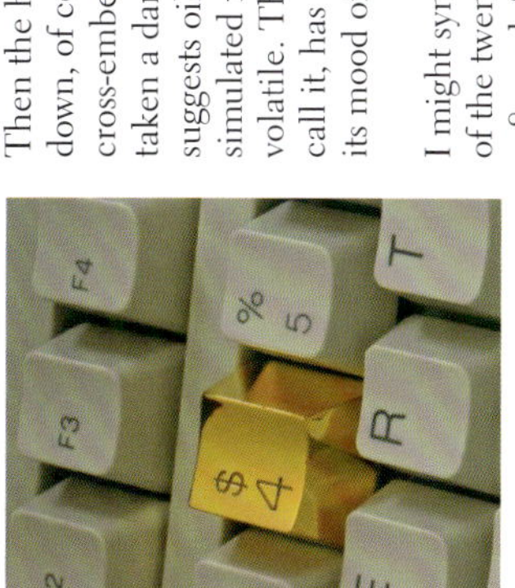

53./

**The Charm of the Lie: A History of Our Unreliable Grasp of the Real**

TEXT BY
NORMAN M. KLEIN

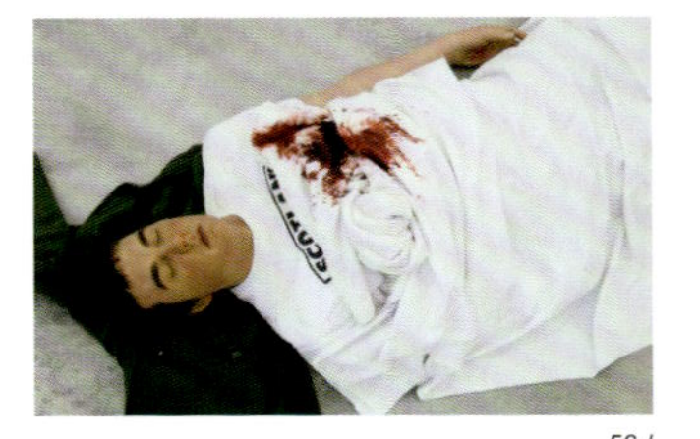

Fig. 56./ Jonathan Monk, *Deadman* (detail), 2006; wax, rubber human hair, oil paint, fabrics; 66 x 22 x 12 inches (167.6 x 55.9 x 30.5 cm); courtesy the artist and Casey Kaplan, New York

56./

Fig. 57./ Resistance is Feudal, from http://toppun.com/Political/Buttons/Resistance-is-Feudal-FUNNY-POLITICAL-BUTTON.html

feudalism. It is probably more like feudalism during the seventeenth and eighteenth centuries, when it also included mass printing and international colonialism. In such a world, with allowances for mobile phones today, the global is increasingly very local. With a weak central government, cities and regions are much more stranded. Sovereignty is practically on auction to transnational investors. Laws become increasingly dispersed, vary more region by region.

We are told that our real crisis is caused by soaring deficits. In fact, to be more accurate, it is caused by unstable revenue (debts uncollected for products already delivered) and, of course, the divine right of the 1 percent not to pay taxes.

But there can potentially be a way forward. Let us remember that a mixed feudalism managed to incubate capitalism, even democracy, for five hundred years. We agree that communication satellites are surely part of this emergent feudalism, this oligarchy, kleptocracy. However, the revolutions of the Arab Spring in 2011 would have been impossible without satellites, just as the Occupy movement has relied on texting and apps to maneuver.

Perhaps feudalism also suggests a new mode of direct democracy? Whenever I type *neofeudalism* as a tag with other words on the Internet (with Occupy, banksters, or Detroit, etc.), I immediately get dozens, even hundreds of sites. Millions of Americans are definitely aware of their new "serfdom." American theories on *industrial* and *corporate* feudalism go back to the 1880s. In the United States, feudalism can be urban, be about slums, and it definitely is capitalist.

That is my final exercise for locating more real circa 2020: search the term *neofeudalism* or *global feudalism*. Americans increasingly assume that we may have to engineer solutions through local and regional planning—a bottom-up kind of Enlightenment. They see this as a return to frontier logic. Mercantilist empires discovered the Americas but in time utterly lost track of facts on the ground. We may split apart into three or four sovereign regions. The new real may be local democracies incubated by feudal oligarchy.

## Notes

1. Norman M. Klein, *Freud in Coney Island and Other Tales* (Los Angeles: Otis Books/Seismicity Editions, 2006), 39.
2. I am conflating various figures identified with the French school of critical theory (ca. 1955–90). It is important to historicize these figures (however brilliant they were) and to wonder why the era that followed them has existed for twenty years without a name. Not since the French Revolution surely have decades passed without labels, like bundles of nameless wires at One Wilshire. The era from 2000 to 2010 is commonly identified now as the lost decade. Indeed, the power to name the present has passed from us. When an empire of this scale ends, no empire replaces it, only regions, dialects, silk roads, Facebook friends in thirty countries.
3. Klein, *Freud in Coney Island*.
4. The term *parafact* was invented by Shuddhabrata Sengupta of Raqs Media Collective, in response to Carrie Lambert-Beatty's splendid discussion of parafiction during a retreat in preparation for this book (see Lambert-Beatty's essay in this volume).
5. Harry Brown (Harrison Telfft Angewynne) appears in *Bleeding Through*, in *The Imaginary Twentieth Century*, and in two more novels to come. For more than fifty years (1898–1953), he was hired by the oligarchs of Los Angeles to erase crimes before they became embarrassing. In order to remain anonymous, for business purposes, he

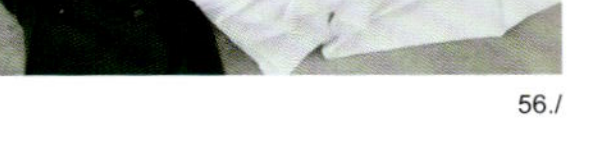


57./

insisted on the name Harry Brown. This had been a family joke for generations: Harry Brown meant someone easy to forget. In 2004 his archive was found in boxes, after decades of being attacked by spores and rodents.

6. Zoe Beloff, ed., *The Coney Island Amateur Psychoanalytic Society and Its Circle*, story by Norman M. Klein, essays by Amy Herzog, Aaron Beebe, and Zoe Beloff (New York: Christine Burgin Gallery, 2009). See also *Albert Grass: The Adventures of a Dreamer* (New York: Christine Burgin Gallery, 2010), illustrations from 1936 to 1939.

7. "In 1926, soon after the Society was founded, its first president and founder Albert Grass proposed that members attempt to recreate their dreams on film and analyze them." Beloff presents a selection of the films on her website. "The Coney Island Amatuer Psychoanalytic Society, Dream Films, 1926–1972," http://www.zoebeloff.com/pages/dream_films.html.

8. John Strausbaugh, "The Case of Sigmund F. and Coney I.," *New York Times*, July 26, 2009. See also Jim Ruland, "Analyze This: Sigmund Freud's Coney Island of the Mind (and Other Cardinal Sins of Therapy)," *Village Voice*, September 26, 2006; Ben Ehrenreich, "Old Haunts Revisited," *Los Angeles Times*, July 2, 2006.

9. Strausbaugh, "The Case of Sigmund F.,". Aaron Beebe is the director of the Coney Island Museum, where this exhibition was shown through the summer of 2009. The museum hosts many events involving ruins, remnants, and fetishes from the history of ludic entertainment. (For example, see also Joanna Ebenstein, "Grand Guignol Spectacular in *The Huffington Post!*," *Morbid Anatomy* [blog], December 12, 2011, http://morbidanatomy.blogspot.com/2011/12/grand-guignol-spectacular-in-huffington.html.) This is very much an archaeological project, while more sites are ravaged on the boardwalk, even in 2011, and the memory of Donald Trump's father continues to haunt what used to be a beach community from the 1910s, which then was torn down in the 1960s.

10. On Huyghe and Parreno's *No Ghost Just a Shell* project, see Elizabeth Armstrong's essay in this volume.

11. For almost twenty years I wrote and lectured about architectural "software" as a manipulation of experience, particularly in *The Vatican to Vegas* (2004). But I am beginning to shift. For example, scripted spaces are identified with themed environments that dominated the globalist expansion of the West but that ended in stages from 1997 on. As of 2012 we are facing an electronic feudalism in the United States that is transforming how the manipulation of experience operates. I have always considered scripted illusion a narrative about power, but now I realize that it is also an *ancien régime*, a sense of being antique, a ruin in the making, the last of the breed, and so on. Thus, scripted spaces are increasingly also about memento mori, dust on the tongue. And the narrative grammar emerging out of globalism is increasingly about the charm of the lie, a much more naked instrument for storytelling than themed environments. We return to the controlled anarchy of the fifteenth century onward.

12. Pierre Bourdieu, *Acts of Resistance: Against the Tyranny of the Market* (New York: New Press, 1998), 102. The book is a summing up at the end of his career, standing in for the sociopathology of the late twentieth century. How indeed do writers speak to power and artists crawl from underneath tourist marketing in this new era?

13. Jean Baudrillard, *The Agony of Power* (Los Angeles: Semiotext(e), 2010), 103.

14. Susan Strange, *Casino Capitalism* (Oxford, UK: Blackwell, 1986). She followed this with *The Retreat of the State: The Diffusion of Power in the World Economy* (New York: Cambridge University Press, 1996), and *Mad Money: When Markets Outgrow Governments* (Ann Arbor: University of Michigan Press, 1998). In the 1980s and 1990s literally hundreds of books and essays noticed the inevitable decline of the Western nation-state under the impact of global capitalism. And yet relatively little policy emerged out of all this, no cognate to Keynesian statism. In the European Union, there was endless concern about returning to the paralysis right after World War II. But Thatcherism and Reaganism set the tone more than these critiques.

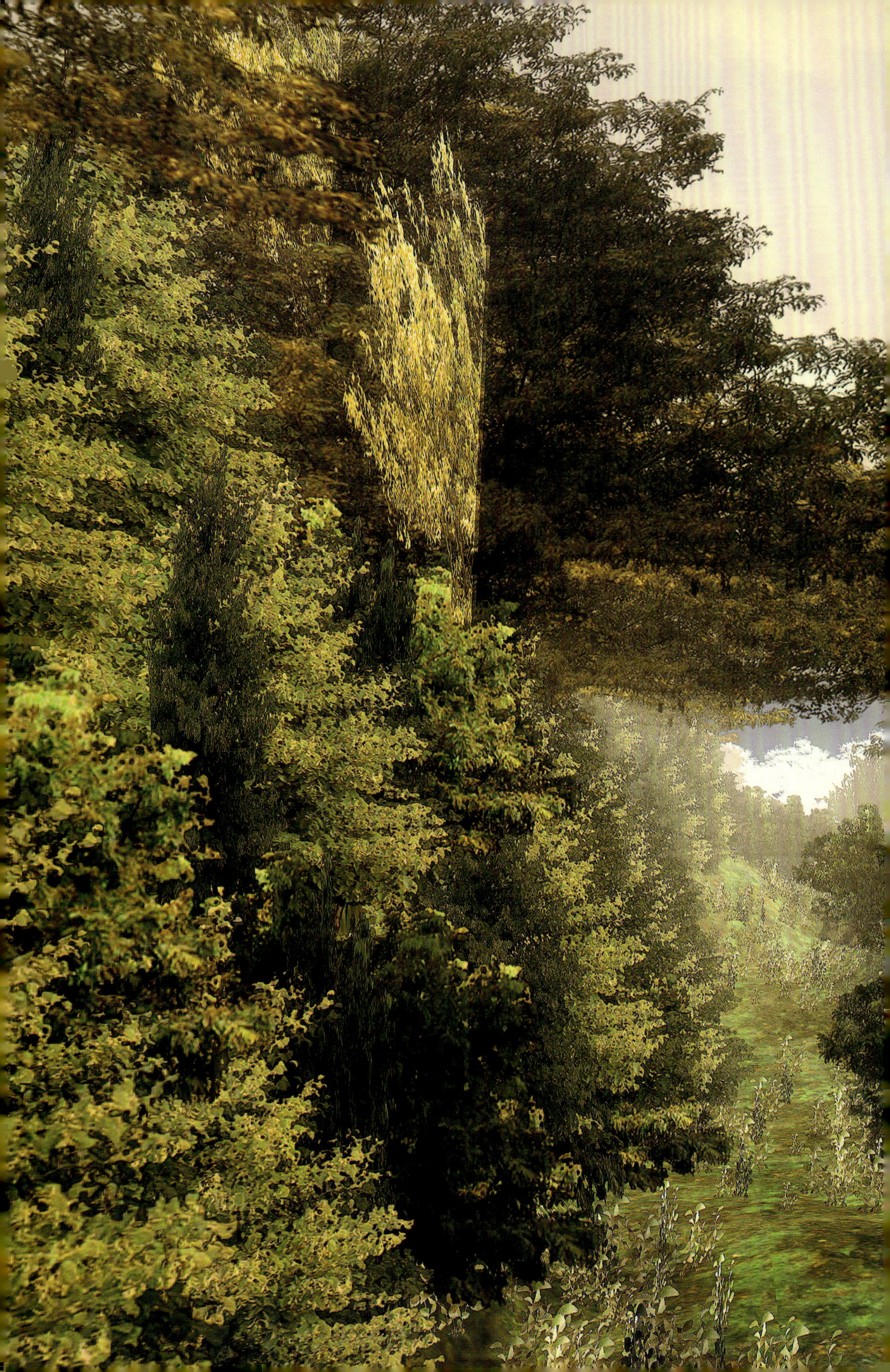

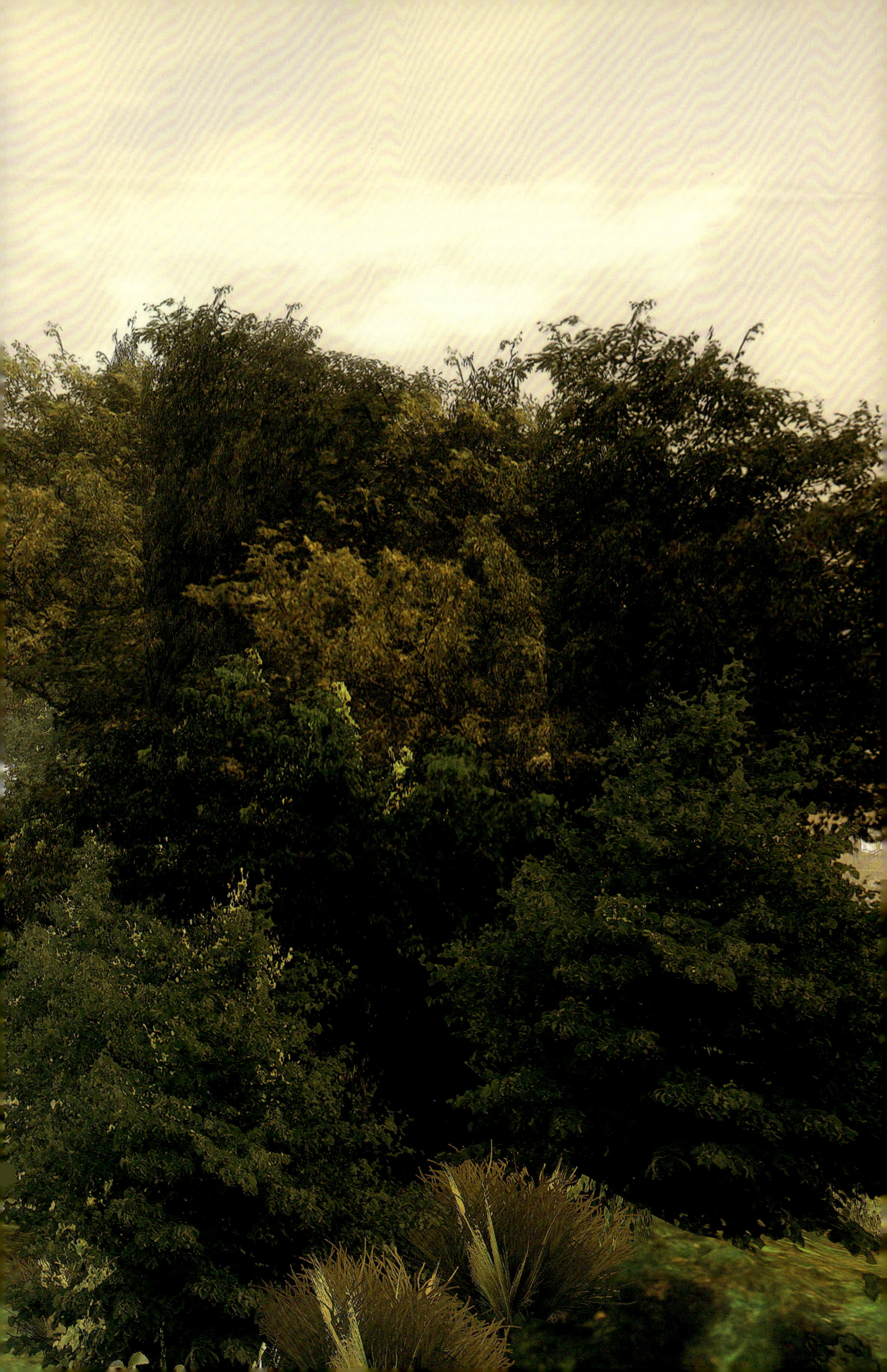

# Ai Weiwei

*BORN 1957 IN BEIJING; LIVES AND WORKS IN BEIJING*

Sculpture, installation, architecture, ceramics, photography, video, the Internet: these are just a few of the mediums that Ai Weiwei has used during an audacious career spanning three decades. Because he has embraced so many means, his work is breathtakingly disparate. He has fashioned irreverent sculptures from disassembled antique Chinese furniture. He installed nine thousand children's backpacks on the facade of a German museum to commemorate those lost in the 2008 Sichuan earthquake. Through his architecture studio, FAKE Design, he has overseen plans for a large urban development in Inner Mongolia and has served as artistic consultant for the design of the stadium for the 2008 Beijing Olympics. He has been a blogger, a publisher, and a curator. What unites all these activities is his deep engagement with Chinese history and culture, both past and present, and his commitment to telling the truth as he sees it. His favorite word, he has said, is *act*.[1]

One of Ai's most notorious acts is the 1995 performance for the camera in which he dropped a Han dynasty urn onto a brick floor, where it smashed to bits. Ai has downplayed the intentionality of his action, saying that he simply allowed the urn—a stand-in for Chinese history, tradition, and culture—to be "grabbed by weight and gravity."[2] Still, the photographs document an act of iconoclasm that is only slightly tempered by the knowledge that an old object was sacrificed in order to create a new one: Ai's performance.

In 2003 Ai began to expand on this theme with the series Colored Vases, which he made by dipping Neolithic clay vases in buckets of Japanese-made industrial household paint. When first confronted with these objects, one wonders whether the vases could possibly be real: has Ai actually painted over dozens of irreplaceable antiquities? But Colored Vases is far more complex than this simple question implies. First, Neolithic pots are fairly commonplace and thus relatively inexpensive, whereas Ai Weiwei's works are highly sought after by collectors. Second, it is far from clear that Ai used genuine ancient vases in the work. When asked directly about their provenance, he has been evasive. One is left to wonder about the status of the Colored Vases—whether they are more desirable as ruined originals or enhanced fakes.

JR

Notes

1. Ai Weiwei, interview with Hans-Ulrich Obrist, in *Ai Weiwei* (London: Phaidon, 2009), 40.
2. Quoted in Dario Gamboni, "Portrait of the Artist as an Iconoclast," in *Ai Weiwei: Dropping the Urn; Ceramic Works, 5000 BCE–2010 CE* (Glenside, PA: Arcadia University Art Gallery, 2010), 86.

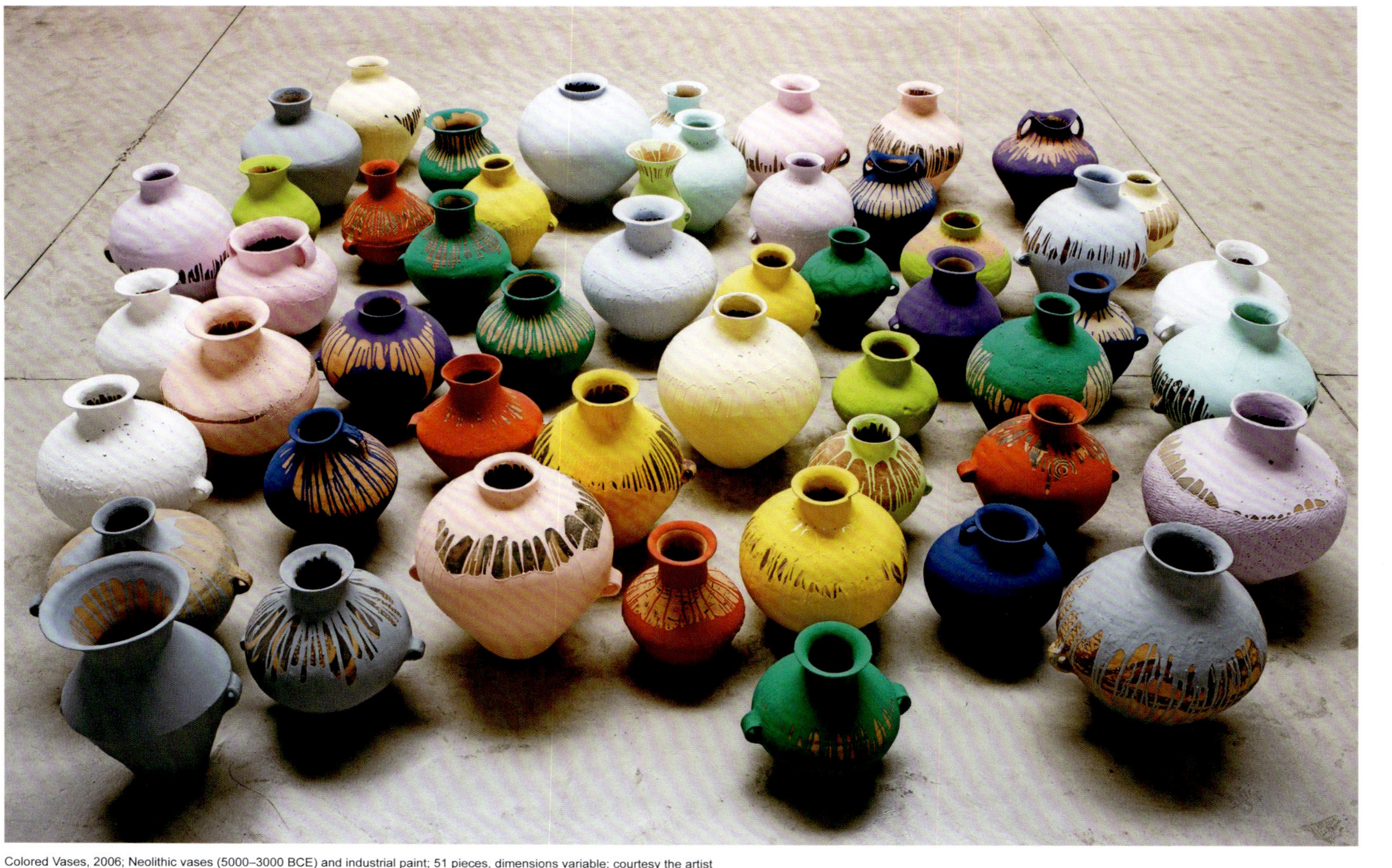

Colored Vases, 2006; Neolithic vases (5000–3000 BCE) and industrial paint; 51 pieces, dimensions variable; courtesy the artist

# Seung Woo Back

*BORN 1973 IN TAEJON, SOUTH KOREA; LIVES AND WORKS IN SEOUL*

"I am a dreamer endlessly floating in my own distorted world."[1] Seung Woo Back has said this of himself, but he could also be describing visitors to Aiins World, a theme park in Bucheon, South Korea. Aiins World is a fantasyland that offers miniaturized versions of more than seventy World Heritage sites and landmarks, some of which feature special visual and sound effects. Visitors can photograph themselves in front of Angkor Wat, the Eiffel Tower, Machu Picchu, or a smoking Mount Kilimanjaro without having to visit the actual sites. But the illusions proffered by Aiins World also contain jarring discontinuities. Tiny Hong Kong junks and ironclad Korean turtle boats float in the waters off Manhattan, where King Kong hangs from the top of the Empire State Building. Concrete backdrops, intended to make visitors' snapshots more "authentic" by isolating the miniature buildings from the city around them, do not completely obscure the modern skyline of Seoul, which sprawls just thirteen miles to the east.

Seung Woo Back has explored the compressed, distorted landscape of Aiins World in his photographic series Real World I (2004–6). As the critic Francis Hodgson has noted, however, Back refused to photograph the park as it was intended to be photographed.[2] His pictures consistently take the "wrong" angle, emphasizing the park's many anachronisms and bizarre juxtapositions and revealing, rather than concealing, the *actual* real world that spreads out beyond the park. In one image, the Great Sphinx and the pyramids of Giza are dwarfed by a banal elevated roadway and nondescript contemporary buildings that loom in the background. In another, a row of trees partially obscures the Louvre; behind it, Manhattan skyscrapers stand shoulder to shoulder with Kuala Lumpur's Petronas Towers. Back emphasizes the oddity of these scenes by adhering to established formal conventions. Like architectural photographs, his compositions are balanced and evenly lit; as with traditional Asian paintings, their elements are gradually "staged" from foreground to background.[3]

Real World I is typical of Back's interest in hyperreal experiences that call into question the relationship between ontological reality and visual reality.[4] A related series, Blow Up (2005–7), came out of Back's visit to Pyongyang, North Korea. Tours of the city are strictly regulated, and visitors who take snapshots must submit their film to security guards for examination (and sometimes confiscation). When Back returned home, he noticed details in his negatives that had escaped the North Korean censors. He isolated and enlarged these details to make the photographs that constitute Blow Up. In both these series, Back commits an act of quiet civil disobedience by insisting that he be allowed to see the world in the "wrong" way.

JR

Notes
1. Seung Woo Back, in *Real World: Seung Woo Back* (Tokyo: Foil, 2007), unpaged.
2. Francis Hodgson, "Seung Woo Back: Real World," *Portfolio*, no. 41 (2005): 4.
3. See the essays by Seung Woo Back and David Campany in *Real World*, unpaged.
4. For further discussion of this topic, see Jean Baudrillard, *Simulacra and Simulation*, trans. Sheila Faria Glaser (Ann Arbor: University of Michigan Press, 2003).

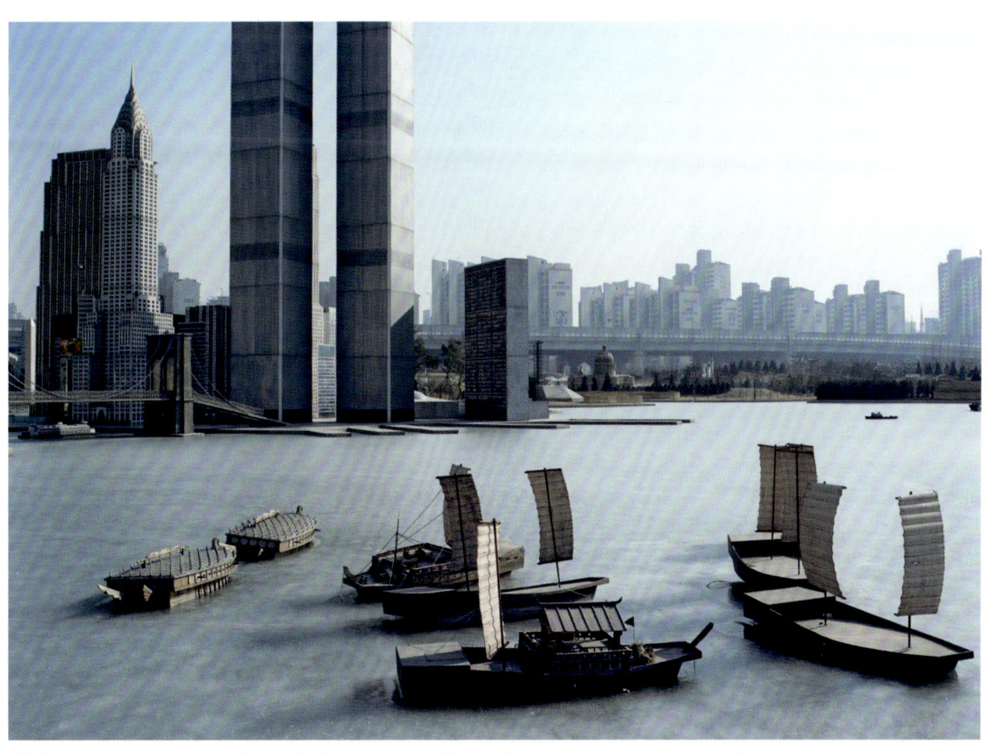

*RW01-001*, 2004, from the series Real World I, 2004–6; digital print; 50 x 66 ½ inches (127 x 168.9 cm); courtesy the artist and Gana Art Gallery, Seoul

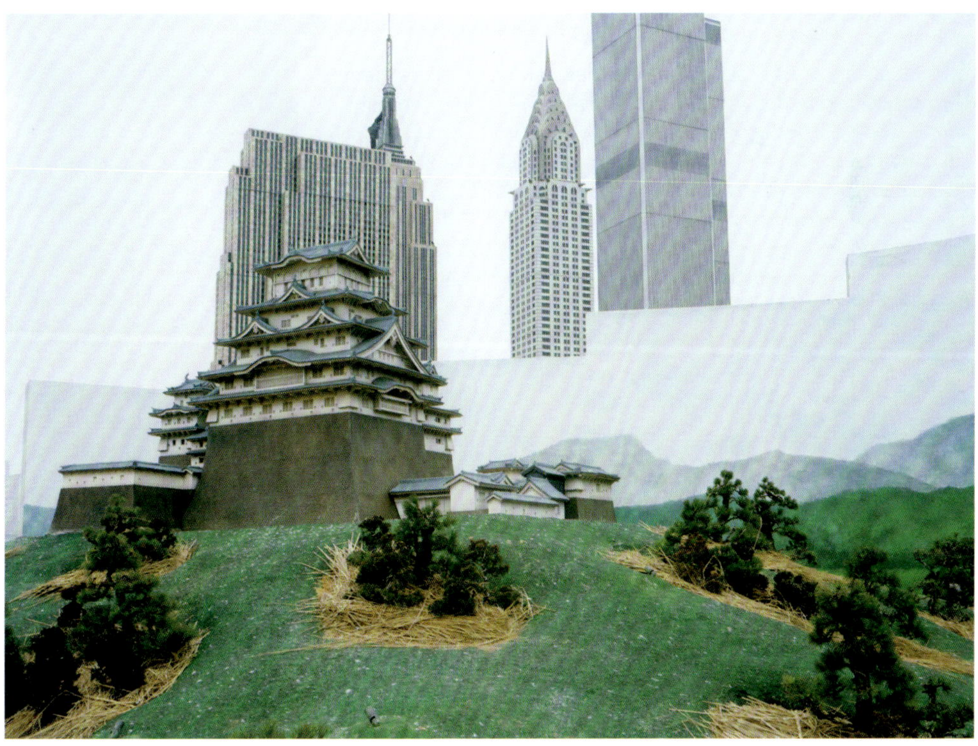

*RW01-002*, 2006, from the series Real World I, 2004–6; digital print; 50 x 66 ½ inches (127 x 168.9 cm); courtesy the artist and Gana Art Gallery, Seoul

# Zoe Beloff

*BORN 1958 IN EDINBURGH, SCOTLAND; LIVES AND WORKS IN NEW YORK*

In her work—which encompasses film, video, interactive media, installation, and drawing—Zoe Beloff looks for ways to make tangible the inner workings of the unconscious mind. She begins each project by choosing a historical document, event, or artifact, usually one that contains elements of both science and spectacle. From there she elaborates, conjures, invents, and fabricates until she has built a narrative that seamlessly merges fact and fiction. Her project *The Somnambulists* (2007), for example, comprises five miniature dioramas into which she projected early twentieth-century films, both real and imagined, of psychiatric patients in the throes of hysteria. In *The Ideoplastic Materializations of Eva C.* (2005), she used stereoscopic images and surround sound to re-create séances held between 1904 and 1912 by Eva C., the celebrated French spirit medium. Beloff has in fact called herself a medium, "an interface between the living and the dead, the real and the imaginary."[1] Her work inhabits the same liminal space.

*Dreamland: The Coney Island Psychoanalytic Society and Its Circle, 1926–1972* began with Beloff's research into the (actual) 1909 visit by the Austrian psychoanalyst Sigmund Freud to Coney Island, New York's storied amusement park. The installation that she eventually created revolves around the purported activities of a group of enthusiastic Freudians and amateur filmmakers, whose archive of drawings, photographs, objects, and short films Beloff "discovered" in the basement of one of its members.[2] One of the project's main components is a working architectural model supposedly based on designs by the society's founder, Albert Grass, who imagined rebuilding the Coney Island attraction Dreamland according to strict Freudian principles. Grass planned five pavilions—arranged around a gargantuan statue of a prepubescent girl called the Libido and linked by a circular Train of Thought— that would give visitors a serious but fun introduction to Freud's theories on the formation of dreams. The society's archive also includes a proposed version of bumper cars called Engines of the Id and the Psychical Apparatus; plans for funhouse mirrors labeled Ego, Superego, and Id; and a cache of short films whose Freudian overtones seemed so purposeful that Beloff deduced that they must have been made by members of the society in an effort to analyze their own dreams.[3]

For this project Beloff combined the roles of curator, archivist, and artist. Where one role begins and another ends is deliberately left vague. Did the Coney Island Amateur Psychoanalytic Society actually exist? "That's a good question," says Beloff. "What do you think?"[4]

JR

Notes

1. See the artist's biography on her website, http://www.zoebeloff.com/pages/biography.html.

2. Beloff describes the genesis and contents of the project in an essay in *The Coney Island Amateur Psychoanalytic Society and Its Circle* (New York: Christine Burgin Gallery, 2009), 51–103. See also "Dreamland: The Intimate Politics of Desire; Zoe Beloff in Conversation with Niels Van Tomme," *Art Papers* 34 (July–August 2010): 26–31.

3. John Strausbaugh, "The Case of Sigmund F. and Coney I.," *New York Times*, July 26, 2009. The so-called Dream Films are actually based on the home movies that Beloff has collected for many years.

4. Ibid.

*Model of Albert Grass's proposed Dreamland amusement park, restored 2009; mixed mediums; 48 x 47 x 48 inches (121.9 x 119.3 x 119.3 cm); courtesy the artist*

THE ARTISTS

# Cao Fei

*BORN 1978 IN GUANGZHOU, CHINA; LIVES AND WORKS IN BEIJING*

One of the most celebrated artists to come of age in post-1989 China, Cao Fei uses video, photography, and performance to explore the profound effects of globalization and hypercommodification on contemporary culture. To make her work, she has delved into phenomena such as video games, cosplay (short for "costume play"), anime, and the online virtual world known as Second Life. All her works address the twin conditions of liberation and alienation that accompany rapid cultural change.

The three-part video *i.Mirror* (2006–7) takes place within the so-called grid, or world, of Second Life. Users create online personas, or avatars, to meet, socialize, and trade goods with other users, often enacting desires that they might repress in real life. In *i.Mirror* we follow China Tracy, Cao Fei's own avatar, as she wanders the grid, which (like the real world) is variously utopian, apocalyptic, deserted, and overbuilt. She encounters another user's avatar, Hug Yue; as their virtual selves explore together, their real selves discuss the appeal of a game in which one's identity is a fluid construct. Hug Yue observes, "There is a crossover between RL [real life] and SL . . . it is hard to separate feelings," and China Tracy wonders, "Is my avatar my mirror?" Ultimately a meditation on loneliness and the difficulty of connecting with others, the video ends with this observation: "To go virtual is the only way to forget about the real darkness."

Following *i.Mirror*, Cao Fei created her own virtual utopia, *RMB City*, within the Second Life grid. Named for renminbi, the official currency of the People's Republic of China, *RMB City* extends the hyperdevelopment of contemporary China into the virtual world of Second Life. Cao Fei's creation is a hybrid of China's largest industrialized cities and iconic locales. Three Gorges Dam flows onto Tiananmen Square, for example, while a Ferris wheel operates atop the Monument to the People's Heroes. The artist has called *RMB City* "a kind of imitation, a dramatic mimicry, an attempt to capture and mirror in a theatrical manner the building and development of an urban center."[1] The site—developed by Cao Fei/China Tracy into an experimental playground for performances, collaborations, and games—extends her own aesthetic sensibilities by conflating past and present, East and West.

JR

Notes
1. Cao Fei, in the video interview "The Building of *RMB City*," on the website for the PBS television series *Art in the Twenty-First Century*, http://www.art21.org/artists/cao-fei/videos.



"

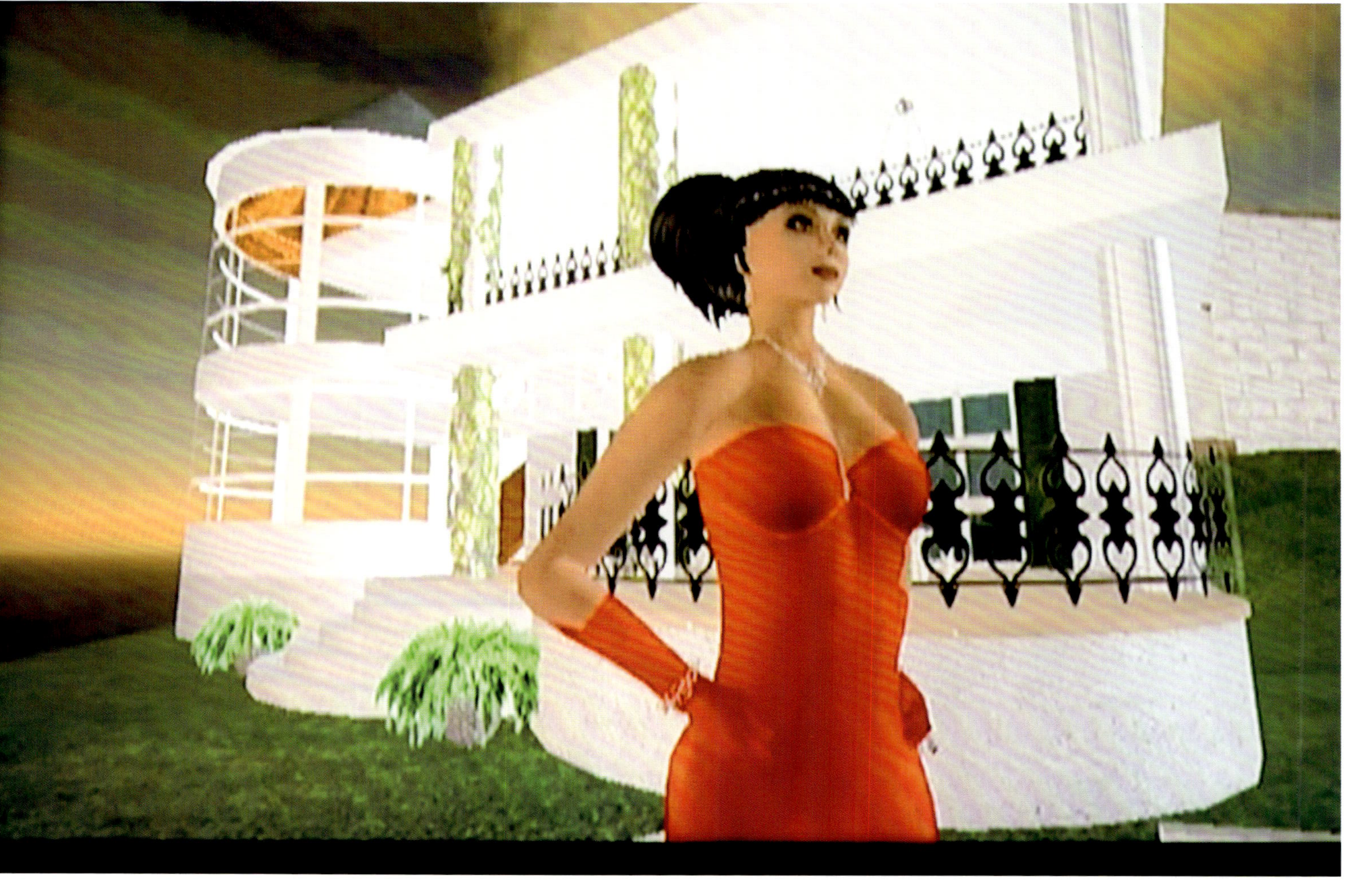

iMirror, 2007; video; 28 minutes; Ella Fontanals-Cisneros Collection, Miami

# Thomas Demand

*BORN 1964 IN MUNICH; LIVES AND WORKS IN BERLIN AND LOS ANGELES*

In his work Thomas Demand plays with the assumption that the camera cannot lie, that what one sees in a photograph reflects a visible truth. His images appear to represent actual architectural spaces, but in fact they depict life-size models that he builds solely for the purpose of photographing them. These sculptures are based on images that he collects from the mass media, but they do not re-create any single image. Instead, they draw on the myriad pictures, memories, and descriptions of a place that have circulated in the culture. Among his past subjects are the corridor outside the serial killer Jeffrey Dahmer's apartment, the interior of Jackson Pollock's barn studio, and Saddam Hussein's kitchen hideout. Regarding his method of choosing subjects, Demand says: "I'm interested in how these images get to me. What path do they take? Why do they get stuck in my head?"[1]

Demand's series Presidency I–V was commissioned by the *New York Times* to accompany Jonathan Mahler's story "After the Imperial Presidency," which was published shortly after the US presidential election in 2008.[2] Demand chose as his subject the iconic seat of American political power, the Oval Office. He began by collecting thousands of images of the space from the media and popular culture. He then mixed and matched elements from those images until he found what he calls "a happy medium between the myth of this room and the reality of it."[3] Using paper, cardboard, confetti, and other ephemeral materials, Demand and his assistants constructed a 1:1 scale model of the hybrid. He then photographed the model from several angles.

Demand's constructed site is both uncannily familiar and strangely bloodless. One might recognize, for example, the drapes used by George W. Bush during his presidency or the flooring that appears in photographs of the Ronald Reagan Oval Office. The rug, which is made of confetti, replicates one used in the television show *The West Wing*. A longer look reveals that certain details have been omitted, such as the stars on the American flag, the facial features in photographs, and the text that encircles the presidential seal. One might see flaws in the construction paper or realize that the furniture is slightly misshapen.

As these features reveal themselves, the truth of Demand's seemingly objective depiction is undermined. The instability of these images suggests the fleeting nature of political power; moreover, because Demand has titled the series after the symbolic office of the presidency rather than the literal workspace, the images also seem to embody the ways in which presidential power can be used in support of a whole range of supposed truths.

NS

Notes
1. Quoted in an interview with Brigitte Werneburg, "Memory Animation," *032c*, no. 18 (Winter 2009–10): 64.
2. Jonathan Mahler, "After the Imperial Presidency," *New York Times Magazine*, November 9, 2008.
3. Thomas Demand, in "Thomas Demand's Presidency," video interview for Deutsche Welle TV, http://vodpod.com/watch/2357729-thomas-demands-presidency.

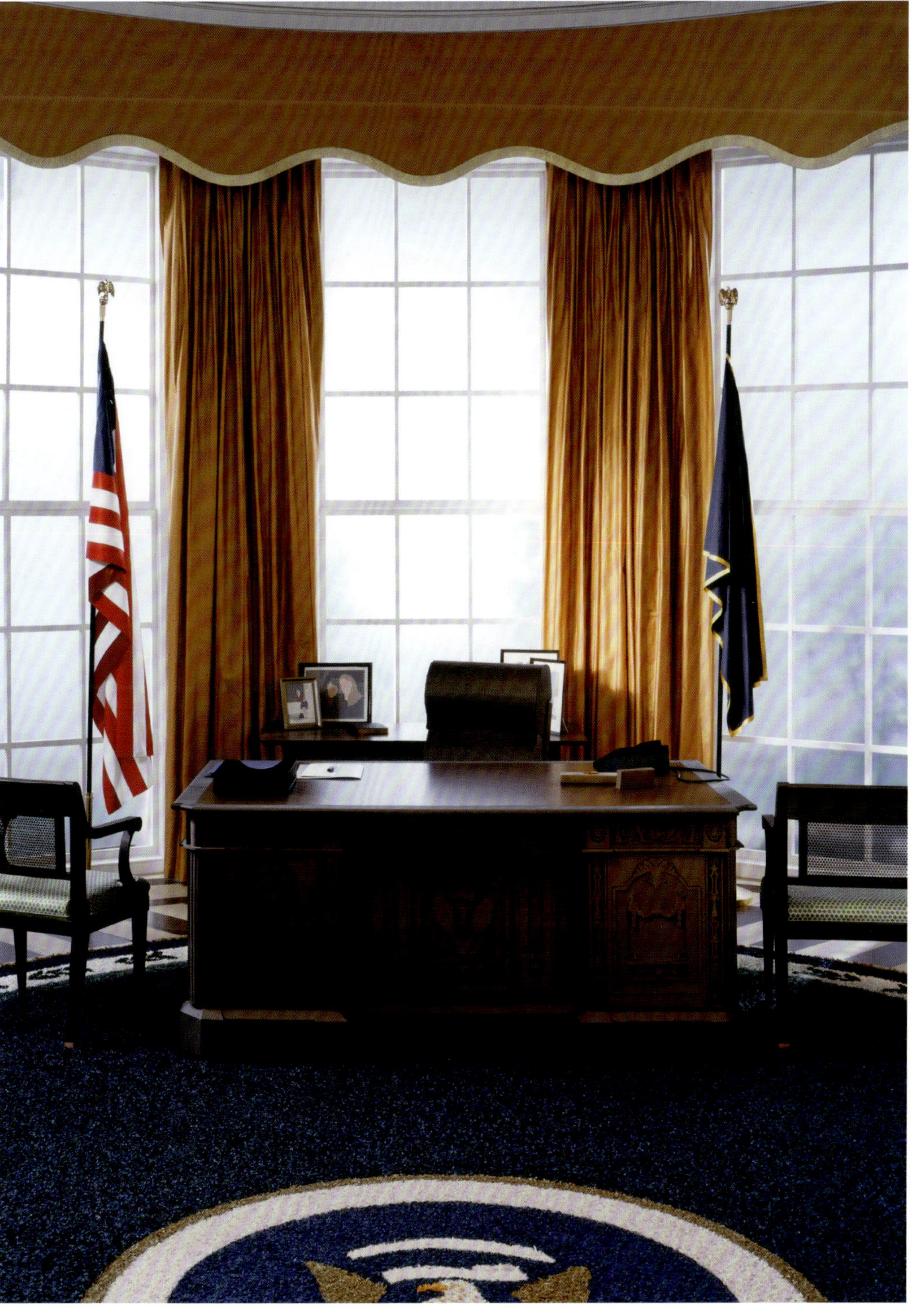

*Presidency I*, 2008; C-print/Diasec 122 x 87 ¹³/₁₆ inches (310 x 223 cm); courtesy the artist and Matthew Marks Gallery

# Mark Dion

BORN 1961 IN NEW BEDFORD, MASSACHUSETTS; LIVES AND WORKS IN NEW YORK

Mark Dion's best-known sculptures are his seductive and often fantastical cabinets of curiosity. Modeled on seventeenth-century *Wunderkammern* (literally, "chambers of wonder"), Dion's displays are filled with animal, vegetable, and mineral specimens along with what appear to be archaeological artifacts and ethnographic curiosities. He arranges these objects according to a system that depends as much on personal taste as on scientific method. By mimicking the syntax of *Wunderkammern*—as well as that of natural history and art museums—Dion brings to light the ways in which the collection and display of objects influence our relationship to nature, history, and culture. His artistic methodology is itself one of mimicry: to make his installations, Dion adopts the roles of scientist, curator, archaeologist, and scholar while never pretending to be a specialist in any one field. Instead, he plays the enthusiastic amateur, the dilettante. In doing so, he has said, "I'm examining the trappings of authority, the signs of authority."[1]

Playing off the signs of authority within the world of academia, Dion created a two-part installation titled *Waiting for the Extraordinary* (2011). Consisting of a waiting room and a small *Wunderkammer*, the work was created for the University of Michigan, Ann Arbor, and is based on a system from the origins of the school in 1816: the "Catholepistemiad, or University of Michigania," in which the university was to have thirteen professorships, each titled with an invented mash-up of Latin and Greek words. Using this system as a starting point, Dion found objects and props that could best represent these classifications of learning and then had many of these artifacts reproduced using 3-D rapid-prototype technology and coated them in phosphorescent paint. Through modern technology, the *Wunderkammer* becomes a hybrid representation of the past and present. But Dion's installation requires visitors who wish to enter to first take a number and wait their turn, simulating the banal experience of waiting encountered in most every institution.

Dion's new installation *Curator's Office* (2011–12), commissioned for the exhibition *More Real?*, adds another layer to his exploration of the ways in which collections of objects are formed and used. In his narrative about the piece, Dion claims that he rediscovered an office used in the 1950s by the first curator of modern art at the Minneapolis Institute of Arts. This office supposedly was part of the museum's original McKim, Mead, and White building but was forgotten after being sealed off during a renovation project. Dion's installation— with its vintage furniture, defunct office equipment, and forgotten artworks—is thus a droll version of the archaeological site that has been discovered intact.

Within the context of a museum exhibition, however, *Curator's Office* also becomes a "period room," an installation of objects, furnishings, and architecture meant to illustrate a historical moment by re-creating its interior domestic spaces. Period rooms are popular museum attractions that are both authentic (in their contents) and false (in their detachment from their original contexts). As such, these displays pose complex museological questions: How does a curator decide which moment in time to re-create? How authentic can a retrospectively assembled room be? How does one maximize both accuracy and educational impact?[2] Because *Curator's Office* highlights the ways in which one person's obsessions, sensibilities, and prejudices shape a museum's collections, it can be read as a metanarrative on the problems posed by period rooms. "Today's museums demonstrate rather than seduce," Dion has said.[3] In *Curator's Office*, he aims to do both.

NS

Notes

1. Mark Dion, in the video interview "Mark Dion: Methodology," on the website for the PBS television series *Art in the Twenty-First Century*, http://www.art21.org/videos/short-mark-dion-methodology.

2. For discussion of these questions and others, see Trevor Keeble, Brenda Martin, and Penny Sparke, eds., *The Modern Period Room: The Construction of the Exhibited Interior, 1870 to 1950* (New York: Routledge, 2006).

3. Lawrence Weschler, "The Irritated Cloud: Mark Dion in Conversation with Lawrence Weschler," in *The Marvelous Museum: Orphans, Curiosities, and Treasures; A Mark Dion Project* (San Francisco: Chronicle; Oakland: Oakland Museum of California, 2010), 23.

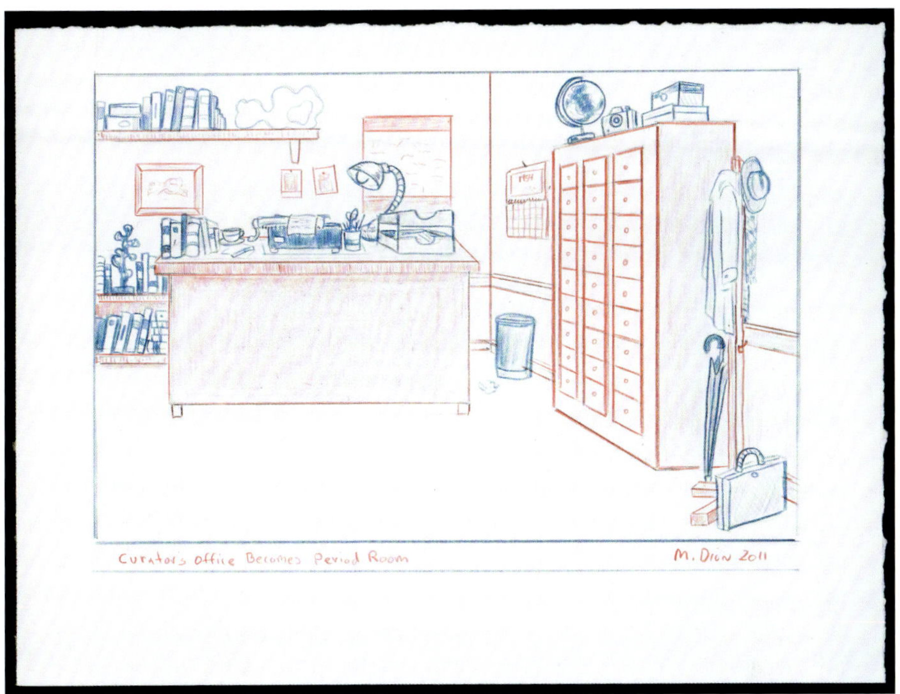



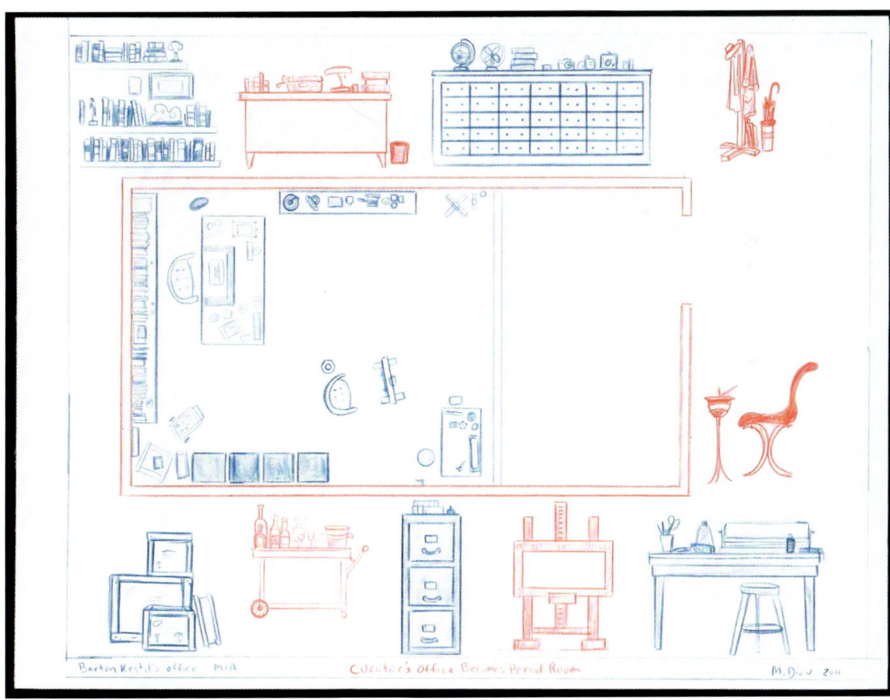



Sketches for *Curator's Office*, 2011; colored pencil on paper; 8 x 10 inches (20.3 x 25.4 cm) each (approx.); courtesy the artist

# Leandro Erlich

*BORN 1973 IN BUENOS AIRES; LIVES AND WORKS IN BUENOS AIRES*

Leandro Erlich produces sculptural mirages. He re-creates mundane architectural spaces or elements in meticulous detail and then somehow disrupts them, offering viewers an uncanny or disorienting experience. Staircases, windows, elevators, and swimming pools appear to defy basic laws of physics, while living rooms, lobbies, and subway cars appear so real that they elicit double takes. In *Rain* (2000), Erlich built a window into a gallery wall, then combined real water and simulated lightning to mimic a thunderstorm raging endlessly "outside." *Swimming Pool* (1999) was a full-size re-creation of a pool that he constructed at the 2001 Venice Biennale. Viewed from above, it offered a surreal scene: fully clothed people appeared to be walking, talking, and breathing beneath the surface of the water. Only when the piece was seen from its lower level was the illusion unmasked. The people were actually mingling in an empty pool whose ceiling was a large, continuous piece of acrylic with just a few inches of water on it. Erlich says that the element of surprise, so critical to his work, functions as "a way to stop the viewer and make them see that things have varying degrees of reality."[1]

Most recently, Erlich has turned his attention to a banal feature of urban life: the elevator. He thinks of it not only as a convenient means of transport but also as a charged entryway to alternate realities in which, he says, "life seems to be suspended parenthetically."[2] He has created a dimly lit, scarred tunnel that mimics an elevator shaft turned on its side; a disorienting maze of cabs fitted with mirrored walls and polished brass; and a full-size cab whose doors open with a chime to reveal a crowd of passengers (actually a video projection) staring out impassively at us. *Stuck Elevator* (2011) is both frankly fake and weirdly disorienting. Although clearly a freestanding sculpture, it also appears to be an elevator cab stuck between floors, its doors jammed open to reveal a glimpse of the interior. Carefully placed mirrors create the illusion that the shaft plunges downward through the floor of the gallery. A discarded newspaper inside the cab hints at a nightmarish narrative of entrapment and escape. Such optical tricks are meant not to deceive viewers but to present them with a visual problem to be absorbed and then resolved. "Reality," says the artist, "is as fake and constructed as the art; it's a fiction. Although it's the fiction that we all agree to live in."[3]

IH

Notes

1. Leandro Erlich, quoted in Elena Oliveras, "Leandro Erlich: Mirages in the Everyday," *ArtNexus*, no. 70 (September–October 2008): 6.

2. Leandro Erlich, quoted in a press release for the exhibition *Two Different Tomorrows* issued by Sean Kelly Gallery, New York, September 10, 2011.

3. Leandro Erlich, in an October 29, 2008, interview with Paul Laster for Artkrush, posted on the artist's website, http://www.leandroerlich.com.ar/exhibitions.php.

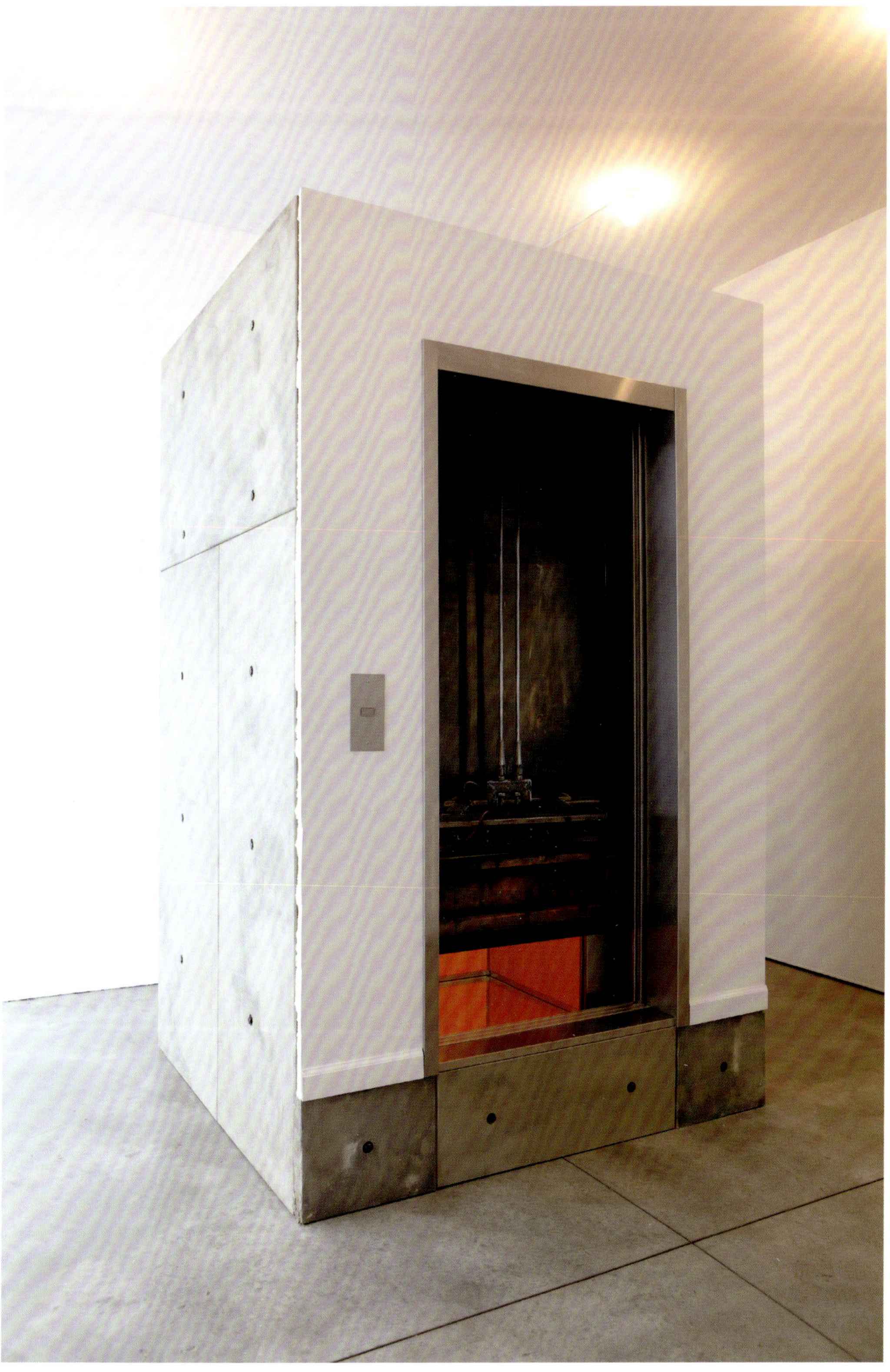

*Stuck Elevator*, 2011; mixed media, metal structure, wood, stainless steel, mirrors, button panel, airbrush painting; 109 1/2 x 68 1/4 x 66 1/2 inches (278.1 x 173.4 x 168.9 cm); courtesy Sean Kelly Gallery, New York

# Omer Fast

*BORN 1972 IN JERUSALEM; LIVES AND WORKS IN BERLIN*

For more than a decade Omer Fast has created video works that investigate the constructs of the documentary form, in particular the way historical narratives are built through a series of authorial choices. His works explore how history is written during the very process of its telling—in other words, "how memory becomes story."[1] Fast uses poetic suggestion to render first-person accounts as, above all, stories, which, he proposes, are fusions of memory and emotion that become intertwined with other memories and emotions. In this way his works reside in the interstices between reality and fiction.

For the video installation *Spielberg's List* (2003), Fast interviewed several Poles who worked as extras in Steven Spielberg's World War II drama *Schindler's List* (1993), which was filmed near Kraków. Some of the interviewees had actually lived through the war and recounted to Fast their childhood memories of the Holocaust. *Spielberg's List* is a carefully edited work in which several layers of reality and fiction intersect to disconcerting effect. The actors' accounts of their experiences working on the film and their experiences during the war are juxtaposed with images of the *Schindler's List* set, which was never completely dismantled and still lies in disrepair not far from the ruins of an actual German labor camp. Watching Fast's video, it is difficult to ascertain which experience the interviewee is referring to at any given moment. Contributing to the illegibility of the narrative are English subtitles that were intentionally altered to present slightly inaccurate translations.

Fast employed similar strategies in the video installation *Godville* (2005), which focuses on three reenactors who work at Colonial Williamsburg, a living-history museum in Virginia. Fast interviewed them both as their eighteenth-century characters and as their contemporary selves. He then intertwined the stories to make a new narrative that creates parallels across time periods. A reference to the Revolutionary War segues to a discussion of the terrorist attacks of September 11, 2001; a black actor's remarks about racism in colonial America resonate with contemporary situations.[2]

While *Spielberg's List* and *Godville* offer multiple individual perspectives about shared experiences and related historical events, other works focus on the stories of an individual. This strategy heightens our awareness of the role that emotional resonance plays in the formation and linkage of memories. In *The Casting* (2007), Fast focused on the memories of an American soldier. His recollections of two traumatic incidents—the accidental killing of an Iraqi civilian and a romantic encounter with a woman prone to suicidal behavior—are edited into a series of new thoughts that conflate the incidents into a single narrative. A dual-sided installation allows for the parallel retelling of the events in two forms. On one side, Fast interviews the soldier, who recounts his memories. On the other, reenactments of the narrated events appear. We learn, however, that the man being interviewed is actually an actor auditioning for the role of the soldier. This revelation destabilizes any assumptions about the concrete nature of the memories portrayed, a project that is at the heart of Fast's work.

JD

Notes

1. Gideon Lewis-Kraus, "Infinite Jetzt," in *In Memory: Omer Fast*, ed. Sabine Schaschl (Berlin: Green Box, 2010), 51.
2. Holland Cotter, "Is It Reality or Fantasy? The Boundaries Are Blurred," *New York Times*, January 7, 2010.

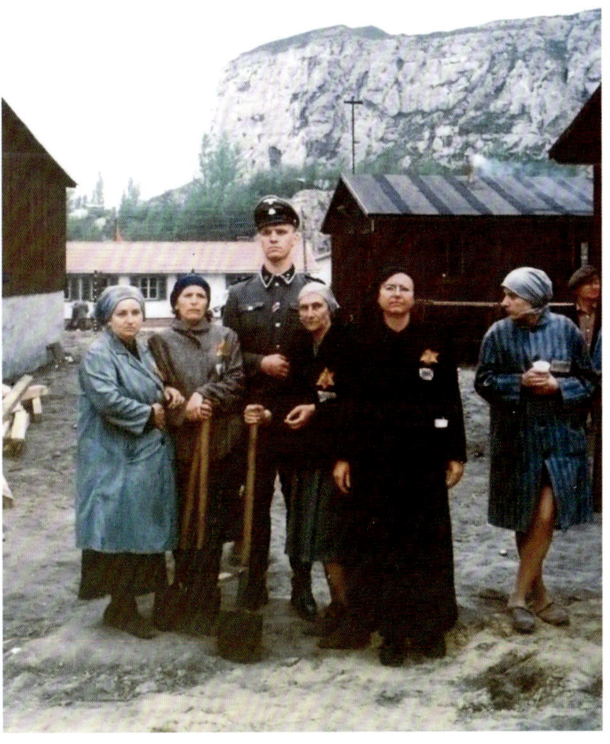

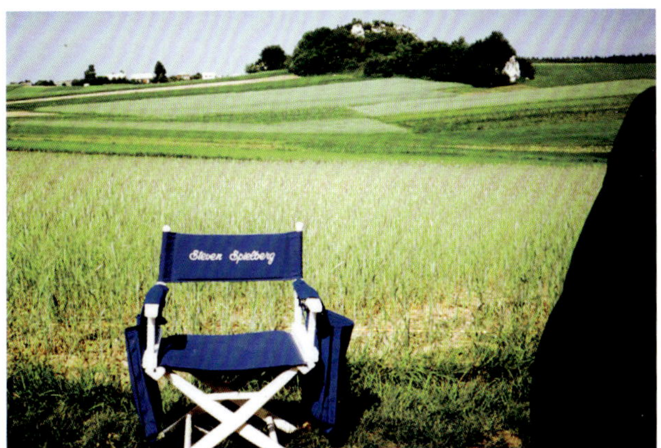


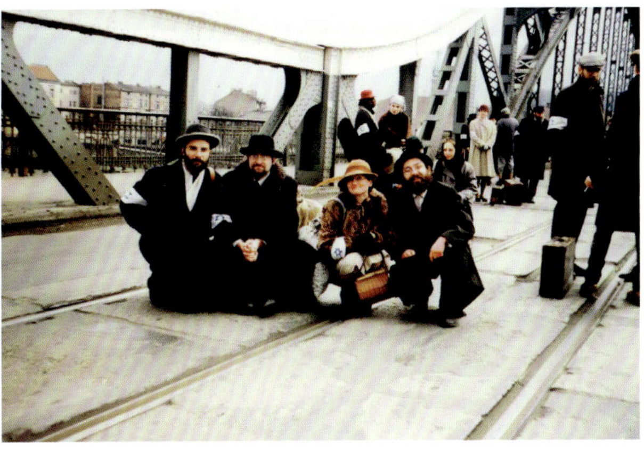

*Spielberg's List: Photos Taken by Extras during Production of the Film Schindler's List*, 1993; snapshots; various dimensions; courtesy the artist

# Kianga Ford

*BORN 1973 IN WASHINGTON, DC; LIVES AND WORKS IN NEW YORK*

Believing that our era is characterized most of all by fictiveness, Kianga Ford makes art that explores narrative as a lived and immersive experience. Her works include interactive audio recordings that blend her short fictions with music and oral histories, as well as immersive sound and video installations that create a three-dimensional story experience. In her projects, which are often site-specific, Ford draws variously on the conventions of cinema and television to explore the ways in which we negotiate and are negotiated through the fictions that we tell about one another.

In 2003 Ford began a series of audio walking tours, gathered under the rubric The Story of This Place, which combine fact and fiction to explore a city's history, communities, and culture. The project so far includes tours of Los Angeles; Winston-Salem, North Carolina; Baltimore; and other cities; the tour of the latter, subtitled *Charm City Remix* (2008), is a forty-five-minute guided walk through Baltimore's Mount Vernon neighborhood. Participants used iPods to listen to Ford's narrative, a fictional history of real places that was based on her conversations with city residents. An original sound track, written by a local composer, accompanied the stories. Ford has described *Charm City Remix* as "a provocation to look at the place you're in in a different way, to look at the people around you in a different way. . . . I want that moment when it all comes together—the light, the music, the narrative, the people—to inspire a sense of, if not awe, then connectedness."[1]

In a piece commissioned for *More Real? Art in the Age of Truthiness*, Ford combines her project series The Story of This Place and You Are Here. The new work is a multipart narrative that guides visitors on walking tours of sites in Minneapolis and St. Paul. The tours reflect on the complex landscape of immigration in the region, which has become home to large numbers of Scandinavians, Hmong, and Somali, as well as other groups, over the past century. Ford's narratives were developed from material gathered during interviews and oral history workshops that she conducted with area residents. Engaging a range of migration and immigration experiences, Ford's new piece "reflects on . . . the different experiences of a visit, which imagines a return; a pilgrimage, which marks a personal life milestone but is never imagined to be permanent; and a migration, which permanently re-orients."[2]

A unique feature of her project for the Minneapolis Institute of Arts is an audio tour that maps a fictional geography within the galleries of the museum itself. As visitors walk through the museum's collections of Asian, African, Near Eastern, and European art, they listen to a story that engages the objects in a way that is more poetic than interpretive. In this iteration of You Are Here, Ford combines fact, fiction, conjecture, and truth to connect the art preserved within the museum to the changing communities that surround it.

IH

Notes

1. Kianga Ford, in "Charm City Remix (Baltimore)," YouTube video, 5:27, posted by MovingBoxStudios, October 2, 2008, http://www.youtube.com/watch?v=RQDxLpu182E.

2. Kianga Ford, undated project proposal for *More Real? Art in the Age of Truthiness*, Minneapolis Institute of Arts files, [2011].

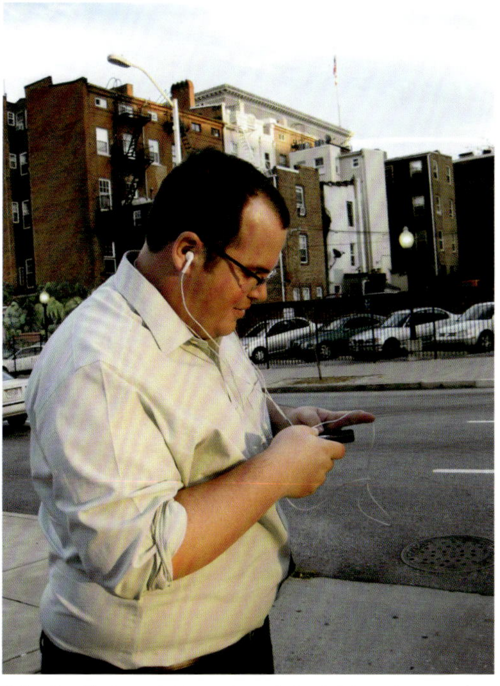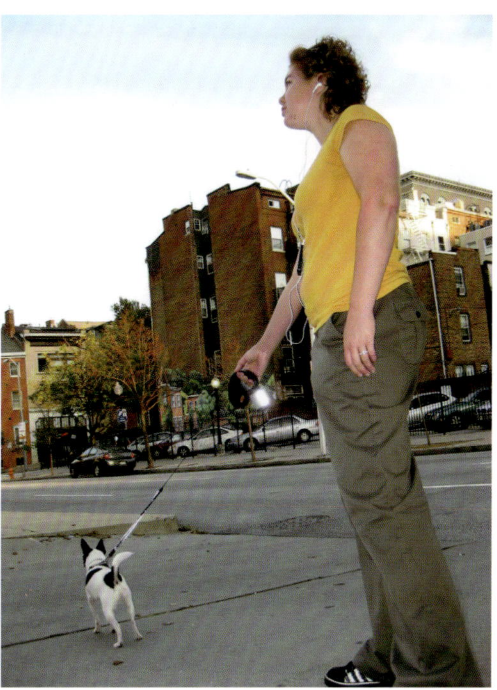

Walkers from *The Story of This Place: Charm City Remix*, 2008; performance at Contemporary Museum, Baltimore; courtesy the artist

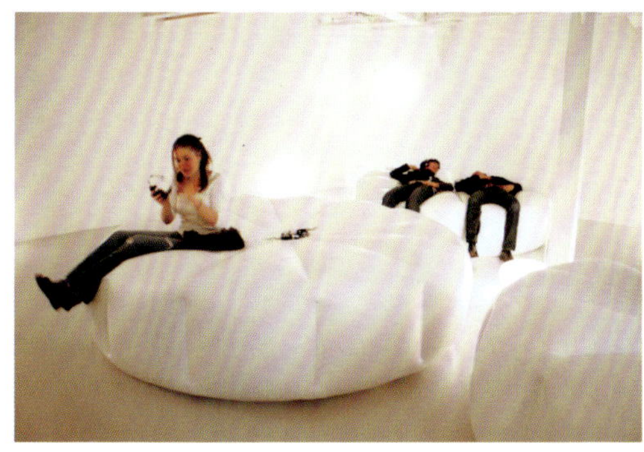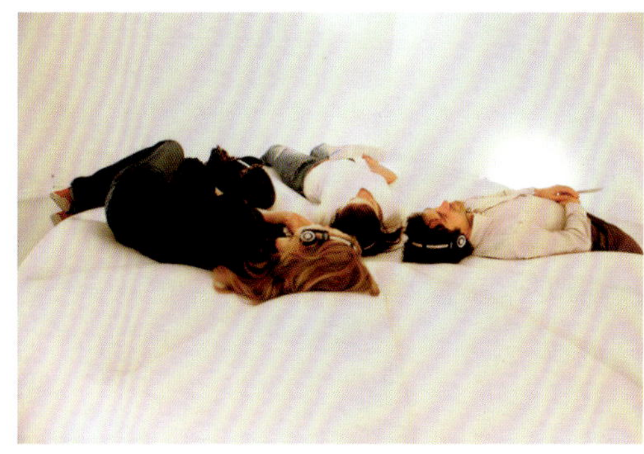

Installation view of *The Story of This Place: Charm City Remix*, 2008; performance at Contemporary Museum, Baltimore; courtesy the artist

# John Gerrard

*BORN 1974 IN DUBLIN; LIVES AND WORKS IN DUBLIN AND VIENNA*

Each of John Gerrard's astonishingly realistic digital projections begins with the thousands of still photographs that he takes at specific locations all over the world. With the help of a producer and an animator, he then turns the images into computer-generated, real-time 3-D animations that are exacting simulations of the real world. Within these uncanny realms, something happens: an oil derrick stoops repetitively to the ground, trucks arrive at a pig production facility to take the animals to slaughter, a dust storm sweeps across a barren Texas landscape. While each of these small dramas is completely plausible, Gerrard's animations are more than just well-constructed digital fictions. Each one plays out against real-time atmospheric conditions, such as changes in the weather, sunrise, sunset, and the phases of the moon. Gerrard makes graphic translations of these conditions and programs them into the work. Viewing his work, one is thrust into a liminal world in which what one sees is both true and false.

Looking at Gerrard's *Oil Stick Work (Angelo Martinez / Richfield, Kansas)* (2008), one is struck by the precise rendering of the grain silos, the landscape, and the weather, which reflects the local atmospheric conditions as they are happening in real time in Richfield, Kansas. What is not always visible in the work is Angelo Martinez, a computer-generated man who mounts a ladder every morning to cover one square meter of the silos with black oil stick. At that rate, the silos will not be blacked out—and the piece will not be completed—until sometime in 2038. "The 30-year trajectory [of the piece]," Gerrard says, "is not an accident. The general understanding is that the replacement of petroleum as our main energy source will happen in that period."[1] In contrast to the fast pace and instant gratification offered by many video games, this piece foreshadows a moment of reckoning; it is a waiting game that unfurls slowly.

Some of Gerrard's newest works have begun looking at how the military uses simulations and the fascinating links between video game technology, landscapes, and basic training. Before American soldiers are introduced to live ammunition exercises in the field, they are trained using "full immersion" simulators that have been reformatted from game consoles. Basic-training exercises are combined with the immersive environments and team combat strategy used in first-person shooter games to simulate some of the physical and logistical stresses of being in battle. Gerrard's *Infinite Freedom Exercise (near Abadan, Iran)* (2011) takes inspiration from a photograph by Henri Bureau in which an Iranian soldier watches a pair of oil refineries burning in Abadan, in southwest Iran, during the first Iran–Iraq war, in 1980. In the foreground the figure of a soldier dressed in generic army fatigues performs an ongoing set of actions. Derived from 3-D motion capture and assigned to the figure in real time, these movements mimic the poses of American soldiers reacting to mortar fire in military exercises, principally in the Gulf region.[2] A related work by Gerrard titled *Live Fire Exercise (near Djibouti)* (2011) is sourced from a military database of videos in which military vehicles are destroyed in a massive explosion.[3] As the blast erupts over the span of a day, the viewing experience becomes a conflation of the simulated danger, aestheticized destruction, and embedded yet distanced spectatorship that we are now accustomed to when experiencing war coverage. Gerrard's work has all the sensuousness of beautiful graphics but also contains a commentary about the limits of virtual environments that is deadly serious.

CA

Notes

1. "How John Gerrard Is Sculpting the Future," *Sunday Times* (London), March 14, 2010.
2. Paula Naughton, Simon Preston Gallery, New York, e-mail correspondence with Elizabeth Armstrong, March 11, 2012.

3. Djibouti is home to Camp Lemonnier, the primary base of operations for US Africa Command in the Horn of Africa, and is home to Commander, Combined Joint Task Force—Horn of Africa. It was established as the primary base in the region for the support of Operation Enduring Freedom. See "Camp Lemonnier, Djibouti," on the Commander Navy Installations Command (CNIC) website, http://www.cnic.navy.mil/cldj/.

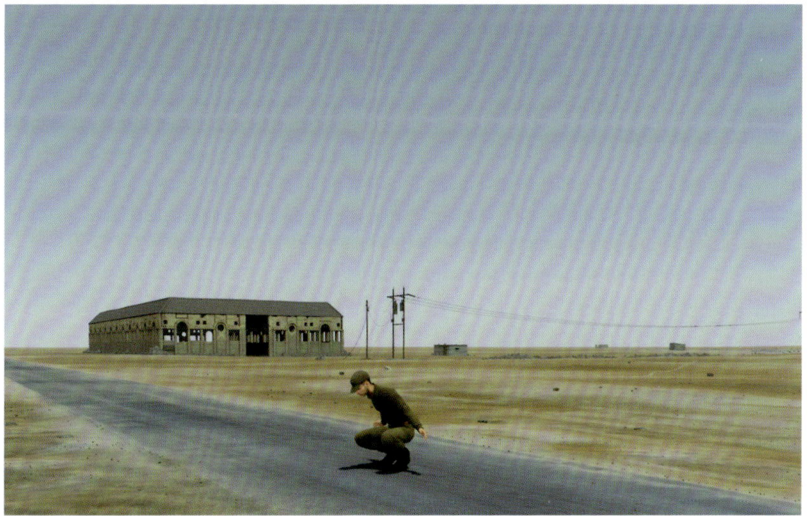

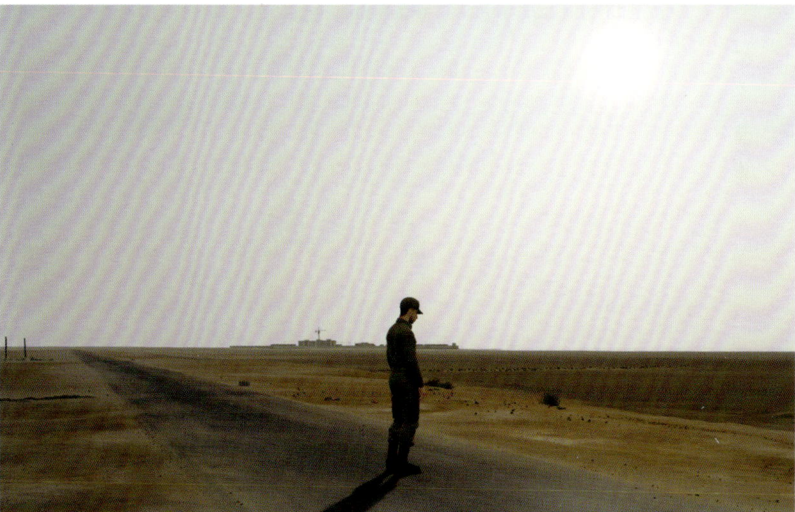

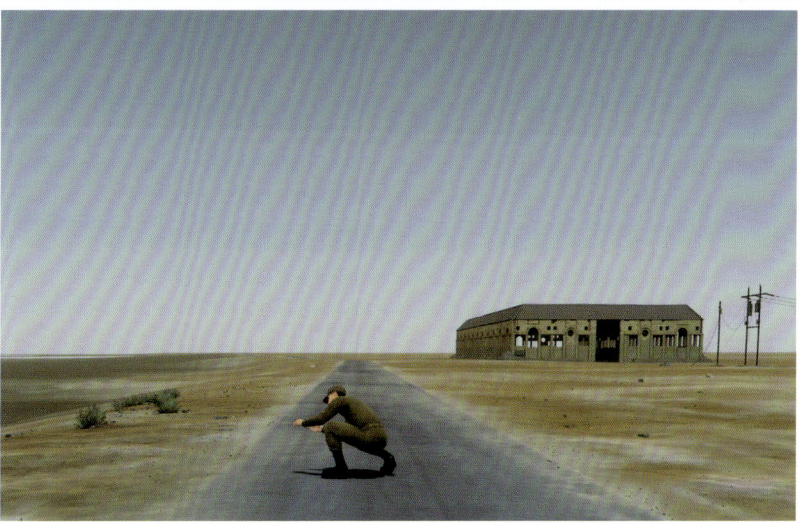

*Infinite Freedom Exercise (near Abadan, Iran)*, 2011; real-time 3-D software; dimensions variable; courtesy the artist; Simon Preston Gallery, New York; and Thomas Dane, London

# Johan Grimonprez

*BORN 1962 IN ROESELARE, BELGIUM; LIVES AND WORKS IN BRUSSELS AND NEW YORK*

In his film and video work, Johan Grimonprez uses the tools of mass media to explore the ways in which those media shape our perceptions of reality. "Fictions always proliferate," he has said. "And at one point they tip over into reality or vice versa. I am interested in how that tipping over occurs."[1] He has been especially interested in television, which brings a steady diet of disaster and death into our living rooms, thus creating a populace that is both addicted to fear and subdued by it.[2]

One of Grimonprez's best-known works is the video *Dial H-I-S-T-O-R-Y* (1997). It is a mesmerizing collage of explosions, shootings, airplane crashes, and interviews with skyjackers and victims, punctuated by short "commercial breaks" cut from Hollywood films, cartoons, and TV commercials. Phalanxes of reporters wield telephones, cameras, and microphones as they scramble to get the story; skyjackers and victims alike vie for a few minutes on camera to tell their stories. "Nothing happens until it is consumed," states the video's narrator.[3] *Dial H-I-S-T-O-R-Y* critiques this society of media spectacle by reminding us that events are woven together from many perspectives and that every reading of history is mediated by influences from the larger culture.

Grimonprez continued his investigation of the ambiguous relationship between fact and fiction in the eighty-minute film *Double Take* (2009), which "stars" Alfred Hitchcock as a paranoid history professor who gets caught up in the Cold War. Like *Dial H-I-S-T-O-R-Y*, the film is a collage of found footage. But its focus on slippages—of memory, identity, and reality—creates an ambiguous narrative in which news footage appears to be fiction, excerpts of Hitchcock's films look like news, and Hitchcock himself, in clips taken from his TV program *Alfred Hitchcock Presents*, confronts a doppelgänger played by a professional Hitchcock impersonator. The notion of the double also gives Grimonprez a metaphor with which to explore the absurdity of Cold War politics as enacted by its twin protagonists, the United States and the Soviet Union. As the film's Hitchcockian voiceover warns, "They say that if you meet your double you should kill him, or he will kill you; two of you is one too many."[4]

In a more recent work, *I may have lost forever my umbrella* (2011), Grimonprez treats the theme of the double in a manner more poetic than political. Grimonprez writes: "The footage used in this video was shot with an iPhone [camera] recapturing images found on YouTube. The project quoted from the work of the Portuguese poet Fernando Pessoa, called *The Book of Disquiet*, but aimed to erase the author's existence and present alternative personas. Pessoa himself used different names depending on the kind of works he created, and the complex structure of the video imagery was intended to express these various personas."[5] On the sound track of the video, a Portuguese writer reads excerpts from Pessoa's book, a "factless autobiography" published under the name Bernardo Soares, one of Pessoa's many fictive personae, or heteronyms.[6] The moving images relate to footage that Grimonprez found on YouTube of the devastating earthquake and tsunami that occurred in Japan in 2011.[7] In its status as a work by multiple authors—Pessoa, his alter ego, and the pseudonymous YouTube videographers, not to mention Grimonprez himself— the project quietly discredits the notion of art as self-expression. Both its text and its images—of earthquakes, floods, and displaced wild animals—suggest fragmentation, loss, absence, and memory. "No one will tell me who I am, nor knows who I was," begins the sound track, as a deer struggles in neck-deep water. It concludes, "Even if I held the world in my hands, I'd exchange it all for a tram ticket back to Rua dos Douradores."

JR

Notes

1. Johan Grimonprez, in Niels Van Tomme, "Constructing Histories: Johan Grimonprez Discusses *Double Take*," *Art Papers* 33 (May–June 2009): 26.

2. See Grimonprez's comments on subvertisement at http://www.zapomatik.com/justdoit.swf.

3. The line comes from Don DeLillo's novel *Mao II*, one of the works that inspired *Dial H-I-S-T-O-R-Y.*

4. See Nancy Princenthal, "Think Again," *Art in America* 97 (May 2009): 75.

5. Johan Grimonprez, e-mail correspondence with Elizabeth Armstrong, March 19, 2012.

6. Richard Zenith, ed. and trans., *Fernando Pessoa & Co.: Selected Poems* (New York: Grove, 1998), 8.

7. Johan Grimonprez, e-mail correspondence with Elizabeth Armstrong, March 19, 2012. See also Grimonprez's statement on the piece, posted at http://www.art-action.org/site/en/prog/11/paris/prog_11_21.php.

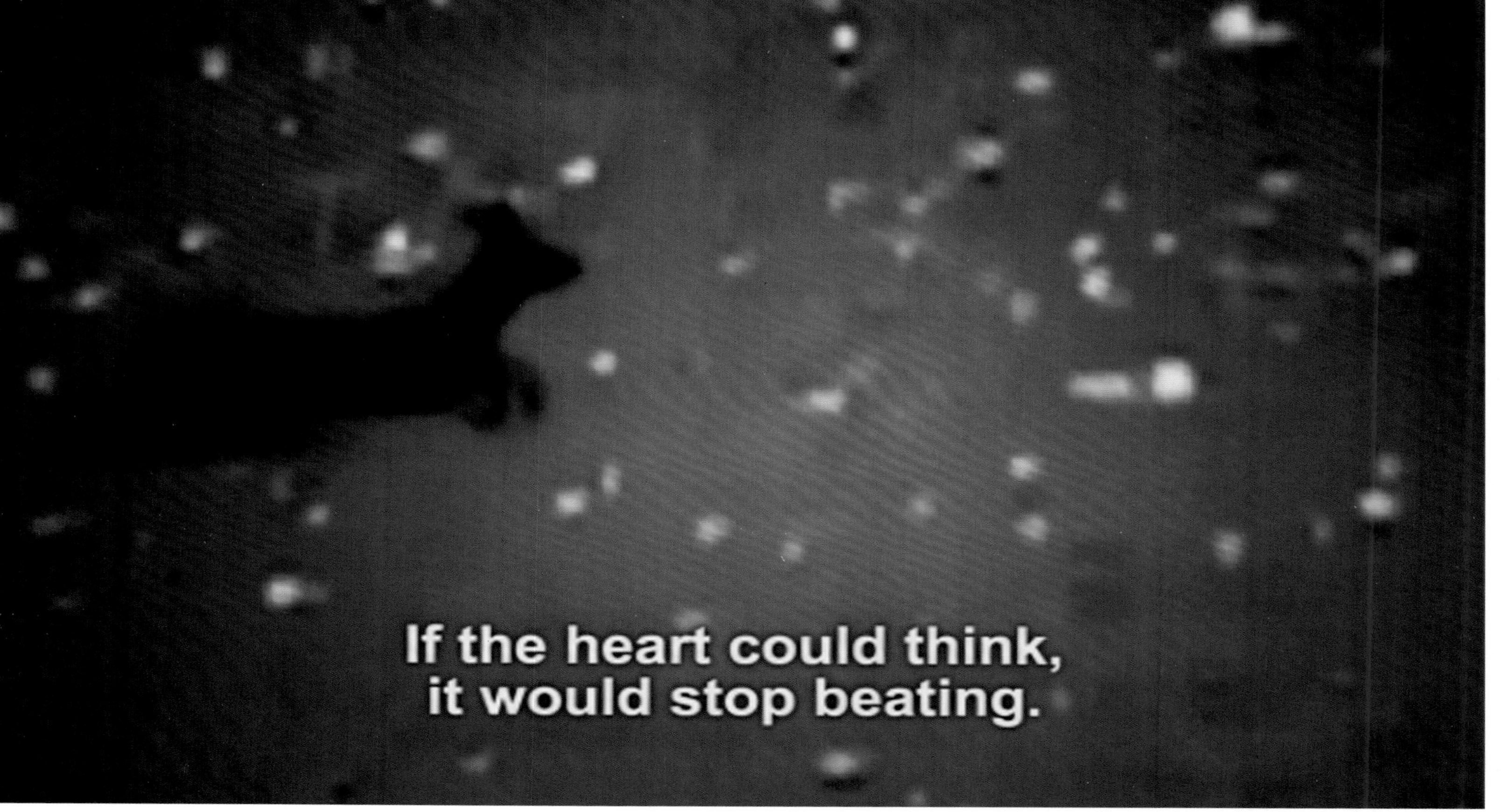


*If the heart could think, it would stop beating*, 2011; still from *I may have lost forever my umbrella*; experimental video (HD cam, iPhone cam), color, sound; 2:54 hours; courtesy the artist and Sean Kelly Gallery, New York

# Iris Häussler

BORN 1962 IN FRIEDRICHSHAFEN, GERMANY; LIVES AND WORKS IN TORONTO

Iris Häussler's narrative installations, which range from the sweeping to the succinct, revolve around fictitious histories. Each project begins with a detailed biography of an invented character, which Häussler drafts with a novelist's eye for detail. She then builds objects or environments that her characters might have used or made, and opens them to the public. Her best-known projects, *The Legacy of Joseph Wagenbach* (2006) and *He Named Her Amber* (2008–10), were elaborately theatrical, often unsettling environments in which viewers were guided through displays of sculpture purportedly created by characters named Joseph Wagenbach and Mary O'Shea.

Because Häussler is interested in the distinctions between fiction and reality, she does not immediately reveal to viewers that her installations are artworks. On the contrary, she goes to great lengths to ensure that they first experience her historical fictions as truth (later, through various means, she reveals their actual status). Although she is sometimes criticized by people who feel that they have been duped, Häussler remains committed to a gradual unfolding of her works that begins with "naïve, childlike fascination" and ends with a reconsideration of the work in its new context.[1] The entire process raises issues of authorship, artistic intention, and the constantly shifting boundaries between art and life.

Häussler's latest project concerns a character she calls Ellen Stanley, who was stricken by an unidentified mental illness shortly after giving birth to a daughter in 1923. Stanley spent two years in an insane asylum before returning home and settling into a seemingly pointless but soothing routine: she filled her bathtub with clay, then dug holes in the soft material with her hands and filled the cavities with molten beeswax. Once hardened, the objects were excavated and displayed in her room. In order to maintain a continuous supply of wax, her family periodically removed and melted down the sculptures. At the time of Stanley's death in 1931, only five of her works remained. These, along with a conical wax sculpture that inspired her, make up the work *Ellen's Gift* (2011).[2]

In addition to the themes raised by Häussler's earlier projects, *Ellen's Gift* delves into the cultural issues embedded within women's histories. Stanley's mental illness (or "hysteria") is linked to childbirth, which is in turn linked to her domestic art-making practice. "My fictitious characters use art as a private method to cope with their condition," Häussler has written.[3] Ellen's method—filling a void and then extracting its contents—symbolically reenacts the processes of conception and birth.[4] The equation between art making and childbearing raises additional questions: What is the exact nature of Ellen's gift? For whom is it intended? In conflating her life with that of her invented (female) character, Häussler performs a doubling that further erases boundaries between history, fiction, reality, biography, and art.

JR

Notes

1. Cecilia Aldarondo, "Hidden in Plain Sight: Iris Häussler's *He Named Her Amber*," *Art Papers* 33 (July–August 2009): 35.

2. Iris Häussler, "The Bequest of Ellen Stanley" and "Ellen Stanley, 1985–1931," unpublished texts. The conical wax sculpture that inspired Stanley's work was by Mary O'Shea, the protagonist of Häussler's project *He Named Her Amber*.

3. Iris Häussler, "Haptic Conceptualist Manifest," January 2009, statement on the artist's website, http://www.haeussler.ca/iris/hapticConceptual.html.

4. Häussler has described Ellen's practice as "sculpting the void." Iris Häussler, e-mail correspondence with Elizabeth Armstrong, August 16, 2011.

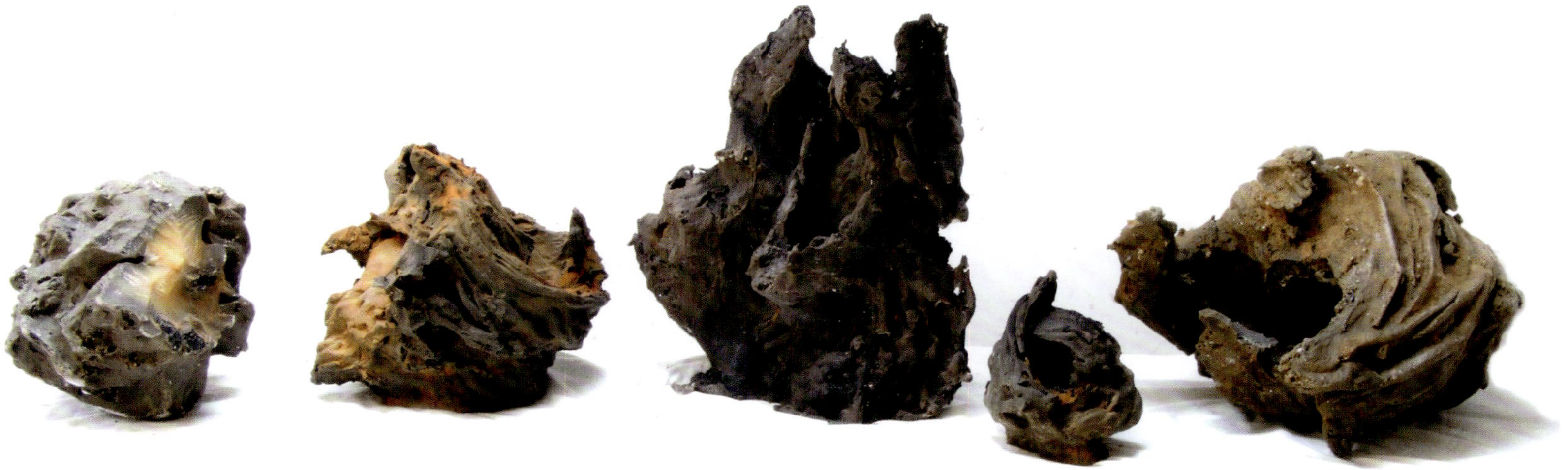

*Ellen's Gift*, 2011; beeswax, pigment; dimensions variable; courtesy the artist

# Jonn Herschend

BORN 1967 IN BRANSON, MISSOURI; LIVES AND WORKS IN SAN FRANCISCO

Jonn Herschend uses the familiar tropes of instructive media—the documentary film, the orientation video, the infomercial—as the basis for narratives about emotional confusion, interpersonal relationships, and the seeming impossibility of locating truth in everyday life. His performances, videos, and installations draw viewers into situations that begin as straightforward nonfiction and quickly go astray, often into narratives fraught with absurdity, doubt, and bathos. In the performance *Unreliable Narrator* (2005), for example, Herschend gave an artist's talk—a standard event at galleries and museums—that devolved into an awkwardly personal confession of lust, yearning, and confusion. In the video *Everything Is Better Now: The Importance of Ambiguity in Life* (2007), a philosophical infomercial about reality (it is "just a tool waiting to be manipulated," says one of the hosts) quickly derails into an argument between the two narrators that ultimately proves their thesis. And in *Embrace of the Irrational* (2010), a public television–style program about the Romantic tendency in art, Beethoven's *Pastoral* Symphony swells in the background as the narrator quotes the poet Percy Bysshe Shelley on the virtues of faith, confusion, and doubt. Almost immediately, technical and personal crises cause the production to fall apart.

Most of Herschend's works are, like those described above, both poignant and hilarious. On the one hand, he seems to suggest that the human experience will forever be defined by both ambition and failure and that life is inherently ambiguous and unpredictable. (As if to underscore this worldview, he has at times called his video production company by the name Not Working So Well.) On the other hand, he delivers these sobering messages with humor. In fact, Herschend feels that contemporary art has become "too austere."[1] He wants comedy, in the broadest sense of the word, to be a respectable genre for serious conceptual artists, not just for Hollywood studios and mass-market fiction writers. "I do feel that, as artists, we gave a lot up to the powers that entertain," he told an interviewer in 2011. "Anything that smacked of narrative or smacked of entertainment—well, there was already a place for that and that's where people went for it."[2]

For *More Real? Art in the Age of Truthiness*, Herschend was commissioned to produce a "site-specific fiction" for the exhibition.[3] Billed as an introduction to the themes and works in the show, this short video will be installed in a screening room near the main entrance to the galleries. Most visitors will likely assume that the video is what it purports to be, and why wouldn't they? That, after all, was Herschend's intention. But after the program introduces the ideas of "more real" and "truthiness," the host becomes lost in memories, and what should have been an orientation video degenerates into a disorienting, wayward—and funny—fiction.

JR

Notes

1. Jonn Herschend, in an interview with Bad at Sports, *Art Practical* 2, no. 14 (April 2011), http://www.artpractical.com/feature/interview_with_jonn_herschend.
2. Ibid.
3. See Herschend's description of *We are not having any trouble in our department despite what you've heard* (2011), http://jonnherschend.com/projects/welcome-to-den-frie-videoinstallationperfromance.

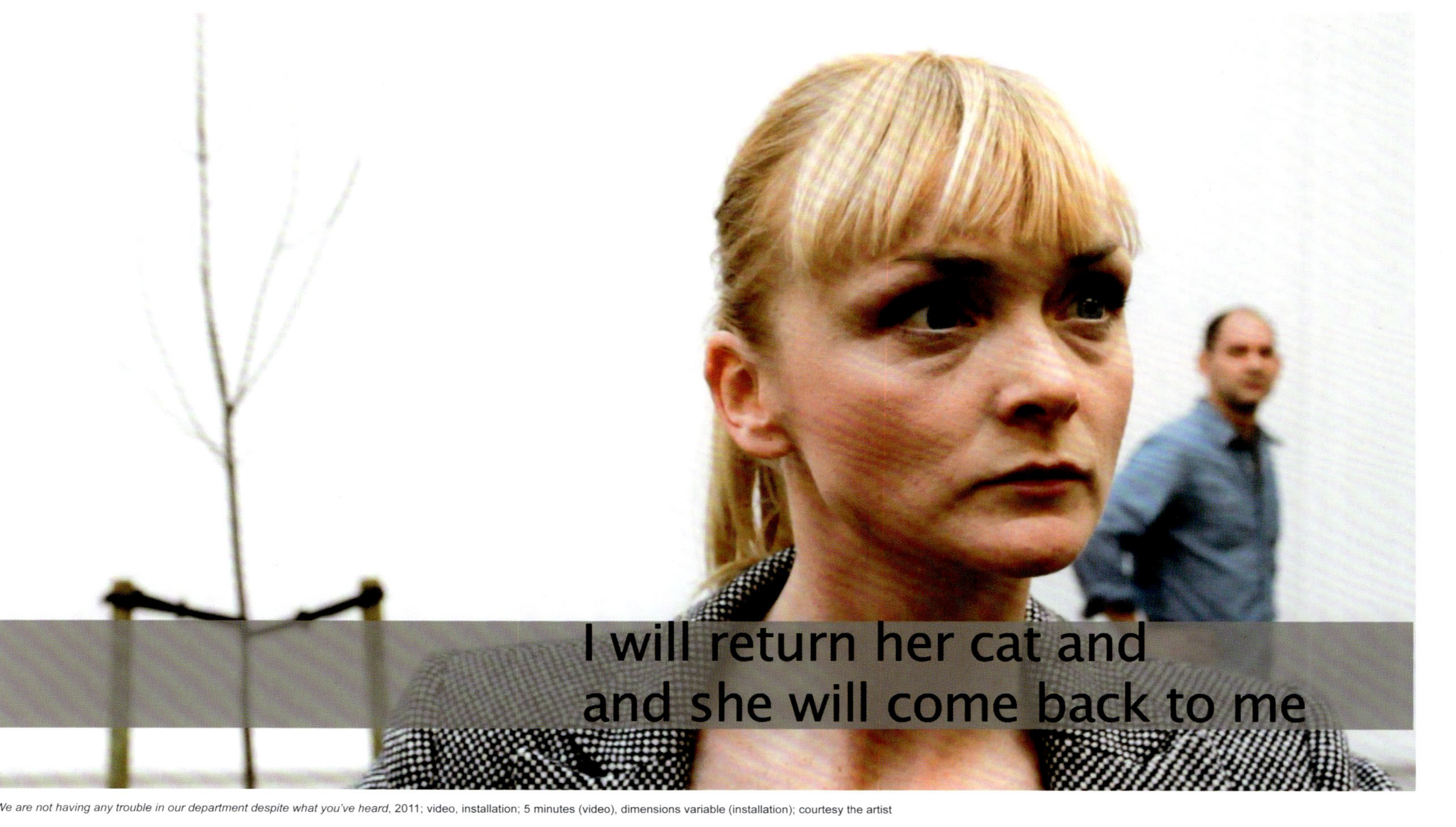


We are not having any trouble in our department despite what you've heard, 2011; video, installation; 5 minutes (video), dimensions variable (installation); courtesy the artist

# Pierre Huyghe

*BORN 1962 IN PARIS; LIVES AND WORKS IN NEW YORK*

Pierre Huyghe's multimedia works use video, performance, sound, text, architecture, and even puppetry to explore "the circulation of stories and how we can tell stories to each other."[1] His narratives, however, do not follow a standard storyteller's arc. Rather, they blur art and life through the use of such tactics as dubbing, translation, reenactment, and transposition. In *Remake* (1994–95), for example, Huyghe made a low-budget version of Alfred Hitchcock's *Rear Window* with a troupe of amateur French performers and a minimal set. Every shot and line of dialogue is copied from the original, and yet there is a fissure between the two versions that can never be mended. It is this "zone of non-knowledge," as Huyghe calls it, that interests him.[2] In *The Third Memory* (2000), he projected Sidney Lumet's film *Dog Day Afternoon* (1975), which was based on the 1972 holdup of a Brooklyn bank by John Wojtowicz, next to his own video of the bank robber reenacting the heist twenty-eight years later. As Wojtowicz acts out his memories, he comments on the veracity of the film version of his life. *The Third Memory*, whose title references Roland Barthes's seminal essay "The Third Meaning" (1970), proposes that when popular culture intersects with real events and personal recollections, a third narrative is created, one that is both true and false.

In 1999 Huyghe and the artist Philippe Parreno jointly purchased the rights to a "blank" manga character—a two-dimensional figure without name or biography—from the Japanese company Kworks. Rather than use the character in a manga comic or cartoon, as intended, Huyghe and Parreno reworked it as an animated 3-D video figure, which they named Annlee. They then "liberated" the figure, initially by inviting a series of artists to use it free of charge in their own artworks and later by legally transferring to Annlee ownership of her own copyright. This final gesture, made in 2002, effectively ended the project, which Huyghe and Parreno titled *No Ghost Just a Shell*.[3] As a whole, the work raises questions about authorship, intellectual property, ghostwriting, and the sale and circulation of images, among other topics.

The video installation *Two Minutes Out of Time* (2000) is Huyghe's contribution to *No Ghost Just a Shell*. In it Annlee stands before a gray void, her eyes blank, and delivers a monologue about what it feels like to be a "deviant sign" detached from its original context as a cartoon character. As she speaks, the narrative point of view shifts from first person to third. The scholar Tom McDonough has pointed out that, in using these strategies, Huyghe seems to have been determined to "liberate" Annlee from attachment to any context whatsoever, thus eliminating her ability to communicate meaning.[4] As Huyghe himself has said, Annlee is nothing more than "a character talking about the condition of being a character."[5] In other words, she is just a shell.

NS

Notes

1. Pierre Huyghe, in the segment "Pierre Huyghe in 'Romance'" on the website for the PBS television series *Art in the Twenty-First Century*, http://www.pbs.org/art21/artists/pierre-huyghe.

2. Ibid.

3. The title of the project refers to Mamoru Oshii's iconic anime film *Ghost in the Shell* (1995).

4. Tom McDonough, "No Ghost," *October*, no. 110 (Autumn 2004): 114.

5. Pierre Huyghe, quoted in Amy J. Elias, "The Narrativity of Postconvergent Media: *No Ghost Just a Shell* and Rirkrit Tiravanija's '(ghost reader C.H.),'" *SubStance* 40, no. 1 (2011): 184.

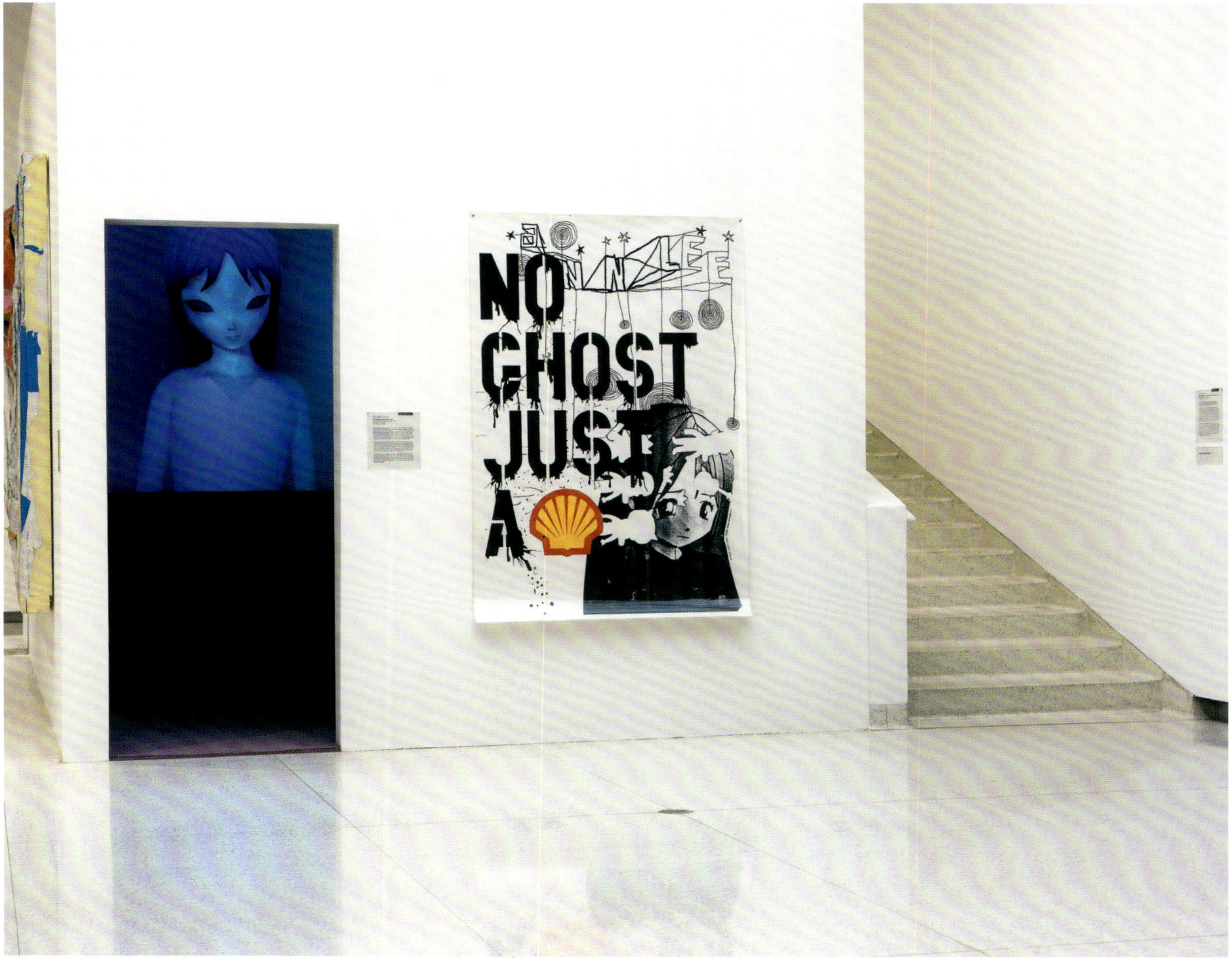

*Two Minutes Out of Time*, 2000; mixed media, digital videodisc, screenprint on paper; dimensions variable; Walker Art Center, Butler Family Fund, 2001

# Bertrand Lavier

BORN 1949 IN CHÂTILLON-SUR-SEINE, FRANCE; LIVES AND WORKS IN PARIS AND AIGNAY-LE-DUC, FRANCE

Bertrand Lavier's sculptures, paintings, and site-specific works have been called mutant objects, a phrase that suggests the semiotic ambiguity that characterizes his work as a whole.[1] Rather than inventing things, he conceptually repositions those that already exist, using strategies such as transposition, juxtaposition, and reiteration. For example, he has arranged colored neon tubes to remake Frank Stella's 1965 stripe painting *Empress of India*. He has covered a white refrigerator with a coat of thick white impasto, converting an everyday object into a painting of itself, so to speak (and one that still functions as a refrigerator). He makes his "stack" sculptures simply by placing one found object on top of another. Confronted by a sofa on top of a freezer, a space heater atop a safe, or a roll of kraft paper standing vertically on a file cabinet, one is forced to consider the symbiosis between sculpture and pedestal as well as the relationship between art and life. Such basic binary concepts as these—as well as high/low, true/false, and original/reproduction—are at the heart of Lavier's work. Ultimately he is interested the "very small translation" that transforms not-art into art.[2]

Lavier's series Walt Disney Productions was inspired by a 1947 cartoon in which Minnie and Mickey Mouse visit a museum of modern art filled with abstract paintings and sculptures whose sinuous curves, wild colors, and strict geometries proffer a generic version of avant-garde art.[3] With the help of a computer graphics specialist, Lavier created large-scale, three-dimensional versions of the fictional works, using commercial materials such as polyester resin and ink-jet printing. Their heightened colors and uniform surfaces allude to their origin as cartoons, while their forms evoke handmade objects by early modernists such as Jean Arp and Piet Mondrian. Looking at these works, Lavier has said: "You're in a parallel world, in front of real paradoxes. . . . These are reproductions of artworks that don't exist, that are sublimated."[4] When viewers step into an installation of Walt Disney Productions, past and present collapse as they reenact Mickey and Minnie's museum visit in real time and space.

In his essay "Travels in Hyperreality," the Italian philosopher Umberto Eco proposed that Americans seem to want the past to be preserved and celebrated "in full-scale, authentic copy." This desire, he writes, "dominates the relation with the self, with the past, not infrequently with the present, always with History, and, even, with the European tradition."[5] Lavier's Walt Disney Productions are just such "authentic copies," full-scale fabrications that link American popular entertainment with European high modernist art. "It's the world turned inside out," says Lavier, "starting with Mickey Mouse's décor."[6]

JR

Notes

1. Pascaline Cuvelier, "Name Games: The Art of Bertrand Lavier," *Artforum* 36 (March 1997): 69–71.

2. "C'est une toute petite translation qui fait l'oeuvre d'art." Bertrand Lavier, quoted in Catherine Francblin, *Bertrand Lavier* (Paris: Flammarion, 1999), 15.

3. A later version of the comic, published as "Traits très abstraits," in *Le journal de Mickey*, no. 1279 (1977), provided Lavier with the source material for this series. See "Walt Disney Productions de B. Lavier: L'art réalité dépasse la fiction," *Pmspg, le blog des fans de BD Disney*, July 4, 2008, http://pmspg.over-blog.com/article-20726860.html.

4. Bertrand Lavier, quoted in Cuvelier, "Name Games," 71.

5. Umberto Eco, "Travels in Hyperreality," in *Travels in Hyperreality: Essays*, trans. William Weaver (New York: Harcourt Brace Jovanovich, 1986), 6.

6. Bertrand Lavier, quoted in Cuvelier, "Name Games," 71.

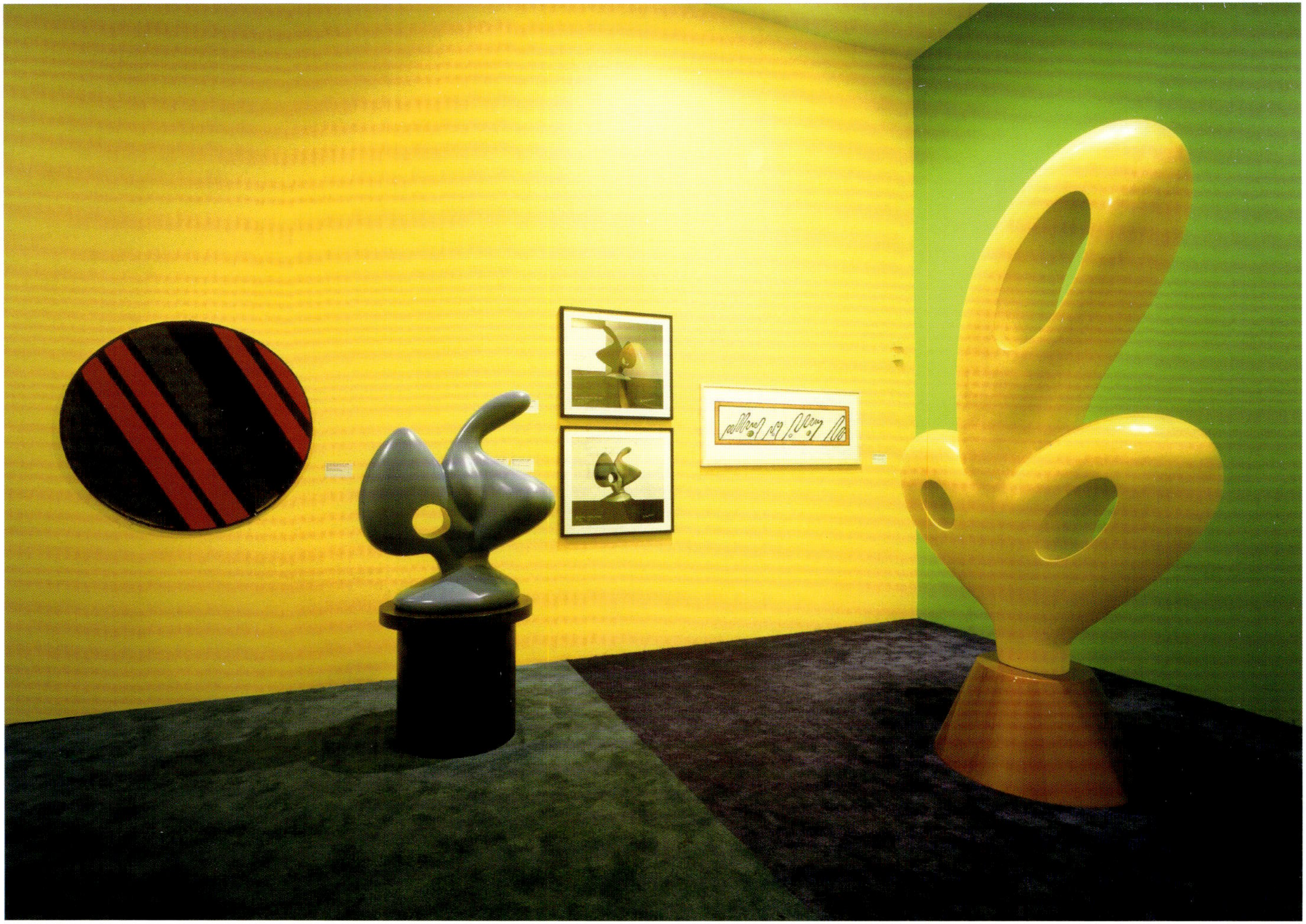

*Walt Disney Productions 1947–1995*, 1998; installation view of *Premises*, Guggenheim SoHo, New York, 1998; courtesy the artist and Yvon Lambert, Paris

# An-My Lê

BORN 1960 IN SAIGON; LIVES AND WORKS IN NEW YORK

Born in Saigon during the early years of the Vietnam War, An-My Lê grew up in the shadow of violence. She and her family fled the country in 1975, the final year of the war, and settled in the United States as political refugees. Her early experience of life during wartime provides the fodder for her work as an artist, which often explores the myriad ways in which military conflict is represented in American media and popular culture.

Commenting on her series Small Wars (1999–2002), Lê has said, "Instead of seeking the real, I began making photographs that use the real to ground the imaginary."[1] The series seems to depict actual battles but in fact documents Vietnam War reenactments in South Carolina and Virginia. The events, staged by veterans and amateur historians, are meant to be as accurate as possible, even down to the smallest details of costume and setting. To get permission to photograph them, Lê had to agree to actively participate in them. According to the artist, "I added to the authenticity of the event, and they would often concoct elaborate scenarios around my character."[2]

The attacks of September 11, 2001, and their impact on the country led Lê to shift her focus from past to present. Her first impulse was to go to Iraq as an embedded photographer to shoot the conflict there. Unable to get approval for that mission, she turned instead to the Marine Air Ground Combat Center in Twentynine Palms, California, where Marines undergo training before deploying to Iraq. Live fire exercises and artillery, tank, and close air support training are among the operations conducted at Twentynine Palms, which also features a two-acre fabricated Middle Eastern village staffed by native role-players. In the series of photographs Lê made there, 29 Palms (2003–4), the chaos of military war games is softened by the calmness of the California desert landscape.

Lê's images are a paradox. On the one hand, their subject matter and straightforward compositions suggest that we are looking at quintessential documentary photographs. And so we are. On the other hand, what they document are real simulations of war rather than actual combat. Her use of a large-format, 5 x 7 view camera and extended exposures contributes to the sense that what we are viewing is theater, while the black-and-white film suggests history, memory, and objectivity. As Lê has pointed out, however, black-and-white is in fact completely removed from reality.[3] In the end, her images both are and are not what they seem.

JR

Notes

1. An-My Lê, quoted in Richard B. Woodward, "Essay," in *Small Wars* (New York: Aperture Foundation, 2005), 119.

2. Hilton Als, interview with An-My Lê, in *Small Wars*, 121.

3. An-My Lê, in the segment "An-My Lê in 'Protest,'" on the website for the PBS television series *Art in the Twenty-First Century*, http://www.pbs.org/art21/artists/an-my-le.

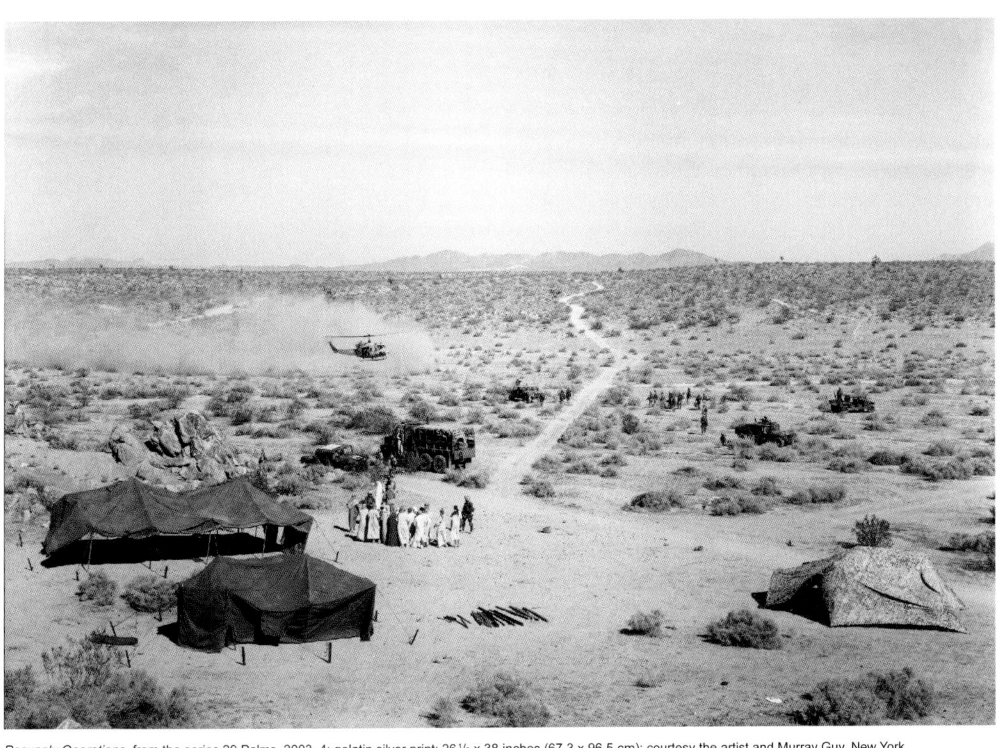

*Resupply Operations*, from the series 29 Palms, 2003–4; gelatin silver print; 26 ½ x 38 inches (67.3 x 96.5 cm); courtesy the artist and Murray Guy, New York



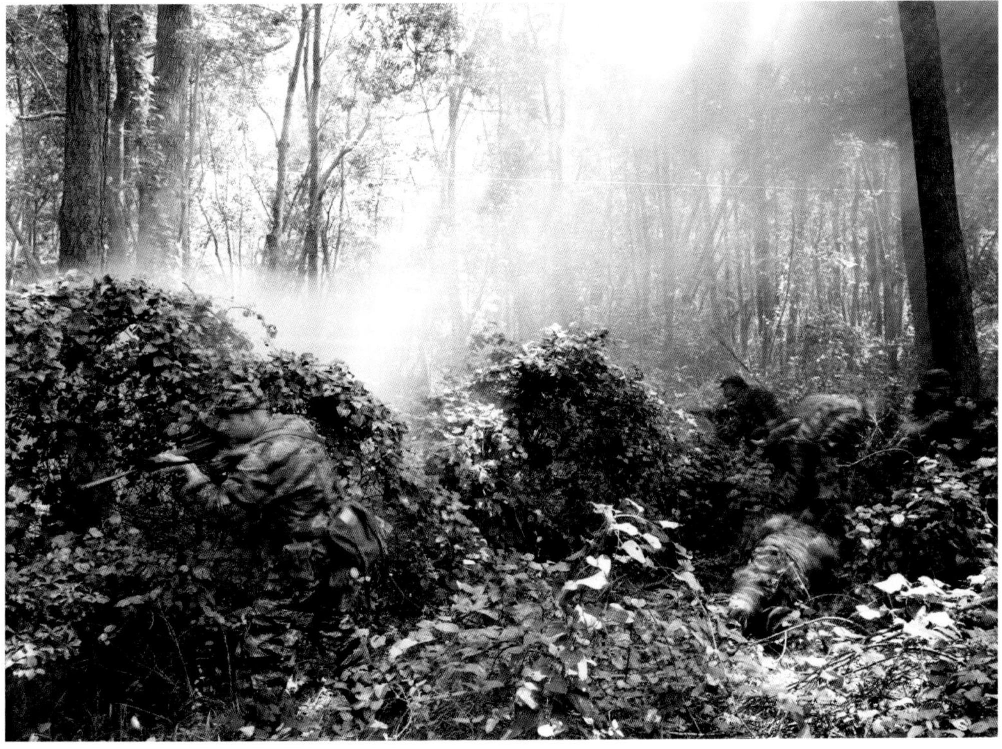

*Ambush #1*, from the series Small Wars, 1999–2002; gelatin silver print; 26 ½ x 38 inches (67.3 x 96.5 cm); courtesy the artist and Murray Guy, New York

# Joel Lederer

*BORN 1971 IN CHICAGO; LIVES AND WORKS IN NEW YORK*

Until recently the relationship between reality and its imitations has been transparent. During the nineteenth century, for example, English gardens were built to mimic those depicted in landscape paintings of the day. During that time, as one writer has noted, "the boundaries between natural/artificial, real/virtual, even nature/culture were blurred . . . but they still were experienced as real."[1] Today, however, the lines between the two realms are far less defined. A middle zone of "real virtuality" has emerged.[2] Joel Lederer has explored this phenomenon in The Metaverse Is Beautiful (2009), a series of large-scale photographs that document the digitally constructed landscapes of the online virtual world Second Life. The project's title points to the metaverse, which Lederer defines as a "virtualized environment" in which we interact with others through digital proxies such as cell phones, e-mail, online role-playing games, virtual worlds, and the World Wide Web.[3]

Like our real-world environment, the Second Life landscape, or grid, is in constant flux as independent users change and shape the spaces. Lederer has said that one of his main challenges in doing this project was determining how best to document a landscape that was constantly changing. He ultimately decided to approach it "with the pioneering spirit of an explorer, wishing to return to civilization with a visual record from a new land."[4] His images, created with the aid of a screen-capture program, are dazzling in their variety and draw on the same established image genres—from cartoons to conventional landscape paintings—that were used by the creators of the Second Life grid itself. Their titles, each a string of numbers that indicate the dates and times of the individual screen captures, reinforce the nature of these landscapes as "nonsites" that can be visited only in virtual space. Through this mirroring and layering of visual syntaxes, Lederer challenges the viewer to determine where one visual trope ends and another begins.

NS

Notes

1. Donald E. Jones, "I, Avatar: Constructions of Self and Place in Second Life and the Technological Imagination," *Gnovis* 6 (2006): 11; http://gnovis-journal.org/files/Donald-E-Jones-I-Avatar.pdf.
2. Joel Lederer, e-mail correspondence with Elizabeth Armstrong, May 4, 2009.
3. See Joel Lederer, "The Metaverse Is Beautiful" (artist's statement), http://www.joellederer.com/the_metaverse_is_beautiful/metaverse_statement.html. The term *metaverse* was coined by Neal Stephenson in his sci-fi novel *Snow Crash* (New York: Bantam, 1992).
4. Lederer, "The Metaverse Is Beautiful."

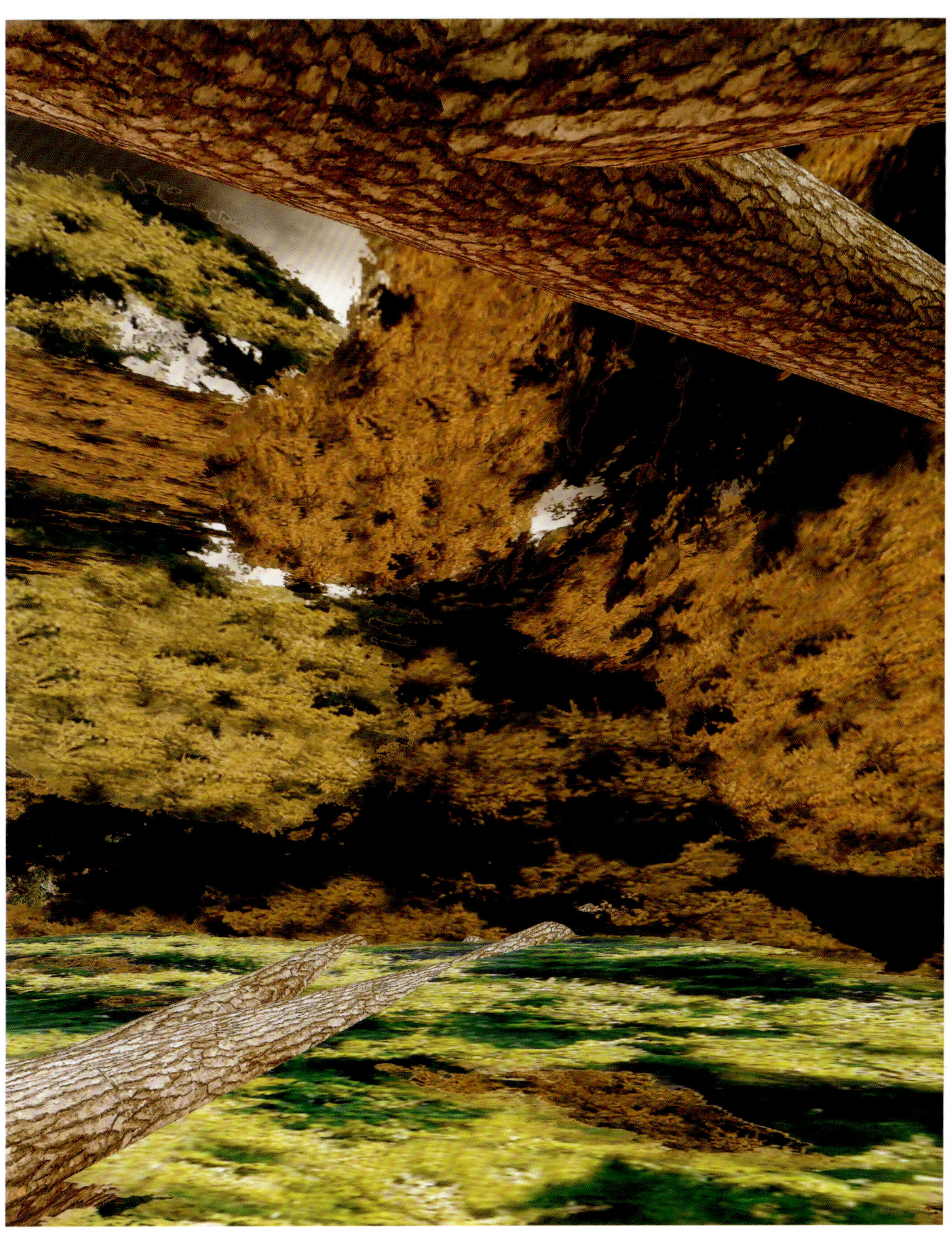





*200805262351*, from the series The Metaverse Is Beautiful, 2009; archival ink jet on paper; 50 x 40 inches (127 x 101.6 cm); courtesy the artist

# Sharon Lockhart

*BORN 1964 IN NORWOOD, MASSACHUSETTS; LIVES AND WORKS IN LOS ANGELES*

Sharon Lockhart has long been interested in the ability of film and photography to undermine reality and alter our perceptions of everyday life. Her meticulously composed photographs have a staged, cinematic feel, almost as if they are film stills. Their theatricality is heightened because Lockhart's subjects are often engaged in codified behaviors, rituals, or contrived situations. She has photographed, for example, a girls' basketball team doing practice drills; children reenacting a scene from a François Truffaut film; factory workers taking their lunch breaks; and Japanese museum guards changing their posts according to a strict schedule. Both her films and her photographs—with their expressive quietude and exquisite, hyperreal detail—have much in common with the work of the seventeenth-century Dutch painter Jan Vermeer. But Lockhart's practice is a thoroughly postmodern one that explores both the act of seeing and the condition of being seen.

These themes are central to the four-part photographic work titled *Lunch Break Installation, "Duane Hanson: Sculptures of Life," 14 December 2002–23 February 2003, Scottish National Gallery of Modern Art* (2003). At first glance, Lockhart's images seem to depict five laborers within a white gallery space, some of them at work and others resting. Attentive viewers might notice, however, that only two of the men change position from one image to the next; the other three remain motionless. The work's title provides a clue as to what is going on here: Lockhart's piece depicts *Lunch Break*, a work by the realist sculptor Duane Hanson, as it was being installed by two art handlers for an exhibition at the Scottish National Gallery of Modern Art. Lockhart had engaged with Hanson's work before. In the diptych *Maja and Elodie*, also of 2003, she added a live model to Hanson's sculpture *Child with Puzzle* (1978), posing her to suggest that she and the child are working the puzzle together. The diptych's two photographs are almost identical but not quite, creating a visual puzzle that invites viewers to search for the differences.

Although they are still photographs, both *Maja and Elodie* and *Lunch Break Installation* play with duration, that basic element of cinema. The former does so by drawing attention to the slight change in the woman's position that took place between the making of the two images; the latter suggests the time that passed as Lockhart shifted her camera's position to circumnavigate the installation in progress. Most important, in these works Lockhart sets up situations in which life imitates art imitating life. She thus complicates our understanding of the relationship between the two, showing that they are not distinct realms but related states of being whose boundaries are constantly shifting.

JR

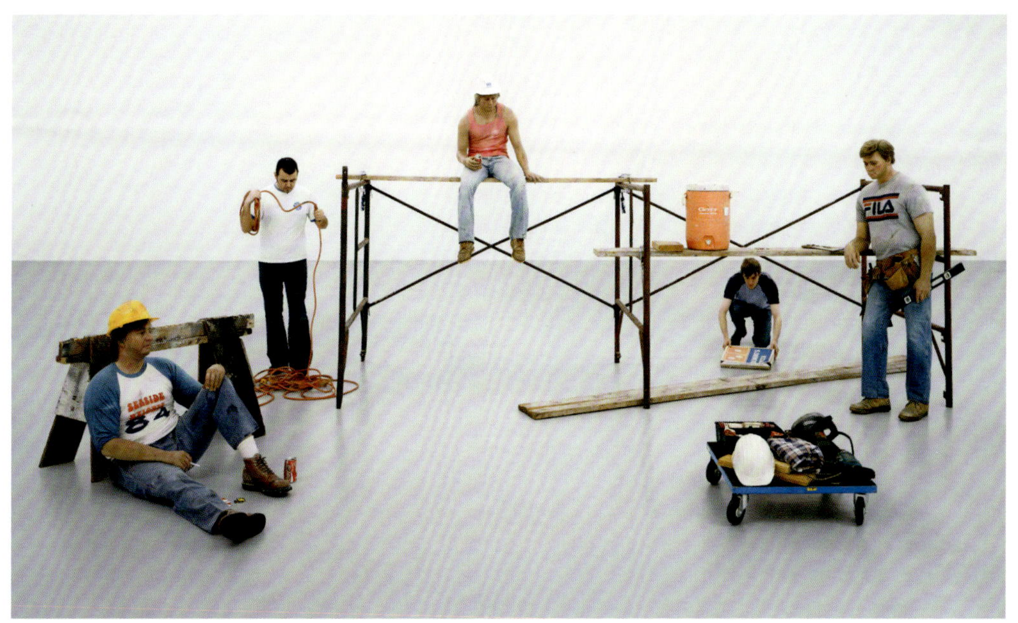

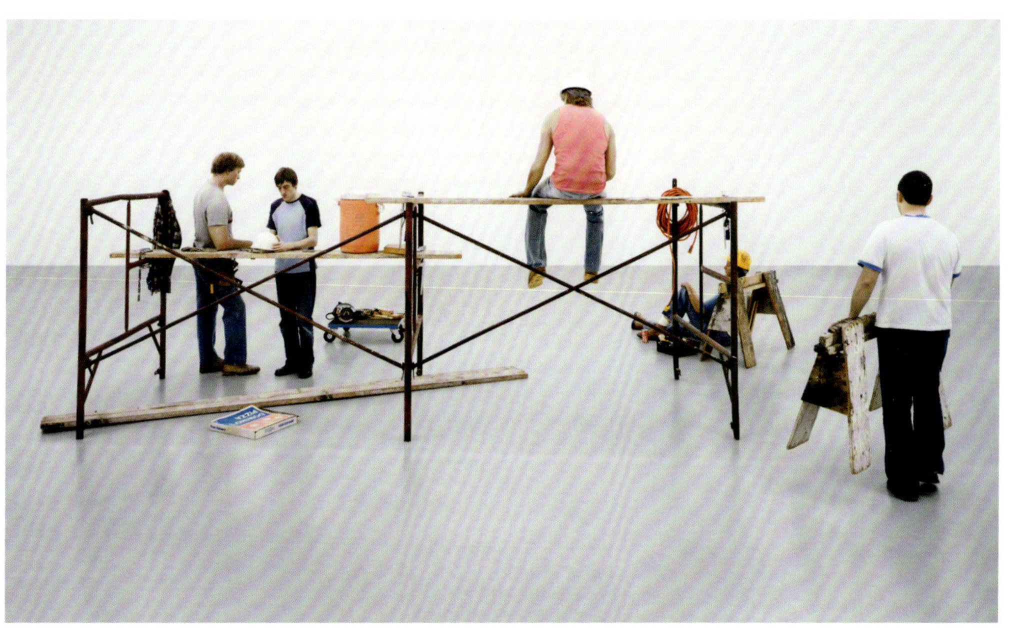

*Lunch Break Installation, "Duane Hanson: Sculptures of Life," 14 December 2002–23 February 2003, Scottish National Gallery of Modern Art,* 2003; chromogenic print; 72 x 121 inches (182.9 x 307.3 cm); Broad Art Foundation

# Iñigo Manglano-Ovalle

BORN 1961 IN MADRID; LIVES AND WORKS IN CHICAGO

Working across multiple disciplines, Iñigo Manglano-Ovalle creates seductive images and objects that address the urgent issues of our time. He has made colorful portraits of DNA strands that interrogate racial identity; a video installation, set inside a sleek Mies van der Rohe house, that explores economic and social class structures; and monumental titanium and fiberglass cloud sculptures that marshal references ranging from climate change to the impact of a nuclear explosion. While all his art is socially engaged, none of it is didactic, for Manglano-Ovalle deliberately keeps his own position on the issues in the background. "If art for me is a platform from which to speak, but not tell you something, that's good," he says. "And if that's a way in which I give you a platform from which to think and debate it, that's even better."[1]

One of Manglano-Ovalle's most ambitious and provocative works to date is *Phantom Truck* (2007). He got the idea for the work while listening to a speech given in February 2003 by Secretary of State Colin Powell to the United Nations Security Council.[2] Powell's speech, titled "Iraq: Failing to Disarm," presented "evidence" that Iraq was manufacturing chemical weapons and moving them around the country in mobile labs concealed inside trucks and train cars. The speech was illustrated by computer-generated renderings of the trucks that were based on satellite images, "eyewitness accounts," and "firsthand descriptions."[3] Powell's presentation helped to justify the invasion of Iraq one month later by a US-led military coalition. Once on the ground in Iraq, however, troops were unable to locate any of the purported weapons of mass destruction. Powell's trucks proved to be a fiction.

Manglano-Ovalle decided to build a real version of the Bush administration's fabrication. Using as his source the US State Department renderings that Powell had shown during his speech, along with Powell's verbal descriptions and photographs of trucks taken after the invasion, Manglano-Ovalle fabricated a full-scale aluminum version of the elusive weapons lab. This monumental sculpture resembles an open container filled with a collection of geometric forms that the artist describes as "formally reductive, smooth simple shapes that suggest Platonic forms, minimalist sculpture, and containers of unknown industrial-chemical nature."[4] For the artist, it is essential that *Phantom Truck* be shown in a darkened gallery. Staged in shadow and barely visible, it becomes a metaphor for the political camouflage that enabled a fiction to help launch a war that was all too real.

IH

Notes

1. Iñigo Manglano-Ovalle, in the segment "Iñigo Manglano-Ovalle in 'Ecology,'" on the website for the PBS television series *Art in the Twenty-First Century*, http://www.art21.org/videos/segment-iñigo-manglano-ovalle-in-ecology.
2. Iñigo Manglano-Ovalle, in the video interview "Iñigo Manglano-Ovalle, 2008 Richard H. Driehaus Individual Artist Award Winner," YouTube video, 4:34, posted by Driehaus Foundation, March 19, 2009, http://www.youtube.com/watch?v=0JWtgkAnWDQ.

3. The images are posted online, along with a transcript of Powell's speech, at http://www.globalsecurity.org/wmd/library/news/iraq/2003/iraq-030205-powell-un-17300pf.htm.
4. Iñigo Manglano-Ovalle, quoted in Edward Kanerva, "Iñigo Manglano-Ovalle: *Phantom Truck + Always After*," Power Plant Contemporary Art Gallery website, http://www.thepowerplant.org/SwitchOn/Features/February-2011/Inigo-Manglano-Ovalle.aspx.

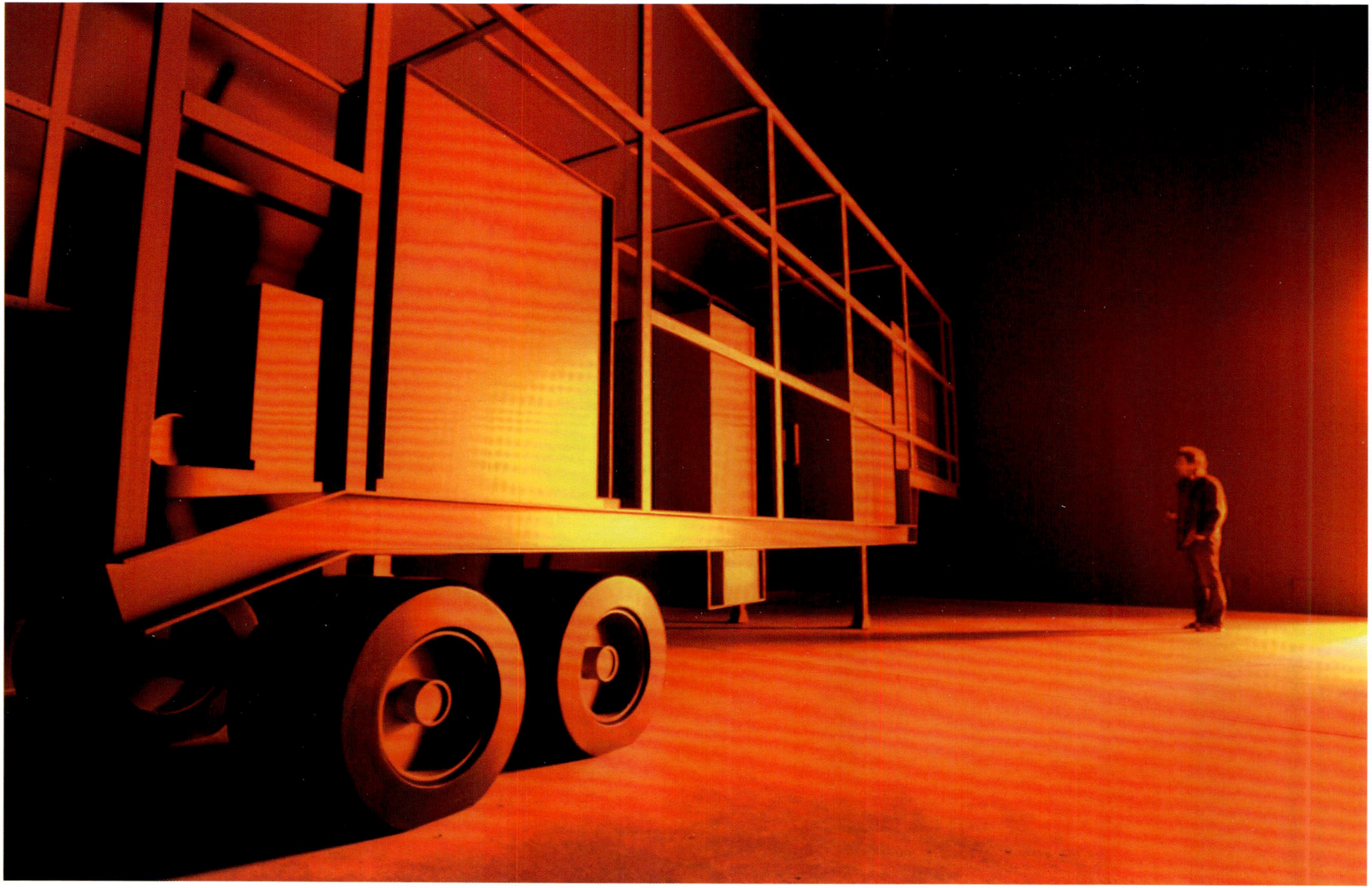

*Phantom Truck*, 2007; mixed mediums; 393 x 98 x 156 inches (998.2 x 248.9 x 396.2 cm); courtesy the artist and Galerie Thomas Schulte

# Eva and Franco Mattes

*BOTH BORN 1976 IN BRESCIA, ITALY; LIVE AND WORK IN BROOKLYN*

Eva and Franco Mattes are art provocateurs whose work appears in galleries and museums as well as online. Their earliest works leveraged the versatility of Internet technology to hide their identity behind aliases, online avatars, and fictional artists. Their projects, which range from disturbing to entertaining, question "the need for material objects, the authority of institutions, the uniqueness of an artwork, and the distinction between reality and simulation."[1] If there is a common denominator among their works, it might be their interest in culture jamming—graphic and technological interventions that draw attention to the ways in which economic and commercial institutions have tarnished social and civic values.

In 2007, for example, they restaged Chris Burden's seminal performance *Shoot* (1971) within the grid of the virtual world Second Life. Eva's avatar, or proxy, takes careful aim before shooting the left arm of Franco's avatar; within the virtual realm of Second Life, the act of shooting another person is completely demystified. The Matteses' revision removes the aspect of shock from Burden's original but at the same time opens up new territory for remixing and archiving past performances.

The Italian artist Maurizio Cattelan, who is also mischievously engaged with the relationship between fiction and truth, has twice been the target of the Matteses' provocations. In 2010 they created an online performance that riffed on his controversial 2003 sculpture of three hanging children. The Matteses staged their piece, *No Fun*, on Chatroulette, a popular social media site that randomly pairs people from around the world in web-based conversations. But when some participants logged on, they were paired not with a live conversation partner but with a live image of Franco hanging from a noose in a dirty apartment. The random nature of the software used to create video chats was a perfect tool for staging such a spectacle. As Franco has said, "If you really want to get people you have to do it when they least expect it."[2] Surprisingly, many of the comments left by participants were disaffected, and only one called 911 to report the suicide (which was of course staged). *No Fun* suggests that social media can create emotional distance and apathy through extreme hyperconnectivity.

The Matteses also have taken advantage of the speed with which information circulates through social media. In 2010 they grabbed a random image from the Internet and used it as the model for a sculpture, which they called *Catt*. They then exhibited the work at a Houston gallery as a new piece by Maurizio Cattelan. Interest in the piece was intense, and photographs of it were circulated widely on Facebook. "We wanted to make a work about Internet's overflowing creativity vs. high art fixation with originality," Franco has written.[3] Just as *Catt* began with an image pulled from a website, it was transformed back into to a digital piece shared all over the world.

CA

Notes
1. Press release for the exhibition *Reality Is Overrated*, May 15–June 19, 2010, issued by Postmasters Gallery, April 2, 2010.
2. Domenico Quaranta et al., *Eva and Franco Mattes* (Milan: Charta, 2009), 106.
3. Franco Mattes, statement on *Catt*, posted on the artists' website, http://www.0100101110101101.org/home/catt/index.html.

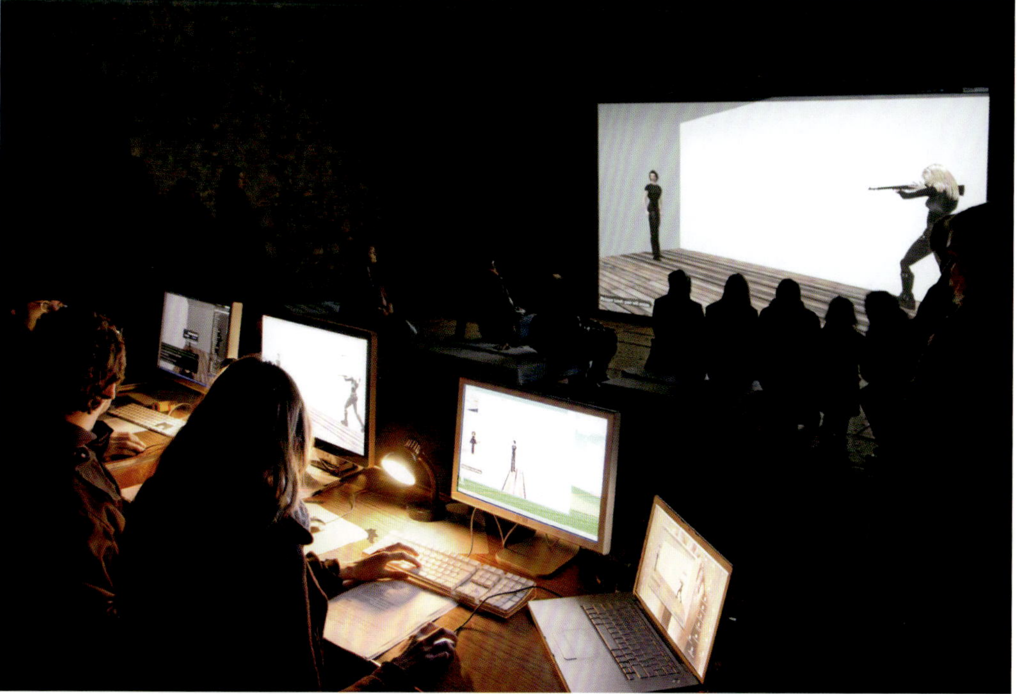

Reenactment of Chris Burden's "Shoot," 2007; synthetic performance; 1:02 minutes; courtesy the artists

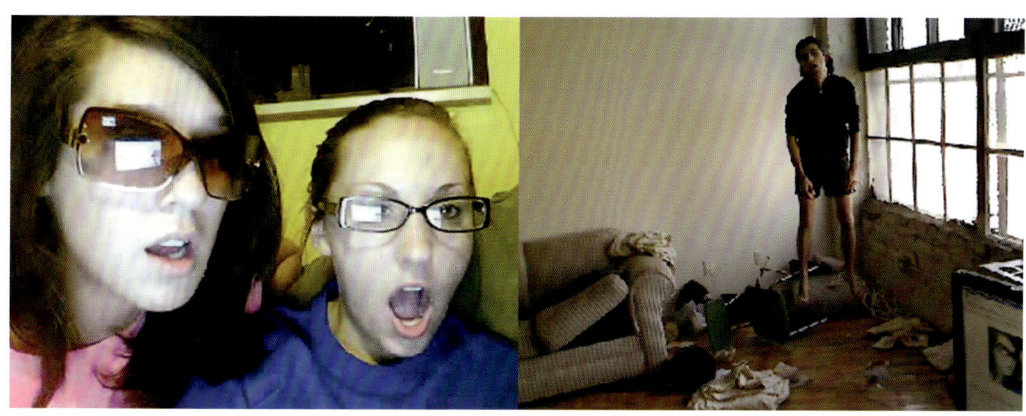

*No Fun*, 2010; online performance; 9:58 minutes; courtesy the artists

# Jonathan Monk

*BORN 1969 IN LEICESTER, ENGLAND; LIVES AND WORKS IN BERLIN*

Jonathan Monk has based his artistic practice on the reuse and re-presentation of works by other artists. "I realised that being original was almost impossible," he has said, "so I tried using what was already available as source material for my own work. . . . I always think that art is about ideas, and surely the idea of an original and a copy of an original are two very different things."[1] His work takes many forms—installation, photography, film, sculpture, and performance, among others—and much of it turns on deadpan humor that is both affectionate and teasing. In *None of the Buildings on the Sunset Strip* (2002), a series of pictures showing gaps between buildings in Los Angeles, Monk riffs on a celebrated artist's book by Edward Ruscha. In 2009 he showed a series of stainless steel sculptures that appear to be deflated versions of Jeff Koons's iconic balloon rabbit.

The French critic Nicolas Bourriaud has proposed that aesthetic practices like Monk's—which depend on remixing, reproducing, or reexhibiting other people's artworks—might be called "postproduction." The practice, as Bourriaud defines it, goes beyond appropriation because it focuses on works already in circulation as cultural products. Artists who situate their own works within that of others, he writes, "contribute to the eradication of the traditional distinction between production and consumption, creation and copy, readymade and original work."[2]

Monk's *Deadman* (2006) is a Bourriaudian remix of two notorious performances by Chris Burden: *Shoot* (1971), in which Burden enlisted a friend to shoot him in the arm, and *Dead Man* (1972), in which he lay on a roadway covered by a tarpaulin and flanked by safety flares. In both works Burden flirted with the real possibility of death: the bullet might go astray, or he might be run over by an inattentive motorist. Monk imagines both outcomes in this one work. A wax figure resembling the young Burden, eyes closed, lies on the floor half covered with a blood-spattered sheet. Monk appropriates the images of Burden's performances (which exist today only as documentary photographs), but he also refigures their historical context. Both *Shoot* and *Dead Man* were created during a period in American history marked by violent riots, demonstrations, and assassinations. Photographs of Burden's actions evoke in particular the iconic news photo from 1970 of a student lying dead on the campus of Kent State University after being shot by police during an antiwar demonstration. Monk's wax figure alludes to that history even as it concretizes the brutality of our current age.

NS

Notes
1. Jonathan Monk, quoted in a press release issued by Casey Kaplan Gallery, May 2009, http://www.caseykaplangallery.com/press_release/2009/jonathan_monk_2009.pdf.
2. Nicolas Bourriaud, *Postproduction: Culture as Screenplay; How Art Reprograms the World*, trans. Jeanine Herman (New York: Lukas & Sternberg, 2002), 7.

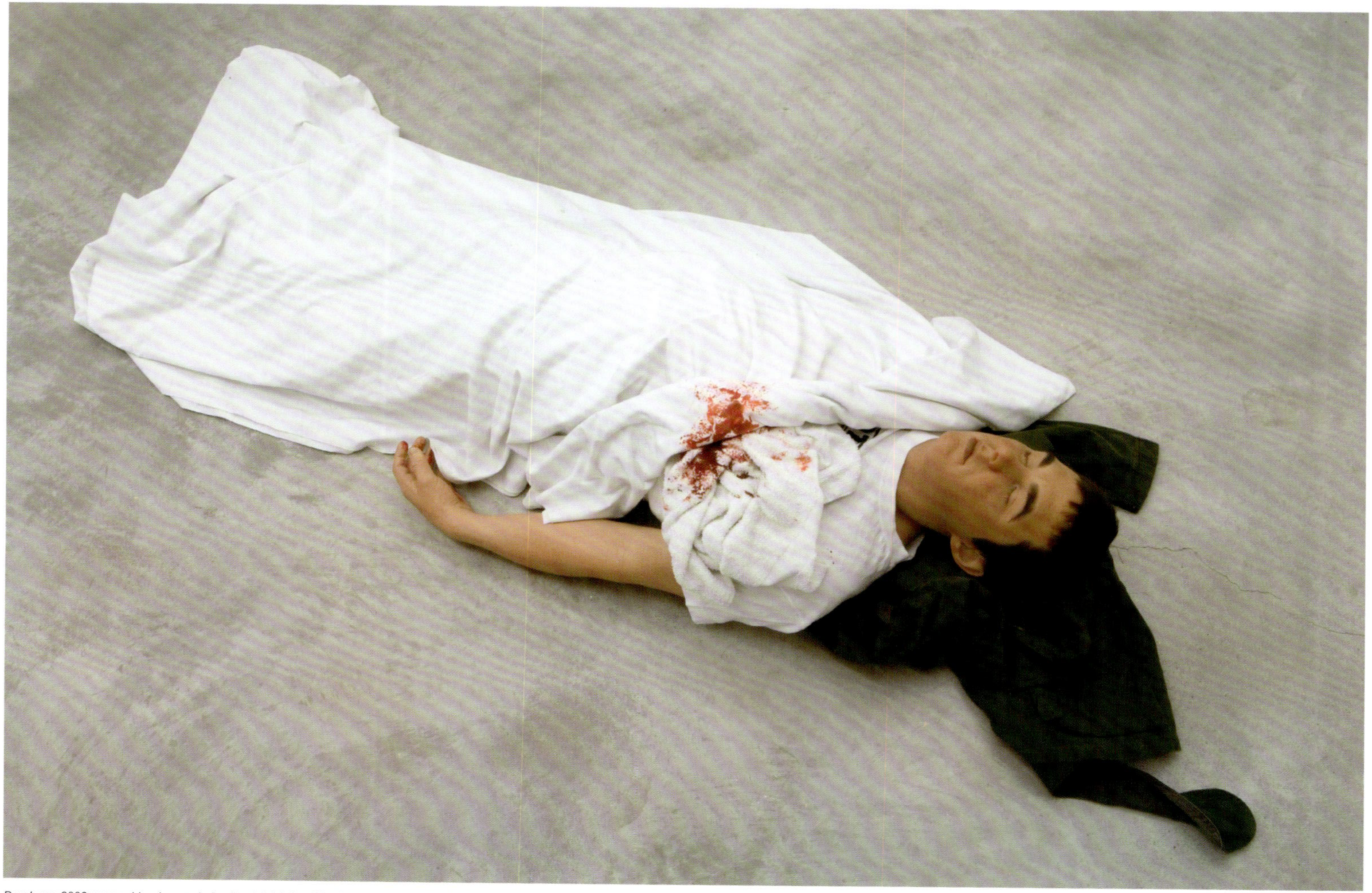

*Deadman*, 2006; wax, rubber human hair, oil paint, fabrics; 66 x 22 x 12 inches (167.6 x 55.9 x 30.5 cm); courtesy the artist and Casey Kaplan, New York

# Vik Muniz

*BORN 1961 IN SÃO PAULO; LIVES AND WORKS IN RIO DE JANEIRO AND NEW YORK*

During his twenty-year career, Vik Muniz has created photographic and sculptural works that question the processes of representation. He often renders familiar images in unlikely substances such as dirt, chocolate, and caviar and then photographs them, seeking to interfere with the easy consumption of images by pointing out that a photograph is not a one-to-one representation of an object in front of the camera. Rather, it is an artifact of the interaction between an object and the photographic process.

Muniz's work also exhibits an interest in the social life of representation. This is evident in his series Sugar Children (1996) and Pictures of Garbage (2008). In the former, he made portraits in sugar of children whose parents and grandparents worked as sugar cane harvesters on the island of Saint Kitts and then photographed the portraits. He used the same methods in the latter project, using trash to depict the *catadores*, or trash pickers, who frequent a massive garbage dump on the outskirts of Rio de Janeiro. In both series, the unorthodox materials point to a reality outside the images themselves and provide information about the lives of the sitters that would not be communicated through a straightforward portrait. Muniz donated his proceeds from the sale of Pictures of Garbage to the *catadores'* collective, which used the money to support the building of housing, a library, and other projects.[1] In this way the photographs are both artifacts and instigators of a larger social process and cultural experience.

In 2008 Muniz made a series of works that merged his dual interest in the fabrication of illusion and the social life of objects. Versos presents replicas of the backs of some of art history's most iconic paintings, including Grant Wood's *American Gothic*, Vincent van Gogh's *Starry Night*, and Edward Hopper's *Nighthawks*. Usually seen only by museum curators, art handlers, and conservators, a painting's verso makes visible its structural support as well as its history, as evidenced by the labels and annotations that are applied each time the piece is exhibited. "The back is real," says Muniz, "and that's why when someone wants to know if something is authentic, the first thing he does is to look at the side that is never seen."[2]

Muniz began his series by choosing paintings that he believed were so familiar that they "could be imagined simply by hearing someone whisper their titles."[3] He photographed their backs, then used the photos to make meticulous re-creations of them in three dimensions. These sculptural "fictions" reveal certain truths about the paintings that are usually hidden from the average museumgoer: a work's travels, the history of its ownership, its "use" as an object. The Versos are exhibited leaning against the wall on blocks, adding another layer to their exploration of illusion by suggesting that one has walked into a gallery in mid-installation.

JD

Notes
1. Carol Kino, "Where Art Meets Trash and Transforms Life," *New York Times*, October 21, 2010.
2. Vik Muniz, quoted in *Vik Muniz: Verso* (Milan: Charta, 2009), 19.
3. Ibid., 18.

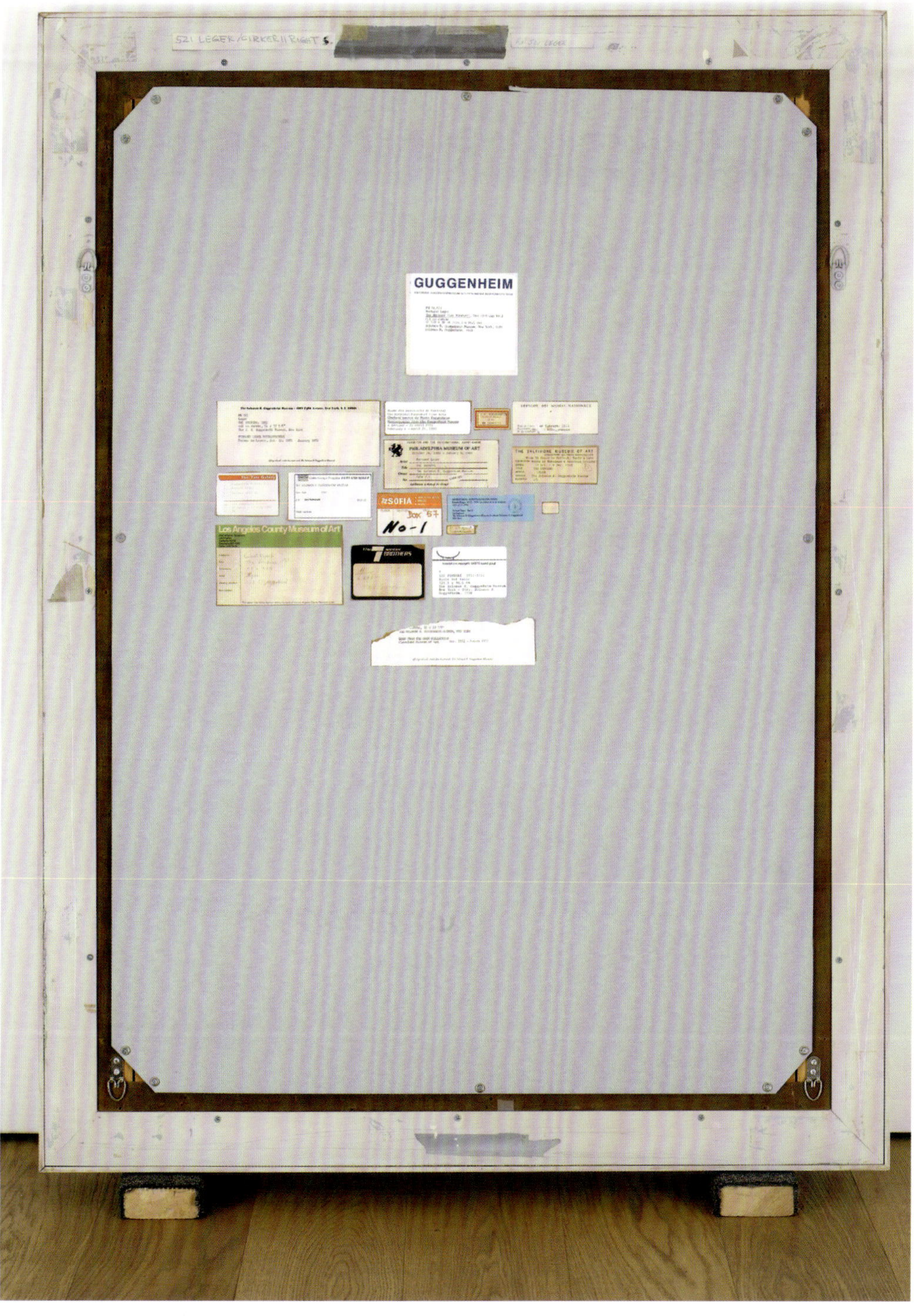

*Verso (The Smokers)*, 2008; mixed media; 53 ⅝ x 40 ¼ x 9 ½ inches (136.2 x 102.2 x 24.1 cm); courtesy the artist and Sikkema Jenkins & Co., New York

# Trevor Paglen

*BORN 1974 IN WASHINGTON, DC; LIVES AND WORKS IN BERKELEY AND NEW YORK*

> We also have to work, though, sort of the dark side, if you will. We've got to spend time in the shadows in the intelligence world. A lot of what needs to be done here will have to be done quietly, without any discussion.
>
> —Vice President Dick Cheney[1]

For the past eight years, the artist and writer Trevor Paglen has been pointing his long-range camera lenses at the US military's international network of black sites: bases, prisons, and research facilities that are unacknowledged by the government and do not appear on any map. They are protected by miles of restricted land, and their furtive government funding is estimated to be as much as $56 billion.[2] Yet, during the US war on terror, they have been positioned at the center of debates on the rapid expansion of military power and human rights violations.

Because of the black sites' remote locations, the photos in Paglen's Limit Telephotography, an ongoing project, are shot miles away from these bases in places like the Nevada desert. Distance and heat convection combine to create abstract images that are hard to decipher. It is when we read the titles, such as *Reaper Drone (Indian Springs, NV; Distance – 2 miles)* (2010), that the photos start becoming clearer. Although they will never be totally legible, neither will the black sites and their operations ever be fully acknowledged. Still, it is hard not to believe that Paglen's images are "real" and to speculate about these locations and their clandestine operations.

Pointing his camera upward, Paglen has also made a series of astrophotographs titled The Other Night Sky. Using a specially designed camera mount and software model, he is able to track the flight paths of panoptic satellites that endlessly orbit the earth. As they pass overhead, the beautiful streaks of light, like those captured in *LACROSSE/ONYX II Passing through Draco (Radam Imaging Reconnaissance Satellite; USA 69)* (2007), become abstractions that Paglen has said could just as easily be described as shooting stars or scratches on a film negative. But if we accept his assertion that his astrophotographs are in fact images of satellites, we might be moved to reflect on the elaborate systems of surveillance that are behind them. Who is watching? Who or what are they looking for? Where is this data being stored, and how will it be used?

The combination of Paglen's extensive academic research and his photographic documentation brings these "hidden geographies" into the light, making the invisible visible and the speculative real. While the exact functions of the bases and satellites may never be disclosed, his images become a record indicating that they do somehow exist, if only as places where state secrets are confronted with photographic facts.

CA

Notes
1. Dick Cheney, in conversation with Tim Russert on the NBC News program *Meet the Press*, September 16, 2001.
2. Noah Shachtman, "Pentagon's Black Budget Tops $56 Billion," *Danger Room* (blog), *Wired*, February 1, 2010, http://www.wired.com/dangerroom/2010/02/pentagons-black-budget-tops-56-billion/.

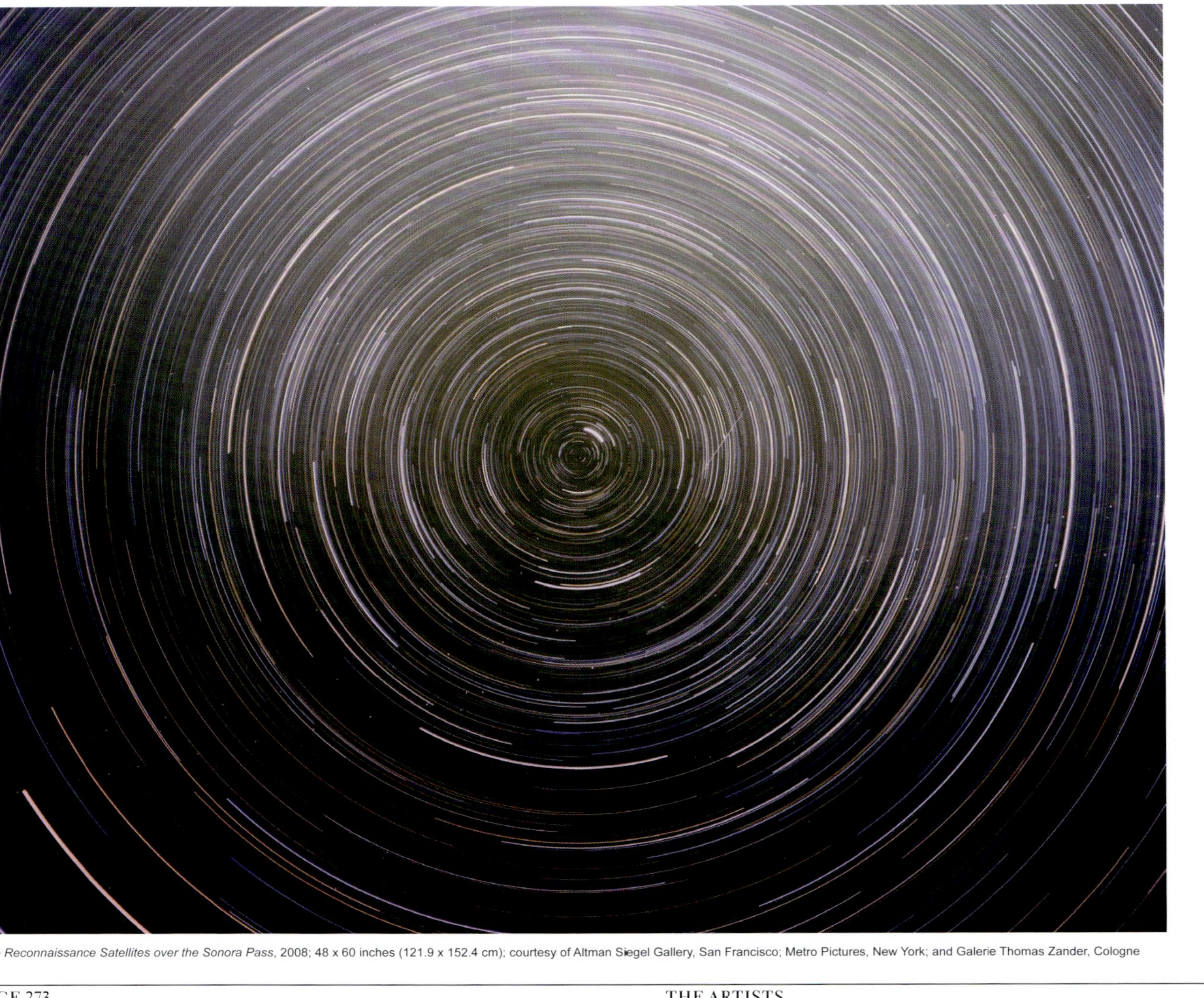

*Nine Reconnaissance Satellites over the Sonora Pass*, 2008; 48 x 60 inches (121.9 x 152.4 cm); courtesy of Altman Siegel Gallery, San Francisco; Metro Pictures, New York; and Galerie Thomas Zander, Cologne

# Walid Raad

*BORN 1967 IN CHBANIEH, LEBANON; LIVES AND WORKS IN NEW YORK*

The focus of Walid Raad's artistic practice is the history of Lebanon. For much of his career he has been specifically engaged with the events of the country's devastating civil wars of the 1970s and 1980s, during which thousands died or were displaced and many more fled into exile. He has often approached the topic obliquely. For example, from 1989 to 2004 he made his work under the rubric of the Atlas Group, an entity of his own invention whose mission, he said, was to form an archive of research related to the history of the Lebanese wars.[1] The group's holdings, all of which were fabricated by Raad, deal with real historical events and include photographs, videos, notes, and documents supposedly produced by individuals on both sides of the conflict. With such a complex provenance, the Atlas Group archive cannot be understood within what Raad refers to as "the conventional and reductive binary of fiction and nonfiction." He proposes that its holdings be seen instead as "hysterical documents," fantasies built from his culture's collective memories.[2]

Among them is a short video titled *I Only Wish That I Could Weep* (2002/2001). It was shot on the Corniche, Beirut's popular seaside promenade, purportedly by an intelligence officer in the Lebanese army whose job it was to watch the area for signs of covert activity. With his camera hidden inside one of the food trucks that line the boardwalk, this officer performed his assigned task daily, except for a brief period every afternoon when he focused on the sun as it set over the Mediterranean. When he donated the footage, the officer told the Atlas Group that he had always longed to watch the sun set from this spot, but during the war years he had been barred from leaving his East Beirut neighborhood to come to the seaside in West Beirut. In his video, figures are reduced to shadows that speed by in fast motion as the sun's orb sinks into the sea. The writer Judith Schwarzbart has observed that the narrative framework Raad invented for this video "permits [the sunsets] to represent the freedom, of movement and spirit, that was stolen from the population during the civil war—a freedom which this agent reclaims."[3]

Raad has said that in creating the Atlas Group archive he intended to raise questions about the ways in which history is written.[4] How are official historical narratives formed? What gets omitted and what included? Where, in the end, do such narratives reside? Raad offers no answers. But he suggests that the only way one can possibly understand what happened in Lebanon during its civil wars—and, by implication, any history—is to enter a space in which fact, memory, fantasy, and fiction mingle comfortably.

JR

Notes

1. See the Atlas Group website, http://www.theatlasgroup.org.

2. Walid Raad, quoted in Alan Gilbert, "Walid Ra'ad," *Bomb* 81 (Fall 2002), http://bombsite.com/issues/81/articles/2504.

3. Judith Schwarzbart, "Walid Raad: I Only Wish," *SUM* 1 (December 2007): 9.

4. Alice Pfeiffer, "Paging Atlas Group," *Art in America* website, posted November 4, 2010, www.artinamericamagazine.com/news-opinion/news/2010-11-04/walid-raad-whitechapel/.

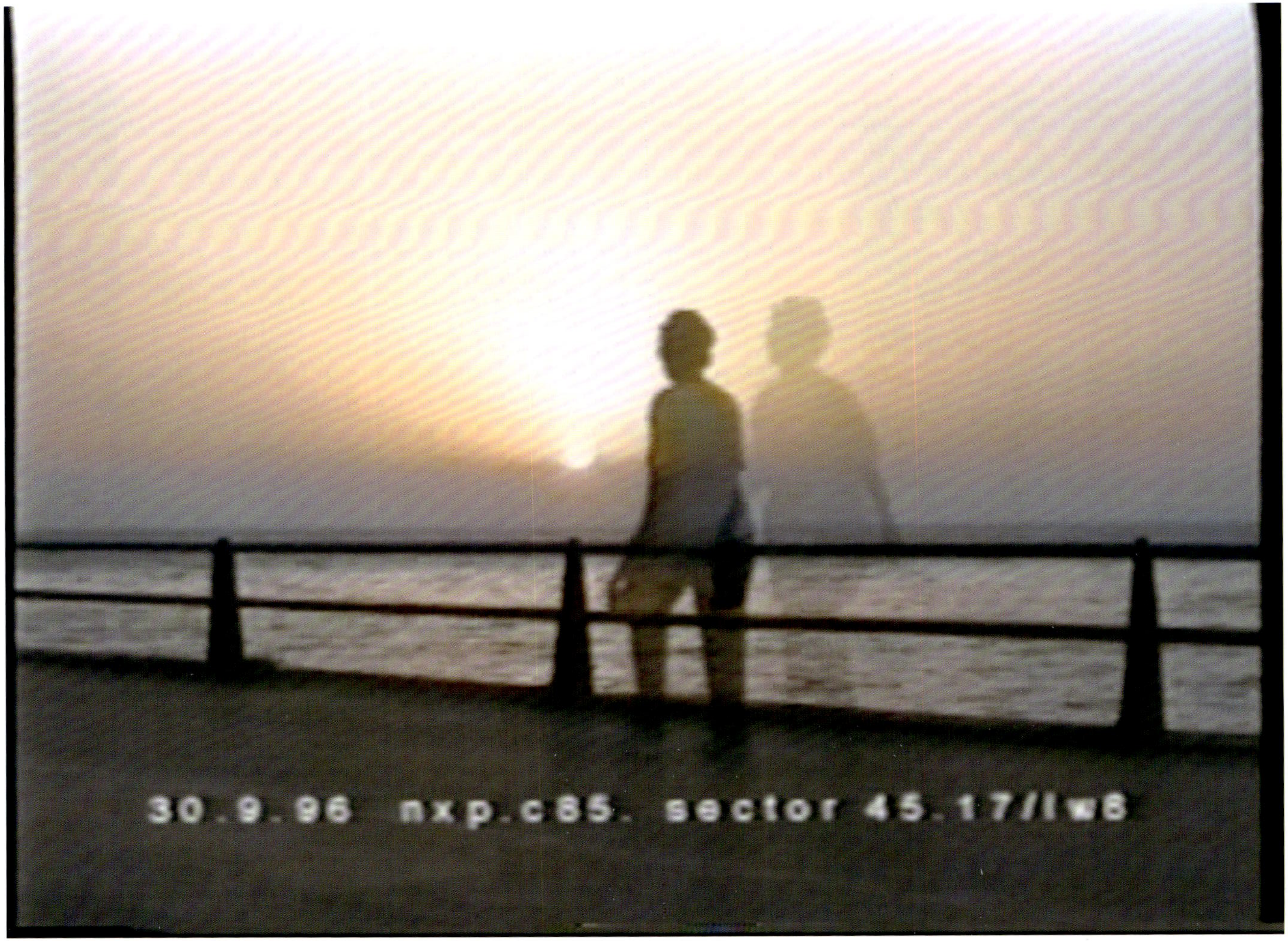

*I Only Wish That I Could Weep*, 2002/2001; single-channel video, color, silent; 7:40 minutes; courtesy the artist and Paula Cooper Gallery, New York

     THE ARTISTS

# Dario Robleto

*BORN 1972 IN SAN ANTONIO, TEXAS; LIVES AND WORKS IN HOUSTON*

Through his art, Dario Robleto looks deeply into the human experiences of loss and mourning in order to connect with what he calls "the truly extraordinary aspects of humanness . . . a sense of wonder and re-enchantment with the world that in a sense counterattacks the effects of extreme grief."[1] Because he believes that music has transformative, healing powers, he has developed a studio practice that is not unlike that of a DJ: he samples and remixes preexisting materials, creating a new context that incorporates the materials' previous history and meaning. Among the artifacts that he has repurposed are audiotapes of the voice of the last known Union soldier from the Civil War; bacteria cultured from the grooves of recorded Negro prison songs; and World War II–era surgical suture thread.

Robleto calls himself a "materialist poet" rather than a sculptor. Before he begins a piece, he writes out a narrative for it, and only after that does he set about looking for the objects and substances with which to tell the story.[2] The narratives that underlie each work can be inferred from their titles and lists of materials, which are given on labels that function almost like album liner notes. The battered pair of boxing gloves titled *The Melancholic Refuses to Surrender* (2003) was made from cast and carved bone charcoal, broken male hand bones, lead salvaged from the sea, horsehair, dirt, ground coal, pigments, string, rust, and a melted vinyl LP of Lead Belly's "The Titanic," a song about the ironic luck of blacks who were barred from sailing on the doomed ship. *Deep Down I Don't Believe in Hymns* (2001) comprises a nineteenth-century American military blanket on which Robleto sprinkled dust from hand-ground vinyl recordings of "Cortez the Killer" by Neil Young and Crazy Horse and "Tainted Love" by Soft Cell. By "infesting" the blanket with microscopic vinyl particles, Robleto refers both to the history of the American Indian wars, during which soldiers gave the native people "gifts" of blankets that were infested with smallpox, and the healing properties of music.

At times Robleto's process seems almost alchemical or even magical. To make the sculpture *Men Are the New Women* (2002), for example, he ground into dust a bone from a woman's rib cage, then cast and carved it into a facsimile of a bone from a man's rib cage. Physically the object is a simulation created from the dust of the real; symbolically it inverts the Christian story of creation. In both ways, it blurs the lines between fiction and reality and plays with our notions of authenticity. He hopes that works such as these ultimately kindle hope for the future even as they carry and mourn the past.

NS

Notes
1. Dario Robleto, "Artist Statement," posted on the website of the Artist Foundation of San Antonio, http://www.artistfound.org/awards/artist.cfm?id=56.
2. Robleto, in a video interview posted on the website of Human Nature: Artists Respond to a Changing Planet, http://www.artistsrespond.org/artists/robleto/.

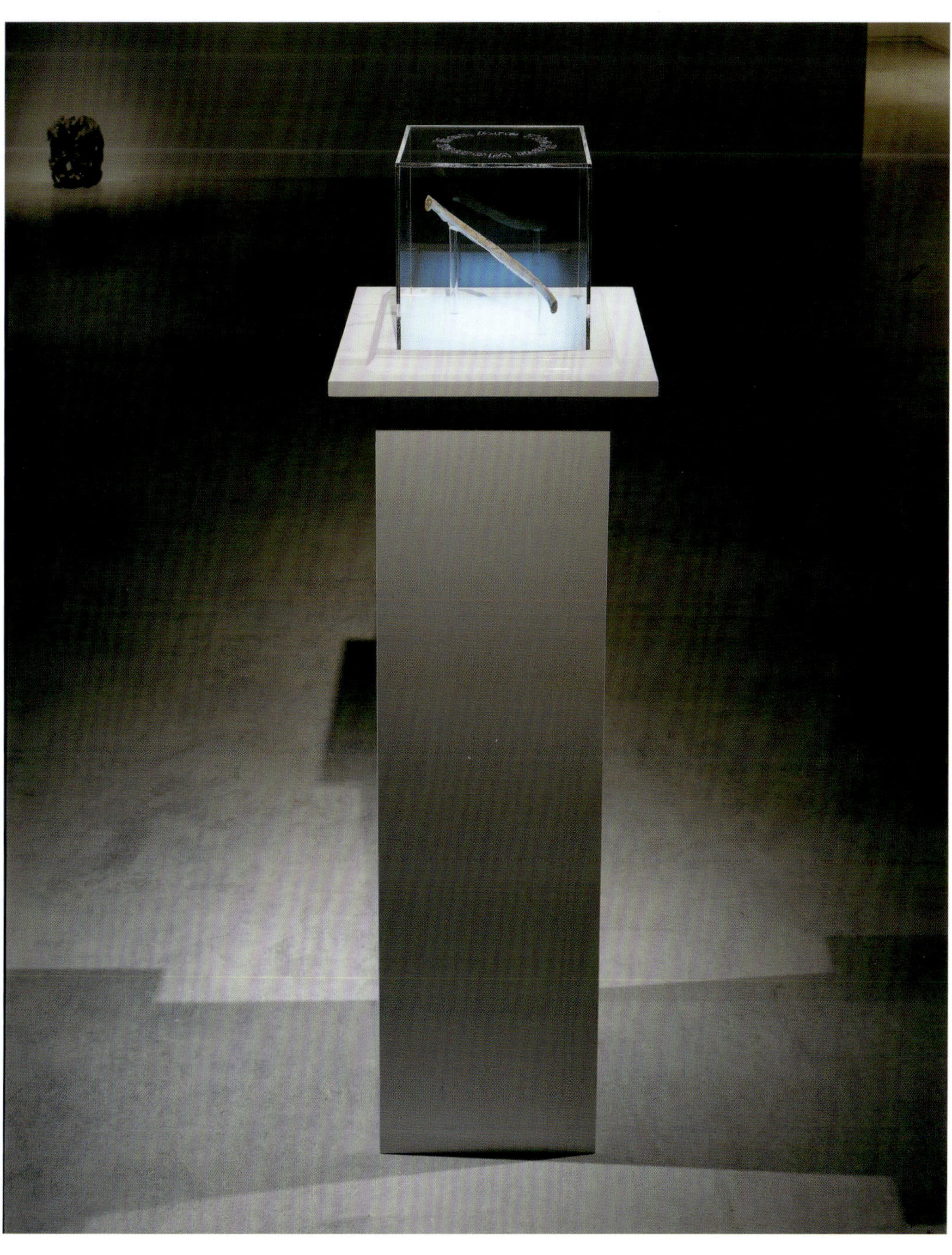

*Men Are the New Women*, 2002; bone dust, carbon, water-extendable resin, pigments, dirt, engraved Plexiglas, polyurethane, wood, light ("A female ribcage bone was ground to dust then recast and carved as a male ribcage bone"); 50 3/4 x 15 x 15 inches (128.9 x 38.1 x 38.1 cm); Linda Pace Foundation, San Antonio, Texas

# Eve Sussman / Rufus Corporation

*EVE SUSSMAN: BORN 1961 IN LONDON; LIVES AND WORKS IN BROOKLYN. RUFUS CORPORATION: FOUNDED 2003*

*89 Seconds at Alcázar* (2004) was inspired by the artist Eve Sussman's first encounter with *Las Meninas* (The Maids of Honor, ca. 1656), Diego Velázquez's iconic portrait of members of the Spanish royal court. The canvas, which has been the subject of much art historical debate and discussion, depicts Velázquez in the act of painting the Infanta Margarita, Philip IV, Mariana of Austria, and their attendants. By placing himself and his subjects in the same pictorial space, Velázquez seems to imply that the artist—and, by extension, the art of painting itself—has been elevated by the presence of the monarchs.[1] Sussman has written that for her the figures in the painting "seem real, psychologically arresting, physically frozen in a snapshot that predates photography by almost two hundred years. It seemed obvious to look for all the other snapshots."[2]

This was the starting point for *89 Seconds at Alcázar*, a video that imagines the moments leading up to and immediately following the scene depicted in Velázquez's masterpiece. Created under the auspices of the Rufus Corporation, a loose collective of artists with whom Sussman works to realize ambitious projects, the piece uses actors to play the royals and their servants and reproduces with extreme care their elaborate baroque costumes and the setting inside the Alcázar (the Hapsburg Palace). Sussman worked with a choreographer to block the actors' movements, which gave weight and purpose to every gesture. One is never unaware that this video is a constructed fiction, yet it is impossible not to become fully subsumed by its gorgeous cinematic illusion.

Sussman and the Rufus Corporation have since collaborated on several projects, including *Rape of the Sabine Women* (2005) and *whiteonwhite: algorithmicnoir* (2009–11), that draw their inspiration from icons of Western culture. The former is an eighty-minute video that reinterprets the Roman myth—the subject of Jacques-Louis David's 1799 painting *Intervention of the Sabine Women*—as an operatic period piece set in 1960s Berlin and Athens. The latter, named for Kazimir Malevich's painting *White on White* (1918), was inspired by "the Suprematist quests for transcendence, pure space and artistic higher ground."[3] The film's continuous, constantly changing narrative is edited live in real time through a custom-designed computer algorithm that draws on three thousand film clips, eighty voice-overs, and 150 pieces of music. Although the experience of these works is very different, the productions of Sussman and the Rufus Corporation are marked by an interest in gesture and human interaction, and a self-conscious engagement with cinematic illusion.

JD

Notes
1. Jonathan Brown, *Velázquez, Painter and Courtier* (New Haven, CT: Yale University Press, 1986), 260.
2. Eve Sussman and the Rufus Corporation, *89 Seconds at Alcázar* (Brooklyn: Rufus Press, 2006), unpaged.
3. From the press release for the film posted on the Rufus Corporation website, http://www .rufuscorporation.com.

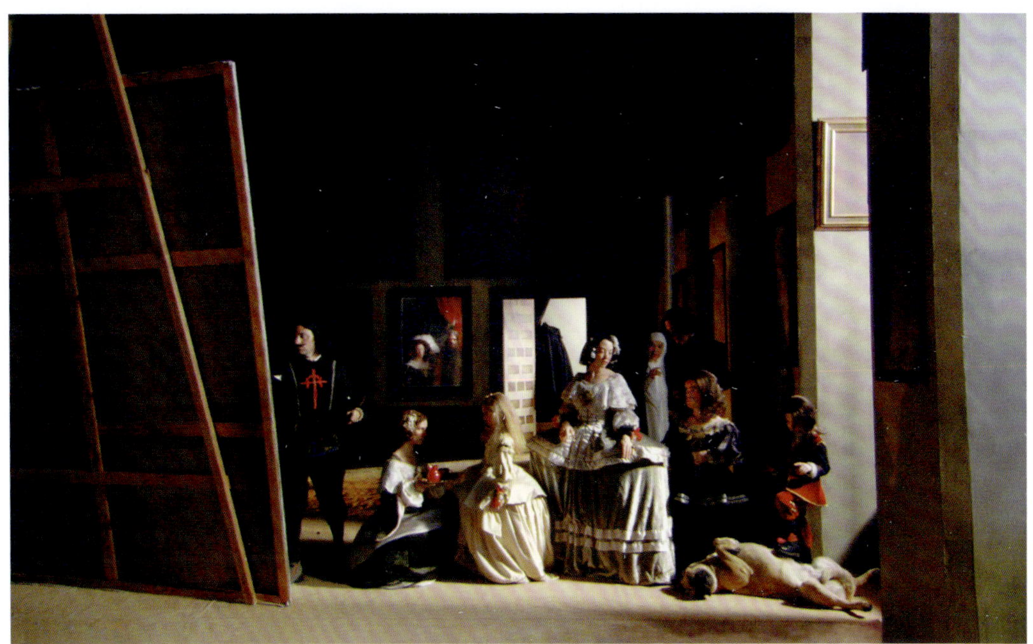

*Dog Rolls*, 2004; video still from *89 Seconds at Alcázar*; collection Jeanne and Michael L. Klein

# Mary Temple

*BORN 1957 IN PHOENIX, ARIZONA; LIVES AND WORKS IN BROOKLYN*

Mary Temple says that the primary subject of her art is doubt. Whether she works in drawing, site-specific installation, sculpture, or painting, "themes of trust, transparency, and truthfulness" are her constant concern.[1] Her Light Installations, a series begun in 2002, get at these themes through trompe l'oeil paintings of shadows and sunlight that seem to merge with the architecture on which they are painted. While completely believable as sensory data, the paintings depict situations that are architectural or meteorological impossibilities. *Forest for the Sea* (2006), for example, was a twenty-five-by-sixty-six-foot image of soft shadows seemingly cast by large leafy trees as sunlight streamed through the windows of Brooklyn's Smack Mellon gallery. But the shadows did not change with the movement of the sun, the leaves did not move in the breeze, and visitors' bodies cast no shadows as they traversed the space. "As viewers began to solve the visual puzzle [of this piece] and understand the reality of the environment," Temple has written, "they may have realized they were taken in by a simple illusion—that their senses were surprisingly untrustworthy."[2] But Temple is not out to trick viewers; rather, she wants to give them the chance to "enjoy not knowing" what precisely they are looking at.[3]

More recently, Temple has created light installation "fragments" on small sections of wall and floor. *IT MUST BE TRUE (fragment)* (2011) comprises a panel of white drywall that leans against the wall and abuts several interlocking hardwood planks assembled on the floor. A painted shadow of the hopeful phrase "It Must Be True" rakes across the drywall and onto the floor panels. The piece has several layers of perceptual truth and fiction. It is made of actual building materials, so one could imagine that it is a fragment taken from another, disassembled room. The piece casts actual shadows in the space in which it is installed but also seems to have brought with it a patch of sunlight and shadow. To those familiar with Temple's work, *IT MUST BE TRUE* might seem to be a section of one of her larger trompe l'oeil paintings. Its title allows for all these possibilities to be true while simultaneously suggesting that seeing should not necessarily be believing.

IH

Notes

1. Mary Temple, statement on the artist's website, http://marytemple.com/texts.

2. Mary Temple, statement about *Forest for the Sea* on the artist's website, http://marytemple.com/detail/light-installations/148/forest-for-the-sea.

3. Mary Temple, statement about light installations on the artist's website, http://s139022.gridserver.com/media/files/light-installations-2009.pdf.

*IT MUST BE TRUE (fragment)*, 2011; acrylic paint on drywall, wood stain and urethane on hardwood, acrylic gel; 39 x 46 x 45 inches (99.1 x 116.8 x 114.3 cm); courtesy the artist and Mixed Greens, New York

# The Yes Men

The culture-jamming duo known as the Yes Men has become notorious for witty mass-media hoaxes that are meant to raise public awareness of unscrupulous corporate behavior. Led by media artists Andy Bichlbaum and Mike Bonanno (also known as Jacques Servin and Igor Vamos, respectively), the Yes Men use various tactical media strategies to perform "identity corrections," which they define as "impersonating big-time criminals in order to publicly humiliate them. Our targets are leaders and big corporations who put profits ahead of everything else."[1] In 2011, for example, during National Asthma Awareness Month, they launched coalcares.org, purportedly under the auspices of Peabody Energy, America's largest coal company. The site, which promised to "make coal cool" for asthmatic kids, featured asthma-related games and offered free Harry Potter– and Justin Bieber–branded inhalers to children living near coal-fired plants. Another of the Yes Men's targets, Dow Chemical, was spoofed by the duo's fake announcement, on BBC television, that Dow intended to clean up the site of the deadly Bhopal gas leak, provide medical care for the victims, and fund research into other hazardous chemicals.[2] The Yes Men's guerrilla activism takes full advantage of the reach and openness of the Internet, where fact and fiction are easily blurred.

In November 2008 the Yes Men engineered one of their most visible hoaxes. Playing on the country's optimism after the election of Barack Obama, they issued their own special edition of the *New York Times*, created by a team of some fifty associates over a period of six months. The paper's front page trumpeted "Iraq War Ends," and inside were fourteen pages of hopeful headlines, such as "USA Patriot Act Repealed," "Washington Redskins Renamed," and "All Public Universities to Be Free." Using real-world information and details, each story provided a fictional history of how these changes had been effected. Yes Men operatives handed out the paper for free in New York, where it was distributed at subway stations during the busy morning rush hour, as well as in Los Angeles, San Francisco, Chicago, Philadelphia, and Washington, DC.[3] To accompany the print edition, the Yes Men created a sham *Times* website with the same content.[4] Overall the spoof is estimated to have reached more than eighty thousand people across the country. One of the Yes Men's collaborators on the project, Steve Lambert, said: "We wanted to experience what it would look like, and feel like, to read headlines we really want to read. It's about what's possible, if we think big and act collectively."[5]

NS



Notes

1. See the group's website, http://theyesmen.org.

2. After the announcement Dow's stock fell by $2 billion, and the Yes Men issued a retraction that read in part: "Dow will NOT commit ANY funds to compensate and treat 120,000 Bhopal residents who require lifelong care. . . . Dow will NOT remediate (clean up) the Bhopal plant site. . . . Dow's sole and unique responsibility is to its shareholders, and Dow CANNOT do anything that goes against its bottom line unless forced to by law." See http://www.dowethics.com/r/about/corp/bbc.htm.

3. Sewell Chan, "Liberal Pranksters Hand Out Times Spoof," *City Room* (blog), *New York Times*, November 12, 2008, http://cityroom.blogs.nytimes.com/2008/11/12/pranksters-spoof-the-times.

4. See http://www.nytimes-se.com.

5. See http://theyesmen.org/hijinks/newyorktimes.

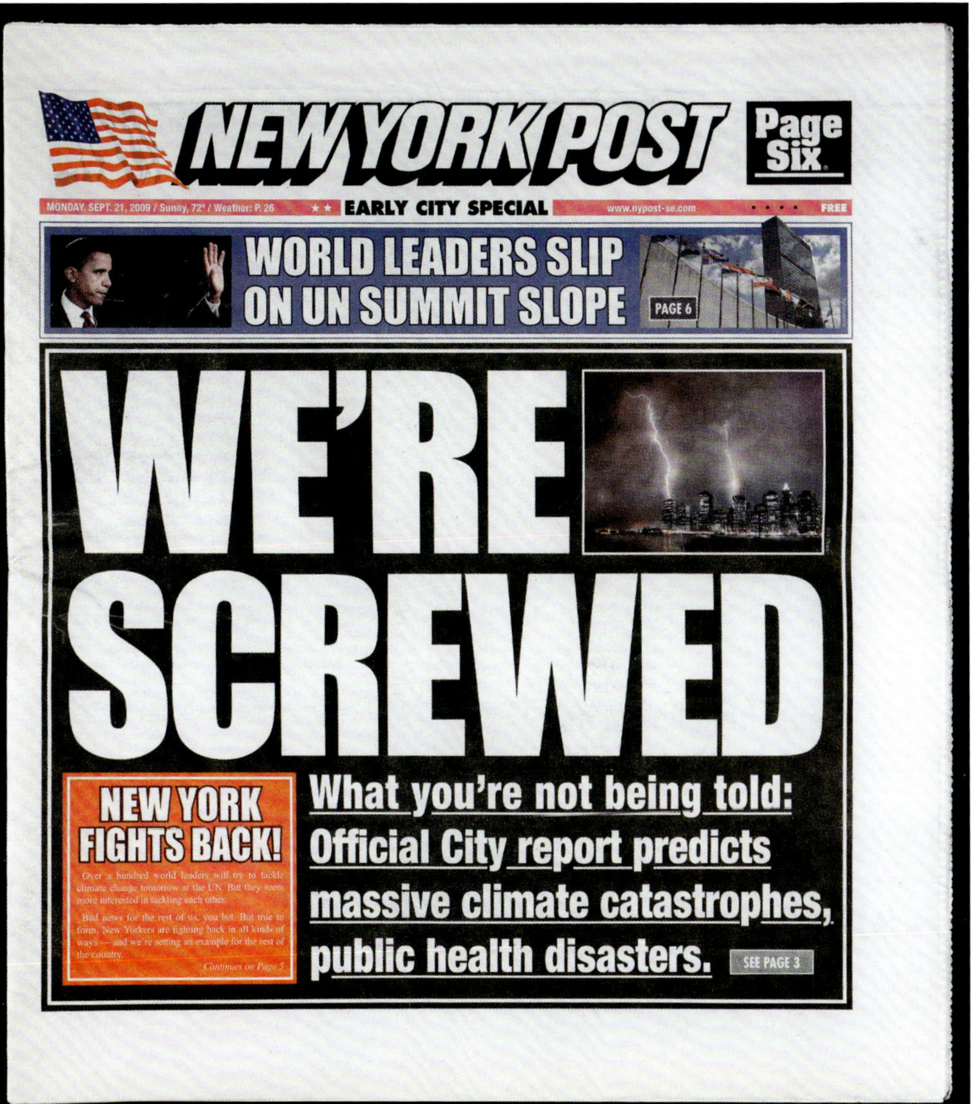


*New York Post Special Edition*, 2009; newspaper; 13 1/2 x 13 3/4 inches (34.3 x 34.9 cm); courtesy the artists

ISBN 3-7757-0993-2

9 783775 709934

Infligh

# NO MAN'S LAND

> ZAP A PLANE
> WEAPONS GAVE ME WORDS
> INVADERS FROM THE WILD WIDE WEB
> CREDIT CARD CAPERS
> MAN IN SWIMMING TRUNKS

COMPILED BY JOHAN GRIMONPREZ

# WHAT TO DO WITH A STOLEN BOEING 777

# Trevor Paglen

**news and updates** | **visual projects** | **written projects** | **media/reviews** | **odds, ends, and blog** | **bio** | **contact**

## Limit Telephotography

A number of classified military bases and installations are located in some of the remotest parts of the United States, hidden deep in western deserts and buffered by dozens of miles of restricted land. Many of these sites are so remote, in fact, that there is nowhere on Earth where a civilian might be able to see them with an unaided eye. In order to produce images of these remote and hidden landscapes, therefore, some unorthodox viewing and imaging techniques are required.

Limit-telephotography involves photographing landscapes that cannot be seen with the unaided eye. The technique employs high powered telescopes whose focal lengths range between 1300mm and 7000mm. At this level of magnification, hidden aspects of the landscape become apparent.

Limit-telephotography most closely resembles astrophotography, a technique that astronomers use to photograph objects that might be trillions of miles from Earth. In some ways, however, it is easier to photograph the depths of the solar system than it is to photograph the recesses of the military industrial complex. Between Earth and Jupiter (500 million miles away), for example, there are about five miles of thick, breathable atmosphere. In contrast, there are upwards of forty miles of thick atmosphere between an observer and the sites depicted in this series.

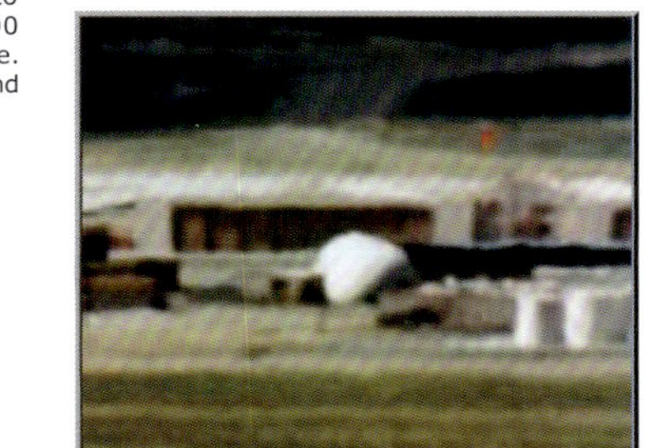

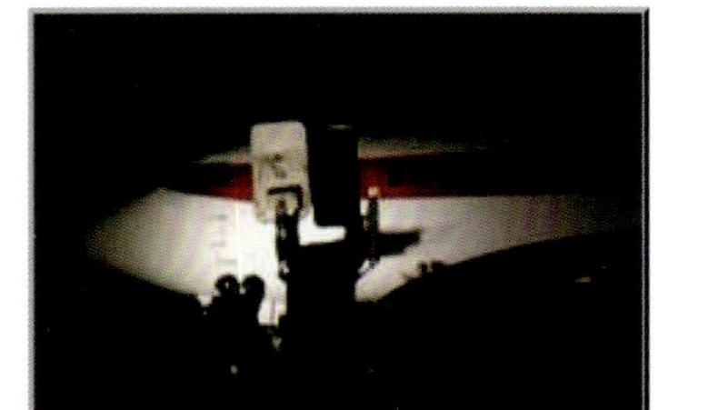

EDITION: U.S.
CA Canada  Québec  FR France  US United States  UK United Kingdom

March 8, 2012

**HUFF POST** POLITICS

THE INTERNET NEWSPAPER: NEWS BLOGS VIDEO COMMUNITY

Like
115k

CONNECT
Search The Huffington P

## Van Jones

Environmental Justice Activist; Founder, Green For All

Posted: September 1, 2005 04:13 PM

## Black People "Loot" Food … White People "Find" Food.

Mississippi Governor Haley Barbour said it best. He noted that the Hurricane Katrina disaster had "brought out the best in some, the worst in others."

I assume that he was talking about the media, which keeps broadcasting the same "Black people looting' scene, over and over.

The racial biases of the reporters in New Orleans has been on full - and shocking - display, since Tuesday.

Repeatedly, reporters refer to white victims clinging to life as "survivors" and "residents," while African-American victims doing the same things are called "looters" and "criminals." Disproportionately, the humanizing, "heart-breaker" stories feature white victims and families. Meanwhile, images of African-American crowds are almost invariably in the background during discussions of "criminal activity."

Yahoo.com's news page provided one of the most blatant examples of this kind of bias.

The website featured a photo of two white residents, wading through the water with food. The caption read: "Two residents wade through chest-deep water after finding bread and soda from a local grocery store after Hurricane Katrina came through the area in New Orleans, Louisiana.(AFP/Getty Images/Chris Graythen)"

Then there is a photo of a Black youth, wading through water with food. The caption reads: "A young man walks through chest deep flood water after looting a grocery store in New Orleans on Tuesday, Aug. 30, 2005. Flood waters continue to rise in New Orleans after Hurricane Katrina did extensive damage when it made landfall on Monday. (AP Photo/Dave Martin)"

You can see the images yourself below:

This is the kind of shameful bias that keeps the country divided, even during awful tragedies like this.

## More in Politics...

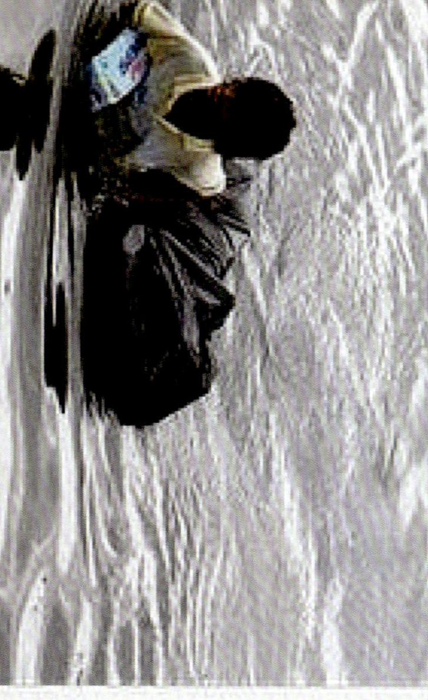

**AP** Associated Press  AP - Tue Aug 30,11:31 AM ET

A young man walks through chest deep flood water after 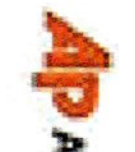looting a grocery store in New Orleans on Tuesday, Aug. 30, 2005. Flood waters continue to rise in New Orleans after Hurricane Katrina did extensive damage when it

✉ Email Photo    🖶 Print Photo

**RECOMMEND THIS PHOTO** » Recommended Photos
Recommend It:    Average (138 votes)
☆☆☆☆☆    ★★★★☆

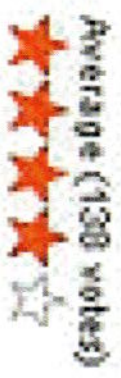

**AFP**    3:47 AM ET

Two residents wade through chest-deep water after finding bread and soda from a local grocery store after Hurricane Katrina came through the area in New Orleans, Louisiana.(AFP/Getty Images/Chris Graythen)

✉ Email Photo    🖶 Print Photo

**RECOMMEND THIS PHOTO** » Recommended Photos
Recommend It:    Average (211 votes)
☆☆☆☆☆    ★★★★☆

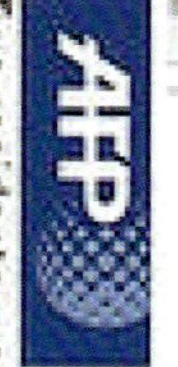

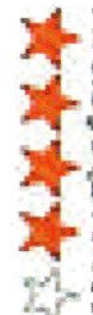

**RELATED**

• Katrina's Effects, at a Glance AP - Tue Aug 30, 1:26 PM ET

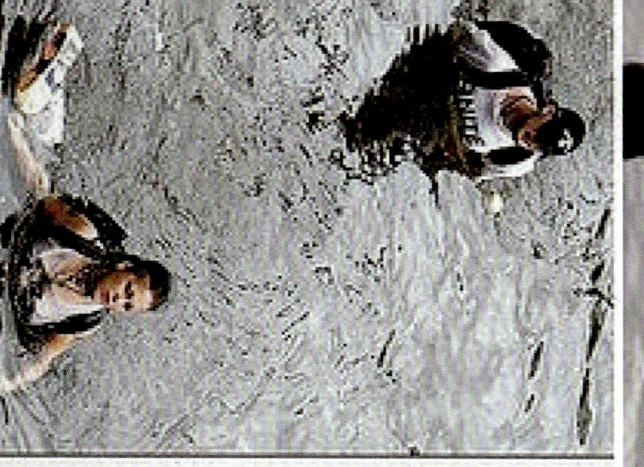

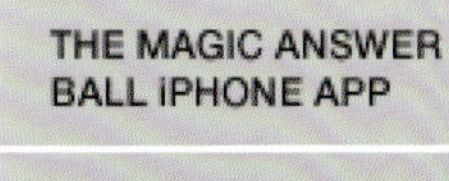


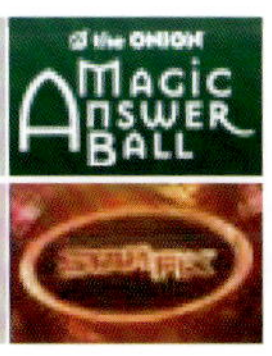


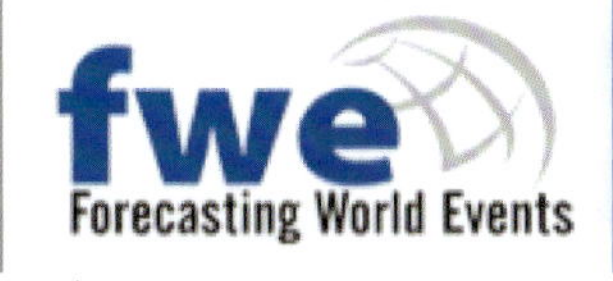


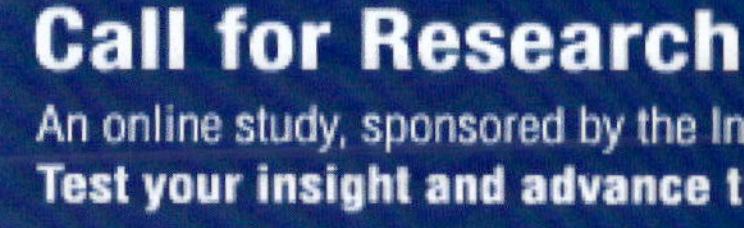




# NEWS

# Evolutionists Flock To Darwin-Shaped Wall Stain

SEPTEMBER 5, 2008 I ISSUE 44·36

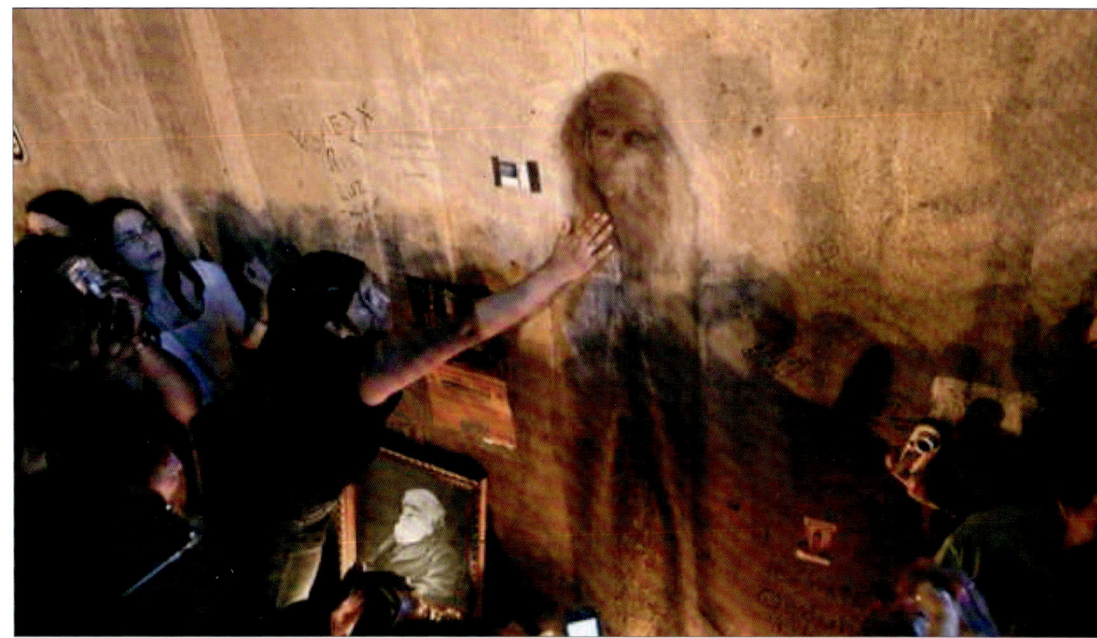

Darwinic pilgrims claim the image fills them with an overwhelming feeling of logic.

DAYTON, TN—A steady stream of devoted evolutionists continued to gather in this small Tennessee town today to witness what many believe is an image of Charles Darwin —author of *The Origin Of Species* and founder of the modern evolutionary movement—made manifest on a concrete wall in downtown Dayton.

"I brought my baby to touch the wall, so that the power of Darwin can purify her genetic makeup of undesirable inherited traits," said Darlene Freiberg, one among a growing crowd assembled here to see the mysterious stain, which appeared last Monday on one side of the Rhea County Courthouse. The building was also the location of the famed "Scopes Monkey Trial" and is widely considered one of Darwinism's holiest sites. "Forgive me, O Charles, for ever doubting your Divine Evolution. After seeing this miracle of limestone pigmentation with my own eyes, my faith in empirical reasoning will never again be tested."

Added Freiberg, "Behold the power and glory of the scientific method!"

# VANITY FAIR

culture ▶ web exclusive ▶ killer riffs

*February 9, 2009*

## This Is Even More Spinal Tap

For the March 2009 issue, *Vanity Fair* sat down with the members of Spinal Tap, whose genre-defining mock-umentary (directed by Marty DiBergi) just turned 25. Here is an extended remix of the interview with Nigel, David, Derek, and Marty—with audio. *Related video:* "The Tap Sell Out."

by Michael Hogan

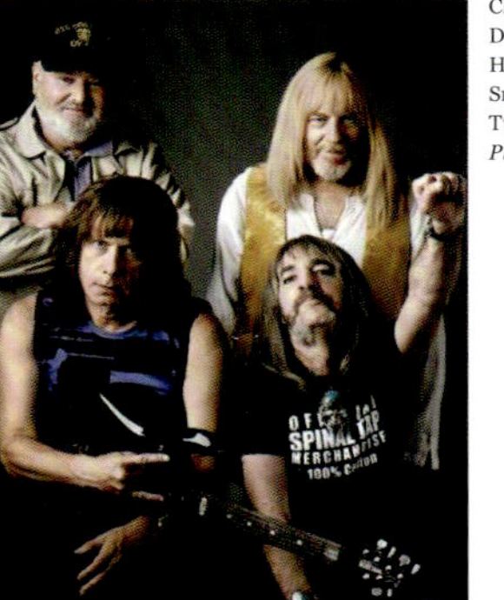

Clockwise from top left: Marty DiBergi (Rob Reiner), David St. Hubbins (Michael McKean), Derek Smalls (Harry Shearer), and Nigel Tufnel (Christopher Guest). *Photograph by Art Streiber.*

*Listen to the interview.*

This is Even More Spinal Tap by Vanity Fair

I t's been 25 years since *This Is Spinal Tap* lugged the big-bottomed rock of David St. Hubbins, Nigel Tufnel, and Derek Smalls onto the screen, and the band is keen to celebrate—just as soon as they find enough corporate brands to fund their arena reunion tour. "We want to be the most heavily sponsored group in the history of rock 'n' roll," says Smalls, the bassist famous for his improvised solos on "Jazz Odyssey." That could take a while in this economy, so the trio's real-life alter egos—**Michael McKean, Christopher Guest,** and **Harry Shearer**—are kicking things off this summer with an acoustic concert series titled "Unwigged, Unplugged, and Undead." There are also plans to release the film on Blu-ray and place a song (may we suggest "Nerve Damage"?) in a new video game. Michael Hogan sat down with the boys from Squatney and *This Is Spinal Tap*'s director, Marty DiBergi (who bears a striking resemblance to **Rob Reiner**), to talk about the anniversary, the new tour, and the triumphs and travails experienced by rockers of a certain age.

**David and Nigel, how has your relationship developed in the 25 years since the**

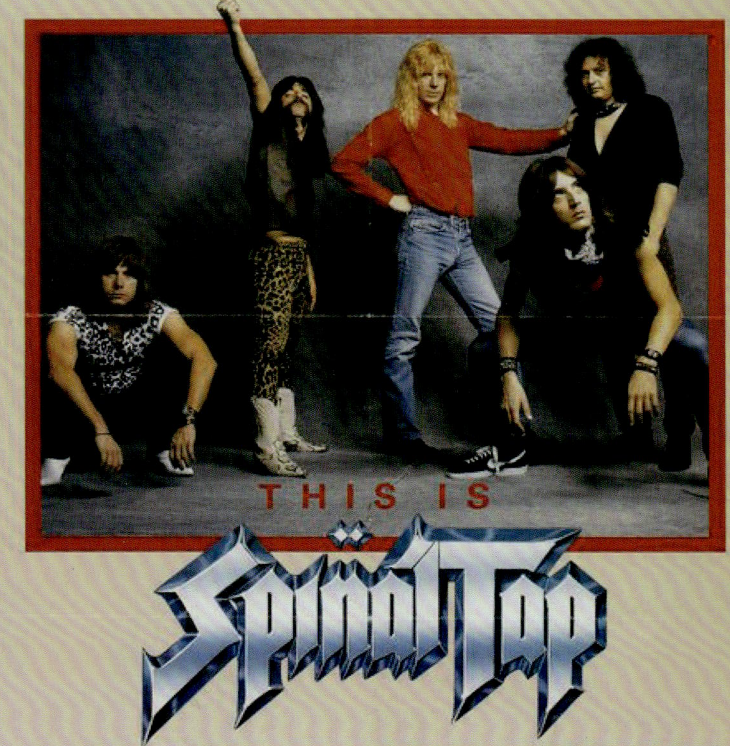

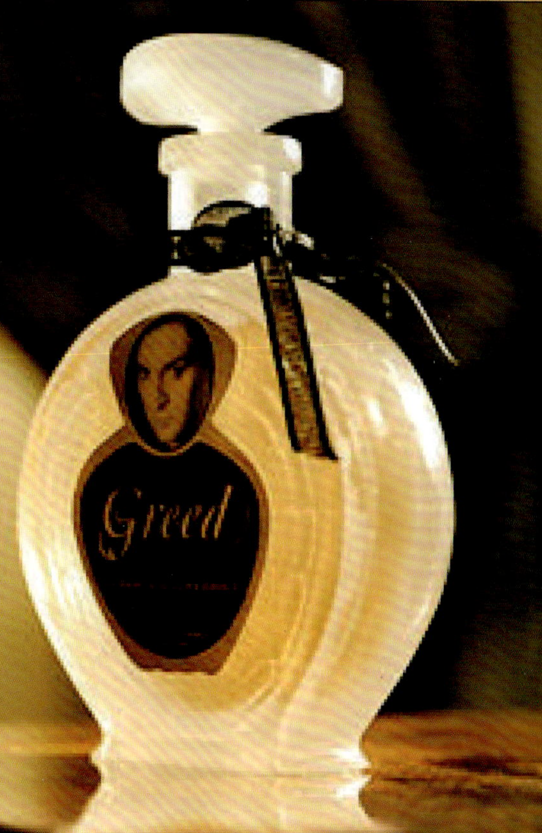

FRANCESCO
VEZZOLI
Greed
THE NEW FRAGRANCE

Greed

FRANCESCO
VEZZOLI
Greed
THE NEW FRAGRANCE

COMING SOON

Greed

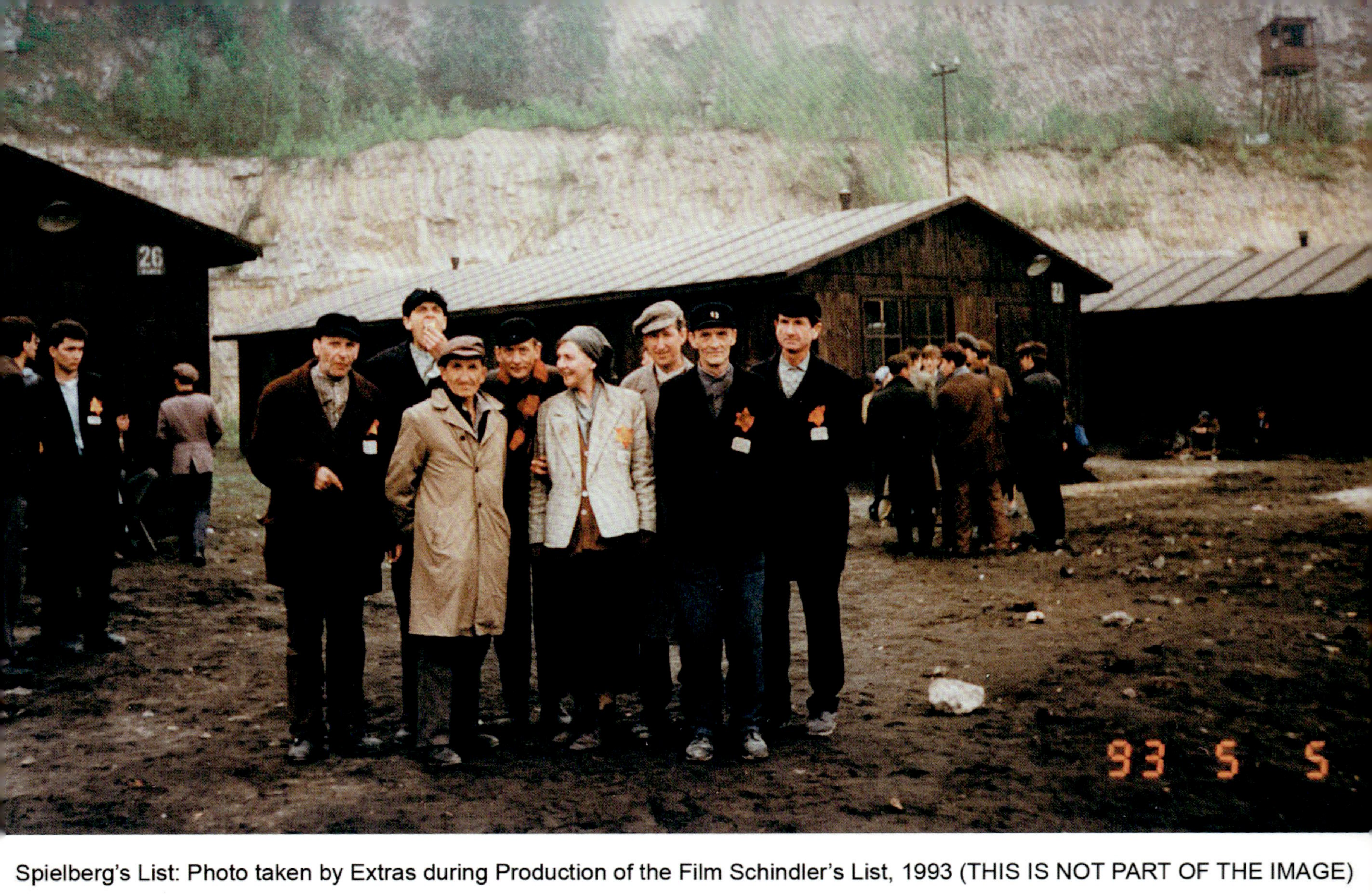

Spielberg's List: Photo taken by Extras during Production of the Film Schindler's List, 1993 (THIS IS NOT PART OF THE IMAGE)

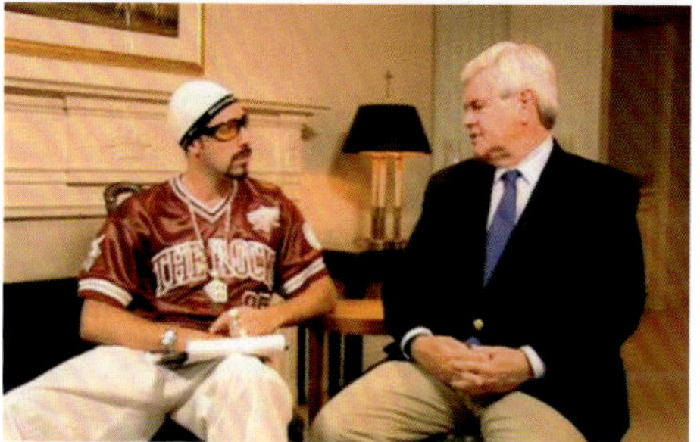



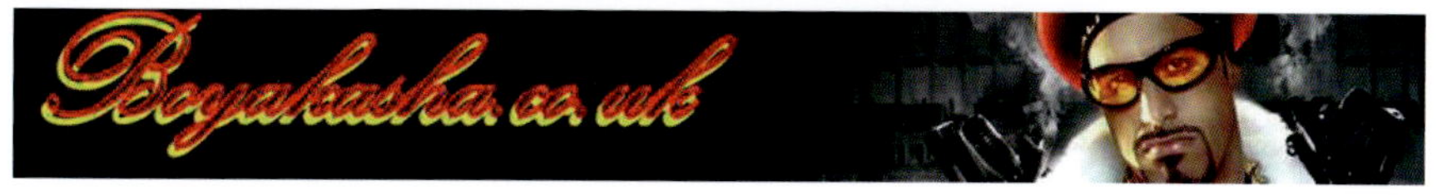



Homie     Sacha Baron Cohen     Ali G     Borat     Bruno     Azamat Bagatov     News archive

Search Boyakasha.co.uk

# Ali G information

**Ali G Info**

Everything you need to know about the main man... Ali G

**Birthplace**
Staines Hospital

**Home**
Langley near Barkshire, his nans house in Staines, old biddies home, 2 flats in Elmslea estate

**Massive**
West Staines

**Dave** (Ali's Mate)
Dave was put down for a 14 year strech for finding a use for the kilo, now he has still got about 12 years to go. About 8 years ago Dave got jiggy with Ali's Julie, and Ali still remeber. Ali received his swimming badge when Dave told him that there was a brick of hash at the bottom of the pool. Dave has a gun and says hes killed someone, but me dont dont know if thats true. Dave also tried to join the army.

**Ricky C** (Ali's Mate)
Ricky C is ALi's best mate, and if he stopped going out with a girl Ali would leave 3 weeks before boning her.

**Rainbow Jeremy** (Ali's Mate)
Aint got no techmology (check out his website if you dont believe)

**Jezzy F** (Ali's Mate)
No Info

**Old friends from school**
Shemfye Tow – Came from Vietnam. Hactually, he came from China. He got hung up on a hook at school.
Zoe Lewis – went to Alis school. She is rank and charged 25p for fingers and thumbs.
Tashid Bagey -went to Ali's school. Has nice skin and charged 75p for a touch outside the clothes.

**Bitches**
Julie
Mary
Ethel (from da old biddies home)

**Enemies**
East Staines massive

**Relatives**
Uncle Jamal
His mum
His sister (who is rank, even his mum cus her, call her a slag)

**Clothes**
Mainly Tommy Hillfigger (even his p.j's!)
Fubu* (see bottom)

**Turf** (see map for details)
Swings in Larecroft park

571
Follow

## The Boyakasha Vote

**Will Sacha Baron Cohen make a good Freddie Mercury?**

○ Aigh, for real!

○ Ish dont fink so.

○ Dont know.

Vote

View Results
Vote results archive

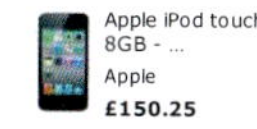

Apple iPod touch
8GB - ...
Apple
**£150.25**

Apple iPod nano

## Selected Bibliography


Abramson, Julia. *Learning from Lying: The Paradoxes of Literary Mystification*. Newark: University of Delaware Press, 2005.

Adamson, Glenn. "The Real Thing." In Torchia, *Ai Weiwei*, 48–55. Glenside, PA: Arcadia University Art Gallery, 2010.

Adorno, Theodor W. *The Jargon of Authenticity*. Translated by Knut Tarnowski and Frederic Will. Evanston, IL: Northwestern University Press, 1973.

Aisemberg, Paula, ed. *La Maison Rouge, 2004–2009*. Paris: Archibooks + Sautereau, 2009.

Amarasingam, Amarnath, ed. *The Stewart / Colbert Effect: Essays on the Real Impacts of Fake News*. Jefferson, NC: McFarland, 2011.

Arestizábal, Irma. *Leandro Erlich*. Rome: Museo d'Arte Contemporanea Roma; Milan: Electa, 2006.

Armstrong, Elizabeth, Arthur C. Danto, and Boris Groys. *Peter Fischli and David Weiss: In a Restless World*. Minneapolis: Walker Art Center; London: Serpentine Gallery, 1996.

Barliant, Claire, Kris Douglas, and Yasmil Raymond. *Iñigo Manglano-Ovalle: Blinking Out of Existence*. Rochester, MN: Rochester Art Center, 2007.

Baudrillard, Jean. *America*. Translated by Chris Turner. Rev. ed. New York: Verso, 1989.

———. *Simulacra and Simulation*. Translated by Sheila Faria Glaser. Ann Arbor: University of Michigan Press, 1994.

———. *Simulations*. Translated by Paul Foss, Paul Patton, and Philip Beitchman. New York: Semiotext(e), 1983.

Bell, David. *Cyberculture Theorists: Manuel Castells and Donna Haraway*. London: Routledge, 2007.

———. *An Introduction to Cyberculture*. London: Routledge, 2001.

Beloff, Zoe, Norman Klein, Amy Herzog, and Aaron Beebe. *The Coney Island Amateur Psychoanalytic Society and Its Circle*. Edited by Zoe Beloff. New York: Christine Burgin Gallery, 2009.

Benjamin, Walter. *Illuminations*. Translated by Harry Zohn. New York: Schocken, 1968.

Bichlbaum, Andy, and Joseph Huff-Hannon. "The Three Greatest Pranks of 2010." *Huffington Post*, April 1, 2010. http://www.huffingtonpost.com/the-yes-men/the-best-pranks-of-2010_b_521594.html.

Blais, Joline, and Jon Ippolito. *At the Edge of Art*. London: Thames & Hudson, 2005.

Borchardt-Hume, Achim, ed. *Keeping It Real: From the Ready-Made to the Everyday*. London: Whitechapel Gallery, 2010.

———. *Walid Raad: Miraculous Beginnings*. London: Whitechapel Gallery, 2010.

Bordaz, Jean-Pierre, ed. *Laurent Grasso*. Paris: Centre Pompidou, 2009.

Bourriaud, Nicolas. "The Reversibility of the Real." *TATEetc.*, no.7 (Summer 2006): 76–83.

Bouwhuis, Jelle. "Nettime—Interview with Norman Klein on the New Canon—10.02.07." *16beaver*, October 2, 2007. http://www.16beavergroup.org/mtarchive/archives/002324print.html.

Bouwhuis, Jelle, Ingrid Commandeur, Gijs Frieling, Domeniek Ruyters, Margriet Schavemaker, and Christel Vesters, eds. *Now Is the Time: Art and Theory in the Twenty-First Century*. Rotterdam: NAi, 2009.

Brighton, Shane. "Waiting Games: Tragedy, Time, and Technology in the Work of John Gerrard." In *Dark Portraits: John Gerrard*.

Burckhardt, Martin. "The Art of Immersion." *Passages*, no. 54 (2010): 24–27.

Burnett, D. Graham. "The Art of Deception: Aesthetics at the Perimeter of Truth" (syllabus), Princeton University, 2011. http://www.princeton.edu/history/people/data/d/dburnett/profile/teaching/BurnettDG_HUM598_2011_Spring.pdf.

*Cao Fei: PRD Anti-Heroes*. Sittard, the Netherlands: Museum Het Domein, 2006.

Castro Cortiñas, Beatriz, and Silvia Fernández. *Florian Maier-Aichen*. Madrid: La Fábrica, 2008.

Colbert, Stephen. *I Am America (And So Can You!)*. New York: Grand Central Publishing, 2009.

Crone, Rainer, ed. *Similia / Dissimilia*. New York: Rizzoli, 1988.

D'Agata, John, and Jim Fingal. *The Lifespan of a Fact*. New York: Norton, 2012.

*Dark Portraits: John Gerrard*. Dublin: Royal Hibernian Academy, Gallagher Gallery, 2006.

Debord, Guy. *Society of the Spectacle*. Detroit: Black & Red, 1977.

Deitch, Jeffrey, ed. *Form Follows Fiction*. Milan: Charta, 2001.

Demand, Thomas. *La carte d'après nature*. London: Mack, 2010.

Dietrich, Lucas, ed. *60: Innovators Shaping Our Creative Future*. London: Thames & Hudson, 2009.

Duncombe, Stephen. *Dream: Re-imagining Progressive Politics in an Age of Fantasy*. New York: New Press, 2007.

Durgin, Frank H. "The Tinkerbell Effect: Motion Perception and Illusion." *Journal of Consciousness Studies* 9, no. 5–6 (2002): 88–101.

Eckmann, Sabine. *Sharon Lockhart: Lunch Break*. St. Louis: Mildred Lane Kemper Art Museum, 2010.

Eco, Umberto. *Travels in Hyperreality*. Translated by William Weaver. New York: Harcourt Brace Jovanovich, 1986.

Elkins, James. *The Domain of Images*. Ithaca, NY: Cornell University Press, 1999.

Ferraris, Marco. *Karen Kilimnik*. Venice: Fondazione Bevilacqua La Masa, 2005.

"Fictional States." Special issue, *Cabinet*, no. 18 (Summer 2005).

Finch, Charlie. "Jean Forgotten: The Prophet Baudrillard." *Artnet Magazine*, April 2008. http://www.artnet.com/magazineus/features/finch/jean-baudrillard4-28-11.asp.

Foster, Hal. *The Return of the Real*. Cambridge, MA: MIT Press, 1996.

Frampton, Hollis. Introduction to *Fictcryptokrimsographs: A Book-Work*, by Les Krims. Buffalo, NY: Humpy Press, 1975.

Frieling, Rudolf, ed. *The Art of Participation, 1950 to Now*. London: Thames & Hudson, 2008.

Fuchs, Martina, ed. *Iris Häussler: Ich War's Nicht / It Wasn't Me*. Munich: ISART Galerie, 2001.

Fuery, Kelli. *New Media: Culture and Image*. New York: Palgrave Macmillan, 2009.

Gadamer, Hans-Georg. *Truth and Method*. Trans. Joel Weinsheimer and Donald G. Marshall. Rev. ed. London: Continuum, 1989.

Getlein, Mark. *Gilbert's Living with Art*. San Francisco: McGraw-Hill, 2006.

Goldberg, Ken. *The Robot in the Garden: Telerobotics and Telepistemology in the Age of the Internet*. Cambridge, MA: MIT Press, 2000.

Gopnik, Blake. "Couple Stole More Than Other Artists' Ideas." *Washington Post*, May 17, 2010.

Grafton, Anthony, and D. Graham Burnett. "Deception as a Way of Knowing." *Cabinet*, no. 33 (Spring 2009): 69–76, and related correspondence in *Cabinet*, no. 34 (Summer 2009): 57.

Grimonprez, Johan. *Inflight*. Ostfildern, Germany: Hatje Cantz, 2000.

——. "Maybe the Sky Is Really Green and We're Just Colourblind: On Zapping, Close Encounters, and the Commercial Break." In Grimonprez, Detalle, and Asselberghs, *It's a Poor Sort of Memory That Only Works Backwards*, 33–57.

Grimonprez, Johan, Benoit Detalle, and Herman Asselberghs. *It's a Poor Sort of Memory That Only Works Backwards*. Ostfildern, Germany: Hatje Cantz, 2011.

Groom, Simon, Karen Smith, and Xu Zhen. *The Real Thing: Contemporary Art from China*. Liverpool: Tate Liverpool, 2007.

Groys, Boris. "Art in the Age of Biopolitics: From Artwork to Art Documentation" (2002). Translated by Steven Lindberg. In *Art Power*, 53–65. Cambridge, MA: MIT Press, 2008.

——. "On the New" (2000). In Groys, *Art Power*, 23–42.

Grundberg, Andy. "Photography in the Age of Electronic Simulation." In *Crisis of the Real: Writings on Photography since 1974*, 222–30. 2nd ed. New York: Aperture, 2010.

Gunning, Tom. "An Aesthetic of Astonishment: Early Film and the (in)Credulous Spectator." In *Viewing Positions*, edited by Linda Williams, 114–33. New Brunswick, NJ: Rutgers, 1995.

Hansen, Mark B. N. *New Philosophy for New Media*. Cambridge, MA: MIT Press, 2004.

Hansen, Miriam. "Benjamin, Cinema, and Experience: 'The Blue Flower in the Land of Technology.'" In "On Weimar Film Theory." Special issue, *New German Critique*, no. 40 (Winter 1987): 179–224.

James, William. "Pragmatism's Conception of Truth." In *Pragmatism: A New Name for Some Old Ways of Thinking*, 76–91. New York: Longman Green, 1907.

Jana, Reena, and Mark Tribe. *New Media Art*. Cologne: Taschen, 2006.

Kakutani, Michiko. "Outdone by Reality." *New York Times*, September 1, 2011.

Kennedy, Pagan, "Rewiring Reality." *New York Times Book Review*, January 15, 2012, 1, 8.

Klein, Norman M. *Freud in Coney Island and Other Tales*. Los Angeles: Otis Books, 2006.

——. *The History of Forgetting: Los Angeles and the Erasure of Memory*. Rev. ed. London: Verso, 1998.

——. *The Vatican to Vegas: The History of Special Effects*. New York: New Press, 2004.

Krauss, Rosalind, and Jane Livingston. *L'Amour Fou: Photography and Surrealism*. New York: Abbeville, 1985.

Lambert-Beatty, Carrie. "Make-Believe: Parafiction and Plausibility." *October*, no. 129 (Summer 2009): 51–84.

Latour, Bruno. "From Realpolitik to Dingpolitik—or How to Make Things Public." In *Making Things Public: Atmospheres of Democracy*, edited by Bruno Latour and Peter Weibel, 14–43. Cambridge, MA: MIT Press, 2005.

——. *Pandora's Hope: Essays on the Reality of Science Studies*. Cambridge, MA: Harvard University Press, 1999.

Latour, Bruno, and Peter Weibel, eds. *Iconoclash: Beyond the Image Wars in Science, Religion, and Art*. Karlsruhe: ZKM, Center for Art and Media, 2002.

Lebovici, Elisabeth. "From Homer to Omer Fast." *Afterall*, no. 20 (Spring 2009): 29–34.

Lee, Pamela M. "Open Secret." *Artforum* 49 (May 2011): 220–30.

Levine, Robert. *A Geography of Time*. New York: Basic Books, 1998.

Lévy, Pierre. *Becoming Virtual: Reality in the Digital Age*. Translated by Robert Bononno. New York: Plenum, 1998.

——. *Collective Intelligence: Mankind's Emerging World in Cyberspace*. Translated by Robert Bononno. New York: Plenum, 1998.

Lister, Martin. *New Media: A Critical Introduction*. London: Routledge, 2009.

Lockhart, Sharon, ed. *Lunch Break Times: Special Edition*. St. Louis: Mildred Lane Kemper Art Museum, 2010.

MacKay, Gillian. "Brilliant Disguise: Iris Häussler's Fact-Meets-Fiction Odysseys." *Canadian Art*, no. 25 (Winter 2009): 82–87.

Mantagne, Orange. *Metaverse Manifesto*. San Francisco: Studio SFO, 2007.

Matino, Lucia, Iris Häussler, and Christiane Meyer-Stoll. *Iris Häussler: Pro Polis*. Munich: Goethe Institute; Milan: Municipal Gallery, 1993.

McGonigal, Jane. *Reality Is Broken: Why Games Make Us Better and How They Change the World*. New York: Penguin, 2011.

McGrath, Charles. "How Many Stephen Colberts Are There?" *New York Times Magazine*, January 8, 2012, 20–25, 36.

McLuhan, Marshall. *Understanding Media: The Extensions of Man*. Cambridge, MA: MIT Press, 1994.

Mitchell, William J. T. *Iconology: Image, Text, Ideology*. Chicago: University of Chicago Press, 1996.

——. "Looking at Animals Looking: Art, Illusion, and Power." In *Aesthetic Illusion: Theoretical and Historical Approaches*, edited by Frederick Burwick and Walter Pape. Berlin: Walter de Gruyter, 1990.

——. *The Reconfigured Eye: Visual Truth in the Post-photographic Era*. Cambridge, MA: MIT Press, 1992.

Molesworth, Helen. *Image Stream*. Columbus: Wexner Center for the Arts, 2003.

Morris, Errol. "Seven Lies about Lying (Part 1)." *Opinionator* (blog). *New York Times*, August 5, 2009. http://opinionator.blogs .nytimes.com/2009/08/05/seven-lies-about-lying-part-1/.

———. "Seven Lies about Lying (Part 2)." *Opinionator* (blog). *New York Times*, August 6, 2009. http://opinionator.blogs.nytimes .com/2009/08/06/seven-lies-about-lying-part-2/.

Mosley, Joshua. *Dread*. Philadelphia: Institute of Contemporary Art, 2009.

Muhle, Maria. "Omer Fast: When Images Lie . . . About the Fictionality of Documents." *Afterall* 20 (Spring 2009): 37–44.

Nash, Mark. "Experiments with Truth: The Documentary Turn." In *Experiments with Truth*. Philadelphia: Fabric Workshop and Museum, 2004.

———. "Reality in the Age of Aesthetics." *Frieze*, no. 114 (April 2008): 118–25.

Nelson, Mike. *Kristus och Judas: A Structural Conceit (A Performance in Three Parts)*. Edited by Sven Bjerkhof. Translated by René Lauritsen. Copenhagen: Statens Museum for Kunst, 2009.

Nelson, Mike, Peter Eleey, and Nato Thompson. *Mike Nelson: A Psychic Vacuum*. New York: Creative Time, 2009.

Nieuwenhuyzen, Martijn van, and Femke Lutgerink. *This Is for Real*. Amsterdam: Stedelijk Museum, 2000.

O'Reilly, Sally. *The Body in Contemporary Art*. London: Thames & Hudson, 2009.

Paul, Christiane. *Digital Art*. 2nd ed. London: Thames & Hudson, 2008.

Perceval, Sophie, and Adeline Pelletier, ed. *J'en rêve*. Paris: Fondation Cartier pour l'art contemporain, 2005.

Plato. *The Republic of Plato*. Translated by Richard W. Sterling and William C. Scott. New York: W. W. Norton, 1985.

Quaranta, Domenico, Maurizio Cattelan, RoseLee Goldberg, Eva Mattes, and Franco Mattes. *Eva and Franco Mattes: 0100101110101101.org*. Milan: Charta, 2009.

Raad, Walid. *Scratching on Things I Could Disavow: A History of Modern and Contemporary Art in the Arab World, Part I_Volume 1_Chapter_1 (Beirut: 1992–2005)*. Los Angeles: REDCAT, 2009.

Rabottini, Alessandro, ed. *Permanent Mimesis: An Exhibition about Simulation and Realism*. Milan: Electa, 2010.

Rhee, Wonil, Peter Weibel, and Gregor Jansen. *Thermocline of Art: New Asian Waves*. Ostfildern, Germany: Hatje Cantz, 2007.

Rich, Frank. "Facebook Politicians Are Not Your Friends." *New York Times*, October 9, 2010.

———. *The Greatest Story Ever Sold: The Decline and Fall of Truth from 9/11 to Katrina*. New York: Penguin, 2006.

———. "Happy Talk News Covers a War." *New York Times*, July 18, 2004.

———. "Operation Iraqi Infoganda." *New York Times*, March 28, 2004.

Robinson, Julia, ed. *New Realisms, 1957–1962: Object Strategies between Ready-made and Spectacle*. Cambridge, MA: MIT Press, 2010.

Rose, Zac. "An Analysis of Artist Thomas Demand's Oval Office Series Presidency, Published in the *New York Times Magazine*." *032c*, no. 18 (Winter 2009–10): 54–61.

Saltzman, Lisa. *Making Memory Matter: Strategies of Remembrance in Contemporary Art*. Chicago: University of Chicago Press, 2006.

Sante, Luc, Eva Respini, and Vik Muniz. *Vik Muniz: Verso*. Milan: Charta, 2009.

Schiff, Jeffrey, and Nancy Princenthal. *Double Vision: Transactions of the American Philosophical Society, Held at Philadelphia, for Promoting Useful Knowledge*. Vol. 2. Philadelphia: Pope's Head, 2011.

Scholte, Tatja, and Paulien 't Hoen, eds. *Inside Installations: Preservation and Presentation of Installation Art*. [Amsterdam]: ICN, 2007.

Schwartz, Hillel. *The Culture of the Copy: Striking Likenesses, Unreasonable Facsimiles*. New York: Zone, 1998.

Scott, A. O. "How Real Does It Feel." *New York Times Magazine*, December 12, 2010.

Shanken, Edward A., ed. *Art and Electronic Media*. London: Phaidon, 2009.

Sharp, Jasper, ed. *John Gerrard: Animated Scene*. Vienna: Schlebrügge, 2009.

Sharp, Kevin. "Harnett's Paint Box." In *The Reality of Things: Trompe l'Oeil in America*, 10–21. Vero Beach, FL: Vero Beach Museum of Art, 2007.

Sheehy, Colleen J., ed. *Cabinet of Curiosities: Mark Dion and the University as Installation*. Minneapolis: University of Minnesota Press, 2006.

Shields, David. "In Writing, Art, and Music, Everybody Steals." *Huffington Post*, May 28, 2010.

———. *Reality Hunger: A Manifesto*. New York: Knopf, 2010.

Siemons, Mark, and Ai Weiwei. *Ai Weiwei: So Sorry*. Munich: Prestel, 2009.

Sirmans, Franklin. *Maurizio Cattelan: Is There Life before Death?* Houston: Menil Collection, 2010.

Smaby, Gary. *Thinking about Things*. Smaby Group. http://smabygroup.typepad.com/ Essay%20PG%203-6.pdf.

Smith, Karen, Hans-Ulrich Obrist, and Bernard Fibicher. *Ai Weiwei*. London: Phaidon, 2009.

Smith, Roberta. "In Shards of the Past, the Present Is Revealed." *New York Times*, November 19, 2004.

Stam, Jos. "Photography Changes What We Think 'Reality' Looks Like." Smithsonian Institution Archives. http://click.si.edu/Story .aspx?story=465.

Steiner, Wendy. *The Real Real Thing: The Model in the Mirror of Art*. Chicago: University of Chicago Press, 2010.

Strausbaugh, John. "The Case of Sigmund F. and Coney I." *New York Times*, July 26, 2009.

Sugimoto, Hiroshi. *The Day After*. New York: Pace Gallery, 2010.

Suskind, Ron. "Without a Doubt: Faith, Certainty, and the Presidency of George W. Bush." *New York Times Magazine*, October 17, 2004.

Tinari, Philip. "Postures in Clay: The Vessels of Ai Weiwei." In Torchia, *Ai Weiwei*, 30–47.

Torchia, Richard, ed. *Ai Weiwei: Dropping the Urn: Ceramic Works, 5000 BCE–2010 CE*. Glenside, PA: Arcadia University Art Gallery, 2010.

Turkle, Sherry. *Life on the Screen: Identity in the Age of the Internet*. New York: Simon & Schuster, 1995.

———. *The Second Self: Computers and the Human Spirit*. 20th anniversary ed. Cambridge, MA: MIT Press, 2005.

———. *Simulation and Its Discontents*. Cambridge, MA: MIT Press, 2009.

Van Tomme, Niels. "Dreamland: The Intimate Politics of Desire; Zoe Beloff in Conversation with Niels Van Tomme." *Art Papers* 34 (July–August 2010): 26–31.

Varnelis, Kazys. "The Immediated Now: Network Culture and the Poetics of Reality." http://varnelis.networkedbook.org/the-immediated-now-network-culture-and-the-poetics-of-reality/.

Vergine, Lea, and Valerio Terraroli. *Art of the Twentieth Century, 2000 and Beyond: Contemporary Tendencies*. Milan: Skira, 2009.

Virilio, Paul. *The Vision Machine*. Bloomington: Indiana University Press, 1994.

Wang Chunchen. *The Myth of Displacement: Li Wenfeng and Liu Lining's New Works Exhibition*. [Beijing]: New Millennium Gallery, 2009.

Wasserman, Tina. "Duplicated Replications: The Interventions of Omer Fast." *Afterimage* 37 (March–April 2010): 6–9.

Wavrin, Isabelle de. "Paradis des loisirs ou cauchemar climatisé? Un weekend à Dubaï et à Abu Dhabi." In *Dreamlands: Des parcs d'attractions aux cités de futur*, edited by Claude Pommereau, 45–49. Paris: Centre Pompidou, 2010.

Werthein, Judi, and Leandro Erlich. *Turismo: La Habana, Cuba*. New York: Kent Gallery, 2001.

Weschler, Lawrence. "The Irritated Cloud: Mark Dion in Conversation with Lawrence Weschler." In *The Marvelous Museum: Orphans, Curiosities, and Treasures; A Mark Dion Project*, 19–31. Oakland: Oakland Museum of California; San Francisco: Chronicle, 2010.

———. *Mr. Wilson's Cabinet of Wonder*. New York: Pantheon, 1995.

Woolley, Benjamin. *Virtual Worlds: A Journey in Hype and Hyperreality*. London: Penguin, 1993.

Wu Hung, Wang Huangsheng, and Feng Boyi. *The First Guangzhou Triennial: Reinterpretation; A Decade of Experimental Chinese Art (1990–2000)*. Guangzhou, China: Guangdong Museum of Art, 2002.

Zhang Hongxing and Lauren Parker, eds. *China Design Now*. London: V&A Publishing, 2008.

Žižek, Slavoj. *The Parallax View*. Cambridge, MA: MIT Press, 2006.

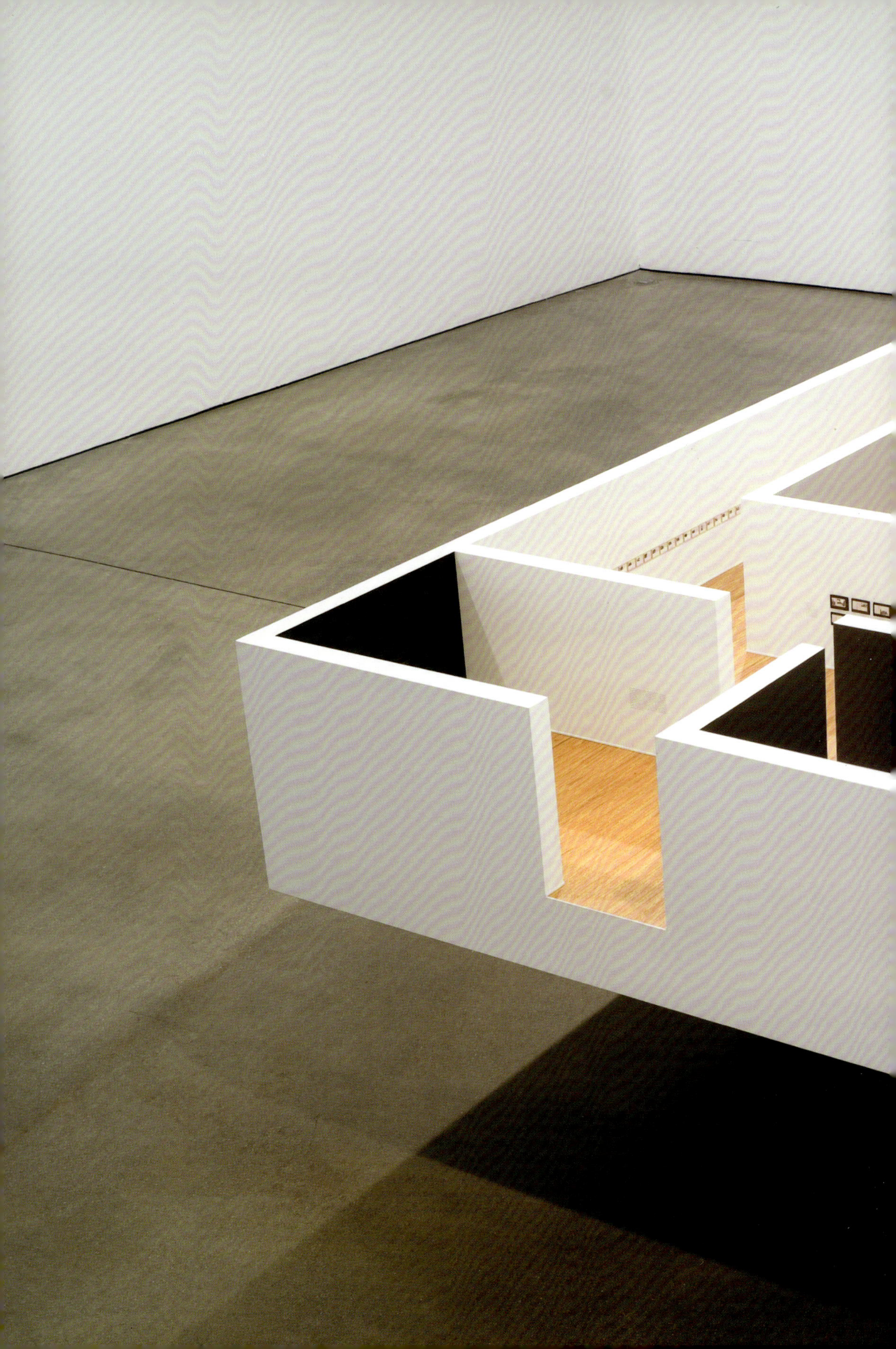

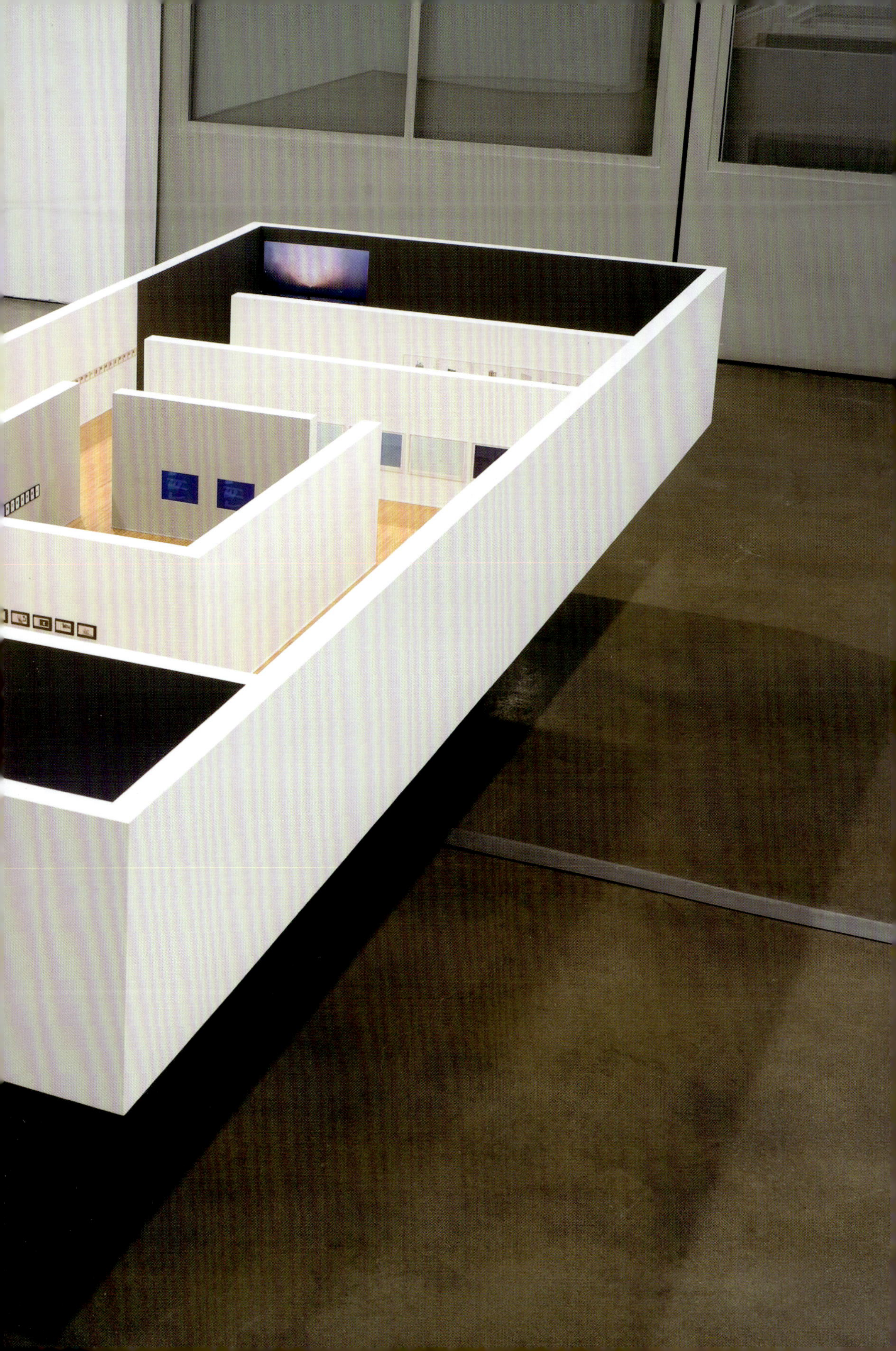

# Contributors

**Elizabeth Armstrong** is curator of contemporary art and director of the Center for Alternative Museum Practice (CAMP) at the Minneapolis Institute of Arts. Prior to joining the MIA, she served as deputy director for programs and chief curator at the Orange County Museum of Art. She has also worked as a curator at the Museum of Contemporary Art, San Diego (1996–2000), and the Walker Art Center (1983–96). She has organized more than thirty exhibitions, many with major catalogues and tours, including *In the Spirit of Fluxus* (1993); *Peter Fischli and David Weiss: In a Restless World* (1996); *Ultrabaroque: Aspects of Post–Latin American Art* (2000); the California Biennial (2002–6); and *Birth of the Cool: California Art, Design, and Culture at Midcentury* (2007), which was awarded the American Association of Museum Curators prize for best exhibition catalogue in 2007.

**Christopher Atkins** is coordinator of the Minnesota Artists Exhibition Program at the Minneapolis Institute of Arts. Previously he taught art history and museum studies at the Minneapolis College of Art and Design, College of Visual Arts, and Macalester College. He received his MA and MRes degrees from Goldsmiths College, University of London.

**D. Graham Burnett** is a professor of history at Princeton University and an editor of *Cabinet* magazine. Trained in the history and philosophy of science, he is the author of four books, including *Descartes and the Hyperbolic Quest* (2005) and *Trying Leviathan: The Nineteenth-Century New York Court Case That Put the Whale on Trial and Challenged the Order of Nature* (2007), which was awarded the 2008 New York City Book Award and the Hermalyn Prize for Urban History. With a New Directions Fellowship from the Mellon Foundation, Burnett is currently working on problems at the intersection of technology and the arts, with an emphasis on issues of deception and forgery.

**Janet Dees** is an assistant curator at SITE Santa Fe, a position that she has held since 2011. From 2008 to 2010 she was the Eugene V. Thaw Curatorial Fellow at SITE. She has cocurated several exhibitions at SITE and is curator of *Linda Mary Montano: Always Creative*, which will premiere at SITE in 2013. She is currently a PhD candidate in art history at the University of Delaware.

**Tom Gunning** is the Edwin A. and Betty L. Bergman Distinguished Service Professor, Department of Art History, Department of Cinema and Media Studies, and the College, and chair of the Committee on Cinema and Media Studies at the University of Chicago. He is a fellow of the American Academy of Arts and Sciences and received the Distinguished Achievement Award from the Mellon Foundation in 2009. In his nearly one hundred publications, Gunning has concentrated on early cinema, as well as on the culture of modernity from which cinema arose. The issues of film culture, the historical factors of exhibition and criticism, and the spectator's experience throughout film history are recurrent themes in his work.

**Irene Hofmann** is the Phillips Director and Chief Curator of SITE Santa Fe. Prior to assuming this post, she served as executive director of the Contemporary Museum, Baltimore, from 2005 to 2010. From 2001 to 2005 she was curator at the Orange County Museum of Art in Newport Beach, California, where she co-organized the 2002 and 2004 California Biennials and the national touring exhibition *Girls' Night Out* (2003). From 1997 to 2001 Hofmann served as curator at the Cranbrook Art Museum, where she organized numerous exhibitions with accompanying catalogues, including *Weird Science* (1999) and *Iñigo Manglano-Ovalle* (2001).

**Norman M. Klein** is a professor of critical studies at California Institute of the Arts. A cultural critic; historian of architecture, media, and culture; and novelist, he is the author of many books, most notably *The History of Forgetting: Los Angeles and the Erasure of Memory* (1997) and *The Vatican to Vegas: The History of Special Effects* (2004). He also coauthored *The Freud-Lissitzky Navigator* with Lev Manovich and developed *Bleeding Through: Layers of Los Angeles, 1920–86* (2003), an interactive CD with accompanying book, in association with the Karlsruhe Centre for Art and Media, and *The Imaginary Twentieth Century* (with Margo Bistis), a historical science-fiction novel and interactive data field.

**Carrie Lambert-Beatty** is the John L. Loeb Associate Professor of the Humanities and director of graduate studies for film and visual studies at Harvard University. Her articles focusing on art since 1960 (performance art, minimalism, and postmodern dance) have appeared in *Trans, Art Journal, October*, and other publications. Her book *Being Watched: Yvonne Rainer and the 1960s* (2008) was awarded the de la Torre Bueno Prize for scholarship on dance in 2009. Lambert-Beatty is currently working on a new project on recent intersections of art and activism.

**Mark Levy** is a professor of art history at California State University, East Bay. He has written many reviews and articles for national and international publications and two books, *Technicians of Ecstasy: Shamanism and the Modern Artist* (1993) and *Void/in Art* (2005), about the significance of emptiness in Eastern and Western art. He is currently completing a new book, *Tantra, Art, and Anarchy*, and is designing a game for the iPod and iPad with graduate students from the multimedia department at California State University, East Bay, based on the Tibetan Book of the Dead.

**Glenn D. Lowry** has been the director of the Museum of Modern Art (MoMA) in New York since 1995. Prior to his time at MoMA, Lowry was the director of the Art Gallery of Ontario in Toronto (1990–95) and curator of Near Eastern art at the Smithsonian's Arthur M. Sackler Gallery and Freer Gallery of Art (1984–90). A scholar of contemporary and Islamic art, he is the author of numerous books and articles, including "Gained in Translation" (*Art News*, 2006), *The Museum of Modern Art in This Century* (2009), and *Oil and Sugar: Contemporary Art and Islamic Culture* (2009). A strong advocate of contemporary art, Lowry conceived and initiated MoMA's merger with P.S. 1 Contemporary Art Center in 1999.

**Joan Rothfuss** is an independent writer, curator, and educator based in Minneapolis. From 1988 to 2006 she was a curator at the Walker Art Center, where she managed the permanent collection and oversaw the publication of the Walker's collection handbook, *Bits and Pieces Put Together to Present a Semblance of a Whole* (2005). Among the exhibitions she has organized or co-organized are *In the Spirit of Fluxus* (1993); *Joseph Beuys: The Multiples* (1997); *2000 BC: The Bruce Conner Story Part II* (1999); and *Past Things and Present: Jasper Johns since 1983* (2003). She is currently at work on a biography of the performing artist Charlotte Moorman, to be published by MIT Press in 2013.

**Nicole Soukup** assisted with research for *More Real? Art in the Age of Truthiness* as an intern and assistant in the Department of Contemporary Art at the Minneapolis Institute of Arts. She holds an MA in art history from the University of Florida.

# Index